# WALKING ON WATER

# WALKING ON WATER

## BLACK AMERICAN LIVES AT THE TURN OF THE TWENTY-FIRST CENTURY

RANDALL KENAN

ALFRED A. KNOPF
NEW YORK
1999

THIS IS A BORZOI BOOK
PUBLISHED BY ALFRED A. KNOPF, INC.



Owing to limitations of space, all acknowledgments for permission to reprint previously published material may be found following the index.

Library of Congress Cataloging-in-Publication Data
Kenan, Randall.
Walking on water: Black American lives at the turn of the twenty-first century / by Randall Kenan. — 1st ed.
p. cm.
ISBN 0-679-40827-4. — ISBN 0-679-73788-X (pbk.)
1. United States—Race relations—Anecdotes. 2. Canada—Race relations—Anecdotes. 3. Afro-Americans—Interviews. 4. United States—Description and travel. 5. Canada—Description and travel. 6. Kenan, Randall—Journeys—United States. 7. Kenan, Randall—Journeys—Canada. 8. Afro-Americans—Race identity. I. Title.
E185.615.K375 1999
305.8'00973—dc21 98-41730 CIP

Manufactured in the United States of America
First Edition

*To the memory of my friend,*

*The Reverend Richard Elias Wimberly, III*

*and to Mama,*

*of course . . .*

The old people in a new world, the new people made out of the old, that is the story that I mean to tell, for that is what really is and what I really know.

—Gertrude Stein, *The Making of Americans*

Black women have been
walking on water for 300 years.

—Toni Morrison

". . . They just turned, my gran' said, all of 'em . . . and walked on back down to the edge of the river here. Every las' man, woman and chile. And they wasn't taking they time no more. They had seen what they had seen and those Ibos was stepping! And they didn't bother getting back into the small boats drawed up here—boats take too much time. They just kept walking right on out over the river. Now you wouldna thought they'd of got very far seeing as it was water they was walking on. Beside they had all that iron on 'em. Iron on they ankles and they wrists and fastened 'round they necks like a dog collar. 'Nuff iron to sink an army. And chains hooked up the iron. But chains didn't stop those Ibos none. Neither iron. . . . They feets was gonna take 'em wherever they was going that day. . . ."

—Paule Marshall, *Praisesong for the Widow*

# CONTENTS

## IV OUR STILL-FRONTIER



## V PROMISED LANDS



## VI NIGHT SONG AFTER DEATH



## VII HOME TO A VERY STRANGE PLACE

# PREFACE

I must say, before I even begin, that this work—in the end—is a failure. Its seed—to chronicle, chart, eviscerate, enumerate, analyze and explain the nature of blackness—was, and is, an arrogant proposal, honest and sincere in its origins but doomed at its inception by the physical and intellectual impossibility of capturing successfully 36 million souls (to borrow heavily from W.E.B. Du Bois, as I do throughout this book).

This book took dramatically longer to write than I had originally intended. My earliest years were spent in training to become a scientist, and scientists are bewitched by those things called "facts." Facts are fetishes for a scientist: a firm belief that the world can be expressed in numbers and relations. However, over time, I came to understand that the central question I was asking—What does it mean to be black?—cannot be expressed in numbers or equations. In the end, this is an essentially spiritual question, involving belief, myth, desire, longing, some history, much faith. As I grew, as my travels in my own country grew from one year to two to three to four, I came to understand that men and women cannot be tallied and summed up. For those reasons, this book changed from what I wanted it to be into what it wanted to become. This volume has become a personal response to all the people and places I have met over the years of my travels across North America. It has become a subjective response to a subjective question; an existential answer to a query about being. In short, it is one man bearing witness.

After it was too late for me to really do anything about it, I realized that this is a very bookish book. But I am a very bookish person, and it stands to reason that my faults would reflect my nature. I don't feel like apologizing for this particular shortcoming, for if I were to pretend to be other than I am, I would be being dishonest, and that would make seven years' worth of work worthless.

Penultimately, I realized that what I was attempting had more to do with my own fears and dreams and prejudices and anguishes; that in the end, my sojourn in North America had more to do with my sojourn in myself, into my own dark soul, and that I had used—perhaps selfishly—

the multitude I encountered to reckon on my own being, my own notions, my own heart, more than it had anything to do with my folk. My people? That was the dynamic that informed this work: Do I have a people? Do I belong? And to what? More than a book of answers, this is my book of questions. More than a book of analysis, this is my book of soul searching. I am asking who am I perhaps more than who are we, where do I belong more than where do we belong. From the beginning to the end, this is more a book about me than anyone else, and I beg tolerance and understanding in this chronicle. Proffering, I pray, a testament that will, I hope, help illuminate rather than obscure; a meditation that might lead others to the real questions and the real roots of the question of not only what it means to be black in America, not only what it means to be an American, but what it means to be a human being.

> "Who knows but that, on the lower frequencies, I speak for you?"
>
> —Ralph Ellison, *Invisible Man*

# WALKING ON WATER

One

# PROLOGUE:
## Come Out the Wilderness

. . . I can hurt
You with questions
Like silver bullets . . .

—Yusef Komunyakaa, "Venus's flytraps"

"You North American blacks, you make me so angry," she was saying. "You set yourselves off from the rest of the Diaspora. As if your experiences were somehow *better*. 'We suffered more.' When, in fact, the slaveocracy of the Caribbean was much more brutal."

We were in a cafe in Greenwich Village, arguing over coffee about the nature of Black America. "But you miss the point entirely," I said.

She was African. In fact an Ethiopian princess, a direct descendant of Haile Selassie, now studying anthropology at the University of Colorado. Her mother worked for the United Nations and she had spent a great deal of time at their family estate in Antigua, where they were watched over devotedly by Rastafarians, who consider the last emperor of Ethiopia to be their Messiah. Moreover, her family had married into an old black North Carolina family—thus she felt more than qualified to declaim on African Americans.

"What you say is true," I said, "but what separates us is not just the psychological shackles of slavery, but the extent to which our bloods have intermingled . . ."

"Bullshit." She laughed and shook her head in disbelief. "You think that there was no other rape and that there aren't Creoles throughout the world? That doesn't make you different, make you *better*."

"No one's saying we're *better.* Just different."

"But you all act that way."

"What? I don't think American black people think they are any better than Africans or West Indians, but we do recognize that our experience has been markedly different. Look," I said, "we've become a part of this country in a way that no other black group has become a part of their country. I mean, we made this country. We still do. Why was slavery instituted here in the first place? Free labor. And look what that labor has created, materially, for better or worse. Moreover, we've contributed to every aspect of American life, scientifically, legislatively, militarily, artistically . . ."

"Oh, God, I don't want to hear anymore about black music . . ."

"It's not just black music. It's everything. Hell, we are America. We have more claim to this country than anyone other than the Native American. We've been here for over three hundred years, for Christ's sake. I don't mean to disparage the diaspora, but how can we ignore our blood-and-sweat connection to this land? This very land here?"

"What I'm talking about is just that attitude, that your experience is somehow better . . ."

"Not better, different . . ."

No one won the argument that warm spring evening. Yet the discussion haunted me for years afterwards, not because I had not thought of these ideas before, but because I had not realized how deeply I felt about being an American, an African American. Nor was it the beginning of a search for my identity, but a turning point, a turning point which led me to the decision to explore firsthand the idea and the reality of what it means to be black in America. To question what it means to be an African American.

What does it mean to be black?

In discussing Black America, on whatever level, be it politics, economics, music, food, I often use the word "we." Aside from the necessity of sometimes making broad generalizations about broad groups, the more I think about African America, the more I cannot help but question what I mean by "we." I'm not the only black person who does this. All through my growing up my relatives did it, my teachers, my ministers; in school, at work, whenever or wherever I encountered black folk talking about black folk—even when speaking to nonblack folk—the word "we" was used.

Do we mean race? Do we mean culture? Do we mean skin color? The more I thought of it, the more problematic the idea became—even as I persisted in using the word, becoming ever more uncertain of what I—what "we"—meant.

Did I mean race? If I did I was a hypocrite, because I don't believe in "race" as a fact of nature. Biologically speaking there is only one human species, and though tremendous amounts of time and money have been spent on the classification and subdivision of human beings, classifications that go beyond mere skin color, no one has succeeded, scientifically, in demonstrating any significant difference between people who look different from others. Consider cats: A Siamese, a calico and a tabby are actually of different genus—that is, they have specific genetic codes (even though they can mate); whereas Koreans, Botswanans, Apaches and Swedes are all within the same genus. We humans are all calicos, despite visual persuasions to the contrary. But as a rule, human beings don't think that way. Since the time the noted anthropologist Franz Boas wrote:

> Where is the proof of the development of specialized hereditary capacities? Where is the proof that such capacities, if they exist, are recessive? How can it be shown that such specialized characteristics in selected mating will be bred out? Not a single one of these statements can be accepted

no one has presented any compelling evidence to the contrary. Where race is concerned I feel very much like Henry Adams when he wrote: "And yet no one could tell the patient tourist what race was, or how it should be known. History offered a feeble and delusive smile at the sound of the word; evolutionists and ethnologists disputed its very existence; no one knew what to make of it; yet without the clue, history was a nursery tale."

Race is better explained by what historian Barbara Jeanne Fields calls "an ideological construct and thus, above all, a historical product." As a great many historians have noted, "race" is far more a mythology than a reality, brought about first by the proponents of slavery as a way to create a caste system in the United States. It is a melding of class with pseudo-biology in such a way as to make and maintain an inferior, unequal group of people, a people both socially and economically on the lowest rung of the ladder. "During the revolutionary era," Fields writes, "people who favored slavery and people who opposed it collaborated in identifying the racial incapacity of African Americans as the explanation for enslavement."

For two centuries "race" has become more and more deeply ingrained in the American imagination, and in some cases has taken on a life apart from its original intentions. Today the word "race" has profound currency. Be it in politics or mass culture, the buzzword "race" elicits for the American ear a panoply of meanings or "realities." Polls are tallied in terms of "race"; the U.S. Census Bureau divides people by "race"; on television talk shows and news broadcasts, on the front pages of newspapers and on the covers of magazines, the word "race" is used with great surety and finality, as if it were a scientifically quantifiable trait. Americans know what they think they know, and in that knowing lies tremendous power.

As Lorraine Hansberry has a character in her play *Les Blancs* say:

> Race—racism—is a device. No more. No less. It explains nothing at all . . . I am simply saying that a device is a device, but that it also has consequences: once invented it takes on a life, a reality of its own. So in one century, men invoke the device of religion to cloak their conquests. In another, race. Now, in both cases you and I may recognize the fraudulence of the device, but the fact remains that a man who has a sword run through him because he refused to become a Moslem or a Christian—or who is shot in Zatembe or Mississippi because he is black—is suffering the utter *reality* of the device. And it is pointless to pretend that it doesn't *exist*—merely because it is a *lie!*

In that same way, to be an American is to be shaped by the "device" of "race." Whether one believes it to be reality or mythology, whether one is white or black or something entirely other, to live in the United States is to be shaped on some level by "race."

Yet race is only one element of being black, only one side of the multi-sided rubric of understanding who "we" are.

My first concept of what it meant to be black came from Chinquapin, North Carolina, 1963 through 1981, in the years, as James Agee so aptly put it, "that I lived there so successfully disguised to myself as a child." It would take me years to truly appreciate the plain yet endless beauty of the lowlands of North Carolina. The fields of corn and soybeans and tobacco; the forests bisected by narrow dirt roads, full of oak and sassafras and long-leaf pines, brimming with squirrels and possums and wild cats. Here were the men in coveralls on tractors and the women with snuff tucked deep in their bottom lip. Here was a land little changed since the 1950s by the time I went to high school. Here I inherited a vision of being black.

What did it mean to be black? In the beginning of my life, in my mind, it meant a pointillism of culture. Collard greens. "Amazing Grace, How Sweet the Sound." Grits and tote. Quilts and pig's feet. Thundering preachers and prayer cloths. It was head rags and chitlins, "Chain of Fools" and "Swing Low Sweet Chariot." Ultra-sheen, Afro-sheen, neck bones, cornrows . . . These signs and symbols were the air I breathed, the water I drank, the ground upon which I walked. Rituals, cuisine, fashion, music, language . . . Oh, the rhetoric and the vocabulary, the syncopation of old men at the barber shop, the women at the tobacco barn—this was music in itself—all formed my culture, unbeknownst to me. Culture, for the insider, is wound round about and worn daily; unless one leaves a culture, one never really sees it for what it is: the blueprint for living. Culture says: Live this way. Moreover, for me—and I'm certain this is true for anyone in any culture—these particles of being were a portrait of endurance, of strength, of love, of community, and of respect. On many levels one could witness this affirmation, bold and subtle; hear it in the reprimands and the pet names; see it in the old women's stitches and the old men's whittling; taste it in my mother's pound cake and in my uncle's scuppernong wine; smell it in the sweat of men working in the fields—or this was my assumption, spurred on by the talk and the subtext, the slip and the grip of this world in which I grew.

We were never given to define or dissect our blackness. And for what reason would we? Being black—or Negro or colored—was something taken for granted. When my great-great-grandaunt Erie or my cousin Norman told stories of "the old days," of the difficulty of breaking new ground with nothing but an axe, a shovel, and a mule and plow, of community barn raisings, of dealing with the KKK through stealth and steely will, of old-time revivals that went on for days at a stretch, of midwives and pickled cabbage—I took for granted that this tapestry, this ever-reaching-back fabric was what being black was all about. To think in terms of being authentic or unique, for me, as a child, was utterly inconceivable, for the perception was the reality. Why would it be otherwise? Indeed, in my youth, if I had met a black Nigerian or Rwandan or South

African, the idea that he or she did not think exactly as I did would have been shocking—and I am certain it would have been so to most blacks in my hometown as well.

Moreover, this perception of what it meant to be black was mysteriously corroborated by watching *Sanford and Son* on TV or reading *Ebony* magazine when it arrived in the mailbox each month; by those textbooks that, every February, served up those timeworn heroes of every God-loving black American—George Washington Carver, Booker T. Washington and Harriet Tubman. (Did any of us children suspect there could have been black male insurrectionists? How dangerous a notion—to teach black boys about Gabriel Prosser or Nat Turner.) When I was a child even *Superfly* and *Dolemite* came to the local movie theater. This was blackness we knew, we accepted, we understood, we celebrated: Black was seamless, undifferentiated, defined—as far as we were concerned. Whether you were in New York City or Chinquapin, North Carolina, Chicago, Illinois, or Savannah, Georgia, there was only one black culture, from Mary McCleod Bethune to Martin Luther King, Jr. We had the same icons, the same language, the same food, the same politics, the same beliefs. And we were certain that all black folk felt the same as we did; if, indeed, they were black. If they thought otherwise, then, of course, their blackness was highly suspect.

This was the fallacy; this was the lie. A persuasive black-think, a monolithic sameness, a we-ism. This was the ideology which, in my late twenties, I had dashed against the brick wall of reality.

What does it mean to be black?

Indeed, who is black? In the United States, for well over a century, "a black is any person with any known African black ancestry," writes F. James Davis in *Who Is Black?* "In the South it became known as the 'one-drop rule,' meaning that a single drop of 'black' blood makes a person black." Or "one black ancestor" or a "traceable amount." The fact that the definition of what it means to be black is still on the law books is enough to give any thinking person pause: Where does genetic heritage end and cultural heritage begin? What do we mean when we invoke "black culture"? Does black culture belong to anyone who is genetically defined as black?

Many people who hold with the idea of a black race also hold with the notion of an essential blackness, an inherited culture embedded within the genes of every black man and black woman. An essentialist view of blackness goes hand in hand with the idea of race as a fact—where defining culture becomes inextricably bound up with the idea of a "race." The cultural critic Michael Eric Dyson has defined racial essentialism as "black intellectuals oppos[ing] the strangling of black culture by caricature, offering instead cultural standards to help define racial authenticity." Others have traced the idea back to the mid-nineteenth century, noting it in the writings of Langston Hughes and W.E.B. Du Bois as being an appeal to sentimental tribalism, something to do with mystery, primitivism and soul. Indeed, this view of essential blackness is in no way limited to intellectuals, for too many times have I listened to people testifying to the inherent "soul" of black people, exemplified by, but in no way limited to, soul music and soul food. One part propaganda, one part mysticism, this view of blackness, especially when used in a positive light, is seemingly irresistible; this view appeals to an unspeakably attractive connectedness, solidarity, a larger-than-human consciousness, Jungian in its telepathic zeal. Truth to tell: I thought this way for much of my life, saw my blackness as irreducible, inalienable, inherited.

To be sure, many people might view my dismissal of essentialism as blasphemy; my rejection of race as treachery. In fact, the first person to get me to see otherwise was a black woman at college who, as a founding member of SNCC and a sociologist, could not have been more committed to African American culture. It was Sonya Stone who first got me to see how powerful a thing culture is; how rhythms are philosophy, ritual is history, language is art. How, in fact, the idea of a biological explanation of "race" diminished the human achievement of culture. In fact, she was the first person who told me I should become a writer.

"Cultural evolution," according to scientist and writer Stephen Jay Gould, "can proceed so quickly because it operates . . . by the inheritance of acquired characters. Whatever one generation learns, it can pass to the next by writing, instruction, inculcation, ritual, tradition, and a host of methods that humans have developed to assure continuity of the culture."

Culture. But what exactly is African American culture? Much ink is spilled yearly trying to pin down that ever-moving, ever-self-defining phenomenon. From condemnation in attempts to pathologize black culture by using it to explain away crime and single-parent births, to celebration in attempts to propagandize black solidarity or uplift black morale by praising Nobel prize–winning fiction, scientific invention and jazz, black culture has a way of being many things to many people. But the one perplexing question for which I found no satisfying answer was: With so many people spread over so vast a continent, can there be one black culture anymore? Has television and technology and expansion robbed black culture of any inherent meaning?

Initially, for me, this problem of perception, of apprehension, of acceptance, had to do with real estate.

I first came to New York City in 1985, fresh out of college, the prototypical country boy aloose in the big city. I was intimidated, ambitious and eager, and I found a job with a major publishing house fairly quickly. After living for six months with relatives in Newark, New Jersey, I moved to the Upper West Side. Then Queens. Then Brooklyn. Then the West Village. Then Hell's Kitchen. For ill-paid editorial assistants finding a place to live in New York occupies an inordinate amount of time and energy. Much of the decision about where I lived had more to do with my wallet than a choice of neighborhoods; with sublets that fell through; with rent going sky-high.

Moreover, there was a social consideration. Coming to a large city, knowing no one, means that your social circle will be largely dictated by who you work with. For me, this meant that most of my associates were white. Over time, my circles grew and my friends were black and white and Indian and Japanese and Native American—a polyglot potpourri of multiculturalism. To better partake of this cross-world living, I tried to live as close to the nexus of work and social fun as I could: I very much enjoyed living in New York.

Except when I complained to my family about rents and having to move so often. Their response was: "Why don't you just move to Harlem? Surely you can find a nice cheap place up there." Many of my relatives had lived off and on in Harlem from the early twenties until the mid-seventies. As a child I remember visiting a grandaunt who had an enormous apartment on Edgecomb Avenue, or Sugar Hill. Why, indeed, did I not just move to Harlem? Ah, the secret, silent monsters in us all! . . .

It took me years to admit to myself that the question made me uncomfortable, that it picked at a psychological welt I would prefer to avoid. I had visited Harlem on a great number of occasions; regularly visited the Studio Museum; attended the Abyssinian Baptist Church, the Apollo, the Schomberg Library; visited friends on 135th and 149th and all over; tutored kids in East Harlem. The history of the 1920s' Renaissance or Cultural Revolution resonated in my bones; all my cultural heroes from

Duke Ellington to Zora Neale Hurston to Countee Cullen to Alaine Locke dwelt within the historic aura of the Cotton Club and the Negro Ensemble and the Theresa Hotel. Yet deep within me welled a strong resistance to the idea of living in Harlem in the 1980s. This resistance resulted in a hidden feeling of guilt and shame.

I had logical reasons, I told myself. The few apartments I found—when inclined to look there—were, when nice, unaffordable; and when affordable, far from nice. Unspoken were fears of crime and concern about distance from work and my social life. Perhaps even a fear of stigma. In my early twenties I had begun to deal with a social reality that I had successfully kept at bay till then.

My academic world had always—except for kindergarten—been integrated, and from high school on, more often that not, I was the only African American in my classes. At college, a predominantly white school where the black population was around 4 percent, this continued, and I countered it by attending black church services on campus and off, singing in the gospel choir, taking Afro-American history classes. Though, perforce, I had white friends, my closest friends happened to be black. Even then—though I did not realize it, had no way to realize it—I was struggling to be a "real" black person. I feared that so much contact with white folk, studying so much European culture, living with, eating with, and sometimes sleeping with, white people, would in some way put my Negro "soul" in danger.

Ironically, in my moving here and yon in the New York metropolitan area, I had lived in an all-black neighborhood in Newark; a veritable slum in Queens; in Spike Lee's neighborhood in Brooklyn; and, in 1991, just before this crisis of identity came to a head, in Hell's Kitchen, which, if I had taken the trouble to research, I would have discovered to once have been the heart of black New York at the turn of the century. To be sure, my discomfort had little to do with the reality of my living situation and more to do with the *realty* of my mental state, with the real estate of my mind; the unspoken fear that the farther I lived from black folk, the farther I lived from my own blackness; that, ultimately, I was assimilating. Growing up I had been taught to always be proud of being black, and to be ambitious and committed to my work. Somehow in this New York, the two were clashing. Though in no overt way, one seemed to be pushing out the other.

Looking back I now see how ill-founded was my fear, personally; how much youth and insecurity and life choices, present and future, were in play. Yet, how real the possibility had been; how precarious a thing is identity. However, at the time, I had to keep asking myself: What is black identity?

What does it mean to be black?

In the 1970 movie *Cotton Comes to Harlem,* based on the novel by Chester Himes, a leitmotif is the recurring question: "Is this black enough for you?"

Is this black enough for you?

Much of the tumult in the social revolution of the 1960s and early seventies, amid the civil rights movement and the demand for economic equality and opportunity, was the internal definition, or redefinition, of what it meant to be black. In this period the phrase "Black is Beautiful" became popular. (Though Du Bois had said it decades before.) Afrocentric garb and hair became popular. Radical became chic. The black middle class—which had initially led and underwritten the Civil Rights movement through all the preceding decades—had become supplanted in the public eye by Afro-crowned and dashiki-wearing young men and women, from all kinds of economic backgrounds; the idea of middle class or bourgeois values, long a part of the very fabric of the African American community from Los Angeles to Atlanta, became suspect. (And in those days, due to segregation, no one had to question what an African American community was or meant.) A profound shift in identity, politics and social thought took place very quickly, dovetailing with the overall youth-engendered rebellion against the status quo: to be black was to be poor, disenfranchised, to live in an urban slum (or what became "the ghetto"), to distrust "the man" and to be very, very angry. Of course this is a rank oversimplification and disturbing distortion of what really happened to African American culture during the '60s and '70s; yet it speaks to the larger American perspective, to what it means to be black in America at the turn of this new century; it speaks to a perception affecting both black and white alike.

Though the black middle class, economically speaking, grew in historic numbers in the intervening years, and though doctors and lawyers were graduated, good marriages were made and kept, and businesses flourished—the image of black identity in the popular media never overcame the trauma of riots and assassinations and marches of the past decades. Nor did the black middle class successfully come to terms with that time; as more African Americans rose above the poverty level, they abandoned the old neighborhoods—or so the new mythology reads today.

Moreover, the idea of being black and middle class (or upper class as some would have it) has always carried an element of stigma within black communities. Historically, to be middle class was to have some ostensibly "white" blood, i.e., light skin. This circumstance was another of slavery's many legacies, the caste system within a caste system that awarded privilege to the lighter and more hardship upon the darker, just as the house-slaves of the antebellum myth and reality were the mulatto offspring of miscegenation and the "field niggers" were the darker, more African-looking men and women. After Emancipation and Reconstruction a society of light-skinned privilege emerged; those with lighter skin had education, professional jobs, their own cotillions and balls and clubs. Neither white nor black, they were a Creole society suspended in time.

Or at least this vision of the black middle class, the black middle class before the Civil Rights movement, became a galvanized force in the American imagination. In reality, though some of this version of social history is accurate, it ignores the larger question of what most African Americans held as goals and ideals, how they defined themselves, and what their values were. A great many dark-skinned African Americans became doctors and bank presidents and college professors; and not every light-skinned black person was born with a silver spoon in his or her mouth. Moreover, what most Americans deemed "middle-class" or "bourgeois" values were as much a part of poor families as of the well-to-do: For my own grandfather and great-grandfather and great-great-grandfather and no doubt his father before him, family came first, then God, then the community, and then economic prosperity. They were churchgoing—how otherwise could the African American church have become such a powerful force?—and largely "conservative." Which is not to say their politics was anything like that of the neoconservatives of our day. They were also unable to vote, sent to substandard schools, relegated to the back of the bus, lynched and partitioned—their conservativism was a form of survival, both physical and spiritual, a combination of common sense and shrewd logic. Religion had more to do with how they lived their lives and how they thought than we now could ever really imagine.

But after the necessary and largely successful battles for civil rights, though the reality was not replaced, the image of what black identity consisted of was forever altered. (Ironically, Martin Luther King, Jr., the scion of a well-to-do family, was of dark hue; Malcolm X, son of a minister and sharecropper, was light-skinned with reddish hair.) "Is this black enough for you?" and "Black Power" were slogans of positive affirmation; dark men and women were not only in vogue, but their beauty, long a mark of derision, became a sign of affirmation. To be black became defined by "the struggle" and if you weren't down with the struggle, who were you? And though Gil Scott-Heron declared: "The revolution will not be televised," in the end it was. Televised, broadcast, filmed, photographed, written about. The most curious manifestation of this "revolution"—far from the type of Marxist revolution dreamt of by the Black Panther Power Party—was the blaxploitation films of the '70s. These films—*Shaft, Superfly, The Max*—exemplify, if not typify or even account for—a strange collusion between African American culture and the mass culture. Being black no longer arose from the reality of day-to-day existence, and upon dreams of equality, and health, and education, and a reasonably good life. Being black—no longer colored, no longer Negro—black, came to consist of a deluge of images, largely negative, of violence and drug dealers, prostitution and poverty. And though no one would argue that these elements existed, their preponderance and intensity far outweighed the actual numbers of decent working folk, quietly working, voting, raising their children. These images of glorified gangsterism clutched not only the African American imagination, but also the American imagination as a whole, especially in places where despair could take hold. Though, in truth, a great many factors entered into the equation—economic policies, the slow collapse of the industrial base and modernization, eroding urban infrastructures, chronic unemployment, rising tuition, etc.—as far as identity and perception of what being black is composed, media affected fashion, language, music, food, personal relationships, religion and education in extraordinary ways.

From the natural to jherri curls to shaved heads; from break dancing to rock; from platform shoes to Reeboks; from large church congregations to empty Sunday schools; from Jack and Jill to the Bloods and the Crips; from Shirley Chisholm and Jesse Jackson to Al Sharpton and Colin Powell; from Motown to Def Jam Records; from *Good Times* to the *Jeffersons* to *In Living Color;* from *Soul Train* to *Yo! MTV Raps*—these outward manifestations have become signs of the ways African Americans perceive their culture, themselves. To ask in 1886 or 1966 or 1996: Is this black enough for you? would yield a profoundly disparate set of inferences and commonalities, implications and significations, becoming more and more uncertain, inexact, curiously diffuse—even as mass culture assumes it understands the question and knows the answer, as if the answer were not only self-evident, but also, in many ways, inevitable.

Is this black enough for you?

. . .

What does it mean to be black?

Upon first reading James Baldwin's *Notes of a Native Son,* I was deeply disquieted. Intellectually I understood exactly what he was talking about, and the language, the language of the Bible and its prophets, rang in my head; yet on a gut level I felt, ironically, alienated from his vision. Baldwin grew up poor and struggling in Harlem, harassed by the police as a young man, convinced that the American Republic was hell-bent on his destruction. Though he was a prophet of love, race pervaded his writing. I, on the other hand, had grown up on land that had been in my family for five generations; my grandfather was a successful businessman and my cousins were college professors and colonels. I had known racism of the most visceral sort, but nothing as hellish as what Baldwin had encountered, nor were my scars anywhere near as painful.

I spoke at length with my brother-in-law who had grown up in Harlem, and with friends, and with teachers. Despite having grown up in what Baldwin himself referred to in "Nobody Knows My Name" as the land of "this dreadful paradox" where "the black men were stronger than the white," I felt in some way not black enough, somehow—ridiculously—inauthentic; that, because of his struggles, James Baldwin was somehow closer than I to being a real Negro.

By and by I came to understand, intellectually, how wrongheaded and stupid I had been. Nonetheless I became more and more preoccupied by the idea of blackness; by what people said, what people meant, and how things were. And perhaps more importantly, where I fit in amid the fantasy and the reality. When I came to New York, my confusion over how to define my own black identity simply mounted; especially as talk in the media and even in conversation threw the words "race" and "black" about with such reckless abandon, as if they were saying "apple" or "salmon."

Perhaps the most arresting definition I would find of what it means to be black came from Ralph Ellison's essay "The World and the Jug":

> It has to do with a special perspective on the national ideals and the national conduct, and with a tragicomic attitude towards the universe. It has to do with special emotions evoked by the details of cities and countrysides, with forms of labor and with forms of pleasure; with sex and with love, with food and with drink, with machines and with animals; with climates and with dwellings, with places of worship and places of entertainment; with garments and

> dreams and idioms of speech; with manners and customs, with religion and art, with life styles and hoping and with that special sense of predicament and fate which gives direction and resonance to the Freedom Movement.

He went on:

> More important, perhaps, being a Negro American involves a *willed* (who wills to be a Negro, I do!) affirmation of self against all outside pressures—an identification with the group as extended through the individual self which rejects all possibilities of escape that do not involve basic resuscitation of the original American ideals of social and political justice.

"*Willed* affirmation." "Perspective." "Identification." These words were powerful, yet I still had to ask myself: Affirmation of what? Perspective on what? Identify with what? Though Ellison made supreme sense, I still felt that the country, the world, had undergone such dramatic changes since the segregated 1950s that it was important to rediscover those countrysides and cities, to revisit the places of worship and entertainment, to see afresh the manners and customs. Before I could affirm or identify, I had to go beyond my narrow world and see Black America. Then I ran across a passage in an essay by Zora Neale Hurston:

> The realistic story around a Negro insurance official, dentist, general practitioner, undertaker and the like would be most revealing. Thinly disguised fiction around the well known Negro names is not the answer, either. The "exceptional" as well as the Ol' Man Rivers has been exploited all out of context already. Everybody is already resigned to the "exceptional" Negro, and willing to be entertained by the "quaint." To grasp the penetration of western civilization in a minority, it is necessary to know how the average behaves and lives . . . For various reasons, the average, struggling, non-morbid Negro is the best-kept secret in America.

Though she wrote this in 1950, I felt more than forty years later it still spoke the truth. In fact, considering what I was seeing on television, reading in the newspapers, hearing on the radio, the need was even greater in 1991. And even though she was speaking to the majority culture, I felt a personal need to discover this "best-kept secret" for myself. To calm my soul, I needed to set out, to see for myself, as I wondered about the nature of my own blackness, to take my question on the road. For, according to the U.S. Census Bureau, African Americans live all over this country. I wanted to know what they thought, what they felt about these questions; I wanted to see, in Minnesota and Maine, how black folk lived; I wanted to understand, in Alaska and Arizona, how black folk defined themselves, what they felt their culture was. If, indeed, they felt they had a culture. If "we" were "we." Perhaps even to witness ways of being African American that I had never dreamed of.

Mindful of Du Bois's admonition "to car window sociologists, to the man who seeks to understand and know . . . by devoting the few leisure hours of a holiday trip to unraveling the snarl of centuries," I decided, just the same as he had done, to travel the country, with the intention of devoting nine months to a year to the endeavor. My plan was to trust in fate and serendipity, to plan little and find what I found, to avoid the obvious places, the places written about ad nauseam; to look at the map and follow my curiosity—little did I know it would take years.

Preparing for my journey, I noted with intimidation that in the year of my birth the estimable novelist John A. Williams had set out on a similar task. "Late in September, 1963," *This Is My Country Too* begins, "I set out in search of an old dream, one that faded, came back into focus, and faded again. The search for my America." Reading his account, from Syracuse to Seattle, from Arizona to Louisiana, I—so much the product of integration, affirmative action, the "New South," a Child of the Dream—could not help but be awed and terrified by how he, a man of African descent, was viewed and in turn viewed the United States of America; how he was treated miserably, refused service in restaurants and hotels, witnessed some of the most outrageous discrimination in housing, jobs, education; how perniciously strong were the soon-banished Jim Crow codes. Reading his account, for me, was like reading about another planet, a planet remarkably transformed in the space of my lifetime. But how much had it really changed?

For me there was only one way to find out. With all these questions in my mind, and in my heart, in the summer of 1991, I girded up my loins and my wits and my courage, and packed my bags and books into a quintessentially American jeep—that I named Bucephalus, for though I am not an egomaniac, I am not unambitious—and, heading north on I-95, set out to discover for myself what it meant to be black.

# I

# IN THOREAU'S BACKYARD

> I am writing for myself and strangers. This is the only way that I can do it. Everybody is a real one for me, everybody is like someone else to me. No one of them that I know can want to know it and so I write for myself and strangers.
>
> —Gertrude Stein, *The Making of Americans*

Two

# ONCE UPON AN EDEN

## Or, Looking for the "Old Guard"

*Martha's Vineyard, Massachusetts*

When I asked Dora Grain about the "middle class," her reaction was a few notches short of violent: "What kind of class? I don't know what you mean when you talk about *classes.* What do you mean by that question? Describe to me what you mean by that. Or what the different classes might be." Her voice was deep and throaty, and it had a natural theatricality, aided by her articulateness and righteous passion. "Since you asked the question . . ."

"Well, I'm using the general American perception of . . ."

"You mean somebody who is financially well off?"

"Well, yes. Income, education . . ." The truth is, at this point, I didn't really know what I meant.

Sitting on the sundeck of her Vineyard Haven home, wood-shingled with blue trimming, in wooded seclusion, off a path off yet another path, amid begonias and chirping birds, I felt far away from the frenzied hubbub of downtown Vineyard Haven, almost in a small Eden of Dora Grain's own making.

I had come across Mrs. Grain's name in an article that appeared in a 1983 *Vineyard Gazette:*

> Mrs. Grain was on Main Street, Vineyard Haven this summer. "A man was collecting signatures for [Congressman Gerry] Studds. So on the top is the Vineyard Haven petition. He comes to me and immediately moves the Vineyard Haven petition and brings up the Oak Bluffs petition. Well, I resented that. I said to him, 'Why do you assume I live in Oak Bluffs? Why don't you ask me where I live?'. . . I go into a bank in Vineyard Haven, this is 1976. And I ask

> about safe deposit boxes. And they say to me, 'Wouldn't it be more convenient to get one in Oak Bluffs?' This may sound small. But I consider it a racial assault. It is a major stereotypical attitude."

Almost a decade later, when asked about that statement she says: "It has nothing to do with living in Oak Bluffs. There are some gorgeous areas in Oak Bluffs. I happened to look at some land that was available in Vineyard Haven. What I resent is the idea that 'In New York, all blacks live in Harlem.' I don't care where they meet you, they ask you about Harlem. That to me is a racist assumption. All blacks on Martha's Vineyard do not live in Oak Bluffs. That is not an assumption you should make at all. It's like saying all Jews live in Israel. Not so. They were born in Norway or wherever. It's a racist attitude."

Martha's Vineyard is an island off the coast of Massachusetts and Rhode Island, a part of the archipelago that includes Cape Cod, Narragansett and the Elizabeth Islands, twenty-three miles long and nine miles wide. Long a summer enclave of the northeastern well-to-do—the Kennedys, the McNamaras—far less ostentatious than Newport, yet considered by most to be a socially impeccable place to spend summers. Oak Bluffs, one of the townships on the island, has become known over the years as an enclave of well-to-do blacks.

Mrs. Dora Grain had that intangible but instantly understood quality known as presence. Her hair a silvery mist, her face blushing from the summer sun, she greeted me that August morning in a pink jumpsuit and with an air of regal authority. I felt very much in her domain. To me, though it may be a tired expression, it seemed Dora Grain knew exactly who she was.

"I identify strongly black," she once told a reporter. "I have been active in the trade union movement, in the black movement and the NAACP, and in civil rights causes when it wasn't totally popular. I have been a political and community activist all my life."

Dora Grain had been born in Sumpter, South Carolina, she told me, and moved to Brooklyn at thirteen. Shortly after high school she joined the staff of the CIO labor union (Local 65), which she described at the time as being "very progressive—I guess you would call it a left-wing union." She worked there for ten years, first as secretary to the vice-president, then for organizers, and later for the newspaper.

"Now that was when the war started," she said, "and the editor of the union newspaper was left with no assistant editor, nothing, no one. So I went to help him out, and he taught me so much. I had to go to press with him. Proofread. I wrote headlines. I wrote caption for pictures. Then the next thing I knew he was sending me out on feature stories, and all kinds of assignments, inquiring photographer—I wasn't the photographer, but I was the inquirer. That was a marvelous experience. I interviewed W.E.B. Du Bois just before he went to Africa."

Eventually she became an organizer herself. "I was involved in organizing the unorganized and in strikes and handling grievances between the workers and management." She looked back on those halcyon days with relish, yet with a remarkably clear eye. "There were very few blacks on the staff. But you know, I talked to you about these marvelous young people—yet racism was rampant. As marvelous as they were. I'm looking back at those beautiful years with those beautiful people, and I can cite chapter and verse of racial incidents and racial attitudes coming out of these beautiful people that I loved so much," she said, her voice tinged with a bit of incredulity, a bit of hurt, yet resignation and wisdom.

Perhaps that was the most appealing thing about Dora Grain: this emotionally deep, yet fiercely commonsensical approach to life. Especially when she was discussing her proudest achievements, her children. She had three: Peter, Gail and David. She spoke of how Gail overcame adversity in a predominantly white school in Queens ("I don't know why, but some black kids are embarrassed to be black—somehow it wasn't a problem with her. Black was beautiful. She accepted that, and didn't resist at all. I'm very grateful for that"); how Peter, now a neurosurgeon, "bends her ear" over the phone, talking about his cases ("I said to him, sometimes you sound more like the nurse than the doctor—he's so caring. And this is why patients want him. I have letters from patients to me, thanking me for raising a son to save their life"); how David, now an investment banker, played the timpani in high school ("I wasn't even listening, I was watching him. He was so dramatic. Drama. He's just dramatic at anything. And somehow or other he gets publicity, wherever he is. Somehow photographers or the newspapers, they find him—I just love my kids!"). There is about Mrs. Grain that quintessential maternity so easily stereotyped, so readily attributed to the "black matriarch." But I felt a profound individuality of character, born not so much of hen-like nurturing, but of a continuing wonder at the fact that these three people, her issue, were indeed separate human beings, people she actually liked, when all was said and done.

Nonetheless, I got the strong sense that this joy in her children came after many years of vigilance and work. "My first born, Peter, was in high school during the Civil Rights movement. But Peter was a very studious young guy, and a reader and very interested in all kinds of things. He was never an activist. I was an activist. I was very active in my community, very active in my trade union, very concerned politically. My mother worried very much about the kinds of things I was doing when I was in the union, because I was on picket lines, and I was out speaking on street corners and doing all kinds of things in the early '40s. She couldn't stop me. But for some reason I was concerned about my son. I wanted my children to be intellectually committed to the needs and the rights of black people. But I was scared as hell to have him involved as a Black Panther member. There were some people who were. You'd go into some houses and the parents were shaking in their shoes. But they did what they did. Peter didn't really, I don't know why. I wanted him to feel and understand, and I wanted him to support some of the things these people were doing. But I couldn't bear to have him in danger in any way, and it was dangerous, as we all know. Police were going in shooting Black Panthers for no reason at all. And accusing them of whatever they wanted.

"My youngest son, David, hearing me talk to Gail about black being beautiful, it rubbed off on him. We would read, we would talk. His complexion is darker than Gail's, and when we'd come up here, three days in the sun, that kid would be—as he said one day when he looked at his arms—'Wow! I'm blue-black, and that's fine, because that's my favorite color.' And he took off. When I heard that, I said, 'Bless his heart.' He went into first grade in Gail's school that year, and he came home to me and said he'd met a new friend. I said, 'You met a new friend? He just came to school?' He said, 'No, no, he's been in school since September.' I said, 'How did you meet him?' He said, 'He came up to me today and he said, "You're black." And I said to him, "Yes, and you're white, what's your name?"' And that knocked me out. Isn't that beautiful?

"But David slipped a few times in attitude. The first semester of his senior year in college, he was an intern at the EEOC with Clarence Thomas. And he came back feeling that welfare was bad. I don't know why he did that. I don't know if he had conversations with Clarence Thomas. I don't know what the story was. Or whether he was asked to read certain materials down there. He was at Holy Cross, and Clarence Thomas is a Holy Cross alumnus. But in any case, that was very worrisome to me, because by the early part of his senior year he was already interviewing for jobs, and he was going to work in the investment banking business. It has no relationship to the black community whatsoever. And I was concerned about him, how he might fare in that industry. I had read an article about their attitudes, attitudes toward the poor. This is a *business* industry. It has nothing to do with the poor, blacks or minorities. And I was concerned about him. I saw no reason that he should not go for any job he wanted in any industry, but it was important to me to know who he was so that he could survive and not get lost and not get hurt. I had read an article by a couple of guys in that industry, black guys, and they were talking about their experiences. And I had given it to him. I said, oh, boy, he's not ready to understand who he is and where he is. And how to protect himself. Anyway, he's coming around now. He's fine. He's beginning to understand a little more."

The Grains moved to Martha's Vineyard in 1974. She had first come to the island in 1948, and in the '50s and '60s she had come infrequently, renting from 1965 to 1972, when they decided, after her husband's retirement at age fifty-five from the Postal Service and the sale of his trucking business—and after she herself, at age fifty-three, had received her B.A. in history, the same year as her eldest son—to leave New York City. Their youngest son, David, attended high school on the island. She notes how David fit into the island easily, working in the summers as a tour bus driver, a summer policeman, teaching windsurfing. "I guess he was the 'unusual' black. There were very few off-island blacks living here year-round. He was, and he still is, quite a young man."

Nonetheless, she recognized that though her son seemed welcome, that did not necessarily mean the going would be equally easy for other black folk living in this high-toned Eden.

"Oh racism still exists. We can have an incident in one of the schools anytime now. White parents are not raising their children to respect all people. I guess somebody might accuse me of racism. I have a very hard line on this issue. I'm extremely sensitive to this. I've had a white friend say that I'm defensive. I'm not really being defensive. I am just expressing myself. But whites are not raising their children to respect all people. Not today. And the black community is still filled with self-hate. There is still the old slave-master mentality about color. Still today. No question about it. Among my friends—who I would expect at this point in time to truly believe that Black is Beautiful—no way! It's a little subdued; it's a little less open. But we have a self-hate and they have the racism."

As Mrs. Grain saw things, it was not possible for a black person to be a racist. "Define racism and you'll see that no black person can be a racist. What we are, we are—and I am—reacting. We react viciously to racism. But that doesn't make me a racist. Blacks will call other blacks racists. That is a misnomer. That's a contradiction in terms. We react to racism. We have self-hate. Our self-hate manifests itself in this thinking that a certain color, or straightness of your hair, or what have you, is better. Light is better than dark, or the closer to white you are the prettier you are, the better you are, and so on. That's baloney, that's absolute baloney. And that will stand in our way; that keeps us separated."

In learning to arm her children against racism, Mrs. Grain relied on advice from an interesting source—a good friend who was a professor at a prestigious university, a black man, married to a white woman.

"I talked to him. I had a lot of respect for his opinion and his analysis of things and his way of dealing with some of these things. I asked him: 'How do you keep your children from being destroyed by racism? Is there any way?' He said: 'Of course you can keep your kids from being destroyed by racism.' I said, 'How?' He said: 'Teach them from the time they can hear and understand.' And he went through all these various relationships that one can have with a white human being. Teach them to never trust them—he didn't say don't expect too much, because he was very bitter—and I believe that. When he said it, of course, it was shocking to me. And I said, 'How can you say that when your children have a white mother? How can you when you're at the dinner table or when they're babies, two years old, teach them to hate?' He said: 'You did not listen to me. Did I say hate?' And he repeated it again. *Teach them to never trust them.* And it made a lot of sense. It truly made a lot of sense. Do business, socialize, work with, live with, do all of these things. But don't expect too much. If you don't expect too much you won't be hurt when this dear friend, this person you care a great deal about, exhibits some racist attitude. You will not be hurt—you see, when you get hurt it's when you expect them to be more: 'Oh that was my friend, he would never do this to me.' But if you understand that this can happen, then you won't be destroyed, and it won't even affect the relationship, or the friendship. I told my children that. I worked on the basis of that. Racism is something that we can't get rid of. Even when the struggle is strong it seems to come out."

I was curious to know Dora Grain's take on the so-called black elite living on the island, especially a well-known and influential social group known as the Cottagers, a group thought by some to be the vanguard of Martha's Vineyard black aristocracy, and whether she was a member.

"No, I didn't own a cottage. When I first came, I was renting," she said with a subdued sarcasm.

"Oh, that was prerequisite?"

"I don't know whether I could have joined. You know, it seems to me that's what it's all about. And then when I moved here, I was not interested in summer activities: selling tickets to the fashion show, selling this and selling that. That was not why I came here. I did not feel like a Cottager. I became active in year-round activities and other things. They are too busy in the summer for me. No, I'm not a Cottager. I know a lot of those folk, most of those folk. I have a lot of friends—one of the reasons for feeling so comfortable coming here is because we didn't come to an isolated community."

As I drove away from the Grain home, I felt at once buoyed in spirit and perhaps a little confused. I would come to remember this interview with Dora Grain with a particular personal poignance—she was the very first in a long line of interviews. I was naive, fresh, asked a lot of stupid questions. The fact of the matter was, I had only a vague sense of what it was I was after and how to go about it. I will always look back with gratitude to Mrs. Grain, and bless her for her patience. Though I should not have been, I found myself surprised to have encountered someone like Dora Grain right off, on this island—someone so committed, liberal, dynamic; someone with such a strong resolve and sense of meaning and purpose. But what had I expected to find? Had I been guilty of stereotyping?

Martha's Vineyard in summer is a hubble-bubble of activity, a spectacle of financial privilege and Veblenesque consumption: The Vineyard Haven harbor, with its many boats, aligned in rows and rows like sweet treats, their masts candy sticks in red, blue and green; the lines of little girls hiking down Beach Road; the boys swwooossshing by on bikes; the young women honking the horns of their twenty-nine-year-old Volkswagens; the men toting fishing poles; the kids running, screaming; the mothers shaking their heads and handing out ice-cream cones. A mile down the road, in Oak Bluffs, down Circuit Avenue, the main drag, the crowds were thick in the card shops, the dress shops, the drugstores, at the hot dog, fish and sandwich stands. Over by the water, where Ocean Avenue formed a large and graceful arc overlooking a semicircular park on Nantucket Sound, fronted by quaint Victorian cottage after quaint Victorian cottage, the porches were full of people; and the park was full of Frisbee-throwing people and sunbathing people, and the street was full of more cars and more people, chasing dogs, talking, carrying suntan lotion, walking toward the ocean.

Though it is still a remarkably beautiful island (twilight on the southern side, near Chillmark or Gay Head, away from the stampede in Oak

Bluffs and Vineyard Haven and Edgartown, can be resplendent), the soothing calm of a peaceful beach was nowhere to be seen. Human beings apparently love to be crammed together; they travel far and wide, from the hubbub of Boston and Philadelphia and New York and Hartford and Washington and Chicago and Los Angeles for yet more of the madding crowd.

In Oak Bluffs, to my eye, black people were everywhere, along with others of all shades and hues and nationalities. But the presence of black folk was distinct and apparent: grey-haired ladies munching hot dogs with copies of the *Vineyard Gazette* folded neatly under their arms; sun-visored men with tennis rackets slung over their shoulders; and teenage boys and girls in tee shirts and long shorts and Reeboks, lugging boom boxes playing rap music a bit too loudly; and also, to the eye, the archetypical buppies and preppies and BAPs (Black American Princes and Princesses).

Though many doors were being slammed in my face, figuratively, over the phone ("You've really chosen a bad time; my brother's children, my husband's cousins, my daughter's friends, are visiting." "I'm preparing to go off-island. Closing up the house, sorry." "I've already spoken with two reporters this summer, enough is enough, I'm sorry."), I nonetheless began to get a clearer notion, through casual conversations with this shop owner, that sales clerk, this innkeeper, that visitor—of the sort of people who came to the island. Suzanne de Passe, the ever-elegant president of Motown Productions, scion of an old New York family, held court in Oak Bluffs during the summer. The former Senator Edward Brookes, until recently the only black senator since Reconstruction, had a house just off the Campground. Adam Clayton Powell's first wife had a house in East Chop. Walking down the street one day, I saw Franklin Thomas—then the president of the Ford Foundation, the largest philanthropic organization in the world—a black man from Brooklyn. Many spoke of film director Spike Lee's arrival as a harbinger of a new black elite. This record producer, that real estate magnate, this actor, that actress. And on and on.

I had come to Martha's Vineyard with a mission: Find out if there is or ever was a Black Aristocracy.

When I was in high school I was fascinated with a book by Stephen Birmingham called *Certain People: America's Black Elite*—much to the bewilderment and dismay of my mother. Birmingham had made a career of writing about "elites" of various and sundry groups—Jews, WASPS—and *Certain People* enumerated and enfabled the richest and "most successful" African Americans. Perhaps my fascination had to do with my being an American boy and taking great pleasure in reading the oversimplified Horatio Alger boosterism, myth-made-flesh stories; and perhaps, more importantly, at the time, there were precious few book-length works available to young black boys about black men (or women) who had attained wealth and influence, while white boys—maybe even to their detriment—were bombarded with white success stories daily. Nonetheless, here were publishers and manufacturers of cosmetics and high-priced surgeons and advertising executives living the life of Riley. But Birmingham's focus was not so much on business and money as it was on "class" and "hierarchy." Reading his book was the first real exposure I had to what some called the black Old Guard.

Here was revealed the world of an aristocracy in exile in their own land; a people who perpetuated within their circles all the codes and manners of a bygone time: printed invitations, white-gloved cotillions, dressing for dinner. Here was a world where light skin was more valuable than gold, and a congenital connection to Thomas Jefferson or George Washington or Peter Stuyvesant—or at least to be the descendant of an antebellum freedman ("My people were never in bondage!")—was considered priceless. To be sure, I saw this world as ridiculous even at the time, and twenty-some years later, I hoped it was extinct. Yet even as a teenager, I recognized how inherently sad it would be to belong to such a world, reveling in a culture that at base despised you, and being in turn despised by those dark brothers and sisters you had no recourse but to despise back. But the confusing and alarming aspect of this middle (or upper-middle or upper) class was the component that constituted their right to gentry. Was it money? Was it lineage? Was it skin color? Unlike the European aristocracy on which this Old Guard assiduously based itself, there were no king and vassals, no titles and money and land being handed down from marquis and viscounts, with order apparent and understood.

For within the American ideology few things other than race incite so much discomfort, so many heated denials and trite dismissals, as "class"—not the class of style and grace and manners, but the class of caste and place in society. You often hear: "Of course there is no such thing as class in the United States. It's a free country. You can become anything you want to become. Be who you want to be." Just as race is fraught with economic, political and cultural land mines, so too can the discussion of class blow up in your face. And in the end, though money has a lot to do with it, class is about values, received, assumed, adopted, reported, cherished and despised. College education, the type of car you purchase, the brand of clothing you wear, where you vacation, whether you are Episcopalian or Free Will Baptist, Republican or Democrat, play golf and tennis or bowl and play basketball, all pertain to class. Of course many of these "values" have to do with whether you can afford them, but ultimately, regardless how superficial or deeply rooted, America (with its heroes from Andrew Carnegie to Jay Gatsby to Michael Jordan) is a society obsessed with stratification, with "upward" mobility. As literary historian and essayist Paul Fussell insightfully points out: "Despite our public embrace of political and judicial equality, in individual perception and understanding—much of which we refrain from publicizing—we arrange things vertically and insist on crucial differences."

In his book *Class,* Fussell sets out with great perception and humor to define and debunk the American caste system. He divides American classes into: low, middle and high proletariat; low, middle and high middle class, and upper class, old and new (read: old money and *nouveau riche*). In America, he believes, class is an amalgam of many factors, including money, inheritance, geography, religion, education, occupation, and that the hypocrisy of Americans of all classes is the denial that we make these distinctions. Often having little to do with reality, these social myths are how people categorize themselves, consciously and unconsciously. Among African Americans the concept of class is fraught with damnable complexities and ambiguities and misperceptions. This reality is especially true of the black middle class.

Perhaps the most damning indictment of the black middle class is E. Franklin Frazier's 1957 *Black Bourgeoisie: The Rise of a New Middle Class in the United States.* "Gertrude Stein would have been near the truth" he writes,

> if she had said of the black bourgeoisie what she said of Negroes in general, that they "were not suffering from persecution, they were suffering from nothingness," not because as she explained, the African has "a very ancient but a very narrow culture." The black bourgeoisie suffers from "nothingness" because when Negroes attain middle-class status, their lives generally lose both content and significance.

The sociologist and chair of Howard University's Sociology Department, after years of tabulating data, especially on the black middle class of Washington, D.C., Frazier concluded that though they were obsessed with money, they owned little. Though they ran organizations supposedly dedicated to the uplifting of black folk, they puffed themselves up in their own press, swirling over the heads of their less fortunate brothers and sisters, while being only a few feet from the basement themselves. Here "a class structure slowly emerged which was based upon social distinctions such as education and conventional behavior, rather than upon occupation and income." Beset by insecurities, self-hatred, and guilt, "excessive drinking and sex seem to provide a means for narcotizing the middle-class Negro against a frustrating existence." Frazier condemns them for a "spirit of play or lack of serious effort" which has "tended to encourage immaturity and childishness on the part of middle-class Negroes whose lives are generally devoted to trivialities."

Frazier had much to say about the negligible size of African American business in the 1940s: "the average volume of business of 3,866 Negro businesses in 12 cities was only $3,260." He notes that over 90 percent of these were retail and service establishments—grocery stories, barbershops, auto-mechanics; and that the total volume of sales for food stores, 37 percent of black business, was only $24 million, "or less than two dollars for each Negro in the United States"; that the remaining 9 percent—newspapers, cosmetics firms, banks, insurance companies, etc.—had an aggregate value of sales and assets of below $75 million in 1940. Moreover, the median income for African Americans was 51 percent of whites', with less than 1 percent earning equal the amount of the majority of white white-collar workers, about .001 percent of all Americans. Such statistics led Frazier to conclude that black business was "insignificant" and able to "wield no political power as a class."

Clearly Frazier was disgusted by what he saw as a spiritually, psychologically and emotionally bankrupt group of people who, "Lacking a cultural tradition and rejecting identification with the Negro masses on the one hand, and suffering from the contempt of the white world on the other," had "developed a deep-seated inferiority complex." And, having "accepted unconditionally the values of the white bourgeois world: its moral and its canons of respectability, its standards of beauty and consumption . . . the members of the black bourgeoisie in the United States seem to be in the process of becoming NOBODY."

Needless to say, *Black Bourgeoisie* became instantly controversial upon its publication in France in 1955, and even more so when published in English in the United States. Though many angrily dismissed the work out of hand (the NAACP leaders called it superficial, and some accused Frazier of playing into the hands of the enemy by giving them more ammunition to fire upon black people), a number of Frazier's fellow sociologists recognized that the work was serious and not so easily dismissed—though their praise for his years of work and mountain of data was not unqualified or without strong criticism.

Frazier was accused of failing to use enough "empirical" data to have done an adequate job. He was taken to task for not substantiating his claims of "suffering psychological effects," and for overlooking many of the positive aspects in the lives of the black middle class of his day. Moreover, one critic pointed out that if the word "black" were taken out of Frazier's book, we would be left with a portrait of the general American bourgeoisie—which leads to an entirely different set of questions.

By the 1990s, of course, the financial footing of the black middle class had shifted dramatically. According to the U.S. Census Bureau, over 54 percent of African Americans in the 1980s earned over $25,000 a year, making them effectively "middle class." One in seven black families was considered to be "affluent" or earned over $50,000 a year. Today, the largest "black-owned" company, TLC Beatrice International Holdings, Inc., has sales of over $1 billion dollars and collectively black-owned businesses earn over $13 billion combined, and the personal fortunes of Dr. William H. Cosby, Jr., Oprah Winfrey, Shaquille O'Neil and Russell Simmons alone point out how different a world Black America has become since the days of Dr. Frazier's study.

All that said, it must be noted that economically the average African American's situation is far from healthy. As of 1989 the poverty rate was over 30 percent for African Americans, and almost another 30 percent of African Americans own no comparably significant assets whatsoever. The gap between the median net worth of blacks and whites is almost $40,000. Black business is dwarfed by the combined revenue of American businesses at $2.8 trillion in 1995; and though African Americans as a group earned over $300 billion in 1990—making them the tenth largest "market" in the world, the total citizenry of the United States earned $3.6 trillion. (Though not "insignificant," as Frazier deemed the financial clout of black America in the 1950s, it is certainly small by comparison.)

Yet so much else has changed since those times, changes that are not all economic. As Martin Kilson wrote in "*The Black Bourgeoisie* Revisited," in the early '80s: "Frazier's view . . . attribut[ed] too much significance to social class as such." And Frazier failed to identify the complex influences wrought by racism on the self-image of his subjects, nor did he discuss those families who cultivated "strong black ethnocentrism in their children."

The difference between the black middle class now and then is "fundamental," Kilson writes, "the old black bourgeoisie faced a fierce ceiling on its professional and social mobility; the new black bourgeoisie, while still confronting residual racism, takes over much of the professionalism and mobility dynamics of the white bourgeoisie." Today with the Congressional Black Caucus (though with only one African American senator), with blacks on the boards of major corporations, as presidents of professional associations (like the American Medical Association) and foundations, as secretaries of entire government cabinet-level departments, and chairs of national political parties—political and economic power for African Americans is neither insignificant nor vestigial. Though some may disagree, Kilson believes a "deracialization" is afoot, and, as a result, the need to "ape white 'high society'" is no longer important to the black bourgeoisie. "The energies and resources that generate black upward mobility now can be harnessed in behalf of bona fide influence and power in the American mainstream—though racist constraints, while weakening, have by no means disappeared and must be dealt with."

Whether or not that is the case, for me the whole debate boiled down to the comment of one of Frazier's contemporaries, Lewis Towley, who mused: "There are, after all, Negroes who are aristocrats in the true meaning of the term, which has nothing to do with the genteel or the snobbish. They are gentlemen and gentlewomen in their cultural appreciation, intellectual achievement, and civic responsibility. Is it impossible that in time they will come to be the models to emulate?" Is this not ultimately what is at issue? I asked myself.

As I bumbled about Martha's Vineyard in search of this mysterious thing called the black middle class, this antiquated aristocracy, I slowly came to understand how beside the point and in vain my search was; that though this rarefied world might still exist, in the end the mythology and reality surrounding class and race made its existence less compelling than the very real changes being wrought all around it, and around me, in the stewing soup that is American society.

Originally called Noe-pe (Algonquin for "amid the water"), Martha's Vineyard, like most of New England, exists uneasily amid the waters of Native American and English and American history. A quaintness born from an overzealous need to hearken back to England, a tenacious clinging to a prettified history masking how the land came into European hands, and a uniquely American blend of individualism, capitalism, social stratification and denial. Religion in particular—as in all America—played a significant role in shaping the Martha's Vineyard of today.

After invasions by the Portuguese and the Dutch, the English took possession in 1602, and Bartholomew Gosnold renamed the island after his daughter, Martha, and for the abundance of wild grapes found there. Thomas Mayhew, in 1642, was made Lord Governor, and the former missionary, heaven-bent on "reclayming and civilizing" the Pokanauket people ("I have alwaies Judged myselff uncharitable enough to the Indians & too apt to take offence against them, though it has been usually apprehended to the contrary"), set the island on its curious course of merging religion with capital. In the late seventeenth and eighteenth centuries, along with the building due to the whaling boom, came a group known as the Exhorters. Beginning in 1835 these "unorthodox" Methodists would pitch tents on the northeastern part of the island, preaching, praying, crying beneath full moons in an open-air tabernacle of oak trees, near a swampy, landlocked pond. Their revivals grew year after year, and fifty years later, that pond became a harbor, and Campground, as it became known, was taken in by Cottage City of America, a resort-by-the-sea, named thusly due to the multitudes of Victorian gingerbread homes that sprang up all around the harbor. The resort officially broke with the old whaling town of Edgartown in 1906 to become Oak Bluffs.

As the American religion transformed from crying after God to pining after money, so did Oak Bluffs evolve from a febrile prayer meeting into the popular pursuit of life, liberty and happiness.

There existed in Martha's Vineyard a significant black population as early as 1765. A number of freedmen settled on the island, many marrying among the Chappaquiddick and Wampanoag. Laborers, sailors, craftsmen came; some were even drawn by the religious fervor on the northeastern shore. Black ministers came to preach at Campground. In 1856 Father John F. Wright of the Colored People's College of Ohio (now Wilberforce) preached and raised money for his school; in 1858 Joshia Henson (the model for Harriet Beecher Stowe's Uncle Tom) came to visit and "exhort"; in 1867 the Reverend Allen A. Gee came asking for funds to build a school for Negroes in Tennessee. And though no blacks were allowed to purchase houses in Campground until the late 1970s, many settled in a section of Oak Bluffs called the Highlands. Most survived by doing the laundry, cooking, cleaning, and caring for the children of the white folk.

Adelaide M. Cromwell, in an article entitled "The History of Oak Bluffs as a Popular Resort for Blacks," argues that there are three groups of Island black folk: the year-rounders, a close-knit group, by necessity, who survive on the local economy; those who come for summer work, either as employees or for entrepreneurial pursuits; and the third group, who started showing up in the 1890s, the monied leisure folk, who gave Oak Bluffs its current reputation. Upon this latter group was founded or projected or extracted the grandiloquent notion of the black elite of Oak Bluffs.

"I started my own business in Springfield," Mr. Graves was telling me. "A machine shop. We never thought we'd ever move down here. But a friend of ours was in the real estate business and he called us when we were coming for a weekend to get away from this business. He said, 'Well come on down, I've got a house for you to look at.' He showed us this house which we're living in now. We were waiting to get off Island, it was a holiday, George Washington's Birthday, and we didn't have reservations, so you had to wait in line to get off of here, and we got stuck in Vineyard Haven all day, and there was a sign on this building down there at the marina that said 'Machine and Marine,' and I said, 'Wonder what the Machine means?' So I went and looked and the place was closed, but there was an old gent working on his boat in the back, who happened to be the father of the guy who owned the place. And he said, 'Yeah, there's a machine shop in there, but my son don't know nothing about it and he don't want to do nothing with it.' So he gave me his name; and I called him and we put our heads together and me and him hit it off real good. And God—two months later we were here."

Mr. Robert Graves was a huge, bearded, Santa Claus of a man, with enormous hands, which, at the time I spoke with him, were stubbornly stained with grease. He was the color of fine blond oak, a complexion he shared with his wife, Mrs. Shirley Graves, though her face sported girlish freckles. Graves Tool & Dye, the family concern, was housed not too far from downtown Oak Bluffs. The structure itself was something of a cross between an old country store (the Graveses also sell tackle and bait) and a garage. Outside were gas pumps.

The interior of the Graves Tool & Die Company had the cluttered, dusky look of many a shop. Mrs. Graves's desk, where she helped with paperwork, was not far from her husband's, which was next to the door that led to the main floor, full of chains and pulleys and metal and tools. Above Mr. Graves's desk was an arrow. He shot his first deer with it. You could see the dark blood still on the tip of the arrow. Mr. Graves liked to hunt: deer, geese, rabbit. "He loves to fish," Mrs. Graves told me. "I just loved the island, and he just loves to fish. Here he'd have the two of them: he could work here and fish whenever he felt like it."

Business was going quite well for the Graveses. Their contracts to make tools came from North Carolina; Tennessee; Annapolis, Maryland; Boston. Contracts for small parts, fittings. "They send me prints and I quote on them; and subsequently they award it. And if I get the job then I do it, get the steel and make the parts."

They told me about their decision to move to the island. Apparently, early on, Mrs. Graves became emotionally attached to it: "I use to cry when I had to go home. I just loved this place. And Robert talked to Mr. West, the father, and we worked it out. It's pretty good. They have some problems like you have anyplace else. But the things that people talk to us about, I can't say it's all racial. I mean, we have people talk about their jobs, or something like that. Where they might have been let go from their job. But when you investigate and look right down deep into it, part of it was their fault. Some people will try it, you know: 'He did it because I was black.' But after you look into it. I don't think we've had any case where we really thought that that was the sole reason."

"It's here," said Mr. Graves, "but it's under . . ."

"It's under, yeah . . ."

"It doesn't surface hardly at all."

"I think though," Mrs. Graves said after some reflection, "it's a problem in itself. I really do. And in school. I think there are a lot of little racial slurs and things among the children."

"There aren't very many black children out here," said Mr. Graves. "Most of your black people on the island are retirees."

"Many of them."

"The ratio is largely toward the retirees, than they are toward the young couples bringing families out here."

"Yeah, because there's no jobs," Mrs. Graves observed.

"There aren't jobs, unless you've got your own business or a profession. It's not an easy place to live."

"Finding year-round housing is sad," his wife added. "You have to buy a house. And kids don't have the money to buy a house. So what happens is that the people who were born here, they're like nomads; they move twice a year. It's what you call a winter rental. You go in in September or October, but they have to be out by May. Because everybody starts renting their house by the week. And they can't afford it."

"Some of them have been doing it all their life," said Mr. Graves. "They don't own any furniture, they own nothing."

Mrs. Graves said: "So therefore, the kids, when they get out of high school or college or something, they don't settle here. They go on. They come back for summer or holidays or stuff. But very few settle here; and there are very few young people who come with children. So there are a very small number of black children on the island. Like I said, I think they will have more problems than the adults, I'll say our age or older."

The Graveses had been married for forty years. Mrs. Graves was related to the arctic explorer Matthew Henson. Her great-grandfather had been a slave who escaped to Canada on the Underground Railroad. Both had roots in Columbia, South Carolina, where Mr. Graves's mother had been born, and their families had been close in Springfield, Massachusetts, where they married, and raised eight children (six boys and two girls). They would bring their children to Martha's Vineyard on vacations. Now four children live on the island. One son died, and they buried him there.

Mrs. Graves was a registered Democrat. Mr. Graves was registered as a Republican. Though, "I seldom vote Republican," he told me.

I wondered aloud about how much contact the Graveses had with the rich and powerful summer residents of Oak Bluffs.

"Well they have all of this stuff, you see," Mrs. Graves told me. "Their dances and their parties and stuff happen only in the summertime, because they don't live here year round. And in the summertime we're busy working, plus having people come to visit. You don't really get into going around."

Mr. Graves said, "We don't socialize with the upper-class blacks. We know 'em; but we don't go to the parties."

"That's particularly because of that happening during the summer," said Mrs. Graves. "Now during the winter there aren't that many things going on. They do have the cocktail parties and so on. But most of the people who live here, they're working or they've got company, people coming to visit. And how're you going to go to somebody's house with six more people?"

"We never got mingled in with a lot of them," said Mr. Graves. "We know a lot of them. We know a lot of the wealthy, professional people. And everybody knows each other, especially those New York people, they all know each other. They socialize together. And once in a while we'll go to a function or something where everybody is together. A lot of them have been coming for years and years and they've known each other for years and years. It's a pretty close-knit little group."

"They spend a lot of time with their friends," Mrs. Graves said.

Mrs. Graves went to the local Catholic church. Not because she was Catholic—she was Episcopalian—but because she found most Protestant churches on the island "very cool." Mr. Graves didn't attend because there weren't any predominantly black churches on the island. "No good ole foot-stomping, Baptist churches, and I ain't going into any of them. There are some nice Baptist churches and stuff, and I've been to them. Back home, you know, the choir, the good ole foot-stomping preacher up there, breathing fire and brimstone and whatnot. I do miss that. When I say I miss it, it's not like I went to church that much. But when I went that's where I would like to go. I miss that part of it."

Mr. Graves sometimes listened to country music. "And she makes me feel guilty. Because they're all white. 'Listening to them rednecks', she says. That's why I feel guilty when I listen to them. I do like some country and western."

"Not just me," Mrs. Graves said, "the kids too."

They both despised rap music. "Terrible," Mrs. Graves said. "There's no depth." "Some of it's filthy I guess," Mr. Graves said. "When they first started it they had something to say, you know? Now all they're doing is yakking. It ain't singing, it ain't music as far as I'm concerned."

Mr. Graves told me that when he first started out, the tool- and dye-making trade was closed to black folk. "I finally got a Jewish fellow to hire me. He taught me the dye-making trade. I learned the rest on my own. My father was a tool grinder; he always wanted me to be a tool maker. 'If you ever get a chance to get that trade, learn it, no matter what kind of crap you got to take, or what you got to do, learn it. Once you learn it, they can't take it away from you,' he said, 'and eventually, you know, you'll work at that trade.' And it worked out that way, exactly that way. 'Cause war hit, the Korean War, then they had to look over your color, they had to look at what experience you had. Then I started getting good jobs. I couldn't work my way up in these places to be boss or nothing. But I was qualified and as good as anybody else that was walking around, any place I went. It started getting better, when they started making them open up government work. As I worked along I got into all the trades, I mastered all of it, dye making, toolmaking, gauge making, and I went into every aspect of it, I learned all of it, you know. And like I say, I was never out of work for a day in my life."

"Never collected any unemployment," added Mrs. Graves.

"Never collected any unemployment; we never were on welfare. I raised eight kids; a stubborn wife." We all laughed. "And eventually we got to a point where I could start my own business, and this would have never happened, you know, before the 60s. It would have never happened."

Our conversation ranged far and wide that afternoon, from "reverse discrimination" (Mr. Graves: "There's no such thing! Now that we're getting our rights, and everything is due to us, then they're using that 'reverse discrimination' to halt it. Affirmative action is the only way we got a chance to get jobs and opportunities."), to mixed marriages (Mrs. Graves: "I go along with it as a kind of something that's done. But to me I don't understand how in all of these people in our race, you cannot find another person, in your own race, to marry. I just don't particularly like it. But as I say, I have some friends that are in mixed marriages that are very nice. I guess you have to take it one person at a time."), to the problems facing the black youth of today (Mr. Graves: "Every kid should have a chance, every black kid in America should have a chance to use their mind. Instead of watching drug dealers on the corner. I feel so sorry for our people in the city, they're going right down the drain. Two generations of this crap. They haven't got a chance. They haven't got a snowball's chance in hell, except school. You got to teach them, let the schools take responsibility to show them what's right and what's wrong. That's all you can do." Mrs. Graves: "But they have to have the support at home, and in the churches, to make sure that they know . . ."). We even discussed the term "African American."

"I like it better than black American," Robert Graves said. "'Black' never set good with me. Period. 'Cause when I grew up, 'black' meant fight. If somebody called you black you fought them. It was next to nigger. It never set with me right. And it's not because I'm light skinned or anything. It's just because I didn't like it. And when they started that 'black is beautiful' crap, we went along with it, you know, but . . ."

"Well," Mrs. Graves interrupted, "under those terms black *is* beautiful. Trying to be proud of yourself, you know, I can understand that."

"I like that African American. I like that much better than anything we've called ourselves."

"Yeah, we've run the full gamut."

I genuinely hated to leave the Graveses' good company—though I was keeping them from work. I found it difficult not to be taken by their warmth and decency and an openness that made me feel more at home than I could have imagined on a place with a reputation like Martha's Vineyard—balm to a lonely traveler. I wanted to go fishing with Mr. Graves, and eat the catch with some of Mrs. Graves's potato salad and baked beans.

Through the days, among the crowds and crowds, biking, moped-ing retirees and college loafers and high schoolers and screaming babies that punctuated virtually every hour with noise—I noticed a lot of exposed skin, especially on the beach by Beach Road. Bronze and teak and pink and cream and mahogany and beige, of all hues and shades, textures, and densities. The sight uplifted me; it reminded me how beautiful—not just black people—but all people can be, in their skins, together.

I couldn't help thinking of a legend I had recently read:

Moshup, a god of Native American lore, was supposed to live in the west of the island, somewhere near what is now called Gay Head. One legend says that Katama, the beautiful daughter of a shaman, fell in love with a man of another station. She sought out the god, who was smoking at the time. In answer to her plight Moshup reached over to his left side, emptied his pipe into the ocean, and, after a great commotion, there arose Nantucket Island, a place for the young lovers.

The gods, I contemplated, had no problem with difference. Why does man?

I had been warned. I had been told that it would be next to impossible: "She's very busy, you know." "She doesn't really see many people these days. A bit hounded, you understand." I even hesitated to call; I didn't want to be a nuisance. But I knew I had to at least make the effort; I knew I would never forgive myself if I let the opportunity to speak with a living legend get away without even a try.

Strangely enough, her number was listed. I called, and Dorothy West herself, the "last survivor of the Harlem Renaissance," answered.

Dorothy West visited Martha's Vineyard in 1909 for her first birthday, and lived on the Island since 1943. At the time of my call she had been the author of a single novel, *The Living Is Easy,* which is considered a classic by many.

In an interview with Edie Clark in *Yankee* magazine, she speaks of her father, Isaac Christopher West: "My father was born a slave, and he was freed at the age of seven, and my grandfather was born a slave. I never thought to ask them how was slavery. I think it's because I know what a slave was."

In his maturity her father would become known as Boston's "black banana king." After opening a restaurant at age ten with his mother in Richmond, Virginia, and hopping a train, in his teens, to Springfield, Massachusetts, where he ran a fruit stand, in his early twenties Isaac began what became a successful produce business in Boston's Haymarket Square. Though he did not die a wealthy man, while he lived he provided handsomely for his family. And in "a fragile black community in the North, where janitors and caterers were the leaders and blacks who could afford it hired Irish maids," Mr. West held a most esteemed position.

She remembers, in an essay entitled "Fond Memories of a Black Childhood":

> We were Black Bostonians on a train full of white ones. Because we were obviously going the same way, laden as we were with all the equipment of a long holiday, we were subjected to intense speculation as to what people with our unimpressive ancestry were doing on a summer sojourn that was theirs by right of birth. . . . The early blacks were all Bostonians, which is to say they were neither arrogant nor obsequious. Black Bostonians were taught very young to take the white man in stride or drown in their despair. Their survival was proved by their presence on the island in pursuit of some happiness.

Heiress to a rare black Bostonian tradition, Dorothy West chose an even rarer, and sometimes stranger path. After attending Girl's Latin School and Boston University, she went to Columbia University and stayed in New York. This was the 1920s. "She had grown up used to having whatever she wanted," one article says. "In New York she lived on frankfurters and pineapple juice." While writing and editing for the New York *Daily News* and the *Saturday Evening Quill,* she became involved with writers and poets and singers, and the broad array of African American artists and luminaries who were flourishing at the time.

Even before she came to New York she had been exchanging love letters with Countee Cullen. Langston Hughes called her "the Kid." She was doted upon by the great spiritual singer and composer, Harry T. Burleigh. She borrowed Zora Neale Hurston's apartment once. And when in London she stayed with Paul and Eslanda Robeson. ("We didn't know it was the 'Harlem Renaissance'! It was called that *afterward.* We were all just struggling, trying to eat, and some of us were dying of TB. But the important thing was we were all young," she wrote in *Yankee* magazine.) But she was no slacker. Along with her editorial work, she was publishing stories left and right, and at seventeen she won a national literary award from the Urban League.

At twenty she auditioned for *Porgy & Bess,* and though she didn't get a speaking role, she went to London (in 1929) as an extra and later would go with Langston Hughes and other artists and artistes to Russia to make films about "the unfortunate lives of Black Americans" in 1932. Russians came from miles away, excited to see black people. "They were lovely and friendly and sang and danced for us."

She had intended to go on to China, but word reached her that her father had died, and she returned to Boston instead. Though he had been well-to-do for most of her life, her father's business reversals left Dorothy West with no grand inheritance. So she worked for two years at what was called then Home Relief (the Public Welfare Department). When West returned to New York in the mid-'30s she discovered that the "Renaissance" was over. Zora and Langston were gone; America was in the deepest depression in history; and most of the artists she had known were decamped all about the country. As a response of sorts Dorothy West founded *Challenge* in 1935, a magazine devoted to the writings of old "new" Negroes—James Weldon Johnson, Eslanda Robeson, Claude McKay, Arna Bontemps, Countee Cullen, Zora Neale Hurston, Frank G. Yerby (Ms. West wrote under the pen name Mary Christopher). It became *New Challenge* in 1937 and Richard Wright was its associate editor.

*Challenge* was indeed a challenge, but remarkably, this supposedly pampered Bostonian "child" (the writer Wallace Thurman wrote to her: "You are as naive as ever . . . *Challenge* lacks significance or personality—it is too pink tea and la de da . . . too high schoolish") nonetheless ran her enterprise with no financial backers other than herself. She could not pay her writers, yet many of her fellow black writers sent praise her way. Zora Neale Hurston "rejoiced that she had learned at last the glorious lesson of living dangerously," Adelaide Cromwell wrote in an afterword to *The Living Is Easy.* However, sometime around 1937, a serious threat came from—of all places—the American Communist Party. They made it clear to her—perhaps misinterpreting her trip to Russia—that they wanted *New Challenge* under their sphere of influence. When she understood that their intentions were quite real (a similar pressure drove Richard Wright from Chicago), in a Medea-like gesture, she killed the magazine rather than lose control.

After a stint with the Writer's Project of the WPA, she returned to Oak Bluffs to be with her aging mother, Rachel. "Because as a child, I thought it was always summer here, and no one ever called me nigger."

In 1948 Houghton Mifflin published *The Living Is Easy,* one of a handful of books published by black women in the '40s.

Ms. West began working with the *Vineyard Gazette* in 1965, handling subscriptions and billing; a few years later she began to write columns, at first under a pseudonym ("The Highlands Water Boy"); later she would write a weekly column about the black "summer colony," and in 1975 it was turned into a column called "Oak Bluffs" covering the year-round activities of that community. During the period I spoke to her, between May and October, she had a job as a restaurant cashier to supplement her income, and in the winter, between and around work for the newspaper, she was working on her second novel.

Speaking with her on the phone, I came to understand that the newspapers weren't the only thing keeping her busy these days. "Oh, dearie," she said, "I've just come back from Radcliffe; and this woman has sent me this questionnaire for a piece she's doing on the Harlem Renaissance, and I'm working on a novel, and I really need to . . ."

The litany, the gentle brush-off, was reminiscent of certain women publishing executives I'd known in New York: genteel, considerate, rapid, direct though sweet.

"I don't know, darling child . . ." Her voice held that quality which assures you its owner will suffer no indignity, strong, self-assured. This woman was no pushover. It reminded me of that axiom of my youth: dignity and respect beget dignity and respect.

Ten years before our conversation, *The Living Is Easy* had been reissued to acclaim from scholars of both women's studies and African American letters. For years she had never left Martha's Vineyard. But now, she told me, she was being given awards and honors and attention and invitations—invitations that, though gratifying, now crowded and intruded upon her life.

The home of Dorothy West's childhood was down by the harbor, where Our Market stands now. A big Victorian, during the summer it housed cousins, uncles and aunts from Boston. (Her father hated the Island and never came with the family.) The house burned down in 1912. Instead of rebuilding, they moved to a smaller cottage, inland, on a quiet road. It was here, in the early '40s, that Dorothy West wrote her first novel.

To this day *The Living Is Easy* remains singular and unusual within the African American canon, for it deals with a world little visited in American letters—the Boston black middle class of Dorothy West's youth. Cleo Jericho Judson is the wife of Bartholomew Judson, "The Black Banana King." He is twenty-three years older than his wife, who is characterized as a sly, manipulative schemer who even calls him "Mr. Nigger." Certainly at the time of publication, and for decades after, Cleo was unique in black literature. Personally empowered, dominant, beautiful, and well-to-do, she is more victimizer than victim; more daughter than mother; more beloved than lover. Admittedly a roman à clef, figures from the black Boston of West's youth are readily recognizable: aside from her father—and other members of her family—there is the activist Monroe Trotter, and J. H. Lewis, the black man who ran what was to become Filene's department store. Dorothy West takes on the entire milieu of Boston "Colored Society"—the color consciousness, the insularity, the scandals of interracial marriage, gambling, failure—all of which she eschewed long, long ago. "I'm a writer and I guess my thing has always been, well, we'll go it alone."

I wanted desperately to speak with Dorothy West. ("Really, I think we'll have to do it some other time, darling child." *Darling child!* I was utterly charmed and disarmed.) I wanted to ask about this world that she knew perhaps more intimately and accurately than anyone else alive; this world of the so-called black bourgeoisie that she had seen personally from top to bottom; this world where she had no doubt witnessed the grandeur and the self-hate and the pettiness and the politics of skin and pedigree; a world she would have been able to articulate and penetrate to the very heart, I was sure. But it was not going to happen.

"Maybe if you can come back in the off-season . . ." Nonetheless, I felt somewhat blessed to have at least spoken, so to speak, with history.

Ironically, four years later, after forty-two years, in her early eighties, Dorothy West published her second novel, *The Wedding,* which went on to become a national best-seller, even hailed by some as a masterpiece. (Ms. West's editor, to whom the novel is dedicated, was none other than Jacqueline Kennedy Onassis, who had a summer house in Edgartown.) The next year she published a book of stories and reminiscences, *The Richer, The Poorer,* and in these two volumes, she answered all the questions I would have asked her that day, perhaps even some I would not have known to ask.

*The Wedding* is the story of Shelby Cole, from the complicated and well-regarded black family of a wealthy physician from New York, a family who summers at a cottage in Oak Bluff's Highland area. Shelby's dilemma (engaged to an "approved" white man, yet tempted by a social-climbing black man) lays bare—as only fiction can do—the spider's web of prejudice and snobbishness, of light-skinned-mindedness and class consciousness: all dynamics I was struggling to understand. Dorothy West was saying, with all the wisdom and pathos and assured comprehension of Euripides, to me, to the world: Yes, darling child, this world exists, lives are wrecked, hearts are broken, fortunes lost, on the shoals of ugly and petty illusions, just as everywhere else: Beware and pity anyone who follows this silly path.

Dorothy West died in 1998.

I had tried desperately, for almost a week, to reach the renowned Vera Shorter, president of the famous Cottagers, Inc., but to no avail. I left messages, called often, beseeched others for help, but the aforementioned frenetic activity of the Cottagers had locked Mrs. Shorter up and away. Near the end of my stay on the island, I did reach a voice on the end of the line. I thought I would leave a message again, would attempt to find a time in Mrs. Shorter's schedule. The woman with whom I spoke, much to my surprise, had strong words for the Cottagers, calling them "siddity" and "uppity," much to my surprise. I was trying, and trying very hard, to keep an open mind about what I encountered; understanding how people would regard certain social functions, social circles; I had not met this woman, who had access to more than I, yet here again I was confronted by visceral opinion. What was I to do?

1:30 a.m. From my open window I hear loud voices. I go to the window. A black woman and a black man are trying to cross the street. A white man, I can see in a car, is discourteous, has said something I couldn't hear. The woman yells back at him. The white man says, "Get out of the road, nigger." The black woman is furious. The black man pulls the woman from the street, trying to calm her. "Hey, check this out," she keeps saying. "Check this out!" She is as angry with her friend as she is with the white man; she wants to fight.

Eden, too, of course, is a myth.

"Come on, Randall, it's beautiful. How could you want to be anywhere else?" We were in a coffee shop, A Taste of Italy, up high in a wooden complex on the harbor. The sunset was so arresting we stopped and went to the balcony to look.

I had no intention of arguing. The idea of arguing with Marla Blakey seemed somehow philistine. As prepossessing as the sunset, she was a fiery beauty with bewitching green eyes and truly bronze skin. Marla wore no shoes on the Island; Marla never took her keys from her car;

Marla never locked her door. There was something wild and cynically savvy about Marla Blakey, even electric. I was hoping to tap into that heady brainscape, hoping to gain a little more insight into the people on the Island who happened to be black.

When asked about the Old Guard and the Island's reputation, I was somewhat surprised by her answer.

"Maybe because I've just been around that type of stuff all my life, I pay it no mind. It means nothing to me. Because as far as I'm concerned, I don't care if you're black, white, green or yellow, if you want a Mercedes, then buy the damn thing. It doesn't make you any better than me, or less. There are people up here that drive Mercedes; they are people that ride around in their little raggedy cars—like me. It exists here only because they take themselves very seriously; which is unfortunate. As far as I'm concerned I'm more than happy to be around successful black people that are doing things, their own things, owning homes, and sending their kids to Harvard—I think that's marvelous. So it exists here, and it also exists in every other part of the country. You know, it's a myth that this whole island is full of people like that.

"You know what it is? I guess it's because I know them all. They're all just regular old people. It's just that some of them take themselves a little too seriously, that's all. You can walk out on that beach any day of the week and Ron Dellums will be sitting out there with everybody, chewing the fat. I have a hard time with this whole color thing. It doesn't exist here anymore, and I don't think it did. I don't want to talk about something that I don't know about. It probably was, but it's not anymore.

"I really do think that we're all in this mess together. And no matter how much money you have today, it could be gone tomorrow. So I don't take myself seriously and I don't take any of this seriously. Some people are here for the social thing. And there's nothing wrong with that. These people work hard. They want to come here and drink and act like complete fools, and hang out on the beach and bake and carry on and hoop and holler, and see who's who, and be with the chichi crowd. Let 'em do it. What the hell? This is one of the few places left in the country where black kids can come up here and meet other black kids, and go out and marry them and go off to college together and feel safe and not be harassed, not be beaten up by the police—but you know what I'm saying.

"My friend who lives in Edgartown was called a nigger last summer. I think it was a bunch of college kids, who really didn't know that anyone black owned a house up here. The woman they called a nigger, she's owned a house up here for sixty years. Sixty years. Her father was a doctor, came up here and bought the house for two thousand dollars. How were they to know that? Maybe they would be a little more respectful. Maybe not.

"They're a whole bunch of regular folks up here, with a regular kind of gig, making minimum wage. Trust me when I tell you—that little tight circle is very, very small. And I think a lot of them get drunk and they start rattling about how fabulous they are. So they think they're bourgeois, but they're really not."

Marla's father was the jazz singer Ruble Blakey, who worked with Lionel Hampton for many years. Born in Washington, D.C., she came to Boston at seven, and she first came to the Island when she was fourteen.

Marla had been a choreographer and stager for recording artists. Before she left the industry she had worked with the likes of ZZ Top, Randy Newman, David Bowie, DeBarge, High Energy, Linda Ronstadt, Sting, Manhattan Transfer, Run DMC, Max Headroom. She choreographed *Motown Returns to the Apollo* and *Bette Midler on Broadway.* In Los Angeles she had been on a very fast track, and though she said, "I was very, very lucky to get as much work as I did," she let me know very quickly that, "Yeah, I paid my dues. I worked nightclubs in Atlantic City for years. Army bases all over Europe. I did go-go dancing in New Jersey, and do you know what that's like? Holy Jesus! Paterson, Hoboken, Weehawken. I paid my dues."

But somewhere around 1987, something changed. "I woke up one day, and I said, 'There's something wrong with my life.' And I took a long look at my personality." She didn't like what the recording industry was taking from her, "playing the game. To keep that momentum going. There was no sense of family, the motivation was tough out there, because there's so much competition. And I just felt that there were some things that were more important to me." She called it a "spooky decision," but she decided to move to Martha's Vineyard. Her mother, who had died recently, owned a house there, "and it turned out that I realized—barring heaven—this is where I want to be."

She was of two minds now about the influx of people. There are too many, she thought, but "who the hell wouldn't want to come here: it's beautiful. There's all sorts of people that come here."

I asked her about what was referred to as the Inkwell.

"The Inkwell? It's the beach where black people go, but they don't all go there. They go to Edgartown; they go to Gay Head; I go to Menemsha. They don't all go there. But it's okay. And it's a marvelous area for children too, because they are being watched by everybody else. Family. You can literally leave your kids and go to sleep on that beach. It's not rowdy. You know what it is? There are some kids there, younger people there with ghetto blasters, and rap music. But that's where I saw Ron Dellums—can we talk?—it's a place to hang out. Plain and simple. Deals have been made on that beach. Houses have been bought. If I ever need to find anybody, I go up there, that's where they are. My mother spent her whole summer on that beach, hanging out with her girlfriends, talking. We're talking judges, black women judges, schoolteachers, school principals. Hanging out, sunbathing, talking, hugging, prancing, whatever the hell they were doing, the music blasting. White people go to that beach too. That's the wonderful thing about this Island. There is such a mixture of people. All up here together."

Currently Marla was working on a musical play called *The Dancers,* a play about dancers which she admitted to be a 1990s version of *A Chorus Line.* But her play would be a bit different. "Let's tell the audience about AIDS in the dance world, anorexia, drugs, racism, sexism. Let's let people know that this is not all fun and games." She was encouraged to pursue this production, and others, after having enormous success with another play a few years ago. She had done Ntozake Shange's *For Colored Girls Who Have Considered Suicide/When the Rainbow Is Enuf.* "We updated it and we opened it at the Whaling Church, in Edgartown." The actors wore leather pants, African garb, "sisters in dreads." "It was a massive success." Much to my surprise, she had "cleaned it up."

"I didn't use the word 'black.' I used 'Man' in place of 'that nigger.' I took most of the profanity out . . ."

"Really," I was taken aback, to say the least. "Don't you think that would take a lot of the bite out of the play?"

"I kept it where it was going to bite. A bit. I made it very sensitive so that you could understand—in a different way. I said there was a lot of anger, yes, but we just took out 'motherfucker,' we took out 'nigger,' we took out—Jeez!—it was marvelous."

For some reason this disturbed me more that it probably should have. I had directed a version of the play in college, and counted it as one of my favorite pieces of literature. The idea of altering such strong work, of "sanitizing" the poet's vision seemed to miss the point of the work, the point of the poetry.

"But I didn't rewrite it. You have to remember that I was trying to update it. I was bringing it into another state and time. A space that I'm in . . . I tried to get past some things . . ."

"So you thought,"—and I was really trying to understand—"it was a violation of your vision of the play?"

"There was lots of anger. But I thought it would alienate some people. There was major, major crying, major anger, major laughter. I just made things wonderful with music and dance when it wanted it; and then I made things tough and angry and painful when it wanted it. I cleaned it up, for my own purposes."

We went back and forth for a while, me trying to understand how you can do *Colored Girls* without the words "nigger" and "motherfucker"; Marla saying it's not about "nigger" and "motherfucker," it's about doing something else, something new, something wonderful. But, as I said, arguing with Marla Blakey is akin to arguing with the sun. I bit my tongue, leaving the idea of "cleaning up" something that is supposed to be funky, and even offensive, alone.

Then Marla Blakey rushed off to a party, sccming to leave a storm of incense and glitter in her wake, leaving me perplexed and amused and, as per usual, confused. I was to leave Martha's Vineyard the next day, and, after a week, I had to admit that my understanding of the place—though perhaps broadened, though perhaps deepened—remained an irritating mental itch. These questions of class, of skin color, of social mores, of power, would haunt me in different ways for the rest of my journey. Yet somehow Oak Bluffs was emblematic of a very particular lacuna in the general discussion of black American life, a cultural phenomenon which was destined—at least for me—to remain a mystery and a vexation, hidden not so much behind the well-trimmed doors of Victoriana, but closeted within the human heart itself. Some of the men and women I had been raised to consider "black" actually considered themselves a bit different from me. Some based that conviction on a dubious genetic heritage, some on the lightness of their skin or on the darkness of mine, some on their bank accounts having more zeroes than the digits of a telephone number—some because of all these factors. The fact that such thinking existed was no shock or surprise; in many ways that way of thinking has always been the fundament, the stirring spoon of American society—a person would have to be extraordinarily naive not to know this reality. What bothered me, what saddened me, what confused me, was how black folk with benefit of even a little education and exposure to the world could convince themselves—and remain convinced—that this vision of themselves had any validity at all.

Three

# WHERE TWO OR THREE ARE GATHERED IN MY NAME

## Or, By Twilight's Last Gleaming

*Burlington, Vermont*

"What to Do When You Don't Know What to Do." That was the title of the Reverend B. J. Perkins's sermon that morning. "What to Do When You Don't Know What to Do." Her voice had a high edge to it, somehow like the pinging of high-voltage electric wires. A short, wiry, dark woman, with a stylish hairdo, the Reverend B. J. Perkins was pastor of New Fellowship Baptist Church of Hudson, New Hampshire. Her congregation was visiting that morning with the congregation of New Alpha Missionary Baptist Church of Burlington, Vermont—the first and only black church in the state of Vermont.

I had arrived late, not easily able to find the chapel on the Redmund campus of the University of Vermont in which the congregation met. The scriptures had just been read, and now the choir began singing "Leaning on the Everlasting Arms." The healthy crowd of sixty, youngish folk raised a joyous noise to their Lord. Later, during the gospel song "It is Jesus/I have told the world . . . ," the church engaged in call and response, clapping, crying: "Come on, now," "All right, now." Tambourines chimed; the organ piped; a piano jangled; drums thumped; folk stood and "felt the spirit." A prayer was delivered with the same rhetorical flourishes I had heard as a boy. Announcements were read (Bible study times, summer schedules, choir practice, a picnic); visitors welcomed.

All in all, New Alpha felt very much like the churches of the South which I knew so well—sans the southern accents and the presence of elders. And when the combined church choir sang "God Is Able," I felt very much at home: the improvisational nature, the spirit of "keeping on keeping on," the informal yet very formal atmosphere.

The Reverend Perkins's text came from 1 Peter 5:6 ("Humble yourself therefore under the mighty hand of God, that he may exalt you in due time . . ."). The Reverend was obviously very big on discipline; she even called back some New Fellowship members who had walked out. In her sermon, she spoke of respect, equating it with *agape,* Greek for unconditional love. Her sermon held much fire and lightning and thunder, taking on those old rhythms, the measured iambs, punctuated by "ah," with the congregation getting into the act—"Yeah" "Weeeell"—in a singsong fashion. The Reverend Perkins worked up quite a sweat. At one point one woman "got the spirit," a thin slip of a woman dressed in white, and crashed into the drums and cymbals. It took two people to subdue her, until she collapsed on the floor.

The Reverend Rodney S. Patterson, the pastor of New Alpha, officiated over the altar call and the benediction.

Afterwards the congregation adjourned to another building on the UVM campus, where we were treated to a meal of barbecue chicken, casseroles galore and salads. A group of eighteen people played volleyball in the August sun; a group of young boys and girls threw softballs; a group of girls played double Dutch; and yet another group of men were burning to play basketball, trying hard to round up enough people. I spoke with a number of the folk that afternoon. Some worked for the university, and many worked for companies like IBM and GE that had recently built huge complexes in a new industrial park just outside of Burlington. Almost to a person, the black people (mostly having arrived within the last few years) all resoundingly said they found Burlington pleasant to live in, a clean and an excellent place to bring up their children—the ones who had them. The only drawback—almost all agreed—was said to be the harsh winters; those who had just arrived that summer seemed to worry, and those who had experienced them mostly shrugged it off as just one of those things. Few said they had had any major problems with racism.

They also spoke of how important New Alpha Missionary Baptist Church was to them, especially the young people—the majority—who had moved to Vermont so recently from New York and North Carolina and Georgia and Illinois. For them this was practically the only place where black folk could gather in or around Burlington. More than a religious need, New Alpha was fulfilling a strong social need.

Watching the children at play and the men and women hitting and missing the ball and laughing and having a fairly good time, I pondered that need, that curious human desire to be among others like ourselves, the need for commonality.

Of course that "need" played a significant role in getting New Alpha Missionary Baptist Church founded in the first place.

The next day in his office, the Reverend Patterson explained how he got involved with founding New Alpha while he was first considering taking the job of Director of Multicultural Affairs at the university in 1988. "The first two people I interviewed were two black women on campus," he said. "One was in admissions, and one was in affirmative action. That was maybe the third question I asked them, 'So where's the black church?' They said, 'Pardon me?' 'You know, the church where black people go?' And they said, 'Oh, you have to go to Plattsburg in New York,' which is across the lake. I said, 'There's not one in the state, you mean?' And they said, 'No, there's not.' "

By the time he returned he had decided that in order to make the move to Vermont, he would take the initiative to organize a church. He began speaking to different people on and around campus. The man who would eventually become the church's piano player started putting the word out. The Reverend told me: "There was also a Black Professional Network Organization and I got ahold of their mailing list. I visited their meeting first and told them of my idea, and they ate it up. We started having choir rehearsals about a month before the first service. The first one—I can't remember exactly how many came—it was between four and seven, I think. After that, we sent out information to the black folk on campus too. We had some handbills made up and started passing them out in the community about our official opening service. I think we had about fifty people that Sunday. It was the third week in September. Then the first Sunday of February—the reason we chose that date was that it was the beginning of Black History Month—my pastor from Chicago came, and we had what we considered a christening ceremony."

I noted that the first few services seemed to generate a lot of ink. He sighed and said the entire affair was "tiresome." "Yeah," he said, in an admirable basso profundo full of woe in remembrance, "it made me real leery of reporters. But it wasn't just that. The first week I got here in this capacity, I was on television and on the front page of the newspaper—students had taken over the president's office prior to that. They knew that the person in this position was going to be a figurehead, so they were biting at the bit to find out what my vision for the future was, and how I felt about being here and what have you. It was okay then, because after that it just died down. But my fear was, 'Oh no, I don't want to become a media figure—everywhere I go people saying, "That's him!"'" Rodney Patterson laughed.

"When the church thing happened, one of the reporters on campus asked if she could do a story for the faculty-staff newspaper, and I said sure, and she was nice enough to publicize our events. She did a nice story, but she asked her editor if he'd be willing to share the information with the Associated Press. At that point I was thinking, 'Sure, it's not a problem; it's not a big deal.' The guy came and asked who we'd be interested in having it shared with and I told him. Well, it was most significant to our community, so people like *Jet* and *Ebony* are the ones we'd be more interested in having it. Then he asked about the *New York Times,* and I said sure, that's okay. So the *New York Times* called and came down and did a story. When it got coverage in the *New York Times,* one of the local *Jet* photographers came across it and called here personally and asked could he come up and take some pictures. He told me he couldn't guarantee that it would become a story, but there was a pretty good chance. So I met him at the airport, and we had breakfast, and he took pictures, got some clippings of what came out locally, sent them to *Jet* in Chicago, and they called, did an interview over the phone, and about a week or two later it was a *Jet* article."

After that, Rodney Patterson told me, things "snowballed." He became annoyed by a great many inaccuracies and wasting of time. He said: "Some of the local people became a nuisance. When my pastor came, I had a meeting with a series of people, the president of the university, the mayor, we were scheduled to meet the governor, and some others just to make sure that we were building a solid community that wouldn't have to deal with problems down the road. And all of them were saying, 'We don't foresee any problems. Pull full steam ahead, we're backing and supporting you a hundred percent. If you need any other assistance, just give us a call,' that kind of thing. One reporter was asking, when she found out what the itinerary was, if she could follow us around to all of these meetings. I told her I didn't feel that was appropriate, snooping around all day. I didn't feel it was that big of a deal to begin with. But somehow she decided that she would check with each of these people, especially in the legislative circles, and maneuvered her way in to be a part of those meetings. So the night before the opening services, Friday, the last night that we had choir rehearsal, reporters wanted to show up for that, and I told them that we didn't have a problem with them taking pictures as long as they were inconspicuous. And before I knew it they were *click, click, click,* you know. I stopped rehearsal and told them they had to leave."

The Reverend told me the sheer act of exciting people in a spiritual way was exhausting. He also pointed out another difficulty—changing faces. In three years the congregation had gone through three "core groups." "This is the most transient place I've ever been in in my life," he said. "I've found part of it is the university; I think part of it's IBM, Digital and GE and them hiring young black professional people. And then this being a good starting place, but not a place to settle. One thing I think about Vermont is that it's a bit too small for an ethnic community. Geographically, as well as its landscape, in terms of numbers, there's not a whole lot of people here. At one point in the '40s and '60s cows outnumbered people. The quality of life is definitely better here than a lot of places because you don't have gang warfare, you don't have drugs, you don't have to worry about theft. Even racism is not as overt as it is in a lot of other places. In that sense, it's not bad at all. As a matter of fact—especially with the aesthetics of this place—it's real refreshing. And that part of you makes you hate to leave it; but the other part of you, the part that has more to do with your social outlets or your religious experience, and just little things like clothes—I go to Michigan to get a haircut."

Which reminded me: "You know I was wondering: Where do you get your hair cut around here?"

"You can't," he told me. "Little things like that make people feel like it's a good launching pad, but no more than that. I'm not too sure how I would feel about raising children here. I want my kids to have the African American experience, and that's going to be hard to have here. So I think people come and they say, 'Good place to start,' and they stay roughly three to five years and then they go. That seems to be changing now because there's an influx of African Americans that are coming for a lot of different reasons, but some of them are coming as settlers rather than transients. We have a lot of outreach to do."

He said there would be three phases in order to really establish the church: First, a full-time pastor; second, to get their own building off-campus and to be seen as a part of the larger community; and third, a lot more outreach into the outlying area, to replenish the constantly shifting "core group."

"You must be a busy man," I said, and he broke into laughter.

"To some degree, probably *too* busy. There's just too much to do. Some weeks it's just literally too much. I tell people I feel like I have two and a half jobs."

When I asked if it had been difficult to adjust to living in Vermont, he said, "No, not really. Not for me it wasn't. I think the hardest thing for me was being this far away from home. And not having any support. But it was a very welcoming place for me. I think the other thing was that people thought it was so important for me to be here; so they did everything they could to makc me feel comfortable."

My initial reaction to Burlington was: clean, clean, clean. Alpine and remote. Green and village-like. Technology encroached in the form of excellent highways and the nearby industrial park, but the timbre and the lay of the land was fresh and inviting. (One night I saw a deer amble down Main Street.) I felt almost as if I were in Canada, rather than still in America—most signs are in French and English, and the television picks up the CBC and CTV—the nearest "big city" is Montreal.

But as I drove around, I realized that Burlington had two very distinct faces, like every other place: One of pristine opulence and one of squalor. I passed through a poorer section and realized that the booming economy had not touched every hovel and den. The sight of scruffy teens in black leather and boots and bandanas contrasted mightily with the evergreen splendor, and I remembered graffiti, on a concrete wall down by the lake, telling me: "Don't shed tears for the Children of Hell."

From downtown, Lake Champlain, on whose shores Burlington is situated, seemed deceptively minor, appearing smallish and long, though nonetheless gorgeous. The mountains in the background receded row by majestic row, disappearing in the distance as steely purple-blue phantoms.

I wandered around downtown Burlington, falling into conversation every now and again with a shopkeeper or a waiter, and I was struck by how everyone seemed to find the absence of black folk humorous, and the fact that I had come to the "Whitest State in the Union" to investigate black life a curiosity.

Later that night I happened to catch a PBS documentary on the late, great Millicent Fenwick, congresswoman from New Jersey with her corncob pipe and firebrand ways. One thing she said in an interview stuck with me my entire time in Vermont: "I don't believe in tolerance," she said. "Who am I to *tolerate* anybody? No, it's not about tolerance, it's about respect and understanding."

Vermont's total population was a little over five hundred thousand souls, and the number of African Americans was less than two thousand—less than one-third of 1 percent, with the largest concentration found in Burlington. Overall, the smallest percentage of any state in the union, thence the curious moniker "Whitest State in the Union." I wondered if this fact happened by some design or by some other happenstance. I found many articles enumerating the results of such a situation—the blatant acts of racism, intolerance, indifference—but few gave me insight into the larger question: Why? Moreover, Vermont's history had been one of tremendous "tolerance," to say the least. In 1776 Vermonters elected the first black person in any state legislature, and Vermont was the first state to outlaw slavery. I found a number of essays which suggested answers. Robert Mitchell sums it up best: "Perhaps the best explanation for the state's tiny . . . black population is its rural character, since 75 percent of the national population of blacks live in urban areas and 97 percent of those in the Northeast are city dwellers." Indeed the presence of people of African descent went back to Vermont's beginnings—a great many black folk escaped to Vermont on the Underground Railroad. One scholar, Marion Metivier-Redd, suggests that many of those former slaves settled and intermingled with the white folk, in effect "bleaching" themselves out of existence, but leaving their legacy.

I wondered, in truth, how white Vermont actually was.

The day I got lost on the University of Vermont campus on the way to church, I met Jack Guilles at the University of Diversity.

The university campus looks like the quintessence of an American land grant school, all red brick and malls, statues and tall steps leading to the halls of higher learning. That morning, already fifteen minutes late for church, I walked around the campus hoping to inquire as to the whereabouts of New Alpha. The few people I did encounter looked at me as if I were a Venusian—but were nice enough. They had no idea what I was talking about.

Then I spotted this mess on the mall. The university mall is a series of grassy lawns, descending, terrace by terrace, from the pillared main buildings. On the lowermost plain, off to the side, squatted these huddled tents and chairs and blankets and what appeared to be garbage—like a hobo camp in the midst of this ivory tower setting. I went to investigate and found a brochure tacked to a tree which read:

> DIVERSITY UNIVERSITY
>
> *Statement of Purpose*
>
> When the "Waterman 22" took over the UVM president's office, many of us gathered together to support the occupation and the demands for a university free of racism. During the three weeks of the occupation, our support group developed into a democratic body: in nightly assemblies, we discussed ideas, planned strategies, and made decisions together. One decision was to expand and develop our educational and political ideas by building a shanty town on the UVM green and opening a free school, called Diversity University. We make no demands on UVM. By working in co-operation with the people of Burlington, our free school will do the work that UVM should have done long ago.
>
> The liberal ideal of education divorced from politics is elitist, cynical, and inevitably corrupt. Education is political no matter what ideals we hold . . .

The manifesto went on to explain how UVM behaved more like a corporation than a place of "high ideals." How the school refused to offer classes in "Native American History, Radical Sexuality, Visionary Art, and Gender Politics." How the school engendered an atmosphere of "Do your work, don't ask questions." "DU has no president and no peons: it has as many teachers as students, as many bodies as heads." It ended:

> We are not here just to educate ourselves. We are a cooperative part of the Burlington community, and we invite everyone to participate in our educational and political meetings. If there is something you want to learn or teach, then write it down and post it in Malcolm X Lounge, and you can arrange to work with others. Even if you don't have a clear plan, come and see what other people are offering: you might be amazed. If you have a contribution or question or disagreement with our school, then come and talk with us and join our nightly (7pm) meeting. Diversity University is free and open to all.

I felt silly right off, not recognizing the place instantly as a shanty town, seeing as how students at Vassar and Sarah Lawrence where I had taught had done similar things. Political action seemed to be in the air on college campuses in 1991. I certainly wanted to talk to these students, but there were no signs of life and I was late, so I turned to go when I beheld this six-foot-one thin but muscular blond man in green camouflage army fatigues and a tee shirt and great big black boots, stomping in my direction.

"Yo, homie, what's up?" He looked enormously happy to see me.

I gave a halfhearted smile, annoyed, yet again, to be addressed as what my friends in Washington describe as a "Yo": That to be a youngish black man meant you spoke and identified with the slang of the street. Moreover, here I stood in my Sunday-go-to-Meeting best, with my bright new tie of which I was particularly proud, my mind set churchward.

"You looking sharp, homie. Where you heading?"

That comment saved him from my wrath. I told him what I was searching for, and to my utter surprise, he told me how to find the church. I thanked him and prepared to leave—writing him off, straightaway as a young liberal/radical/progressive wannabe who had no real knowledge of black folk, but who meant no harm.

"Yeah," he said, "I usually like to go, but I was out late last night. Got to hang with the folk. And I'm a Muslim anyway."

"Uh-huh."

"I miss my brothers and sisters, man. I'm from the city."

"Oh, really."

"Yeah, man. I grew up in Brooklyn and shit."

"That's nice."

"Ain't many of us here, man."

He kept talking, but I had stopped listening, latching onto that word: *us:* looking at his unmistakably yellow hair and reddish white translucent skin and profoundly Teutonic features; he could have been a Viking.

I interrupted him, trying hard not to sound offended. "Waitwaitwait—What do you mean 'us'?"

Without a pause, he said, "I'm black, man."

"Oh, really? Do tell."

He told me his name was Jack Guilles. He had been born in Toronto and his parents had moved to New York when he was very young. He described his parents as "problems." He ran away from home when he was five and stayed with a friend in the Bedford-Stuyvesant section of Brooklyn, and his friend's parents allowed him to stay, and eventually made him their son. The family was black and also members of the Nation of Islam. Growing up in Brooklyn, according to Jack, looking as he did, was no cakewalk. He told me of being chased and of even being shot when he was seven, and that sometime around the age of twelve, the people in the "hood" just accepted him, "forgot," and treated him like a black person.

I must say, in all honesty, initially, I did not believe one word of this Americanized neo-Dickensian tale of reverse Oliver Twist–hood. Yet for the life of me I could not shake this feeling that he spoke the truth. And his body language—which, for lack of a better word, I can only describe as black—was strangely well executed, seemingly effortless, a part of him, and perhaps most importantly, he really *sounded* like a "black person," which is not to say that only his vocabulary and sentence structure were African American; no, the very marrow of the sound, the timbre, where the utterances emerged, how the color of the language married emotion and fluidity, had a depth of culture I had never encountered in one who looked like this man. If I had closed my eyes I would have sworn he was as dark as I.

My mystification turned to fascination, and I wound up spending a good deal of time with Jack. We had supper, and he showed me the town. On two nights he took me to the university radio station where he was working on a jazz demo tape—at the end of the summer he intended to move to Chicago to join his girlfriend (a black woman) who had just graduated from UVM, and his plan was to get a job as a disc jockey.

The more time I spent with Jack, the more I came to believe his unusual story, to believe that he was not trying to pull one over on me. And, indeed, if he were, his acting alone was of the utmost skill and penetration, and his motivation, in and of itself, a profound curiosity. All of which, inevitably, led me to all sorts of questions about the nature of blackness.

Was Jack black?

"Woman from California called," Representative Francis Brooks told me, "and got one of the secretaries here out front. And she asked the secretary did we have any African Americans here. And the secretary said, 'No. But we have two colored representatives.'"

Francis Brooks seemed much more the high school physics and chemistry teacher he was, than the Democratic Majority Leader in the Vermont State House. He was good-natured, soft-spoken, contemplative; I could not detect one ounce of the bombast most of us take for granted in our politicians—none of the self-importance or the pomp.

The morning I met Representative Brooks, the state of Vermont had just learned that their governor had died the night before. We were in a conference room in the Capitol, and the representative himself had not long ago heard the news.

Governor Richard A. Snelling had been sixty-four years old and had served as governor from 1977 to 1985. He had run for his fifth term in 1990.

The representative explained the state's new situation: "Well, today changed the legislature drastically in that the Senate was 15–15. The lieutenant governor is a Democrat. The governor was a Republican. So with the death of the governor, the lieutenant governor becomes governor. In our constitution we do not replace the lieutenant governor until the next election, so that means that the president pro tem of the Senate, who was a Democrat, will now have to be the presiding officer, which means that the working vote on the floor of the Senate is fifteen Republicans, fourteen Democrats. So it alters the composition on that side in a significant way."

Mr. Brooks seemed particularly contemplative about matters both governmental and social that morning. "It's just a strange state, Vermont, in the sense of its closeness. Again, don't misunderstand me: The shock of the governor's death goes beyond just the governor. I mean, I knew the man personally. Okay? I didn't know him personally because I'm a big shot; I knew him personally because of the way the state runs itself. As an example, his last term in office eight years ago and my first term, I'm a freshman, I'm a little guy, nothing. The phone rings, one time, I was away from home. My wife answered it, she took the message, she never put the two together, and she said to me when I came back, she said, 'Do you know a Dick Snelling?' I said, 'No, I don't know a Dick Snelling. Whoa, whoa, wait a minute. I know a Dick Snelling, but that's the governor. He wouldn't be calling me.' She said, 'Well, here, this person, Dick Snelling wants you to call him.' So it's a strange state. You don't have that kind of pompous isolation that you have in many big, big states. I'm sure that right next door in New York State, there's probably a member of the House of Representatives there who has never even shaken the hand of the governor. That doesn't occur here."

Originally, Francis Brooks was from Alexandria, Virginia. After prep school for two years in Cambridge, he came to Vermont in 1963 as a student. He graduated in 1967. For the last fourteen years he had taught in the local high school, and in 1981, he ran for the Montpelier district seat in the state house. He was the third black person to be elected in the twentieth century, the second in fifty years, the last being in the early '40s. At the time there was one other black representative, Lavinia Bright of South Burlington. When I spoke with him, he was in his fifth term.

Eight years before, the Democrats had taken control of the State House. And even though they didn't have the numbers, they succeeded in electing a Democratic Speaker of the House. Six years later, the representative told me, they finally achieved a numerical advantage, and he replaced the former minority leader as Democratic whip and assistant party leader, where he served for a year. When the majority leader ran for the U.S. Congress, Francis Brooks became the Vermont Majority Leader in the State House. At the moment, the House was tied, "75–75," he told me. (Technically the Democrats were in the minority: seventy-five Republicans, seventy-three Democrats, and two independents—but they usually sided with the Democrats.) "So, technically," he said, "I'm the minority leader. It doesn't make any difference to me. Personally, I would put myself as a moderate, but maybe I can't judge. I would say that they'd probably put me as a liberal. But as a Democrat, generally we're the ones who are fighting for education or fighting for welfare reform or fighting for the state minimum wage or whatever."

"How much has the issue of race affected your political career?" I asked. "Clearly you've done well in your five terms."

"It has never been an issue. It has never been an issue," he said.

"Never?"

"Never been an issue."

"Never been used against you in campaigns?"

"No. No," he said, clearly without reservations, much to my amazement. "There have been times, certainly, in ten years, that I thought, 'Isn't it too bad that Francis Brooks has to be recognized, introduced, specifically, as the third black representative, or something?' But it has never been used in any manner, way, shape, or form remotely close to anything like in North Carolina with Jesse Helms. It has always been issue oriented, personality oriented. Whenever it has been brought up in the media—which is seldom now—generally my comment is that I certainly don't have to tell you that I'm black."

We talked about church life: His late father had been a minister. The representative told me: "The church means a lot to me. I went to several churches. I went to the one that I wanted to join and stated such. I have been a member of that church since 1967. A member of its board of trustees, a member of its board of Christian ed, a member of its deacon board."

I wondered if his church experience, as a lay minister, had been different from the church he had grown up in. "There are some traditions, and there are some styles," he told me. "I like a true and correct well-thought-out sermon that is not just whooping and hollering. Here you have those aspects. For instance a hymn sung as the notes are written and whatever. That doesn't say that you cannot then put in some of the emotion, which has been the criticism, the supposed lack of emotion. My point is, give them something that they may be lacking but do not exclude what is also correct in terms of the proper way to form and write a sermon and all the other kinds of things." He did confess to missing—at times—the black Southern tradition, the call and response; what he called a more "personalized" approach.

Mr. Brooks had two children, one eighteen-year-old who had just graduated from high school and one sixteen-year-old. Eric and Maria.

"How do you feel they fared in this environment?" I asked. "Obviously you didn't think it was a detriment."

"No. No," he said. "First of all, you have two different personalities. So I won't group them totally together. I think, in essence, they have the sensitivity about race to be aware. At the same time, hopefully, I have inculcated in them that you do not automatically judge anybody to be good or bad by what color they are. Every black person you come in contact with is not automatically good. Every white one is not automatically bad. Hopefully, they will just be able to gauge people from that perspective. Culturally, their generation is more of a melting pot culture than the specific culture that I grew up with. I grew up in a black neighborhood. I went to segregated schools. I didn't touch or dance with anybody outside my race until I went to prep school, until I was eighteen years old. I was lucky enough to come out of a home that was able to prepare me for that kind of thing. So I would say, if you're looking at culturally saving something, it's last with them. In terms of their exposure. Although they're quite interested in several kinds of things, it's got to be less than mine, and mine's less than my daddy's."

"Does that worry you?" I asked. "Or do you think it's just inevitable?"

"Some things, some aspects of that could worry me," he said, "Do we lose anything spiritual? That kind of heritage? That kind of thing. It has to be of great significance, and not just because it's black. But on the other hand, things just change. They change, and I don't know any way around it. Who are my kids going to marry? It doesn't make any difference to me. From the point of view of things like race or creed or color. When it comes down to marrying somebody, for their lifetime, that they're going to live with, I want them to marry somebody who's honest, somebody who's ethical, somebody who's kind, somebody who's good, okay? Then we'll worry about whether they're a Japanese who's Greek Orthodox."

The Reverend Alexander Lucius Twilight was elected to the Vermont State House of Representatives in 1836—fifty years before the next African American (Benjamin Arnett of Ohio). An odd, mystery-shrouded man, he was born in 1795 on a farm in Corinth, Vermont. There is much speculation as to whether his parents were escaped slaves or whether they were part white—but he was certainly among the first, if not *the* first, black man to graduate from college in this country: Middlebury College in 1823. (Perhaps Amherst graduated the first in 1826; or perhaps Bowdoin in that same year.)

In 1829 he became preceptor of the Brownington Academy in the Orleans County Grammar School in Brownington, Vermont, and on a fifty-dollar-per-twelve-week salary commenced land speculation and, over the next seventeen years, bought and sold land perhaps thirty times, transactions amounting to thousands of dollars. Some say he borrowed the money, some say his wife—a white widow from New Hampshire—footed the bills. No one is certain.

Regardless, in 1836, land was given personally to Alexander Twilight as a gift to the school on which to build a boardinghouse for students. Again, much mystery surrounds the construction of what became known as Athenian Hall, as Twilight named it—called Stone House by the locals—a building still standing, 36 by 66 feet, 24 feet high, 41 feet at the gables; granite walls, bricked and plastered at a thickness of 20 inches. Four stories tall, with a dining hall, a music room and a large kitchen, and it had enough room for more than forty students. Of the many stories regarding how the structure was made, all seem to involve an ox. The most arresting tale, as recounted by Vincent Nicolosi in his essay "Twilight Mystery," suggests

> that an ox turning a bull wheel lifted stones to a temporary platform on the inside of the walls. As the stones rose, the platform also rose with the ox on it . . . When the building was complete, there was no way to return the ox to earth, so it was slaughtered on its wheel above the hills, the meat providing a feast.

Clearly a productive and intriguing man; who as the stories go, was probably contentious, and headstrong—at one point Twilight fell out with his board of trustees and moved to Canada, just over the border in

Richmond, Quebec, where he founded Twilight's Academy. Eventually he returned to Brownington.

Over the years Twilight educated more than three thousand students, including boys who would go on to become mayors, missionaries, a college president and a railroad magnate. "He was respected for his ability to discipline wayward boys, sometimes with a yard-long leather strap; it was said that if anyone within a hundred miles had an unmanageable boy, he was sure to be sent to Brownington." Nonetheless Twilight seems to have been beloved, known also for great humor and "contagious laughter." He died in 1857.

Today the hall remains as a museum and historical society, rescued after decades of neglect.

How curious that Vermont's history contains such a figure. How sad that so much of his mystery remains a mystery. How illuminating it would be to peer through that shroud and behold the man, and his "supreme control." How precious would be his nineteenth-century knowledge in this twentieth-century world.

I had lunch with Dorothy Williams at the Winnoski Mall in nearby Winnoski, Vermont. Once an old water-run mill, it now was one of those deceptively rustic shopping centers, quaint with wood floors and too many trinket shops; Vermont maple syrup by the barrelful. The restaurant served excellent fish, and we chatted by a window situated adjacent to an authentic babbling brook.

"I like it here. I like my job. I like the area," Dot Williams later told me in her office at St. Michael's College. "But the most ironic thing is that I have a life up here that I didn't have in the Mississippi delta. I mean, a social life. You know, doing things with people of the opposite sex. No! No! I didn't say that!"

We both almost died laughing at her mock contrition. Perhaps that is what I almost instantly adored about Dot Williams, her warmth and spontaneity and irrepressible humor. There was something about her at once nurturing, interested, and nigh devilish.

Originally from Greenville, Mississippi, she came to Vermont in an extremely roundabout way. "My life is evolving," she explained to me. "Because it did not go in a straight line, and I'm very curious about that, as I go back home and see friends who went in a straight line and have done their thirty years of teaching and are about to retire. I'm just fifty and not wanting to retire, but even if I did, I couldn't."

She worked for many years in California "when the government was really giving money for seminars and so forth, and you got to meet people and it was wonderful—when Johnson was president." She taught for a while at Fisk University. Returned to California. And then "bounced to Las Vegas," where she received a masters degree and stayed for eight years. And "bounced back home." She taught at a small black college. She received her Ph.D. in 1988, taught some more, and in 1990 accepted a job as director of minority student affairs at St. Michael's College.

A Catholic liberal arts school, St. Michael's, at the time, had a population of about seventeen hundred, of which seven were African American, five were Asian, two Hispanic, and none were Native American. She points to higher forces in bringing her to this small, though not inexpensive little college in Winnoski, Vermont, something to do with her Catholic faith and something to do with determination.

Dorothy Williams firmly believed in St. Michael's vision of its educational mission, and what she saw to be the vision of all Catholic education, "to have more of an open-door policy as far as blacks are concerned," she said. "Students who would not ordinarily have the finances to attend a college of this caliber, who did not have the expected SAT scores or did not have the best academic record." But with a caveat: "When idealism and pragmatism clash—I trust I don't sound unkind—does the school have the will to do that? Does it have the support system to bring X number of students who don't fit 'the profile?'" She saw her role as an attempt to make that vision work.

Dr. Williams spoke of the ongoing attempt to integrate black students and others into the largely traditionally white school. "It hasn't been all pleasant," she said. "There have been mistakes, not from a malicious standpoint, but mistakes have been made. Mostly it has been being unaware. Not realizing what is considered insensitive or improper or inappropriate when it hits our ears. For example: For a student who has applied for a position and someone looks at their grades, and says, 'Oh!'—like in total amazement, 'You have good grades!' A lot of that. But of course, if you mention that R word, then people gasp, 'Not I! Good Catholic person that I am, and look at all this wonderful work . . .' That's what I got hit with when I first came here. I'm hoping to bring in a man, a white man, who's in psychology, who does a presentation called 'Racism Among the Well-Intentioned.' It's getting them to understand that even though you may be a very good person, and I know that you would not stand on a building and shoot me, and you may not incarcerate me, and certainly you would have me over for dinner, and we might go out for a movie, you still may harbor ideas that we consider racist. It's trying to get them to understand that that doesn't mean, 'I hate you,' or 'I think that you're a person with horns,' or whatever. But that we do have to find a way for you to understand what to say and what not to say, and how even your body language and your tonality and all that can contribute to my being uncomfortable when I'm visiting here in your home."

All that will evolve, Dot Williams said. "But when they first came, a lot of those slips of the tongue were made. I was just talking to a student, and I was saying to him—because he had overheard me saying to another student that he can't come back—(they're all from the same town) and it really hurt him, in fact he had tears in his eyes, and I said to this student, 'You all have got to study, study, study, study!' You know, it's tough up here. I used the thing about roller-skating, cause that was his big thing. Big man on campus. He'd organize these roller-skating parties every week. I said, 'Look at the time you are using to get that together. Put that aside. People will be roller-skating after you get your degree. It ain't going out of style, and all this partying . . .' And he's like, 'Well I haven't seen a movie in three days!' So? These city kids! You've got to change their mind-set. They say, 'Nag!' But you have to say over and over and over again to use the genius that God has given you and to go against the stereotype, 'Oh, you cannot succeed; you don't write well; you cannot think,' and the whole nine yards about our intellect. You disclaim that kind of thing by doing just the opposite: Make an A; make a B. And that makes people sit up and notice. Maybe on the other side of the thing, they're saying, 'I was stereotypical. So the second year is going to be interesting. We've been through the fire.' "

In general, Dot Williams felt that people didn't recognize—or even know about—the history of black folks in Vermont. "A wonderful history in terms of helping," she said. "Our heritage here, in this state. What has happened also is that there has been a lot of racial assimilation. Lucy Terry is a sister who lived here, was married to a black man, who lived here. And she wrote some poems. She stands out in history as a woman who went to court and was her own advocate about a dispute in a land division between her and a neighbor. An extraordinary woman who did not have any formal education, but had that black genius and that raw assertiveness that black women just have. And won her case. This is the seventeen hundreds. Now she gets overshadowed by Phillis Wheatley, because Phillis's poetry was more published. She even fought very hard for her sons to go to college in the state. She didn't win those battles because they were denied just on their race. But that's the kind of fiery woman I'm talking about. She didn't just roll over and play dead. Three of her sons married white women. A lot of that probably went on, and so you see, you get lighter and lighter and lighter, and then, after two or three generations, you are all the way over on the other side. So it comes across that there are no blacks here or very few. Even though you sometimes have to look deep to see Mother Africa—and I do that all the time—you see some very physical things: the fuller lips; no matter how straight the hair is, sometimes it's a little crinkly; and of course the high behinds, like we see at home."

Now, she said, she sees so many black and white couples together, that "when I saw the first black couple here, I just stared at them—a black man and a *black woman*—together! Husband and wife? A couple?" She laughed.

"So, we are here," Dot Williams said. "And we have been here. But because we have not been here in recent years, maybe in the last century in such visible numbers, people that look like you and me, that are very identifiable, white people have assumed: 'Well, it is not important.' People get comfortable. And it works on both sides of the fence. I was talking to a sister who recently attended a conference at Hampton, and she said there were ninety-nine African Americans and four Latinos, none of anybody else. And she said she actually went into culture shock when she came back—she was down there a week. It was just a love-in, just being yourself, you know, being around the folk—and she thought, 'Lord, if we could just be like this 365 days a year!' But then the party was over, and she had to come back to her job at UVM."

After a year, Dot seemed to be feeling at home. "My life had gotten very routine. And I came here not expecting too much. Not only have I developed very wonderful relationships with the students here, I have made contact with a lot of black people. When someone asked if I could put together a directory of blacks in the area, I said, 'No, I've only been here less than a year.' He said, 'Well, just give me what names you have.' I came up with seventy-five names. I had no idea I had that many."

I mentioned how, earlier in the week, I had encountered a middle-aged black couple in a restaurant and had wanted to speak to them, and how they failed to acknowledge me, so I backed off.

"A lot of them will try not to make contact," she told me. "It's like, 'Okay, don't do that. I'm up here now.' You kind of get that feeling. 'Cause a lot of times I've passed by people in a grocery store, or something, and I'm wanting to say hello, and they look straight ahead. Like 'No! Don't you dare!' That's something I've observed."

Later Dot showed me her house and some places in the area she found particularly attractive, and I left Dorothy Williams with the feeling that Vermont's future might not be as white as I had somehow been led to believe.

I met Sonya at a bookstore in downtown Burlington. In my bold and bumbling fashion I explained to her what I was about and asked if she would have coffee with me, to which she agreed.

A student at UVM, she had spent three semesters at Emerson College in Boston, but the prohibitive cost brought her back to Vermont. She had wanted to take creative writing, but since it was not offered, she was concentrating on English literature. She regretted that there were no courses in African American literature, though she was reading a lot of work by black authors on her own, particularly by black women writers.

Sonya had a sunny smile and a sunny laugh and a sunny face; her complexion, though brownish, also held a lemon-like hue.

She never knew her actual parents, though she knew that her mother was classified as white, and her father as black. And she had been adopted by a white couple who, as she put it, "did their hippy thing." They had lived in France for two years when she was younger, and in Michigan. "But my parents bought land here with some friends they had met in college. They were going to do a kind of commune," which apparently didn't work out. That was in 1982, just before her eleventh birthday.

For her, the years in Vermont were uneventful and "normal." "Nothing has really happened to me. I don't know why. I don't know how I escaped. My brother's had a few incidents, mostly because he was younger."

Also adopted ("His parents were just the opposite. His mother was black, his father was white. We're not blood related."), he seemed to have a much more difficult time than Sonya. "He moved here when he was younger, he was seven, eight, nine. He didn't pick the right friends, right away. So he had that kind of trouble. So he kind of hung out with losers. When he got older it developed into, you know, 'I'm black and what am I gonna do about this?'

In many ways this seemed to affect the whole family, Sonya told me. "My dad wasn't happy with his job, my mother wasn't happy, and we lived in a trailer. They were going to build this magnificent house to be made from a bridge. And then we moved to Underhill, like about forty minutes away. And again, my brother didn't pick good friends. So he's out of high school, but he's got no clue of what he wants to do."

I wondered if I could meet her brother, talk to him.

"He's in cello camp right now."

"Did you say, 'Cello camp?' "

"Yeah, he's been playing the cello for about eleven years. He's in the Vermont All-State Orchestra."

"Cool."

"Yeah, he's basically one big contradiction. He's kind of punk, I guess. He's got a big Mohawk, and wears combat boots. Plays the cello and is actually a very sweet kid. He's not so punked out now. I don't think he'll ever give up his boots, but that's about it. At first it was just adolescence, and then it was identity crisis on top of adolescence. And then a day-by-day crisis. Living in Vermont. So that was just triple fold."

"And how did you escape all this?" I asked.

"I have no idea. My parents wonder about this. I know high school was just . . . Well, nothing happened in high school, but it was one of the worst things that ever happened to me. I hated high school. It was a small school, with like 170, 180 people in my grade. When I was a freshman, there were two other black kids in the school. By the time I was a senior there was one freshman who was just coming in. It was a small redneck school."

"And how did you deal with that?"

"I don't know, really. I picked good friends. I don't know. No clue. I never had any incidents, but my brother—someone tried to run him down in a car."

"You're kidding," I said.

"No," she said, "They were having some big feud with some other group of kids, and he was the only black in the other group. So they focused on him. They threatened to burn a cross in the yard, but they didn't. My mother called the police but nothing happened. There are no great horror stories."

For which, I said, I reckon we all should be grateful.

"I've been called some very strange things. But the thing is you don't call me that in front of my friends. 'Cause if you do, you ain't going to be talking to anybody. You fuck with one of us and then you have all of us out there. Well, the thing is there are so many more of them than there are of us here."

I was sitting with Jack Guilles on a knoll overlooking Lake Champlain, just talking. Twilight approached.

"What have your experiences been with folk here?" I asked.

"Oh shit. The rednecks? Damn, they're a disgrace. These people right here are like, they're like a gnat on a dog's dick. They're just annoying."

"What did you say?"

"They're like a gnat on a dog's dick."

"A gnat on a dog's . . . ?"

"A gnat on a dog's dick. You never heard that before?"

I lost it, and broke down in a fit of laughter. He took me by surprise.

"I'll let you breathe for a while."

"No, I never heard that one before," I said with tears in my eyes, my sides hurting.

"Straight out of the ghetto, man," he said. "They're like a gnat on a doggie's dick; they're annoying as all shit. I told them that, too. I'm like, 'You're a gnat on a dog's dick,' and they look at me like, 'What? I ain't never heard that before!' But, I don't know. You know what it is to say, 'I want to peel someone's cat back?' You know what that means, right?"

"No."

"It means you're going to go get their fucking ass, right? And they start to laugh when they hear you saying, 'peel your cat back.' 'What does that mean?' Sometimes the way I'll say something, something perfectly normal. Or sometimes people try to talk like me, right? But then there are some people who just, they hang out with me for a while and they start talking just like me. I don't know why that is. I don't know, is it catchy or what? They'll be around me for about five or six hours and they'll start doing the same thing. There's this head-banger, all right? He'd, like, listen to thrash metal, death core, and all that shit. While I was at the college, I had a radio show, and I had something on, a feature called Malcolm X Forum, right? And he used to come up and say, 'I want to do the Malcolm X Forum with you.' Cause he was a Malcolm X reader. He really liked Malcolm X. This blond-headed, blue-eyed, trash, long haired—*long* hair, too. Long, blond hair. Blue-eyed, thrash metal, leather-wearing—I can't think of a name for him. Damn, that's the first time I ain't never been able to think of a name for somebody.

"Anyway, he was like, 'I want to do it.' I was like, 'All right.' But it was surprising that this guy wanted to do it."

"And did you let him?"

"Yeah, I did."

"How did it work out?"

"It worked out pretty good, 'cause he'd read just about as much Malcolm X as I had. He was full of mud, though. Right? He read all that Malcolm X, and it changed his mind about things. Right, he decided he better get with it. He's expressed interest in going to Harlem. Personally, I think the minute he stepped out of the car, he'd get his ass kicked. All the way down the block. You know, they have long-ass blocks in Harlem." Jack took a long drag off his cigarette, devilishly contemplating the sight in his mind.

"Yeah, and another thing is the people get upset with me here because of a lot of things I have to say. 'Well that don't got nothing to do with me, cause it's not about the ghetto,' right? And they like, 'What do you mean *ghetto?*' I give them the explanation I gave you, and some people say that when I get going, I get going fast and furious. When I start talking about it, when I start explaining it? That I tend to get a little angry. I haven't noticed it, but they say that I do. And I get me some scary look on my face."

Jack had told me earlier that he was no longer a practicing Muslim. I asked why.

"My questioning? Well, I do my meditations and all that business, but I don't feel like it's giving me any more at all, and it's supposed to, but it doesn't. I like going to mosque. I learned a lot through the Nation of Islam, but what I'm going to do is not forget what I learned. Always use what I learned, and let that remain who I am. But still also believe in Christianity. I'm not going to denounce the lessons I learned in Islam, but I'm also going to believe in Christianity. Do you know what I'm saying? I'm not going to believe in Islam so much, I'm just going to take the lessons from it. So . . ."

I wondered what it was about Christianity that appealed to him.

"I notice Rodney Patterson seems to have something," Jack told me, "to have an air about him that not many people have, and I think that might be it. So . . .

"Anyway, I got to get to Chicago and get out of here. Chicago would be a totally new start."

"You've been before?"

"No. That's why I'm going. I ain't never been to it. So. I never seen Chicago. That's why I'm going. Start out fresh. Good people. Positive people."

"I suspect that's as good a reason as any."

I actually hated leaving Jack behind in Burlington, for aside from being this most curious of anomalies—this white black man—he was hilariously funny: one of the “blackest” people I had ever met. What did I mean by “blackest”? The more I tried, and try, to define what it was about Jack that made him seem black, and so real to me, the more vague and confusing the question becomes. To be sure, it could have been an act; I could have been fooled and my initial assumption true: he was a white boy “acting” like a black boy, what some would call a “wigger.” He had clearly studied the walk, the talk, the warp and weft of the culture; moreover he would have had to do what actors call “emotional research.” A lot of work, and why? Some psychosexual, Fanonesque head trip? Or simply to be different? But he could be on the level, he could be a phenotypical, blond-haired descendant of Danes and Brits and Russians, for that matter, who had been soaked and pickled in African American mores—who identified with us dark folk enough to live and die with us. Yes, you might say, but would he hold on to that gig when the chips were down and the cops had Jack up against the proverbial wall? Of any of these possibilities, past or future, I could not know. All I had been left with was a feeling, and with mind-twisting questions on the nature of authenticity.

Was Jack black?

To this day I have no idea whether or not Jack was telling the truth, and it no longer matters, really. Whether I wanted to admit it or not, thanks to Jack, my idea of a black man had been rearranged and broadened. For in some unexpected and unplanned way he was a timely messenger for me; he got me to thinking more and more of how being an African American was larger and deeper than skin color, that the power of culture infects and takes hold; that the bond of solidarity depends on something greater than blood, something more than the human body, and more spiritual than mere words.

What if Huck were black and Jim white? What if Bigger Thomas were a rich white boy from the suburbs and Nick Adams the black scion of an old Mississippi family? What if Invisible Man were white and Jay Gatsby black? Impossible you say. Then the books would be radically different. Yes. But, stop and think again. The room for said possibility exists.

The mind flips, the heart skips, and all that's old is new again.

I left Burlington feeling that my original questions were indeed valid—there was more to being black than nappy hair.

“When I first moved to Vermont, I was just angered by the fact that right here in this area, in Marshfield, there was a mountain called Niggerhead Mountain and a Niggerhead Pond. What amazed me was that it took people maybe six years or more to finally get the town to see the reason to change the name. People would say, 'Well, you know, it gets so dark up there, you know,' and they said that the trees, if you look at them in the dark, they look like black people's hair. 'Looks like nigger's hair.' "

On one level Paige Wadley-Bailey reminded me of those women who surrounded me in my youth, like Miss Nellie Mae and Miss Clem—strong church women who could do almost anything, you suspected. However, on two counts Paige was remarkably different. One, she had a splendid head of dreadlocks, decorated with cowrie shells and beads; and two, though the good church ladies were lifelong Democrats, Paige Wadley-Bailey was the very essence of a radical. On every front it seemed.

"Vermont was very, very active in the whole Underground Railroad movement," she told me. "As a matter of fact, this Marshfield parish house has an underground, a place where they used to hide runaway slaves. They've since renovated it, but right here was one of the places for the Underground Railroad. And some slaves who decided not to go on to Canada, they would settle like in pockets, and, of course, stay among themselves. Throughout Vermont, you'll find Nigger this or Nigger that. You know, Nigger Cliff, Nigger Mountain, Nigger Meadow. Because ex-slaves were concentrated there."

Paige didn't take these curious historical markers in stride. "When I was a student at UVM I was working as an intern, and I'm talking on the phone, and I'm looking at the map, a map of Vermont, and it says, Niggerhead something. This was in Lincoln, Vermont. I dropped the phone. I was shocked. I dropped the phone, you know, and I went over and I got a black professor. I said, 'Bill, you're not going to believe this. Come and look at it.' By the time he looked at it, I was in tears, because I was working for the Center for World Education. We were doing a lot of stuff around trying to develop a more comprehensive, multicultural educational plan, for the education school master's program in education. And then looking at me, was this. So Bill went to the bank that had the map made up, to find out if that name was an old name that just wasn't taken off that particular map. And come to find out—they checked with the town—it was still officially the name. Then we got Kwanzaa involved in it. Kwanzaa is a predominantly black group that deals with Third World cultures, issues, cuisines, celebrations and the whole bit. And did some talking with some people in the town. There were a couple of white students who lived up there, who could also kind of talk with the town about it. They very quietly, very quietly, changed it to Lincoln Hill. That was just about six years ago."

Plainfield, Vermont, is the home of Goddard College, famous particularly in the 1960s as the ultimate in radical education, attracting a great many people, over the years, interested in wholistic living, interested in beginning communes, which many of them went on to do; it taught wholistic medicine and yoga as well as writing, the Goddard Nonresidential Writing Program being quite well known.

Paige Wadley-Bailey moved to Vermont from Connecticut in the late seventies to go to school initially. She brought along with her her two boys, and her daughter came a year later. "People were friendly. I had a good base. I had the faculty right at Goddard. It's not like I came up here with nothing. And I found some women who were interested in continuing the work that I was doing in New Haven." Paige worked for the Center School Play Group, a parent-run nursery school. "We're in the process of writing a grant to Haymarket [a progressive foundation] to develop a comprehensive antibias, multicultural curriculum, that hopefully we can take to a point where we then become the teachers of other nursery schools throughout central Vermont."

Paige told me that there were about a dozen black folk in Plainfield, out of a population of one thousand. One Japanese family. And that there were a number of white couples who had adopted black and Third World children. Remembering Sonya, I asked how they fared in Plainfield.

"Actually, I was on the board of Root Wings, which brings in kids from the Third World because they said they're the hardest to find placements for. It's not so easy. People want white babies. Is it because they can't get white babies, that they go and get black babies? As a matter of fact, now they're going over to Lithuania, wherever it is that they had that big AIDS epidemic. And they're getting them from over there, AIDS or no AIDS, and they're white. You see what I'm saying?

"There are some legitimate cons on that, okay. But the pro for me is: Do I keep that kid running from foster home to foster home or institution to institution, while I'm trying to work out the fact that it's because of the white man's shit that they're in these places in the first place? In other words, do I wait until they're grown, or do I say, well, meanwhile, get these kids exposed. I'm talking about heavy-duty exposure, because some of these folks around here got some money and they have access, and they got stability. When the kid reaches a certain age he wants to begin to identify with his culture, he's got to have a lot of skills to do that.

I would much rather see a child in a loving home, even with those new problems, than to be shifted and shunted and kicked about from foster place to foster place. Some about every two weeks. So when black social workers talk about, why don't white people adopt white people, instead of stealing black kids, I try and tell them, why don't they take the money and deal with the reason why the mother can't keep the child in the first place? They're dealing with the effects of racism, not the causes.

"But a lot of these kids—boys especially—run into a lot of trouble when they reach teenage. Then white mothers become afraid of them, because, for all their liberal shit, they believe in the myth of the black rapist. And that's some heavy-duty shit. The kid is going through a whole lot of identity stuff and growing stuff as it is. Because he's a male, he's more threatening. The teachers are more threatened by them, and harass them more than they do the little girls. Because they can paddle the little girls. You see what I'm saying?

"So that adopted black kids with white parents have a hard way to go, especially the males. I mean, black males have a hard way to go, period. Here's this kid, stretched out here, who's detached from his culture, who's going through physical stuff. I mean, he's having more wet dreams, his dick's getting bigger, you know I mean, all that shit. Come on, let's face it. Right? And then the white girl that he's been playing with in the sandbox all of a sudden—you understand what I'm saying? *Badoop—Bing.* Hey. So that's a hard thing."

Paige had founded a group called POMOJA to help black males deal with coming of age.

"That shit is real. From the time they come out of the womb, maybe even in the womb, they are affected. They begin to learn that stuff. You got to see yourself reflected back, otherwise you're going to be crazy."

I felt I could learn a lot from Paige Wadley-Bailey; she seemed so on top of things, and so wise and for real in a refreshing, earthy sense—something I was finding became rarer and rarer. She showed me around outside, and we stared at the ancient cemetery just behind the old house, everything New England and late summer green. "But you know," she told me, "it's exciting dealing with this stuff. This cabin, I hope like in two years to turn into a black, Native American and Third World reading and reference room. People can come here, do some research. Organize some actions. You know, boom, boom, boom. The whole nine yards. And this ceiling's going to be raised. All these walls'll be filled with books.

And that loft upstairs, the dormer, books. That little room in there, books. We're talking reference room, you know."

As I took my leave I confessed how, though Vermont was beautiful in the summer, I felt I would never survive the winter. "You might surprise yourself," Paige told me, almost in a prophetic trance. "You learn to make friends with the cold. You have to get out into it." It's a different mind-set, she told me, you think of the cold in an entirely different way. She told me how she learned cross-country skiing and how wonderful the land looked, all covered in snow and frost. A magical wonderland, she called it. Now she enjoyed the winter much more than the summer.

Looking back I remember how excited I was to be finally talking to folk, getting other people's thoughts; yet I also remember a level of fear: I had set out to figure out for myself what it meant to be black. The few people with whom I had spoken did share some obvious notions, and yet they were also at times wildly at odds with my own, and with each other. What the hell was I trying to accomplish? These questions I had been asking were not going to arrange themselves in neat little files. In fact, I intuitively knew what I would find was going to get much more complex and confused.

Of one thing I was certain, on my way that day, east to Maine: Being black, understanding blackness, was an awfully complicated matter.

On my way to Bangor, Maine, I crossed the White Mountains of New Hampshire and felt twinges of the splendor in store for me in the months ahead out west. I stopped to visit my friend, the historian Nell Painter and her new husband, Glen, a statistician from Kansas, at her summer home in East Stoneham, Maine, a place she calls Camp Armageddon after one of her books. A house on a lake overlooked by Rattlesnake Mountain—it remains one of my very favorite places on earth.

Before going off to bed I had a cup of tea with Nell and I confessed how apprehensive and uncertain I was about this project, this nebulous notion I had of searching for this thing called blackness. I was worried that this voyage was all stuff and nonsense; that I was chasing after a phantom of an idea. She spoke of her own growing up in Oakland, California, and how she herself, at one time, felt detached from black culture. How some people had considered her a pseudo–black person; how all over the country there were young kids in the suburbs who learn about being black from white kids. She reassured me that I was not chasing after a phantom; that I had a point; that I was looking for something real.

Four

# MANY HUNDREDS GONE

*Bangor, Maine*

Why on earth did I choose Bangor, Maine?

The truth is two part. On the surface I figured that Portland, Maine, was too much like Burlington. For, like Burlington, Portland is picture pretty and newly done up, the largest city in the state, New England to the bone, the center of all commercial, cultural and educational activity. But that is not the real reason I chose Bangor, Maine.

I will not lie. The real reason was Stephen King. Stephen King lived in Bangor. I read *Carrie* when I was in the seventh grade. It had just been released in paperback, and Stephen King became a boyhood hero. Always an easily frighted child, paradoxically I could never get enough of vampires, werewolves, Bigfoot, the Monster of Boggy Creek, ghosts, goblins—I was just dying for someone, something, to scare me to death. And no one, but no one could write of ghouls and the bogeyman and stuff that goes bump in the night the way Stephen King could. As a fourteen-year-old I ate it up. Even re-reread his novels. I remember vividly reading *'Salem's Lot*—which is about vampires taking over a small town in Maine: Jerusalem's Lot—just before the funeral of my Cousin Petsey, and it was autumn, and it was autumn in the book, and the book was about people dying and being buried, and here, in real life, people were dying and being buried. Moreover, I could not get over the impression of how much the small-town Mainers seemed—from King's writing—like the small-town North Carolinians who surrounded me; and I had always wondered, from age fourteen on, in the back of my mind, how black people in places like Castle Rock and 'Salem's Lot fared. In all honesty, though there were a few, there were not many black characters in King's novels.

I wanted to see for myself.

. . .

As one approaches Bangor from the south, as one enters the town, off the interstate, there stands a massive statue of a lumberjack, a statue perhaps as famous as Bangor is famous.

Bangor surprised me as being clearly and predominately a blue-collar town. The University of Maine at Orono is just up the road, and the hospital seems fine and fancy enough. But Bangor exudes the feel of men and women coming home from work tired; the houses look comfortable, warm, humble (even Stephen King's house, though it is enormous, is painted red with white trim, like a barn, like a place where kids could play in the yard, approachable, surprisingly human), and very old in a quiet and unself-conscious New England way. I found downtown Bangor to be quaint and dusty; the library a Greco-Roman relic, yet somehow inviting. Stores seemed out of a dream of the '40s and '50s (I fell in love with the bagel shop on Main Street, with wooden floors and old-fashioned screen doors and their gigantic sandwiches and hard bagels—"strictly kosher"), not like the prettified brass and "Ye Olde" signs and whitewashed and sandblasted and acid-treated brick and stone of downtown Portland: Bangor was very much what it appeared. A mixture of basic architectures curiously yoked, interrupted by the rapid and rushing Penobscot River, running through the middle of town.

The night I arrived in Maine, Hurricane Bob followed me, and while I was talking on the phone, the lights winked out and the phone blinked dead. In the dark I felt the great winds making the building sway. Later I would learn that the eye of the storm had passed directly over us. The very next morning the dissolution of the Soviet Union was announced, and up the road at Kennebunkport, George Herbert Walker Bush was announcing the end of the Cold War. The two events played together in my brain, like an equation demanding a solution. The storms of change, and here I was in Maine.

Having absolutely no idea how to find black people—I had yet to see any—I did the logical thing. I found the NAACP's telephone number in the book and punched in the number. Directly I was speaking to the chapter president, a gentleman named Duff Gillespie who agreed to see me the next morning. So pleased was I with myself that I treated myself to a steak and a movie.

The next morning I arrived at Duff Gillespie's home—and a fine home it was; in fact, one could even call it a mansion, Victorian with mansards and gables—and this tall, silver-haired, good-looking, smiling white man greeted me, introducing himself as Duff Gillespie. He invited me in and I explained my mission, and he offered me tea, and he gave me the names of a few people. Didn't know many younger black people, he allowed, or I think he told me he didn't know any. But I should check at the university. I asked about old black families, and he pointed out that the few names he had given me fit that description, but in truth—though at one point Bangor had a sizable number of African American residents—most had moved away. (I would later discover that the black population "peaked" in 1963 at 439, and had been dropping ever since.) I told Mr. Gillespie how obliged I was and went on my merry way. To this day I still wonder if he knew that I fully expected him to be black; and I still reckon the whole thing remains more amusing if the silent understanding of my faux pas remains silent. Rich.

"Well, we always say 'down east,'" Mr. Sterling Dymond was telling me. "They're 'down east,' but they're really north. North is east of us. So we say 'down east.' That's an old Maine habit. Down east, yeah."

We were sitting in Mr. Dymond's kitchen, that evening, after Duff Gillespie had given me his name. Sterling Dymond was a native Mainer.

"Were there many other blacks in Bangor when you were growing up?"

"Oh yeah, lots," he told me. "At one time they say there was 500 or 600 here in Bangor. Right up to the 1940s, you know. World War II came in then. Went in the service, and they got better jobs and moved away and didn't come back. Ones in the service didn't come back. Most of them stayed away and married and they settled down in other places. They left.

"Back in the 1800s, early 1900s, they worked in the woods, they were woodsmen. And on the timber drive, course the drive came down into Bangor with the pulp, and a lot of them stayed here, and made their homes here. Was a big wood port. And they used to go up in the woods and work. And during the winter they would come back and have them drive them home. And they built homes here and they lived here and had families here."

I remarked how I had searched all day at the university for the history of blacks in Bangor and Maine and how I had found precious little.

"Lot of those people you see in the university don't even know themselves," he said. "They don't come from here. They come from upstate. They don't know the local people. We had quite a community here in the '20s, and early '30s."

I asked if there was ever a black church in Bangor.

"No, we never had a black church, not what they had. They went to all different churches. I'm Episcopalian. They had a Baptist church and Methodist church and some went to the Pentecostal church. They never all went to one church. Never crossed our minds. Never thought about having a church of our own. Not until we got grown up, you know, after the war, that's when they first encountered black churches. But Portland always had a black church.

"Back then in Bangor they had the Masonic lodge, and they had the Elks lodge here too. And the women, they formed what they called a mothers' club. They all got together once a month and had meetings and had sewing circles and things like that, you know, and then they would put on extra big dinners and what not. They even had a hall in the downtown, where they used to hold dances and things like that, you know. When the lodge was flourishing. Always had a New Year's Eve dance, Easter dance, and things like that. At Christmas time they had what they called a Christmas tree, for all the kids, and everyone all over the territory came to it. They had the tree, and we were singing hymns that you probably wouldn't see no more. Lived out in the country. Native farmers. Then in the summertime, they had two or three picnics they would all go to."

I wondered how things were between blacks and whites in those days.

"Never had no trouble until after World War II started, when they had a lot of Southern soldiers, white Southern soldiers come here. And that started a lot of the problems here. When they came in. And it seemed the black soldiers that were there had hard times getting rents. But I blame that on the commander of the base. Then they built a place for the GI's to live, so they didn't have a problem after that."

Sterling Dymond's maternal grandfather had come from Liverpool, England. His own mother had come from Fredericton, New Brunswick. "My father, he didn't know where his parents came from." Mr. Dymond's parents were married in 1904, and he was born in 1920, number nine of ten children.

"My parents didn't talk much about the younger days. They didn't. I know my mother was brought up on a farm outside of Fredericton. Her father had a big farm there. He had a good life. My mother's family. My father, I guess he worked, like from a youngster, right up through his life.

"I was brought up to be strong. My mother just brought us up not to take anything from anybody. 'Nobody's better than you are.' And she was a proud woman. Nobody was any better than she was. Not even the

Queen of England. I think this was passed down to her somehow. Probably from her father being an Englishman. But we were brought up to be proud. I had a lot of people say, 'You Dymonds think nobody any better than you. You think you're the best people in town.' I says, 'Yes, we are.' " Sterling Dymond laughed. "But you'll find that the people who were brought up here, and know the black people in this city, they all have a good word for the blacks in this city."

I begged Mr. Dymond to tell me more about what it was like growing up in Bangor. For instance, What was Sunday dinner like?

"Sunday dinner was either you had roast chicken or you had roast pork. We had roast of beef. And you had the whole works, potatoes, and you had vegetables and dessert and the whole nine yards. See, Canadians, we have a breakfast, then we don't eat again till about four o'clock in the afternoon. Only two meals for the day. Yeah, that's all we ever had. And, you'd eat your breakfast and go to church, and you'd come back and you might have a doughnut or glass of milk or something like that to hold you till dinnertime. And I still have the same thing. And holidays, you know, always had the big meal. Thanksgiving, when I was a kid, we had chicken. We didn't have turkey supper. People didn't decide to have turkey around here till during the war. Turkey was more like a rich man's dinner. Because we raised our own chickens, when we was young. Right up to, I think about 1945, we stopped raising chickens."

"That was right in the town?" I asked.

"Yeah, them days, you could raise chickens right in town. As long as we cooped them. They were all fenced in.

"And Christmas was the same thing. We had roast of pork and you had roast of chicken. Then you'd have mashed potatoes, you'd have squash. You'd have carrots, and green beans that were put up, preserved for the winter. And then you'd have your plum pudding. And your pies, apple pie and squash pie. Then afterwards, later on, you would always have made these cakes during the fall and we'd have them all winter long. Fruitcake. And tea, later on in the evening.

"New Year's Day, Mother would generally have either fricasseed chicken or something like that, you know. With the full meal. Mince pies. Always had mince pie and squash pie and apple pie and pumpkin pie. Because Easter was for ham and eggs, always. Had the big ham. Fourth of July we always had salmon, Atlantic salmon. Well, that's what the Canadians always had. We would have steamed salmon and potato salad, or else we'd have the new potatoes, and we would have the egg sauce over the salmon. Then we'd have green peas, always had new peas. Then we had fresh strawberries and strawberry shortcake. And I have the same thing right today. Got to keep my kids into that tradition. I like traditions."

I wondered about social activities, school, whether he felt hindered or isolated.

"All my life I've been around black people. After we got to high school, we always had our own little parties. Dances all the time, so, it didn't seem strange to me at all. I was surrounded in high school, six blacks graduated in my high school class. And year before and after that was six more. When I went to high school, there was at least a dozen blacks in the school. Well, over a thousand kids in the high school probably. Hell, there'd probably be about four blacks and be about half a dozen or more whites all go to school together, and meet up here on the corner of Third Street and all walk to school together."

I said I assumed that the blacks and whites got on quite well in those days.

"Well, we didn't socialize together after that. When you get to high school, that's when, you know—you may go to the same places, see everybody there, but you really didn't socialize that much with each other. You all went to school and back together, or basketball games, football games and what all. But when you went partying, we went to a party by ourselves, they went to a party by themselves."

Sometimes they would go to Portland to have fun. "Back in them days, it was a long ride. But you always had the trains. You could jump on a train, go anytime. Always was somebody had a car. Get a bunch in a car and go down, so we got to know all the people in Portland, and they knew all the people up here. Some of them were relatives."

Mr. Dymond had been a draftsman for the Soil Conservation Service, from which he retired in 1985. He graduated from high school in 1938. "Right during the Depression, so was no going on to college." He went to work right away. First at the nearby air force base, Dow Field, where he worked for six years. "I was the foreman for brake detail crews. Then I went to the railroad, worked for the Great Central Railroad. I worked for B&A Railroad for a year in a dining car." After he was laid off in 1959, when passenger service began to decline, he worked in construction for a year, after which he went to the university. Eventually he joined the Soil Conservation Service in 1968. "I worked up to technician and I retired as an engineering technician."

He married in 1959. I asked how he met his wife.

"We always went down to Fredericton, during the fall, to see business people down there. She lived in Woodstock, New Brunswick, and I went to go through Woodstock and stopped off to see her when I first met her. She was a nurse at the hospital. Till she retired. She only retired six months before she passed away, that's all. Takes a lot out of your own retirement."

"I guess you guys had planned to do a lot during your retirement."

"Yeah. So don't never plan—do," he told me. After a pause he said: "Well, we did a lot. Oh, yes, we did a lot. Took our kids everywhere, Boston and New York and Washington."

The Dymonds had three children: two girls, Nancy, who still lived in Bangor and worked for the university; Claudia, who worked as a hospital consultant in New York City; and Sterling Dymond III, or Chip, who had just graduated from the UM-O, and was now a swimming coach in San Antonio, Texas.

"See," Mr. Dymond told me. "There's very few black people my age here. They all went away. The young people, once they get out of school, move away to better jobs. Which are not here. Yeah, they are moving away, so imagine: one of these days, you're going to see even fewer blacks here."

Why were folk moving away?

"One thing is job opportunities. If you're a professional, you do okay. But it wasn't until the '60s come along, and the civil rights and all this started, that the blacks started getting in better jobs, like in the telephone company. It's the big companies, not the small companies, the big companies that had to hire blacks, you know. Opened up. I don't think today there's problems in finding rents, as long as you got the money. And I know a lot of blacks work up at the malls, in the stores, whatnot. But there's certain jobs that they still can't get. They don't come around saying, 'Oh, we don't hire because you're black.' They'll say, oh they hired somebody else."

Still and all, Mr. Dymond told me, "it's a good place to raise a family. One thing I liked about it. Good place to raise a family. What more can you ask? Exactly. That's what it comes down to."

Mr. Dymond was very much involved with his Prince Albert Masonic Lodge. There were about twelve members, all black men. "We don't segregate nobody. If some white person wanted to join, they'd be welcome." At Christmas they have a tree for the children and bring presents, and have a summer potluck. In February they have a black history night. In the summer a cookout. October is a soul-food dinner. "Last time had about 250 people there."

I wondered if Mr. Dymond felt part of a larger black community. If he felt any kinship with blacks in other parts of the country.

"I really don't think much about it. I'm used to it now, because during World War II most of the blacks here were from the South. And I was round them all the time. So to me it was just meeting another brother, that's all. We got to know each other pretty well. And I'd been used to seeing a lot of blacks in my house here. When I worked for the railroad, when I was in high school, I'd be seeing the guys, always a lot of railroad people. See a lot of chauffeurs, who used to come down to Bar Harbor, drive these really rich folks down there. We had a lot of blacks down there in the summer, matter of fact, we used to all go down there in the summertime to parties. Yeah, we used to go down there Thursday afternoons and Sundays. We all worked for all those rich people. Rockefeller, and all of them, they all had black help. We used to see a lot of blacks come here, visiting people who lived here. We had a lot of black people brought up here, but they went away and was working, some were teachers in the South and whatnot, and they used to come home for the summertime. My mother always had them by the house for dinner or something. I've been around a lot of blacks all my life."

I asked Mr. Dymond what he thought of the term "African American."

"Well, when they first started out with 'black' you know, I kind of had it a little hard. Always been used to saying 'colored,' or 'Negro.' I didn't have a problem remembering what to say." He laughed. "So I got used to black. Hell, I think it's wonderful now. But this Afro-American, I don't know why they want to be called 'Afro-American.' I know why. But where's it going to end? First there was 'colored.' Then there was 'Negro,' then there was 'black.' Now it's 'Afro-American.' But hell, I mean, we don't know no more about Africa than what we read and what we see on the TV. Years ago, somebody called you 'African,' you want to fight them. Or if they called you 'black' you'd want to fight them. I am not going to be called 'Afro-American.' I ain't going to call my kids 'Afro-American,' but if they want to be called 'Afro-American' it's up to them, I guess to each his own. I'm very independent that way."

We talked about a number of things, politics: ("People come sit up here and complain all the damn time on account of the vote, they vote—but they don't vote with their heart. Course they don't vote with their head neither. I don't know what the hell they vote with really. They're doing a hell of a poor job. Country's in bad shape, especially up here. We feel it more here now than we ever have."); and relations between blacks and whites: ("I think there's too much hatred. Blacks have towards whites, whites have towards blacks. We've got to stop having hatred, if we expect to get by and be peaceful. When you go out in the world today, you've got to work, you've got to work in the white man's world. And in order to work in the white man's world, you got to learn to get along with them. They're trying to group people. Like they say, 'All blacks are this and all blacks are that.' And we say, 'All whites are this and all whites are that.' But it's not that way. There's a lot of good white people and a lot of good in the world too. If there weren't, it'd be a hell of a place to live. I don't think that the world's going to change as long as we have this hatred all the time. You don't hear about the good things black people do. You always hear about the dope. And having children, babies all the time. On welfare. TV does that. And every time they talk about welfare, they show people, black people on welfare lines. You don't see the blacks getting the education. You don't show some of the fine homes they have. Some of the good jobs they have. You don't ever see that. Hell I bet you there hasn't been six people on welfare in all the time that I've been here. In this city. One woman who has both her legs off, she's on welfare. Well, she deserves it.").

I now realize it was a silly, biased question, but I asked Mr. Dymond if he felt he had missed anything by staying there in Bangor.

"Oh, I might have missed a lot of good parties," he said. "What did I miss, really? We had parties here. Our culture was just the same as culture anyplace else. We missed seeing big plays, the operas, things like that, you know. Ball games and stuff like that. You had to travel probably to see that. I was in Washington, D.C. way back in the '40s. Visit my sister, and went to her church, and heck, she goes to the Episcopal church, and it was just the same as the service I had here. I was very disappointed. Just like being in my own church here.

"We always thought being in a small town, we didn't miss a lot of things. When we'd go to Boston, we found out that things were no different than they were here. They would just be having little parties where they lived. They'd go to some little bar or club, right in the neighborhood. So they weren't doing any more than what we were doing here. They just had more people to socialize with, yes. But on a day-to-day basis, the city people aren't going out that much.

"I don't know. I might have had a better job, but maybe I wouldn't have. I figure from the education I had, I think I've done all right. But I made sure my kids were educated though. I made sure my kids went to college. Or had the chance to go to college, which they did. Maybe if they was in the city, they wouldn't have got that chance."

As I was about to go I asked if Mr. Dymond enjoyed hunting or fishing, since Maine is legendary for its great game and forests and shores—after all it is nicknamed the Vacation State.

"I used to hunt but now I'm golfing. My thing now. Yeah, I'm a golfer."

"Pretty good at it?"

"No," he said, matter-of-factly. "Getting worse all the time. I just can't get rid of bad habits. Can't keep my head down. Always got to peek up, see where the damn ball's going. And that's my death. Hitting right on top of the ball. But I have a good time. Have fun. Yeah."

I had left my grandfather's house in North Carolina in mid-July. It was now almost September and I had been a week on Martha's Vineyard, a week in Burlington, and I needed a haircut in the worst way. I asked Mr. Dymond where I could get my hair cut, and he told me about his nephew who was a barber. I reckoned if it was good enough for Sterling Dymond, it would be good enough for me. The next day I made an appointment for that very afternoon.

Across town, I found the house out of which the gentleman performed his services, a big house, and old and sturdy.

In I walked, and the gentleman greeted me, and I knew from the beginning things were just not going to work out. He was a nice enough fellow; in fact, he looked like a younger, jollier version of Mr. Dymond. However, there was a woman sitting in his chair. There was a woman cutting and fixing yet another woman's hair. And there were two women sitting, reading magazines. Waiting to be operated on. The women were all white.

He took a look at my head, and asked me what I wanted done. I told him, and he said, no problem. He had two heads to get to before me. Have a seat. It would be about twenty minutes. I sat down and tried to read a magazine.

Now I see myself sitting there, in the back of my memory, and I see myself being an absolute wreck. I see myself without any real consciousness of my state, but being aware, at the time, of a strong sense of alienation and agitation and primal testosterone vulnerability. In the most Socratic of ways, I think I know myself: I am not a bigot or a racist or a misogynist or a fool. Call it a man thing, call it a black thing, call it a sex thing, call it a Southern thing, call it a dick thing. Call it anything you like, but the thing is, I had to go.

Just as I had made my decision, and was thinking of a way to exit gracefully, two more women entered. These women were black. The gentleman introduced them to me, since they were from Wilmington, North Carolina, and were in Bar Harbor with the people for whom they worked. They made an appointment to get their hair done and left.

I probably sat there no more than ten minutes, fidgeting and shuffling my feet, smiling at the women who surrounded me, probably good working people who had absolutely, positively no notion, no comprehension—no way of comprehending—my profound discomfort. I rose, and told Mr. Dymond's nephew that I had made a mistake, that I remembered I had an interview scheduled in less than thirty minutes, so I'd go, and probably come back later. Knowing in my heart that there was no way in hell I would be back. In retrospect, the excuse was probably so lame that I bewildered the poor man. Or perhaps he didn't give it a second thought.

I practically ran from the house into Bucephalus, and drove away in a cloud of a sigh of relief.

Now why did I do that?

Why did I react so bizarrely to that situation? For years I have been puzzled by these feelings. As soon as I left, it bothered me that I was so bothered. Was it because I was getting my hair cut among women? Was it because the women were white? Of course this goes against the grain of everything I believe in, practically. So I had to dig deeper into the issue for myself. As some of my friends would say: I had to go there.

Upon reflection I realized that getting a haircut has always been a source of anxiety for me, and it probably is for most black men I know; though I'm not certain they are aware of it, and, if they are, I'm not certain they would admit it.

Consider the archetypical barbershop: Historically, black men—who often felt and largely were, in fact, emasculated, daily, in society—gathered in the barbershop and felt a rare moment of solidarity and unity, as men. Here men gossiped, men debated politics, men lied, men laughed, men revealed intimacies they probably would not have revealed even at the poker table or at the bar. The barbershop represented an institution, provided a ritual. Power was laid down in the barbershop; the barber was given the power, over each man, turn by turn, to be shaped; a man was given the responsibility to shape another man's appearance for the rest of the world. (It is an interesting fact that two of the largest black-owned and black-run institutions in the world outside of African nations—North Carolina Mutual Insurance Company and Atlanta Life Insurance Company—were both founded by barbers at the turn of the century.) The barbershop, especially for most of the black men I have known, was always a male bastion.

My first memories of barbershops—my great-aunt said I cried my first time, though I remember it dimly—were always fraught with mystery and ritual. My first barber was Mr. Cleveland Kelly, and he cut hair for the military and worked on the weekends in a barbershop in a nearby town on Back Street, where many black businesses thrived—and the barbershop was the center of the hub. Black men gathered there even when they weren't getting their hair cut. On Saturday, if you wanted to find someone, one of the first places you might look was the barber shop. Another barber in the community was Mr. Jarvis Stallings, who did very well, and I remember sitting in his chair, watching the aquarium he kept there full of guppies and neon tetras and seaweed. He was a deacon and trustee of the church. Barbers were among the most respected of men. (The connection between barbers and Masons is historic.) Several ministers in the area were also barbers. I am certain this was not just true of the South. Even in African American literature I can think of a great many stories and plays that explore this most masculine of institutions, made masculine by the men who populate them.

Think of Samson: Delilah cut his hair; he lost his power. I know it to be a myth, but perhaps men attach more to the power invested in the shearing and shaping of their mantle than they realize. Perhaps there is a singular moment of vulnerability in placing the head in the hands of another; perhaps who men give that power to and where that power is given, speaks more loudly than any speech.

Moreover, there is the insecurity of appearance. For me, and I'd hazard to guess that for most men, especially black men I know, women, especially mothers, sisters, aunts, and lovers, exert a powerful control by their ability to critique men's looks. Indeed, in the world in which I grew up, so much of "looking nice" was abrogated to women. This was a cultural matter—in every aspect, every relation—mother/son, wife/husband, teacher/student, employer/employee, girlfriend/boyfriend. To be sure, other men's tacit approval, and verbal comment, was felt, welcomed, prized—but the final word, the power and the glory, existed on the lips, in the eyes, within the nod of certain women, collectively and independently. Hence looks became the shoals of insecurity, the fragility of vanity, the very essence of what make us civilized: mutual need, psychic touch, approval.

Therefore, that place, that neutral ground where vulnerability could be set down at the door, this place where we could remake ourselves, held an air of the sanctum sanctorum. The place itself had a power of its own by virtue of that laying down of power among men—power was no longer an issue; power is suspended, and therefore the black barbershop became in a way sacrosanct.

I reckoned my reaction had much to do with these unreasoned, unreasonable, unspoken, unreflected demi-urges within me, compounded, doubly, by the fact that these women were white. Unconsciously—for I did not think any of this then—the idea of laying down my power alongside their power set off all my instinctual alarms. It was as if my training had hardwired me to react that way. Certainly at the time, these feelings were not thoughts; and even now I am neither proud nor clear about how I feel. In the end, however, this is neither a question of wrong nor right, but of the way things were and are. My reaction was silly, I admit. But in looking at my behavior, it made me begin to think of myself in a different light: I was not even conscious of certain cultural attitudes I held. Or maybe, as James Baldwin would have put it: I'm just an uptight cat.

Gerald Talbot was elected to the Maine legislature in 1972. "If you're black in places like Maine, you can lose your identity if you're not careful," he once commented to David Sharp, a reporter for the *Bangor Daily News.* He was the first African American elected to the state house. The Talbot family descended from Abraham Talbett, a slave who served as a private in the Revolutionary War. He wound up in a small black community called China, Maine, in the late 1700s.

At the time a great many African Americans found their way to Maine, especially to Portland, where they found work in the shipyards and docks. In 1800 there were approximately 818 black folk counted in Maine; the 1840 census counted 1,355.

The town of China (near Augusta) had a small settlement on the eastern side of China Lake, off a road called "Nigger Road." The 1820 census counted twenty-four "colored people" there at the time.

Abraham Talbett either owned or managed a brickyard for years and sired eight children. He collected a monthly pension of eight dollars, and one day, in 1840, on a trip to Augusta, he dropped dead. His wife, Mary, lived to be ninety-five years old.

For generations the Talbots worked as chefs and caterers in and around Bangor, where Mary moved in her later years, that work being practically the only work available for African Americans at the time. "Younger Talbots were cheered on the basketball courts," a *Maine Sunday Telegram* article reports, but quotes a Talbot as saying, "snubbed by their high school classmates when it came to choose sorority and fraternity members."

Abraham's great-grandson, Charles Alvin, built a delivery business in Bangor, using a horse and buggy. Sterling Dymond knew him, "He owned three or four houses. He had a cow up there in his pasture. He was a shrewd old man."

His son, Charles Rainsford Talbot, graduated high school in 1906, and would become a navy cook during World War I. Later he would work as a steward for thirty years at the exclusive Kenduskeag Canoe Club. He became president of a black social club called the Tarragona.

Another Talbot, Pansy, became a caterer, and a rather well-to-do woman by all accounts. Each year she bought a new Plymouth; she gave away free theater tickets she had been given by her employers; in her home was a library full of books.

W. Edgerton Talbot became chef of the Bangor House, a hotel of some renown, having hosted over five presidents, many potentates and dignitaries, and several state conventions. His son, the future state representative, remembered hanging around the kitchen as a boy watching his father create the most elegant of meals almost effortlessly. Gerald Talbot seemed to have bittersweet memories of his days growing up in Bangor: "There was just a little something that said you were different . . . You knew something was wrong, somewhere, but you just couldn't put your finger on it. And nobody was really talking about it in so far as sitting you on their knee and saying, 'This is what's going on.' " Matters of race relations, remarkably, were never discussed in the Talbot household.

At times Talbot said he resented the way the hotel took his father away from him; though he would eventually work at the hotel as a pot washer and eventually a short-order cook. But one day he witnessed a manager of the hotel dressing his father down ("ridiculed him for whistling"): Gerald Talbot removed his apron, walked out and never returned.

In the fifties and sixties he went to work for Gannett Publishing Company, where he worked for more than twenty-five years, but he also became an activist. President of the Portland chapter of the NAACP in 1964, he involved himself with many court cases and protests, and was present at the historic 1963 March on Washington.

Though Talbot's father was a bit bemused by his son's activism, W. Edgerton Talbot was reported to have been proud when his son became the first black man elected to the Maine legislature—but his father did not live to see his son sworn in.

In the early 1980s, Gerald Talbot became more and more interested in his family history, and spent considerable time uncovering what was lost from memory, some things practically erased. The home in which he grew up in Bangor, more than 200 years old, was seized by the city at one point and about to be sold. Talbot purchased it for $3,132, and found in the attic, "ledgers from his great-grandfather's delivery business, old photographs, a dance program from a black social club . . . and lots of other memorabilia." In retirement, in his early sixties, Gerald Talbot continued to piece together the lost remnants of his family's remarkable history, hoping one day to write a book about blacks in Maine.

"I asked where you lived," I explained to Professor Herbert Heughan, referring to some people I had encountered down the way, "and they didn't know your name, but they remembered you as the 'black fellow.' They said they hadn't talked to you in about two or three years."

"Well, it's true," Professor Heughan said. "They go by and they wave. I don't even know who they are. Because all these people around here, they're new. They weren't here when I was growing up here. There were no houses across the street. I don't know how much they know about us. Unless you live with them, you don't know much about the black community here. Kind of cute: One day I was out here mowing the lawn, and a guy stopped, wanted to know if I thought the people who owned the house would want to rent it? I said, 'Well, I own it.' He says, 'A schoolteacher comes up here, he owns it.' I said, 'That's me.' But he didn't realize that you could be black and be a college teacher."

The professor gave a knowing laugh. "They all try to get the place, want to buy it."

Herbert Heughan retired as chairman of the Math Department at North Carolina Agricultural and Technical University in Greensboro in 1981. I asked if he was *emeritus.* "When I retired, I retired." He had been born and raised here in Hamden, Maine, about twenty miles south of Bangor. I met him and his wife at their white farmhouse amidst summer fields of corn.

"My family came from Canada. New Brunswick. Both my father and mother. My dad was ten years old when he came, and I guess he'd be about a hundred now. My mother came over here to work, and then they married and settled down over north of Maine Junction and started a family. My mother's people came through on the Underground Railway. Must have been 'round there. She remembers her grandfather talking about it. But my father, his people, they won't say anything. We don't know where they came from. They just say 'don't know, don't know anybody.' "

The professor felt they tried their best to forget about all that. "Because they wouldn't even talk. My mother said that a lady brought my great-grandfather in her arms and they wouldn't talk about where they came from or anything. They picked up the culture of Fredericton. Or New Brunswick, I guess. And that was it. Lost all track of anything else."

Professor Heughan's growing up in Maine was a different experience from that of Sterling Dymond's in Bangor, as his parents and six siblings lived miles out in the country. "Bangor was a ways away then. Horse and buggy days. As children, we would probably go down just once a month. Something like that. As we grew older, we hitchhiked. We never had a car. So you're going to go to a dance, and then hitchhike a way back up."

His father farmed the land. "My father had a team of horses. And he used to mow hay. I guess he'd be somewhat a day laborer. And he farmed for himself at night. Nothing to sell. We didn't sell anything. Just the potatoes and cucumbers and things, you know. But he worked out plowing and doing other people's gardens. My mother was a domestic. She worked in Bangor for the wealthy people."

I wondered if they were a part of any black community out in Hamden or Bangor. "No, we were always too busy. Really, here. Dad didn't plan that. We saw people at school, we saw people at church. But as far as visiting house to house, we didn't. They didn't take too much part in community affairs. But there wasn't too much out here in the country. Even in the city, I don't recall anybody taking too much interest in anything; the NAACP wasn't even active when I was coming up. My parents were raising a family and making a living. That's what they did."

"My mother raised a lot of chickens," the professor told me. "We ate the hens, the ones that weren't laying. We kept the laying ones, you know, to sell eggs. But when they got a little older and tougher, we killed them. Ate them boiled. Then we always had a pig, cooked, killed for the winter. We had most of the vegetables that they eat in the South. We didn't have chitlins. We didn't bother with all that stuff. Pig's ears, and . . ."

"Pig's feet?"

"Pig's feet, and all that stuff. No, we didn't do that," he said, laughing at the idea.

"What happened to that part of the pig?" I asked, being a country boy from an area where hog meat is a staple.

"Well, my mother made head cheese. She made the loaf, you know. I guess the kidneys she must have thrown away. But we ate a lot of potatoes, baked beans, that was a staple, still is with me. I have baked beans every Saturday. Even now, I take baking beans when I go back. And cucumbers, and we raised just about everything they raise in the South. We didn't use much rice or things of that sort. A lot of pies, cakes. And in the wintertime, we couldn't get in to town. We had barrels of flour in the pantry, and barrels of sugar, and that sort of thing. And most of us could cook."

The family attended the nearby Baptist Church. "That was the only church available. There was an Advent church, we went to that in the afternoon. But my parents were great churchgoing people. In church all day Sunday. Dad sang in the choir. My mother had been Episcopalian. I don't know what my dad was."

I wondered what relations were like between blacks and whites in those days.

"I hear a lot of people talk about all the problems they had. I did not have those problems. Even though we were the only black family. I was the only one in school, in high school. And I had no problems. In fact, I was the only one in our graduating class who went on to college."

"Really?"

"There was just twelve of us. And I was the only one that went." But apparently there was little socializing, or going to one another's homes. "I understand there's eight of us living, of the class. And two of them come by to see me every year in the summer. I'm ashamed to say, I don't go to visit them, but they always stop by when they see me here, and chat, you know. But I haven't seen the others. If I saw them, I probably wouldn't know what they look like, because, see, I finished high school in '35. They've changed a whole lot of things in fifty-six years, you know." He laughed.

He attended the University of Maine at Orono in 1936.

What was it like in '36? I asked. "How many black students?"

"Well, nobody lived on the campus. I didn't live on the campus. I lived in a house that a man ran. It was a boardinghouse, but it had been an old fraternity house. I lived there, and I worked; I cooked while going to school." He remembered two or three or maybe four other black students, but "they traveled back and forth. I stayed up there."

What was it like? Did he encounter much difficulty?

"I didn't." He named a black woman who was in school at the same time. "She wrote a letter to the school, and she said she had all kinds of problems, but I didn't. I didn't have any problem at all. She said that the teachers didn't think she was intelligent, and all that sort of thing. I don't know how she could have felt like that, because I didn't run into that. Of course, I was busy all the time. I didn't have much time to take in any of the activities on the campus. I went to football, the sports, but not the dances. You know, blacks didn't belong to their fraternities, so I didn't do that."

I asked about the size of the black community in Bangor and Maine in those days.

"Goodly number. Goodly number, yeah. Guys and girls. But we were related. There were quite a few. We did a lot of house parties."

After graduating from the University of Maine, he went "directly to Hampton." The Hampton Institute in Virginia. I wondered what kind of experience that had been for him.

"Pleasure," he said. "That was the first time I'd ever been around black girls who were not my relatives." He gave a chuckle. "It was a pleasure. It wasn't too much of a shock, because the constitution of Hampton says they've got to have half and half races on the faculty and staff. So many of the teachers were from New Hampshire and Maine, you know, those places. And we didn't leave the campus very much for anything. Everything was right there. Restaurants were there. The cleaners were there. The shoe repair place was there. Everything was there. All the dances and parties. Yes, I enjoyed it for two years.

"I didn't know anything about Negro culture. At all. I'll never forget—I was elected president of the dormitory where I lived. And we had a gathering, and on the program was written: Start off with the Negro national anthem. And I didn't even know we had one!" He laughed. "I couldn't sing it. I didn't know. But I ended up by taking a lot of courses in Negro literature and Negro history. I determined I'd just have to work in the South anyway because I was a teacher. They didn't have any black teachers up here. So I tried to get all I could while I was at Hampton. Before I went on to teach."

The professor told me he liked the music in Southern churches, but he "didn't like the preacher. I couldn't stand it. I couldn't stand that shouting and hollering. I didn't mind the crowds, but I couldn't handle the ministers. By the way, we went to church because at Hampton you had to go to church. That's required. And as I got into teaching, it was pretty much a requirement. They wanted to see you in church. On Sunday. But I loved the singing."

After graduating from Hampton, Professor Heughan eventually moved to North Carolina, and has remained in Greensboro. He and his wife spend their summers at this homestead in Maine, from June to October.

"In fact, after we're here a short period of time, we get homesick, you know. Because there are no parties we go to up here. We go to Canada to visit relatives, and they come to visit us. Then we start thinking about home. That's how it is. Yeah, very much so. Soon as it starts to snow, my wife says, 'Let's go.' She doesn't like that snow."

But in his heart Hamden, Maine, was home. "I just like it. One thing I don't like about the South is the summer. I've spent many summers down there, and I don't like sitting in the air conditioning. And up here I just feel like it's out in the country, and of course, there we live in the city. Out here in the country, you can sit back and enjoy yourself.

I asked him to speculate on why so few black people chose to settle down and remain in Maine. "If you're talking about blacks, you don't find any black professional people here. Those who went on to college left. Here there was nothing for them. There are very few natives. We can count them. But I understand there are quite a few blacks here now who joined the army, and they decided to stay. Then of course the University of Maine has hired some. I think one or two of the other business colleges had one or two. So they are here now, but they're not natives."

Just the day before there had been an article in the Bangor paper about African Americans living in Maine. One woman in particular, who was a native of Mississippi, and had come to Maine in the late 1940s, seemed absolutely put out by black folk in Maine: "Black people are not together up here. I don't know what their minds think. I really don't understand them," she was quoted as saying. The article, which included a few black people in Portland, was entitled "Maine Blacks Seem to Lack a Strong Sense of Community." I asked the professor about the article.

"My wife liked that article, because she's from down there. I didn't. I thought this woman—well, this lady was a cook. She sounded like she probably was not a highly educated person. She was looking for a black community and there is not a black community, and we don't hang out together. We didn't have a common religion. We didn't have a common language. We don't have common color. We have nothing in common. Like whites have. A common church or something. We're all different religions. All different colors.

"I think lots of people coming up from the South look at it a little different than those who are here. To me, I would rather be in the South now, because I've been there over half my life. I went south when I was twenty-three. Now I'm seventy-three. The first five years I lived in rural Virginia, and although I had fun, I really wasn't too happy with what I saw. The way the whites treated the blacks. What was there for blacks? I didn't see anything there for them. Dingy little beer parlors and pool halls and things of that sort. Even the schools were inferior. Now the teaching probably wasn't, but the buildings certainly were inferior, and the school books, and that sort of thing. I drove a school bus—the one that the whites had gotten rid of and passed down to us. This sort of thing kind of irked me. North Carolina Agricultural and Technical was a little different. I mean, the town's a little different."

I asked Dr. Heughan about "bleaching."

"There's been a lot of it," he said. "On the quiet, you know. I know my uncle married white. This is before I was even born. Couple of boys married whites. Quite a few have married whites, I'd say, and the children have all gotten lighter and lighter. Sometime we have a get-together, and we go to one of those places and you can't say who's who. I guess, just like other places, the whites would have blacks working for them. They had children by them, and give them some name, and that was it. So they're there, even the ones in Fredericton, they're all mixed up in color and all. Nothing in common. Least the ones I've met and I've met quite a few relatives up there, but they have nothing, nothing in common. They picked up the group's culture. Very few of them go in for business. Or pick up a profession or anything like that. They just go ahead as common laborers."

I asked Professor Heughan to prophesy about the future of black folk in Maine.

"In this area, they're all going to turn white. They're doing it now. We have very few real, what you call, 'real black people.' Because they've intermarried, they've mingled together, and they've taken on the white culture, and they're nothing like they are, I don't think, in the South.

"I don't think blacks can stand this weather," he said through laughter. "Really I don't. When I was teaching in college, we would try to place students in different places. They didn't want to come here. No farther than Boston. They don't want to come. They said the weather. And they didn't want to come because of the social life, because that's one thing you look for. Social activity. You don't find it up here." He mentioned a student at the university who was the daughter of one of his former students. He said recently he teasingly had asked her about her boyfriend. "She says, 'Don't I wish.' And I said to her, 'There are a lot of blacks up at the university.' And she says, 'Yeah, but they're all going with white girls. They don't want us.' That's what she said. Now that's a black girl talking."

Professor Heughan mentioned that he had recently become interested in finding out more about his family genealogy. But his remaining sisters asked: "Why do you want to know?"

"What about your nieces and nephews?"

"They don't care. They could care less."

Maine's major majesties are its lakes, its forests, its rugged, rocky, recalcitrant coast. Vacationland, U.S.A. Land of arctic winters and Vanderbilt yachts, deer hunting and tents from Sears, L. L. Bean, duck boots, long-distance runners, and a whole lot of poor folk.

When I talk about black folk in Maine to most people—black and white—what I usually get is laughter. In fact, that goes for most of New England, outside the obvious urban areas—which Vermont, New Hampshire and Maine simply do not have. The reason there aren't a lot of black people in these states is quite simple—it has a lot to do with the fact that, comparatively, there aren't that many people living there. Period. (Which is also why I didn't find that many black folk in Stephen King's novels in high school—so I answered that question at last.)

Yet what I continue to glom onto is the way most people react to the idea of a black New Englander: "Black people? In Maine? Come on, all two of them?" The very possibility goes against the grain of what the nation would believe of black folk; as if to be black came with an agreement; as if having origins—or a livelihood—geographically located outside an agreed upon, fixed, predictable location, somehow makes one less than black. Were Mr. Dymond, Professor Heughan, Sonya, Dot, Paige, less than black? To me, it seemed, there was something suspect in the way the nation continued to construe this thing called being black.

Heading west, I wondered about those ancestors of the Dymonds and the Heughans and the Talbots. These men and women didn't have the luxury to worry about such matters as who they were—they were too busy trying to survive, wherever, however. How terrified and brave they had to have been, launching off into this strange land of beauty and cold and harshness. I fixated particularly on the image of Professor Heughan's great-grandfather being carried in the arms of a woman running from slavery. How did it feel to arrive in Canada? She must have been so very, very tired. Could she taste freedom on her tongue? What does freedom actually taste like? We, who take freedom so much for granted, no longer truly taste it. Can we ever understand how she felt? I thought of the weird paradox that is the American South and the American North: One once a place to flee, now a place of promise; the other now a land of ghosts.

# II

# THE GREAT BIG MIDDLE

Autumn's end—
how does my
neighbor live

First winter rain—
I plod on
Traveller, my name

Come, let's go
snow—viewing
till we're buried.

—Bashō

Five

# LAKE EFFECT

*Buffalo, New York*

Vladimir: Perhaps we should help him first.
Estragon: To do what?
Vladimir: To get up.
Estragon: He can't get up?
Vladimir: He wants to get up.
Estragon: Then let him get up.
Vladimir: He can't.
Estragon: Why not?
Vladimir: I don't know.

—Samuel Beckett, *Waiting for Godot*

"You know, the chickens would shrink. We didn't know that." Mrs. Estelle Anderson was telling me about their days as chicken sellers.

"I've never heard of chickens shrinking," I said.

"Well, just a little," she told me. "If you have 500 chickens and they all lost maybe a fourth of a pound, you're losing so much per pound. You see. So if they shrink more than that, and you add it up, five, six hundred chickens, you've lost quite a bit of profit."

One of my closest friends in New York, the jazz disc jockey Sheila E. Anderson, had spoken to me often of her family, who were a remarkable lot of people. While in Buffalo, I was fortunate to be the guest of her parents, Arthur and Estelle Anderson. After their children—they had four: Arthur Jr. (Chips), Michael, Michelle and Sheila—had all left home, they had moved from a grand house in the Parkside section of Buffalo into a smaller, more manageable apartment downtown. Mr. Anderson, now a retired attorney, was a man with many careers behind him, including court reporter, educator, and college founder. But perhaps his most colorful was his earliest: merchant. When he was nineteen ("too young to sign the deed") Mr. Anderson had been briefly known as the "Chicken King of Buffalo," selling all manner of produce and foodstuff, but especially chickens. ("Frozen food didn't exist in the '40s.") A series of untimely disasters, however, forced him to abandon the business in 1947 and start anew, which he did by going to law school, which led to a host of other involvements over the decades. He married Estelle Hood, who had been born and raised in Terre Haute, Indiana, in 1922. She both raised her children and taught in the public schools for years.

"But my husband has done some interesting things, I think."

Mr. Anderson entered the room.

"I told him how when we went in business—that Thanksgiving—what went wrong with those chickens that you lost?"

"Oh, no—" said Mr. Anderson.

"Did they get a disease or did they? . . ."

"No, they got coxsilliosis. I went into a deal to ship chickens into Hamilton, Ontario."

"Oh, I didn't know that. That's when they fell over?"

"Yeah," Mr. Anderson said. "They just fell down and died. And so we had to destroy them."

"Yeah," said Mrs. Anderson. "Our money was tied up in our house. And then Christmas, you thought you'd make it up, and what happened to the chickens then?"

"I don't know, but some kind of—"

"I thought you said they shrank, but I know he didn't make it up. We never recovered. We never recovered."

"So—"

"And then I told him how you went to that agency and had that job. It was through your attorney, who recommended you. Now is that right?"

"Yeah. So—"

"And we had not registered Democrat or Republican."

"No, we hadn't registered until I got the job."

"In order to—"

"Yeah."

"I told him how your aunt was a little disturbed because you were Democrat. But really Democrats were not very popular."

"Yeah, they gave me a job that lasted. Didn't turn over Democratic until the early 1930s, when you had the rise of the welfare state, and the black social workers and the white social workers became intellectual icons of the society, then you had the blacks beginning to go Democratic. Because that's all they could see in the White House. Welfare and a cup of coffee."

"Oh, Art, you're so hard on those guys. I mean, he put food on the table for people."

"Yeah, and that's when the blacks started going—"

"Oh, Art. Absurdities!"

"Not at all. No. I mean—"

"Always hard on Roosevelt. Because see, his people they didn't have to depend on Roosevelt."

"No, but I mean, the point is though—"

"Because his father always had a good job during the Depression."

"But what I'm saying is—"

"He was one of the few blacks with a good job."

"Now see, what I think happened is like before the onset, most of your black political people were independent of businessmen."

"Oh yeah, oh yeah," Mrs. Anderson said. "They were independent."

"Then you had the rise of professional politicians. Who did nothing but hoodwink people."

"No, they didn't have a business," said Mrs. Anderson.

"Didn't have a business," said Mr. Anderson.

"They didn't have a job."

Mr. Anderson said, "The black social workers, if they couldn't find a need, they created one. The black politicians became professionals who lived by their representation."

"If I could play devil's advocate," I said. "What about somebody like Adam Clayton Powell, Jr.?"

"He had a church," said Mrs. Anderson.

"But his father was a very wealthy man," I said.

"Sure he was," said Mr. Anderson. "But there you have independent livelihoods. If you can survive outside of the white sphere, then you're unique."

Mrs. Anderson said, "If you make your living on black people, like a black preacher."

"Or a black doctor or a black undertaker, or a black printer," said Mr. Anderson. "But once your income comes from the whites, you are not independent."

Mrs. Anderson said, "Oh, and like around here, the whites give these black politicians big money to run. So, they owe their allegiance to the white people."

"No black can be independent, not if he's dependent on whites for his livelihood he can't. There's no independent black I know of who is dependent on whites."

"Do you know what was interesting?" Mrs. Anderson said. "Back when Art was a court reporter, he was making good money. All of our kids have always been in private schools. They were like the first blacks in expensive private schools. And we had no trouble with the tuition. We had two cars."

"That's right."

"And Art would take Michelle and Chips to their school. I would take Sheila and Michael to their school, and then I would go to teaching. Art did a lot of work for Allstate. He had a white Oldsmobile and they thought he had a Cadillac. So then this professor—I mean, really—"

"I was doing some outside work," Mr. Anderson said. "So he says, 'How do you find time to do this, with your law school work?' I said, 'Oh, it's not hard to do.' That semester he gave me a D."

"Isn't that something?" said Mrs. Anderson. "And you had been getting all good marks."

"I'd been getting all good marks. So I go to him and I say, 'What's with the D?' He said, 'Well, you can't work like you do.' I said, 'That's it.' "

Mrs. Anderson said, "And his wife, all the law wives, were just as bad. I would go out to their homes. I made a mistake of wearing a very expensive knit dress that I had purchased. So this man's wife had on a knit dress—not like mine—but the same knit fabric. And she knew that my outfit was very expensive, like hers. And my goodness, did she look at me like, 'How can you afford that with your husband in law school?' I'll never forget it. And another man's wife came in with, oh, an ugly bag and looking bad. But she knew better than to go out there dressed. So the next time I went to one of those meetings, I wore the same outfit. And she looked at me like, 'Well, I guess that's all you have.' Then the next day I wore it again. But I was teaching and I had taught during the summer. That's why I say, I thought I had reached a land of freedom when I came to Buffalo. But then I realized they had a different way of keeping you down, and reminding you that you're black."

Mr. Anderson said, "I have seen guys actually working with the Buffalo Common Council, where they really zeroed in to destroy somebody. If you can't destroy them by jobs, the DA will indict. Even though they know they can't convict. They bend it enough to destroy a person. It took me all my life to find out that things have basically not changed in this society. In fact, it has taken on a more subtle tinge, but the white arrogance and the white racism to a certain extent has stayed the same."

"Oh, yeah," Mrs. Anderson said. "I think so."

"It has stayed the same," Mr. Anderson said. "In fact, the thing that gets me about black intellectuals—they really think they are superior."

"You're talking about yourself," Mrs. Anderson said through laughter.

"No, no, I mean, actually they really think they are superior human beings."

"Did it take intellect to get through law school?"

"No."

Arthur Anderson was descended from a long line of exceptional Buffalonians. His great-grandfather, Benjamin C. Taylor, was the first black physician in Buffalo's black community. During the 1849 gold rush, Taylor ventured west to California with a friend, Robert Talbert. They were said to have returned successfully with fortunes with which they purchased a great deal of land in Buffalo and all over western New York. (Robert Talbert was said to have purchased more than thirty houses and 600 acres of land—later the Talbert family descendants would be duped out of their fortune; and Mr. Anderson told me he had "no idea" what happened to the legacy of Dr. Taylor.) Dr. Taylor had four daughters, including Arthur Anderson's grandmother, who married Gustavus Anderson. Arthur's father, James, became a district manager for the Courier Express, and his uncle Gerald became the first black person to work for the Buffalo post office. Perhaps most remarkably, his aunt Amelia Grace Anderson graduated from Syracuse University with a Ph.D. in Liberal Arts. Amelia was Secretary for Du Bois's Niagara Movement. When Mr. Anderson told me about his aunt—who in later years became more and more "eccentric," a mysterious spinster living in the large house originally owned by Gustavus, a woman who was never seen after dark, and who escorted visitors to the door at a precise hour—my imagination was captivated. I wish I could have met her.

But the spirit lived on in Michelle (who had clerked with the legendary jurist Constance B. Motley) and Sheila (who at a very early age sat on the national board of the NAACP as a youth member) and Michael. Chips had graduated from Harvard before he died. I reckoned it was bred in the bone.

Mr. Anderson told me how he got involved in the formation of a small college in Buffalo.

"I told you how we picked kids to go to the state university. On the corner of Jefferson and William. I'll never forget. We had a car with a bullhorn, 'Do you want to go to college?' And I said, this is ridiculous. Bunch of liberal whites wanted it that way. Then they proceeded to lay the grounds for the future disasters. And they did it step by step. When they organized the SEEK program—it stood for Search for Education Excellence and Knowledge—the instructions were that all of the counselors were going to select students with the lowest grades and the worst economic positions. Which means an ideal student was one with a 59 average and their parents were on relief. My question was, What about a young black fellow whose father works in the post office and has eight children, and the kid takes papers in the afternoon, and has an 89 average? The answer was: He's not to apply. So my idea is, why don't you use the same standard that you do with the whites? Get a transcript from high school, look it over and pick the best? They didn't want that."

Ultimately, Mr. Anderson told me, he ignored those guidelines. As he saw it, the educational system was designed "for the failure of blacks."

"That was in the late '60's. I had been a counselor at SEEK, and I was doing court reporting too. That's when I ran into that law professor who caught me doing court reporting. 'Hey, you can't do this too.' That was it. I had to leave the SEEK program and apologize for putting in the effort."

After law school Mr. Anderson got a job with education officials working out of SUNY-Buffalo, who had been given $2.5 million to establish an alternative college. They looked to Arthur Anderson to organize it. He arranged for the housing of the Cooperative College in downtown Buffalo, and commenced ordering supplies.

"Within two days, we had committed the university to like $350,000. Then one of my co-workers said to me, 'Let me call up and see how much more we're authorized to spend.' So he calls up. 'Oh, my God. Oh, my God.' I said, 'What?' He says, 'We only have your salary, Dick's salary and $10,000 for our office supplies!' He told them we had spent $350,000, and that they were stuck with the building, so they had to put it to use." At this point, Mr. Anderson was laughing so hard he broke into a coughing spell.

"But the point is we had to organize a staff and begin to enroll the students. Now this was August. So they agreed to start with about 300 students. Then I get a call from Albany, about the end of August, they said, 'Can you get 600 students in there so we can hit the legislature for more dough?' So again, it wasn't the interests of the students they had in mind. It was conning the legislature for more dough. And we had a program in order. So then we had to hire a staff, and take in the students all at once. But we opened on September 20th with 600 students and a staff. So we organized the whole school in about six weeks."

But after the death of SUNY Vice-Chancellor Emil Rivera, a man Mr. Anderson had great respect for ("He was a very dynamic man; he was sufficiently strong; we knew we were safe—when he died everybody was gone in six months."), things changed. The school was now the Educational Opportunities Center; "What they do now is help people get their GEDs—business courses, cosmetology, that kind of stuff." Understandably, Mr. Anderson had strong opinions about the New York State educational system. "You find that education has been the care and feeding of the education bureaucracy, not the education of students. Students have nothing to do with it. But to educate them—*Bah!* And the thing that's interesting is: it took the drugs. Not until it brings down the country sufficiently to where it affects the general population—meaning the whites—will there be a real crisis. Now it's almost approaching that point, because the white kids are coming up short too. They can't perform on jobs. I don't think it'll become a real crisis soon. I give it about ten years.

"You've got, on the one hand, a welfare mentality, and on the other hand, a mentality that says we should have it because we're black. There's no emphasis on economic priority. There's no emphasis on educating them. And where is your black leadership?

"It gets so bad—like for instance, the way that they treat the black inmates in the state prisons. Do you know who was one of the biggest contributors to the black office holders? The correctional guards. How can they protest? I met with two guys who were at Attica. They had been sent from Greenhaven to Attica, because their job was to make the black guys look bad. Then these two had a twinge of conscience, and they decided that they didn't want to be a part of it. So somebody decided to kill them. I had a hearing before a Superior Court Justice. To show how somebody was trying to kill these two men. By putting razor blades in their apples. That kind of stuff. The judge found no grounds. I knew the United States District Court judge. So one day I get a call from one of the black guards, they said, 'Anderson, they're going to move your guys out tonight at six o'clock and at eight o'clock one will be killed for trying to escape.'

"So I called the federal judge. I said, 'Judge, I hate to disturb you so late in the afternoon, but they're going to move my guys out this evening.

And one will be killed about eight o'clock trying to escape.' He said, 'Aw, Anderson, they wouldn't do that.' He said, 'They just appointed a new corrections commissioner in the state, and he wouldn't allow that. But I'll call you back.' So I said I'll work till he called me back and he said, 'Well, they were going to move them, but they changed their plans.' So the guy didn't get killed.

"One day I decided to go down to Attica, and they told me, 'You can't see your clients. You can't come in here.' I go outside and I call the head of the state prison. I can't get him on the phone. So I drive back to town, and draw up the papers, an order to demand that I have a right to go in to see my clients. I called up the state attorney general here. He says, 'Art, where do you come up with this bullshit?' The assistant state attorney general came over to the office. I said, 'You guys work this out. I couldn't get in to see my guys.' He said, 'Art, there must be some mistake.' He wouldn't address the issue. Two days after that, I go down to see my clients. As soon as I hit the front gate, the first guy said, 'Hey, did you see how your guys fought the guards the other day? Man, they were terrible.' Every guy I saw on my way in, this guard, this guard, every guard said, 'Boy, your guys were terrible.' By the time I finally saw them, they had been so badly beaten they probably couldn't have walked. So then I figured I can't possibly continue to represent these guys alone. I figured, Hey, I know what I'll do. I'll go to the head of the Baptist Ministerial Council. So I took a transcript to the head guy. He said, 'I'll see what I can do.' I never heard from him. Any of them. So I didn't know if the guard had been killed or what. Because I couldn't afford to represent any one of them. And the ACLU wouldn't come in because they would get no publicity out of it. After all, when you're poor and black you have no rights. When you're white and poor you have no rights either."

Later I spoke with Mrs. Anderson about growing up in Indiana.

Mrs. Anderson told me, "Course, in my family I knew in first grade I had to go to college. And I don't know why, I was always so sad when I heard the word 'college.' The first grade teacher said, 'Oh, you look so sad. What's wrong?' I said, 'I have to go to college.' And she said, 'You'd better work on first grade right now.' And I couldn't understand her, and I was so worried about college. Going to college. It was stressed so much in our family that maybe I figured, gee, it sounds awful to me. I don't want to go. I was a little strange anyhow because Mama was always asking us what we wanted to be when we grew up. We had been somewhere, at some church, and Mama and I, we were walking home together and, we were just talking, she said, 'Well, what do you want to be when you grow up?' I said, 'Mama, I want to be a sportin' woman.' And she said, 'Well, what is that?' I said, 'Well, Myrtle told us not to tell anyone, but she told us about these sportin' women and I don't see anything wrong about telling you.' And I said, 'Myrtle said that they get all dressed up and look real pretty and the men come in to see them.'

"And Mama kept quiet. And we kept walking. She said, 'Well, now, when you're old enough to go on that side of town, don't ever let me hear of you going by Myrtle's house.' See now, in our town, they had a red light district. It was legal. It was just in one section of the town. Our Methodist church was on that side of town, but it wasn't near the red light district. Now Myrtle's mother worked for the biggest whorehouse in town, and it was gorgeous. So when I got older, I found out. They had a little house that they lived in down the street from the whorehouse, which was in the red light district. So Mama knew that eventually I would probably go by bus over to church for rehearsal and she just assumed that Myrtle lived near this sportin' house. Mama didn't know her people at all.

"I'll never forget, when I got my bicycle, and I was in maybe seventh, or maybe sixth grade—but soon as I got my bicycle, I made a beeline for Myrtle's house. Because she had a bicycle too. She had everything. And she wore the best clothes and all like that, you know. And oh, did we have a ball, riding all over the neighborhood. And that's where I saw Madame Brown's place. The big whorehouse on the hill. I'll never forget. It was a yellow brick house. With a great big picture window, and it was on a corner lot. And then in the front, big picture window. We went in Myrtle's house, and she fixed something, because her mother was working down the street.

"I'll never forget. When I got home, it was at dusk. Mama was so mad. She didn't ask me where I had been. She had assumed I was in the neighborhood, but she said, 'Don't ever let me catch you riding your bike, and we don't know where you are.' She never dreamed I was with Myrtle. Over in the red light district!

"And so I think I was grounded for a few days, for taking my bike out and just riding. Now, when I got to eighth or ninth grade, I realized where Myrtle lived, that it was the red light district, and that these sportin' women were just plain old whores. Oh my God! I said, 'I hope no one who knew me saw me,' because everybody knew our family. And if they saw us anywhere that we weren't supposed to be, they would send word home. 'They'll tell Papa, and I will get a killing.' I never went back. I didn't see Myrtle from that day on. Myrtle evidently dropped out of school when we were sent to the white schools, because most of the black kids did. They just didn't go to school anymore. I wasn't in her neighborhood, and I had to go to my neighborhood school, which was in a white area.

"And I often think of that. You were not permitted to drive through that neighborhood, not unless you were there for business. So when I got to college, a bunch of us took the car. (Mama couldn't drive, and by that time, Papa was working at Purdue University, and he didn't use the car, so it just stood in the garage; he'd come home on weekends.) So one night we figured we'll go for a ride. The kids came by the house, and I told Mama, 'I'm going to take them home. Is that okay?' She said, 'Yeah, but you make sure you come right back.' I said, 'Oh yeah.' So we made a beeline for the red light district!

"So the girls put on the boys' hats, and we drove slowly. And I saw Madame Brown's house, all lit up. And these white women, they sat in these chairs with their legs crossed. They had on satin gowns, and they were sitting there. There were like two in this picture window, sitting. And two in the other front window. And the lawn was beautifully landscaped, and it had a wrought-iron fence around it. And as we drove through, we got down to these little shacky-looking houses, where the blacks were, and they had a little red light in their window. And they almost knocked over the wall trying to get us to stop.

"So I told them, 'We'd better get out of here.' So we rushed out, and I hit a railroad track, and messed up something on the car. I didn't get home until real late. I don't even remember how I got home. I don't know if I had to leave the car. I just don't remember. But Mama wanted to kill me. But I could always talk her out of something, because she always thought I was so honest. I very seldom gave her any trouble. I wasn't like my sister next to me. She was always doing something. But I wasn't like that. She could trust me, pretty much, she thought.

"But it was interesting to think that that little tiny town had a red light district. When the war broke out, they did away with it because there was an army camp nearby. And it hadn't always been there. And my mother was very upset when they closed it down, because she said, 'Now it'll spread all over the city. You won't know who you're living near.' "

Mr. Anderson said, "So the point is: we have not made progress as a group, but we have made permissible progress."

"Well, you know, this is awfully depressing," I said. "What advice do you have for me and my generation? Can things be fixed?"

Mrs. Anderson said, "I'll tell you about my husband. It's always doom and gloom with him." She laughed. "And I think you should stop that, Art. Because some good has come with a lot of the noise that the young people made in the '60s."

"Oh, some good has come," he said. "But like a friend told me one day. He was talking about what happened in the '60s. He said, 'It's like when your house catches fire. You turn on all the water, the hose and everything else. The main thing to do is to put the fire out. But now the cork's back in. My idea is, it boils down to the best you can do day by day. Develop whatever potential that you can. But when you get an overall change, it will be brought about by an unpredictable catalyst."

"I don't think any form of government is perfect," said Mrs. Anderson.

"No form of government is ever organized for the benefit of all the people."

"I really think the opportunities are there."

"Oh, they are there, sure."

"And a few blacks will make it," said Mrs. Anderson.

"A few, yeah," said Mr. Anderson.

"And I don't think that when you make it, all the other blacks are going to say, 'You've left your community. Why don't you reach back and bring others along?' I don't think you can do that, really."

Mr. Anderson said: "No, no, no, no, it isn't doom and gloom. It's looking at the range of possibilities. Who was it who said, 'The worst curse that could come to any man is to be able to see both sides of the question.' And I always think that's true. You've got to be this way or that way. I mean, if you can black out your mind and be a revolutionary, it's one thing. But if you try to see both sides—"

"Well, I think these are some exciting times," Mrs. Anderson said.

"Oh, they are exciting times."

"Because there's so much that a young black can take advantage of."

"Oh, sure, really."

Mrs. Anderson said, "But, gee, I look back and see all these things open to these people and I read about these young men who were in fashion. Of course they die out young, but I mean, they've made big bucks. They've made their way. Of course I don't know if a female—I don't hear much about them. But I would have loved to have gone to—"

"Oh, I mean," Mr. Anderson said, "there are a lot of opportunities now that did not exist before."

"There's been progress made," Mrs. Anderson said.

"But the thing is though, those in control have erected a wall of the mind. Like for instance, you must have had in school psychology experiments with rats. You put food here and have them run toward it, then you close down the gate. And they hit the glass. And you do that six or eight times. Then you put the food there, you don't put down the glass, but they never run for it."

"But the only thing, Art, it isn't fair for you to group all whites together. That's what they do to us. Because if it hadn't been for some good white people during slavery, we'd still be—"

"Oh, no, yeah, no, no, it isn't all whites, but those who control." Mr. Anderson said. "As long as there's an echelon that you are not exposed to, you can say at least up there, there's a degree of justice—"

"You know what, Art?"

"—the unfortunate part is to be among them."

"When Art was a little boy," Mrs. Anderson said, "he grew up in a white neighborhood. I grew up in a white neighborhood. We were about the only black family on our block. And traditionally here in Buffalo they were friendly with their neighbors and talked to each other. They were the business people on Williams Street. But where I grew up, Mama dared us to ever be caught in any of their houses. And evidently, the parents of the white kids were told the same thing. I don't ever remember a white kid coming in our house. Of course there were only two kids in my age group on my block. Two white kids. We could play outside and talk, but never go into their homes. We were only friendly with two families, the people who lived next door. They were German. We would talk outside. The girls, they were older than myself and my sister, next to me. And then two doors down, these kids. We did not communicate, we didn't go to school together. Now, Art went to school with all the kids. We had to go to a black elementary school. Then in high school we were with the white kids, who came from all over. In fact, there were thirty-two black kids in my first grade. And only two of us went to high school and finished, and two of us went to college and finished.

"Art remembers the kids he went to school with. But when I got with the white kids in junior high and high school, we just didn't talk. It was just like I wasn't there. And I didn't expect them to talk to me. So when I went to state teacher's here, I would sit and not talk to anyone. And we had one of those silly teachers who was always joking. And I wasn't interested in laughing at any of his jokes. They weren't funny to me. And a girl nudged me, and she said, 'Why don't you laugh? Why don't you laugh?' I just figured they were like the white people at home. They're not going to talk to me, so I accepted it. Then I found out that they were friendly, so I relaxed a little, and I became friendly. But see, Art didn't have that experience, and I don't know why he is so doom and gloom." She nudged him and started laughing.

"No, no, no," he said. "The point is, it isn't doom and gloom. Back in the old days, it would have been impossible to do what you do."

"Me?" I asked.

"Yeah," he said, "But now the times have changed, see. So I mean from a collective standpoint I don't see any improvement. Individually, you can do it."

Mrs. Anderson said, "You're talking about the masses."

Mr. Anderson cited a number of cases where individuals ran afoul of the establishment ("You see a selective prosecution"), and one black woman judge in particular who was ultimately taken off the bench for not "playing the game." "I think the tragedy comes from not being aware of your own limitations. If you associate with enough white people, you'll think there are no limitations on you either. As blacks go higher and higher, they hit the glass ceiling and you have more frustration. You hit the ceiling, but you can still see the sun. So you're deluding yourself into thinking that you can also share the rays. Before that, we didn't even have a chance to rise. Now you do. With a little imagination, and a little push, what cannot be done?

"But the main thing is the thrill of something new. But when it comes to my attitude about education and law, like I said to one of the guys one day, 'You know, the only field that's worse than law is education.' He said, 'Why?' I said, 'Because if you push a lawyer a little bit, he'll admit he's full of shit. But an educator never will. Educators delude themselves into thinking they were called by God to destroy kids.' Deal with the hierarchy, Albany, the central office, talk to the educators here, like the Board of Education. When they refer to the central office, it's like they're talking about heaven. In awe. The image is the essence. See, and also—"

Mrs. Anderson interrupted, "But Art, I think you're looking for perfection in education."

"No, no, no, no. I'm not looking for perfection. I'm looking for a degree of sincerity."

"Yeah, but—"

"As a country, collectively, you have to have some principles to build on. As a race, you've got to have some principles."

"Well, Art, really now, let's be fair. You weren't in it that long."

"Yeah, but I can see where people develop the art of writing satire. You find out that it's universal, no matter what field. To me, it's an endurable existence from the standpoint that it makes no sense. There's an old saying, and down here it's true: When a deer is trapped, and he knows he can't escape, his heart explodes. Have you ever heard that?"

"But I really don't understand," Mrs. Anderson said.

"What?"

"Your attitude."

"What? Why?"

"Because you didn't grow up in such a hostile environment the way I did."

"Being black," Mr. Anderson said, "I'll tell you, if you don't start out being aware of it, experience will remind you. It's an advantage being brought up being aware of great obstacles. Rather than thinking there are none, and finding out they were there all the time."

"Well, see, you didn't think there's—"

"No, I thought there were none. See; I figured you could—"

"He thought he was white. He thought he was a Jew."

"Yeah, sure, really."

"And you know where he really got a jolt? There was one lady who owned the Ten Cent store on Williams Street. She and her husband. Very friendly."

"Very friendly."

"Very close as a family. So when her husband . . . was it her husband, Art?"

"Yeah, Al dropped dead."

"Art went way out in the suburbs, she wouldn't even speak to him."

"Yeah, I walked in and she looked around and kept on talking. And I had known her since I was a little boy." He paused in reflection, and then said, "If you learn how to walk step by step, appreciate each step."

"Do you think I'm as angry as this kid?" Mrs. Anderson asked me, patting her husband's hand, regarding him with affection and a touch of bewilderment.

"I'm not saying a word," I said.

"No, I mean, I'm not angry." Mr. Anderson said, "If you can only keep the bright ones dreaming. You got to help them with their dreams."

In 1832 Buffalo became the first city in the western portion of New York State to incorporate as a municipality. It would become one of the country's most vibrant and exciting cities for decades. Anthony Trollope, traveling in 1861–2, was very taken by the grain elevators ("as ugly a monster as has been yet produced. In uncouthness of form it outdoes those obsolete old brutes who used to roam about the semiaqueous world, and live a most uncomfortable life with their great hungering stomachs and huge unsatisfied maws"); but in the end, he said of Buffalo: "It is a fine city, like all other American cities of its class. The streets are broad, the 'blocks' are high, and cars on tramways run all day, and nearly all night as well." Thanks to Andrew Jackson and his Erie Canal, Lake Erie and Lake Ontario helped make Buffalo one of the busiest hubs—if not the busiest—in this frontier nation, and Buffalo was preeminent among those rising American cities. By the time Mark Twain gave up adventuring in the Wild and Bad West, and married a wealthy socialite of old Buffalo stock, the city—which he found intolerable at best—was the very epitome of "civilization," rivaling even the old money of Gramercy Park. Indeed by the time the Astors and the Vanderbilts began building what Twain would lampoon in *The Gilded Age,* Buffalo was already long secure and firm in its grand heritage.

Among, around, beneath, behind, alongside those benighted robber barons were of course black folk. In 1828 there were 60 African Americans in Buffalo; by 1855—twenty-five years after the Erie Canal was completed—there were 700. Though blacks would not establish neighborhoods recognized as black neighborhoods until the turn of the century, the first black churches were established in 1831 (the Buffalo A.M.E.) and in 1836 (the Michigan Avenue Baptist Church). When public education began in the 1830s, blacks wanted to send their children as well, but met with resistance. Most of the children were sent to what was known as "the African School" on Vine Street, which received inadequate funds from the city and state. The black folk of Buffalo fought steadily against the segregation and lack of support (Dr. Benjamin Taylor is listed among those engaged in the battle), a struggle that was effectively won in 1881.

Buffalo also became an active terminal and station in the Underground Railroad. Much of that information has vanished or is deeply hidden or simply lost, but much is still known: the creation of the Buffalo City Anti-Slavery Society (founded in 1834—New York State did not abolish slavery until 1841); the secret passageways and rooms used to hide slaves can still be seen in the Michigan Avenue Baptist Church; Mary B. Talbert, a relative of Robert, was at Harriet Tubman's deathbed.

In truth the number of blacks in Buffalo dropped dramatically in the 1850s. Many historians explain that fact by pointing toward the Fugitive

Slave Act which included the federal government in the searches for runaway slaves and the 1857 Supreme Court Dred Scott decision which held that slaves were still slaves, even in a free state. By 1895 there were said to be fewer than 1,000 black people living in the city.

Later, steel would become Buffalo's backbone—Bethlehem Steel et al—and by 1910 several thousand sons and daughters of the South would make their way up to the factories, finding all manner of work. Those few old families, like the Andersons and the Talbots and others, were mightily overshadowed by the throngs of new folk finding work. In the 1990s, 70,000 of Buffalo's 328,123 people were black—and unemployment was close to 10 percent. (In 1950 Buffalo's population was almost 600,000, and unemployment was less than 1 percent.)

Driving around Buffalo, it became apparent to me how much effort—and money—was being put into its redefinition. Downtown was under renovation, with new buildings amid some of the oldest and most influential commercial architecture in the nation; a trolley car had been refurbished and reinstalled; high-toned developments were going up down by the lake. (Though in the Fillmore section—once famously Polish but now practically all black—Buffalo seemed physically frozen in the midst of an economic collapse. It seems the new development had yet to spread in that direction.)

A city of ups and downs, by the mid-nineties Buffalo looked as if the worst of its economic woes were behind it. Along with the rest of the Rust Belt, the city on the lake was struggling to reinvent itself for a new millennium. Newer, lighter industries were being encouraged and growing; the city fathers were rethinking Buffalo's place in the New York economy and in the economy of the world, just as Pittsburgh and Allentown and Youngstown had. However, the way black folk would fit into that new equation was not completely clear.

I took a trip out to the old, now-defunct steel mills on the shores of the lake, near Lackawanna. Many were abandoned altogether, vast, rusting, ghostly hulks. These hangar-like behemoths of decay, all black and brown and ominous, would have elicited Trollope's most vehement response, considering what he thought of the grain elevators. Nonetheless, I found in them a compelling sort of beauty—in their abstract deterioration and crumbling collapse—and I could not help but wonder how they might have looked in the days when steel made Buffalo a true power, and when it was not a city rushing to catch up with the present.

. . .

Ken Holley was director of the Lutheran Unemployment Center, and he also ran a bookstore, Harambe, near Fillmore. A seemingly mild-mannered, thoughtful man, he took time out of his schedule to talk to me at his store.

He told me about a new novel by Connie Porter, called *Allbright Court:* "It's about growing up in Lackawanna, which is a suburb of here." The novel recounted the lives of the men who worked for Bethlehem Steel, and their families, and how, when the steel mills started laying off the men, "the whole thing changed," Ken Holley said.

"Pittsburgh and all these places had these gigantic steel mills going full blast in the '50s and stuff, and then all of a sudden, they were really obsolete. You know, the foreign steelmakers. Suddenly everything just went dead on them."

The effects on the men who worked in the mills were devastating to many, Ken Holley told me. "You'd see them starting to abuse their families. And the other thing is how, in the '50s and '60s, we tried to appease white folk. How their mothers always told them they had to be clean. 'You can't smell. White folks don't like this.' That kind of mentality. When men came here and worked in plants, they got pretty good-paying jobs. Got the car and everything. Black men started to go back home in their cars. Call on the family in their big car. Go South, show all the relatives what they're doing. And when all that stopped, it was like disaster for the families and the whole community, because all the people really had ties to Bethlehem Steel. It was really, really hard."

The entire economy of the Rust Belt was changing dramatically, he told me. "Those same young black men are not going to be a part of this new thing that they got. And if they do become a part of it, it's in the lower service end. So a lot of men could have been making more in 1960 than they're making today. And still have to raise a family and everything. Their sons may never make as much as they made, and that's all kind of sad, when you stop to think about it. Their sons may never have a job for an extended period of time like their fathers had. Even though they were laid off, a lot of these men were there like twenty or thirty years. Where their sons are now doing service jobs. Anything from McDonald's to working in a hotel as laundry aides, housekeeping. Jobs usually that you don't want to stay in and that you don't stay in. And jobs that you can't have no pride in neither."

Young black men from the South were still arriving in Buffalo, Ken Holley told me, full of expectation. "They can't believe it when they get here. Because down there they were working sometimes, because the welfare system's so bad down there, you got to do something. You're going to starve down there, especially as a single black man. They want to give you nothing down there. So they were doing some kind of service job, and up here they're struggling even to get into that. It's a whole different ball game. But like I said, these are symptoms. And when you get these young men who feel that they can't do any better, you're going to have trouble in this community. The streets are not going to be safe. Most people don't feel safe, let's say. It's not like being in L.A. or somewhere, but most people do not feel safe in the black community in Buffalo."

I commented on how so much seemed out of whack in Buffalo to me. And I wondered if there was any infrastructure at all in the black community.

"Well, it depends on what area you're talking about. If you talk about politically, I would say yes. As far as trying to pull everybody into the political system, and getting people out to vote, and doing the basic thing for people. It's probably a vacuum after that. If you're talking about a social infrastructure, there's probably none. Even the black church here has gone inward, for their own survival, rather than trying to be a community resource for people. Maybe it's more because of economic times, and the type of ministers that are coming. I know in the few churches that were at one time community-based, the minister has now taken a very much more spiritual outlook. In other words, they wanted to separate themselves from community services. That's a major problem—you're leaving out most of the buildings and most of the structures where you could do things if you eliminate the churches."

Ken Holley told me that now Buffalo had a lot of people "on the fringe," who simply didn't have much to donate. A lot of storefront churches had opened, and schisms had developed in many of the older congregations. Just keeping some of "these buildings" going—with reduced and poorer populations—was a drain in and of itself. "I think the power base is still out there because there are so many of them."

Had the black church seen its best days as a base of power?

"Not really," he said. "If we go back, the black church has always been built on a community base. The black church has been the place where people come for meetings, start schools, and as recently as the '60s, it was the backbone of the whole Civil Rights movement. When it goes back to that, to being its natural self, it will become a power base again. Just recently in New York, a minister and his wife, who used to be here, have started an independent school out of their church. And that's being done all over the country. It just takes a rethinking, to go back to what they really were when they came into being. The service. It wasn't just the spiritual needs. A lot of times what's happening now is the ministers are forgetting that."

I asked if the Nation of Islam and other groups had established a foothold in Buffalo.

"Islam's growing," he said, "Islam's growing on two fronts now. Islam's growing under Prophet Muhammad. And also Islam under Elijah Muhammad—which is now Mr. Farrakhan's thing. So you got it growing on both fronts, especially with young black men. And if you get a lot of young black men, they pull young black women into it. Because young black women, no matter what anybody says, they want to be around black men. Especially when they determine that they're standing up and acting like men, what they perceive men should be. So the two forces combined, they're really pulling a lot of people into Islam, yeah."

I shared some of my observations with Ken Holley, some of the things other black folks were saying about the problems facing black America as a whole. I wondered if he thought a lack of parental involvement might be the cause of many problems among black youth.

"I don't think that's the cause of their problem, really," he said, "the parents working hard. I think what's happened is, Europeans are frightened. It's happening all over the world. The same thing is happening in Canada, to African people of Caribbean descent, and over in Europe to Africans from the continent. That fright is coming from white men vying for the jobs, vying for positions. Traditionally, no matter where we are in the world, we get what's left over. And when the countries are going through good times or prosperous times, there's jobs running all the way up to the middle class that are left over for us to take. But when things go bad, white men are saying, 'Lookit, you can't come over here. You can't take our jobs.' So racism really comes down. It's open warfare on people of African descent all over the world when that happens."

What about the high level of dropouts? "Can we blame that on racism?"

"It's definitely racism," he said. "It's almost like the church again. Children usually learn from what they see and what they experience more so than what you tell them. So if a black young man goes in a school system, and he behaves like he's been taught for the first five years on the street, and what he sees other black men doing, when he goes in the school system, he's going to have problems. Another thing is that most of the teachers are going to be female teachers, so he's going to have a double problem. I think if you're going to turn it around, you really have to get some radical solutions to a radical problem. What you have now is a few of us get through the system, and everybody points to the few that get through, the few that go to Harvard, the few that go to Yale. But the mass of the system is really set up for the mass of us to fail. For the masses of young black men not to get through high school even, for them to see the street crowd there and be attracted to it and never go to school. The way they think, school is for somebody else. It's not for them."

But again, I asked if the burden was not still on black folks.

Ken Holley said, "Saying things stem from racism is not saying that we are powerless, or we should lay down and do nothing. But we have to recognize racism for what it is. It's a powerful system, and we've got to deal with it. As a matter of fact, once we recognize that, it should even make us more active, and more enthused to do something, instead of less. Once you identify a problem, that's halfway to solving it. But for some reason, once people start saying it's racism, that means that it's over. There's just nothing that can be done about it."

I asked what he thought our options were.

"As individuals or as a people?"

"Both, I guess."

"Basically what you got to do," he said, "is you got to start with your own situation, because what we do as a people, we see it as this big gigantic problem, that we can't do nothing with. Because if you can't do nothing with yourself, you can't do nothing with nobody else. Black men have to become involved in family again. I think that's key. If we're not involved in family, that means we're going to be involved in all kinds of other stuff. None of it is very positive, usually. That's a starting point. If we could start building for the family, for the community, for the nation at large. You must say, 'What can I do?' Instead of looking for this messiah figure just to pop up. Everybody's waiting for a Martin Luther King, a Malcolm X. Not realizing if you read history, all of these men were struggling at the time of their deaths. Asking the same question you're trying to answer. What do we do to solve this problem? How do we come together? There's no panacea out there. It's going to take a lot of work, and it's going to take time too. And that's the other thing, do we have the time? That's the major question I ask myself."

I found Ken Holley a thoughtful, sincere and, I felt certain, a good man. We talked for a while about African American history, and he shared his worries about how drugs were being used to eliminate so many black folks ("Who lets these drugs curiously go on, in certain areas of the city?"), and he lamented the breakdown of the extended family ("In my day, ladies we used to call 'Big Mama' didn't work usually. They were home."), and how welfare was designed not to uplift, but to disrupt, and how some females were having babies too young, and some males had no notion of responsibility ("No values"), and how the nuclear family was "never a reality, even going back to Africa. It was always more than just that."

"But I don't think the problems are insurmountable," he said, "I think it's just going to take a lot of individuals. Most of us want to only focus on one little area. When that doesn't work, we're ready to give up."

In the end, it seemed, Ken Holley had tremendous faith in African Americans. The hope, the possibilities, lay in North America, not Africa. "Even when I go to the continent, I see less and less a sense of their own identity. I see European thought running rampant in Africa. Some people say the hope is in Africa; I don't see it myself."

"I see the hope with us," he said. "We've got more time. In Africa, you got so many people—some of them just survive. Whereas if we ever get our thing together, we got time to study and think. I really think the hope of our race, no matter how bad it looks worldwide, is here. I think on a big level, we're going to understand our American thing, our identity as African Americans. Not just as Americans. I think we got to understand who we are, all the way. Just take the American experience, first of all. You got to start with slavery for most of us and that's a bad way to start out with any people. That forgets how you became enslaved. You didn't come here as slaves, but you were a slave. How you lost so much. How come everybody else still has some understanding of what language they spoke, and what group of people they belong to and stuff like that? You got to understand that you are African American. People want to say they're just African. But I tell them, you can't tell me you're just African when you miss a McDonald's hamburger. You can't say this experience doesn't affect you. This experience affects everybody. There's no way you're going to escape America. I don't care who you are. Because most of us intellectually don't believe that opportunity is there for us to do this. But I really believe it is."

Ken Holley introduced me to a gentleman named Tim Smith. He was in his mid-eighties, but he had the physique and the energy and the exuberance of a man decades younger, and his voice was profoundly resonant. He told me, at a great clip, of his days as a union organizer. "I knew all the big boys," he chuckled, as he showed me picture albums and clips of his days at the great conventions. Meany and Hoffa stood by his side.

The day he met with me he wore midnight-black shades that he never removed, and had a bandana tied around his head, topped with a hat. I wanted to talk about the life of the mill workers and black folk in Buffalo in those days, but he had his own program.

"My dream," he said, and handed me a mimeographed paper with that old purple ink. It read:

> Attention!!!! Attention!!!!! Attention!!!
> The UNITED STATES IS IN TURMOIL SO
> WE BEING THE ANCESTORS OF KUSH MUST CORRECT
> OUR PROBLEMS OF COMMUNITYS.
>
> THE WORKERS UNITED MOVEMENT BRANCH #3
> ARE SEEKING STABLE YOUNG BLACK MALES:
> Strong in mind and faith.
> Tired of the present situation in our communitys.
> Able to work together as one.
> Being able to EDUCATE our PEOPLE and our CHILDREN.
> LEARNING about our ORIGIN (where you came from).
> Energy to work on task no matter what obstacles we encounter. . . .

Another handout was headed: "The Cushite Organization." "ITS BASE: To teach its theory and deal with needs of self identity." The goal of the organization was to establish a cooperative with the "continent of Africa." "With clothes, shoes, work clothing, with farm equipment for light and heavy farming." "It will correct most of their problems in this country until they exist back in their mother land of their ancestors."

"We will never be nothing in this country till another 100 years," Mr. Smith told me. "Till you decide to put your mind to all. Calamity is coming to this country, I'm sorry to say. The white man is going to pay."

Mr. Smith took me out to his car, and opened up the trunk. There he showed me African sweet grass: wispy, bright green, seemingly delicate. And he spoke of the plant's miraculous properties, its multitude of uses, especially for the body. It seemed something of a panacea in his mind.

I made it as far west as Lorain, Ohio, where I had intended to snoop about (the hometown of Toni Morrison, a town she once described as "too small to be segregated," just sixteen miles from Oberlin, famous for being a major hub of the Underground Railroad), but I fell ill with the flu. From a motel on the shores of Lake Erie I lay abed and watched the Senate ratify Clarence Thomas's appointment to the Supreme Court—52 to 48—the largest number of votes ever cast against a confirmed justice. That very night a storm roiled the great lake and winds shook my flimsy building, as Senator Byrd of Virginia made mystic and classical references in favor of Anita Hill, and the faces of Ken Doggit and Arlen Spector merged in my fevered brain. Peering across the icy graveyard of Lake Erie, I imagined I saw Canada. And it occurred to me that if we all had a bit of the juice of African sweet grass, perhaps we would all feel better in the morning.

Six

# THE SNOWBIRDS

*Idlewild, Michigan*

I came rolling into Idlewild, Michigan, late of an evening in mid-October, on Route 10 from the east. As per usual I had no idea where I was going to stay. Indeed, I only had a small notion of what I'd find in this small town I could barely locate on the map. The dark was the inkiest I remember—of course, when you are lost, the dark always does seem darkest; I could barely make out houses obscured by shadows; I could hear leaves whish and whorl, crackle and crisp, as Bucephalus careened down those small roads. After taking several wrong turns, thinking I had been lost and imagining that I had run across Sasquatch and whatnot, I happened upon the Party Store, and there I met its owners—Calvin and Patricia Cormier—who to my delight were black. They told me there was no lodging in Idlewild, and took me down the road to Baldwin, where I got a room in a hunting lodge.

The kindness of strangers.

After I checked in, the Cormiers stopped by to chat.

"I left Texas awhile back. A long time ago," Calvin Cormier told me. A large, sturdy man with a large mustache, he lacked pretention, and his mirth and decency were instantly apparent. "Texas City, Texas. I left in '58." They had been living in Pasadena, California, until two years ago, when they made the move to Michigan. "In '90. And she happened to find some friends she followed up here. She started this place, and she came back and said, 'Hey, this is the place. We're going to—' And I was kind of skeptical. I said, 'Oh, I don't want to go to Michigan. I tell you what, Honey. You go ahead.' She was retiring the next year. So it was '88. So she retired and came up and left me there in California all alone. I said, I'll work another five years, you know. And I started coming back and forth. I must have made at least six trips up here, back and forth, within that period of time, and the store became available. And she said, 'Well, hey, we have the opportunity to buy the little store.' So I said, 'Well, maybe, just maybe.' I came up and when I came up, it was just about this time of year. And there's snow on the ground already. And I didn't like it at all. I said, 'No way. Uh-huh.' Milling around, walking in the snow, and the longer I walked, the colder it got, so I said, 'No, no part of this.' We were at her friend's house, and she said, 'Calvin, why don't you go out and warm my car?' But I didn't know I had to go out and *find* the car. This is the truth. Snow. The car was covered with snow. This is October. But the longer I stay here, I guess it's wearing on me. It's just becoming a habit to get up and put on your long johns. It's something that I haven't been used to doing. I get up now, I'm comfortable. I put on two or three layers of clothing and get out here and it's okay. I don't miss Los Angeles. I don't miss California at all. I don't miss it. The longer I stay here, the better it gets. It's good. It's a different feeling altogether. You know, it's wide open space."

Patricia Cormier was neither a small nor delicate woman; she was at once feminine and strong. She smiled while remembering her first impression of Idlewild: "Aaaah, I'm sitting here having breakfast, looking out the window and watching the squirrels run up and down the trees and the rabbits running across the lake. I know they thought I was just joking. Just sitting and drinking coffee and looking out the window. To me that's as close as you can get."

"I came here," Mr. Cormier said, "I saw turkeys running across the street, walking across. Wild turkeys. Deer. This is bow season and small game now. We're talking, the rabbits, the squirrels. I'm learning a lot, you know. I figure by this time next year, I'll have my suit on and my tag on my back and a-hunting I shall go." He laughed.

"We kept stopping on the bridge," Mrs. Cormier told me. "They had the trout. I've heard fish stories, but I had never—"

"The salmon run upstream," Mr. Cormier said, "and right at the bridge you cross right there. We're talking 50-, 60-, 70-pound fish. And you ought to see them when they run up. The river is going down, they're coming up, they're swimming up and you'll see them, swimming just to get up."

"Oh, that must be beautiful," I said.

"Imagine every township has a trout farm built, right? And you can imagine how many cities that these fish pass through just to get up river, to spawn. That's a thought. I mean, they're strong fish, and they have to fight the currents and everything. Just to get up there."

"We could stay there for hours watching them," said Mrs. Cormier.

"Just like you see it on TV," said Mr. Cormier.

"Just like something new."

"Yeah, you see it on TV," Mr. Cormier said. "You're sitting in southern California and you're looking at this, and say, 'Aw.' But then you get up there and living in it, it's altogether different. Brand-new experience. I'm becoming a part of it. What is it, what am I now? A Mishu what?—

"Michigonian?"

"I'm a Michigonian." Clearly the idea delighted Calvin Cormier. We all laughed.

"Was it a tough decision?" I asked. "Were you looking to move somewhere? And did the fact that this place had a history, a black history, figure into it?"

Calvin Cormier said: "Well, to tell you the truth, I didn't know anything about this place at all. I'd never heard of Idlewild, Michigan, in my life. In Texas City, Texas, I went to an all-black school. I'd been in segregation. I left in '58, and they closed the school in '60, I think it was 1960, and they integrated. Well, I spent my life in California. I was a young kid. I didn't know anything about Idlewild. I didn't know that the blacks couldn't go here or go there. Hey, segregation was just a part of life. I never did think about—where'd the entertainers go? I thought they'd go home. I thought maybe they had a break, and they would go with the whites, something like that. And my wife brought home some material and the more I read, it kind of opened up my mind to think about, when I was a kid, what happened to these people. And come to find out they was all right here. They was all right here, living a good life. Just all black."

Patricia Cormier had been raised in Lafayette, Indiana, "home of Purdue University." "And there was about, four or five hundred blacks. We had a segregated grade school." And while the segregated grade schools had offered her teachers like Mrs. Millen ("By the time we left that grade school, we knew algebra. I always made an A in algebra. I really appreciated being in segregation, because they taught us that we had to be better than. That's something that doesn't happen now.")—for high school, she had been sent to the predominantly white school across town: "Like in my graduating class, there was 242, I'll never forget it. And there were three black girls. I'm one of the three." Mrs. Cormier told me it was a often an awful experience: "You sit there, and they're saying 'nigger' openly in class. It never registers in their minds that you're as bright as they are."

And though she felt she carried those memories ("Sure I carry them. I carry them right now."), Idlewild held a bright promise for them both.

"Nineteen eighty-three," Mrs. Cormier told me. "I think it was, first time, my friend started talking to me, she'd say, 'Girl, I found a three-bedroom house for $8,000.' Now, I said, 'Naw, naw.' And she lived next door to another girlfriend of mine, and I said, 'She's got to be telling a tale.' No kind of house . . . She said, 'There's a house. $8,000. You've got to come.' I could hit her. When I came, she had told about three other people, see, I didn't know this. So when I got here, the girl who had the store before me, had bought this little place. I can't get over it. It is so cute. Right down from the church. Ooof. But anyway, I said, 'I don't believe it. $8,000? I'm going.' So I flew up here, and she drove me all around, after she told me it was gone, and showed me a place, and told me about the history. And I said 'Well, I don't understand. How could all those stores have been here?' She gave me a brochure with Bill Cosby and all of them that had been here. I said, 'I can't believe that they left this place. But integration caused it. They just left and integrated. And this place just went to pot. I think if there was any way that I could contact any of these people, I would certainly tell them that this is an injustice against your own race."

"That's exactly what we're trying to do now," Mr. Cormier said. "I figure if I can get someone to publish something, and these people, they read, they read *Jet,* they read *Essence.* They read all the black literature that's out. If they just picked it up, 'I've been there. Let's fly back,' or 'Let's see what it looks like.' If I can just get one to come and see, maybe they'll start coming in. Sometimes, you get where you're going, but you forgot where you been. I mean, all you have to do is turn your head, look over your shoulder and say, 'Okay.' I think that's what happened. Lot of these people are gone now. But even Redd Foxx was here. Well, Jackie Wilson used to live right around the corner from the store. Even, what's the lady star?—Della Reese."

"And had a good time here," said Mrs. Cormier. "This is all they had. How can you leave something that was all you had at one time?"

Mrs. Cormier pointed out how the older retirees seemed hell-bent on keeping Idlewild underdeveloped, to hinder young people from moving in. "They're old and they don't want all these kids."

Mr. Cormier said: "Well, it can't be like that. In order to raise it back up to its glory, you have to have life. How the hell can you raise anything that's dead? You have to have life. You got to put life in it. If the tire's flat, you got to put air in it. This place is flat. Needs some air, needs fresh air. It's just that simple. Common sense'll tell you that, you see. You have to get young ideas, young adults. You have to get fresh blood in here to bring it up."

Apparently there were class problems involved as well.

Mr. Cormier said: "You have certain types, certain little cliques they call it. And you just don't do that, it's not done."

"They have that here," said Mrs. Cormier.

"They have it," said Mr. Cormier, "but it's on a different level. It's not being educated, it's on a different level altogether. Believe me. Well, you have your bourgeois and then you have your lourgeoise and then you have your niggers. You deal with color in all races, in all ethnic groups, you're dealing with color. That's just like now, our last name is Cormier. Okay. Cormier is French. When you talk on the phone, say, 'Cormier?' Well, they're putting Cormier with light skin. And green eyes. And sandy hair."—He gave a belly laugh—"Well, now, my dad was like that. My dad was a Creole. He came from Cuba and Germany. And my mom came from Barbados and Haiti. You understand? Now I'm Cormier. I can't help it because I'm reddish skinned. And I have black eyes. I'm Cormier. And I'm just as real."

"There is a woman," Mrs. Cormier said, "that lives on a lake and one of her other friends, who lives on the far lake, came over and she said, 'Cormier. I expected you to look like something else.' I thought: I *got* you. So that's what some of the ladies think. The snowbirds, they're in the city and they come by the summer. They have cottages. With the lake view."

"Well, that's all right," said Mr. Cormier. "But they all eat gumbo and jambalaya and crawfish and bo-dandy. And they all eat it with their fingers. The same. They're all the same."

One of the earliest and most eloquent boosters for the resort community that would become Idlewild was none other than Dr. William Edward Burghardt Du Bois. Writing in *Crisis* in 1921, he waxed romantic:

> For sheer physical beauty—for sheen of water and golden air, for nobleness of tree and flower of shrub, for shining river and song of bird and the low, moving whisper of sun, moon and star, it is the beautifulest stretch I have seen for twenty years: and then to that add fellowship—sweet, strong women and keen-witted men from

> Canada and Texas, California and New York, Ohio, Missouri and Illinois—all sons and great-grandchildren of Ethiopia, all with the wide leisure of rest and play—can you imagine a more marvelous thing than Idlewild?

So in love was the sociologist and historian that he himself purchased a number of lots in the area (though he never actually spent much time there; the idea of participating was enough for him). He went on to write:

> It is worth a great deal more than most people paid for it. The present price of $100 a lot is very cheap, but hundreds of lots sold for ten and twenty dollars. White men developed it because they knew how. We pay for the experience, but we pay a very low sum. Our hats are off to the Idlewild Resort Company . . . The lots are nearly all sold. It is our duty to develop, beautify and govern it. It must be a center of Negro art, conference and recreation. Its whole future is being turned over to a democratic Lot Owner's Association, composed exclusively of colored folk. Behold the day and the chance!

In 1912 six white men—Erastus Branch, Adelbert Branch, Wilbur Lemon, Mamye Lemon, Alvin E. Wright and Madolin Wright—purchased 2,700 acres (including a lake) roughly seventy miles north of Grand Rapids, Michigan, in rural Lake County. They formed a corporation, the Idlewild Resort Company (IRC), and aggressively sold the land, according to John Hart in the *Geographical Review,* in "small plots 25 x 100 feet in size with a price tag of thirty-five dollars each—six dollars down and one dollar a week" to black folk in Chicago, Detroit, Cleveland, Fort Wayne, Gary, throughout the Midwest and wherever else they could. The black media of the time picked up on the news and spread the word with hyperbolic zeal, so appealing was the idea of an affordable resort for African Americans. The IRC employed black salespeople throughout the country, exhorting them: "Undoubtedly you have friends who would be interested in securing lots . . . All you have to do is to get your friend interested, then call or write our nearest agent or communicate with the Chicago office. If you can handle the sale yourself, a location will be sent you." Many sites were sold sight unseen. The little community grew, quite literally, by leaps and bounds. Old-timers speak of how bungalows were hastily constructed, eight by ten feet, one door, called "dog houses," containing "two cots, a crude nightstand, a pitcher and bowl, a kerosene heater, a night pan usually stored under the small beds, a bucket for drinking water and a vintage hot plate." Though the conditions were primitive, again, the idea of an affordable, poetic, rural vacation spot brought in droves. There are photographs of crowds pouring out of buses and throngs at the shores of Lake Idlewild. In later years more suitable structures were built. Lela Wilson, one of the earliest salespeople, purchased eighty acres of land and called it Paradise. She built a store, a hotel, and what would become the Paradise nightclub. In later years she would be thought of as the preeminent Idlewild matriarch.

Helping Idlewild's reputation in the early days was the arrival of one of America's most prominent men—an arrival many Idlewilders are still surpassingly proud of—Dr. Daniel Hale Williams, the first surgeon to perform open-heart surgery. He purchased a large section between the years 1917 and 1925. Later he created the "Daniel Hale Williams Subdivision" and sold lots to the likes of Madam C. J. Walker, the millionaire of hair-care fame; Lemuel L. Foster, president of Fisk University; Louis E. Anderson, Chicago politician; and the North Carolina novelist, short story writer and lawyer, Charles Waddell Chestnutt, author of *The Conjure Woman* and *The Marrow of Tradition.* Here, Chestnutt's daughter Helen wrote, he "relaxed in the clear, pine-scented, health-giving air. He spent his days fishing, sitting in an old willow chair at the end of his little pier, absorbing the golden sunshine and catching a bluegill now and then with a bamboo fishing pole." Or he would row on the lake; or "sit before the log fire in the living room and read or play solitaire."

Whether it was the presence of distinguished folk or just the idea of a black resort, all sorts of people started arriving in Lake County, from minister to bootblack, from pharmacist to factory worker, from small businessman and teacher, to chauffeur and domestic—all came to enjoy those same rustic wonders.

The Idlewild Lot Owners Association took over the property in 1921, giving the IRC a $20,000 profit (the ILOA meets in cities all over the country to this day); and all manner of businesses began to spring up from dry cleaners to grocery shops—a veteran of the Spanish-American War, Sgt. Johnson, established the Clover Leaf Ranch for horse riding and outdoor enjoyment in the late 1920s. By the 1950s enough nightclubs and venues had been built for Idlewild to become an official stop on the Chitterlin Circuit—nicknamed by some the Fountain Blue and the Summer Apollo. Moms Mabble, B. B. King, Aretha Franklin, T. Bone Walker, Brook Benton, Betty-de-Bop Carter, Bill Doggett, George Kirby, Sarah Vaughan, Jerry Butler and Jackie Wilson were among the many who came through and performed at the Purple Palace, El Morocco and the Paradise Club.

By 1950, of the 5,257 people who lived in Lake County, 1,300 were "Negro." Some even did a little farming, but a small percentage. As can be expected, tourism was the helium that kept Idlewild afloat.

The next morning Mrs. Cormier took me to the township office where I met Audrey Bullett, the town manager, who not only had a very bad cold and problems breathing, but who had been up most of the night fighting a fire. Ms. Bullett's family had moved to Idlewild in 1954 from Chicago, when she was fourteen. She waited tables at all the nightclubs—all of which had closed by the late sixties. When her husband died, in the 1970s, she attended university and worked at the Lake County courthouse in various positions. She became Supervisor of Yates Township in 1984, of which Idlewild comprises practically all. In 1991 the population of Idlewild was around 583—the summers saw the population double.

Ms. Bullett didn't have much time, as she had to run off to Reed City. She spoke with me briefly regarding the community; how it now saw itself as a retirement community, and how it was much more integrated—65 percent black, and 35 percent white. She spoke of the historical significance of the place, stressing the presence of Dr. Daniel Hale Williams ("Dr. Dan").

After she left, I stopped by the shop of James Cox. A retired policeman, Mr. Cox had been a friend of the Cormiers from California. He was a huge man, with a shaved head and a greyish Vandyke beard, who wore tinted glasses and a piratical golden earring. Like Mr. Cormier, he saw enormous potential in Idlewild.

"They had the clubs," he told me, "and you couldn't pick up a *Jet,* an *Ebony* or *Hue* or *Color*—any black periodical that you picked up every week—you'd see something in there about Idlewild. Diana Washington was here, and Count Basie was here, and Duke Ellington was here. Aretha Franklin. All of them got their start right here in Idlewild. Four Tops and all of them. They had the Flamingos on. They had the Paradise over there. And bourgeois blacks, the middle class, the doctors and lawyers, they all played, and they had places around the lakes and whatnot. All the people used to come up here—B. B. King and Sammy Davis and all of them. And all the stuff that was happening up here then. If you go back, man, and see, even when I was in the navy, understand? In the fifties, I used to read about Idlewild. And I can remember my dad said,

'Dr. So-and-So was coming from California or from New York, or attorney so-and-so and his family was in for the summer.' Ella Fitzgerald was playing here. They had nine nightclubs up here then. And people would come all the way from Grand Rapids and Luddington, whatnot, to come up here to hear the jazz. The white folks come to the clubs, and never was any incidents. Nothing happened at that time. So people just come from all over, man. People from New Mexico and from Arizona, from Texas and Florida and all of them that had places up here. During the earlier days, I guess up until maybe the '40s or something, before they got main highways, the people used to come from Detroit. It would take them a couple days, because there was no highway, to get up there sometimes. There was a stopover in a couple places. Maybe Flint. Somewhere that they would go and they would stop overnight at some of these boarding houses that blacks used to have. But after it took them a couple days to get up here, it was mostly the wealthy that could stay. And that's what this was geared for.

"They would have nightclubs and whatnot. And people'd be sleeping out in the cars. They'd say it was so packed with campers. Whatever they could get. Man, when those people came up, hotels and motels and stuff would fill. Even now, when they have Idlewild Week, people come, and all the cottages generally during the month of August is filled up, man, people come and just hundreds more people when they have the festivals. And they start off with the picnic. And every day there's about three or four different activities. They'll have an African day and an Asian day and this kind of thing. They have parties and brunches and breakfasts and whatnot. All through the month of August. But it's concentrated during what they call Idlewild Week, which culminates with a fashion show."

James Cox described Fashion Flair, with food and drink flowing, and the show itself, with door prizes and dancing afterwards at the Lot Owner's Club. In October comes the Closing of the Cottages which is made into an event.

I was thinking about Martha's Vineyard, and asked if there were any overt class problems here, in his opinion.

He told me, "A lot of people here allow the status quo, man, and they want to keep it like it was. But there's a lot of changes. Like I said, when they started, it was all black. Now you got 30 percent white. Most of them, because it's a depressed area, are from all up through Lake County, but as I begin to see, in the last six years or so, there's been a migration of people to retire here because it's economically a lot cheaper than other places. With all the vacant houses and units here, it's a lot cheaper to live. So there's whites that's moving in here, because Idlewild is a beautiful area. It's the only public beach out here for several miles around. They got 156 lakes in Lake County. And 46 trout streams. But a lot of the lakes are surrounded, they're private."

He first came to Idlewild in the 1950s. "It was beginning to decline a little bit, I think around 1964. After the Civil Rights Act allowed blacks to go anywhere they wanted. I'd only been up here one time prior to that. But like I say, my kids used to come up all the time. I can remember reading about Idlewild. I said, 'One day I'm going to get me a place up there.' So when I came up here in '64, I said, 'They need something to give them a shot in the arm.' So we came up and bought a place. When I started putting them houses down, my wife opened up the shop here. I've talked several people into coming up here, just come up to visit."

He had just purchased his store from the township, that year. "Hopefully, we're going to make this the hub of things. So I talked Calvin into going in with me to buy the bar. It's the only one for five miles to Baldwin, and fifteen miles east. They'll stop at the bar before they even get to their cottage." He laughed. The previous owner was closed down. But his real dream, James Cox's ultimate Idlewild vision, was "to get a dude ranch, where families bring the kids up. Lot of people ride horses, and there ain't no place to play tennis. Riding bicycles, and this kind of thing. So I wanted to get twenty or thirty acres or so, and put cabins where people could come with their kids, and pay a minimal price, and they got the cooking facilities there and they'll have a place that they could go and cook and bring their food, and it's a convenient spot there, that they could rent some horses, at a minimal charge. Rent some bikes—so this is what I want to do." He said he'd been checking into the feasibility of the matter and researching and investigating since 1988, "but I need about $100,000. All I would need is $100,000 and all that wouldn't have to be paid at one time. I could pay down on them. Because this'll make money, summer and winter."

When I asked Mr. Cox's opinion on why Idlewild had fallen into decline, he told me, "We had a big part in it. There's a few people that held tight," but the prospects of the newly opened Atlantic City or Palm Beach or Las Vegas, dulled Idlewild's once-shimmer. "Then people began to explore and go to these other places." All entertainers found they could get booked in larger venues, and "I guess everybody wanted something a little better than what they had. I feel that was the ultimate."

However, Mr. Cox was most definitely an optimist. He felt the area could recapture its former appeal. It could be different, new; it could reinvent itself.

How long would that take? "The next five years ain't going to see it." But ideas were afloat, and opportunities were certainly there.

Driving around Idlewild left me with a mixed yet wonderful impression. The leaves were past peak, and mostly dun-colored and expired, interrupted every once and again by bright brilliant yellows. I went to see the Robert H. Rittle Youth Center, on the lake, cinder block, painted green, with a brown trim roof, all oblong shaped, and closed. I drove out to Williams Island, to see the site of the Paradise Club, long torn down. (The Flamingo Bar was the only remaining club.) The water of the lake was placid, almost brackish, dotted by dead leaves; nonetheless there was a quiet and still beauty about the place—it seemed so very far away from everything. Magnificent houses could be seen on the shore of Idlewild Lake—some peeking out from the curves—most of those apparently closed down for winter. Perhaps that is what pervaded the air and my mood: the sense of a ghost town. Yet Idlewild was not dead.

I visited the library, which was a squat, squarish building that had been once a school and now housed offices for tax assessment for Lake County and Yancey Township; the library itself was one largish room with a sad number of books—one wall and a half—and an even smaller number of books by and about black folk. Margaret Ray was the woman I spoke with that day, a lovely lady with perfectly coiffed, translucent angel hair, immaculately dressed. She told me of coming to Idlewild ten years ago from Chicago. She told me about her sons—one was a doctor, one taught law—and her daughter who also taught. I found her own past quite interesting: born in Montreal; her father from Nova Scotia; her mother from western Ontario.

Mrs. Ray told me her grandson called her Dugan, and his mother was Italian. Often he had rung her up and told her he wanted to come and live with her, because she was black. This was when he was seven. She told me about racism around Lake County. "Idlewild is a strange place," she said. "Some of the most wonderful people you would want to meet in the world; but it's a strange place." She spoke of the interaction among African Americans there and of how discrimination existed—"not so much discrimination, but problems between classes"—and "If you haven't got what I've got, then I won't talk to you, etc." She told me she was concerned about blacks not reading, and of how she herself was an exceedingly voracious reader, and how if she didn't have a book, she felt sick. We sympathized on that. She also spoke of how the funds for the library were running low, and how difficult it was to get new books, and she questioned whether it was worth it because people weren't using the library anyway. Margaret Ray gave me a great deal of information about the history of Idlewild, Michigan.

Later I went to visit the Wattses. I had seen Mrs. Watts at the library. Mr. Watts—an older man, wearing a cap—was working in his yard. At first he was mightily suspicious of my motives and really didn't want to talk to me. He told me: "I've given up on talking." He told me how some reporters came from a radio station wanting to do a story on Idlewild and after he talked to them for a long while, after he had given them all sorts of history, ultimately what they used from him was the statement "Idlewild is not the place for young people." And he was so dejected by the notion that all the media wanted to do was "portray the worst about us and never anything good." After I tried to convince him that that was certainly not my intention, he agreed to speak to me *but* he was cold from working outdoors all afternoon. He told me to come back tomorrow while he would be putting on a septic tank cover, and I said fine. He never showed up.

Back at the Cormiers' store, I met a woman who had moved to Idlewild from Detroit in 1989. She had visited Idlewild before its decline and she said, "It's night and day." She talked about "how wonderful it had been to be in a town where after you got off Route 10, all you saw was black faces. It was like coming to another world, a black country." People were trying to outdo one another in yard work, she said; it was absolutely stunning the way people kept their houses. She felt that the current black leadership was trying to sell the town out. When blacks came to buy land, they were only shown certain areas and she felt they were pushing for more whites to buy into the area, which she thought would ultimately expel the black folk. She felt very strongly that there was still potential, and "the reason we died is not so much from integration, but our own thinking. We didn't reinvest in the property." She told me what a wonderful party place Idlewild had been; how she got here on Thursday night and prepared herself for a long string of parties, parties that went on well into the wee hours of the morning, and then breakfasts, "breakfasts all over the place."

. . .

"Now, some of these books are so fragile. They're old."

"I understand," I said.

"This is from the beginning."

Mrs. Griffin "Trixie" Aldrich was sharing her photo album with me. "Yeah. 1919. You read some of these, and see what parts of it you can use. These are of the organization that first came up here. And of course, you can look at the attire and tell how old." She paused, her finger on the photograph of a stern-looking woman. "She's dead now. She was our mounted policewoman."

"Really?"

"And—let's see. I think I have—this lady right here, that's Miss Bullett. She was my waitress." Mrs. Aldrich let out a laugh. "She's quite a knowledgeable woman now though, believe me. So this is years back. And of course, that's me down there. So this is a long time ago." She laughed again.

Griffin "Trixie" Aldrich had been a showgirl at the Flamingo, and then she became a manager and producer in the 1950s. She had made Idlewild her home for a great many years.

She pointed to a photograph of a group. "Like this group here, they're gathering there. That's the way it looked at that time. And there were only some cottages over on that island, which we call Williams Island now. Across the street from the Club Flamingo. Of course, there was no such thing then. No streets or nothing. They just saw the beauty of the place, and they started putting up these little cottages, and I think we bought lots at that time from a girl who graduated with my sister. We didn't even know where they were. Didn't even know where Idlewild was. That's what they called this, Cottage City"—reading: "*If you buy lots in Idlewild, the payment within your reach, six dollars cash. A dollar a week, and the price is only $35,*" she rocked and laughed. "That was for lots 25 by 100 feet."

"I came up here in '40," she told me. "They had a club sitting right on that corner as you make the big circle coming back around the lake. It was called the Purple Palace. I came up here as a dancer. Mr. Giles had been my road manager, oh, for a couple of years, then, and he came up here, and he was another one that fell in love with the place. And there was very little going on. The Paradise Club was over here. It was a supper club, more or less like, for the firemen and the few people that lived up here at that time, but it was not a nightclub. They could have their parties there and whatnot. And then the Purple Palace was on that corner. Mrs. Hopper was running it. And Mr. Giles told her she needed a dancer in there on the weekends and during the summertime. People had begun to come. At that time, I happened to come up here. And oh, Mr. Giles decided to invest. He stayed up here—I think his first purchase was the hotel. And then, Mrs. Hopper was ill, went in the hospital, and that license became available. The beer, the club license. And he bought it, bought the license, not the building. He bought the license, and where that nightclub is now, he had just a little tavern there. It was a log cabin. He called that Film Charles. I didn't start working for him up here until he decided to build a nightclub. I was working at the Purple Palace, and after he bought the hotel, he put two boats on the lake, and I drove the boat—"

"Were these sight-seeing boats?"

"Uh-huh," she said. "Oh yeah. He took people out sight-seeing. One was chrisCraft, and the other one a—a—hmph. Forgot the name of it. But I used to drive one. I don't know if there's a picture in here of me with the boat. I have one in my basement somewhere. But during the day, that's what I would do. And at night I was dancing."

"Were you by yourself, or were there other dancers?"

"No, I was by myself at that time."

"What sorts of routines did you do?"

"Well, I did interpretive," she told me, "most all kinds of dance. And then after Mr. Giles got the club up there, and I started bringing the shows up, I had my own course. I didn't dance up there. I produced the shows. And then managed. I broke my leg up here. Course, that didn't stop me from dancing. I kept dancing a long time after that. But later years I gave it up and started working on the road with my own group. I carried my dancers, but I didn't dance. I just taught them, and I did narrations for exhibition basketball, and carried my dancers as part of the show.

"And I was still coming up here in the summers. Oh, we had all kinds of acts. The Club Paradise had the beautiful show. Because this was an investment for Arthur Bragg. He was in business elsewhere, when he took over the Club Paradise. As I said, that was a supper club, but he made a nightclub out of it, and called it the Fiesta Room. And he imported shows from Mexico and he had fabulous shows . . ."

Also present that afternoon was Mrs. Aldrich's sister, Master Sergeant Blanche C. Moon, United States Army, Retired. She was telling me—at the same time—about her work with the townspeople. "I learned that from a commanding officer. About four phases. The master plan." She was speaking of codes and ordinances that had to be established to make

Idlewild a fit place to live. "To get simple resolutions, such as no outhouses permitted to be built. Things of this type, because, 'good enough for my grandfather.' Hey. That was the answer we got."

The sergeant definitely had a commanding presence, and that day her attire had a more than vaguely military appearance. The cap she wore was certainly standard army. All of which contrasted sharply with Mrs. Aldrich's more matriarchal appearance—she had on a lace collar—but she was far from a pushover herself.

"This was in the 70s?" I asked the sergeant.

"The resolution," the sergeant said, "I can show you two or three seniors that thought it was all right. We still have some that's got off. You see, there's no law that says you have to tear privies down. I just won't permit you to build another. You know, die like an old soldier." She laughed, a hearty laugh. "I was just looking at that, and half of the planning commission members now are dead. I was just looking into how the membership has been going. And how hard it was for us to get things done, because you had to hire brains. You had to hire your legal consultants, and then you had to hire your architects and your this and your that, for the maps and surveying the land. All this costs money. But the people who had to vote on the utilization of this money were illiterate, the majority of them. That's what I was trying to say to you.

"So I coined the phrase 'You have to knock on every door.' And 'Terry, explain to Miss Jones why I need her to mark X on this line.' That's what we had to do. It took us, it took us years. I've got somewhere a copy of the first resolutions that we pushed through at a general meeting, and getting everybody to come out and listen to it verbally. What was being said and why they couldn't have this. Now they understand because we're having pollution in some of the lakes etcetera. But twenty years ago, they didn't understand. 'My grandfather's been here, bluh, bluh, bluh. Hey. Good enough for me.'

"So this is what you're up against when you start to change a man's way of life. It's funny. But it was done, and I don't know how much Ms. Bullett bent your ear, but she's so capable of explaining everything that went down. Step by step. Such as the first monies we got from federal funding, what we did with it and so forth and so forth and so forth."

"Has it been derailed?" I asked.

"This is a picture of the Club Fiesta," Mrs. Aldrich said, pointing out another picture.

"Let's put it this way," Sergeant Moon said to me. "It's not derailed. I'll put it this way. Now, why? Because the people in general, as you grew, as the community came forward, in accordance with it, there was no enticement factor for brains to be concerned. As they got to be your age, from 1920 on, and they were able to participate and they had to leave. So why did we not have a continuation of this planning? Because the youth that found themselves in a position to do something had to leave, to survive. No industry here. To put anyone to work.

"So a standstill, because they failed to reckon with that. It's still beautiful. And it needs to be updated. The first time I used that term, I was still on the planning commission. This'll give you the level of IQ that we had on the planning commission. You know what they said? They would ask me, 'Miss Moon, what do you mean by updating?'

"So if the planning commission was at that level of thinking, that I'll have to tell them what I meant by updating, replacement was almost impossible, because their children had grown up and gone. So after a few phases of a master plan, where do we go from there?"

"This is a picture of the interior of the Flamingo Club," said Mrs. Aldrich.

"It's hurting, isn't it?" Sergeant Moon asked me.

"Yes," I said.

"But it's the truth," said the sergeant.

"I had a picture in color of the Fiesta," said Mrs. Aldrich. "I wanted to tell you something about the Paradise/Fiesta Club. It was most fabulous. This is one of the older photos, and of course, being in black and white and it's faded, you can't see. That was just one of the shows at nighttime, the Fiesta Club, it was right at the end of Paradise on the lake right up there. And of course, it's gone."

"This is what it looked like? That's astonishing," I said.

"Can I get you something?" the sergeant asked her sister.

"It's almost five o'clock," Mrs. Aldrich said, peering at her watch.

"All right." The sergeant nodded to me. "She's diabetic, and can't wait and then realize she hasn't had anything to eat."

Mrs. Aldrich asked if I had seen the new clubhouse. I told her yes, and she sighed. Watching her as she turned the pages, and listening to the timbre of her voice, I got the sense not merely of nostalgia, but it felt as if she were lamenting an unspeakable act that could have been avoided. She spoke of "trends" and attempts to rebuild that were either thwarted or wrongheaded: "When I came, I was here for the first rebuild. And as soon as the credit card and integration hit, it was all over."

"The credit card?" I said. "That's interesting. How?"

"Working people may have a few dollars, but you can't accumulate what it would take to go spend two weeks in Hawaii, but with the credit cards, you can do it and pay later. That's the way it happened. The credit card and integration, just like that. It killed this place. Because all the people that had been coming up here were satisfied with a cottage and just *reading* about the summer resorts. We are a race of people that just will make do as long as we can talk about it. They never bothered about making hotels comfortable. We had summer cottages people rented. The motel was nothing. They said, 'Okay, I got a room here, and you got one at the end of the hall, and we share the bath.' But they got used to going to the best with the credit card. And so they chose not to be satisfied with this anymore.

"I remember when my sister came out of the army and was talking about buying. I was still in Detroit. And I came up here and I said, 'Bea, it's all right. But this is a big house. It's going to cost a fortune just to heat it.' I had lived in it in the summertime. We had the club, and we needed a comfortable place during the summer. But then she said, 'No, I don't think I'm going back to the city. I'm going to live up here.' That's how she bought. And then I decided I was going to leave the city. Of course, my husband's health had a lot to do with it, and then she needed help also—this is too much house for one person. So we came."

Over the years, Mrs. Aldrich says, she had been "involved in everything. What we need is people, of course," she said. But Lake County lacked industry, and even the children who were raised here were forced to go elsewhere. ("I don't care how much paper they got out of the university, it takes money to live.") The area "cannot afford the best," she said, and pointed to Ms. Bullett as a rare exception. "She would have never gotten through college if the mortician hadn't seen leadership qualities in her. He took her into the business over there. And he insisted on her going to school. Her graduation night, they had a convoy going down there to Ferris. But she didn't stop there."

"We are still a race of picky people," Mrs. Aldrich told me. "You can't never do it right. But Idlewild is beginning to thrive again."

"Yeah," said the sergeant. "What was that word you used a while ago? The word? I said no it isn't. I say it's—"

"Derailed?"

"Yes! derailed. I don't know who told you that, but it sounds sort of like one of the old-timers." She named a name. "He should be marking X on the line, based on his knowledge, which is zilch. And he's a strong talker with no knowledge and it sounded like it possibly came from him.

He's the type, if there's ten things to be done, and you do nine and don't quite have time to finish that tenth one, he will make a podium speech about what you didn't do, that tenth. He don't say nothing about the nine that you did do. He's that type."

"That's right," said Mrs. Aldrich.

"That's why," Sergeant Moon said, "I don't like go to town to a meeting, because 90 percent of them in there are in there to bitch and complain and make it uncomfortable for those who are trying to accomplish something. And I don't go, because I get up and I shoot them down."

"Blanche," said Mrs. Aldrich.

"And then that makes it bitter, so I don't do that. I stay away."

"Blanche," said Mrs. Aldrich.

"And I can understand someone saying that. 'Derailment.' That's because nothing, as far as they can see, which isn't far, has been done that's positive."

Mrs. Aldrich said, "You make my sandwich or you ain't going to do nothing."

"Well," the sergeant said, going toward the kitchen door. "I hope I sort of rebutted it a little bit, it's definitely not derailed, it is at a standstill because it has not had viable, physical input from the generation that should have followed. You see what I'm saying?"

"Yes he does," said Mrs. Aldrich, "but don't come back in here till you fix my sandwich."

"You two have a good time, don't you?" I asked through laughter.

"We're two opposites," said Mrs. Aldrich. "So we get along. Even as children, she was an athlete, and I was—my husband died up here."

The sisters had been born in Alabama, and their parents moved to Detroit "before we were school age. Our parents died in Detroit. Mother in '32. Father in '34." Blanche Moon was in the army for twenty-one years. And Griffin Aldrich went into "the entertainment field because that's what I could do."

("Believe it or not," the sergeant told me later, "she had to start working at sixteen. I was fifteen. Because we didn't have any parents. And we were under age. She couldn't work in a colored club because they'd close them up. So she worked two jobs. I stayed in school. This shows you how close we were. Even after we were grown. We're two different types of individuals. She goes one way, and I go another. I'm parks and recreation in Detroit. And she's a dancer, floating all over the world and the United States. Up until she moved up here, I don't think we had ever lived together closely. Since we were grown.")

Mrs. Aldrich started telling me about Idlewild in its heyday again. "Oh, the stars. The Club Paradise had more big names than we had. Flamingo Club was the largest club. But Mr. Bragg, as I say, he was a person that had never been exposed to show business or anything. Mr. Giles asked him to come up here and open that club. Business was flourishing, and there were times where we had people standing in line. And he said there's enough up here for two clubs. And at that time it was.

"He and Mr. Giles were friends. But a lot of times, we had to help him make payroll, because he got over his bounds. We tried to have good shows, a star now and then. Mr. Giles didn't have any money when he got in the business so he was after making a dollar. He started just from the bar, and then he built a patio. This is the summertime, that you have business. But the patio didn't work. The nights are too cold for a patio. So he said, 'Okay, close it up. Put the roof on.' But he did it with a mind for endurance. He put steel in the roofs, like that. Like the government said, the only bomb shelter in Lake County was the club."

Sergeant Moon had returned without Mrs. Aldrich's sandwich. "That's right. The demolition. One phase of the master plan, really it was the first phase, but the government, you know how they try at first to give you a little piece of money and see what you do with it. And then if you do all right, then I'm going to let you have this big piece. Well, that's what they did. The first phase was our Lincoln Park. We took that, and I mean, right down to the penny, $30,000, all they gave us, and that little Lincoln Park was cultivated. Then came demolition. Demolition meant tearing down all the shanties, and believe me, I don't know if they gave you these figures, but it's in the master plan—278 or 287 homes were earmarked. Those were homes that had been left by generation after generation. Nobody wanted them, couldn't be lived in, but they were owned properties. So we went through a demolition phase, and that was the big bucks. Two hundred and seventy-eight I think it was what we tore down, because that was contracted, etcetera, etcetera. Legal paperwork for somebody; most of the people had never even seen it when they inherited it. The next was the island. Acquisition. We had to acquire the island plot by plot because it belonged to all the individuals. The only building the engineer said 'I'm not tearing down' was the Flamingo Club. They went in it and said, 'Let it stand, if you can utilize it.' That's why it's still standing there now. That was in the demolition phase."

"My sandwich?" Mrs. Aldrich turned to me. "I don't have to tell you, I'm the cook around here." The sergeant left the room, laughing, and Mrs. Aldrich called after her, "Oh, dear, I appreciate it though!" She turned to me. "Now, back to the Club Fiesta. You hear them talk about Bill Doggett, Prysott, Demeter Joe, the Four Tops—that's where the Four Tops started. Della Reese. Oh, gosh, just go on and name—"

Mrs. Aldrich told me all the many problems and fun of managing the clubs, of the time the blind singer Roy Hamilton arrived in Grand Rapids and no one was there to meet him, and how she got him to Idlewild in time; of getting the ventriloquist act Willie and Lester to come before he became a famous entertainer ("I was paying him ten dollars a day, out of my pocket"), and how people were lined up "a block away from the club."

When the sergeant returned with Mrs. Aldrich's sandwich, she regaled me with tales of Jackie Wilson, "Well, he upset this place."

"He upset the place?"

"Well, he was excellent," said the sergeant. "I tell you, he was so wild, but he was so talented."

"In a nice kind of way," said Mrs. Aldrich.

"In a nice way," the sergeant agreed. "But he was *wild.* You ever been to Detroit? Just picture a big city, and picture a downtown section, the major section. And we were riding downtown, major section, and all of a sudden Trixie had heard somebody yell, 'Trixie!' I looked back at this convertible, and Jackie Wilson stopped the traffic, and was standing up behind the steering wheel, getting out, downtown Detroit. Oh my God. That kind of wild. Everybody liked Jackie."

Mrs. Aldrich said, "He was at the Fiesta Room. He would come over to Flamingo because all the kids played on the beach. He'd get a gang of them out there in the parking lot and they would be singing and dancing. You'd think the show was going on outside. And that was Jackie Wilson."

They told me the only entertainer to actually buy property in Idlewild was a member of the Four Tops. "They wanted to buy the club," Mrs. Aldrich told me. "But the people who had purchased it at the time, they were the kind of people that are grabbers. They just grab things and do nothing with them, but they won't let you have them."

The sergeant said, "'I ain't going to let you have it. I ain't going do anything with it either.'"

Mrs. Aldrich continued, "Before they put their money on that place down there in Detroit, on the riverfront, the Duke came up here and he rented a little cottage right down on the corner. And he wanted to purchase that, because that's where they started.

"The property was for sale at that time, but he couldn't get anybody to outbid the people that were trying to buy it, and they didn't do nothing. It finally had to be condemned and torn down."

I listened to the two reminisce some more. And eventually they came round to the present and the problems facing Idlewild. Particularly the recalcitrant folk who were full of apathy, Mrs. Aldrich said. "I walked from door to door, trying to get a group of kids together for Christmas. We have a lot of snow. I wanted these kids to walk, do Christmas carols. We were to light candles, and write the words 'Merry Christmas' on the Island. I had people saving milk cartoons—for the candles (milk cartons don't burn; and the kids can't get burned, see)—for months, from the summertime. I got a contract with Dial-a-Ride to pick them up at the library. I arranged for hot dogs, potato chips, hot chocolate. And chaperones, which state law requires—one for every ten or eleven children.

"The time approaches for me to do this. I'm getting the kids, we're going to practice these Christmas carols. I did not have one mother. Not one. Not one mother.

"'Well, I got to do so-and-so and so forth. I promised my daughter I was coming down—.' All kind of excuses. I had to go and cancel the contract with Dial-a-Ride. It took me months to get rid of all those milk cartons. I gave up on it. I gave up the council. I was just absolutely floored."

The sergeant said, "I have turned back more money for this township than from any. Now some of the councils spent all of it. Different area, different concept of thought, different people, they do different. The composition of people that was here, and their way, their way of thinking, they don't believe in blending together: I'll help you and you help me. They don't believe in that, and it's hard to get anything done. Other communities, you could just pass the word, and everyone shows up at town hall. 'What's it about tonight?' But that's not the way it is here."

Surprisingly (but upon reflection, far from surprising) these two Iron Ladies were not pessimistic. "It's hard," the sergeant said. And Mrs. Aldrich said she was busier now than when she rehearsed all day and danced all night.

"It's changing all over the world," she said, "and we're getting some of the change. So this place is going to revive again."

"Oh yes, it is," the sergeant agreed.

"But it's not going to be the city. I hope not. It's not going to be like the big city."

Seven

# SOMETHING LIKE THE FUTURE

*Madison, Wisconsin*

Despite small numbers, the sources and characteristics of the black migration to Milwaukee were similar to those of other northern cities. Upper south, border, and mid-western states contributed the bulk of newcomers to the city. In 1870, migrants from the Upper South and border states of Virginia, Tennessee, and Kentucky, collectively, made up 34.7 percent of the city's black population. In 1910 blacks from Kentucky, Missouri, Tennessee and Virginia provided the largest single percentage (18.1) of newcomers to the city. The second most important contributing states were Illinois, Ohio, Indiana and Michigan, with 15.6% of the total. Only one deep south state, Georgia, significantly contributed to Wisconsin's black population and that was a mere 3%.

—Joe William Trotter, Jr., *Black Milwaukee: The Making of an Industrial Proletariat*

In 1980, the black population in WI numbered 182,592, or 4 percent of the state's population.

Forty-six percent of Wisconsin Blacks were born in the state, compared to 77% of the total Wisconsin population.

Blacks are a highly urbanized population—95% live in large cities in Wisconsin, mostly in the Southeastern corner of the state. The vast majority live in Milwaukee County.

—Doris P. Slesinger and Pilar A. Parra, *Blacks in Wisconsin: A 1980 Chartbook: A Demographic Profile of the Black and Total Population of Wisconsin*

For a number of reasons, I desperately wanted to profile a high school in Madison, Wisconsin. My idea was to interview a black principal, black teachers, and black students, especially boys—as I felt thus far I had spoken with too few young African American males.

After finding a black principal, I was told to speak with a member of the school board, and then the board of education, and before I knew it, I became embroiled in a nightmare of bureaucracy and dithering and phone-tag and exhaustion. I wasted days trying to get this accomplished, and in frustration realized I had to abandon this little mission.

Near the end of this bafflement and befuddlement, a friend, a native of Madison, took me around that benighted midwestern capital, so formidably well laid out, with a shiny brass-domed capitol smack dab in the middle; the massive university on the shores of Lake Mennoda; we took in Joel Gershman's production of a play he had written about the famous Wisconsin serial murderer and cannibal, Edward Gein. At the Essenhaus—a frightening establishment full of very loud Germanic folk, literally guzzling beer from human-sized glass boots—I lamented my wasted time, and my friend looked at me with a little awe, and said, "You know they did it on purpose, don't you?"

I was dumbfounded.

"The last thing these people want is a black man writing about things around here. You've got to be kidding."

A wise man once told me, the more you know, the more naive you get.

I happened to meet a black graduate student in history at the university—Darryl Graham, from back east, from New York. And his wife, Dainah, and their new daughter. The Grahams had me over for supper before I left, and invited a native Wisconsiner named Greg. Greg had grown up in Eau Claire, and now lived in La Crosse. "La Crosse is full of teachers." It is the home of the Teachers College of Wisconsin. Madison is not so bad by comparison, he said. He told me he had worked in a steel mill in Illinois for a year. "Nice money but no future, not what I wanted."

Presently we fell into talking about the souls of black folks.

"We're always looking for precedents," Darryl said. "We need to make choices. Why do black folk have to be around a city? Why are we waiting for one person to lead? A lot of it comes from education. As we become more educated hopefully we can make choices to draw us into the American dream."

"Racism is not important," Greg said. "What our folks did after slavery is something to be proud of. Why aren't we doing it now? We have thrown away the things that benefit us. We've got to spread out and know where we are."

I wondered if the fabled middle-class departure from black neighborhoods actually had anything to do with the creation of this so-called new underclass.

"No," Greg said.

"It's about choices," Darryl said.

Dainah said, "I'm certainly not going back to where I came from."

"Cities really do break spirits," said Darryl. He noted how when he spoke to his friends in New York, he noticed a new coldness. "I see something happening."

Dainah noted that she was the only one in her family who hadn't been mugged. "Two brothers, one sister and my mother. My mother was mugged at knifepoint. We are in a crisis situation."

I noted the use of "we" and asked if there is such a thing anymore.

"What is it that is holding us together?" Greg asked. "It could be skin color, but that's too superficial. We may be an anomaly in the whole world. We may have to redefine who we are."

"Because of the rhetoric," Darryl said, "it was about skin color."

"Our culture is a culture of poverty," Greg said.

"Be careful about that," Dainah said. "We are too ready to give up. We gave rap away. What is the story which holds us together? Is it slavery? I think it's more than that. When I was growing up, it was something to do with the language, the games, the rituals."

"Well," Greg said. "If it falls apart too easily, then it's not a culture, is it? The main thing that might be a culture might be the adapting. Maybe we're watching the demise of the culture."

Dainah said, "We need to defend our own culture and we need to learn not to follow white folk."

"How do we know we have a culture?" I asked.

"All we have in common is blackness," Greg said.

"Well, what is that?" I asked.

Darryl said, "In the post-1960s—a black urban creature who knows nothing about the South. The things to hold onto versus consumerism. The point at which we lose culture." He spoke of the McDonaldizing of the Martin Luther King holiday.

Greg said, "On one hand being in the Midwest is a negative, and on the other hand a positive—it gives me a push."

Darryl thought blacks in Madison "really don't seem to be alive." "Back in the late '70s black men focused on the youth. The pecking order has been reversed: We are failing our youth. We have allowed the white world to reverse the course. You are left with the media and us. Your elders are of no use. No respect."

"We make excuses for youth too readily," Dainah said.

"I won't go so far as to say we don't have a culture," Greg said. "But I am at a loss to say what that culture is."

"Americans are looking back for a history that doesn't exist," Darryl said. "What if African Americans look more toward the future. Maybe there was never a true black culture. We were forced together. The language of black intellectuals has always been decades behind." He pointed out that most black communities he had seen were all poor. "You can tell a black community because of the poverty."

"Are we a culture of poverty?" Greg asked again.

"We have to get out of the cities," Darryl said. "And get out of the old shell and become a part of the American culture. *If America is fucked then Black America is fuckeder.* There is no sense of empowerment when you remain in the city. When they say minority, we are no longer in vogue; that was the mistake—civil rights was not for blacks only."

"Integration versus reparations."

"We need to get in touch with the flow of capitalism," Darryl said. "Not your culture will be pulling you out, but knowing about interest rates, housing markets—"

"Reparations?" asked Greg. "Is that the only thing we want to do? And that's not a gimme and an owe me. This is a debt to be paid."

"Now you're talking about a guilt compulsion," Darryl said. "My colleagues paying for the sins of their ancestors. With integration they were buying something they didn't want. They weren't going into something negotiable. You can't force integration. If you want to see what will happen, look at the kids." He used by way of a metaphor the "Sand People," the desert bedouins from George Lucas's *Star Wars:* scavengers, despised people, "people on the outside." Computers give you access, he said, without moving. In the future, couldn't black people place themselves closer to the center of things through "access to information?"

Greg said: "If blacks want to make it, they are going to have to start making things and owning things. There is nothing in this country that really belongs to us."

"Southerners keep land linkages," said Darryl.

Greg suggested that the group work out something along the lines of "bulletproof posterity," so that assets stayed in black hands.

"William Julius Wilson says we should go back to live with the underclasses," Darryl said.

"We don't have the resources," countered Greg. "A significant number of black folk seriously want to do something about it. They are not fleeing. They don't want to turn on black folk, but do they have the will?"

The souls of black folk.

Eight

# MY OWN PRIVATE CHICAGO

*Chicago, Illinois*

All I could think of was Carl Sandburg, and warmth. "City of the big shoulders. . . ."

The Chicago skyline is shocking; the very embodiment of *Will to Power*—to see those monstrous towers at the foot of Lake Michigan is to see Will to Power personified. (Did Friedrich Wilhelm Nietzsche ever see Chicago?) Unlike New York, which is awash in the effluvia of entitlement and romance—"On that Isle"—to look at Chicago is to see a hardness, a determination, a refusal to look down. Such a spirit, a hard and pragmatic spirit, is not fun; for rarely do such spirits allow themselves to be complicitous in the pursuit of merriment.

While in Chicago I stayed at a place called the Brent House in Hyde Park, at the University of Chicago, a restored mansion, run by the Episcopal Church, and I was happy for their hospitality. Unlike the University of Wisconsin at Madison—which seems to be a city within a city, or McGill, magically apart and separate, while in the middle of the city—the University of Chicago and Hyde Park are like another planet, distinct from Chicago. In the midst of Chicago's South Side it sits, the lake to the east, with old-world manses, and its neogothic architecture—Oxford by way of Duke University; bookstores by the handfuls. But beyond its boundaries exists a more conventional time-space continuum, a sight to make eyes sore, made all the more improbable and problematic by the approach to the campus from downtown. Through Kenwood into Hyde Park, one drives past the homes of Muhammad Ali and the Honorable Elijah Muhammad now owned by Louis Farrakhan—eastern-inspired, neo-Alahambra-like gems, strange guideposts between the two worlds. Around the university I found people to be not so friendly (at least towards me). And October was coming to an end, and it rained every day. The sky was damnably dim, and as Halloween approached, I found myself disenchanted and bitter about Chicago.

I saw Gus Van Sant's motion picture *My Own Private Idaho* in Chicago, and it made me exceedingly sad. Though a good movie, I found it particularly hard to watch. Cold and nasty. Like Chicago. One scene where River Phoenix's narcoleptic character tells the Keanu Reeves character he's in love with him and is rejected, I found particularly painful. It dredged up all sorts of feelings of thwartment and botheration and unrequitedness and shamefulness and vulnerability and coldness and aloneness. And here I was in my own private Chicago. More than anything, the film made me dread going to Idaho. Would the people be as detached and detachable as these poor pitiful white boys? Is this the American reality? I wondered. The end result of our manifest destiny? Our individualism? To be utterly and finally alone?

So lonesome I could cry.

> Life is only a *means* to something; it is the expression of forms of the growth of power.
>
> —Friedrich Wilhelm Nietzsche

There is a room in the DuSable Museum of African American History—on East 56th Place, the museum is the brainchild and love child of the artist and activist, Dr. Margaret Burroughs, dedicated to black history and art, an ancien régime edifice of austere presence that had just turned thirty—a room with 287 awards and plaques and citations (plus more in storage at the Chicago Public Library) awarded to the Honorable Harold Washington, the forty-second mayor of Chicago, from 1983 to 1987, and its only black mayor. The room included, among other things: a plaque from the Chicago *Tribune* acknowledging his reelection; scissors from a ribbon-cutting of Walgreens' 1,000th store; plaques and citations from the Chicago City Service Taxi Association, the Chicago Housing Authority, the American Institute of Street Custodians, from Latinos for Political Progress, the Baptist Ministers' Conference of Chicago, from La Sociedad Civica Mexicano; a Man of the Year award; the Goodwill Industries Politician of the Year award; awards from the Polish Welfare Association, Escuela de Consejo Moral de Puerto Rico, Inc., the United Way, Asian American Coalition, Philippine Chamber of Commerce, Chief Earl Old

Person, Tribal Chairman of the Blackfoot Nation: "Say No to Drugs" Award. . . .

There is something prototypical and definitive about Chicago and African American life. It shares with Harlem being a northern terminus in the great migration of black folk from the rural south to the urban north. (Los Angeles figures into that mythography, but its comparative youth and western situation make it a separate and particular and different story.) The central idea of African American culture—essentially, primarily a southern culture, influenced by African retentions and syncretisms and techniques of survival and making a way in the lower former colonies—is made manifest in Chicago. Nicholas Lehman's *Promised Land* is almost exhaustive in tracking the back and forth movement between Illinois and Mississippi (particularly Clarksdale in the Delta), examining the forces—economic, political and social—that shaped Chicago's black life.

Chicago is middle west. Something about that midwest ethos has been responsible for the fact that the Windy City is responsible for at least three definitive institutions in the broader black scheme of things: the Johnson Publishing Company, the Johnson Products Company, and the Nation of Islam. (I should include, at this point, Oprah Winfrey, a true postmodern force, but she's much too tricky to assess, too much of a moving target to pin down.)

It was time to get a haircut, and I found a barbershop on the South Side. In truth, to me the South Side of Chicago did not look so much threatening as it did drab and sad and run-down. A woman I assumed to be the owner was there, a compact, ginger-skinned woman, with a cigarette poised in her mouth. She chatted with the man who went to work on my head, and I felt very much at home.

By and by, a man, who could have been homeless but who certainly looked derelict, came in the door. He asked if anyone could spare some change.

"You know better than to come in here," the woman I reckoned to be the owner said.

The man asked again.

"I said get the fuck out," she said.

"Just a little something to get something to eat."

The woman I took to be the owner reached down by her barber chair and unhooked a straight razor. "I told you to get out!"

The man mumbled something, and she charged toward him. The man's eyes grew big and he almost ran into the door. She chased him out.

"Goddamnit," she said, puffing on her cigarette, which she had not removed.

City of the big shoulders, indeed.

Perhaps my earliest memories of Chicago come from Richard Wright's *Native Son,* and his unredeeming and unredeemable vision of how a hellish environment can produce a Bigger Thomas; how circumstances model and shape individuals, like Pavlov's canine, to follow trails and paths they have no recourse but to follow; and perhaps along with that memory, in the back of my mind, was Bigger's own Pavlovian labyrinth: Chicago. Of course I had the gift of being of the generation after the generation after the generation of Richard Wright; I had the responses of Ralph Ellison and James Baldwin and John A. Williams and David Bradley and Charles Johnson to color and amend my thoughts. And though *Native Son* was—is—important, monumental, in its day groundbreaking, serious, thoughtful, artful, commercially successful, I never cottoned to that book; I found it terribly chilly, lacking soul. His short stories, *Uncle Tom's Children,* and his autobiography, *Black Boy,* moved me differently and deeply, and I reckoned that, like me, being a country boy himself, Richard Wright never cottoned much to Chicago, and *Native Son* was his assessment of that city. In truth he had not spent that much time, proportionally speaking, in Chicago. His ten years there—from 1927 until 1937—were marked by the Depression, communism, and hunger. Though he found his voice and his identity as a writer there, I never sensed that Chicago did much more than "depress and dismay" him, as he writes in *Black Boy.*

While I was on the road, a study was released from the American Demographic Association, which listed Chicago as the United States' most segregated city. Not New York (in fact Queens is listed as the most diverse); not Los Angeles; not St. Louis; not Miami; not Durham—Chicago. Friends I know who visit Chicago often speak highly, rapturously, of Chicago, of its restaurants, of its museums, of its architecture. When I ask if they visited the South Side, I get a puzzled look, often a bewildered, hurt look, as if I were being impolite or just plain dumb, as if to say: *How could you ask that?* From which I can only infer the meaning: *Are you stupid? Of course not.* I, on the other hand, spent the majority of my time south of Garfield Boulevard, and would like to think that the time I spent in Chicago—not long I admit—treated my eyes and senses to a world not so adorable or attractive. Unlike Harlem, the buildings on much of the South Side do not reflect, despite neglect, a once-splendorous past; they are uniform and mercantile, large tenements and bungalows. So many blocks were drab and grim; the majority of the streets on which I drove were pot-hole-ridden and bad. Of the many buildings on the many streets that were not condemned, many looked as if they should have been. In all honesty there were in that area perfectly lovely, well-kept neighborhoods that gave off no odor of either poverty or strife, but unfortunately they were overshadowed, at least in my brain, by the other places, and a great many liquor stores, with kids hanging out on the street, and some destitution—although, to be fair, homelessness not as visible as in New York or Washington, D.C. Perhaps it was the rain; it rained every day I was there. And I grew powerfully tired of the dreariness, dreariness reflected in dreariness.

Don't get me wrong: Black life in Chicago, the black history of Chicago, is immense and impressive. The first settler—after the Potawatomi—in Chicago was a black man, the trapper Jean Baptiste DuSable; there were also John Jones, nineteenth-century businessman and Underground Railroad conductor and activist and city legislator; the ninety-year-old Chicago *Defender;* the cosmetics empire of George E. and Rita Johnson of Johnson's Products, and of John H. Johnson, one of the wealthiest black people in the United States, and his Johnson Publishing Company, publisher and owner of *Ebony* and *Jet;* Fashion Fair Cosmetics, radio stations, and more—plus the only black company to have a skyscraper on the Chicago Loop; artists, musicians, educators, doctors, the first black woman ever elected to the United States Senate; and my favorite poet of all, Gwendolyn Brooks and . . . No, Chicago's black history, in many ways, makes one wonder why Harlem has received so much more ink. A rich past so vast and deep that I felt crushed by it.

I felt crushed, particularly, by the weight and significance of what colored so much of black life in Chicago, namely the mass influx of black folk from the first decade of the twentieth century until late in the 1960s from Alabama and Mississippi and other southern states, the archetypical African American move from the South of despair to the North of despair. It has been documented that the move is turning around—more blacks are returning to the South than are leaving. Yet many more remain. Perhaps that is what gave Chicago this sense of the last stop.

Of the black people I've known from Chicago, most remembered it fondly. But their nostalgia was acknowledged as such. They often had a hard, clear vision of that past, tainted with horror stories about both blacks and whites; and were themselves often hard and practical and eager to prove themselves. (One friend, to whom I had figured I was close, I offended with one sentence, and he never forgave me. That may say absolutely nothing about Chicagoans, but it always haunts me, and is inextricably bound up in my mind as a way of looking at the world.)

Perhaps I am prejudiced; perhaps I am too influenced by the old views of Upton Sinclair and stories of Richard Daley and the reception Dr. Martin Luther King, Jr., received in 1966; perhaps I was not yet ready to shed my own tainted vision of the place, to rework the details and come up with a fresh notion; perhaps it can't be done. Perhaps I failed.

Or perhaps Gwendolyn Brooks—Poet Laureate of the state of Illinois, Pulitzer Prize winner and longtime Chicago native—said it best when she penned in her novel *Maud Martha:* "The weather was bidding her bon voyage."

I am probably a romantic at heart. I define a romantic as someone who seeks the good despite the external reality. (A dear friend once told me, "You're like Jay Gatsby: You would remake yourself for love." Which may be the truth, but unlike Jay Gatsby, I pray I am (a) not doomed, and (b) not quite so shallow.) My being a romantic notwithstanding, I have, however, always seen romanticizing the truth to be a sin. The thing that moves and captivates me about the best writing is that it strives to tell the truth: those sentences and passages that make us stop in a moment of recognition, because we have glimpsed what we once thought to be ineffable, suddenly, freshly, put into words.

Too often, in writing about black folk, I have read what is romanticizing. It is much too easy: to make poverty holy; to make ugliness beautiful; to make violence valiant; to make weakness charming; to make stupidity wise; to make arrogance comic; to make disease health; to make squalor exotic; to make meanness noble; to make cruelty ingenious; to make stink perfume; to make laziness expression; to make anger pride; to make debauchery art; to make nothing something; to make blindness sight; to make evil good.

I have visited the country of poverty, and personally, I never want to return: I didn't have enough money to enjoy it; and I have known black folk intimately and long, and though I have insights and deep knowledge of white folks, I always suspect that, though I know more about the majority culture than it suspects I know, there are topics, attitudes, secrets, intimacies hidden from me. Yet black folk have been revealed to me since I had eyes to see and ears to hear and a nose to smell and a tongue to taste: I have been behind the door. I have been beaten up, lied to, cheated, stolen from, hated, betrayed, disappointed, shunned, and heart-shattered by black people, and—both statistically and commonsensically—if I am killed, it may well be by a black man. But by that same passage, all that I know to be good and honest and noble and self-sacrificing and self-disciplining and powerful and loving emerges from what I know about black folk. In sum, my vision of humanity arises from that intimacy of knowledge and experience: I am black; nothing black can be alien to me.

Perhaps that is why I felt so pained in Chicago. It would have been much too easy to haul out a paintbrush of vibrant colors to touch, to blotch, to blackwash, what I saw.

That would be a sin.

Haki Madhubuti was born in Little Rock, Arkansas. "As John Oliver Killens says, 'We moved up south.' Detroit, Michigan, and stayed there for my formative years, grade school. My father lived in Chicago so it was kind of a single parent home most of the time. We would come back and forth between Chicago and Detroit. I have a sister. My mother passed, kind of early. So I've been on my own since I was sixteen. After she passed, I just decided to move to Chicago. I finished high school here. I did a degree in the army. And then have been here ever since."

I met Haki Madhubuti in his office at the bookstore (Third World Books), publishing company (Third World Press), community center for research and resources (Institute of Positive Education), and school (New Concept Development Center), on Chicago's South Side, on South Cottage Grove Avenue. The old building could have been an antique shop or an accounting office from the outside, but once in the door, I was met by books and books; and, as I had hoped, I found copies of books by Gwendolyn Brooks that I had not seen anywhere else in the country. Upstairs, the offices were cramped, full of desks and computers and file cabinets and keyboards clacking, and phones ringing, and people rushing about—the atmosphere was of things being made and work being done.

Poet, essayist, publisher, college professor, father—as he said, he wore a great many hats—Madhubuti had, a few years before, published a volume of essays in answer to the infamous volume *What Every Blackman*

*Should Know About the Blackwoman,* by Sheherazade Ali, with *Confusion by Any Other Name: Essays Exploring the Negative Impact of the Blackman's Guide to Understanding the Black Woman*—which assured him of being put up against the pit bull Ali on many a television talk show in the late '80s. But Madhubuti (who originally began publishing under the name Don L. Lee) had published close to twenty books by the time I met him, and had received a number of awards and honors.

In all fairness, I should say that, as I've already noted, I came to the offices of Third World Press that day more than out of sorts and not simply because of my perception of Chicago. By this time I had been on the road for a solid three months, from Massachusetts to Wisconsin, and though I had encounted a number of people full of hope and good faith, I could not ignore or shake off the many negative situations, the utter sense of entrapment and doom, hanging over black folk in America. As I say, it might have been the weather, but nonetheless, I came to Madhubuti, perhaps unfairly to him (he had no notion of the fact), casting him as a griot, a wise man, a guru: an older black male writer whom I respected and looked up to; who had made such a profound statement, not just in his work, but in his institutions, in concrete influence within his neighborhood—unfairly, I say, for I knew he couldn't answer all my questions: here I was a grown man, asking like a little boy why the sky is blue: looking for a hero. I knew he hadn't made the world, nor had he put African Americans in their present situation. But perhaps he might know more about this than I did.

I had known his work from my college days, reading his poems from the sixties, and I was curious to know how he got involved in writing. "Books in my home were about as scarce as money. I was introduced to literature, probably on my own, via the Detroit Public Library. Detroit, at that time, had a very good children's library, which is behind the general library. I began going there early because it was a kind of a peaceful haven. My life was, my family life, was a state of turmoil. Like really poor families, always short of everything, from money to energy to patience. So it was a way up for me to find a place of virtue, which I found in the library."

Perhaps it was projection on my part, but there was something priestly about Haki Madhubuti, soft-spoken, gentle in demeanor, his eyes dark and penetrating, his well-trimmed beard making him seem wise; and it did appear, to look at him, that he understood certain mysteries, certain hidden secrets about the earth. A poem he wrote called "Possibilities: Remembering Malcolm X" began:

it was not that you were pure.
your contradictions were small wheels.
returning to the critical questions:
    what is good?
    what does it mean to be black?
    what is wise?
    what is beautiful?
    where are the women and men of honor?
    what is a moral-ethical consciousness?
    where will our tomorrows be?
    what does a people need to mature?

"I started writing, primarily, I think as a lot of writers start out," he told me. "Not having that major literary influence, I just started jotting things down. Read the poets, and said, 'Well, I can do that.' I really didn't take it seriously until I went into the service. When I came out of high school, there weren't any jobs for us. The major 'boy job' was the military, and so I ended up in the army.

"In fact, the summer before, when I came out of high school, I couldn't find a job. So I ended up selling magazines in a group. We traveled from Chicago, down through Illinois, into Missouri, stopping at small towns, knocking on doors, going from door to door, selling magazines and lying about working our way through college.

"The interesting thing about this is that it was the first time that university education ever flitted into my brain at all. (I came through high school pre-integration. There weren't any kind of programs for us to go to college or university. No one ever talked to me about it. I didn't have a family to rely on.) I was going through some small town in Nebraska, I don't remember, it may have been Galesburg, it may have been Omaha, but I knocked on the door, and a brother answered, an elderly man answered the door, and I went into my spiel. 'Trying to work my way through college, and will you buy these magazines?' And he said, 'Well, what college are you trying to work your way through?' And I don't know even what I said, but he knew I was lying."—Haki Madhubuti laughed—("I've never been a good liar, even when I was young").

"So he asked me to come in, and he said, he'll take a couple of magazines, but he wanted to talk to me. And he did. He said, 'You really should think about going through university.' He was a college graduate himself. I was about 131 pounds, six foot one. Very thin. He knew I was hungry too. He gave me a meal, and then with the meal, he gave me a lot of advice. So what happened when I left his home, I went up to East St. Louis and I got very sick, just because of the pressure. Everything I owned I had with me. I got sick, and so the people—and this was a black group—they left me in the Booker T. Washington Hotel, I'll never forget. Two-fifty a day. In order for me to get out of there, I had to go through the poor man's bank—the pawn shop—and pawn all my clothes. At this time, I was trying to play the trumpet. I pawned my horn, and took half the money and went to a doctor. Sent the other half to my sister. And went and joined the army."

Prior to that, he told me, he happened upon Richard Wright's autobiography, *Black Boy.* ("*Black Boy* influenced me a great deal. Primarily because, here was a man who came from poverty, even far greater than my own poverty. But at the same time, he was able to open me up to ideas which I'd never ventured into in my own vision at all.") That experience led to other books by Wright (as well as Chester Himes, Langston Hughes, Margaret Walker). "I went away to basic training, and I was reading *Here I Stand,* by Paul Robeson, and his picture was on this edition. You know, big, black, very serious, and when we got off the bus, a white drill sergeant saw the book and snatched it from me. And said, 'What's your Negro mind reading this black Communist for?' Robeson's picture had been plastered all over the country in terms of being a nutty-thinking, left-wing person. And he told all the recruits, he called us 'ladies.' 'Ladies, you line up against the desk.' And then he put the book over his head and tore the pages out and gave some to each recruit for toilet paper.

"Now, I said, 'Well, look at this. This is really something. This is just a book.' What it confirmed for me, at that time, was the power and the importance of ideas. That ideas, creators of ideas, run the world."

Luckily, he said, at the time he was also reading John Oliver Killens's *And Then We Heard Thunder,* about black men in World War II, a book that gave him insight into his own circumstance. But he didn't stop there, he began a "systematic" study of black literature. He would read a book, and for himself, write one or two hundred words about that book. "I used those three years to really pull myself into some level where I could begin to write."

Music, he said, also figured largely into his style and his thoughts, and his ideas.

Ideas not only led to a shelf of books by Haki Madhubuti, but led him to create organizations.

He told me that the Institute of Positive Education had been originally founded in 1969, and that its primary focus was education and communication. The school had full-time classes for children aged two to eight; Third World Press was created in 1967, and now had several hundred books in print, and this bookstore was one among four that his organization ran in the metropolitan Chicago area; they also published a magazine about current African American letters, *Black Books Bulletin,* and a paper, *Wordsmith.* Among his many motivations to create these institutions was the fact that so many works by black writers tend to go out of print. "If the writer's work is to live, then you have to have institutions that are going to make sure it stays in print." He never hesitated to begin what he dreamed of, he told me: "I came from serious abject poverty. I did not have a fear of failing. If you come from nothing, then all you can go back to is nothing."

Madhubuti spoke of his influences: Dudley Randall, whose Broadside Press had once published Madhubuti's work out of Detroit; and Gwendolyn Brooks. In fact, as Professor Madhubuti at the Chicago State University, he was director of the Gwendolyn Brooks Center. "Gwendolyn Brooks has been probably the shining light in my life. She came along at a good time for me, being young, much younger, having had military service, and just evolved into this very angry—and still angry—man. What I learned from Gwen was to begin to channel the anger in a much more positive way. It's been a twenty-five-year-plus relationship. It's like a mother-son relationship."

All in all, when he reflected upon his life and what he had seen and been able to create, he felt, "It's been a good life, a difficult life, but a great life."

Nonetheless, Haki Madhubuti found his many operations at times difficult to keep afloat. ("It's more than a notion to pay fifty-one people every two weeks. You can't write a poem for extra money.") A practical world called for practical solutions. In fact, Madhubuti had been writing and lecturing extensively about what is called, in lieu of black capitalism—an idea that smacked too much of profit and gain and exploitation—black entrepreneurship. To him it was another form of activism.

"I came through the '60s as an activist," he told me. "I have to maintain activism in the community. I think we have to be involved in the whole enterprise system. One of the problems with black people, in terms of trying to get into business, is trying to get capitalization. We need to develop new, other, ways to get people to invest in what you're doing." The stock market, he said, is not the only route. "I can't depend on General Motors or Ford or Dow Chemical. What I advocate is that you look throughout your community and see what is needed. If we are serious about being African Americans, and we're serious about helping our people, then what we need to do is reinvest in ourselves. Why is it we cannot develop homegrown businesses?" He mentioned the many goods and services, from McDonald's to entertainment products, that could be provided locally. "What I find is that there's a lack of vision. And what happens with our businessmen: they come in talking millions and millions of dollars. So if you ain't got a million dollars, you can't do nothing. My approach is: I don't have a million dollars. I'm saying that at one point, you've got to find things that excite people. And in this excitement, we can make a living. My children know that, when I die, they're not going to be well off. We use what we make in order for us to try to have a decent life while we're here. Not only us but for other people. The point is that you build a community, within the context of the community you're a part of. A large argument that I have with black capitalists is that they're basically just duplicating white capitalists. That's why I prefer the term entrepreneurship, or even 'freedom'—even though I don't believe it exists."

As I had read Haki Madhubuti's work over the years—especially in the eighties—a phrase kept reappearing, "Afrikan Humanism" ("In spelling Afrika I use 'k' rather than 'c' because for many activists the 'k' represents an acknowledgment that 'Africa' is not the true name of that vast continent"). In one essay he writes:

> In order to survive, one had to give up something, and if that something was not the body, the only explainable substitute was the mind; it goes, snaps like steel under intense heat; the mind, once fire and light, snaps under the force of ocean and darkness seeking peace in forgetfulness . . . Reconstruction of the Afrikan self was to be just about impossible. . . . Yet, there remain important elements of Afrikan culture to which the people hold tight such as Afrikan Humanism, a deep spirituality . . .

"I think Afrikan Humanism is probably the major factor in our survival," he told me that day. "And our ability to not dwell on the evil that's been done to us. If any people is going to rise to the level of even their own expectations, first and foremost, they have got to depend upon themselves. Otherwise, you will always be a slave and in slave relationships—a master-slave relationship."

I confessed to Haki Madhubuti that after a few months on the road, and reading and talking to people, a great many negative issues and facts kept nagging my consciousness. "The message I keep hearing is that black culture is dead. And if it's not dead, it's dying. You yourself have made some strong cases here—that we're in trouble."

"Oh yeah," he said. "I think we're in trouble, but I don't think that we're dead."

"Do you think it can be reversed?"

"Well—yes."

"Determined not to be a pessimist?"

"No," he said, "I say I'm a realistic optimist. That's why I stick with our children, we're dealing with early childhood education. Let me just give you some glimmers of hope. When I started publishing, back in 1966, there were probably eight black bookstores. Now we've got 250. When I started publishing back in 1966, there were approximately three or four, if that many, black publishers. Might not have been that many. Now we have 89 to 100 black publishers. In the '60s when I started sending my material out to magazines, you really only had about three or four magazines. Now you got *Essence,* you got *Black Enterprise* and *Callaloo* and the *Western Journal of Black Studies,* and *Wordsworth,* so many major magazines. Let me give you another example:

"I've been in higher education for twenty years, which means that anytime a student comes to me, he or she is going to be conscious when they leave. They're going to be angry, or conscious. Sometimes, it depends on whether they know something about women's books, Malcolm X, something about our history. But most importantly, they're going to know something about themselves. Now multiply me by, say, a thousand. I'm talking about Sonia Sanchez at Temple. Toni Morrison at Princeton. Maya Angelou at Wake Forest. Gwendolyn Brooks at Chicago State. Major universities in the country. Now you going to at least find one of us who's conscious. We're touching the cream of the crop." He pointed out the number of black women who are college presidents and in other roles of leadership.

"I'm saying that it's easy to dwell on the negative circumstances. If you've seen the black community, the black churches, they're doing a major work and I'm not 100 percent for that, but I'm just saying that we do live on. And we do seem to grow. We're now strong enough that we're coming back at every level, stronger.

"Look at the black film industry. That's the one industry, at least, that's thriving. Spike Lee, John Singleton, Julie Dash. Just look at black media, period. We own radio stations, a couple of television stations, newspapers all across the country. Sure, we're in serious difficulties, but, I mean, even yourself, doing this kind of book.

"I just cannot and will not take the pessimistic view. I served on the National Commission on Crime and Justice last year, which was set up by the American Friends Service Committee—the Quakers. And we studied the criminal justice system, and mainly the prison system, and so I had the opportunity to travel around, visit prisons, all across the country. And if you want to see the bottom of the barrel, that's where you go. You got over 70,000 black men and women in prison in this country. More black men in prison than in the university. That's enough just to knock you out. I receive two or three letters a day, if not more, from black prisoners, who have been influenced by our work, read my books, black books. But even more than that, we have a prison literature program, so a lot of the royalties on some of our books go into this literature program, and we just send free books to prison.

"These brothers tell you, boom: my problem was nobody never introduced me to ideas that were life-giving and life-saving. For the first time in my life, here I'm in prison, I got nothing else to do but think, and I really didn't realize how precious thought was until I had to do it. I just need some literature to keep feeding my mind. So that's the option."

One of my mentors at school always warned me: There is no such thing as balance. Balance is a mathematical concept, dealing in equals and proportions: Human beings are simply incapable of living up to their highest ideas, balance being one of them. Balance is a form of perfection: we ain't perfect.

In fact scientists are telling us nowadays that the universe itself is an unbalanced place; that there is order in asymmetry; and determinacy in randomness. Perhaps in chaos lies many a truth.

Oh, I had big—enormous—plans for Chicago. I would write about Cabrini Green (which I did visit, but found so depressing I told myself I'd come back later—and did not); the Johnson Products Company (I would interview people who worked in the factory—mixing Afro-sheen and Ultra-sheen); the *Chicago Defender* and Supreme Life Insurance Company; I wanted to interview executive Barbara Proctor Gardner, advertising pioneer; and kids on the street; and visit an all-black boys' school; and yes, the food, and the music, and the sociologist William Julius Wilson, and the extraordinary novelist Leon Forrest; I would go to mosques and talk to black Moslems, perhaps members of the Fruit of Allah, that famous security force—maybe even reprise Baldwin's encounter with the Honorable Elijah Muhammad, meeting with the current leaders of the Nation of Islam; and, if she wasn't too busy, my heroine Gwendolyn Brooks—indeed, my plans were so ambitious, so encompassing, and so impossible that they would have filled a volume even larger than this one; and after a time, I began to realize that the reason I had so much material was exactly because I had been reading about Chicago since I was in high school. Why add to the trillions of words when so much of the country had yet to be written about?

Ultimately my grand designs collapsed of their own weight, as any good engineer would predict. Also, I realized, Chicago was the first site I have visited on this mission that contained literally millions of black folk, and I was taken back to my original, staggering puzzlement: How do you define so many souls?

I decided to go.

On All Souls' Day I fled Chicago in a rush of blue wind and rain and thunder and lightning, feeling blue myself and out of time and space. I longed to be away from it, away from cities altogether.

I know Chicago must be a better place than I perceived. Yet I could not get Carl Sandburg out of my head: "Hog butcher to the world . . ." And all those messy, mean, mercantile images housed in the back of my eyes . . .

Nine

# WHAT IS THE QUESTION?

*St. Paul/Minneapolis, Minnesota*

How odd, the way events echo from one part of the land to the other. In this case from Nova Scotia to Minnesota. In truth the parallels end rather abruptly. In Halifax there was a community called Africville, predominantly black, that, after a lot of threats and acrimony from the city, was destroyed, its residents often cheated, often left with little. In St. Paul, there was a black community called Rondo, and in the 1960s a number of government agencies decided that the new Interstate 94 should run smack-dab through the middle of Rondo. Of course it was the straightest route . . .

The parallel really ends there, although a number of voices cried racism and unfair practices, and pointed to a larger conspiracy. When so many black neighborhoods are being destroyed by interstates and the placement of antisocial facilities, the question must also be asked: Is this common occurrence a sin before the fact or after the fact? When one considers that historically most black neighborhoods are not placed in the most desirable of areas—not the hillside nor the lake front nor the picturesque river view—it stands to reason that when highways and airports and dumps are needed, the least becomes the first, and the "quaint" history of certain people is seen merely to stand in the way of progress. So places like Rondo might be considered from the very beginning to be "high risk" areas.

In truth, Rondo—that was the largest black community in St. Paul from the 1920s until the 1960s when construction of the highway began—was not completely destroyed. Some of the most powerful and influential institutions still remain: Pilgrim Baptist Church, the oldest black church in the State of Minnesota, and the AME Zion Church, the second oldest, and a few other buildings. However, a great many businesses and homes were made to vanish, and as a result the idea of a center of black life in St. Paul no longer exists.

Often when I spoke with St. Paulians, their memories of Rondo were vague, nostalgic, often augmented by Evelyn Fairbanks's memoir of her years there, *The Days of Rondo,* in which she reminisces about a time in the 1930s and 1940s when the area around Rondo Avenue and Arundel Street radiated with life. She speaks of how it was known as "the colored district," which meant it was integrated, for the numbers of African Americans in St. Paul—and Minneapolis for that matter—were never large enough to dominate any area. An orphan, abandoned in Omaha, Evelyn Fairbanks was adopted by two black Minnesota natives. Hers is a sentiment-laden account of a midwestern upbringing in the middle of the century, being a girl before the war, being a teen during the war, and perhaps most intriguingly, what it was like to be black in urban Minnesota during those years. She also describes working as a secretary at a prison in which her brother was an inmate. In the end she does not wail and gnash her teeth over the dissolution of Rondo, rather her tone is melancholy and almost wistful. She writes:

> The community that I wrote about is gone. It was erased by the highway department and "progress"—other people's money . . . From 1970 to 1989, when it closed, the Faust Theatre showed movies unsuitable for children. The neighborhood storefronts on Dale and Selby, where I paid ten cents for paper dolls, suffered and closed when the corner became a high-crime area, then began a process of renovation . . . There is busing now, so kids don't necessarily go to the same school as their neighbors, forming lifetime bonds. The black population has grown so large that we don't all know each other. We weren't the first generations of blacks born in Minnesota, but we think of ourselves as FF's (First Families) now. The hunger for the old days is so great that in 1983 a group of St. Paul people started an annual celebration called Rondo Days in an effort to remember and re-create at least the atmosphere of our community. I share that hunger. It makes me write stories.

Though Evelyn Fairbanks may hunger for Rondo, for that old-time sense of community, after my stay in St. Paul and Minneapolis, I came to conclude that neither in history, nor in food, were many black Minnesotans without much to eat.

. . .

The day Bucephalus drove into St. Paul, over thirty inches of snow had fallen. My first real blizzard; and I loved it. I remembered intensely Paige Wadley-Bailey's admonition: To survive winter you must enjoy winter. And winter was so formidably present, I had no earthly other choice. Never had I imagined seeing so much snow, everything so impossibly blanketed and white and dangerously, incredibly transformed—at least, I imagined the cityscape had been transformed, for I had never visited Minnesota before and had nothing to compare it to. My good friend, the novelist Don Belton, was living in St. Paul at the time, and teaching at MacAlester College. He asked me to come and take him to run errands—ironically, I had a four-wheel drive, and he didn't. As I turned into Warwick Street, the drifts covered yards, and streets were carpets of compact snow—it seems even the ever-ready state of Minnesota could not keep up with that icy deluge.

My one big hope while in Minneapolis had been to interview the music maker once known as Prince. Of all the pop musicians currently on the scene, Prince Rogers Nelson was the one I most admired. Back in college, as a freshman, Prince had just released his *Controversy* album and he came to Chapel Hill to do a concert. A friend played the record for me and I hated it. Nasty, unchristian. I didn't listen so much as recoil. I turned off my ears when people described the concert. A year and a half later, and something obviously had happened to me, for when his album *Purple Rain* was released in the summer of 1983, I was blown over, away, up, down and around. This dancified, electrified, funkalicious, soul-fierce music had me on the edge of each rift and on the curve of each spiraling note—I dwelt in the album all summer. More than feeling sheer esthetic bliss and enjoyment, I downright admired his ability to merge so much of not only African American musical expression but American musical expression in any way he damn well pleased. In his music there was eighties' rap, seventies' funk, and sixties' rock and even the teens' ragtime; in his music, and in his lyrics (often as cryptic and inscrutable as Zen koans), met Little Richard and Bootsie Collins and George Clinton and Louis Armstrong and Bob Dylan and Holland, Dozier and Holland and Marvin Gaye and Joni Mitchell and Thomas A. Dorsey and—perhaps most spookily and reverently—Jimi Hendrix, whose music was a similarly enigmatic fusing and blending and wreckless, careless merging of all those things within American musical expression that make it dangerous and virtuoso and gloriously impossibly romantic and forever young. *Scuse me while I kiss the sky!*

I don't remember when I found out that Prince had grown up in Minneapolis and still lived there (perhaps when I saw the movie *Purple Rain*); but I do remember that I thought more and more about how growing up in that part of the Midwest might have influenced him; and wondered more and more in what ways being black there had affected him. As subsequent albums came out, *Under the Cherry Moon, Paisley Park,* and so many others, I kept wondering: What gave him his devil-may-care defiance of borders and boundaries? What allowed him to seemingly effortlessly partake endlessly of the American musical smorgasbord? Was it Minnesota?

Before I even took to the road, I knew that His Highness did not give interviews. But I did hope to interview perhaps an employee at his recording studio, Paisley Park, or a friend or—I was told over and over again, that all employees of His Royal Badness signed agreements that they would not speak to the press; and that the only person known to be close to Prince was God. In short, forget it kid.

I discovered that the hip record producers Jimmy Jamm and Terry Lewis operated out of Minneapolis as well—they who gave Janet Jackson new umph and zap in her albums *Control* and *Revolution.* Perhaps, with one or both of them, I could discuss the much-touted "Minneapolis sound." Indeed, in the albums that they produced, I did hear borrowing and mixing and timbres similar to those of the soon-to-be "glyph" musician (and known even later as "The Artist"). But the producers were surrounded by a staff fiercer than Cerberus guarding Hades, and they wanted me to send copies of my work and a statement of my intentions and I reckoned, like the Ghost of Christmas Present, that my life on this globe would be brief.

However, I did belatedly discover, much to my wonder, that the singing group who had bucked me up, elevated my soul, rocked me over sadness many times during my travels with their gospel-good, drumbeat-drunk, hallelujah music, the Sounds of Blackness, were from St. Paul.

I would discover also that a large number of the choir—which had begun at MacAlester College in St. Paul in the early seventies as the campus black gospel choir—had grown up in Pilgrim Baptist Church.

Pilgrim had been founded in 1863. And I had been told that this church had one of the largest and most affluent black congregations in the state of Minnesota. The morning I attended services there, I noted the stained glass windows, a row of images on the west wall, of the forefathers of the church. Solemn-looking icons, including that of the founder, the Reverend Robert T. Hickman, an escaped slave from Missouri. The sanctuary was enormous, almost cathedral-like, with a fellowship hall downstairs, and I would later discover very well-appointed offices and chambers; the organ with great silver pipes loomed; and above and behind me was a balcony; before me, and the congregation, were both the American flag and the Christian flag.

There was a lot of singing that morning, beginning with "Give Me That Old Time Religion," and the associate pastor read from Psalm 100 and the choir marched in, quite stylish in their robes, all full of joyful pomp and circumstance, and they stopped among the congregation awhile, singing "Stand Up for Jesus" as they went, in a modern rendition whose rhythms and rhymes—like the Sounds of Blackness's—were potent with rhythm and blues constructions, and they took their places behind the pulpit. The associate pastor read Romans 8:28 "Liken unto spirit also . . ." and Children's Hour was had, with all the little children coming forth, and they were questioned as to what they were looking forward to in the coming Thanksgiving season: "Spending time with family." "To have brunch." "To carve the turkey." "Thankfulness," they answered.

(I noted that there was an unusual amount of standing up and sitting down, up and down, up and down, for prayer and such, and I almost felt as if I were in a Catholic church.)

The welcome was given by one of the members, and the visitors present (I never have stood in church when they ask, "Are there any visitors present?"; I always found it too embarrassing) stood and identified themselves, and it was noted that several members of the University of Minnesota basketball team were present as well as a few members of the professional basketball team the Timberwolves.

The minister entered at the appointed time, aflow in a white robe with burgundy stripes, and he presided over the "baby dedication" of two children. The pastor left shortly thereafter.

A nine-member male chorus "favored us with a selection"—"Fix Me"—which craftily segued into "Never Alone" (and, as they say, rocked the church), and I felt I was beginning to get a clue about the intensely musical nature that had spawned the Minneapolis sound. Later the larger choir as a whole, their red robes swaying with their rhythms, sang a spiritualized gospel (as opposed to a gospelized spiritual—spirituals are the old songs prior to ragtime and the explosion of the blues, more austere and with specific musical constructions; gospel music is an essentially twentieth-century creation, largely attributed to the influence of Thomas A. ["Georgia Tom"] Dorsey's songwriting and arrangements) version of "Love Lifted Me," initially a capella and measured, featuring a tenor solo. But soon, along came the guitar and the drum and the piano and the organ and, again, they rocked the church.

I sensed an almost competitive nature in these choirs, seeing who could conjure forth the most powerful spirits. And I could see how much emphasis was being placed on "making a joyful noise," which is fine, which is dandy. But it bemused me greatly when there was applause after most numbers, and at one point a standing ovation. At First Baptist Chinquapin, such things just don't happen; they are seen as taking the emphasis off the worship and placing it onto the worshiper . . . but then again, I'm just a naive country boy. Who was I to judge city folk? And in the Midwest to boot.

Enter again the pastor, who based his sermon on Romans 8:28: "We know that in the end God works for good." "*We know,*" he emphasized.

His sermon was entitled: "For those who believe, every situation can become a blessing." And upon that rock, he built his sermon, a cadenced, at times intellectually challenging piece of oratory, and ultimately, rhetorically rhythmic and old-school—I would discover later that he was from the South.

After offertory, "Do You Know Jesus?" was sung, and the church became afire with standing and dancing and shouting—it was, after all, a Baptist church, even though it felt almost Pentecostal, and I was a bit surprised, but ecstasy had been achieved.

Later on that day five people joined the church: a doctor from Minneapolis, his wife from Ghana; a man from Belmont, Wisconsin, his daughter; and a woman from New York who was already singing in the choir. As they had all been baptized they were merely given the "Right Hand of Fellowship," which meant all the members of the church came down in a line and shook their hands, thus making them members.

That day the congregation looked all finely dressed and proud (though I did see a boy or three jacketless and without ties—about which I thought, When will I get over my own upbringing?). And there were a good number of white folk present, I would estimate as high as 10 percent of this crowd of several hundred.

Anthony Johnson worked for the church and the next day he was kind enough to speak with me for a spell. At the time he was twenty-nine. I asked what his title was and he told me facilities manager. And I asked what that meant.

"'What do that mean?'" He laughed. "It means you're a janitor. But it's much more to it than just cleaning," he said. "You got to schedule rooms and stuff like that. Make sure everything is working."

Anthony told me he had grown up in the church; this was his neighborhood. Rondo had been destroyed before his time.

"My parents often tell me about it. Because the house I grew up in used to be right down here on Western, before they built the freeway. People talked about Rondo used to be this street and all that, and then I have some of my older friends who grew up in Minnesota talk about how they used to get lost. They used to go downtown and get lost. They knew their way home by walking where they built the freeway. They just said, 'We just follow this, we'll get home.'"

Anthony Johnson had been working full-time for Pilgrim Baptist Church for about a year. Prior to that he had worked part-time at a five-star restaurant called the Blue Horse, and spent the rest of his time as a sound engineer—which he felt was his true calling. He had worked with a number of bands, and gospel concerts, and he continued to do it part-time. Recently, he had been working with a group called Mint Condition. "Real new. R & B, funk." They were on the Jamm and Lewis label. We started talking about the "Minneapolis sound."

"Lot of people say, 'Well, the Minneapolis sound is a mixture of jazz, rock, a little bit of country.' Far as I can tell, growing up in Minnesota, we've never really had a black radio station. All right? We had like the radio stations that the sun goes down, they're off the air kind of thing. So basically, you had to create. You weren't in no hallway or nothing. You were just open. And there were artists before Prince. I guess he just worked harder." He mentioned jazz singer Roberta Davis, and the singer Rocky Robbins. Also, he pointed out, Bob Dylan had been from the Twin Cities. "Minnesota's always had talent. It's just that Prince—he got the foot in the door. He's just strange, you know. When you listen to his music, you say, 'This man is strange.'"

In the end the Minneapolis sound was "different people from different kinds of backgrounds. People were trying to copy the Minneapolis sound, and all that. In other parts of the country, the drumbeat and all that, the rhumba beat and all that. We never really had anybody else from Minnesota before him who could be copied." But the music of Minnesota could not be limited to one artist, he told me, and pointed to the strong interest in gospel music.

Pilgrim Baptist Church, he told me, had seven choirs. "Choir A and Choir B, Spirit of Christ Youth Chorus, the Chancellor's Choir, the Men's Chorus, the Women's Chorus, and the Rase Majestic Choir." The latter had been named after a much-beloved director who died in the 1970s. That choir had made an album, he told me. Much of the credit went, he said, to the Reverend Miller, who created a new youth department when he came to be Pilgrim's pastor. "Reverend Miller said he wanted a kids' choir. And they got so big they had to split into A and B. And then they split into age groups. I think it's like seventy kids or more. The male chorus is called the William O. White Heritage Singers." Mr. White, he told me, had a beautiful baritone. The group had been named in his honor. The Chancellor's Choir was the "older choir," Anthony told me.

"It's powerful, man," he said, "when you hear the kids sing and perform. They sound good, it's not just put together. They enjoy it. You know what I mean? They come to rehearsal every Friday, they contribute, they listen. All that. Fellowship's really improved."

Anthony Johnson told me the church built the townhouses immediately around the church (he called them "projects," to which I said, "you've got to be kidding, they're lovely," to which he replied: "Yeah, well, see, you're in Minnesota now"), but they were eventually sold to the city. The church also had a credit union. "Credit union is only like, I'd say—ten years old at the most. It was a black thing. We don't really support that like we should. That bothers me a little, because we should. We have enough members in the church making over $20,000 a year that our credit union should be just pounding. But they don't support it. I don't know why. But they don't. You have a lot of brothers who start stuff and have stores. You know what I mean? And don't do it right. But it is strong. As far as blacks go. You just have to build up. We're not as vast like Chicago and all those places, and some of the southern states. But we're getting there, we're getting there."

Anthony had been born and raised in St. Paul; but his mother had been originally from Mississippi, his father from Arkansas. He pointed out that a number of Pilgrim members either had ties to the southern states or were themselves recently moved from there to work for the large companies in the area, to go to school, for internships.

The current dynamism that existed in Pilgrim, Anthony felt, was due to the Reverend Miller, and the Reverend Amos Brown before him (both, he pointed out, were originally from Mississippi). The Reverend Brown had been the local NAACP president, worked with the Urban League and the city council, and with the governor. "Being a minister at Pilgrim is kind of like being pushed into the community." The Reverend Miller had also been involved with the same organizations. "It's a very, very powerful church." He mentioned the many organizations that came out of, or that were directly influenced by, the church. "Pilgrim is just amazing."

Though it was always a powerful entity, Pilgrim's reputation in the black community of the Twin Cities was somewhat mixed. "You talk to your friends, and they're like, 'You go to Pilgrim?' Because their parents are like, 'Pilgrim's an uppity church.' Years ago they used to have two choirs. One was called the Gospel Chorus, and they sat in the balcony. The more lighter-complected, educated ones who could read music sat in the Chancellor's Choir."

"Get out of here," I said.

"No, straight up," he said.

"This is in your lifetime?"

"No," he said. "Late '50s, early '60s. Reverend Brown, he's the one that got rid of that." The pastor prior to the Reverend Brown, Anthony said, had made the church, "real strict, real quiet. Then Reverend Brown came and he ended that. I guess it's not important. It's over with. It's done. But if you talk to people about the history and all that . . ."

But those days in no way resembled Pilgrim's current situation. "A lot of everyday people come here. More poor people. There's still a lot of everyday plain old people. We have your 3M employees, your doctors, your teachers, lawyers. If somebody came along with enough money and business skills, we could have our own 3M. Doctors of chemistry, medicine, dentists, you name it. We got it. There is a member in this church that does it."

In Anthony Johnson's view there was no reason a black student in Minnesota should not excel. "Because we have the people to prep them. People who are fresh out of college could help these people. That bothers me a lot. If we put our energies together we could control a lot of things," he said. "When I was in high school, they said, 'SAT tests will be given at such and such an hour.' I tried my hardest not to be in school, because I didn't know what it was. Nobody had told me. You know what I mean? My counselor, if I saw him today, I'd probably punch him. He knew I wanted to be in electronics, so he let me take all the wrong classes. I went through photography, choir, band, and then I had to take the required stuff like English courses and government and all that. That's all I took. He knew I wanted to be in electronics and all that, but he never forced me to take a math class, at all. He was white. And see, my parents were older. So they weren't really hip to what was going on." Unfortunately, when he took the vo-tech entrance exam, though he did well in English, he was not successful with mathematics. "I didn't have a learning disability, it was just that I was never told, 'If you're going to be in electronics, take this.'"

He told me that of two schools he could have attended one was predominantly black, and one predominantly white. "And I never had no black history. Only black person I knew about was Martin Luther King. I heard of the Malcolms. Those type of people. The few people they put in the history books, and then Reverend Miller came. And he said he wanted to start a black history thing here. I was home with his daughter at the time, and she was like, 'So who are you going to write about?' And I was like, 'I'll write Martin Luther King.' She said, 'Write about somebody else.' 'What do you mean, about somebody else?' She just started running on about, 'You know, a black man did the first successful open-heart surgery. A black man created the plasma thing and didn't die from it. And the stoplight, the gas lamp.' She just went on and on. It was like, 'You're lying.' You know what I mean? Never told that. Never."

Anthony felt his elementary and junior high school experience had left major gaps in his knowledge. This also led to other problems.

"When I went to summer school, I didn't know how to mingle with black kids. I was like, 'Dang.' It was like a whole different culture, as far as school goes. I just sat in my corner. They'd be talking about stuff and they all knew me, though. But I just didn't know how to interact with them."

Circumstances took a turn for the worse at his high school, Wilson. "And that's when all of them came together, boom. I got to sit with the people I knew from school, who were white people. I got called every name in the book. I kicked many a butt. It's just that they didn't know how to interact with the white people either. Some of the older kids used to throw me in the garbage can. They used to be vicious. But they did the other brothers that way too, though, that went to Gallatier. Finally, after that year, after I started meeting more of them, I just ended up hanging with both. By that time, they had learned to react with the white people by just being in class with them. Being in shop with them."

Anthony told me he also learned a great deal when he began working with the St. Paul Oxford Boys' Club. "I went to Oxford, it was like—whoa. A whole different type of black people. It was the other side of the bridge. They were a little bit rougher, more black, basically. Much rougher than what I was used to. More poor families went to Oxford. Like in basketball games, they used to almost get in fights. And stuff like that."

I asked Anthony Johnson: "You said, 'more black.' Is that what you associate being black with? Being rougher?"

"No," he said. "More black means they haven't been around white people. If they have a painting of the Last Supper. And a black guy did it, when I look at this picture, I see a black guy who probably didn't see a white person until he was older. Because the lips are there, the nose—it looks like a real black person. It's not like somebody that took it and painted it and just made the lips bigger and the skin and all that. This looked like a real black person. You know what I mean? Like for instance, I'd never drunk Kool Aid, growing up. That kind of stuff. My mother wouldn't let me drink Kool Aid. When I go over to my friend's house, they're like 'You want some Kool Aid?' I said, 'No.' You know, that's from being around those Anglos, going to school with them, talking, eating lunch with them. So when I say more black it's not meaning it's rougher, it's just that their culture's more solid. I was an only child also. Now that I've become more aware, I went through that stage. For a while there, I didn't hang with no white people. Like in high school, after ninth grade, I didn't really hang with no white people. I still knew them all, but see, the same thing with them. We stopped associating with each other. As far as like going to the movies and doing that stuff, that all ended."

He told me of a black friend who had been adopted by a white family, "They treat him nice. He's never been around blacks. So when he met me, he was scared of me."

"Scared?"

"I'm really mild," Anthony said. "And he was actually scared of me. He told me later."

Anthony had worked with this friend at the restaurant. "And all he dated was white girls and all that, and he had this attitude, 'All white girls are going to be nice to me.' Because all the people in his community were nice to him. He said, 'Black people backward.'" Later, on a different job, the friend had run into problems with the management; felt he was not being treated fairly. "And he's going, 'Why are they doing that to me?' I said, 'Are you the only black there?' 'Yeah,' he said. And I said, 'That's why.' He said, 'No, no, no, no, no.' And later he found out that's why they were treating him that way. That was like a real culture shock to him."

Anthony Johnson felt it was much more practical and positive to be in the situation to understand both worlds, as he felt he did. "I get along with white people. And I get along with black people." However, he had slightly different feelings about marriages between white folk and black folk. The white folk were generally intrigued and well versed in things like black music and black vernacular. Sometimes "there's an identity problem, with the kids. I would never put myself in that situation. Who am I going to invite to a wedding? All my black female friends? They would probably kick my butt and the white girl's butt too, if they saw me."

He told me he had dated a white woman once. "We kept it secret. And I was like, 'Wait, this isn't working. We're not getting the full relationship. Christmastime, I broke up with her. She dated another black guy and this black guy fell in love. She almost got kicked out of the family. For real. It does happen. That is the real truth."

Again he said that until the intervention of the Reverend Miller, he had little notion of his own identity. His parents raised their children well, Anthony told me, but "as far as everyday dealing with the world, Reverend and Mrs. Miller" were crucial in his development. He mentioned how a man had come to the neighborhood, and had been playing basketball with some kids. His beeper went off, "and they said, 'What are you, a drug dealer or what?' 'No, man,' he said, 'I'm a surgeon.' And they're like, 'A surgeon. A black surgeon? Go ahead.' That's what we need. We need our black people who have all that, to let the kids know that they can achieve that too. And help them achieve it. You know what I mean? That's what Minnesota lacks. As a whole. But like I said, it's coming. It's a lot better than it used to be. A lot better."

> On November 1, 1854, St. Paul, formerly known as Pig's Eye, was formally organized as a City. It was not until 1890, however, that a detailed census was taken.
>
> St. Paul's Black population since the 1890 census has remained rather static percentage-wise. The total population at that time was 133,156 with the Blacks comprising 1,524, a little over 1 1/2 percent. In 1970, the total population was 309,823, with the Blacks comprising 10,930, approximately 3 1/2 percent. So, over an eighty year period, the Black population rose only two percent . . .
>
> On October 25, 1892, James H. Burrell, a former pullman porter, was appointed to the St. Paul Police Department. (20 years before the first Black officer was appointed in New York City.) This was twenty-nine

> years after the Emancipation Proclamation of 1863. As far as can be documented, Officer Burrell was the first Black officer on the police force. . . .
>
> —James S. Griffin, *Blacks in the St. Paul Police and Fire Departments: 1885–1976*

James S. Griffin, at the time, had been the highest-ranking officer in the St. Paul police force. He was Deputy Chief of Police from 1972 until his retirement in 1983. The day I drove out to his house in St. Paul, I got lost in the drifts and was sadly late; in fact I had to call twice to get new directions. When I arrived, apologizing profusely, he seemed in no way put out, and full of understanding. Mr. Griffin instantly struck me as one of those large, solid American citizens, good-humored, fair-minded, optimistic, hardworking, the sort of man who could talk to anyone and make it a pleasant experience. With his expansive face and Poseidon-like hair, swept back and steel-colored, his personality seemed encased and complete. This was not the sort of man who spent a lot of time wondering and worrying about who he was: He knew.

His comfortable home was full of awards and honors and citations. I noted one from St. Paul mayor George Latimer, declaring August 30, 1988, James S. Griffin Day.

"I think in every city, you have to have a time frame," James Griffin said after settling back in his easy chair—though I can remember few who could achieve such a state of animation while sitting. Mr. Griffin was a demonstrative speaker.

"Each city has different times, and different problems. And one of the reasons why we probably have more civil rights in Minnesota than most places is because there are so few of us. We weren't a threat to the population. So they didn't mind. And I hear people say there aren't many blacks here. From my perspective, we're loaded with blacks here now, compared to what it was when I was a boy. Or when my parents came here. There's a different philosophy now.

"When I was a boy, if you'd go downtown to St. Paul, and you saw another black person, you took another look at him. There were so few. In the '20s, there were less than 5,000 blacks in the whole state of Minnesota. We were never segregated in schools, or the streetcars, or the parks or the theatres, or things like that. But once in a while, we'd have issues, and as a rule, they were subtle. We've never had hard-core prejudice. It's more subtle."

He told me his parents came to Minnesota in 1906. "I can trace them all the way back to before slavery." His mother had been from Chicago, and her mother from Kalamazoo, Michigan. His father had been born in Kentucky, and his family had taken him to Cincinnati. (He "left home and travelled around, worked, and ended up in Minnesota by way of Denver.") His parents were married in 1911. Mr. Griffin used this information, he told me, when he ran for the school board: "I said, 'My grandson's in public school in St. Paul right now. He's the fourth generation of my family to attend public school in St. Paul.' I said, 'I go to St. Phillip's Episcopal Church. My grandsons are there, the fifth generation in that same parish. At that time there were two black members on the St. Paul school board. At that time, we made up 4 1/2 percent of the population."

He had been born and raised in St. Paul. Mr. Griffin told me, "I think there's no question about it, in my humble opinion, the St. Paul–Minneapolis area, is very unique. They talk about Rondo. Makes a difference how long you've lived in St. Paul to really know Rondo. One of the things I think is necessary to say is this: 75 percent of all blacks in Minnesota, anyplace in the state, 75 percent of them have been here less than thirty years. And the people who migrate here, they think nothing happened till they arrived."

Mr. Griffin began to tell me a few of the many things of which he felt proud. From the recently deceased Chancellor of New York City Schools, Richard Green ("Richard Green was the superintendent of schools in Minneapolis before he went to New York. As a matter of fact, there's his picture right there on the wall"), to Pilgrim Baptist Church and St. James AME Church, and the fire department.

Mr. Griffin told me: "First black police was appointed 110 years ago. June 1881. Jesse Townsend. See, in those days, they didn't have the squad cars and things. They would go walk the beat. Another thing about black police here, for years, most black police worked in the low social, economic white areas. I was on the police department for about two years before I arrested a black guy because I was never was in a position where I could police black people. I was placed with poor whites. I walked the beat. When I first went on, I walked the beat on Skid Row. I didn't have particularly any problems. And another thing is that they wouldn't put me in a squad car. Of course, all those years you had black detectives. Hell, we had black detectives back in 1912, in Minneapolis, same thing. Never had any supervisors. I was the first black guy to be a sergeant. I was the first black guy to be a captain. See, everything was done by civil service examination. And I was fortunate to be ranked high enough. I took the examination in 1939. A thousand guys took the test. I ended up getting the job. But see in '39, the city didn't have any money. So they didn't hire anybody. They extended the hiring for a year. Nineteen forty came and went and they didn't hire anybody. (You ever heard of John Dillinger? He used to hang out here; they had a lot of scandal in the police department in the '30s. So they cleaned up the department and one of the things they were going to do was take the politics out.) So in 1941 they hired sixty-seven guys in three different groups. And I was one of them. Another black guy, he was ahead of me on the list. He got appointed. World War II came up, and he left and never came back. When I was up, they horsed me around. The first time I went down there, they said I had an overlapping toe, had albumen in my urine, and I was running a temperature.

"Went to my own doctor and he said, 'Hell, there ain't nothing wrong with you, son, you go down and take that again.' And they turned me down. They said my temperature was down and the albumen was gone, but I had an overlapping toe. Doc says, 'Keep going back.' I was considered kind of a wild kid, I guess. So-called conservative black leadership, they weren't pushing it too hard. One guy said, 'Hell, if they get that Griffin boy on there, they'll never have another black policeman.' Anyhow, I kept going. Finally, the guy who was commissioner of education, his son and I had gone to school together. Kids played together. We hadn't had a black schoolteacher in about fifteen years. He appointed a black schoolteacher too. So when I walked into his office, he looked at me, he says, 'Hello there, son, how are you?' He said, 'You used to play with my boy, Axel, didn't you?' 'Yes, I did.' He lived about three blocks from me. He asked me how my family was and all that sort of thing. 'So what's on your mind?' I told him my problem. He says, 'I'll call the police commissioner about that.' I said, 'Thank you very much.' That's all he said. Next time I went down to take that test, there was nothing wrong with me." James Griffin slapped his knee and laughed. "We were friends for years. I've known him all my life. The whole family. Now right in this little old town, this place, kids that grew up here in St. Paul never had trouble. I used to hear people say that they're culturally deprived and all that b.s. Well, I didn't know I was culturally deprived till some black guy told me, and by that time I was forty years old, I was a sergeant in the police department and had one kid who had already graduated from college.

"When I got in the contest over the deputy chief's examination, I was number one. That's where I got in a hassle. They appointed this guy who was number two. And of course I got a little hot about that. The chief and

I had a few nasty words. I said, 'Dick, I'm past fifty-five. Thirty years on this job. You've got to be kidding.' Said, 'Hell, I'll take this to court.' He said, 'Go ahead.' I said, 'I'll take this damn thing to the Supreme Court of the United States.' And we got in a hassle. People started writing into the paper about it. Here's what started it off. People started writing, and it was on the TV. Finally, the newspaper editorialized. Got headlines in the paper. And the union supported me. Only three black guys in the union when that happened. They threw in the sponge after about sixty days.

"I got appointed deputy chief in '72 and I stayed deputy chief, till I retired in '83."

James Griffin had been a basketball and football official for many years. "I used to work college basketball, small college basketball games, high school games. I went all over the state. I wrote down all the towns that I worked in, officiating basketball and football, 135 towns in the Midwest. Went as far northwest as Danforth, North Dakota. As far east as Hot, Michigan. All over Wisconsin. As early as the '50s. There were only two black guys doing that at the time. I think that I'm probably the best-known black guy in the whole state of Minnesota."

A popular notion of the Midwest, perpetuated by the media in the East and West, is one of vast farmland, a great many Germanic farmers, with dull, Bible-bound lives, and faithful wives and harsh winters and fields upon fields. Its history is not well known, other than the quaint farm tales, *Little House on the Prairie* and the robust stories of outlaws on their way to the Wild West.

One of the first things that struck me about St. Paul and Minneapolis was how wealthy those towns were. Thanks to a curious bend that the Mississippi River takes there, and the confluence of the St. Croix River and the branching of the Minnesota River, it became an ideal crux in the Midwest between Chicago and Denver. Here, thanks to the cultural backgrounds of many of the settlers, and to necessity, Minneapolis became an extraordinarily affluent part of America. Some of the largest privately owned corporations in the country are there, with the multibillion-dollar, multinational, one-hundred-year-old, agricultural, food, steel, and money-trading Cargil Corporation being among the first—a company few Americans have ever heard of, yet which affects some aspect of their daily lives; and there is Pillsbury and 3M—the Minnesota Mining and Manufacturing Company—and General Mills, a host of insurance companies, banks and, in general, capitalism at its U.S. best. This state also produced

F. Scott Fitzgerald and America's first Nobel laureate, Sinclair Lewis—the one having nothing to do with the other, but an occurrence that speaks to the wide, contradictory, far-ranging nature of the place. Minnesota also gave us two vice presidents, which probably does have a lot more to do with its business might than most realize.

But this industry and hard work was also evident in black folks, going back to 1857, when a white surgeon from Missouri, named Dr. John Emerson, brought with him one slave, named Dred Scott, to the military post Ft. Snelling from 1836 until 1838. At the time Minnesota was a territory under the Northwest Ordinance, which prohibited slavery. Ten years later, Dred Scott sued for his freedom, based on his stay in Minnesota, and the case was appealed all the way to the Supreme Court, and resulted in the infamous *Dred Scott* decision, which said slaveholders could take their property anywhere they wanted, and that "Negroes had no rights which white men were bound to respect." In effect, the law tightened the Peculiar Institution even more. However, that was one of the few African American defeats in Minnesota. For the most part, Minnesota has had more than its share of triumphs.

One of the earliest black families to live in the land that would become Minnesota were trappers and traders named Bonga. It is said they were much beloved by the native Chippewas. George Bonga, whose father was freed in 1794, was part Chippewa and was married to a Chippewa woman. In 1856 he was described as being a "thorough gentleman in both feeling and deportment . . . very popular with the whites . . . a man of wealth and consequence." When Minnesota applied for statehood, African American suffrage became a divisive issue between the Democrats (against) and the Republicans (for). The Republicans traded away that right in 1860, but attempted to pass voting legislation in 1865, and again in 1867, succeeding in 1869, two years before the Fifteenth Amendment to the U.S. Constitution made it a national right—at least for men. Segregation was done away with in Minnesota in 1869 also.

The number of blacks in the area continued to grow, and more churches were built, and a sense of community developed. According to the U.S. Census Bureau, the combined black population of Minneapolis and St. Paul went from under 500 in 1870 to around 2,000 in the 1890s. By the 1880s, two men in particular, Thomas H. Lyles, former barber, real estate dealer, mortician, and funeral parlor owner, and James K. Hilyard, also in real estate as well as insurance and used clothes, were both noted in the press as men of influence and power. Together and individually, these two helped initiate or were involved in the founding of

Masonic lodges, the Robert Banks Literary Society, the newspaper *Western Appeal,* and brought other black professionals to the area, like Frederick L. McGhee, the state's first black criminal lawyer, Dr. Valdo Turner, the first known black doctor and a slew of others. Lyles is said to have influenced the hiring of the first black police officer that James Griffin spoke of. The first blacks served on juries in the 1860s; were serving in the fire departments and had their own city militia in the 1880s; were elected to the legislature in 1899; and they began political organizations such as the Minnesota Protective and Industrial League, the Afro-American League, the Minnesota Citizen's Civil Rights Committee, and the Twin Cities Protective League—all moving more and more toward national challenges to Jim Crow laws and civil rights. Two active Minnesota men, the lawyer McGhee, and the editor of *The Appeal,* John Quincy Adams, participated in the Niagara Movement, and were national representatives to, and charter members of, the local chapter of the NAACP.

During the early decades of the twentieth century, large successive waves sent African Americans out of the South and to northern urban areas. For many reasons, some known, others only speculative, the Twin Cities did not see a dramatic increase in their black populations. The numbers grew—by 1920 there were almost 9,000 African Americans in the state—but not by leaps and bounds. Some point to the restrictive housing codes both cities enforced, hence St. Paul's Rondo and Minneapolis's North Side and Seven Corners. There were other areas, but, again, due to the small numbers, these areas were never predominantly black, simply integrated. During these years a large number of community centers were created, like the Hallie Q. Brown Center and the Phyllis Wheatley House. During the height of the Depression, the Black Neighborhood Cooperative Store was created, and by 1937 that institution issued loans and extended credit to make up for the difficulty most blacks had with majority-owned financial institutions.

And while the labor leader A. Phillip Randolph successfully cajoled Franklin Delano Roosevelt into issuing the executive order which barred discrimination on any federal contract, in the early 1940s, in Minneapolis, major boycotts were organized against the four largest breweries: Schmidt, Gluek, Grain Belt and Hamm. Though those boycotts were not successful, the fact of organization and activity does demonstrate a strong sense of political community among African Americans in the cities. (However, other companies not only capitulated but went beyond expected norms: Federal Cartridge not only hired over 1,000 black folk, but it allowed them into every aspect of the business—at one time they were said to have employed around 20 percent of Minnesota's black population.)

The black population of the Twin Cities is very like, and yet very different from, the rest of America. By the early nineties, Minneapolis and St. Paul were home to one of the most affluent black middle classes in the country; they participated in every level of government from president of the city council to members of boards of directors, to the legislature and the judiciary, to a wide variety of professions—in a state where their percentage was less than 2 percent. And yet, a similar number of African Americans in the Twin Cities were either unemployed or members of what is called the "working poor" or involved in criminal acts or incarcerated (among males)—in essence, barely getting by. Thus the problem; thus the conundrum. But considering Minnesota's history, I could not help but ask myself, first: Why? And second: Considering what the population had achieved, couldn't black Minnesota become a true success story as well?

If someone had told me that Nellie Stone Johnson was in her early fifties, or even late forties, I would have been thoroughly convinced—and might even have suspected her to be younger. For to look at her, you could never possibly suspect that the woman before you had been a part of Minnesota history for over eight decades.

She grew up on a farm in Hinkley, Minnesota. ("It's quite a bit north, a hundred miles north of here.") But she had spent the larger part of her life in Minneapolis.

"I knew St. Paul just by visiting, because of an uncle and aunt that lived there. I've been more familiar with Minneapolis, you know, and my mother and father both lived here before they were married."

I met the nimble and energetic Nellie Stone Johnson at a bagel shop on Nicollet Street in downtown Minneapolis. She told me about the family farm:

"It was good land and good country for what they wanted to do. They settled on a farm about twenty miles south of the city here. That's where I was born, in Dakota County. My dad wanted to go deeper into dairy, and his family was getting bigger, and the farmers in those days always felt you have to have enough milk cows to accommodate the kids. So we moved up to Hinkley there, and we took twenty-five milk cows with us. I forget how many boxcars we had of all the stuff we were moving from the farm, machinery and stuff like that. And horses and cows. We had some sheep. Not too many. And we moved up there in 1919, acquired a bit more property. Wasn't long before we doubled the milk, and that was a part of his idea anyhow. We were east of Hinkley; it's only seven miles from the St. Croix River, which is the dividing line between Wisconsin and Minnesota right there. That's known as Wisconsin dairyland country so we were very close to that whole area, whether it's in Minnesota or Wisconsin—dairyland. Pretty much our prime income was dairy."

She told me hers was the only black family there. I asked what it was that gave her father the pioneering spirit.

"Well, it really wasn't pioneering to him," she said. "No, he was raised on a farm in Dalton, Missouri." Her mother had been from the small town of Carrolton, Kentucky, and had gone to what was then Louisville Teacher's College. "They lived on land pretty close to a farm. My uncle, the one that I'm named for, was a racehorse breeder, beautiful thoroughbred racehorses. They both were really, for all practical purposes, farmers. But there was no question about him wanting to come here; this was an ideal place for him. I don't think he thought of it as pioneering. He had bought a farm, not a very large farm, when he was quite young, in Green Bay, Wisconsin. He sold that after he met my mother, and found some property that he liked better. We still have a home farm up there. We rent it out. We rent the land, you know. And the buildings were getting pretty bad, one old building's almost a hundred years old. And we tore all that stuff down, and now it's almost like a trailer town. Everybody in the family's got a trailer up there. We keep five acres, right in the center, where the road kind of hits the main road, and we rent all the rest of it out. The other farm then, the little farm we call 'Eighty Acres,' we just rent that out, period. We don't even have a trailer on the place."

I had earlier spoken with a young man who had known Nellie Stone Johnson all his life. And he described her to me: "This is a woman who's in her eighties. I walked with her for about—God—a couple of blocks this past summer, and had to almost run to keep up! She just won't mince words. Her personality, her reputation as somebody who would talk straight to you, won't bullshit you—she's just quite a character."

Participating in the organized labor movement as early as the 1930s, Nellie Stone Johnson was the first woman vice president of the Minnesota Culinary Council and the first woman vice president of Local 665 Hotel and Restaurant Union—in fact she helped organize them. She was elected to the library board in 1945; in 1947 she led the Minneapolis Central Labor Body, the Hennepin County Council, and the NAACP to include the Fair Employment Practices Act as a city ordinance. She served on national committees for organizations including the NAACP, the National Council of Negro Women, and the National League of Women Voters. Nellie Stone Johnson was an early mentor to Hubert Humphrey, and later Walter Mondale, and intricately involved in the 1955 act which ultimately led to the creation of the Minnesota Human Rights Department. She served on the Democratic National Committee in both 1980 and 1984. Her awards could fill a museum, and in the early eighties she became a board member of the Minnesota State University System. Nellie Stone Johnson still ran her sewing shop, Nellie's Alterations, which was around the corner from where we met. I paid a great deal of attention to Nellie Stone Johnson's every word. You can imagine why.

I asked how she got involved with the labor movement.

"Well, I tell you," she said, "that kind of comes from my background too, because my father was very active. He was elected to the school board, Dakota County, before I even started school, 1913. And being as my mother was a schoolteacher too, they kind of thought in terms of higher education all the time. My father was very active in a farm organization that was a very strong organizer for the family-type farmer. What the price of the products was going to be; how honestly people weighed their milk or your corn, your oats, or whatever, as you were selling it, and things like that—you had to have an organization. I know that he used to say that the Farm Bureau was too conservative. He didn't like that, he didn't like the Grange. Before I knew it, there was a farmers' union that had developed. And that's still going strong, and I work with them and the Department of Labor. So when I came to town, and went to work, and was going to school at the same time, I remember, I went home, because I used to drive home every other week. I just couldn't get too far away from the kitchen table. One morning I called my dad, I said, 'Looks like you're going to get a union.' And he said, 'Look, there's nothing wrong with that.' And I said, 'Well, I'm helping to organize.' And he said, 'Good.' So I had a lot of support. And it was a function of health plans, vacations, and more money. And the whole Civil Rights movement that a lot of people take credit for in the '60s and Martin Luther King, that's not true. Black labor helped to really put together that whole civil rights thing. And the great leadership of a person like A. Phillip Randolph, the Brotherhood of Sleeping Car Porters. I knew him quite well. He was in New York and we were back here, but every once in a while, he was here, and then I worked on the NAACP committee, worked on labor committees, and within the Democratic Party. And all of that, he was a part of that too. There's hardly one of the leaders, black leaders, that I haven't worked with."

"Getting people jobs."

"Yeah, that's the root of everything," she said.

I asked if she felt that was the root of all the problems that existed for African Americans now.

"They exist because a lot of our middle class, which us peons helped to get jobs for, didn't pay anything back to the community. Oh, sure, they'd get out there and march and jump up and down, and honor Martin Luther King, Jr., and like that, but not the hard things that you have to do politically or by way of your own organization, to put people to work. I think the generation probably before you just got caught up in the picture of what middle-class thinking was supposed to be, without understanding and knowing. I have some cousins and we used to argue about that middle-class thing. See, the difference in my family and myself, we were born into a middle class. We weren't hungry. We always had plenty of work. We always had all the things that we needed for a good living, and a very high standard of living. But none of the foolish things. So what we get caught up in is, like with the cousins, somebody has to have a fur coat, or somebody has to have an oriental rug on the floor. Or somebody has to eat steak every day. Or two or three times. All of that kind of stuff. Or drink whiskey, whatever. I like a good shot of brandy, but that doesn't have to be my reason for living."

Nonetheless, she felt hopeful regarding young black men and women of all classes today: "They have a better grasp of the realities of life. Unless the Republicans kill off all of the black people in this country, you will have the so-called underclass of people breaking out.

"I get very disgusted here in Minneapolis, people that have got good jobs, they've rode my back, and people like me, to get the job that they have, and are too uppity to reach back and help anybody. Their own children. Their grandchildren, for that matter. It's a destruction of the whole black population."

"But what about the statistics?" I asked. "The thing that worries me so much is black-on-black crime. The fact that black men are killing one another."

"There's no such thing as black-on-black crime," she told me with emphatic exasperation. "I keep on saying that to our so-called leadership around here, who keep talking about black-on-black crime. I said, 'It's white-on-black.' And I said, 'Black people don't control the jobs and the houses of education. Things like that.' So how in the world can it be black-on-black? And if a black person kills another black person, that happens as a result of the frustrations that take place, because that person who is out of work doesn't know how they're going to feed their family. They don't know if they're going to be cold when the next storm comes along, or what."

As regards drugs she felt that was a purely "economic" situation. "Person gets kicked out of a job, they're not hired, and they're going to go out there and make some money off of drugs, try to feed their family. Same thing. I always call it a drug economy or a drug culture. The people that control things politically and economically are the people that are in control of drug traffic; they built that."

I asked her: "In your eyes, do you see a tremendous amount of change? Have conditions gotten better or worse?"

"Worse, worse. They've been going downhill for thirty years. That's one of the reasons I've come back into the labor structure. And I should not be serving on as many boards as I'm serving either. I should not be doing that much work. I was up this morning on a conference call at seven o'clock. It's because people went around here beating themselves on the chest, talking about 'black is beautiful, black is powerful' and all of that. And no politics, no politics. We have to get out there and work at politics."

She told me about the Nellie Stone Johnson Scholarship Program. "It's the only one in the country like it. Most of the scholarships for minorities are tied to the corporate structure. And most of the people that come out of that can't find their way across the street politically. I'm not saying that in a degrading manner. It just happened that way. I think the parents fall down on the job. I wouldn't be opposed to some of my young relatives taking one of these scholarships, but they would also get a parallel education as to what life is all about, and particularly what black life is all about. It has to be for a long time. It has to be people that are in the movement, because see, a lot of that stuff got sidetracked in the '60s. When they started setting up these African Affairs departments in the various colleges. Well, in 1939, I was plugging then for multicultural history, but not that way. Sure, we can learn our history. My mother taught us all that history. We didn't go to one of those schools. We also learned what we had to do to survive. In this society. Or in the society of the world. I think a specialized education in our culture has to fit into the total culture. They don't have to lose their own culture. I can be the most cultured black person in the world, and not know where I am going to eat my next meal. Or have a place to sleep. That's what I'm talking about. You do those parallel things. And I don't think it's hurt me. I don't have degrees coming out of my ears, but I can run rings around the average general lawyer. So I don't think I've missed too much."

After talking to Nellie Stone Johnson I almost felt guilty. Almost felt the thrust of my entire journey was half-baked, wrong-headed, false. Almost. Questions still burned. But perhaps I had to find a way to recouch the question. Perhaps. Almost.

What was the question?

The two weeks I was in the Twin Cities, Isaac Julien was also in town. Already well known internationally, the black film director had left his home in London to do a local residency for the McKnight Foundation. His activities in the city included a play based on his short movie *Looking for Langston*—a lyric and poetic piece about black gay life during the Harlem Renaissance; a film inspired by Langston Hughes's unpublished poems to a male lover, known only as "Beauty." Isaac's black-and-white film is at once expressionist and impressionist; he uses found footage and photographs and poetry and, at its core, the reenactment of the gay, fancy dress balls held in the 1920s in Harlem, notable for their integrated attendance. His film is haunted by images of ravishingly gorgeous black men—especially the actor who plays "Beauty": if Pygmalion had been gay he would have sculpted this man. My friend Don Belton had befriended Isaac, so we all hung out together.

I attended the play version of the movie, now called *Looking for Langston: Undressing Icons* (in which Don had a minor role). The play, which was in many ways, perforce, different from the movie, took place in different rooms, which is to say the audience walked into different areas for each new scene. And like the movie, its center was the Langston character's overpowering love for the elusive, allusive "Beauty." Isaac Julien's obsession is the "politics of desire." At the same time, the play also dealt with another issue both separate and related to its original theme. The estate of Langston Hughes aggressively and successfully moved to have the film blocked in the United States. And when it was finally shown in 1989, the estate demanded the volume be turned down on the poems. Later, they successfully forced Isaac to remove the poems from the film for a time. It seems that though it has become common knowledge that Langston Hughes had a penchant to fall in love with men—and was moved to write about it—the people who control his estate apparently would like that information to disappear. To address these issues, the issues of copyright infringement and what Julien called "the belated queerness of black icons, such as Langston Hughes," the play included controversial images by the photographer Robert Mapplethorpe and Platt Lynes as well as the unauthorized poems.

I very much enjoyed Isaac Julien's company. A big, dark burgher of a fellow, he had a round boyish face with the deepest dimples imaginable, with hair close to the skull and a laugh that was infectious and always near the surface. I could see also, after a spell, that he might just as easily be brooding and intense and distant. We three had dinners and drinks and attempted to get into Glim Glam, the nightclub owned by his Royal Badness Himself (Prince)—but we were turned away. So we went about downtown Minneapolis to bars and sandwich shops, we three brothers, dark against the ever-hardening ice and snow.

At one point during the second week, Don invited Isaac and me to attend his writing class at MacAlester, as "guest artists." We listened to the students' stories and made our critiques, and I couldn't help but wonder what these well-scrubbed, all-white Minnesota kids made of these three black men, one a Southerner, one a Londoner, one formerly from Philadelphia, expounding on art—perhaps they made nothing of it at all.

A number of Isaac's works were being shown in downtown Minneapolis: *Territories,* a 1984 documentary inquiry into Carnival; *Looking for Langston*; and *This is Not an AIDS Advertisement,* made in 1988, which was about the very thing it said it was not: the aesthetics and politics of safe sex ads; and his latest film, *Young Soul Rebels,* which had already won a critics' award at Cannes, about the London of Isaac's youth in the '70s, in which the main character is a black man in a love relationship with a white man, and dealing with violence, homophobia and racism—a rather heady mix. Isaac Julien could never be accused of making light-minded fluff.

The next week motion pictures by the film collective Sankofa, of which Isaac Julien was a founding member, were shown, including the films *Passion of Remembrance* by Julien and Maureen Blackwood, and *Perfect Image* by Blackwood, and *Dreaming Rivers* by Marina Attile, almost all dealing with the heritage many black folk in Britain have from the West Indies—challenging, beautiful pictures, quite unlike anything being done in the United States. I was particularly haunted by a refrain from one of the movies: "When did we stop laughing? Oh the mess of it all . . ."

After the screenings, Isaac spoke to the audience and answered questions. He spoke of the film collective's objectives and origins in 1983;

of how frustrated they had become and how they "didn't want to have to explain themselves to white people or black people for that matter"; of how many voices were being excluded from British television. And of how under the current "fascist" government, the once progressive Channel 4—which had produced *Looking for Langston*—was becoming more and more conservative; and of how these young black filmmakers wanted to have "an autonomous space to talk about cultural representation, political will"; a space of their own and not to have to respond to a program, and live up to any perceived notion of authenticity. What is black? Isaac Julien asked, and my ears pricked up. He pointed out that so many of the questions were mere pedagogy handed down from the academy. There are other questions that have to be asked, about identity, about the politics of desire, about gender, about so many things, he said, "Questions we've got to deal with." And I noted how very much Isaac Julien liked the idea of "questions," and I felt as if we were kindred spirits.

He used as a prime example the reception of Marlon Rigg's documentary *Tongues Untied,* a celebrated film about being black and gay in the United States. When it was to be shown on the Public Broadcasting System, it was pulled by fifty of sixty channels. Questions needed to be asked, he said, particularly why not a peep was heard from the African American community.

Questions.

Again I was late, but this time—I am ashamed to admit—I had gotten engrossed in a special episode of *Star Trek: The Next Generation* (Spock's return), and simply forgot the time. After I had arrived at Seitu Ken Jones and Soyini Guyton's striking loft in downtown St. Paul, I apologized, and Seitu said, "Don't worry, I was just watching *Star Trek.*" I guiltily admitted that's what I had been doing. Soyini shook her head and said "Boys!" Seitu and I fell into a discussion of *Star Trek,* and I commented on how many black men I knew in my generation were avid for the science fiction series. We figured it was the lack of any racism and disease. Needless to say, Seitu and I got along famously. Having just turned forty, there was still something remarkably boylike and eager about this man, with his wire-framed glasses. Seitu Ken Jones was a visual artist, and the community programs coordinator for the renowned Walker Art Center in Minneapolis.

"I'm just curious," I said to Seitu, "Where did 'Seitu' come in? Is that what your parents gave you?"

"No, no, no, no," he said. "I grew up with, believe it or not, Butch. And people still call me that, people I grew up with. The name I was given was Kenneth Jones Junior. My parents called me Butch. It was a name that I took on during the height of cultural nationalism. Early '70s. It's from Burundi, Hutu. It means artist."

I asked when Seitu first wanted to become an artist. "As soon as you could hold a brush in your hand?"

"No, no," he said. "Not quite like that. I was always doing it. I was really passionate about art and always had that kind of passion, although about the time I graduated from high school I really didn't want to be an artist. Because of all the hype. So many people tried to frightened me away from it. 'Oh, you won't be able to earn a living. It's going to be hard.' You know the rap. Eventually, I overcame, I mean, the passion just overcame that. And sure enough, they were right. Now you won't be able to make a living."

One of Seitu's great-grandfathers came first to Minnesota in the 1870s, to Red Wing. "He came from Kentucky, where he was born in the 1840s. Fought in the Civil War. He ended up here in about 1879." He worked as a porter at the St. James Hotel there. "My father and mother used to go there for long weekends. He was telling somebody that his grandfather had worked there, when he first came to Minnesota. This person went and got this photograph of these black men who were porters, and he wasn't quite sure; it wasn't a good photograph, but it was probably him."

His grandmother's name was Ida Jones. "In fact you can see her name on a plaque in Pilgrim. She came and joined Pilgrim, when she was like fifteen. During World War II. She'd been sent to a boarding school in North Dakota. I know that Dad talked about how much she hated it. How she had been called pickaninny and nigger and everything else. How they used to be physically abused. Beat them. And she hated it. She said it was a horrible experience. I don't know if she ran away or what, but she ended up at Pilgrim Baptist Church."

Seitu and Soyini's loft was right on the river. "Right on this spot, almost straight downstairs, is the lower town. It was the place where you could get easy access to the river, without having to go directly down one of the blocks. The riverboats would come to this spot, the largest ones, this is about as far north as they could go." Right across the street, he said, before the Civil War, was the major trading post for the Red River Valley. Here men would come loaded down with pelts, to be sent down the Mississippi. "This is where the city began. This is where folk settled." And he was certain, of course, that African Americans were among that number.

Pilgrim had been originally located closer to where he lived now, and he remembered his grandmother telling him about those days. Of the current building, "I remember my father saying, how everybody pitched in, literally to help build the church. He said he could remember taking lunches down to my grandfather, as they helped, working with masons to lay the bricks. To set the stones. The people literally built the church. Not just contractors. Fellowship in its truest form."

It seemed that Pilgrim had been a huge part of his life. "For a time period, there's no question. I couldn't get away from it. Every time I go in there, it seems like this monument. It was huge when I was a little boy. Seeing those images in the stained glass of black folk, the founders of the church. That made a big mark, a black mark—" he laughed. "One of those things stamped in there was the image of this black man in the stained glass window. I just assumed that's the way it's supposed to be, in every church.

"I used to spend a lot of time with my grandmother, growing up, a whole bunch of time. She lived on Fuller Avenue. The house is still there. Because one of my aunts lives there. I have the earliest memories of Rondo Avenue. I can vividly remember its destruction. That's what I can remember the most. The construction of that freeway. Being a young kid, it made a fantastic playground. This big vacant lot that stretched for miles. Full of rocks and all kind of trouble."

At the time, Seitu said, people's feathers weren't really ruffled by the disruption.

"Not at that time," he said. "People didn't have that sense of loss that we have now. For a whole number of reasons. One, it was the same time the push for integration began. And many of the houses along Rondo Avenue were really substandard. They were really bad. So people ended up getting more than their homes were worth—more than they might have gotten otherwise—they still didn't get as much as they should have. Or as much as comparable homes were going for. But people were happy to get the money that they got, and many folks moved out of the community altogether. My generation was like the last generation to remember it. And now, I think people have this great sense of loss."

Seitu's father, who had died shortly before, had worked for over thirty years in various government jobs, the post office, the VA hospital. He also owned a liquor store in Minneapolis, Ken and Norm's Liquors. "He was actually trained as an artist. He was good." But because of the climate of his times, Kenneth Jones, Sr., "eventually gave up that dream." Seitu told me, "He didn't want me to go through the same hurt and pain

that he went through. He discouraged me for a while, while I was in high school. But once he saw that my passion really outweighed everything else, he became my biggest supporter. When he retired, I was in another studio. I gave him the keys to my studio, and he would come up there and work. He made a full-time living from making art, painting signs for barbecue joints. I can remember him hand-lettering signs. I can remember trying out the stuff and sitting down with him and watching him and he showing me how to do stuff. I remember all of that. It was all straight commercial stuff. Then, after a while, he started pulling out some of his old paintings. Said, 'I got boxes and boxes of paintings back here.' He was good."

Seitu described his school days in Minneapolis as being "different" in a way, but not that different from other urban experiences. "When we lived on the north side, my earliest memories are these Quonset huts that were put up right along Olson Highway. And from there we moved up in and out of those things into the projects, and from the projects, we moved to a couple of apartments. People aspired to that middle-class lifestyle and wanted to move out to single-family homes. No projects. And so we moved to South Minneapolis in 1958. That's when I had this experience of being the only black kid in my class. But the neighborhood changed so drastically so fast." He said that by the time he got to high school, that school was around 60 percent black. From then on he had a circle of friends both in his neighborhood and his school. He told me he never felt isolated. His neighborhood had become what he called "a black list." A banker lived on his block, and a member of the school board. Several doctors. An architect (I remember admiring his house as a kid; Lloyd Wright, but it was more prairie style). Archie Givens ("who built this nursing home, that became the first in a whole string of nursing homes across the country, and he became Minnesota's first black millionaire"). And Fred "Spike" Jones, inventor of the refrigerated Thermo King truck and hosts of other patents, along with his vintage Studebakers.

Recently Seitu Ken Jones had created an art installation in honor of Dred Scott. "One of the things that runs through my work is the spirit of collaboration," he told me. "I love working with others, sometimes acting just as the facilitator of a process to create a piece. And having many people have some input into this piece. That's something that comes out of the '60s, cultural nationalism. They stressed that artwork should be collective, committed. And that was something that I still maintain in my art."

"I've been working in murals," he told me. "Working in other public sculptures. I've got fifteen pieces, something like that, working right now with another brother here in this building. On a piece, on the Nicollet Mall in downtown Minneapolis. That'll be built into the pavement. It'll consist of this image of the river, for about eighty feet, and inside of it there'll be these shadows, and there'll be outlines of people with text in them. So you'll be able to walk across it. People from Minneapolis's past will be represented, not the robber barons. In fact, none of the robber barons will be in it. They already have enough of their shit. No Daytons. No Pillsburys. None of them. We're going to propose using two living people. One of them's going to be Nellie Stone Johnson. It'll be one way to honor her. I've worked with other artists in units like this, two people. Worked with classes of kids, worked with seniors. Any number of combinations. To give people a real sense of ownership of the piece too. Part of it came up in cultural nationalism. Part of it came from just studying design and not wanting to create pieces that were imposed on people. It was a real process, I don't know where it came from. I guess from a combination of sources. When you talk about this relation to popular culture, I got all these inputs from Bugs Bunny and the Roadrunner to Henry Louis Gates, Jr. Just this wide range of input."

I suggested that this might be a chart of Seitu's own personal trajectory through life.

"Yeah. I graduated in 1969." He told me he remembered the tumult and the spirit of the Civil Rights era.

"So it stuck with you, in a sense?"

"Yeah. It really has."

I asked if he had been involved with any civil protest. Taken over any buildings? Demonstrations?

"We were in high school when that happened. It spread like a ripple, throughout this community. Within the whole student body of our high school. In fact, we ended up blowing up a toilet." He laughed. "Now, it's completely different."

I said it seemed to me—and a number of people who were of age at the time corroborated it for me—that the Kent State affair had been a bellwether of the conservatism to come; a virtual end to mass public unrest had become the norm of the '70s.

"What was a marker to me," he said, "was Jackson State, in Jackson, Mississippi. I went away to school, Morehouse College, in 1969. And that first year, they closed the schools early. There were, I think, four students at Jackson State who were killed in similar gunfire. Kent State overshadowed it in the media. But when that happened at Jackson State, the word spread like wildfire at a black school. Black colleges and universities all across the South closed early for the year in order to defuse the tension in those schools. That's what folks were talking about. It happened so quick, and boom. It's hard to look at one incident or one event as being the linchpin, at least in my life. There were a whole slew of things. Blurred memory. It's a really funny thing, talking with other folks from the time period. It almost sounds like old soldiers talking, you know. 'Yeah, remember back when? Remember that? Blah, blah, blah.' "

To Seitu that era had a pervasive spirit of camaraderie—wherever he went in those days. "All elements of black life, black Christians, black jet plane pilots, doctors, alcoholics and bums—the whole gamut. Even that's changed now. Then I could walk into a community and feel the same thing, fall into a meeting called by some social nationalist somewhere, and know the language and the rhetoric and the literature. The leadership of the time, and all of that was there. And it was just really dynamic. There were a lot of things happening. But to be honest, that's just from my perspective. We're talking about nineteen or eighteen years old. I think everybody probably goes through that. I was just a product of the time. To a point I was aware of it as it happened. I could see something, just a kind of gradual change. You know, washing away, change. Middle to late '70s, and knowing something was kind of obscene. I could kind of see it as natural progression. I'm not exactly sure what it was. I don't want to say it was necessarily apathy, because there are people all along the way who were out of that activist mold, and agitating all the time, agitating all throughout that time."

"Would you put yourself among that group?"

"To a degree," he said. "There were people who were doing that all along. One of the things that happened is that a whole bunch of folks who are my age, my generation, got to the point where they settled into a middle-class existence. People who would change their names, became, you know, Hakeem, now wear suits and drive a BMW."

"The pressures of having families," I suggested, "of having the energy?"

"That's just one of the reasons," Seitu said. "I don't know exactly. I've seen it happen and I've tried to remain true to some of those values. There's no question that I've changed and evolved too. And there might be somebody saying the same thing about me." He laughed. "I don't know. And those folks, there are a lot of them too who will say that they've remained true. From the inside of corporations or government, they have tried to create some sort of change. It's always been incremental."

. . .

Soyini Guyton possessed an absolutely flawless complexion, her skin lustrous and smooth; her face absolutely mesmerizing. Her hair she wore in massive braids that snaked down the back of her head. To me she somehow embodied grace, otherworldliness, a phantom, a spirit: her presence was of one who walks on air. I would even believe her footsteps made no sound—and yet her presence made itself profoundly felt—Soyini Guyton was the sort of woman who makes people wax poetic.

Married to Seitu Ken Jones, and working at an arts foundation in downtown St. Paul, she considered herself a writer. She had published one piece of fiction then. Most of her recent work had been art criticism. Cultural criticism, she told me. Her fiction was "loosely based on my aunt and some people from home." "I'm going to write about growing up in South Dakota. We have all these things about *Little House on the Prairie,* white people growing up on the prairie. But black people have had a midwestern prairie experience too. And there's not a lot of fiction about it. There's certainly no movies. I think it's fascinating—when you read books and see movies about the prairie experience of white people, there are never any black people. Black people have been living in South Dakota for generations. They're not new there. They were pioneers too."

Soyini Guyton grew up in the town of Yankton, South Dakota. "That's what people always ask me. How did you get to South Dakota? But actually my family, they've been in South Dakota since 1901. Yankton is in the southeastern corner of South Dakota. Actually, the first black people moved to South Dakota, I believe, in about 1880. My people came from Missouri. And they migrated there because a black man was already living in South Dakota, trying to recruit southern blacks to come there. They said it was a cold place, but 'freedom would really warm you up.' There was land there. They were also putting in the railroad at that time, so there was work."

Now, Soyini told me, Yankton's population was around 12,000 people. When she was growing up, it was closer to 8,000. "So it's a large city for South Dakota." There was a black Baptist Church and an AME church in the town, established in the mid-1880s. Her grandparents migrated there, and her mother had been born there. At the time, there were eight families there; in her family alone there were eleven children. There were cousins and the other families. "It was just one of those things, all through high school, because of the cousins, they'd get ahead or be behind. Except for my twin sisters. But we were the only black ones in the entire high school. In elementary school you certainly felt—you knew the differences. But because you're all in the playground, playing, it's not felt as intensely. I think as soon as you hit junior high school, the alienation really begins. I don't know if it's because of the onset of adolescence or what, but the social dynamics really changed then. It's very alienated. It's very lonely. I hear people talk about their class reunions, and I've never been to a class reunion." Nor did she expect to go to one, she said. Nevertheless, blacks and whites did associate.

"Intermarriage did happen," she said, "among my cousins. But for the ones who didn't choose that, or see that as an option for them, they left. The ones who stayed there are intermarried. But I think I figured early on that that wasn't something I wanted to do. I wanted to be a part of the social set, but I wasn't going to marry a white man, or I just wasn't going to marry anybody other than a black person. Also there's the dynamic of race and class. I felt the perception was that the mates available for black people were a certain class of people. But that wasn't an option for me. It's not because of the lower social economics, it was just lower class in terms of activity and mind-set and stuff like that."

There was little tension in Yankton, Soyini told me. The largest percentage of the population was Native American, who were largely apart from the rest of the population. She remembered that there were only three Indians in her high school, "and the rest of them went to what they called the Indian School." Discrimination, she told me, she did feel from her fellow students. "We had cousins in one family who'd get into fights. After a certain period, they'd come to respect you and know they can't call you 'chocolate drop,' 'booger,' 'nigger,' and all this stuff—unless they wanted to get their butts kicked."

Soyini told me she owed a great deal to her grandfather's vision. "He had a strong sense of himself, and his relationship to South Dakota and to the universe. And he didn't feel that he was less of a person because he was African American. He decided to leave Missouri because of the way black people were treated in Missouri. He used to say that when he first got there, there were a lot of Germans working as manual laborers. But they had to fight too, to get that respect. I think after a while, the community became accustomed to these African Americans being there. They were working the land, trying just like other people. And in some cases, better off than many of the white people around them. Had stable families. And even though the church congregation was very small, they still preferred to have their own congregation."

In many ways, she told me, when a people are faced with isolation, they hold on to their culture more tenaciously. Soyini remembered her mother reading Paul Laurence Dunbar to her, and other black writers. Her grandmother used to write a column about living in South Dakota that was published in the black newspaper, the *Kansas City Call.* "To me that demonstrated people's need to stay connected. To keep their identity." In fact, aside from friends, the only thing she really wanted, felt she lacked, were horses. "The Indians had that. I remember, I wanted some of those. I wanted a horse." And also the isolation protected her from the many traps she could have fallen into in an urban environment.

Surprisingly, Soyini got wistful about the Dakota plains: "I miss the openness. And I still miss living in the country, the trees and natural stuff, and I miss the stars. The Northern Lights. I really miss that. I've never lived in a small southern black town, but somehow—and this may just be a fantasy—I think it would probably be the best of both worlds. Those natural elements and being able to live in an African American environment."

"I think the '60s have had just a tremendous impact on me. And also helped me to look back on some of it, and especially my experience in South Dakota, and be able to understand what was happening there on the social level. Especially that isolation. When I was growing up, I didn't understand why my grandparents would want to move from Missouri to South Dakota. I understand that perfectly now. My uncle, my grandparents, used to tell this story. My grandfather and a cousin were walking down the street in—I think it was Hannibal, Missouri, or Slater, Missouri, one of those small towns. And suddenly this white man ran up to him and said, 'Boy, don't you ever do that again.' And the kids were looking at some white woman, and that's when my grandfather said to his cousin, 'I'm leaving here.' And the next day he saw this man who was already living in Yankton and had sent flyers up to Missouri, urging black people to move to South Dakota. It was the tension of living under the Jim Crow system. The tension of not knowing who's going to take your life for something you didn't even realize you'd done until it actually happened. It was like a breath of fresh air to be there.

"There in South Dakota, it's mostly farmers. There's really no way for people to say that they got more of a break than another farmer did, because the success of the farm, other than the weather, depends on how hard they were going to work the land. If you didn't work the land, you didn't have a crop. They were successful as farmers, and they knew that they built that success themselves. That nobody gave them anything. They didn't have to pay it off. So I think in that way, just living on that land was such an equalizer in that way. Another farmer would never look down the road and say, 'Well, he only got this because he's black or because of equal opportunity.' He got it because he had to work for it. Being a farmer was just luck and skill and weather and all that. I think that once they got there, knowing what they knew of where they lived in Missouri, the isolation didn't bother them. It was probably welcome, not to have an eye always trained on every move you make."

What resulted was a space to learn her culture: "Urban black people especially think people who come from isolated places are just strange. Even beyond strange. It's like well, 'How did you survive? Or how do you know anything about being black?' Well, you're coming from a black family. It's not like we're adopted into a white family. It's not so much where you grew up, but what you learned, what was passed on to you, culturally. You may grow up in an urban community with lots of black people, but if there's no one passing on the culture, then you really don't get it anyway. Even though it's right down the block in the library. They take it for granted. My mother always used to read these black poets to us. So I knew those people. Church anchored our existence in so many ways. We knew the spirituals. We had black preachers who preached that old singsongy call and response. My grandfather's parents were slaves. Connections are passed on, and some certain kind of mannerisms of southern people. They were stubborn, and they passed that on to my mother, and passed that on to us. Sometimes it's not about always being surrounded by culture."

Ironically, by comparison, she felt Minneapolis–St. Paul "just feels real white. And I'm not saying that in a negative way. It's just that's the truth." Some days, she said, she could spend days downtown without having any contact with another black person. Rarely did she see motion pictures with black faces in them. "Sometimes I wonder if white people even realize that. I open the papers and everything is white. All the pictures in the paper, the advertising supplements. It's just frustrating."

Recently, her seventeen-year-old nephew, who had grown up in South Dakota, came to St. Paul, and became very self-conscious about his speech. Within a year he had altered his language. "His grammar and everything had deteriorated. I said, 'You're insulting black people, because you're saying that's the way black people sound. All black people don't use incorrect grammar. And have that—whatever you call that voice.' He thought that he was being more black. I said, 'You just sound ignorant.' He didn't want to sound white. He wanted to sound black." But it wasn't real, she said, it was an idea without foundation or understanding. "It's just something I think you grow up getting—identity. It's something that you certainly can't purchase. It's not something that you can tack on. It's real. Internal." Soyini also spoke of a cousin back in Yankton who joined the white Church of Nazarene. "She always wanted to be white. She's a black dumb blonde. You know, high squeaky voice, saucer eyes, all this sterile kind of expression—the whole thing. Had she been a white girl, she would have been perfect. She ended up marrying a white man. And she's still at it. We'd always laugh at her. But it wasn't funny. See, people like that don't value their identity. They'll shed it. Just like a snake sheds its skin.

"They don't question their identity in the way they carry themselves, in their choices in life. Especially the older black people in my grandfather's generation, I never felt that they were dissatisfied being who they were. That part of their identity was the land, and being able to provide for themselves in a certain way. That's just what black people did for their families. That's how black men could care for their families. That pride in being able to keep your house together, your kids disciplined. Projected themselves in a certain way. I didn't feel that we were in any danger, which is why I said, under the circumstances, after my parents died, that it was better that we were in South Dakota. We weren't in danger."

Before I left, I had to ask Soyini about the eastern notion—perhaps myth—that midwesterners lacked a sense of irony, which is such a staple part of black culture as I had known it all through my growing up. I wondered if she saw in the midwestern black folk she had known a sense of irony.

"No sense of irony? Well, I think almost the fact that we're living here—" and she laughed "—is irony. Especially when it snows the way it snowed just recently; I trek through the snow, and I'm black as I am, and the snow is white as it is. Whenever it snows real hard like that, I always think of the first Africans to come to this country and to have to experience that and just what they might have thought. Just the sense of desolation that they were going through, a sense of deprivation, being pulled away from your family and your loved ones, and people treating you cruelly, and on top of that, having this white stuff coming down. And it's cold. And it's all white people. I think, to me, that's the ultimate sense of irony. You know?"

As I drove north from Minnesota, I felt, for the first time in a long time, that I was beginning to ask the right questions.

Ten

# "HOW OLD WOULD YOU BE IF YOU DIDN'T KNOW HOW OLD YOU WAS?"

*Grand Forks, North Dakota*

Someone called it PraireEyrth.

Flat earth with nothing to impede the eye. Soil so rich and black it could be crude oil. Freshly turned fields after the two-week quick harvest of potatoes and sugar beets; and the wheat all gone. I was told the growing season in North Dakota was nigh-perfect. In summer the days stretch from 5 a.m. to almost 10:30 p.m. when dusk just begins.

I am afraid that even after having my head crammed with prejudice—about the cold, about the bleakness, about the lack of any distraction other than the flatness and the alcohol and the cold, about the very lack of a reason for NORTH DAKOTA to exist—that I came at once to adore the prairie. God knew what She was up to. There is, in the seeming monotony, like a calm sea, something at once terrifying and cleansing; a wonder about the grandeur of pure space, and the inevitable and humbling knowledge that you are a mote on some vast gameboard. For a dweller from multifaceted farmlands and rolling fields and canyons of steel and glass, this effect was a drug.

On the first day—was it the first day?—I drove onto the campus of the University of North Dakota at Grand Forks, and before I could even ask anyone, I saw there the Era Bell Thompson Center.

Who was Era Bell Thompson?

"What in the world was a nice Negro girl like you doing in that godforsaken country in the first place?" was what Bell Thompson had been asked so often. She had been an associate editor at *Ebony* magazine in the mid-forties, and from 1951 until 1964, its managing editor, and international editor for all of the Johnson publications until she took semiretirement in 1986. Back in the forties—before she came to work for Mr. Johnson—she had applied for a Newberry Fellowship to dispel myths about her home state, North Dakota. Her autobiography, *American Daughter,* was published in 1946. Fascinating for its many rich accounts, it tells her own and her family's story from 1914 until she left in 1931, when her father, a restless man, finally moved his family to a farm near Driscoll, North Dakota, and then to Bismarck ("Bismarck was a beautiful prairie town along the banks of the muddy Missouri. Less than twenty of its ten thousand people were Negroes, all living south of the tracks where the streets were unpaved and the sidewalks were broken and crumbling; Ed Smith's young son and I were the only colored children in town"), where her father worked as the governor's messenger; and of Mandan, North Dakota, which "marks the beginning of the real West. It is here Mountain time begins, here the Indians come from the reservations to greet the tourist trains and dance at the big rodeo; here, on this side of the river, live the rattlers; and farther to the west, in the Bad Lands, is the town of Medora, once the ranch home of Teddy Roosevelt and his fabulous friend, the French nobleman, The Marquis de More."

Thompson speaks of befriending her neighbors of Russian and Dutch and Norwegian and Germanic backgrounds, of busting broncos and rodeos, of picnics, of the chinook and footraces, of working her way through the University of North Dakota, and, ultimately, what it was like to face the inevitable discrimination and prejudice one assumes she had to face. Yet despite those obstacles one gets the impression that Era Bell Thompson possessed a rare, adventurous, unstoppable nature—or, as they say in my family: That sister was tough.

She would go on to write articles and the book *Africa, Land of My Fathers,* and coedit others. In 1969, the University of North Dakota gave her an honorary doctorate; and in 1979, a cultural center was named after her.

The Era Bell Thompson Center was located in a three-storey house, right at the center of campus, on University Avenue. I wondered who had lived in it before. Without much trouble, I soon met the woman who would aid me so much during my two-week stay: Toni Scott. Toni, originally from Rhode Island, had been the director of the center for a few years. Part black, part Narragansett, Toni, I quickly discovered, seemed to know everybody, and before I could turn around, she was giving me contacts from Nevada to Oregon. I got a tour of the center—whose rooms now served as offices and meeting places. I was particularly taken by the Jack Mayfield Room on the third floor. Mr. Mayfield had been a boxer in his early years—and an entertainer, a masseur and a cook. He had sparred with Jack Dempsey. He died at 106 in Minneapolis, but had lived in Grand Forks for some years. Newspaper articles practically papered the walls. The Grand Forks *Herald* had run articles on Mr. Mayfield on Feb. 28, 1953; Nov. 16, 1969; May 19, 1970; May 4, 1976; Nov. 12, 1978; Sept. 30, 1979; Feb. 11, 1979; Oct. 5, 1981; Oct. 2, 1983; Oct. 6, 1984; June 23, 1985; May 13, 1986; June 7, 1986; and June 10, 1986, as if they were waiting for him to die, as if he refused to give them the satisfaction.

At the entrance to the Jack Mayfield Room, I noticed, upon exiting, a quote from the great baseball player Satchel Paige, who was uncertain when he was born. "How old would you be if you didn't know how old you was?"

T. Scott Pegues was a busy man. A very, very busy man. "Well, wow, I'm really involved in like eight groups. That's the way you define people around here. I came to North Dakota because there's lots of opportunity. And I'm in public relations, and there's a lot of people going into PR and you need to have experience. They want you to have experience. They want you to start with three years of education. Three years of experience. And you say, 'Well, how the hell do I do that?' So I believe in cocurricular. I don't believe in extracurricular. Cocurricular activities are just as important as academic studies. Without one there is no other. And you say, well, you come here and you pay money for school, yes, I do. I do well in that, but I need to devote the same amount of time to actively practicing what I learned in class, because learning—this is my quote: 'My learning does not stop when I cross the threshold on the way out of the classroom—it begins.' You can read Aristotle and Plato and Shakespeare and I. M. Pei and P. T. Barnum till you turn blue. It's not going to do any good unless you can actively play a part, and if you're going to wait four years until you get a job and then make an attempt, it will not work."

That year, his junior year, T. Scott Pegues was president of the Black Student Association and two fraternity councils, on one executive board, and a public relations chair. "I'm the national liaison for the Public Relations Student Society of America; I send letters and read letters and pass phone calls and things like that." He was also active in his fraternity. "I pledged like two years ago. I have a pledge. I'm on lots of committees over there. I was the vice president. That was like a couple terms back. I was vice president of administration. I was second in command. And I was still a freshman, I had been initiated on Saturday; I was an officer on Monday. I was top ten. Now I'm on the risk management team. I'm on the scholarship committee. I'm on the rush committee. And I'm a big brother, which is the program for pledges week. It's like a mentor; it's a mentoring thing. I'm in the university leadership mentor program where we start with new students and get them involved with leadership things. For student government, I'm on standing committees; one's the university program council and below that I'm on a subcommittee that's called the Zoo. I'm one of the managers there—the Zoo is a nonalcoholic dance club, and it has the largest, and the best, and most expensive light-and-sound system in the state. And it's only open every other weekend. So I'm manager for that. I'm one of four managers."

"Sometimes I need a calendar to remember everything," Mr. Pegues told me.

As I said, T. Scott Pegues was a very busy man.

I wondered about the origin of the name "Pegues."

"It's French. That's what I know. It's just misspelled in the English language. I don't know. I guess my original family moved from Africa to Portugal to Spain to France, Portugal to Spain, back to Africa, and then over here. I know there's two Pegues families in the United States."

His father was from Selma, Alabama, and his mother from Detroit, Michigan. But he had lived in St. Paul all his life.

"I was born there, raised there. My mom moved to Minnesota, I would say like in '65. With her whole family. They all came from Council Bluffs, Iowa, where the rest of her brothers and sisters were born, and then moved up to the Twin Cities. And then they all left and went to Denver, except for my mother. It was kind of a traveling thing."

There were forty-two black students in the Black Student Association, which included about all the black students on the UND campus—there were about ten non-black members. Recently they had changed the name from the Black Student Union to the Black Student Association. "We had a problem with the name. It was very separatist. To us. And to the community. It was just perceived as really odd. So we changed it to Association. We could have been Alliance, but we wanted something that sounded more open. I'm a PR major. We think about word meanings and things. Association was the term."

I asked about the Black Student Association's activities.

"I think the most important things are the informal things. You know, we just meet and know each other, which is very important up here, because there aren't that many black folk. There's point zero, zero five percent. So if people can come to a Black Student Association and talk—whatever the business is—a homecoming float, or a program we're going to put on. The programs and things are important too. But at that meeting, other black students can meet other black students. And after the meeting, they might see each other on the street. And they form a friendship.

"We're really cautious, and now we're starting to bring in more entertainment kinds of things. We do programming for black history celebration month, and for the Martin Luther King holiday. And before, really traditionally, the Black Student Union was the only place doing the Martin Luther King holiday in the state. We felt wrong in doing that because it's not a black holiday, and by us doing the only programming, being the Black Student Union, we were perpetuating the idea that it was a black holiday. So it was kind of a catch-22. Do we just not do anything, when it's not celebrated? And if we do something, we're put in a kind of a compromising situation. Now we just do a portion of it, and we help coordinate. We involve everyone we can from the Chamber of Commerce to the Department of Communication. It's statewide. I'm very proud of that." Adding dance and music became a controversial issue. Certainly black students didn't want to reinforce stereotypical notions. "Black people are intelligent. They can lecture. They can think deeply. We need to warm the community up to the fact that they do classical music and they do jazz, and they've created many things that people don't really know about."

The year before, the Black Student Association had initiated "edutainment" events. "I can tell you how many people come up to you and say, 'I just want to know. I feel kind of ignorant, I don't mean to be offensive, but how am I supposed to know if I'm not told.' And I find the campus and the community to be really receptive to new stuff, because they haven't had any exposure. I mean, we've brought in forty-four different countries across the world with the international programs. We're bringing in blacks and Hispanics and Asians. They don't just naturally occur in North Dakota and these people are coming from places like Fertile, Minnesota, eleven miles to the east with a population of a hundred. Maybe they had never even seen a black person before."

According to Scott, there was no natural social interaction between the black students and the Native Americans—largely due to mutual ignorance. But their respective student organizations were holding joint meetings and progress was being made.

But now T. Scott Pegues was more concerned about his future, elsewhere. "So I have to remain involved. I keep myself busy and I'm a very busy person. I like to be busy. My calendar is like this"—he showed me a Filofax calendar inked all up with different colors—"I panic like if it's not like this, this is the way it should be. I should go to bed at three in the morning and get up at 9:30. You know, and be busy. I should only be home when I sleep. That's my personality."

"And you go to school part-time," I joked.

"No, I'm a full-time student. I take fifteen credits," he chuckled with pride. "And I'm always busy and I like it. I'm not stressed though."

I teased him: "But I'm not stressed, I'm not stressed, I'm not stressed."

"Well, I cut back a lot."

T. Scott Pegues was raised in the St. Paul suburb of Knot Oaks. Only after he reached junior high, he said, did he cease being the only black student in his classes. "Then in high school I think there were twenty-five blacks period. My graduating class was like 10 out of 523." Scott also grew up in Pilgrim Baptist Church—which by this point I reckoned to be as long-armed as everyone suggested. He sang in the choirs and generally partook of its many activities.

Growing up in a Minnesota suburb forced him to make adjustments, he told me. "I really had lots of trouble. I wasn't accepted by the black kids in St. Paul for the longest time. They said I was white. 'You're white, you're white.' And I was like, 'What's black and what's white?'" He said he learned to speak a double language, learned largely when he visited his relatives in Birmingham, Alabama, during the summers. "If you're black you're supposed to talk a certain way, you're supposed to walk a certain way." Also working with city kids during the summer helped give him insight. "I don't even know how I really dealt with it. I was just myself, and knew that this was me. You didn't have to act a certain way. I was always going to be black, and I'd always have the same black heritage as those inner-city children did. But to me they always seemed as if they knew more about being black. Those were probably immature conclusions."

"Do they still hold weight?" I asked.

"Oh, no, not anymore," he told me. "I always probably will be in a white dominant society. But I don't feel any less black. I feel very validated as a black person. And I know my culture and I know my heritage. We all came from the same place. 'Don't you forget where you come from.' They used to tell my parents that, see, 'The city is where black folks belong, so your son will know about being black.' These people in Pilgrim would tell my father that all the time." His parents knew better,

Scott told me. "Of course your parents, as any black, any good black parents should or any other good parents should teach their children about their heritage, my folks did. And when I was in Birmingham and down south, my aunt used to take me around and point and say, 'That Baptist church. When I was little, your father and my whole family, we sat on that bench right over there, and they came by and bombed the church and killed those four girls in my Sunday school class. Touch it.' Okay, now tell me that I'm less black and tell me that I don't have the same heritage. Our family were slaves just like your family were slaves."

T. Scott Pegues: a child of the dream.

Though I was told I had not quite made it yet, I felt damn sure I was in the West. Grand Forks at least had the feel garnered from popular media and books and the imagination: cow towns, pioneers, the frontier, which are associated with the ethos. (Even my motel was made of wood and had hitching posts in front of each room; and the restaurant really outdid itself with decor straight out of a John Ford movie.) But this was the 1990s, and this was not the West, just the center of the continent—quite literally—and with faxes, modems, Federal Express, interstates and airplanes. Grand Forks—despite the dusty-road feel of its old downtown on the Red River, and the buildings, seemingly untouched since the 1890s (North Dakota attained statehood in 1889)—was up-to-date. In fact, most folk in Grand Forks rarely venture into that old downtown now, for like so many modern towns, all the services and businesses and entertainment had been built up outside the old center. (This was before the flood of 1997, which destroyed much of that downtown.)

With a population of just under 50,000, it depended heavily on the airforce base (whose population was said to be almost 10,000) and the university. Indeed the town seemed much larger than the numbers report.

And all during my time there it was *cold.* Not cold, but *cold.* Minnesota had been frigid, especially with the ice, often in the teens, and sometimes single digits; and the nights brought howling windchills I will not report. But once in Grand Forks—where it had not even snowed—some days the temperature did not go above zero degrees. One morning I woke up, turned on the television, and when the newscaster announced that the day's high would probably be minus five degrees, I wondered about the semantics of that statement. Nonetheless, I made a powerful discovery while in this refrigerator world: I did not mind. When southerners think of cold, they think of physically being out in the cold, of the fingers numbing, of the blood slowing. In subzero weather, that is simply not an option. One must be prepared. As someone told me, "You play around up here, you could get yourself dead." I did not play. And as a result, the temperatures didn't phase me, and as I watched the frozen world from the warm insides of Bucephalus, I came to admire how starkly beautiful winter was.

A few nights later I sat in on an African American literature workshop at the center. I was surprised to come in the door and be greeted by five white people, two men and three women, and two black women. The facilitator was a woman named Sharon. She happened to be white. Upon reflection, I don't know why that surprised me; what had I expected in North Dakota? A Major Bill Lee from Alabama (who, when he introduced himself, said, "I'm in the missile business") also joined the group.

Their reading list included Zora Neale Hurston, James Baldwin, Paul Laurence Dunbar, Gwendolyn Brooks, Alice Walker's poetry and her story "Everyday Use," and Mari Evans. That night they were to discuss a 1963 speech by Malcolm X.

The discussion was slow getting off the ground, but eventually one woman confessed that she was "surprised by the cynicism in the speech" and couldn't really comprehend his push for a revolution. Another woman quickly asked what did she mean? "I mean look at Mandela. Look at Harlem." (I wondered if she had ever been to Harlem.) One of the men asked—and I'm not certain how the conversation got to that level—"What did I do? I'm not the enemy." However, the man said, "his style made me think."

Sharon brought up the question of whether Malcolm X felt that reconciliation between the races was possible. And people waffled. Most suspected that Malcolm X only seemed to appear not to believe it was possible . . . but then again . . . The conversation moved on to one of his ideas about land being key to the problems between whites and blacks, and how that was a sticky issue—a part of the discussion that led right back to the beginning about whether or not blacks and whites could get along in this world. Which led to a discussion of the differences between Malcolm X and Martin Luther King, Jr., Booker T. Washington and W. E. B. Du Bois.

Major Lee asked, Do we need a leader? He questioned the entire idea of people speaking with one voice. He asked, What brings people together? War, he said, is a justification for people to be people. The

Olympics. Earthquakes. "These things make people unite." Becoming even more pensive, he asked: "But why doesn't it last?"

One of the two black women present, who had not said very much that evening, quickly answered, "Temporary knowing."

Legend has it that, during the turn of the century, the head of the Ku Klux Klan in Grand Forks was a black minister. The reason, I am told, is that the number of African Americans was so small that they were not considered a threat. The real threats? Jews and Native Americans. Records exist, I am told, verifying the fact. But they are locked away in archives at the university, and only "certain people" have access. I really didn't know if I wanted to see them.

A 1990 census showed that 638,800 people lived in North Dakota. Of that number 605,142 were white (94.5 percent); 25,917 were Native American (4.0 percent); 4,665 were Hispanic (0.7 percent); 3,462 were of Asian descent (0.5 percent); and 3,524 were African American (0.5 percent). Of that number probably 3,000 were attached to the military bases in Grand Forks and Minot or with the university. Many would suggest the reason is obvious—North Dakota is a hard place to live—for anyone. Indeed, of the 600,000 who did make it their home, the strain of that existence is told by the high rate of alcoholism and other troubles. Yet, North Dakota's history yields tantalizing—sometimes seemingly anomalous tidbits.

Since the early nineteenth century, black traders and trappers were known to come and go. (The Bonga family had been well known here.) Relations between blacks and Native Americans were mostly friendly in those days, and a great number of the scouts and translators for whites traveling through the area were black.

Before and after North Dakota became a state in 1889, reports arose that African Americans were trying to gather the numbers to create communities on the homesteads there. The Reverend W. S. Brooks of St. Peter's AME Church of Minneapolis was quoted in *Plains Folk* as saying in 1901: "I have long held the opinion that a colored colony in the northwest would stand more chances of success than a similar undertaking anywhere else in the world. There is good land, good will on the part of the inhabitants, and all that is required is hard work to bring good crops and good times." Certainly he was referring to North Dakota.

A group of seventeen African Americans acquired several thousand acres—160 per man—in 1884, near the Mouse River. They only remained three years. In McKenzie County, in Moline Township, in Larimore, near Grand Forks, attempts were made, in the early part of this century, to establish group homesteads; most of them failed. But individual claims tended to take better root. In 1910 as many as forty-one were said to exist. Among them were men like John Bryant, who farmed in Alleghany for over thirty years; and in Sheyenne, George Pincott farmed and lived for forty-two years; and Blakey Durant, known as "Old Shady" (said to have been a "good friend" of General William Tecumseh Sherman—he had been his cook), who farmed in Inkster until his death in 1894, and was given a full military funeral.

Perhaps the most fascinating was William T. Montgomery. A former slave who joined the Northern navy during the Civil War, he served in the Red River Expedition. Later he would be county treasurer of Warren County, Mississippi (his brother, Isaiah, was a member of the state constitutional convention), and a successful cotton grower. He came back to North Dakota in 1885 where, twenty-some miles south of Fargo, he established a farm of over a thousand acres, with its own grain elevator near the railroad. He went into business partnerships with local merchants, and the town that grew around his operation was known for a time as Montgomery. He eventually sold the farm and moved to Canada and later back to Mississippi, but the town remains, now called Lithia.

From 1900 to the late 1920s, North Dakota flourished, the railroads making more and more commerce possible, and its population grew. Bismarck, Minot, Grand Forks and Fargo actually had well-known "black sections." Farm hands were needed, and for at least the summer, there was a large influx of black folk to work in the increasingly productive fields. It is reported that "Negro baseball" was extraordinarily popular in North Dakota, and in 1935 Bismarck's team won the National Semiprofessional Baseball Tournament in Wichita, Kansas. On the team were Quincy Troupe, Double Duty Radcliff, Hilton Smith, Chet Brewer and Leroy "Satchel" Paige—he had been hired as a pitcher for the 1935–36 season, and it is said he was famous all over the state.

The Great Depression, along with the dust bowl, made North Dakota almost a ghost state, as people abandoned homes and farms and towns. Only around 200 black people were recorded as living there in 1940. With the introduction of machinery, "miscegenation" laws, and the imposition of segregation (some speculate as a reaction to the many blacks who came into the state in the 1920s) by the advent of World War II, black neighborhoods had vanished completely. But though African Americans themselves had vanished, the hostile feelings had not.

. . .

As I mentioned earlier, one of my spiritual guides during this journey was John A. Williams's 1964 *This Is My Country Too.* Of Grand Forks he wrote:

> It was in 1960 that I had heard some ugly stories about Grand Forks, the kind of stories that were so commonplace in America during World War II that after a while they stopped being news at all . . . The town itself was small, misshapen, and gray; it sat upon the plain apologetically. Most of the buildings and homes appeared to be made of wood. I checked into one of those motels that still pay tribute to the old West. There was a corral, hitching posts, and of course the bunkhouse.

Later Williams encounters some black airmen who elaborate their situation:

> The second airman flushed livid. He was dark, and now his skin took on an ugly purple color. He began ticking off on his fingers: "We get the lousiest houses in town. We can only be served in two or three restaurants. Our officers, mostly from the South, don't back us up: they don't even care . . . Nearly all of [black officers] are on the crews and they stick to themselves as if it couldn't touch them. Once in a while some cracker gets drunk and calls them 'niggers' in the officer's club; everybody laughs for a week."
>
> My guide spoke now: "We get the stiffest sentences, bar none, for minor infractions. And don't let something happen with the cops in town. They'd forget all about us out here. The white guys really get upset when we have dances and some of the colored guys bring white girls from Winnipeg. We've had one or two rumbles already. They hush those up right quick. There are no colored women here, except the wives and daughters of the personnel. The single guys go all the way to Winnipeg when they have time off rather than hang around this dog-ass, Jim Crow town."

Williams writes that he was himself fearful for the men; he noticed how profoundly angry they were at their situation, and remembered a time he himself defied an order in Guam and was court-martialed and put in a hellish marine brig for five days. He "felt fatherly," he said, and wanted to see no ill come to these boys. He asked if they had gotten in touch with their congressman. They had written to Adam Clayton Powell, Jr., but the military had told the representative that nothing was the way the men described it. The men were angry. Williams called an editor at *Jet* on their behalf, to get the news out, uncertain exactly what he should do, or could do. Williams went to one of the men's homes for chitlins, and said "He lived in a ramshackle little building; the ceilings and walls were done in cheap paint over buckling walls. The place came furnished, but the furniture must have been carted from England at the height of the Victorian period; there was hardly room to pass between the chair and couch in the living room."

The man told Williams he paid eighty-five dollars a month and it had taken him seven months to find this place. Later, he writes,

> my guide took me around the town, pointing out places whose windows ordinarily carried signs that read: *Indians and Colored not allowed.* But it was dark; the signs were small, and I didn't see them. Only the places where I was told they were. As we walked, we came upon a pinch-faced woman pushing a baby in a stroller. She slowed, as if demanding that we move off the sidewalk. When we didn't, she drew up her skinny frame and came straight ahead, looking neither right nor left. The stroller struck my ankle as she passed. I thought, you bitch!

Most of my notions of a military base came from growing up in North Carolina—home of the army's Fort Bragg, the largest military installation in the United States, if not the world; and Camp Le Jeune, a little over twenty miles from my home, the navy's primary marine base. So like T. Scott Pegues, my feelings about military bases were somewhat creepy. Always thinking that in the event of a war, a nuclear strike might focus terribly close to home. Of course, those North Carolina bases were important, but Strategic Air Command was another story altogether.

Major Bill Lee took me on a tour of the Grand Forks air force base. The buildings were of the most unremarkable design a human being could conceive, low, blocky, clean—lawns well manicured, and plenty of them—the houses nondescript and multiple, down straight streets in a grid, very like a low-end suburb. Everything could see you and you could see everything. (A friend pointed out to me, some months later, that this was exactly where the idea of the modern suburb was hatched: by the men who fought in World War II, who wanted no more chaos, nothing else hidden or strange; everything innocuous and bland and unthreatening—a statement on how powerful an experience it must have been to see that war up close and more than personal. An idea that makes me look upon the suburbs now with more melancholy than scorn.) Yet wherever the major took me that day—surprisingly few jets roaring overhead—I could not forget that not too far way, under the earth, lay the seeds of man's self-destruction. Gigantic and phallic and beyond lethal.

To my mind, Major Bill Lee was two people. One man was the model of the old school Christian gentleman, courtly, gracious, polite, not one whiff of sin on him (if it existed it was well hidden, deeply and well camouflaged); indeed, he was very vocal about his being a practicing, born-again Christian, who invited me to come to church. The other man was the archetypical, postmodern buppie, by way of the Air Force Academy, frightfully efficient, orderly, *precise,* punctual, logical—almost inhuman in his uprightness, his verve, his neat crispness. So in Major Lee's presence I was caught somewhere between charm and intimidation. On the air base, intimidation won out.

The major obliged me with an interview during my visit, and we sat down in a vacant classroom and commenced to talk. I timidly shared my questions about the military—or perhaps boldly, considering who I was speaking to and where I was. And I asked what he thought of being in North Dakota.

"You got two perspectives," he said. "As a major, I plan to do a colonel in the air force or make general. And my thing is why not have that, being the best you can be. That's really the thing. And I look around this base, and a colonel, which is a really high rank, next before general, and I say well, we need more role models and I think that I'm one of the people that's going to be up there. Like a modern-day Tuskegee Airman. That's how I view myself. I really do.

"A lot of people that came here might never have access to those high ranks. Commensurate with that, I think it's very good to be a role model for the blacks as well as be a good officer. That is why I'm here. This is dedication to duty, saluting smartly, doing the do, and really leaving an impact on the community. Everybody will want to leave their mark and their stamp. Not from a selfish reason. Up here, I consider it a more culturally desolate area than a lot of blacks are used to. Me being from the southern tradition, I tell you, it's too cold for me—thirty-four below, six below—it's too much. I came here when I was thirty-two years old, and I'm thirty-seven now. It's just like being a cultural, sociological hostage. A fifty-to-one man-to-woman ratio. Really for the black professional, I consider these prime-time years. For me personally, I never thought in my wildest dreams I'd be in North Dakota during this period of my life."

The major told me the upside to this assignment—among the many he felt were there—was the opportunity "to learn what makes people tick." He was studying North Dakota from its Scandinavian influences to its Native American culture, trying different foods, speaking to people. "The Native Americans are absolutely forgotten. Terrible plight. One of the things I say is I'm here to learn why that is. I think that blacks should be paying more attention to that. Blacks should be aware of federally sanctioned pockets of poverty and dereliction. They call them 'reservations,' and they have a little bit of political autonomy. But what does that mean? That means the federal government has no responsibility, even the state government, to address some of the issues, like food, medical care, some of the basic protections that American citizens should have. I think that a very strong coalition would be successful in our civil rights struggle." These ideas and perspectives, he told me, were a great opportunity for learning. Also, because of the low numbers of African Americans in North Dakota, he felt this was "nonthreatened white America—for lack of a better term." He wanted to see how far he could go.

"Whereas if I was in Alabama, if I was a fast-moving executive, working for IBM, at a commensurate level, which is middle trying to go up the executive ladder, well then I might find more institutional barriers, but here, in a nonthreatened environment, the novelty of seeing me—well they might let their guard down, for lack of a better word, and talk about things. I found this happening especially with a lot of Native Americans. People get comfortable around me, and they talk as though, hey, I'm one of you or them. Kind of like the key to the boardroom."

Being an active role model for young airmen made him feel blessed, he told me: "I've been in about fourteen years, and I've been fortunate in working on the ICBM which is the strategic system."

"The missile business," I said.

"The missile business." He laughed. "And I look at that in an executive fashion. In the missile business—the Soviet Union and the Red Scare and Communists and the Evil Empire, and let's build our bombers and build our missiles—America got a lot of mileage out of that, and the Department of Defense, Martin-Marietta, McDonnell-Douglas, B2 bombers, all these folks. They get a lot of the same benefit out of that. I am blessed. I had a chance to go to the Air Force Academy. To find out what they teach the people they want to be the future senior officers and generals. I've been fortunate to be in the security system, to work with one of the strategic triads—that is, bombers, tankers and missiles.

"That allowed me to go into a lot of the super-secret things, allowed me access to like the Western White House to learn how the political meshes in with the institutional, how corporate America, all that meshes in."

I wondered how William Lee got from Anniston, Alabama, to Major William Lee, stationed in Grand Forks, North Dakota.

"It's thirty-seven years," he said. "But actually it's relatively simple. My father worked in civil engineering for the army. He was born in Alabama, and did a lot of things—helped build some oil wells, and things like that. Very good positive role model for a man. Very positive, very active. Played sports and stuff with the kids, and I had two or three brothers and sisters around. Went to church, and Sunday afternoon we went and watched him play baseball. Here's a man that stood up for black rights then. Eventually, what it led to was he was killed. Killed as a result of some Klansmen not liking him being out of his place."

The family had been on a trip down south. "He was coming back, and we had about ten miles or eight miles to go to our house, and we were running low on gas. There was a station right there, but there was no gas for him. They basically served whites only. Father came up there; they normally had self-service. My father went out there, and they said, 'We don't serve niggers.' Or something to that effect. They were going to get real out of hand. Father, he had his gun, and before the other guy pulled his gun out, Father pulled his gun on the guy. Told him to give him two or three dollars of gas. After that, he gave the guy the money, and he pulled off. He didn't want to mess with him. That's all he wanted, was some gas. Went on about his business.

"Now this was a 'nigger' that was too uppity. Stood out and spoke out, and just wasn't pigeonholed. Who didn't stay in his place.

"So they set him up, it was a fact. We used to live in a rural area. A guy needed some help on the side of the road. He stopped. Helped the guy. They jumped him, they stabbed him, and left him there to bleed to death. He was able to gain enough strength to drive in his car about two- or three-odd miles down the road. Pulled into the first place he could, which was a juke joint. Just a little house that was kind of like a clubhouse. He asked somebody to take him to the hospital. Just take him to the hospital. He said he'd been stabbed and was bleeding.

"The people there were terrified. Absolutely terrified to do anything.

These were all black folks. And they watched him as he was dying in the middle of the floor in a pool of blood. Because they were actually terrified.

"I'm six years old. Christmas, 1960. About two weeks before Christmas."

I sat listening to the major's story, and the profundity of his personal tragedy—to imagine being a six-year-old boy and having to grow up with this story. I realized he had to be an extraordinarily complex man. One of the many results of that childhood trauma—("What did that do? What did that do?" he asked himself quietly, but purposefully)—was to "solidify" his view of his own education and his own dedication. "It gave me a very positive image as far as what a black man should be. And what they should stand up for in the community. Knowing that he was pretty much self-taught, and knowing that he was very industrious, knowing that he was an engineer, and worked on all these nice and wonderful things—it gave me a really good, wholesome and positive role model figure."

He said it would be years before he came to understand exactly what the "ku kux kan" was. At one point, as a boy, he said, Klansmen actually shot into the Mount Olive Baptist Church in Anniston, due to work the NAACP and the SCLC had been doing. His mother told him to get down, but the young Bill Lee wanted to look. "I wanted to stand up and see what was happening. I was just a kid."

He remembered when he was ten or eleven, at a place called B&B Grocery, some Klansman came down and burned a cross, and some black teenagers in the neighborhood "beat him almost to death. Doggone near unconsciousness. Took him, put him in his car, took the burning cross, threw it in the car, and said, 'Get out of here.' Bold move. Never had any problems from them after that. No retaliation, nothing."

The major's mother had worked for a city attorney when he was growing up. "She worked for slave wages. She did maid work for two or three others." For twelve dollars a week. Later, he would see how she was being exploited. "I said, 'No, that's just two or three hours' worth of work!' But she said, 'No, no, no.'" That was another thing, Bill Lee told me, that pushed him to excel. The city attorney offered to pay for his college education. "But I wanted absolutely, positively nothing to do with that. I knew that I could do anything. And I really believe that. And this is from a positive father model and from the community."

He chose instead the military. "The Air Force Academy and the military. That way I could absolutely economically divorce myself and be unobligated to him. Have my own, based on my own merit, and be something in a real positive vein. I had the older brothers that were in the military, but they were enlisted. I wanted to be an officer. And this was the one opportunity. And the thing that really made me want to go in the military—and actually to the Air Force Academy in particular—was a guidance counselor. She looked at me, and I was an A student. My guidance counselor said, 'Well, Bill, you're an all right boy. You got some real good grades and stuff. But I don't know. I think the best you can do is to try for vo-tech. You ought to try for vo-tech. And I think you'd do real good in that.' I wanted to go to Auburn, I wanted to go to Alabama. As a matter of fact, my grades, my SAT scores and stuff were high enough to get into Georgia Institute of Technology on an academic scholarship.

"I said to myself, 'How can she?' And here I was, I had twelve letters, okay—*had twelve letters.* Basically three or four letters every year since the ninth grade. All-state, all-district, everything. On the student council. The corps commander of air force ROTC detachment, junior ROTC. In the 'A Club' and everything else, plus an A student. And this woman says, 'Well, I don't know. I don't know if you're college material. You probably can go to a good vo-tech and do real good in vo-tech.' And I said, 'Hey. I can't believe it.' But fortunately, I had a teacher who was my math instructor, who said, 'Hey, yeah, go for it.' I was in junior ROTC. He said, 'The Air Force Academy is a good thing for that.'

"But those experiences made me determined to go into the Air Force Academy because it was competitive and it was strictly on merit. And when I graduated, I went onto the missile operation track and did very well. I'd say ever since then."

Indeed, Major William Lee was a man full of spunk and determination. I pointed out how the air force, to some, was seen as the elite of the armed forces. Did he foresee a glass ceiling?

That was one of the things that spurred him on, he told me. The jets, the technology, the Space Program, "all this good stuff," excited him tremendously. "I said, 'If somebody—if man—can do it, I can do it.' You can do everything. It's not egotistical. But it's a challenge there, because you're young, gifted and black. Then you can do it, if you have access to it. And doggone it, you're going to die trying. If not, you won't be denied it because you didn't try."

He pointed out that he had surrounded himself with young black men and women in his younger years who thought in the same way. Men and women who were achievers and overachievers. Now doctors and lawyers and such. "I guess they went to the Hill and I went to kill." He gave a guffaw. "We always joke about this. And they say, 'You made general yet?'

And I say, 'No, no, no, no. Not yet. But soon . . .' We're one little, real close-knit bunch."

Major Bill Lee emphasized the importance of pointing out the great many opportunities available to people. "I work a lot with the youth. Black youth." He felt worried about the teenagers he was encountering. Especially in North Dakota. "They have lost the sense of awareness."

As I was leaving, I asked the major what it was like, personally, to be in North Dakota. One of two or three black officers present, at the time. "Well, being a major, I fly," he said with a proud smile.

"Of course," I said. "I forgot who I was talking to."

"I call it thawing out. Once a quarter. I just go to Florida or maybe Chicago or Atlanta or to Dallas. I see different parts of the country."

"So of course you don't feel isolated," I said. "A very nice, built-in safety valve."

He took me by both the Officers' Club and the Noncommissioned Officers' Club to illustrate the environment in which he dwelled. The OC was all white, except for the two of us; in the NCO I saw mostly black and Hispanic faces. Earlier someone had told me that there were two types of black soldier who came to a place like North Dakota: the ones who got involved and out into the local environment and the ones who made the barracks their home. The major agreed. He said there were the couch potatoes, and there were the dynamic ones who went to Winnipeg on their off-duty time. He tried to explain that to the black enlisted men he encountered who felt profoundly isolated. Indeed, he saw his role as a "personal commitment. To keep close contact with a lot of the younger folk who are here." He thought everyone "should have the opportunity to come in the military for four years. They should come in at seventeen until they're twenty-one, and they're out. And they can still do whatever they want. A good, clean reference."

Understandably the men came to the major for advice; and understandably, Bill Lee gave it to them. "I've found that is my role, I'm very much an advocate."

I left the air force base that evening feeling uncharacteristically charitable, and, momentarily, good about the United States. Clearly, here was a man who had used the military, perhaps more than it had used him. I thought about the many definitions of leadership I had encountered on the road so far, from socialites, to artists, to politicians, to businessmen, to labor and to the military, which is itself built on the idea of hierarchy and chain of command. Each of these worlds had a very different meaning for the word "leadership," yet each contained elements of the other: Leadership needed integrity, authority, clarity of thought, forward-looking vision, competence. But unlike the military, African America could not be uniformly fitted into rows of barracks and orderly formations and lined up in hierarchical avenues. Unfortunately, unlike the men who came back from World War II, for the rest of us, living within chaos, formed by chaos, we had individually to eke out a clean, well-lighted place in which to dwell. We could not count on agreement or uniformity. Perhaps therein lay both the answer and salvation. Perhaps individualism would ultimately—after people (re)discovered the Reverend John Donne's sermonic admonition: "No man is an island"—lead people to see the necessity of coming together, if not under some common ideology, or ruler, under some common good, some common order, some common sense, larger than any declaration or constitution: a human order.

Or perhaps, the second law of thermodynamics was correct: We are doomed to fall apart. But we often make the mistake of assuming entropy applies to humankind: the laws of thermodynamics apply to closed systems, systems that get no outside energy. Is our system closed?

Audrey Henderson-Nocho was a tall, statuesque woman, dramatic even when she lifted her finger or batted an eyelash. I could not help but think it genetic: that she was simply the descendant of some African throne. Yes, regal was the word for Audrey Henderson-Nocho. Regal, masterful, formidable. One certainly did not want to be on the wrong side of an argument with this woman.

At thirty-two, her life sounded like a tale Scheherazade told to save her life. She had been born in Sacramento, California. "My father was in the air force. When my father's tour of duty was done in the Philippines, the next base assignment was Grand Forks. And when we got here, the Grand Forks base had just been completed. It was several years after we got here that my mother and father split up. And my father left. Don't know where he went initially, I think over the years we found out that he wound up in California, and my mom stayed here in North Dakota."

When I asked if Audrey and her siblings ever quizzed her mother on why she remained in North Dakota, Audrey said, "We sure did. We sure did. We always complained." But it seemed because of all the violence in the South at the time—this was the turbulent '60s—her mother figured North Dakota, for a single parent with five children, might offer them a better environment. Audrey told me her mother worked hard, "from sunup to sundown. She worked at whatever. I remember her ironing clothes. She was a cashier. She was a custodial person. She was a waitress at the air base." Often simultaneously. "My mother never took a handout. She felt it was in her best interest, and in the best interests of her kids. She was going to provide for them by any means necessary." Audrey also remembered her mother listening to and watching on television all sorts of opera and classical music shows, which the kids hated. Later the children discovered that she had begun training to be an opera singer in her early years.

"She always would tell us, 'Go after your dream, because sometimes things happen where you have to put off your dream for a while.' I believe the reason hers was put off was that she had the five kids. At that point probably she thought there was no possibility of ever trying to make that dream come true. What she did was funnel her dream through her kids' eyes. My mom always kept saying, 'Don't ever do a half-assed job. If you're going to do it, do it right the first time.' "

At present Audrey's mother worked for the federal government, out at the air force base. ("She doesn't look like my mom. She looks like my sister.")

In the early years, the family had lived in a trailer park in Merado, about ten miles west of Grand Forks. She said, "There was nothing there except the trailer court, a gas station, a Dairy Queen, a car wash. And in the town, a school, Johnny's Bar, a post office, a couple of churches, some houses, a grain elevator, a potato warehouse. That was 'bout it."

Growing up in North Dakota was, of course, cold. "I hated it because we had to walk to school. You hear about Abe Lincoln having to walk six miles to school? Well, we walked half that distance, in colder weather. There was no bus. We knew about living in the North. We knew that you had to take adequate precautions. You didn't go out ill-prepared. We bundled up. And we knew when it got cold, you could only go outside and play for a little bit and come back in, because it only takes a second for the wind to burn your skin. It gets cold. We heard those horror stories about people having to have their hands and legs and whatnot amputated, because of the cold. We have our last storm around the middle of March. But I remember one time, there was still snow on the ground in June. Once spring is upon us, then summer comes, and we've got about like three weeks of nice weather, until it rains. When it rains, two days after that, the mosquitoes are out. Look out. Mosquitoes don't discriminate."

In grade school, there were a fair number of blacks since they were close to the base. But her brothers and sisters were the only black children in their high school, in Larrimore, a little closer to Grand Forks. I asked if, outside of school, they had any black friends.

"There weren't any."

Audrey told me there were a few transient black families with children, but it had been clear from the outset that they would not be in North Dakota for long. Otherwise she did develop a few friends among certain white farm kids. She fondly remembered one girl: "Her name was Laurie, and we played basketball on the high school team, and she lived three miles outside of town, and she had some pigs, I remember. She says, 'Guess what. Guess what. My daddy's giving me something to do.' 'What's that?' She says, 'He's got me some pigs. Got to come out and see the pigs.' So I got on my bike and I rode out to her house one day and I saw these little pigs. And when I saw these little pigs, I remembered my sixth grade teacher reading us *Charlotte's Web.* I named all her little pigs. I would visit them throughout the summer. Till one day I went back out there, the pigs were gone. She wasn't there that day, but her father was home and her mom was there. And I asked, 'Where are the pigs at?' They go, 'To the market.' And I go, 'Oh, okay. So they'll be coming back.' I didn't know. I didn't know. When Laurie came home, I go, 'Where are the pigs at?' She says, 'They're to the market.' I go, 'What market?' And I got mad then. I didn't talk to her for a long time. I was mad. I go, 'How could you have me come out, get attached to these pigs, and then take them and sell them to the butcher?' She said, 'I had a hard time too. My father told me never to get attached. You can't get attached to them.' And I guess I was looking at those pigs as my friends. Growing up you only had so many pigs, and like my friends, they were always coming and they were always going. 'Well, I guess I can't rely on pigs anymore.' So pigs were gone."

I asked Audrey about dating as she was growing up. "I had my first date, my first kiss, when I was sixteen." But she had other things on her mind. "I wasn't going to buy into that goody girl Cinderella syndrome when I graduated from high school, get married and all I wanted was a house with a picket fence and a washer and dryer and a couple kids and a dog. No. But at that point"—near the end of high school—"I was disposing of my friends in rapid numbers. If you couldn't accept me for me and you let your parents or your grandparents dictate your life, I don't need you as a friend."

I asked her how she felt about interracial couples, and she emphatically told me it was an individual choice, depending on people's personal values.

"I grew up in North Dakota. There weren't that many black men. Period. I knew one. I wasn't getting married to him, and I also knew that there was a whole world out there. Why should I discriminate? Because somebody told me blacks and whites couldn't go out? Bullshit. It wasn't etched in stone. All right? As long as I wanted to, I was going to. My mom tried telling me, 'You should be thinking about this. You should be thinking about this.' And I took all those things into consideration. It turned out well. Turned out well. My other friends now, 'How'd you ever go out with that white person? How'd you ever go out with that person?' And they ended up being the ones who were prejudiced."

Audrey Henderson-Nocho was the first black person to graduate from her high school.

"So I was told—January of my senior year—there had been no blacks that graduated. 'You will be the first.' So as I went up, my principal says, 'Audrey Henderson. Records indicate that she is the first black to graduate from Larrimore High School, May 22nd, 1977.' And everybody stood up and clapped and clapped and clapped and clapped and clapped. My mom was pissed. She just had this evil look on her face. I was disappointed because my mom wasn't happy. She had this frown on her face and I guess she was saying, 'Well, why did they have to do that?' I go, 'Mom, it's a first.' 'But they didn't have to do it that way.' I think my mom is real private. So I said, 'Well, that's your prerogative, mom, but I asked them.' I looked back that day, in retrospect, on the four years, and the prior eight from grade school, and saw where my life had gone to, and where it was going to, and said, 'Well, after this, I'm on to the next phase.' So when they asked high school seniors, 'What do you want to do when you grow up?' I set some long-term goals. Have some kids. Go to truck driving school and get a license, and travel throughout the United States. That was my goal for life. By the time I was twenty-one I had completed my goal."

"You were a truck driver?" I asked.

"Twelve, fourteen, to fifteen-C, yeah."

"At eighteen?"

"I couldn't drive interstate," she told me. "I didn't go to truck driving school until I was twenty-one. So I went to college fall semester after I graduated from high school. I went to college from 1977 to 1980. I dropped out of college in 1980. Got married the fall of '80. Had my child the fall of '80. When my child turned one, the next year, I applied for truck driving school and went to truck driving school. Got my license, drove trucks.

"I was going to carry an Uzi. I always had it in my mind. My husband said you can't carry an Uzi. I was fearful of the South. I just didn't want any problems to happen. I go, 'Well, if it's an Uzi, I figure I can get off many shots before they can get off one or two, and I got them down.' "

Audrey told me her husband had nightmares when she was on the road. "It's like a woman whose husband is a police officer. It's this never-ending thing that she goes through. This torment and terror that she puts herself through every day, that it's the last day I'm going to see him. Did I tell him I loved him? I think he sort of felt the same way too. Is this the last time I'm going to see her? What happens if a semi jackknifes in the road? What happens if somebody tries to highjack her? And I just said, 'Hell, it's not worth this shit.' So I stopped."

Thereafter Audrey Henderson-Nocho got a civil service job at the base. She had another child and her husband—who was in the air force—got orders to go to Germany for three years. She remained in North Dakota with their children. "I should have gone back to college. But I stayed home. When he came back, he had gotten out of the air force." The long separation had taken its toll on the marriage. Eventually they were separated. But in the meantime, Audrey's fourth child, Allegra, was born, "and I found out that she had some major medical problems. A heart problem."

While battling for her daughter's life, Audrey made a fateful decision. "I had been sitting home, doing nothing except raising kids. And I said, 'This is the last time I'm ever going to do this for anybody.' So I went back to school. Spring semester." The struggle, the battle, the in and out of hospitals, the school work, weighed heavily. "I was going to drop out. But I did well." The second week of November 1986, her daughter died.

"I never recuperated that semester. My grades took a dive. I never recouped. Never recouped. Those grades on my transcript grew to haunt me. And to make a long story short, there were so many obstacles that I had to get over. I had less than a month to grieve before going back into spring semester. I had three children at home that were dependent upon me. I was not about to put myself in a cycle where I was going to be dependent upon the state my whole life. I knew I was capable. I knew I was intelligent. I knew I had the drive to go out and do something. Grieving, and couldn't grieve.

"It meant lots of sacrifices. I fought like hell. I experienced almost every major catastrophe a person can go through, and I did it as a single person. I said, 'Well, I can't sit here and mourn all my life. I need to gather the pieces up and move on.' "

At the time I spoke with Audrey, she was struggling not just for one degree, but two: one in recreation and one in communications.

I asked Audrey, "Do you worry about your girls growing up here?"

"You always try to do better for your kids," she said. "And that doesn't mean always that I got to go live with black people to do better. I do what I want to do. If I choose to pick up and move, I do it for economic reasons. There are things that I want to do for myself. I want to go beyond what my wildest expectations are, and to exceed those. Beyond that, I want to provide exposure and opportunity for my three kids. I don't want any obstacles placed in front of my kids. I'm sure there's going to be some obstacles, but I'm going to try to provide as much as I can."

Audrey said her children had friends of all hues and backgrounds there in Grand Forks, and this was a very good thing. She wanted her kids to appreciate commonalities and differences, and North Dakota was as good a place as any to learn. Nonetheless, she figured in due time she'd be moving elsewhere: "My generation has got to be mobile. In order for me to do the things that I want to do, I have to be mobile. Wherever there are opportunities. This state doesn't economically have enough to whet my palate the rest of my life. It has nice summers. And it has nice springs and falls. There is a cause here that I could take up. I have a number of Native American friends—I could work on Native American relations. That could be a reward in itself."

In the end, however, Audrey Henderson-Nocho felt her fortune lay far beyond North Dakota. She mentioned Russia, she mentioned Alaska. "Wherever." But no, she fully expected to hitch her, and her children's, wagon to a star, and sail to where/whatever the adventure that was her life would take her. I suspected the adventure would be quite a tale to tell.

Before I left North Dakota, Audrey was kind enough to take me to a powwow, to a performance of the American Indian Ballet Company.

She had told me earlier that she had a number of Native American friends, and took me to the Indian Center on the campus of UND and introduced me around. "I get along well with both," she told me. She made trips to the nearby reservations.

"There's uncertainty with any group," she said, referring to interaction between blacks and Native Americans. "Nobody knows who you are, and what you do, until someone out of that group says, 'I know her. She's okay.' I don't want to call that group-think. That's in place. You got to tread water slowly. You don't just jump in and drown."

I noted how in my reading, I had seen historically a strong connection between blacks and Indians, and was surprised to see that it had vanished. Why did she think it had?

"With each generation there's lost information. So the whole cycle has to start back over again, and the education. I'm going to keep the friends I have and try to increase them. Whether they're white, black, whatever. I surely don't discriminate."

A lot of myth surrounded Native Americans, Audrey told me, and people had just bought into that myth. Some people she knew were actually afraid, and had *Dances with Wolves* mentalities. "Ignorance. I think the Indians have always opened the door for them. But nobody will come. No one's ever asked. They just assume."

That night's ballet company performance was something awesome and beautiful to behold. At once athletic, and as graceful, as skilled, as professional, as mysteriously gorgeous as Alvin Ailey or Martha Graham; yet also rich with colors and costumes and sounds—compelling sounds of drums and high-pitched vocals, the stomping of feet. There was the traditional dance, the grass dance, the fancy dance, the sneak-up, the trick song, the fancy shawl dance, the jingle dress dance—of Ojibwa and Crow and Seminole and Cherokee and Apache and Lakota and Navaho and Hopi. I fell instantly in love with a music and a style I had never really seen before, and I regretted that so few Americans had witnessed it. So much their loss.

That night, the auditorium was full, and Audrey reckoned that folk had come from all over the state. I don't know if I saw one white face that night—if I did they were relatively few. The only two black faces I saw belonged to us. And again, I felt a twinge of regret and sadness. I had come from a New York, and an East Coast, awash in talk of multiculturalism, or diversity; had come from young folk so optimistic and idealistic for a future of sharing and dynamic intermingling ideas of cultures. Yet, here, in the true center of the continent, I came to see how very, very far my nation was from that bright new vision; I saw, in a space full of true Americans, how much work lay ahead.

. . .

I had been told of a phenomenon in North Dakota called "whiteout." Since the plains are the plains because there is nothing on them, nothing stands in the way of winds sweeping straight down from the Arctic Circle. Audrey in particular was adamant that I be careful, that I take supplies. There is no warning, she told me, and she was quite serious: One minute clear sky, the next minute you can't see a foot in front of your face. I wanted to laugh; it sounded too primal, but again, no, she said, you don't play with this stuff, and she listed all the things I should have with me, like flashlight, food, proper clothing for subzero weather. Needless to say, I headed west out of Grand Forks with a little trepidation. Almost midway between Grand Forks, which is on the Minnesota border, and Minot in the west is a marker pinpointing the "exact" geographic middle of the continent of North America. I got out and stood there, and thought: From the Arctic Ocean to the Gulf of Mexico, from Maine's coast to Oregon's shore, from the deserts of California to the barrens of Labrador, and the tundra of Alaska to the swamps of Florida, I was smack-dab in the extraordinary center of it all. I was only beginning to come to a realization of how much space America takes up.

The North Dakota Badlands I found beguiling, and recognized within myself a love of denuded, ghostly, ranging landscapes. These areas of the Dakotas are often compared to the moon. I disagree; I could see, in the rare scrub, life there, and the color is not dead-white but an ochre that contains browns and blacks, and the shapes are wonderful, almost humanly round, great piles of inexplicable raw rocks and mounds.

I made it to Miles City, Montana, by nightfall, and felt thankful. (Coincidence would have it that one of my favorite short stories, by Alice Munro, is entitled "Miles City" and has a pivotal moment in a public pool in that town.) The plains were behind me, for Miles City is where the "foothills" of the Rockies begin and I thought: No hill is this tall. Now I was in that curious thing called Mountain time, which to this day I don't fully comprehend.

The next day, bright and early I continued on, and it was bright. Perhaps it is a cliche to say it, but I finally understood why Montana is called Big Sky Country. There is no ceiling there; coming down off the top of a low mountain, you see until you can see no more; mountains scream in the distance and their voices reach you as faint whispers; so deep, so wide is the sky that you can imagine an entire world just there, hovering above you, populated by this earth's billions. To live in such space must do something to the soul, must stretch it and expand it. I know how romantic a notion it is, but to see it is to think it possible.

Midday arrived and, just as the weather forecaster had predicted, so did a storm. However, he had not told me it would be a blizzard. I thought, My first time in this part of the world and two blizzards in less than a month. I crossed the continental divide, higher than I ever imagined, and I could not see it. All I could see were jackknifed eighteen-wheeler rigs in the median divider, or completely stopped, coming round the mountain, waiting, or slowed to a mere creep; and the snow kept falling, and I listened to Tom Waits ("Independent as a hog on ice"), and laughed, thinking back on my drive in the mountains of New Hampshire. Thinking, I guess I ain't seen nothing yet.

Eleven

# FIGHT NO MORE FOREVER

## Or, The Thirteenth State

*Coeur d'Alene, Idaho*

> The name "Coeur d'Alene" was first given to a chief of the tribe who was known throughout life by that name. It was first applied to this particular tribe by French Canadians, in the employ of the Hudson Bay Company. While belonging to the family of Salish Indians, the correct tribal name is Schiguimosh, which means, in the Indian tongue, "an awl's heart."
>
> —Orland A. Scott, *Pioneer Days on the Shadowy St. John*

I don't how many people know it, as a matter of course, but Idaho is the thirteenth largest state in the United States, at 82,413 square miles. It puzzled me why Idaho became known as the state famous for the people who had died there: Hemingway died here; Chief Joseph of the Nez Perce fought, and fought no more, and died here. Of course famous people were born here: Lana Turner; Mrs. Walt Disney; Paul Revere of Paul Revere & the Raiders. But as I arrived in Coeur d'Alene, on the other side of the graceful, green Bitter Root Mountains, just east of Spokane, the incomparable glory of northern Idaho did not mitigate the grave images I had preconceived of the state—the very series of events that had led me to choose Coeur d'Alene to visit—reports of the growing number of neo-Nazis and white supremacist groups in the area, particularly the Aryan Nation whose headquarters were a few minutes away from Coeur d'Alene, in Hayden Lake.

. . .

According to a local paper, the *Spokesman Review,* February 3, 1991, the census figures said Idaho towns were shrinking. But Coeur d'Alene was growing, with a population then of 25,563. (Boise, the king of the state, had a population of 125,000.) I wondered why.

"When I retired from the service, I definitely didn't want to stay in L.A. When I first moved there, I liked it, but then after I got on the sheriff's department and saw what life was really like, I said, I don't think I want my kids in all that. I went to Malibu, and then the Marina, which was a lot nicer, but still kind of bad. It wasn't me. I was just a country boy from New Orleans. So I decided I was going to retire up in this area, because I like the area. It took a few years to get over it, the people. The first thing they wanted to know is what I'm doing up here. After I got to know the people, they realized that I was just another person. And it was just kind of like the thing to do. To just proceed."

Walt Washington was now a real estate agent in Coeur d'Alene. He had that manner of quick affability and ease. A handsome man, with gently graying hair, I could easily see him in a sheriff's uniform as well; but he seemed well adapted to his recent transformation into a salesman. At times, I felt as if he were selling Coeur d'Alene—and of course he was, both figuratively and literally.

"Anyway, I bought a place down in Salmon, Idaho, which was where the rafting trip was. That's like central Idaho. I realized that Salmon was too remote; even if I caught a plane up to Idaho, I'd still have to rent a car, and drive a hundred miles because there were just no airports in the area. So I started looking for a place where I could commute back and forth a lot easier. Because of my family and all of that distance—California and New Orleans now. So I found Coeur d'Alene which was the closest to Spokane, thirty-five to forty minutes. I could catch a plane and come up here and do what I had to do, and still get back down there, if I was working. After I retired, I decided I was going to move up to this area. I started checking on a house and how many telephone poles it would take to get the utilities to the house. And I realized that I was talking $25,000 or so just to start building a house. I bought two and a half acres, a nice little house, barn, stable area, $43,000 at the time I moved up here. Right after things went flat. That was at the end of the flat period. And the following year it notched up, and it's been going up ever since. So I caught it just at the right time. I sold the house three years later for $59,000 and then bought another place over by the golf course. Didn't like city life after living out on this acreage. And I rented that out and had this place a little farther out. After I kind of got my feet wet and found that I really liked the area. And things have been working well for me ever since." Often, he said, if another minority—"Jewish, Italian, Oriental, black"—spotted him in his office, they quickly made their way over to him, "a guy with a black face, if there's any problems around here, he's run into them." He laughed.

"When I first moved up here, the Aryan Nation was around. Oh, 300, 350. And due to the things they did with the bombings and other stuff, half of them are in jail and the other half went away. Maybe I know less than a dozen of them."

"Really?"

"So the area has more of a stigma now," he said, "*about* the Aryan Nation than them actually being here and creating havoc. It's not near as serious. In the time I've been here, I found that the people in the area, the white original settlers, disliked them as much as I did. Because of the name it gives them, and there's a lot of people that can't afford things to get too bad. New people didn't want to come to this area, for fear that they might get snatched up. It made the local people negative toward these groups too. I just kept chugging right along. There's hardly a place you could go in Coeur d'Alene where if you asked about Walt Washington, they wouldn't know who I was. And I'm not bragging by saying that. It's an actual fact. There's so few blacks here, it's really easier to tell who's who. It might be something in my personality as well. I'm kind of a friendly person. That's seems to be kind of the way it is."

Walt Washington's ex-wife and children were still back in California. He explained that the desire to come to Idaho was one of a number of things that contributed to his breakup. "I was kind of an aggressive person so far as getting ahead, and doing things. Trying to buy property. I don't know if it was the different cultures or what. I felt I was pulling by myself . . . I feel we're both better off than we were before."

But now he very much enjoyed being in Idaho. "There's a lot of people here that get up in the morning, and they wash up and they sit down, and that's the start of their day. Here I am, I'm out trying to do something. They eat breakfast and then they eat lunch and then they eat dinner, and they cut some wood and they go to bed. Getting a city person and putting them up here, if they're not ready, they're definitely not going to enjoy themselves. There's not a lot of stuff here that you'll find in southern California."

The real estate market was truly booming, he told me. He said 40 percent of the progress made had been achieved in the last two years. Californians, Washingtonians, Oregonians, Arizonians—but particularly Californians—were gobbling up houses and land. "Somebody can come from California, having sold their house for $350,000, and buy a comparable house here for less than $200,000. Put $150,000 in their pockets. Buy a mobile home if they want to. The median prices of homes has gone from $54,000 to $78,000 in just over two years. In about two or three years, there won't be any more."

He told me about the multitude of resorts opening in the area, especially ski resorts, and even for the summer trade. But the ski traffic was truly the big market for the area. "And now there's hardly space between Coeur D'Alene and Washington state—probably in the next five years, that corridor will be just one city. City-like. So it's really coming about. When things were bad in California and the economy was down, things were still giddy here. It's now to the point where you can't hardly buy an existing home. Most people, I'd say probably 70 percent of the people, at least 60 percent of the people that are now buying homes are buying land, because homes are just not available, and a lot of investors are coming into the area and buying up all of these little shacks and remodeling them, and renting them out. There's a zero vacancy factor here. Two-bath homes go for probably about $245,000 to about $500,000, $600,000."

I asked about the black population. Officially he had seen some statistics that said, "There was like nine blacks here, including me." But he figured there had to be at least twenty, just by the people he knew.

"You know, when I first moved here, I expected—being an ex–police officer, I didn't put my gun away. Just don't do that. It took me about two years to just say, well, I'll put it in there. I expected to get some phone calls about, 'get out of town' or some stuff like that. When I first moved to Idaho, I was working in the yard at the first place I bought. I had a Velcro vest on, a police officer's shield. I didn't know what to expect. I had a rifle at the back door, one at the front. And I kept my gun under my pillow. I'm serious." He laughed. "Because when I came from California, Oprah Winfrey had the head of this white supremacist group on her TV show, and they had just done the bombings, and I'm saying, 'Jesus, crazy.' I don't know what to expect from these guys. So I was kind of like prepared. It took me about four months of actually wearing vests and the other stuff, before I just said, 'Well, if they're going to get me, they're going to get me eventually. I'm just going to get killed.' "

"But you remained anyway," I said. "What motivated you to risk your life to live here?"

"I got injured at the sheriff's department," he told me. "I took several rounds in this vest. But my heart had stopped beating, and I felt that my life had ended. Literally, that was the way I felt. So I was really kind of living, I guess, on borrowed time. I had put a deposit on this place, and I'm not one to run. I was born in the South. I don't know what it was that my parents gave me that was instilled in me. If I felt I was right in what I was doing, then go ahead and kill me, because that's what I'm going to do. When they wound up doing the bombings and stuff, I just decided that I was going to go ahead on through this. This was my plan. I figured, if they did kill me, or whatever they might have done, it would have created more problems for them than just to leave me alone. Because the FBI and everybody was on the case to start with, and then if something like this occurred, I thought it would only be worse for them. I don't know if they realized that, but that kind of put my mind to rest, and I just went on about my business."

"I went to visit some of the local bars and such. Just put on my jacket and went down there and had a beer. The first place I went in was this mining place, this saloon. I was in there about twenty minutes, and ordered a beer, and the next thing, another beer comes up. These people were at the table and sent me a beer. So I drank the two beers, and then before I left, I sent them a beer back to show thanks. I was able to relax because I felt I had been in the worst possible circumstances to create some problems. So it gave me a little more encouragement. I wound up going to the resort and then went to a couple of these dance places, and I actually asked somebody to dance, which took some nerve, for me, because I hate rejection." He chuckled remembering the incident. "I didn't get refused, so I said, 'Well, wait a minute now. All of this I've been hearing can't be totally true.' I thought I would have felt some of the negativism by now. And it just got better for me. I married a white woman. Was an Idaho native here, was in the paper and everything. And I still didn't get calls at my house from people saying, 'Get out of town.' I just went about doing my business, and not worrying about the ramifications of being black in this area, because I tell you, it is quite a charmer. I went to a chamber function that was a dinner. And there was 600 people, not counting waitresses and others. In one room. And I was the only black in the room. I only knew about five or six people total in the room. It was overpowering. You felt like you just wanted to crawl in or something or leave because it made you very uncomfortable. I just dealt with it, and I never ran into any problems. Just take the next step. And that's what I've been doing for the last seven years. I feel like I've taken every step I could possibly take. I feel that if my daughter wants to come up here and go to school or something, I wouldn't have any hesitations or reluctancies whatsoever.

"I really believe that the whole fuss of the Aryan Nation was to discourage minorities from coming to this area. And maybe if they were left as strong as they originally were, they may have. But I think the black eye that this area has been given, for years to come, will cause the average black person to say, 'Well, I'm not going to Idaho, because that's where the Aryans are.' And not realizing that there's only a dozen of them left. I did a surveillance job down in Newhall, which is about fifty, sixty miles north of downtown L.A. where the KKK were meeting, and over 1,600 people came to that meeting. Wasn't even in the paper. Three of these guys get together and stand on the corner, and UPI or whoever it is try to make like it's most of the people in this area. What's starting to irritate me is that I've been here long enough to see that this really does not exist like the media says it does. But I guess it sells papers. These guys can get together and say, 'Well, we're going to have a conference,' like this last conference they had in July. That was about twelve people, I think, about twelve additional people, about twenty-four, twenty-five people, total, that came to it. And across the nation, they were showing these eight or nine people walking down these walkways, on the news. Sixteen hundred people could get together in Los Angeles and have a Klan meeting, and it doesn't make the paper."

When I asked Walt Washington if there was anything he missed about his life in California, he surprised me.

"One of the things I really miss is black people. I've just known you less than an hour, and I feel a relationship with you that with these people took me maybe a year and a half to nurture. During the summer, that's when most of the blacks will come through. I can see black people up the street, and they see me walking by and will wave and may not even stop and talk. You may never see them again, but there's that relationship there. And I think that's what I sort of miss. One of the advantages of being one of the few blacks in this area is that the others who are here are outstanding citizens. I've had a guy tell me that his interpretation of a black guy was what he saw on TV. And so if you weren't a pimp or in jail, a Crip or something, you weren't black. That's what they do, that's who they are. We sat down and talked for about twenty minutes, before he came up with this. And he said, 'You know, come to think of it, I've never talked to a black guy.' In his entire life. He's from Idaho. His image of a black guy is the guy he's seen on TV. And the image of the black guy on TV, other than Bill Cosby, is not positive. He was so enlightened that he gave me his card and told me where he lived and to come see him. And I think he really wanted to project me off on some of his friends who had the same kind of ideas."

Mr. Washington said a number of black people lived over in Spokane, Washington. "If you spent four, five, six hours in Spokane, you'd see, maybe two or three blacks. One out of every thirty or forty people." Mr. Washington reckoned that to the minds of most black people "country living is a poor living," since "most of them came from some kind of country living. To move to a city was an advancement. So to move back to the country is like, 'Why would I want to do that?'" In his excursions to Spokane, he said, "if you find a black in the area, a lot of them are not apt to be very friendly to you."

The reason, he felt, was they were naturally suspicious of other black folk due to the low number; they were wary since another black person could spell bad news.

I spoke with Walt Washington for a while about some of the ideas and issues—about black America—that had been recurring throughout my travels. I was curious to know what he thought and felt. Especially about black youth. Especially with him having been in law enforcement in California. How could some of these problems be reversed?

"I don't know," he said. "As a cop, when you're on the street . . ." He paused and reflected gravely, no more the salesman. Over the course of our conversation, I noticed that his chipper facade had slowly disappeared, and he became more pensive. "I think I'm cynical. I don't know if I could really give you a positive insight on that. Like I say, being a country boy, and good-hearted and all of that, I figured if I find you and you're having a problem, I should be able to set you somewhere that gets you on the right track and gets you going. And it just doesn't happen that way. We are talking about kids in high school having alcohol and drug-related problems. They're trying to find somebody to help. There's nobody there who can help them. All of these organizations they only take kids who have come in contact with the law. So if you want to help these kids, what you really have to tell them is, go out, steal a car, get caught, go to jail, and they'll give you some help. You're telling a kid to ruin his life to get help. If he is just a normal everyday kid, he could go into the police station and say, 'I used heroin. I'm having a problem. I need some help.' And they'll say, 'There's nothing we can do.' Go to jail for four or five years, and he has a record for the rest of his life. It's like you can get rewarded for doing the wrong thing. Or they got him back out there doing the same thing he did when you arrested him, and it took you more time to arrest him and write up the paperwork than it did for him to get out of jail. I feel we're defeating ourselves."

Where did he think it's all headed?

"Boy, I don't know," he said. "I'm just glad I'm here. I tell you. My son works for the Narcotics Bureau of the sheriff's department in California. He tells me about the gangs and how things are going. I can't really say anything positive about the future. From what I can see how things are going, everybody's basically for themselves, and if you find a guy who's doing the wrong things, you kick him out of office and put another guy in there. Two years later, you kick him out too, because he's probably doing pretty much the same thing the other guy was doing. Where does it stop?" He paused a spell, and then said, "I can't give you no positives."

I felt a little bad, a little guilty, for it was apparent that I had brought a cloud of depression, though perhaps mild, to the tone of his boosterism. Shortly, he was smiling and glad-handing again and discussing real estate, and I figured no harm had been done. To be sure, I speculated, whatever drove Walt Washington to leave southern California, with those almost boyhood dreams of wilderness and isolation, that Hemingwayesque desire to be among nature, that Thoreauvian love of peace and American-style freedom was bound up in a past and a set of feelings deep and hidden and his own. And I respected his need and desires to continue to make his own history.

Quiet as it's kept, Idaho has a long and intriguing African American history. Something the white supremacists, be they six or six thousand, hidden away in their aeries of hate, might be surprised to know.

Idaho attracted most of its population through the railroads and mining. In the 1860s gold and silver and quartz and other valuable metals were found in the north of Idaho and in western Montana. One of the earliest claims was made by a black man, near Coeur d'Alene. It became known as "Nigger Prairie." Now it's called Mullen. George Washington Blackman came to Idaho in about 1879, and lived near the Fourth-of-July Creek, it was said, until he was a hundred. The Sawtooth National Forest's Blackman Peak is named after him. A black barber in Silver City,

Lewis Walker, made so much money on his claim that he became known as "Silver Walker." It is said that his barbershop sported hot and cold baths, and that he collected racehorses and ran them throughout the state. A North Carolina sharecropper, Calvin King, drew a number in the homestead lottery in the early 1900s, and moved his wife and seven children to a valley near Coeur d'Alene called Desmet. They built roads, cleared land, and turned several hundred acres into so significant an operation that the area became known as King Valley.

One interesting fact is that in 1899 when strikes at the mines in North Idaho created major unrest, the governor asked for federal assistance. Detachment M of the 24th Infantry was sent to keep the peace. It consisted of seventy-five infantrymen, two sergeants, two corporals, and twelve privates—all black. Except for some officers.

Mamie O. Oliver's *Idaho Ebony: The Afro-American Presence in Idaho State History* enumerates the many black folk who made the state their home over the years. According to Oliver, in 1890 the black population of Idaho was around 200, in 1910 around 650, in 1950 over 1,000, in 1980 2,700, and estimates in the 1990s suggest that close to 5,000 African Americans were living in the thirteenth largest state, which at the time had a little over a million people. Oliver points out the many people—especially in Boise—who had become a part of Idaho, their churches, their organizations, the local chapter of the NAACP, the masonic lodges. Historically, though the population was never large enough to warrant the legislature to write segregation laws, Oliver states that Jim Crow was in place. Black folk, along with Native Americans and Chinese—who were the main target of the Idaho "laws"—were discriminated against and made to live under de facto segregation. The city of Pocatello had a black section going back to 1905, and over the years it had been known as "the Walled City," "Twilight Zone," "the Restricted District," and the "Iron Triangle." In 1960 an incident was reported to the Commission of Civil Rights that "a Negro family of 10 was driven out of the city of Burley in October by hoodlums who threw a flaming oil flare onto the front porch. Some residents helped raise money to send them to New Mexico, but no effort was made to help them remain in Burley or to defend their rights."

Clearly the Gem State, as beautiful as a diamond, could be equally hard and cold. But the African American past in Idaho was not exactly zirconium.

So much for Aryan supremacy. (And anyway, the original word

"Aryan" referred to Indians who lived near the foot of the Himalayas. Did the "Nation" know that?)

"Well, how did you get here?" I asked Ida Leggett in pure, narrow-minded ignorance.

She reared back in her chair and laughed, and sighed, signaling a lesson in history for me—clearly I had touched a nerve. "You know," she said, "whenever I hear that question, I think, 'God, what a waste of energy!' You hear it at cocktail parties and that kind of thing, I just say 'How do you think? I got here the same way you got here.'" To Ida Leggett the question, when posed to her by most, dripped with racism.

But she demurred to tell me that she had lived in Tampa, Florida, when she decided to go to law school. She had expected to go to Florida State when she got a telegram offering her a fellowship to Spokane. After law school, she fully intended to go back to Florida, but was offered a law clerkship with the Washington State Supreme Court. "And I thought, 'Bye, Florida.'"

At the time I spoke with Ida Leggett she was an attorney in Coeur d'Alene. Her current partner had been her moot court partner in law school. After the Supreme Court, she did her stint with the "mega firms" in the Pacific Northwest. "I decided it wasn't me." Eventually, she decided to "get some guy to paint our name outside." Her partner had lived in Coeur d'Alene. Ida had visited the town in the past, and considered it a good place, professionally.

I asked her if she had been aware of northern Idaho's national reputation, to which she said, yes, of course. I asked how she felt about it. Could she give me a sense of the place?

"I grew up in the South. You know, I was seventeen years old or sixteen when the Civil Rights Act of 1964 was passed. In a time when there were signs that said, 'You can't go here, you can't go there, you can't drink here, and you can't drink there.' Or, 'You can't have this job. Can't have that job'—and by the way, they call it North Idaho, not northern Idaho; that's one thing you have to make sure you get right. You say, 'North Idaho' not 'northern,' and I don't know why—but North Idaho doesn't have the signs. That feeling is still here. But it's not all pervasive. I don't think about it all the time. But it's there. There are community leaders who, if not in practice, at least believe in just this thing. On one level, there is this talk about what a wonderful place this is, and how to reach out to bring in people from diverse backgrounds and yet, 'If they come, they're not going to work for me.' One of the selling points, if you look to promote light industry or whatever, 'Well, we won the Wallenberg Award for our human rights activism, and our fight against those guys up the street.' And on another page, one of the selling points is, 'We have a very small minority population.' In fact, I had a guy who was an expert at trial here, and he had one of those packets, very well put together and slick. Real estate development was their main focus, but they had a couple paragraphs on the highlights of the area, squeezed in between the wonderful views and the lakes and the clean air—small minority population. I thought, 'Well, that's pretty good.'" Ida Leggett's humor was wry and sharper than a hypodermic.

I asked about the presence of the Aryan Nation.

"One is here because of the other. That Aryan Nation's here because they feel comfortable here. That group is very small. But there are many, many more, who are not as militant, I guess, not as vocal. The same idea. This place is more and more being populated by people—I call it the white flight from L.A. They speak in terms of crime in the city."

When Ida Leggett first moved to Coeur d'Alene, she came with a son. In fact, she had gone through law school with three children to raise. "It was hard. I wore my youngest son's shoes and I wore my oldest son's jeans and sweater. That's what I wore to law school. I got divorced when my young son was about three months old. I just couldn't do it anymore. At the time I was young, and I looked ten years younger. And this was in the South, so you're dragging through the supermarket, with one kid running in front of the cart, and one kid in the cart, and one kid in the baby seat. And you could feel dreadful. I hadn't done anything wrong. Just trying to do it. When I started to go back to school my kids were older. I had an adviser tell me I had to decide which one I wanted to do. One or the other. And he also told me I was really disturbed because there was something about my grades. And I said, 'Look, I want to go to law school, and I want to go next year.' And he said, 'Well, there's no way in the world you're going to be able to go next year.' I had like two and a half years of college to go. I knew I could do it in a year. He decided that since I had children, I probably should have waited until they graduated from high school, or at a minimum, take three hours a quarter, or something like that. He absolutely refused to be available to me for the registration process. So I did it myself. When I graduated, I sent him a little note: 'You probably don't remember me, but I did it.' It was not because I wasn't that young. And it wasn't because I was a single parent. I think it was more because I was black than anything else. I wasn't supposed to be in that university anyway. And on top of that, I had all these kids. But it works both ways. See, some people look and say, 'Well, she's a black woman. God, she must be good!'" Ida Leggett laughed. "Go to a jury, and they think, 'God, she must really be smart.' I don't think there's a lot of difference from one region to the other."

By the time she moved to Coeur d'Alene, all her other children were grown and gone. "My son was a sophomore in high school at the time. That was an experience." But he was now away in the army. Once, while her son was still in college, her car had been totaled ("decided to run into a concrete wall"). "My son came home from school, and they had given me a loan car, and he was out one night with friends and his friend dropped his wallet. Turned on the light in the car so the kid could find it. Cops came up. Detained them for about thirty minutes. They hadn't done anything. The next night, there were some black kids who played basketball at the college, so he went over, and he was coming home, he'd just pulled off the campus when the cops stopped him again. And then he told me—he didn't tell me the first night—the second night he told me and I said, 'Now, I know you must have done something wrong.' And he said, 'No. I didn't.' So the next morning I got on the phone, and called the police chief and I said, 'What is this? This kid's been home for three nights, and already two nights in a row he's been stopped? Hasn't been cited for anything. Hadn't done anything, not speeding, not doing anything. Why are you stopping him?' The guy said, 'Let me check and I'll call you back.' The police chief called me back, and he told me where it was and what time the kid was stopped. And he said, 'Ida, I'm sorry. They didn't know who he was.' And I went, 'Oh, yeah, that makes all the difference in the world, because the cops didn't know it was my son, it was all right for them to do that. Why was he stopped?' 'Well, he was suspicious, and he was in a vehicle, and he fit a profile of a young black man in a car that fits some kind of a criminal profile. Well, Ida, I told you we didn't know he was your son.'

"The thing that really upset me—he had his little car, but I sold his car when he went to school, so evidently the cops knew that that little car that went whizzing by was his. To the cops, driving a car that apparently fit some kind of description of—I don't know whether it was a pimp or a drug dealer or whatever it was. They pulled him over, and it was okay. They were justified because they didn't know. The man who was in charge of this whole town. He thinks it's okay. Doesn't think there's anything wrong with making a statement like that."

At the time, Ida Leggett's son was in the Persian Gulf. "Last year was a real good year. My mom died at the end of July, and in August my son went off to war."

"Where you going to go?" she asked me, in response to the question why a black person would choose to live in North Idaho. "My response as far as staying here is really, 'Where am I going to go?' I was here and I lived about two blocks from Bill Wassmuth when they tried to blow his house up. And I heard and felt the explosion. I thought it was my car because I'd left my car on the street, and I had been followed and all that stuff. In the weeks before that. And these guys came down from *CBS Sunday Morning,* interviewed me, and when they were leaving, one of the producers said, 'You know, you ought to get out of here. There's no reason why you should stay here. Go to Atlanta.' Two months later we had this guy get killed in Georgia. Yeah, right, uh-huh. I'm going to Atlanta. So that's the thing. Where you going to go? You make the best of what you have, and most days I ignore it. And some days when I can't, you know, I let that person at that particular moment know, and then every year when they drag me out for Martin Luther King Day, I let a lot more people see me." Again she laughed her laugh.

Did she miss anything about being in the thick of black culture?

"Gee, I don't know what that means," she said. "The only thing that I really miss by being in the Northwest is the environment. I took my son to New Orleans, he was seventeen at the time, and when we got out of the plane in New Orleans he said, 'God. Mom, look at all the black people.'" Ida Leggett laughed. "So I do miss that just being a person. Just being one of a lot of people. I'd like to walk in a room and not cause a stir just by walking in. I miss that sameness. I miss that—I don't know what it is, but when my family's all together—it's there. You're just a person. And if you do something, you're doing it for yourself and if you fail, you fail for yourself. You didn't do it for every other black person in town. That's a product of being the only one who's visible. 'God, we can't have any more black people in here. Because they might be like Ida.' Or 'God, we've got to get some more black people like Ida. Ida's different.' I hate this. That's why I don't join in their little groups and task forces. When somebody tells me that we've got to clean up this image because this area's got to grow, and we've got to attract more businesses, and we can't have them believe that we have this racist atmosphere up here—*that* tells me that economics is more important than the underlying reasons. I'm not helping them do that. So there. Anything else? I talk too much because I'm a lawyer but—"

Less than a year after I left Coeur d'Alene, Idaho, Democrat Governor Cecil Andrus made Ida Leggett a trial judge in the Second District Court in Lewiston. Needless to say, the first black woman judge in the state's history—and, I'm sure, like me, she'd think that a highly irrelevant fact; someone always has to be first, but it's the quality, in the end, that counts. The governor was quoted as saying: "Anybody who appears before Judge Leggett can't make the accusation 'You don't understand how tough it is out there in the world.' She knows exactly how tough it is." I figured that if all judges were of Ida Leggett's ilk, this would be an amazingly different country indeed. Woe unto miscreants who come before her.

> A total of 320 hate crimes ranging from cross burning and a racially motivated slaying to defacement of property were recorded from 10/89 to 9/90 in Washington, Idaho, Montana, Oregon and Wyoming.
>
> —*Coeur d'Alene Press,* October 22, 1990

> I still get calls from New York, London, Massachusetts, Toronto and elsewhere in the Northern Hemisphere. People simply want to know what kind of people do we have in our area who adhere to a philosophy of racial and religious superiority.
>
> Folks, these people are revisionists. They think the Holocaust never happened, that the Nazi party was a kind and benevolent political party, that Hitler was God-like and the world's problems could be traced to a Jewish conspiracy.
>
> They believe it; they live it, they go to jail for it and they strike fear in the hearts of many who oppose them.
>
> The Nazis' being here is an area problem that we need honestly to address with a totally hard-nosed commitment of resources—of all people, money, brain power, and energy to help alleviate in people's minds throughout the United States and even the world the perception that the Northwest and the Inland Empire is a haven for people who espouse a philosophy of prejudice, hatred, and bigotry . . .

> For us as a region to ignore the trickle-down effect that this group at Hayden Lake has on Spokane, Coeur d'Alene, Sandpoint, or whatever is tantamount to regional suicide.
>
> —Raymond L. Stone, Mayor of Coeur d'Alene, Idaho, before the Spokane Downtown Rotary Club, May 31, 1990

Whether they were 5, 50, or 500 (which was unlikely), the hate groups were there—neither bogeymen nor haints, but flesh and blood, often skin-headed and Third Reich–attired human beings. To be sure, there is a sensational, emotional element to the idea of white supremacists, white Aryan nationalists, Ku Klux Klansmen and neo-Nazis, whether they be called The Order II or the *Bruder Schweigen* Strike Force. Folk of all backgrounds sit up and take notice; for some, in fear and in loathing; for others, the chance for vicarious bloodletting, and hate-mongering—wherever their sympathies lie. A great many reasonable folk even suggest that to give attention to this "movement" is to add to their mystique, to legitimize them—and, after all, as people are so fond of telling me, "it is a free country." Yes, even Thurgood Marshall would probably defend these folks' right to free speech. Personally, I don't care what anyone calls me as long as they don't touch me or my family and friends, my property, and my ability to go where I want and continue to add to my bank account. However, when people like Phil Jones, author of *The Negro: Serpent, Beast and Devil,* or Aryan Nation founder the "Reverend" Richard G. Butler, in their "Church of Jesus Christ Christian Nation" (huh?), speak of themselves as "holy Aryan warriors," I conclude they have more in mind than talk.

"The Aryan Nation is the militant arm of the Church of Jesus Christ Christian," Butler was quoted as saying in an article by Nancy Bateman. "It is the action arm. It is the one that goes out and makes the declarations."

Declarations? Would that include the 1986 series of explosions in Couer d'Alene banks, federal office buildings, the robbing of a bank and the National Guard Armory and the bombing of Father Bill Wassmuth's home? Is that what led, in 1988, to David and Deborah Dorr and Edward and Olive Hauley of Hayden Lake being convicted on sixteen counts of counterfeiting, racketeering, bombing, illegal possession of automatic weapons, and malicious destruction of federal property? Would that include the numerous hate crimes—whether they were rising or falling—that were still occurring throughout the Pacific Northwest (and elsewhere)?

While in North Idaho, I came across a number of pamphlets and articles, espousing all sorts of lunatic, half-cocked, ignorant, hate-riddled, vile sentiments about blacks, Jews and gays, and spoke with people who had wildly different opinions on how strong this so-called movement was, and what needed to be done about it. I remained uncertain of everything except one thing: While there, at least, I would take them very, very seriously.

When I first met Inez Anderson and her three children—Ayisha (thirteen), Tariq (twelve), and Faheem (ten) Rahman-Anderson—they were dancing. Dancing with a group of other children to Hammer's "Too Legit to Quit," preparing a dance program to be performed at North Idaho College, in Coeur d'Alene. Inez Anderson was the dance instructor for the group.

I had been told that the Andersons had been the object of a number of attacks from white supremacist groups, and that I should talk to her. She invited me to their home for supper, where we were joined by her husband, David, a slim, good-looking, bearded young white man, originally from Wisconsin.

After dinner, we settled down for a chat.

Inez believed there to be around six African American families living in the Coeur d'Alene area. Originally from Chicago, she told me her father was part Sioux and part Cherokee, so her insight into intolerance was multifaceted. During her years in Chicago, she was among a group of students who integrated Gresham High School. "The National Guard used to take us to class, take us to the bathroom, take us to lunch. Walk us out." After some particularly violent episodes, her mother said, " 'That's enough. No more. You're just not going to go. It's not worth it.' I was totally upset with her because of that. It seemed as though she was giving up. But when you're standing in a mother's shoes that was a scary thought, that one of your children might be murdered, for any parent."

For Inez Anderson living in Coeur d'Alene was quite a chore. She mentioned a number of run-ins with people—people she thought should have known better—who challenged her right to be in Coeur d'Alene, who were aghast at the notion that she possessed advanced degrees, that she was married to a white man, and people who confronted her with stereotypical and racist notions. "But our living here has, I think, some point, no matter how small. They're beginning to recognize I'm not going away."

"I agree with that," David Anderson said. "And I think the dancing helped a lot of these people."

Inez said, "Especially after we perform, and we do a lot of benefits. A lot of charity benefits, and I've had people here come up to me and ask, 'Can I have your name and your number? I would really like you to get my child.' Before these children dance, I give the community a background history of why we've come together. So actually, this is not your typical dance group. This dance group has a purpose. When I first started it, it wasn't supposed to be a dance group. It was just something for the children to do, so they wouldn't be on the street. So they wouldn't be bored. I had no idea that it was going to turn into something like this. And then we started to get recognized, people started hearing about it, and the kids started saying things also. We started getting racially harassed. And all of the kids stick together when that happens. Over the summertime, my youngest, Faheem, was outside getting something out of the car—this was like some months before the Aryans had tampered with our car. A bunch of about three or four white children were walking by and said, 'Why don't you go back in the house, you little black nigger.' Well, I had gone to the door to see what's taking Faheem so long, and he goes, 'Mom, they called me out of my name.' Our kids can't even bring themselves to say that word. We teach them that all people are equal. All of the dancers were in the house, and when they all heard that, they went—'Can we go after them?' I said, 'Go get them.' The four boys took off down to the lake. All of the kids ran out of the house. 'Come back here! You're going to apologize!' And that was good. That was good to see. We sit and we can discuss racial issues."

"Yeah," David said. "Twenty years ago, you wouldn't see this."

Inez and David were married in Wisconsin Rapids, Wisconsin. His family seemed okay about the arrangement initially—there was a big wedding, and a reception, over 350 people. But not long after they were married—a week—they felt "a backlash." "The racism was *aarrghh,*" Inez said. "I had my mind made up. I told him I was leaving, with or without him." "I had to quit my job," said David. And they literally stole away from Wisconsin under cover of night. They moved to Spokane, Washington. But directly, his company transferred them to Coeur d'Alene. When he told Inez, her initial reaction was: "No! I am not moving there. You move there. I'm not moving." She had lived nearby during her first marriage, and understood what she was getting herself into. "You did not darken Idaho." But, by and by, she relented.

I asked if I could get bold in my questioning, feeling somewhat uncomfortable asking personal questions in their home. They said they were happy to discuss any matter. I recounted a number of attitudes of black people I had known and encountered. Especially the attitudes of black women with regard to black men marrying white women.

I was surprised to find that Inez's notions about the role of "race" in gender and sex seemed oddly conservative coming from a black woman married to a white man. The more we talked, the more things became muddled and unclear and peculiar to me: White women involved with black men were after the legendary dark phallus, she explained to me; black men did not properly respect black women; black men had low self-esteem and wanted nothing more than prostitutes for their service; white men viewed black women as objects of their sexual fantasies—and on and on.

But, I'd asked, gingerly, was it safe to make such blanket judgments across the board as the norm? Yes, I was told. And when I asked about her situation with David, I was informed that they were the exception to the rule. David agreed.

We went on this way for a time, while I tried to point out the contradictions in what they were saying, trying to find some middle ground. I cited the work of Frantz Fanon and Calvin C. Hernton, acknowledging that such psychology was often at work, yes, but that certainly couldn't be said to define all black and white relationships, could it? I suggested that her ideas sounded a great deal like the fear of miscegenation. I told them that I knew black men married to white women, and black women married to white men, black men with white men, black women with white women, and all sorts of other combinations. (Some, it's true, do it for money, but that's true for all creeds and colors and sexualities—but mostly the people I knew did it for that old-fashioned virtue called love.) To suggest that the overriding reason most people of different colors got together was due to slithering reptiles in their unconscious was not solid ground in my reckoning. I did not state this quite so emphatically, but I said as much.

But the Andersons continued to smile. Though Inez in particular disagreed with me.

We all had a long way to go, Inez told me. When Inez and David went out, they were seen only as a black woman and a white man. And in people's minds, the only thing that mattered was, "Why are you together?" Until such thinking was done away with, these psychological games would continue to persist. However, she did concede people of color were farther along in this acceptance, in seeing people as people.

By and by we returned to discussing their living in North Idaho.

Inez told me: "Living in Idaho, I get a lot on both sides. The black communities in Washington said, 'You need to get out of that state. Why don't you just move over here?' When I move over there, what's going to happen? I still have to deal with the fact that those are my brothers and sisters over there, and they still don't know nothing about themselves. And they still have these mental battles going on. And they still have their own ideologies going on. There is no difference, from me moving from here to over there. Over here, I have a better chance of making a difference, which ultimately will affect over there."

"You're working on a different scale," David said.

Inez said, "Because the people know I'm here now. I've been here for quite a while. They know I'm not going anywhere. They might want me to go somewhere. But the only place I'm going is to the store and home."

The phone rang, and Inez left the room briefly, and I chatted with David. He struck me very much as an earnest man, and honest. His nature was surpassingly mild. And I wondered how he could possibly survive the onslaughts that his marriage surely provoked. But I remembered the old adage about still waters running deep, and how strength does not necessarily advertise itself. He spoke to me about the Midwest and the South. He told me, "I don't feel uncomfortable talking about black issues. I've questioned myself at one time or another. It allowed me to be able to sit and see or hear all these different opinions. It makes me understand better, as a Caucasian." I asked him how that made for life among other white men. "I separate myself from that. I don't feel I'm even part of that. I don't view it as a reality. I guess I kind of straddle both sides. Through my wife I'm being taught some black culture and stuff. I would rather see myself with an open mind." I asked how it made him feel to sit amongst people, absent black folk, who spoke disparagingly of African Americans. "I grit my teeth. It's really hard in that situation. You want to get boisterous, and say, 'Well, gosh.' And when it gets downright derogatory, I'm going to jump in and say, 'Look, you know, it's time you educate yourself. This is the way it is.' "

I asked about our friends over in Hayden Lake. "They don't even look at me. They don't even associate with me."

David worked as a heating and air-conditioning man with GTE, and traveled a great deal.

Later Inez told me, "David isn't usually around when a lot of these things are going on. He'll usually call me and ask, how is my day?"

"I'll keep in touch with her from time to time," David said. "Through the day and stuff like that."

"He'll hear a little anger in my voice," Inez said. "I really have to try hard to not cross over that thin line of hating."

That past summer, the brakes to their car had been tampered with. "The car kept going," Inez told me. "I was pushing on the brake. It was like pushing air." The car wouldn't respond to shifting gears or anything else. The car had been fine that morning. Eventually, "we hit a tree. The car bounced off the tree, and we hit a car that was on the side, after which it slowed a bit." But after she turned a corner, the car began to speed up again. In desperation, she ran into a utility pole. "It was a blessing I didn't go through the windshield." A child was in the car, and her head had been injured, but nothing broken. The next day, "I get a phone call, and you can hear these people giggling in the background. 'Yes, who is it?' You can tell this was a redneck cracker. He goes, 'You can't drive worth a damn, nigger.' I go, 'I beg your pardon?' And the guy said, 'Next time you get another car, we're going to do that to that one too. How does it feel not to have no brakes on your car, driving down a road? You should have been dead, nigger. But we wasn't expecting no white girl in that car. Why did you have that white girl in the car? You black nigger bitch.' I hung up the phone and they kept calling back. I kept getting these sick racial calls. I called the police."

David Anderson said, "Called the police station. Explained to the police what's been going on. And they said, 'Well, okay, we'll put a tap on the phone. We'll check it.' Would you believe after that, no more phone calls. Just stopped, boom."

"Just like that," said Inez. "I'd been getting them for four months prior to the accident."

The Andersons told me that the registration had been stolen from the car. After the accident. The car ransacked. Gloves had been used—no fingerprints. Inez told me, "I found out from the kids, from the dance group, that one of my dancers used to be friends with some of the Aryans. He had stopped being friends with them, but when they found out he was in my dance group, they told him not to come back, told him to quit hanging around those niggers. He said, 'I'm not going to stop hanging around my friends, and don't keep calling them "niggers."' That's when my car got tampered with. They called me and let me know, 'Yes, we did it. And we will do it again. You get another vehicle.'"

Prior to that, the Andersons told me, they had received hate mail, and garbage had been thrown in the mailbox, and junk in the front yard. In 1989 Inez had participated in a march against racism in the area. She assumed that made her more visible than she already had been. In school, she had run-ins with the principal and with teachers, who she felt were allowing bad things to happen with her children. "Kids would have my boys pinned up against the fence, and they would tell them, 'Go home, niggers. Go home, niggers.' And would try to fight them. My kids didn't want to go to school. I said, 'That's it. I'm going to school.' I was talking to the principal, and he said, 'Why are you doing this?' I said, 'What are you doing about these children harassing my kids?' He says, 'We put them on the bench.' I said, 'Really. So when the children call my children a nigger, all you do is tap them on the head and say, Don't say that word anymore?'" That visit, and other visits, Inez told me, led to screaming matches. Attorneys were involved. It seemed the issue had not really been resolved, but the Andersons were intending to pursue it further.

The Andersons also told me of how they had problems with a house they had rented. A landlord resorted to the most obnoxious actions to get them out of his apartment, they believed, once he found out David Anderson was married to a black woman. Eventually they moved out, they told me, surrounded by a lot of ill feelings and monkey business. After looking at over 200 places—("*Two hundred?*" I asked. "I went to two hundred places between Post Falls and Coeur d'Alene," she told me. "I had doors slammed in my face." She almost had a nervous breakdown, she said.)—a couple of non-Idaho residents (the woman being a Native American) happily rented them their current home.

By the end of the evening I had one burning question: "Why the heck are you people still here? I'd have probably killed someone by now."

"I almost did," Inez said. "I'm telling you. I had gotten to the point that I was walking around here angry, and so hateful. I just hated white people. I've acquired high blood pressure. Severe tension headaches. I have to take muscle relaxants. Living here has stressed me out that badly."

I asked my question again. And Inez Anderson fixed me with steely eyes and her jaw clenched: "'Why?' Because I'm not a quitter."

"Yeah," David said.

"Because I'm not a quitter," Inez said. "And I'm not going to let these white people win. I ran from Wisconsin when we were having racial problems. Not again. So I have stayed because I'm a fighter. I'll stay as long as I have to until . . . until I've exhausted every avenue and possibility of a change of some sort. I will stay as long as I know that people are changing. If I know that I can't do any more, that's when I move. We've already made that decision. If we do, we're going to Alaska."

"And when we get our eight million dollars," said David as a joke, "we're going to move to Alaska anyway."

Taking my leavc of the Andersons, thanking them for a good evening, I could not help but think of the Oedipus from Sophocles' *Oedipus at Colonus,* as translated in the musical *The Gospel at Colonus,* telling his daughters: "Live where you can / Be happy as you can / Happier than God has made your father . . ."

A few days before I was to leave Idaho, I had been invited to visit the historian Dr. Frances Heard. A white woman in her nineties, she had devoted decades, I'd been told, to the study of blacks in Idaho. I had put a call in to her in the morning, and she got back to me midafternoon. Saying please come out, she had a great deal of information for me. She gave me directions to her ranch, but before I rang off, she paused and cautioned me. Her home was literally next door to the entrance to an Aryan Nation compound. She advised I be wary. I was to be at her home at four, so I left a little after three, and proceeded, for the first time after months on the road, to get undeniably, unarguably, without a doubt, lost. I knew I was in Hayden Lake, but I had taken a series of wrong turns; and as I was already paranoid about being lost in Hayden Lake—about being in Hayden Lake at all—I was loath to ask for directions, not knowing what I might open myself up to. (As if being a dark man in a jeep, driving around, indeed, circling around, lanes and byways might not in itself open me up to suspicion.)

That very day, before I left to see Dr. Heard, I had stopped by Radio Shack to pick up batteries and cassette tapes. As I searched the shelves, a young fellow, towheaded, rosy-cheeked and lanky, a salesman, no more than seventeen or eighteen, approached me with a wide-open, golly-gee gait, and as guileless as you please, asked, without hesitation or preamble or reservation, "What are you doing here?" Not, "Can I help you." Or "Afternoon." As I inferred that "you" and "here" were not referring to me-customer and here Radio-Shack, I figured he deserved to know. Indeed, I was curious to see his response. I explained that I was writing a book about black people and had chosen to come to Coeur d'Alene, Idaho, of all places. He found that richly amusing. And he enjoyed a fine laugh. I just stared. As he got my tapes and batteries, and was ringing me up, I asked him for directions to Hayden Lake, reviewing what the good doctor had told me—which is probably what got me lost in the first place. He verified my directions, and asked if I was going out there. Yes, I said. He laughed again, and reminisced about a guy he knew, a student at the college, "a colored man who made such a big deal about delivering a pizza in Hayden Lake. He'd go around saying: 'I survived Hayden Lake.'"

Now it was getting dark, since it was early December, and by 4:00 p.m. it was deep twilight. In my mind, I conjured up all sorts of scenarios. Running directly into a grove full of neo-Nazi, skinhead militia men. Perhaps doing a Marx Brothers routine in the face of Israeli-made submachine guns. I was not afraid, as I remember it, just annoyed, just anxious, just amused. For you must admit, it was amusing. And ironic. After all these miles, after devoting so many months to the study of black people, I was coming so perilously close to an oldfangled ending, a cliche, a cosmic joke. A joke in such bad taste that I refused to believe it could actually happen. Not to me. Not that night.

Stubbornly, I retraced my tracks, and as sometimes happens to good little boys, I found a road to a road to a lane to a driveway to a house, that resembled what Dr. Heard had described as her home. For the first time, getting out of the car, I was indeed afraid, for I could still be at the wrong house. The night was pitch-black, and a spotlight illuminated the door. I rang the bell, and stood, waiting, in all my ebon glory before the door. I may have even said a prayer.

"Mr. Kenan?" Dr. Heard's assistant said. "We were afraid you were lost."

"But now I'm found," I said, and apologized for being so late.

# III

# THE ICE MYSTIQUE

. . . Crow wanted to be born—he wants to make the
world! . . .

After Crow made the world, he saw that Sea Lion owned the
only island in the world.
The rest was water—he's the only one with land . . .
Crow rests on a piece of log—he's tired . . .
He wants some land too, so he stole that Sea Lion's kid.

"Give me back that kid!" said Sea Lion.
"Give me beach, some sand," says Crow.

So Sea Lion gave him sand.
Crow threw that sand around the world.
"Be world," he told it. And it became the world . . .

That's the end of Crow's stories. At end he gets tired of
walking around.
So made himself into Raven.
Now he doesn't bother people anymore.

—from "The Story of Crow,"
translated from the Tlingit and Tagish
by Julie Cruikshank and Angelia Sidney

Twelve

# BY THE BIG GULLEY

*Maidstone and North Battleford, Saskatchewan*

Bucephalus pulled into Maidstone, Saskatchewan, at around 9 p.m. on June the 25th, 1992, and the sun was yet high and bright in the sky. I was feeling good. I had successfully made the journey from North Carolina to New York to Winnipeg to Saskatoon to Maidstone—about 100 miles east of Lloydminster on the Alberta border, and about fifty miles west of North Battleford. I only regretted having not spent more time in Saskatoon, which fascinated me, like a northern Denver it seemed, yet more western in feel. It had to be the dustiest town I have ever visited. That summer, the prairie was an ocean of endless green, and the Canadian Highway a straight, uninterrupted shot, so I could go for a score of miles or more without encountering another automobile. Out west, Canada needs no more than a two-lane highway for an interstate. The small towns in which I stopped were inhabited by handsome, sturdy-looking people who treated me with nothing but respect and kindness. I could see what seemed like billions of gopher holes all along the way, and rodents popping their heads up now and again to check the air, and saw more than a few of the critters trammelled on the road, and, as I said, the sun did not set until at least eleven, and I came to adore this strange, plain land.

Once in Maidstone, I checked into the motel, I think the only motel, in the town of around 500 souls (still larger than Chinquapin), and had some supper from the local burger shop, and settled in to watch television. (Oddly enough, most of western Canada pipes in a lot of Detroit stations; the reason being perhaps that Motor City is the largest American city near Ontario, hence, the influence of the East overrides the more logical interest in goings-on below the closer western border.)

The next morning, bright and early, I made my way to the local library to begin my work. And, as I had seen not one black face in Maidstone, Saskatchewan, in my several hours there, I walked into the small one- or two-room building right on the little Main Street, and told the librarian—after saying, 'Good morning'—quite simply: I'm looking for black people. She gave the most sincerely regretful look I can remember receiving in quite a while and raised her hand to her cheek and said: "I'm so, so sorry, but all our *Negrews* moved away years ago!"

Back at the turn of the century, the Canadian government was concerned that they didn't have enough people. Moreover, out west where most of their land mass existed, the land that made them the second largest nation in the world, their populace was scarce. What to do? Give away land. If you give it, they will come. And they did.

Some estimate that upward of 3,000 African Americans made the exodus to northwestern Canada to become homesteaders. Though they came from all over, the bulk came from Oklahoma—which had once been more welcoming than the South, but was now becoming a more and more intolerant place to live (in 1910 the Democrats in the state legislature moved to take away black voting rights; and in 1913 segregation was legalized). Some estimates are that as many as 7,000 black people left Oklahoma in those years. So many, in fact, came to Canada, that the immigration branch of the Ministry of the Interior sent agents, one of whom was black, down to dissuade more from coming. According to a local history of the area, *North of the Gulley,* it appears that black Oklahomans were told northwestern Canada "is desolate, frigid, unsettled, unknown; to which the black people would be climatically unfamiliar and financially unfit." Effectively, the Canadian government quickly put a stop to the influx.

However, by 1911 there were over 200 black folk in and around Maidstone, most living in the Eldon district, twenty miles to the northwest. (Two hundred more continued west to Alberta where they settled in the Amber Valley, 170 kilometers north of Edmonton, and also Wildwood to the east; as many as seventy-seven families farmed in the Amber Valley at one point; in the early '90s as many as eleven were said to remain.)

The people of Maidstone referred to the new arrivals as the Shiloh People. People named Bailey, Beely, Boyd, Cotton, Crawford, Eason, Farmer, Forster, Gaston, Harper, Lane, Mayes, Robinson, Taborn and Wright. They built a church named Shiloh Baptist Church in 1916, and erected a school in 1917. In *North of the Gulley,* it is written: "They found a place where they could live closely together in order to help each other and be socially independent." Here, they would live, not without hardship, for decades.

> Almost I did not see it as we passed
> Along the roadside . . . veiled in grizzled brush,
> Board door hung slanting from one rusted hinge,
> Long grass uncut . . . swept in the summer rush
> Of moving on for no apparent cause
> So that we passed before we realized
> This was the place. With primly folded paws
> A gopher watched us from bright, beady eyes
> Retrace our passage to the brambled yard
> Where sleep the faithful, marked by trees grown tall
> And stone of careful size and shape, unscarred
> By name or date, and hymned by wild birdcall;
> And, gradually, the vision fell in place;
> A dusky form took shape, a dusky face . . .
> "We're here!"
> Out of rough wagons, tired, a wave
> Came tumbling . . . young folk, old folks, babes in arms
> In search of Freedom . . . slave and son of slave . . .
> On wild, alien, unconquerable prairie farms . . .
>
> —Violet M. Copeland, "Negro Pioneer Church"

The librarian placed a call to the Nicholsons, and when I spoke to Mrs. Nicholson, she sounded delighted to hear from me, and offered to come and pick me up and show me the church. Which she did.

The Nicholsons owned a vast ranch of hundreds of acres, much of it in Eldon. They seemingly happily took on the task as de facto caretakers of what was left of the Shiloh People, which, sadly, was essentially the church and the cemetery. That summer day, the grass had recently been cut, and a great spruce tree, one of two in either corner of the churchyard, was as tall as any building in the area—in fact, I had not seen a tree that tall since I had been on the prairie. The church itself had been made entirely of logs and entirely by hand, it sagged at one corner, and it amazed me that it still stood. At the corner one could see how it was constructed with dovetailed logs set by fieldstones; and inside (one door in front, one door in back) it was dimly lit by the sun coming in the ancient, distorted (and distorting) few windows; the pews, also crafted by hand, seemed so uncomfortable to have sat on; yet one could imagine these people found much comfort here. Outside was the graveyard where around forty people were buried. The original markers were all gone, but new white crosses had been placed at each head in 1971. Many of the graves were sunken and a few birch trees and hedges grew among them. As we were leaving, I spied a skunk scurry under the church, and as we paused at the stone marker in the front of the yard, declaring this an official historic site, I wondered how it all would have seemed in 1917. In summer or winter, the bell ringing, all those dark faces coming to church in the morning; I imagined what sermons the minister might have delivered; what songs they had sung and how they sounded; indeed, I wondered how long, and if, they were happy in Saskatchewan. They were, indeed, all gone now.

The Nicholsons, who were quite charming and, it seemed to me, good and sincere people, took me back to their home and fed me cake and coffee. On the way back to their house, they showed me an extraordinary view, peering down from a great slope to the famous Gulley Creek—expanse upon expanse all wheat and green. They spoke of how very difficult it was for anyone—white or black—to make a go of it this far north. They told me that the number of white farmers who left around the same time as the Shiloh People did was also enormous; in those days, the Nicholsons told me, the winters were particularly fierce, subzero temperatures and snowfalls of extraordinary depth—some winters over forty feet. But in the end, the Great Depression was the real culprit; though many blacks tried to hold on to their land, the majority had to let it go and moved to places where it was less treacherous to make a living. They gave me names of people living in Saskatoon and Vancouver and Edmonton and North Battleford.

I had been looking in particular for Murray Mayes, who I had been misled into thinking still lived in Maidstone.

Oh, no, they told me, he still owns the family land, but he's lived in North Battleford for years.

Ah, I thought. And they gave me his phone number, and took me back to town. I contacted Mr. Mayes, and he said he would be glad to talk to me. Contrary to earlier expectations, I got in Bucephalus and headed back east to North Battleford.

I had first learned of Rueben Mayes back in 1987 when he was playing for the New Orleans Saints. In his first year, the twenty-three-year-old running back had led the NFL in rushing with 1,353 yards, making him Rookie of the Year. I noticed in reading an article about him that he was Canadian, and from Saskatchewan. It told the story of his family, starting with his great-grandmother, Mattie Mayes, who was born in 1849 in Georgia; and how she married a Baptist minister after the Civil War in Tennessee, and they moved to Edna, Oklahoma. After a flood ruined their crops, Joe and Mattie Mayes and their thirteen children headed for the northwest, where they homesteaded 160 acres. "People didn't know what blacks were all about," Rueben told *Sports Illustrated.* "They almost starved that first winter." It said his father, Murray, spent most of his childhood in a one-room sod house; and that he sometimes had to go to bed hungry. Mr. Mayes, Senior, left home as a teenager. Rueben had been born in 1963 in North Battleford, the oldest of seven children. He was said to be a "track phenomenon" in high school, clocking 10.4 seconds in the 100 meters. And he went on to win Saskatchewan's male Athlete of the Year Award, and Canada's top black male athlete award, the Harry Jerome Award, in 1985. At Washington State University in Pullman, he upset NCAA records, rushing 357 yards in a single game, with a two-game mark of 573 yards. In two seasons he covered over 1,000 yards. When I met his father in 1992, Rueben was playing for Seattle.

Rueben told the *Saskatchewan Report Newsmagazine:* "I had a really good childhood. I felt that in my little group of boys in North Battleford I was kinda the leader. There were no problems because I excelled in sports and was average on the academic side. They looked up to me . . . I've grown up on my dad's stories. It makes me thankful for what I have . . . Whatever talent I have, I have because both my parents and their families were hardworking."

North Battleford was a small, blue-collar town of around 14,000—people I found, again, friendly and outgoing; or at least the ones I met while staying there were. The architecture is unremarkable, and the town seems spread out and expansive—lots of land; on either side of the North Saskatchewan River run railroad tracks, and the smaller town of Battleford sleeps to the south. The shopping mall was full the day I went there; and I fondly remember while at a McDonald's, waiting in line, this most adorable lad, no more than five or six, I suspect he was Cree, turned and looked at me and pointed. "You are *black!*" he said. And I agreed with him, and his mother started apologizing, and I told her it was okay: The child was just telling the truth.

. . .

"Well, I moved when I was eighteen. And I'm sixty now," Murray Mayes told me. He had been living in North Battleford for forty-two years. "We only had about thirty acres of land broke at the time. And I had to get out and get a job, you know, survival really. My parents stayed there on the farm. Just south of that cemetery, in fact, the next quarter-land, adjacent to the quarter-land that the church is on, is our land. We owned that land. There's a little dugout, a waterhole, there for the neighbors. One of the farmers, a friend, is leasing from us. And he pays us cash rent. So we're quite happy about him being on there, because the land had some hay seeded in there, and that's best for the soil. So we're happy with the way things are. Pays us cash rent, and the land's getting better as time goes by."

Mr. Murray Mayes was a sturdy-looking, dark man, the complexion of coffee without cream, with sharp observant eyes, and the hands of a man who has worked with his hands many a year. His manner was easygoing and gentle. That day in his apartment, he also came across as devout—his conversation was peppered with biblical wisdom and thanksgiving—a devotion perhaps strengthened by recent years.

Mayes Autobody Shop had to be closed, he told me, for two weeks, due to bankruptcy problems. The details were complex and bothersome. "That's part of life, isn't it? Struggles, and some things happen that you don't think could happen. You're surprised, and some of those things are not very pleasant. We just thank God for our life, and we just keep on going. We don't stop."

Mr. Mayes also taught for the government's Manpower Program. He taught welding, in particular to men in need of a trade to get back into the workforce. He spoke of the men's talents and skill quite highly, and seemed to enjoy the opportunity to pass on what he knew.

At the age of eighteen, Murray Mayes left Eldon, and took a job in construction in North Battleford. But of course, due to the weather, construction ceased in Saskatchewan by mid-December in the 1950s. "Then they'd lay you off, and hire you back in the spring. That didn't suit me. I like to be working year-round." The Sharon schools had courses in auto mechanics, and by that fall, he had a job in a local Chrysler dealership where he worked for six and a half years. He also studied in Moosejaw. ("I passed my journeyman's after four years at the technical school in Moosejaw. My marks were ninety and eighty. And seventy is the passing mark.") Got married, had seven children.

He started his auto body shop in the early '60s. "It was City Auto Body Shop Limited, which I originally started up with a partner. We had the farm, and after being in business around twenty years, I expanded with a loan from a development bond. Private banks. And then they called the loan in. Because my wife had left home, and I'm not blaming her, but a lot of things that happened really hurt my company and a lot of shocking things happened—and my business went under. So after struggling with the bank, and not being able to meet my payments and being on the verge of divorce (which did end in divorce)—All that happened at the same time. Without the Lord's help, I couldn't make it, I'm sure. Couldn't make it. But I came through it all, and I was only out of business for two weeks. I reopened my business and I've been going along quite well. My son has helped me, and other friends. Church friends, helped me. So, the Lord's been with me. It appears to be an uphill grind. Through all that trouble, the Lord has been a tremendous blessing to me. Some people never recover. I'm very thankful that I was able to come out of bankruptcy. It was tough, really tough. I really believe that the Lord allowed these things to happen. So I could learn things and I could help others. So the Scripture says that everything works together for good, to those that love God."

Speaking with Mr. Mayes, I was struck by the feeling that I had known him, met him somewhere before. After a spell, I realized he reminded me utterly of my grandfather, who often used similar scriptural references, whose humility was of the same tenor, who, in fact, had not only grown up on a farm and had known hardship, but was a small businessman and father. How odd, from southeastern North Carolina, to western Saskatchewan, the likeness, the commonality. And though my grandfather spoke with a southern accent, and Mr. Mayes's Canadian "eh" punctuated his sentences; the feeling of recognition abided.

"I would go to Maidstone, the little town of Maidstone, and people that I've been working for, picking up rocks, or cutting brush, some of them, not all of them, but an odd one, you'd see on the street. You'd be walking down the street, and they would cut across to the other side of the street. And you'd say, 'Hi.' He wouldn't even look toward you. You'd think, 'Well, I wonder why he didn't say hello to you.' He didn't want to speak to you because he figured you were a lower level of people. I smile at it now, because later, he would come to me, he would be coming to town here, and he'd say, 'Murray, how you doing?'—because your boy's a success—'How're you? How's Reuben?' And you just smile, and you look at that. Some of them are dead and buried now. And I'm not hoping them any bad luck or anything like that. I don't consider myself any better, and I don't consider myself any poorer. I figure I'm on the same level them people are. Some people think, 'Oh, you're way up there.' I know some people say, 'Well, I saw you on television. And I wanted to meet you.' I've had CBC from Toronto and W5 and then CBC here again. Regina News, Leading Polls, the *New Optimist*—all these people that have come. I was going through some of those crises, they'd come to me, and they would talk to me about different things. No, I see myself on the same level, just like everybody else. So I treat everybody the same. Be nice to them, treat them kind, be reasonable. And you never lose, eh? You always win. Always come out on top."

Mr. Mayes took me to church. He attended the Sharon Star Missions, which I had never heard of. He had been involved with that group since his earliest days in North Battleford: "*The Sharon Star* was sent to Maidstone, and I was reading it at eighteen. Began in 1948. That group formed the Sharon Orphanage in North Battleford. There was a revival here, in the early 1940s. Definitely a revival here. And that spiritual revival spread all through the nation. I was moved by it. I became a part of it. In the early '50s, I came here and started to attend the local assembly. That revival is still on."

The church was out aways from the town, and white and saltbox-like. The congregation gathered there were no more than twenty or thirty at the most. The room in which we met was smallish and unadorned, and I noticed all about me the sternest, plainest faces I could remember. Most of these people were descended from Germanic and Ukrainian folk, with a bit of English and Scots—Mr. Mayes and I were the only black folk there. Everyone seemed to know Murray Mayes, and Murray Mayes seemed to know them. As I sat among the women in their plain white dresses, and the men in their stiff suits, I thought: These people must have what it takes to live here; and perhaps the plainness and the sternness are necessary by-products of this atmosphere.

After an elder or deacon read scripture, he began to pray, and the most surprising thing began to happen: Everyone commenced keening and moaning. They were attempting, achieving, some sort of ecstasy. They did not shout or stomp; just moaned and swayed, and I must say I was taken aback and momentarily afraid, for the outward appearance of this group of people had not prepared me for this unusual form of worship.

Back at Mr. Mayes's apartment, I met his son Christopher, who had come home from college for the weekend. He had brought his girlfriend along. An athlete like his brother, he had a truly Olympian body and deeply resembled his father about the face.

Later we talked about Eldon and Mr. Mayes's first eighteen years on the farm. "In my early years, my mom was sick. She had been in a mental institute, because of a bad accident. A horse ran away and mama got hurt, and she was carrying her second child. (Dad had left years before that, and then he came back, and he and my mom got married.) They moved away from Maidstone to Lloydminster. The Depression started to set in, and dad had a tar paper shack in Lloydminster (this was before I was even born), and he worked in a bowling alley. Setting up these pins in the bowling alley and other jobs that he'd get for construction and so on. And mom got sick and she had to go in the hospital in North Battleford here, and dad was told by the psychiatrist that she'd never come out of that hospital. Dad said he was going to try, and he was going to take her out anyway. So the doctor told him, 'Harvey,' he said, 'If you take her to the farm, maybe she will be all right.' Now immediately, his house burned in Lloyd and all these things happening, and he had my older sister. Mom had been in the hospital, so he took her out, and he built a log house on my uncle John Mayes's farm, at the south end in Eldon. And that's where we were raised. Sixteen years I lived in a sod house. The first part of my life, we only had one room. There was nine people. Because there were seven children. I have two sisters and four brothers. She never recovered from this mental breakdown. But she was able to mother us, and after you were about two or three years old, you had to look after yourself. But if you got sick, you were on your own. Mom wasn't able to give us medication because of her ailment. It was tough.

"So I became a man quickly. I figured I was a man at fifteen. No doubt about it. My dad had a rough time of it, because my dad was injured when he was just a little boy. They were digging worms to go fishing in Oklahoma. Before he came to Canada. They were using a grubbing hoe, to dig worms, you see. And my dad was watching the area that was being dug up, he saw some worms, and he jumped down to pick them up, and he got hit with a pick in the head. He just about didn't make it. That injury affected him some. He wasn't able to figure things out like a person could normally. An example of that was when in the fall, we'd haul up a pile of wood, and we'd haul maybe ten, twelve loads. Well, we needed about twenty, twenty-five of those. And he'd look at that pile, and he said, 'Well, that's enough.' And then it'd get colder during the winter, right after Christmas, that wood'd be gone. You see, we'd have to get out and get more wood. Where he should have hauled up a lot of wood in the first place, and then you wouldn't have to go out in the cold. But he was a good man anyway. Hardworking man. He had quite a few brothers, and some of them took advantage of him. They would come for his animals, and so on. And his brothers, they'd come over to my dad's place, and by then he had his own land and everything, and they'd say, 'Harvey, we'd like to borrow your horses.' And he said, 'Oh yeah, that's okay.' They'd be using his horses and they'd have their own horses, but they'd borrow his. That's why they moved, mom and dad. Mom figured she could see what was happening, so she said, 'Well, maybe if we move away from these people, he'll be able to get along okay.' But once he got into Lloydminster, things didn't get any better. Well, he didn't have his land now. He sold out, and he tried to recover from that, and that was very difficult. And then my older brother got killed in a train accident in Ontario. Oldest brother, Otis.

"Of course, if you're working on the railway, as a porter, they'd had to insure you. And with the insurance money, my dad bought the land that we have now. So it worked out. It's unfortunate, a very sad thing that my brother got killed—two of my brothers was in the same accident. Two older brothers. What had happened is that Otis was on leave, he got so many days off, after you go out on a run. And there's a friend that was a porter as well, wasn't feeling very well, and he'd been out late, or whatever. He had been drinking a bit. And he wasn't in no condition to go out on this run, so he asked Otis to go out on this run to Ontario. On that run, my brother got killed. The train had stalled on the track, and it was storming. And this train that my other brother was on hit the back of Otis's train. Two brothers in the same accident. And Otis got tore up so badly because they were in the wooden boxcar, in the sleeper. Him and the conductor, and they both got killed. Sandy we called him—my other brother's name was Sanford—he found my brother's leg. And they had to knock him out to get him back on the train because he was in shock. Mind you, we didn't see him. We had him shipped back and buried him here at the church. Well, that was a bad thing to happen, you know.

"So anyway, those are some of the sad things that happened in our lives. We had a lot of fun, too, when we were going to school, playing ball, in the spring. We'd play hopscotch, and other different games. So a lot of happy times, you know, in our lives growing up. And I had two older brothers, and they towered over me. Then I had two younger brothers, so between us, there was five brothers. Otis was quite tall, and Sandy was taller than me, when we were growing up, and then Stanley and then Willis.

"And then there was Uncle Virgil. Virgil Mayes. He was a really tough guy. I think that the South made him tough. He was one of the original thirteen. Blacks were going through some harassments in the South. Uncle Virg, he turned quite mean, and on guard, and everything. You had to deal gentle with him, because he was a very tough man. Nobody could take him. He'd back down from nobody. And he wasn't as tall as me. But his brothers had to watch how they dealt with him."

"There used to be some severe winters up here. But we don't get those winters anymore. I remember, it used to be thirty-five, forty below. It would last for a couple days, three days, you know. And snow, we used to get snow; we don't get those snowstorms like we used to get, I'd say, six feet of snow, during the winter, six feet. And now we're lucky if we get three. I'll tell you. It's amazing what you do. You can deal with something if you have to. And you didn't know anything better to do. You just deal the best you know how. We'd ride those snowbanks, they'd be, honestly, they'd be seven feet high. So we'd make up some kind of sliding, we'd be sliding on it. Fun, you know. And we'd walk to school. That's why I missed a lot of school because, after the Christmas concert till April, I'd miss school. When the teacher would come and give you an exam, you wouldn't know what it was about. And mom wasn't able to teach us at home or anybody. So you'd miss that and then you'd fail that year, and the second year you'd fail. And then, by the time that things got better, I was getting too old to go to school. That's the way it worked with us. My younger brother, he was the only one who was able to go to high school. You learn things in life, a life of learning."

"In Eldon we were in pretty close community. Most of our relatives was about—oh, two and a half miles apart. But it thinned out quickly. A lot moved. Opportunities other places. They moved to the cities. And they all did better, when they moved. There were some exceptionally good farmers in there. Some did really well. But they'd get older, and their children didn't want to farm. A lot of them sold their farms, and some went for back taxes, and miscellaneous things happened. But we find it with the white people too. They're not staying on the farm either. They grow old and die and some move to the cities and it's no different. So you know, life goes on. Yeah, life goes on.

"Good relations, though, between the black and the white. The only thing is for the blacks, in some cases, the breaks is tough. Like you could go—and everything I told you is the way I feel—and I see that a black person could go to the bank, and approach for a loan, and he wouldn't get it. And the white man could go in there and get it. It's tough. I'm not just joking. It's tough. You got to be better. A better man than the white to make it.

"In the old days, they done well. We ate mostly potatoes. I didn't realize how a diet of potatoes is really good in potassium and of course the starch there. I just wondered why we had to eat potatoes most of the time. But they're good for you, and they were not expensive. Mind you, in the early part of the spring, things would be tough, a tough time because of people's gardens being used up. The first few years that I was growing up, we didn't even have a garden. No horses, no cows. Dad was down-and-out, and it was difficult to get back on his feet because of the Depression. Depression was really bad. And he had no horses, no cows. And no pigs. Just a few chickens. Later, as time went by, he started to buy a few pigs, and then he got a cow. And then some horses. Things started getting better, and then we bought our own land. But one thing he instructed me, 'Never sell the farm.' We still have it. It's quite a thing that. During my years working for the Chrysler dealer in the garage, I would be constantly sending money to my dad. Because he was having a rough time still, you know. Even though he had land, he was still struggling, and so I give him the first car I got. I fixed it up and give it to him, because he had twenty miles to go to town. Later on, I bought a tractor and a few other things. And then I started spending quite a bit of money out on the farm, and I'd help break up some more land. We'd get the Caterpillar to come over there, and Daddy would make a deal with them, and then I'd help him pay, and then we moved a house on there. We put a basement in, and I had a well dug, and different things.

"I spent a lot of money on the farm, from the shop, eh? After several years, my accountants approached me and said, 'You have to pay (I forget how many thousands) several thousands.' He said, 'The reason why you got to pay this income tax is because of that farm, you can't declare it on income tax. Money you spend on the farm you can't write it off.' He said, 'The only way you can write this thing off is put the farm under the company's name.' And so, I thought, 'Well, I'd better check with my parents, and see if this is okay.' My dad said, 'There's no use you paying more money out, when you done spent it on us and the farm.' And so he says, 'Well, sure, do it.' So that's what I done, put the farm under City Auto Body Shop Limited. When I expanded, I'd use it for security, and I'd pay it all back. Paid off the loan. Several times I did this, a couple, three times. Then when I borrowed this money from the bank, and they got looking at this land, and looking at my shop, they thought, 'Well, hey, let's just shut him down and grab all this.' And they just about did. Now, if I hadn't had my brother and sister, I think they'd have took it. The bank tried their best to take it."

But thankfully, the land was still in the family.

Before I left, I asked Mr. Mayes about his grandmother, Mrs. Mattie Mayes.

"She was a fantastic, spiritual person. See, there's quite a difference between spirituality and religion. Religion can be a bad thing. Spirituality is a godly thing. And she was a spiritual person. And so that way, she's a unique person. I'd go and visit her when I come back from school, and she'd tell me a lot of things, a lot of things that happened. A lot of stories of the South and how people were treated. She was treated well but there was others that wasn't. She was a tremendous help to me. Always respected her, because Grannie was such a great person.

"I remember when she was—oh, she must have been around eighty years old. And I used to ride with her. She'd be going to visit someone, with a team of horses and stoneboat. (A stoneboat is two skids, logs that're used, trimmed, were tied in the front so that they don't slide, and they put planks across, and they tie the horses to that, and they slide that across the grass. In the summer. You can use it in the wintertime very easily, but in the summertime, you'd have to make sure it's on the grass because it'd be hard to pull, there's no wheels on this thing, just sliding, eh? So if there's a trail that's been there from wagons, well, you split the trail, you put one skid on the middle where there'd be some grass, and then the other on the shoulder. Mind, you could wear the grass down quite quickly. But you'd always find a new spot where you could drive on. But that's what they call a stoneboat.) And she used to do that, and then she used the buggy. But she was a tremendous person. Everybody thought a lot of her. She was very friendly and she used to be a midwife, for a lot of the whites as well as the blacks in Maidstone. Doctor wasn't able to get out to the residence when the mother was going to have a baby with the deep snow, and the vehicles wasn't so readily available back in those days. Sometime it'd be late at night, and she'd be right there on the job. But she was a terrific person. You heard that she got lost one time?

"She was up in her nineties, and she'd visit, after we had moved to our own land, there would be about a mile, maybe a little better, from her house. She stayed with her youngest son. And she'd walk over there to visit. And on her way back to her residence, she missed the turnoff, and instead of her turning into her son's place, she went down the road, and she crossed into the neighbor's, and she was lost all night. She walked all night. We searched for her, and they got the Royal Canadian Mounted Police, got quite a few people from Maidstone to come out—this was on a Saturday. And they searched. They put out search parties looking. But we were combing the immediate area around our residence. Not thinking about going north, and that's the way she went. She walked all night. At ninety years old. They found her, they used a dog, a German police dog, a tracking dog, and they found her next morning, about I'd say 9 o'clock, in a house, about three-quarters of a mile to the river. She stopped at the house there. Rested there. And she said, 'Lord bless you, doggie.'"

Mrs. Mattie Mayes died in 1953, at the age of 104.

Thirteen

# COLD HANDS AND FIERY HEARTS

*Anchorage, Alaska*

> But the ethereal and timeless power of the land, that union of what is beautiful with what is terrifying, is insistent. It penetrates all cultures, archaic and modern. The land gets inside us; and we must decide one way or another what this means, what we will do about it.
>
> —Barry Lopez, *Arctic Dreams*

A flatlander, I had left my breath in the Rockies that preceding winter, there among Colorado's 14,000-foot peaks, and beneath Montana's topless sky. Nothing could have prepared me for British Columbia's ever-changing and magisterial poetry, heights ever-increasingly high, vastness that robbed the word of meaning—What is vast?—on upward toward the Yukon, up and up. How could I breathe? What does it mean, literally, to be 17,000 feet above the level of the sea? These mountains were the granddaddies and grandmamas of the lower Rockies. Surely, I thought, God made these lands first or last: first, in abandon and flourish, majesty personified; or last, after having made all else, bringing about, at the top of the world, a new wildness, higher than high had been before, and vistas stretching beyond the comprehension of the puny human eye.

The first time I drove to Anchorage, I left Edmonton on Canada Day, full of trepidation, as the western plains took on a more austere countenance, bare, hints of foreboding. I found it difficult to get my mind round the idea of a 1,975-mile journey—one way. I had been warned how rugged most of the road would be, hundred-mile stretches of gravel, falling rocks, moose, buffalo, bears.

I officially picked up the Alaska–Canadian Highway, the AlCan, about 200 miles out of Edmonton, at Dawson Creek, B.C., and stopped at Wonowon, which gave new meaning to "wide spot in the road." From Wonowon it was ten hours to Watson Lake, Yukon, a place known for its exhaustive collection of street signs brought there from all over the world. The next day, 439 miles to Destruction Bay, on the 250-kilometer-long Kluane Lake. It did not seem far then to Tok, Alaska, the next day. At the border, the decidedly southern patrol officer told me when he handed back my passport, "Welcome back to the United States, where the gas is cheaper and the roads are better"—and from Tok, it was a mere seven hours to Anchorage, that northern city of lights.

To use my grandfather's phrase: I ain't never seen nothing to beat it, that drive. It had been a five-day pause from myself, from the world, and back into the world at the other end. I relearned awe and childlike wonder for a time. A friend had told me that once he had seen a landscape so beautiful it made him cry. I cannot testify to having shed a tear, but upon the crest of certain mountains, I surely understood the feeling.

At one point, during a long, seemingly endless stretch through a seemingly endless forest, I stopped to relieve myself. I was wary for I had seen a brown bear a number of miles back. Outside of Bucephalus, I kept smelling what to my mind was soap, and I pondered how the car had gotten splashed with detergent, the smell was so strong. Presently, I realized it was not a man-made infusion; I smelled the real thing; I was smelling the forest. I was smelling evergreen, but more intense than any forest I'd ever smelled before. The realization both boggled my mind and set it free, for that understanding showed me where I was and where my mind had been. To think I had thought of artifice first. Here was wild's wild, fresh's fresh, uninhabited's habitat.

Standing at Kluane Lake, its icy, blue glacial water splashing about in great waves, I felt such a sense of peace that I hated to leave it. Though I knew it was then summer, and that fall and winter could be harsher than harsh there, my soul nonetheless enjoyed an exaltation I have rarely experienced.

Here, in the Yukon and Alaska, I finally felt I understood how all those Native American stories of the great Northwest came into being: to see the raven against the blue sky; to see the bear among the brush. I saw how landscape affects faith: We believe what we see.

. . .

Not until after I had driven the entire length of the AlCan did I find out that my sense of spiritual connection had an African American precedent. To my amazement, but by now not surprise—I learned that most of the Alaska–Canadian Highway had been built by black men.

The U.S. Army took over a strip,
　　A strip of Canadian soil,
They did it without a single hitch,
　　Without creating a boil,
Their engineers went on ahead,
　　Surveyed and staked a trail,
The job was done in record time,
　　No such a thing as fail . . .

—Anonymous, "The Alaska Highway"

It so happened that during my visit to Anchorage an exhibit was running at the Anchorage Museum of History and Art: "Miles and Miles: Honoring Black Veterans Who Built the AlCan Highway," curated by Lael Morgan of the University of Alaska at Fairbanks. ("Deep in a stack of dusty 1943 war records is a wistful quote from a Negro soldier who had been asked what working on the AlCan highway was like: 'It's miles and miles of nothing but miles and miles,' he said," writes Morgan.)

Some have compared the construction of the 1,630-mile gravel road to the building of the Panama Canal. Experts had shaken their heads: can't be done, they said. It took the U.S. Army Corps of Engineers eight months and twelve days to complete the job. A good third of the 10,607 men who built the highway were African American—men who had been originally declared unfit for the job.

There had been talk of building such a roadway since Lincoln had been stuck with "Seward's Folly." Even as late as the 1940s much of the terrain had yet to be charted. Even the Native American presence was comparatively sparse in that part of the world. But the bombing of Pearl Harbor made the need for such a thoroughfare an imperative: Alaska was much too close to the empire of Japan for comfort; the United States needed a way to get supplies from the East to the Bering Sea, just across the straits from Asiatic Russia.

"Certainly the Army has a responsibility in not further complicating the population characteristics of the territory by leaving a trail of new racial mixtures," said General Simon Bolivar Buckner, Jr., son of a Confederate general, according to Morgan. "Buckner's objectives were echoed by top brass in D.C. who worried that Black soldiers would not have suitable intellectual capacity to handle bulldozers." And they were expected to fare poorly in the subzero arctic temperatures.

In fact, the winter of 1942–1943 had been the worst in human recording. At times, the mercury stubbornly sat at minus fifty degrees for weeks on end.

Despite the quibbles, all-black Engineer Outfits—the 93rd, the 95th, and the 388th—were dispatched to western Canada in an agreement with the Allied Canadian government.

White troops worked their way south from Fairbanks; the black troops started at Dawson Creek, heading north.

One of the numerous difficulties in building the road was dealing with permafrost—the layer just beneath the topsoil which never thaws out. In areas with permafrost, the wanna-be road quickly turned into muddy bog as soon as vegetation was stripped. Often heavy equipment would nearly disappear into the quagmire. Logs had to be laid to stabilize the surface—in some areas it took five layers of wood to be effective.

A bridge was erected over the problematic Sikanni Chief River—a river with a flow of glacial waters that rushes at times at the rate of ten miles an hour, precipitous rapids. Engineers predicted two weeks; the black soldiers said they could do it in four days. Wagers were taken. The men accomplished the task in eighty-four hours—working on rafts, defying ice floes "big as grand pianos"—not to mention bears.

According to a 1943 *Yank* article, "Alcan Epic," when that bridge was dedicated, Corporal Timothy Womack of Americus, Georgia, was said to have played "I'll Never Turn Back" on a hand organ, and a record of Marian Anderson singing "Ave Maria" was played. "A colored chaplain, Capt. Edward G. Carroll of Washington, D.C., told the soldiers, 'We have built this bridge as a symbol of service to the democracy which we love.' And he added: 'Unless the Lord builds a house, they labor in vain who build it.' "

Sergeant Walter Simon of Brooklyn, N.Y., is quoted in the same article as having written in a mimeographed newsletter: "We're a lucky outfit, lucky because we are good. If we weren't, we could never have been chosen to do this job. We can't afford to lose all, our reputation, our own personal pride, by 'slipping up.' It's tough going, it will be tougher, but our will to see this 'baby' through, will keep that road going, as the miles flatten out under our D-8 bulldozers. Fort Nelson, see that cloud of dust getting nearer and nearer? That's us building the Alaska–Canada Highway."

The men ate Spam and dehydrated potatoes. They attended roadside church services heard from a loudspeaker anchored to a pile of timber. Ironically, the black soldiers weathered the experience better than their white counterparts, who were often arrogant in their naivete about the cold, losing fingers, ears, toes to frostbite; the black soldiers listened to cold-weather wisdom. Apparently the men also found time for some fun: pitching horseshoes, watching movies. The chaplain was said to have had 500 books in his tent. The men said they were glad when the mail arrived.

On October 20, 1942, the northbound and the southbound regiments ran into one another—(quite literally, one bulldozer almost toppled a tree on the unseen other)—and the official opening occurred at Soldier's Summit on Kluane Lake on November 20, 1942.

"Some day," said General O'Connor, "the achievements of these colored soldiers—achievements accomplished far from their homes—will occupy a major place in the lore of the North Country."

I found it passing curious that in practically all of the literature and material I researched on the building of the Alaska–Canadian Highway, virtually none of it—with a few notable exceptions like *Northwest Epic* by Heath Twichell—made mention of the fact that one-third of the men involved in its building had been the grandsons and great-grandsons of slaves. In one highway souvenir book, there is only one black soldier in "100 photographs," and a videotape I purchased along the way showed not one black face. Not to mention the general absence of acknowledgment of the Native American guides who told the engineers where to go.

It pains me to think that any of these men should go to their graves in relative obscurity. They deserve to be as famous as the road they built.

A reunion of the few remaining veteran African American roadbuilders took place that summer of 1992, in Tallahassee, Florida.

A towering man of impressive build, his hair greying, Walter Furnace had a presence at once easygoing and impressive; competent and generous. He had been elected to the Alaska State House of Representatives in 1982, and won reelection in 1984, 1986 and 1988. In 1983, he had been voted one of the ten outstanding Republican legislators in the U.S. by the National Republican Party. When I met the congressman he was running for the state senate.

Walter Furnace joined the air force in 1962, and had spent the last two years of his four-year tour in Anchorage, Alaska, and had remained for the next twenty-eight years. When he left the air force, his choice was either to stay and make an excellent wager, or return to Texas and work for five dollars a day. "Didn't make sense to go back."

Walter Furnace's wife had been originally from Chicago. They met and married in Alaska. "She came up to live with an auntie. Came up with her sister. She must have been nineteen, and I was twenty-two. We dated for six months or so. Decided to get married." He allowed that his wife's perspective differed a bit from his own. "She works with the school system. A lot of problems. People that want to give her a hard time. She's strong and she knows how to handle them."

"Is she a Republican as well?" I asked.

"I think my wife is a registered Republican. She's an independent spirit so she votes Republican, I'm sure, yeah."

He got married the year he left the military, and his children had all been born in Anchorage.

He got involved in banking, "by invitation." He had attended a local business college in Anchorage, and the owners of the school held him in high regard. They made introductions for him at the National Bank of Alaska, where he began as a management trainee. "I was the only black, and there were about five whites." He went from "a kid on the streets to an assistant vice president in five years," running a branch with a staff of fourteen.

Representative Furnace wound up in the legislature, "quite by accident." Beginning with the local PTA. "I was invited. Three ladies walked into the branch one evening, and said, 'We're from the PTA. And we know you have children in the elementary school up here. We want to know if you would consider being president of the PTA.' "

Though he hadn't been active before, as president of the PTA he found that he could get things done, that he understood politics and was good at it.

Next, he ran for the school board and won a seat and was elected president after nine months. Despite Alaska's flush coffers in those days ("This would have been about '81, '82. The money was really flowing pretty, because Prudhoe Bay was in its heyday then."), the legislators were tight with money. "For the most part there were not very many legislators who had kids in school. And those that did, didn't have a real strong knowledge of education." As president of a school board in the state's largest city, Walter Furnace spent a lot of time lobbying in Juneau, but he found that there was still a lack of support for educational issues; a fact he found frustrating.

When a new legislative district was created in 1982, Walter Furnace decided to run. He found the prospect attractive since there was no incumbent. He resigned from the school board, ran, and won.

"My first year," he said, "had a seat on finance, chairman of labor and commerce. Had a seat on state affairs. Was on a bunch of subcommittees and whatever. Long story short: when it came time for funding for education, in fact, I introduced the supplemental appropriation bill as a freshman legislator, and it was the first bill to pass in my freshman year. It was like 17 million dollars to recover prior shortfalls in education spending. So the progression of me getting into politics started at the PTA."

When I spoke with Representative Furnace, he told me his three daughters were twenty-two, twenty-four and twenty-six. The oldest worked for a mortgage company; one was a loan interviewer; and the other worked for the Salvation Army in the Booth Memorial Home Project. The youngest was also married and had recently made Walter Furnace a grandfather. "My girls are well adjusted, and I don't see any problem. They've got their own lives and are happy within their environments."

I asked if he ever had any concerns about his daughters being cut off from African American culture, having grown up in Alaska.

"No," he said, "they're smart enough to understand. We took them out in 1978. I left the bank in '78. I took four months off. Went outside, bought a motor home, and we traveled through the lower forty-eight states. They were just before high school. So for three months, we visited all the relatives we could find. Now I assume that there would be some colorful shock if they went back. The middle kid went to Manhattan for a concert about five years ago. Went on her own. Coming from Alaska and doing something like that, well, that shows you that they're pretty independent."

"But culturally, it's kind of difficult to assess how well adjusted an Alaskan kid is. Black or white. Particularly the black kids, because first of all, they've not been subjected to the real die-hard racism that some black kids have had, just because of living in an enclosed environment. Their best friends have always been white kids. And yet, I don't think they act white—you know what I mean by that. They've been equally comfortable with their black friends. There haven't been many because there were few black kids around. Our next-door neighbor was a black family, and so the kids grew up together. They were all in the same age range. They have two girls, we had three girls, and they all went to church together. Parties and birthdays and celebrations. But it's difficult to assess how well adjusted they are, and how knowledgeable they are about the human condition. I think whatever setting you put them in, that they would adjust to it. And, if not, there's always Alaska. They can always come back. This is home to them."

I noted that statistically Mr. Furnace—as an African American and as a Republican—was a rare breed.

"Hey, I'm the first to realize that." He laughed again. "I mean, and it's not by design. It just happened. If I were in Texas I'd be a Democrat. No question about it, because that would be the structure that would embrace me. It's geographic. I feel safe to say that had I been a black Democrat, I would not have been able to move through the political system as I've done. No."

Around Anchorage, Mr. Furnace told me, it was common to be greeted as "one of the boys."

"I walk out of here to a grocery store, it'll take me twenty minutes to get out of there, to get a pack of chewing gum. Because invariably, somebody will come up. Want to sit and talk. You give them your time. Whether you know them or not. I might happen to know one guy but hell, four out of five people come to the door. I don't know them. But they know me. And so you got to sit there like he's a long, lost friend. 'How you doing, old buddy? Gosh.' I was out knocking on doors last night, and walked into this guy, sort of recognized him. And he knew me. 'Wow. Come on in. How you doing, old buddy.' 'Great, great, great.' And I asked him for a yard sign. Then I said, 'Well, let me make sure I got your name right.' 'First name again?' Just to be superdiplomatic. If you don't know them, you don't know them. You want to make sure you got it right."

As a physical reality, the state of Alaska beggars the imagination. For that fact alone, it is easy to understand why so little of it is understood or is generally known by the citizens in the lower forty-eight. First there is the size: 586,412 square miles, or 365 million acres. Texas could fit inside the state with room to spare. It is one-fifth the size of the lower forty-eight states combined. Its population is around 600,000, most of whom live in or around Anchorage, whose population is about a quarter of a million. Tallest mountain, largest state park, and biggest earthquake—March 27,

1964: 9.2 on the Richter scale. Still find it hard to get my mind around Alaska.

But these are just numbers, and as all adults should know, size isn't everything. For me, perhaps one of Alaska's most remarkable traits, indirectly related to size, comes in the form of a legal precedent that has powerful ramifications.

In 1971, the United States federal government "awarded" $960 million and 44 million acres, timber and mineral rights included, to that state's almost 100,000 Tsimshan, Haida, Tlingit, Athabascan, Aleut, Yup'ik and Up'ik peoples. Twelve regional corporations were established, and 220 smaller village companies followed, each paying dividends to its shareholders, the native people. Twenty-some years later, the largest of these corporations were among the *Fortune 500*—Cook Inlet with sales of $530 million, Sealaska with sales of $331 million, Arctic Slope with sales of $328 million. But, most importantly, that action had significantly raised the standard of living for tens of thousands of people—plumbing, sewage, heat, food, health care, education. Purists might grumble about the erosion of ancient traditions there as Native Americans become more affluent, but reality is hard. I love Native American culture and arts with a passion; but I am far from a fool. One thing we seem intent on forgetting is that cultures change, and that which does not change is dead. Moreover, we are all guardians of each other's culture, blacks of whites', whites of blacks', reds of blacks', blacks of reds'. Culture is a willed thing.

Not very long ago, Native Americans were the eponymous low(est) man on the totem pole in Alaska. People would even rent to black folk before they would rent to Indians. Barbs and racial epithets were repeated to me that made my ears curl; I could scarcely find equivalents with regard to talk about niggers. Interestingly enough, that's all largely gone now. One teenager told me, "I just know that a lot of them got a gang of money though. You have kids come by school shopping, and these kids, fourteen, fifteen years old, got $2,000 in their pockets. Somebody might have made $15,000, $16,000. Them kids come in, sixteen, seventeen years. They buy anything. I show them Air Jordans. 'Air Jordans, oh, yeah, yeah. We like Air Jordans.' I don't understand them too well. I don't come in contact with them enough to understand them. But they seem to be okay. I guess. I don't know enough about them."

There is a lesson here. Part of it is how much we Americans worship capital; another part is how inextricably bound to capital is the thing called "racism"; and how bound up with both is our sense of identity. I wonder, in twenty more years, how much more *We* will know about *Them.*

Then there was Mahalah. Mahalah Ashley Dickerson, attorney-at-law.

I caught Ms. Dickerson in action in Courtroom G in the Federal Building on I Street and 3rd. She was a tall woman, stately in her tailored blue suit and grey blouse, her hair pinned back; it was hard to imagine that this commanding figure was a few days shy of her eightieth birthday. She was in the midst of a divorce proceeding, representing the husband. The man's sled dogs were a huge bone of contention; the wife said she had paid for most of the dogs' upkeep (sled dogs are expensive). A child was involved. A young boy. Messy stuff. It was almost amusing to watch the wily Mahalah Dickerson in action. The judge at one point spent forty-five minutes reprimanding her. She was reproached for being argumentative. (Later she told me that she and the judge had been friends for decades; she knew him before he even passed the bar.) At the end, she gave an impressive, impassioned plea—calculated, humane, sly: she was not above using her years as a trump card.

We chatted awhile after court was adjourned. First she gave a pep talk to her client who looked a bit hangdog.

After she had graduated from Fiske University in 1935, and after a few years teaching in public schools, doing clerical work, and social research, she enrolled in Washington, D.C.'s Howard University Law School.

"Now had I been Caucasian I could have gone to the University of Alabama, right out of college, and been a lawyer in three years. However, I wouldn't have known as much as I did by the time I became a lawyer. Wouldn't have had the experience of encountering problems and knowing as many people and been capable of understanding as many things."

Mahalah Ashley Dickerson entered Howard in 1945 and graduated in 1948. She had been the first black woman to pass the Alabama Bar Exam that same year. With three other black attorneys, she began practicing in Birmingham in 1949.

"I was fortunate. I was able to get scholarships all the way through because I kept my grades high. We had no such thing as student loans. I had failed at one marriage. I had triplet sons, and by the time I entered law school they were six. So we all entered school at the same time. It was really fun. We were growing up together. My kids may not have learned much from me, but I sure learned a lot from them. My kids are health nuts—exercise, diet and that kind of thing. I think that's one of the reasons I'm still around and still active. I do try to take good care of myself. I never did smoke. I eat too much, but I try at least to eat the right things."

After her second marriage, she moved to Indiana (where she was the first black woman to practice law), beginning in Indianapolis in 1951.

She first came to Alaska essentially on a whim. She had had a pretty good year and said, "I'm going somewhere I've never been before. Where I don't know anybody. And I will sleep for thirty days. I took a thirty-day vacation—but I didn't sleep. I got here, just got a new energy, and I met so many interesting people. People were so friendly and I just loved it. So I decided I would go to the land office and sign up for land. Well I came in, and I was dressed like stateside people. Alaska people are real down-to-earth. And so I said, 'I'd like to sign on to homestead.' And the woman looked at me like she thought I was crazy. She said, 'What area?' I said, 'Oh, something within a hundred miles of Anchorage.' And she said, 'Well, I don't have anything. Only thing we have is Homer, and that's 280 miles.' I was just about to turn away when I heard this voice say, 'Why don't you show her some of that land you've just shown me?' And up stepped this tall, good-looking, Caucasian male, and oh, she turned so red, the woman at the counter. And she reached down and got a map and slapped it down, and walked out of the room. He said to me, 'Now, lady,' he said, 'this is the area you ought to be looking at. Now that's just seventy some miles from Anchorage.' (Now it's fifty because they've made more roads.) He said, 'Here is an area that they just opened up. They opened it up the first ninety days for veterans. And those ninety days are up, and now nonveterans can sign. I see here's one with a lake on it. The way you describe this is, northwest quarter, section 29, range 2, West township 17.' Oh, I was so happy about all this. 'I want this one. I want this one,' I said. He said, 'Now she showed me this. But I don't want to homestead. All I want is a homesite. So I'm getting five acres and birchwood.' He said, 'But this is what you ought to get.'

"And so he left. Wished me good luck. I stood there and stood there. I thought she was never coming back. Finally she came back, and I said, 'I want to sign on this one.' She said, 'You can't sign on it. You haven't seen it yet.' Well, there's no way I could have seen it because it's nothing but woods. I didn't believe her, but I didn't know. So I picked up all the literature that was around and I took it back to my hotel room, and I read everything. Nowhere did it say you had to see it. So I went in the next day, loaded for bear. She wasn't even on duty. It was another white girl, but nice, who let me sign right away. And I paid my $16. The same thing we paid the Russians. That was the beginning. But of course, there were other things you had to do. I had to put in a road. I had to clear a homesite, and I had to build a habitable dwelling and all, before I could actually prove up. But I got my patent the day of the earthquake which was March 27, 1964."

She had staked her claim in 1958, a year before statehood. Which made her one of the last few people to homestead in Alaska.

Mahalah Ashley Dickerson was the first African American—male or female—to practice law in the state of Alaska. And the first black woman president of the National Association of Women Lawyers. "Now that was a grand fight. In order to let them know that I represent the North and the South, I said, 'I'm going to go grey—for the Grey—and blue—for the Blue. I'm wearing my blue suit, and I'll put on this grey blouse to show that I was born and raised in Montgomery, Alabama."

A fact of which she is proud—primarily since her upbringing was not the typical, tobacco-road sort.

"Fortunately my grandfather owned a plantation. And my father inherited it. I understand he bought that land for something like a dollar an acre. But he had 360-some acres. And as I remember looking out—nothing but trees, peach trees, apple trees—Oh, every kind of fruit and every kind of vegetable and cotton, cotton, cotton. Fields of cotton. And he had some tenant farmhouses on it, and my father had this big general store on it. Now that I look back on it, it's more like being in a Western, because people would come in their wagons and horses and everything, and they would just load up with supplies, sides of bacon, big bags of flour and stuff. And of course they would pay for it at the end of the year. Some of them lived on our plantation. Some lived on the adjoining plantations. But the thing that broke my father was the migration, when everybody went north.

"Those blacks who owned a lot in the South, didn't think about going north. I often think about it. When I went to Fiske University, the kids from the North, they sort of turned up their noses at us kids from the South, but the only thing about it, the kids in the South had yards to play in. You didn't have to play on the street. Had houses and were not living in apartments. Growing up for a black child, despite all the segregation, was more wholesome in the South, because you had lots of friends. We had lots of parties. We really enjoyed growing up. We were proud of ourselves. Only when you'd go downtown or something like that, in a place where they'd be snippy, and not want you to try on something."

Mahalah Ashley Dickerson had been a Quaker for many years, partly because she admired their fine Friends' schools, where her children went, and partly because of their long tradition of advocacy, abolitionism and pacifism. She even built a Quaker meeting house on her property in Wassilla. "Every Sunday at 10:30. A small group of Quakers, ranging from about five or six to as many as ten or fifteen. Silent worship. We don't have elders speaking much. Everyone's supposed to be on call. But it's revealing and it's refreshing. I said, after all, Mohammed goes to the mountain, and so it's time I got to be the mountain. Then they will all come to me."

One mistake black people coming to Alaska made, Ms. Dickerson said, was allowing petty slights and insults to get under their skin. "And let the hurt linger. I don't pretend that I don't have feelings. I don't let it linger, because after all, it's only temporary. My dad always said, if one won't, the other one will." She laughed. "That's something that I pass on to you: There are others. We got some stinkers. But there are so many wonderful people here."

After Salt Lake City, Anchorage is one of the most logically laid out cities in America. Brigham Young was responsible for Salt Lake's numbing grid; Anchorage was designed by the ubiquitous Army Corps of Engineers. That said, I found it hard not to have a little admiration for Anchorage. Perhaps it is the Chugach Mountains that ring the east, or Turnigan Bay at the end of Cook Inlet to the west. But certainly it was the people and that "in-country" spirit. Despite technological advances, it takes more than a notion to live in Alaska. This *esprit de place* is reflected in Alaskans' confident, friendly, laid-back manner, their matter-of-factness and close-to-earthness. Yet, unlike New Englanders, their security is mixed with a sense of openness and adventure—a love of thrill and fun. Alaskans seem to revel in the slightly rakish nature of their past, for like Australia, it is a place bad folk have run to, and a place of gold rushes and greed, brawls and feuds, bloodletting, whisky-drinking, whoremongering, gambling, as well as broken spirits and broken bones, fortunes lost, souls crushed. Alaska is west of west.

But it can also be frightfully dull.

I endeavored to get my hair cut in Anchorage, and found a black "hair care" center. It was unisex and unimpressive, and I knew it would be a bad experience when I noticed that everyone had jherri curls—an unfortunate hairstyle already considered ancient history by most black folk by then. My barber was profoundly untalkative, and seemed a bit slow on the uptake. Consequently, I was displeased with the cut I got—a lopsided fade. Damn.

> Before the oil strikes, before the earthquake, before practically everything else that makes Anchorage of interest today—there was Zula Swanson. When Mrs. Swanson, a former cotton plantation worker "disgusted" with the United States, moved up in 1929 from Portland, Ore., Anchorage was a frontier town of only 3,000 inhabitants to which fishermen and gold prospectors came to rest and have a good time in bars and brothels. For $2,000 Mrs. Swanson bought a burned building and a piece of land along the town's one street, and rebuilt the structure into a rooming house. "Anchorage wasn't nothing then," she says. "But the land is flat and you got the Cook Inlet. I could see it was going to be something." In those early days it was easy to buy a lot from a fisherman cheaply, she says, and "I got some of my lots for $700. Nowadays when you want to buy they just rob ya."
>
> —from "Zula Swanson: Alaska's Richest Black,"
> *Ebony,* November 1969

Mrs. Swanson (I cannot find if she was actually a "Mrs.") is shown sitting in her $100,000 home on Goose Lake outside of downtown. She is reported to have been in semiretirement at the time. ("This year she bought a Cadillac Fleetwood so that 'when I want to go down to the grocery store I don't have to bother my friends,' " *Ebony* reported in 1969.)

*Color* magazine, back in 1953, had stated: "Easily Anchorage's 'First Lady' among Negroes and its pioneer citizen of the race is Mrs. Zula Swanson, who has been here longer than any other Negro. She does not claim to be the pioneer Alaskan . . . For many years she operated a hotel, and is one of the largest holders of real estate in the city."

Well, to talk turkey, as the old folk used to say, it appears to be common knowledge that land baron Zula Swanson did more than "operate a hotel." Everett Louis Overstreet, in his *Black on a Background of White,* uses a delightful euphemism: "As legend would have it a variety of services, in keeping with the Alaskan tradition, were available at the hotel."

Earlier, Overstreet refers to those services as "the oldest profession." It is no secret that prostitution did—and does still—flourish in Alaska. When Zula Swanson came to the territory, men outnumbered women 18.5 to 1. Black madams became famous. Black Kitty in Circle City. Black Alice in Nome. Black Mary in Ketchikan. Snake Hips Lil in Dawson City. While in Anchorage I had been told—strictly hearsay—that among Swanson's more well-heeled guests were numbered mayors and governors. What bothers me is that as amusing and ribald and colorful as the "legend" might be, the "official story" may be the truth. And the woman who for a time owned much of what is prime downtown Anchorage may well have made her fortune, not by pimping poor women on their backs, but legitimately as a hotel owner and real estate developer. But Zula Swanson was long dead in 1992, her home burned to the ground, and her fortune heirless and gone, so she could neither defend herself nor confirm conjectures.

But there is one claim I can explode: She was not the first black person to come to Alaska.

As early as 1868, when the U.S. Army arrived at the town of Sitka, 6 of the 391 people living there are recorded as being black. (Three were apparently from the West Indies, two were a married couple who worked aboard a ship, and the other was the servant of a local doctor.)

Even those of us who have read *Moby-Dick* often forget that black men were among the crews of whaling vessels that hunted in the Gulf of Alaska and the Bering Sea, and even the Arctic Ocean. "Colored fellows" are often mentioned in memoirs of the sea. Felix Terry was one man who worked on the *Thrasher* in 1897, and before that the *Grampus.*

Surely the most celebrated black man from those days (though many never knew him to be an African American) was the inspiration for Jack London's *Sea Wolf*—"Hell Roaring Mike," Captain Michael A. Healy, and his parrot, Polly. From 1880 to 1902, Healy commanded several cutters for the U.S. Revenue Service—the *Rush,* the *Bear,* the *Corwin,* the *McCulloch* and the *Thetis.* His job: to enforce the maritime laws and assist ships in trouble. His policing was often extended to land as well as sea, since much of the time he was the only official representative of the United States government in the region. He helped establish the Whaler's Refuge Station at Barrow in 1889, and aided Sheldon Jackson in transporting reindeer from Siberia to western Alaska in 1900.

Healy, the son of an Irish immigrant planter and his former slave, then wife, was from Georgia, and had been educated at the College of the Holy Cross, as had his older four brothers, who all became involved with the

Catholic Church—one, James, becoming Bishop of the Diocese of Portland, Maine.

Joseph Skerrett writes that Michael was "the ideal commander of the old school, bluff, prompt, fearless, just. He knows the Bering Sea, the Straits, and even the Arctic, as no other man knows them."

Gold was found in the Klondike in 1896, and literally thousands of folk made their way to the Yukon and Alaska to make their fabled fortunes. A good many were black. In the spring of 1897, St. John Atherton (you've got to love that name), a former slave from Atlanta, stumbled out of the Klondike with something in the neighborhood of $30,000 worth of gold. He went home.

To be sure, much of the history of black folk in Alaska is the stuff of operas and novels—adventure, sin, greed. But equally interesting, I find, are those hardworking folk who had to have thought themselves crazy when they experienced their first Alaskan winter in October. Folk like Bessie Couture who opened the Black and White Restaurant in Skagway in 1896; or the seven black men recorded as living in Nome in 1900; or Mattie "Tootsie" Crosby, who, in 1911, opened the "finest bathhouse in Alaska" in Flat; or John Cleveland who enrolled, in 1928, in the Alaska Agricultural College and School of Mines (now the University of Alaska) at College (now Fairbanks).

Indeed, black folks received patents for land grants as early as 1915. Yet another great misconception is that any African Americans living in Alaska today came with the Pipeline—the Trans-Alaska Pipeline, that great modern miracle of American enterprise and creator of Alaska's current-day wealth—800 miles long, $8 billion worth of pipe and terminals, carrying 1.8 million barrels of crude oil per day—the Pipeline. Of course, the truth is that just about everyone living in Alaska now came after the Pipeline. Its construction more than tripled Anchorage's population in ten years, expanding from 48,000 people in 1970 to 174,000 in 1980. And the state nearly doubled its population in twenty years. (Alaska remains second only to Nevada in annual population growth.)

All that said, it is important to note that during the preboom years, there were a goodly number of black folk in Alaska, many of them doing more than just getting by.

Blanche McSmith, who moved to Kodiak, Alaska, in 1949, was appointed to the state legislature in 1959, and she had helped organize the local NAACP in 1951. Fairbanks had a black assemblyman, Pete Aiken, in 1956. Summit, Alaska, had a black postmistress, Lois Nicholson, back in 1948. The first black church—Greater Friendship Baptist Church—

was established in 1952. The *Alaska Spotlight,* a black newspaper, was founded by George C. Anderson in 1953.—("RETURN FROM TRIP 'OUTSIDE': Mrs. Margie Hopkins and Sterling Bell returned this week after a short trip 'outside.' They visited, among other places, San Diego, Riverside, and Los Angeles, California, and report a wonderful trip. Mrs. Hopkins is offering some very attractive income property for sale. Mr. Bell will leave in a few days for Mt. McKinley Park where he will work for about a month."—May 23, 1953)

And on and on. The list is quite voluminous—but the message is quite clear: Black people have been in Alaska as long as white people, and they don't seem inclined to leave anytime soon.

In a black bookstore in the lower forty-eight, I happened upon a most curious document: *1992 African Americans in Alaska: Black Community Calendar/Booklet.* A four-color, glossy, handsomely produced affair incorporating a "Who's Who" of black Alaskans, and photographs: masons on snowmobiles; a veterinarian and a violinist on skis; realtors, architects, heavy machine operators; church congregations on a mountain; physical therapists on bicycles at Eagle River; oil industry workers; land management workers; artists with their art on display by a lagoon; children at play. Plus there were lists of churches, community services, photographers, auto repair shops, graphic designers, beauty salons and barbershops, clothing stores, restaurants. . . . I had yet to visit Alaska, but upon seeing this, I had no doubt I should go there. Moreover, with this dynamic array (neither Chinquapin nor North Carolina certainly had such a booklet), I expected to find some fierce folk.

Before I left I phoned up the calendar's makers.

Linda V. Pennywell described herself at the end of the calendar as: "Alaska Resident since she was 6 months old. Vice President of Abram Abraham Prod. & Mgmt., Specializing in Public Relations, she is also a Day Care Owner, a Licensed Barber, a Wife and Mother and she has 10 years of work experience in the Oil Industry (Computer Dept.)."

Her sister, Sheryl K. Bailey: "Born and raised in Alaska. Mother of 1. Employed as an Audio Visual Technician/Quality Control. President of Abram Abraham. Specializing in management. Aspiring to be an Alaskan Talent Scout for a Major Record Co . . . There's too much talent in Alaska going unrecognized. Alaska has a Gold Mine of Resources and Talents . . . and Alaska is way over due in getting recognition from the lower 48's!"

Her mother, Evelyn D. Bailey: "Our Support Analysis. Our #1 Proofer, currently on Hiatus. She is also a Licensed Cosmetologist and Business owner, Mother of 4 and Grandmother and Great Grandmother."

They invited me to come by.

The Bailey home was a large, squat, sturdy, dark, two-storey house with a large porch at the front. Mrs. Bailey ran her beauty parlor there. (Had I known before, I would have had my hair cut there.) It seemed a household accustomed to goings and comings. Here was a family in the larger, older sense, cousins from the lower states, nephews, grandkids, friends, old acquaintances.

The day I arrived Mrs. Bailey was getting a pedicure from a woman who worked there along with her. Watching her relax relaxed me. The Bailey matriarch had a penetrating look, and was quick with a deep wry laugh.

Evelyn Bailey told me: "I've been here since 1952. I have never encouraged anyone to come here, other than giving a family member a vacation. But I never encourage them to come here."

"Why is that?"

"Let me tell you something," she said. "You got to know what you got to do to make it up here. You can't sleep on the streets here. And as quiet as it's kept, Alaska has the highest educational curriculum in the United States. The parents that's up here have got to be strong, to raise children up here, and make sure they know how to stay out of trouble. That's what it's all about. Staying out of trouble."

Don't let anybody fool you, Mrs. Bailey told me, it was rough going for black folk in Alaska. "No blacks worked downtown in Anchorage until the late '60s." In 1957 Joseph M. Jackson had a picket outside Local 341 Laborers and Hod Carrier Union Hall, protesting their lack of African American and Native American members. Later there had been a boycott against Carrs Grocery chain, the largest in Alaska. "Only thing blacks could do at Carrs was janitorial work." She remembered a pimp named Lewis Lee who fed everyone who walked the picket line. "The only person who crossed the line was the man who owned the black newspaper."

By and by, Mrs. Bailey's two daughters, Sheryl and Linda, came by. Both were very like their mother, direct, energetic. Sheryl told me that the origins of the calendar had been pragmatic. They had been building a market for their future line of greeting cards. Sheryl and Linda showed me an unedited version of a film project undertaken by the Black Lifestyles Institute, "Black Pioneers," interviews with people living in the mid-1980s who had been in Alaska for decades.

Joe Jackson recalled that the major commercial street, Spenard Road, had once been known as Miracle Mile: "It was a miracle if you got through safe." He remembered when most people still had outhouses. Mr. Zelmer Lawrence said Alaska was a "runaway place"—a place people ran away to. His first trip to Alaska was in 1931, and the population was around 3,500 people. Only 400 people were at Elmendorf Air Force Base. Helen Gamble came with her husband in 1952; he had a construction contract; she worked for an ophthalmologist, Dr. Mylo Fritz—the only one in Anchorage at the time. Ben Humphries had been president of the Painter's Union. He came up through Ketchikan in the '40s and settled in Anchorage in 1951. He said most blacks who lived in Anchorage spent most of their time at the Rendezvous—a place owned by Miss Swanson ("Not 'Mrs.' Swanson"). He remembered a black man nicknamed "Bushjob Bennie" who lived and worked in Nome. In the early fifties, he said, blacks and Native Americans "would stand and stare at one another." He remembered that the first jazz he ever heard was at a place called the Conjure Hut, being played by Native American teenagers. Etheldra Davis had been the first black elementary school teacher and the first black principal in Alaska. She remembered it had been difficult to find a place to stay in the '50s. It took five years before she taught her first child. . . .

It went on: Osemae McCurry, the first black woman to work in the Anchorage post office (who lived in a tent when she first came in 1950); Richard Watts who owned a nightclub in 1949; Ethel Johnson who lived in Kodiak; Martha Ferry, Vannie Robeson—after a while I became overwhelmed, and to a degree overjoyed, and to a degree disoriented. At that moment, I could have been easily convinced that black folk in Alaska outnumbered the white folks.

Linda's daughter Jasimine sat and talked to me for a while.

"At the beginning there was like two or three people," Jasimine Pennywell told me, "and then a group of people just all of a sudden, over the summer. I went to that school in seventh and eighth grade. Seventh grade, there wasn't a lot of problems. It was just a school and everybody was having fun together, but then eighth grade came, and they came with shaved heads and combat boots. At first there was like two or three of them, then through the whole school year it just kept on, they were a real, real big group. And it was like always white against blacks, always. And wasn't but thirteen blacks in the school.

"At the last day of school, they had to have a police guard escort all the blacks out of the school. They had a bomb threat at our school. Skinheads came, and were waiting around for everybody to get on the bus. They had to escort them off the property, and then they were fighting with one of our security guards, a black guy. It just got to the point where you couldn't really do anything. You had to have someone with you at all times. If you were going to Service Junior High School, you were going to have an escort. You couldn't just walk, or do what you felt like doing. You always had to have someone with you."

RACISM
(Draft)

*by Jasimine Pennywell*

I am a student attending a highly prejudiced school system which has a majority Caucasian atmosphere.

I am an honor roll student of Hanshew Middle School. I am very disappointed and concerned by the racism that I deal with each and every day, here at my so called root of education.

For example the bathroom walls almost every day are covered here and there with "WHITE POWER" and white power symbols. With slogans such as "BLACKS ARE ONLY GOOD FOR BEING SLAVES" and "WHITES RULE OVER BLACKS."

As well as labeling the working water fountains "WHITES ONLY" and the non working fountain "BLACKS ONLY." It's extremely difficult to deal with.

There is an intense amount of stereotyping, as well as hatred floating in the minds and mouths of students and staff of the Hanshew and Service Anchorage School District. I know, by personal experience.

I feel that this is absolutely horrible that the wars that we as a minority (African Americans, Puerto Ricans, etc.) fought many years back have to be refought over and over as the days go by.

It's sad that people can't have their own opinions and approve and disapprove without discriminating others.

It's a shame that there is only two times in life that we as people with skin and culture differences are seen as equals. Those two important days are your first and last day of your life. For example, when you're born and you're in the nursery you're not seen as a white or a black baby. You're seen as beautiful babies. When you die you're not seen as a dead black or white man, you're just dead. . . .

BUT I REFUSE TO BE A PART OF THE PROBLEM! If all I can do is just put the problem in the eyes of the community and the faces of all its students, principals and staff. Then that is "exactly" what I'll do.

It may not stop during my school years, but one day with the help of the community and the Almighty God it will!

Because I am fighting for the respect that I have earned and deserve and most importantly the rights and education of my children. The children of others, African American and Caucasian, because one day we "Tomorrow's Dream" will be a part of "Yesterday's Work Force."

—May 1992

Copies of this piece were made and somehow got distributed throughout the school, among both faculty and students.

"That was just something I had written, just to be writing. I wrote it like in twenty minutes. My mom was talking about sending it to the editorial page of the paper. But it never seemed to get to the editorial staff. The principal came to tell me this, and everybody wanted to interview me, and say do this and do that and no, 'Don't take it to the paper, and we'll deal with the problem.' They didn't want it to get out. That was a rough draft copy. I never seemed to even get enough time to finish it. It caused a lot of problems. I just let someone read it in the school, and it just got passed around. Copies were made and this and that."

Jasimine began to collect odd bits of evidence of racism in the school: notes and posters and graffiti like "David Duke for President," the "White" and "Black" signs over the water fountain; "KKK" or "nigger" scrawled on a shoe. "So if they're going to say, 'No, it wasn't me. I didn't do that,' I have pictures of it. I'll take them down to a whole other level.

"So my piece never had support from anybody though, except for a lot of staff. They caused a lot of commotion. Like, 'Well, I just didn't know this was going on.' And they knew it was going on. Just didn't want to make an issue out of it. 'And you're just such a good student, and you're just so intelligent.' First I was Jasimine Pennywell, 'Oh, there she is.' Not, 'You're in trouble. Oh, what you done now?' But then, 'Oh, you're just such a good student. I just never knew. Oh, I just always knew that there's just something about you.' Well, this—crap. 'Oh, what can we do to help you? Anything you need, just come to me. I'm just there for you.' But I mean, a lot of things went on about it, because a lot of the people in Service came down, saying that they were supposed to beat me up because I was trying to ruin something. They purposely put me in the papers. It was Jasimine. Jasimine, Jasimine, Jasimine is a troublemaker. Everybody knows Jasimine. If they hear 'Jasimine' 'Oh, I know her.' But a lot of them don't know me, what I look like, who I am or nothing like that. There was eight of them at the 7-Eleven, down the street; purposely I get out, they were sitting by the phone booth. I had to use the phone. I just walked over to the phone, and called my house. Knowing wasn't nobody home. Hung up the phone, and they were all scattered right around me. They acted like they didn't even know I was there, and they were the ones supposed to come and beat me up. I was just standing there. Somebody said, 'Oh, I know her name.' They had a paper and they handed it to me. 'I think that girl Jasimine's in the paper here.' I said, 'Oh, I'm Jasimine.' And they all looked at each other, and they looked at me. I hung up the phone and looked around, looked up and down at them, and I left. They knew who I was. But if you don't show fear to them, which is what they want, if you don't show fear, what are they going to do? They're going to get intimidated like, 'Oh God. Gee, she must have a gun or she must know karate or something. She's not scared.' You know?"

I wondered if all Jasimine's experiences with school had been marked by such a strong sense of antagonism and alienation. But she told me that elementary school—she had gone to the Northern Lights Elementary School—had been "enriched." There, she told me, she found challenge and a certain joy in learning. She didn't think of school as being hard then, or of her white classmates as "different." She did remember one incident of mistreatment, but only later did she think it had anything to do with her being black. Otherwise, "I never knew me as being different. I knew black and I knew white, but we were all together. I noticed all these friends. Only people I hang with was a lot of black people. And my best friends in elementary school were black. But I don't ever remember a difference. But if I look back, I notice why a lot of things happened to me."

She remembered the very day the racial animosity began at Service, when a black Canadian professor addressed the school, and certain white students began to say, "'Why do blacks have their own Negro College Fund? Because they don't like to learn anyway,' and things like that. And that was the first time I ever had any racism problems. In elementary school, I went to school with a guy. Now he has 'KKK' on his shirt, on his shoes. He wears grease in his hair and braids it up. Just to make fun of people and do ignorant things. He'll come to school with black on his face, half black or something. He's totally prejudiced now. For no reason. It was just something that they thought was in. That's how they're supposed to act, so that's how they act. I guess it never really took me down and made me feel like, 'Oh, I'm less and I'm a nigger and I just can't get along so I'm going to give up without even trying.' I wasn't going to let that get me down. It's going to always be there. You can't change everybody's mind. That's not going to be a scar on my life or anything like that. It's just going to be a stepping stone."

I wondered whether or not, in the future, Jasimine would want to remain in Alaska.

"There's a lot of Alaska, but there's a lot of things that just haven't increased in Alaska. There's probably good things going on in the state, but I want to move from Alaska because it's too small. Anchorage is too small. Anchorage is just too small."

"Alaska is *too small?*" I laughed.

Yes, she said. "Anchorage is too small. Everyone knows everyone. Where's a person going to go? In other states—if you go to New York you can go to Brooklyn, you can go to Manhattan, you can go to Long Island. Everywhere. Where you going to go? Valdez, Ketchikan? Juneau? There's nowhere else to go. Everywhere else there is just more glacier. More glacier. Eskimos, Indians, whatever. No black people. If I'm in Brooklyn and I'm bored, I can go somewhere else—and there'll be black people there too.

"I'm going. You'll be somewhere. In Youngstown, and there's a concert in Cleveland, you get in a car, and you go to Cleveland. I know there's not going to be any concert in Juneau. Where am I going to go? I want to leave Alaska—too small.

"But I'm not running away from nothing. Everybody says, 'Oh, you got to be running away from the problem.' How can I? They're going to stereotype me anyway. So I mean, everywhere I go I have to prove myself. And that's why I want to leave Alaska, Anchorage, Alaska, period. I just want to go. I'm ready to go. I'm not running away from nothing. Wherever I go, I'm going to have to deal with it."

Jasimine was fourteen; I was curious to know how she would be thinking at twenty-four, thirty-four, forty-four.

. . .

Later I sat down with Jasimine's older brother. Eugene Heflin was eighteen, extremely fetching to look at, and possessed of that go-get-'em, upbeat, can-do spirit that is so outrageously, infectiously, unmistakably American.

Eugene was a salesman at Nordstrom's department store.

"I went to one school, Service. That's out in Hillside, where my mother lives. That's kind of like the upper class one, where most of the wealthier people in Anchorage live. A lot of rich white people there, like that. I had a bit of a problem there. I mean, people think that there's not a whole lot of prejudice here, in Alaska, but there is. I mean, it's just depending on what area and what class of people you're around. But I had a little bit of a problem there.

"Just mostly kind of like teasing and things like that. Petty things. Nothing really, really big or major. But it wasn't just with the kids. It went onto the teachers out there, the counselors. They had a real bad stereotype of black kids, because there were 40 black kids out of 2,500, and so they weren't real familiar with the way black kids are. You know, just in our differences and things like that. How we dress. How we talk. So they didn't like us too much. If we didn't do the things they liked, they didn't like that. We were our own. We hung around together. We sat at our own lunch table. We had a cafeteria with about forty tables. We could fit at one table. And we sat there—all black kids. Every day we sat there. We hung around this one hall together. And so we were real, real tight like that. I would say half were born in Alaska. You don't get too many people here that are really born in Alaska, I don't think. Not too many kids. Even in my generation.

"Before Service, I went to West. That's over in Turnigan. West was a lot better school. It's like a cultural melting pot, that we had. They got Koreans there, they had Filipinos there. They had some richer white kids, and they had some poorer white kids. Which made it a better environment to go to school in.

"I went to Service in the eleventh grade. And then I went back to West my twelfth grade year. So it was much better. I enjoyed my last year. But school up here is a lot, lot better than down in a lot of places that I visited. It's like a whole different mentality. The people down there don't think the way we do educationally. Because I went to Youngstown, Ohio, last summer, and I have cousins who graduated from high school, who can't read and write—and graduated.

"Here I think they're more ambitious, the parents are, because Alaska presents more opportunity, I think, than in the lower forty-eight. I'm eighteen years old, and I'm making over $20,000 a year. That's just simply selling clothes. One of my coworkers, she made over $40,000 last year. And all she does is sell men's shoes. Off commission. It presents a better opportunity, yet we have people here too that sell a lot of drugs. That's becoming huge here. Becoming a big problem. Each summer it gets worse. We started having a lot more shootings. We get a lot of kids shot—a lot of kids with guns. My experience is that you see a lot of black kids selling, and a lot of white kids using it. Not cocaine, but like marijuana, white kids up here. Marijuana up here is like cigarettes. Everybody smokes marijuana. You can't generalize 'everybody'—but marijuana is big up here, in my age group. And cocaine is getting bad up here. Crack is bad. You don't meet that many black kids that are out of school, eighteen, nineteen, twenty years old, that don't sell drugs up here. All the black kids that I come in contact with, like the guys that come and shop at my store. Nordstrom's is more expensive than most. It's the biggest department store in Alaska. And the only ones coming in there to spend are drug dealers. The only black kids that I sell to are drug dealers. And these kids are making a lot of money. But I don't see the point in it, because up here, they have opportunity. It's because it's the easiest. It's an easy way to make money. They don't need no education, they don't need no brains. All you need to know is how to count money. It's kind of ridiculous."

Moreover, there was simply not much going on in Alaska to interest black youth, Eugene thought. There were concerts for the white kids, and many of them could afford to fly "out country." Nonetheless, he also felt opportunities existed in the state if one looked hard enough, opportunities that didn't necessarily exist for young black folk in places like Ohio. Plus, he felt surrounded by a positive vibe. "You're in the land of opportunity here. I like it. But it's just that isolation. If you can't deal with that, don't come to Anchorage, Alaska. But if you like the wilderness, and you like it kind of peaceful like, you can have a simple life. Alaska's a good place."

Eugene told me he enjoyed going to places like Aleyeska and Seward. "You can just get out and drive. I don't really go out too far. I go to Eagle River. That's about fifteen minutes away. I fish. I've never been hunting before. We fish all summer, every summer. My father's a big fisherman. We go out in a big boat and catch sharks and all that. Got nothing but killer whales out here."

I wondered if Eugene had any contact now with the white kids he had gone to elementary school with.

"Hmm-mm. No. I see them now. But they kind of look at me a little bit different. We used to be tight, like best friends, every day, be over at my house. But now it's kind of like they'll say, 'Well, what you been up to, Eugene?' I'm not doing things with them, so they don't see what's up. They think because I went back my senior year to the school I originally went to that I had changed."

I wondered if many black kids became strongly identified with white kids in Anchorage: became black white kids.

"They did. I think up here it's bad. You're like in limbo. It's not like white kids run everything, but their parents run everything. If you don't kind of conform, it's hard. They make it harder on you. Like I was in these advanced placement classes, and it's like you get college credit. And I was just as smart as any of those kids in there, but the kids didn't want to give me an opportunity. The teacher didn't really want to give me an opportunity. You would think a teacher could see these kinds of problems, so then he could help his class deal with them. At Service, I had this AP teacher—the man was smart. He fascinated me. I didn't like those kids in the class. He'd say, 'Okay, partner up.' And they were all buddy-buddy. Then I'd always be like the last one, and if there was an odd person, then that was my partner. It was like that. I mean, you know, they never really said, 'Oh no, we don't want to be with you, Eugene.' But that frustrated me, man. I was always getting pushed out over there in that school, and that kind of made me upset.

"But the teacher really challenged me. I didn't do well. But I think I learned a lot. I think I learned a whole lot there at Service. A whole lot."

Eugene told me he still enjoyed reading, especially about black history, Malcolm X, and Muslims. "The Muslim religion was fascinating because it was neat to see a bunch of black people get together and think the same, and collaborate, and teach, and get smarter. I was fascinated by that, being in Alaska, because up here there's no black community. Black people live here, black people live there. Other side of town."

Eugene told me he loved a good challenge, and that, for him, simply being black was often a challenge. "White people challenge you. Challenge you day to day. They have an expectation of you. They have a stereotype of you. They just see us on TV as rappers and things like that. A big thing up here among black kids was the Californians. A lot of people are infatuated with California. Total opposite from Alaska. My little cousin Johnny, seventeen years old, infatuated with California. Anything from California is the best. If it's a rapper, if it's clothes, if it's anything. Gangsta mentality. Maybe because it seems so far away. I listen to it and everything, but I don't get caught up in it. They just want to live the life Ice Cube lives, and stuff like that. I think a lot of white people see that in black kids, and they don't really want to give them the opportunity up here. There's my point right there. They don't give you an opportunity unless you conform to what they're like. Like my little cousins call me 'White Boy,' but I got more than any of them. I've accomplished more. But I'm kind of like the 'white boy.' "

Why, I wondered, did they call him "white boy"? Because he wore a suit to work every day, drove a brand-new car, had nothing to do with drugs. "I'm not really out there. I used to be out there, but I'm not anymore. They call me 'the spoiled one.' Stuff like that. It's just hard, if you're different. I don't want to say that I've sold myself out at all. I don't date white girls. I date black girls. I don't hang around with white people. But I know how to deal with them on their level. I'm not going to lie. I'm not going to say, 'Well, white people don't do that for me.' They have done a lot for me. They financed my car. They gave me a job. I was the employee of the month in February. I'm only eighteen. I'm the youngest salesman in there. I was sixteen years old when I first worked here. They give me opportunity."

Earlier Eugene had referred to having been "out there." I wondered, for a black teenager in Anchorage, Alaska, what exactly constituted being "out there."

"Bunch of stuff. This was in high school. Stealing car stereos. I was carrying a knife in my pocket my senior year. My grades show it. Believe me. I had a brand new truck then. I had more clothes than any kid my age. I did a lot. I was kind of out there. But I'm doing better now. I'm not going to present myself as being real bad. I mean, it just happened to me in all of about four months."

"Was it through outside influence, or a decision you made?"

"I was trying for a while. It was like I had to prove to myself that I was black. Okay? I got sick of people calling me 'white boy' all the time. Even when I went back to West, I was still white-orientated, and I just got sick of that, man. I just had to prove that I was black. And a lot of the black kids were doing those kind of things. A lot of people didn't really, but the people that were teasing me were the ones that were out there selling drugs. And so I just got caught up with them. I started kind of slowly being around them more and more and more. And some close people came up from the lower forty-eight, and they were doing that, and they had been doing it down there. I got around a lot of bad things. That just proves the point that association brings about assimilation. Because I tell you, I was total opposite, the day before they came. This is just a year ago. But I wanted to be a part of something else."

The turning point in his thinking occurred "when I saw them cats, how they were living in the lower forty-eight. When I went down there, I kept seeing what I was trying to be earlier that summer, and I saw that was the reality of it. I said, 'No. That's not where I want to be. It doesn't make sense for me to be there. Alaska presents too much of an opportunity for me here.' Why should I act like I'm struggling when I'm not? I can understand somebody selling drugs because they have no other means. But why should I do that? I have other means. That's a waste of time. I just decided, 'No, I'm not going to do that.' My mom spent too much money and too much time for me to go to jail. I'm not going to be cellmates with my father. You know. Because my father's in jail."

For a moment I was taken aback: My own father had also been in prison, and it was something even a number of my closest friends didn't know. I never talk about it. Yet, due to the overwhelming number of black men in jail—for whatever reason—perforce there were multitudes upon multitudes of young black men like Eugene and me. All of a sudden, this country boy from the backwoods of North Carolina and this eager-beaver teen from Anchorage, had much more in common than being black: we were both spurred by the "sins of our fathers."

"Yeah. My dad's serving time. I see him once every summer for two days. He's in Terre Haute, Indiana. We write each other about twice a month. We talk about books. You can tell, I can talk. He can talk. He's an intelligent man. He's about to get his degree in English. He's from Ohio State. He does a correspondence through Ohio State, so he's like my inspiration. Sometimes I'll write him a letter and I'll be upset, and he can feel my anger, and he'll write me back a letter, and put some of my pages in there, cut them out, and just point arrows to them, and say, 'Now, what do you mean by this statement here? I don't understand that. Why are you doing this?' Picks my brain. We can have a conversation all day. That's cool. One day, when he'll be out, we'll be together. He's positive now. I think if nobody else has faith in him, I do. I don't even picture him doing bad things. People will say, 'Are you afraid that he might do drugs again?' No. I know he ain't going to do it. We think about starting our own business and stuff like that, and he's cool because he's like, 'Yeah I can understand. I could picture us doing that.' He'll say, 'Well, while I'm in here, you've got this much time to finish doing school.' So it's something to lead up to. 'I'm going to do that, dad, I'm going to meet you there.' You see?

I asked Eugene what he wanted to do in the future. He very promptly answered: "I'm going to be the richest black man in Alaska," and laughed though he was quite serious. "I don't want to be just rich. I don't just want to have a bunch of money in the bank. I want to start something for my grandkids. A family business. The whole family will be a part of it. I want to be like the Carrs and those other Alaskan families." Eugene felt that though he was good at math, and teachers and the like suggested he study engineering, he wanted to study something in business. His dream was to get an associate's degree from the University of Alaska, a bachelor's in accounting from Morehouse University, and an M.B.A. from either Harvard, Stanford or Yale. "And then come back to Alaska. That's what I want to do. But you never know, once you get started, man, all kind of things fall into place. I'm coming back to Alaska. I'm going to be the richest man in the state. I might be governor. This would be good. Improving some of the bad things."

Later he said to me: "What do I want to be? I want to be a role model. That's what I want to be. I don't want to be perfect. I want other black kids to see me and say, 'Man, I used to chill with you, Gene. Look at you now. And that cat's driving around in that Benz. Got a pocket full of money. Got him a nice house. He got a beautiful family. He goes to my church.' I want people to notice that. 'He's one of the biggest brothers in Alaska.' I want the other kids to see me, fourteen- and fifteen-year-old kids, when I'm twenty-eight. But you see what I'm saying? That would be kind of cool, you know."

Since he wanted to be a role model, I asked him who his role models were. At first he said none, and then, the more he thought, he listed his grandmother, his mother, his aunt, his Uncle Freddy, his football champion cousin. He said his father was his inspiration. He added Malcolm and Martin. Then he said: "I don't know. I don't really have too many role models."

"Well, you just named about fifty."

"I think that's why I'm going to make it. Because I got a family, man. I mean, it's the truth. I know I'm going to make it. I'm going to be—" at that moment Uncle Freddy walked in "—you think I'm going to be governor, Uncle Freddy?"

"I think you can be anything you set your mind to," said Uncle Freddy.

"I'll be Governor of Alaska."

"If that's where you want to be. If you want to be the governor, put yourself in the position."

"E. D. Heflin. Governor E. D. Heflin." Eugene laughed.

"Got to learn to be tough, firm, and to the point," his Uncle Freddy said. "Know where you're coming from. You got to stick to your word.

That's right. Don't let them trap you up in your wording. Man, if that word don't mean nothing, you don't mean nothing."

"You've got to be articulate," said Eugene. "Be able to get your point across. Let people know where you're talking from. I think I could be governor."

"Yes," said Uncle Freddy, "this is a young generation."

"You know, that's kind of funny, man," said Eugene in a moment of epiphany. "You know what? You might not even use me in your book. Whatever you do, but you might, you might save this and you might see me at the Democratic Convention. I'm going to be a Democratic governor. You might see me up there and you might remember me."

What a wonderful mental exercise, I thought, to visit the capitol in Juneau, and interview E. D. Heflin, governor of the great state of Alaska.

# IV

# OUR STILL-FRONTIER

NGUZO SABA
*(The Seven Principles)*

1. UMOJA (UNITY)
   To strive for and maintain unity in the family, community, nation and race
2. KUJICHAGULIA (SELF-DETERMINATION)
   To define ourselves, name ourselves, create for ourselves and speak for ourselves
3. UJIMA (COLLECTIVE WORK AND RESPONSIBILITY)
   To build and maintain our community together and make our brother's and sister's problems our problems and to solve them together
4. UJAMAA (COOPERATIVE ECONOMICS)
   To build and maintain our own stores, shops and other businesses and to profit from them together
5. NIA (PURPOSE)
   To make our collective vocation the building and developing of our community in order to restore our people to their traditional greatness
6. KUUMBA (CREATIVITY)
   To do always as much as we can, in the way we can, in order to leave our community more beautiful and beneficial than we inherited it
7. IMANI (FAITH)
   To believe with all our hearts in our people, our parents, our teachers, our leaders and the righteousness and victory of our struggle

—Maulana Karenga

Fourteen

# CITY ON THE EDGE OF FOREVER

*Seattle, Washington*

And the promise of Seattle for the transplant still recalls the dream that hurled covered wagons westward a century ago, the hope for a new start, a clean landscape, and escape from institutionalized ill will. All this may be illusion, the fantasy of a burnt-out Chicago boy still ensorcelled by the beauty of Mount Rainier, but I know one thing: we're going to stay.

—Charles Johnson, "A Kind of Promised Land," *Pacific Northwest*

Why do we remember the past, and not the future?

—Stephen J. Hawking, *A Brief History of Time*

There is a famous episode of *Star Trek*—considered by many to be a classic—in which Captain Kirk and Science Officer Spock must travel back to 1930s earth in a vain attempt to alter the future. They fail. The "device" they use to return to the past is a sentient door called the Guardian. That episode is called "The City on the Edge of Forever," and was originally aired in 1967. I did not know it when I first saw it, but that episode had been written by one of my favorite science fiction writers, the flinty and bizarrely imaginative Harlan Ellison, which made me glad. However, I did not know that the script in question had been the source of a feud between Ellison and the series' creator, Gene Roddenberry.

Apparently, what Roddenberry shot was not what Ellison wrote. Roddenberry died in 1991, and in 1996, Ellison published his original version of the script. In an introduction he writes:

> If it weren't for the money, for that overflowing *Star Trek* trough in which the pig-snouts are dipped every day, no one would give a rat's-ass if the truth about Roddenberry and the show got told. But if you follow the money, you see that river of gold flowing straight off the Paramount lot in boring sequel-series after clone-show, and you see the merchandisers and the franchisers and the publicists and the QVC hustlers and the bought critics . . . and you see the fan-magazine fanatics and the convention-throwers and the endless weary biographies and the huge pseudo-book franchise of useless *Star Trek* novels written by a great many writers who ought to take up flyspeck analysis instead of littering the bestseller lists with their poor excuses for creative effort (not to mention the few really excellent writers who ought to know better, but have gulled themselves into believing they're writing those awful turd-tomes out of adolescent affection for nothing nobler than a goddam *tv show,* when the truth is they're doing it for the money, they follow the money, just like all the other *Star Trek* barnacles attached to that lumbering behemoth); and you see the venal liars and adulterers and con-artists and charlatans and deluded fan-fools who have a vested interest in keeping *Star Trek* sailing along, and all the innocent but naive tv absorbers, and you figure, Ah what the hell, Ellison, let it go! Just forget about it! . . .
>
> . . . If you read all of this book, I have the faint and joyless hope that at last, after all this time, you will understand why I could not love that aired version, why I treasure the Writer's Guild award for the original version as that year's best episodic-dramatic teleplay, why I despise the mendacious fuckers who have twisted the story and retold it to the glory of someone who didn't deserve it, at the expense of a writer who worked his ass off to create something original, and why it was necessary—after thirty years—to expend almost 30,000 words in self-serving justification of being the only person on the face of the Earth who won't let Gene Roddenberry rest in peace.

I have great respect for Ellison and know he is right on the money. But as a "fan-fool," I am largely unrepentant. I often ask myself: Why? Why do I take so much pleasure in *Star Trek?* Moreover, during my travels, I encountered a great many other black males of my generation who were also Trekkies and Trekkers. Indeed, of all the detritus of pop culture, *Star Trek* seemed to occupy a strange and singular status. Why was this?

One of my closest friends at college, Richard Elias Wimberly III, a black man who, alas, died too young, was equally in *Star Trek*'s thrall. We spoke of it often, and when *Star Trek: The Next Generation* came along in the eighties, it was he who finally convinced me to watch the show. Mind you, my dear friend was in the top of his class at Chapel Hill, made the dean's list a number of times, graduated from Duke Divinity School, was an ordained minister, and was one of the most intelligent and beautiful souls I have ever encountered. But there were days when I could not get Richard to stop talking about *Star Trek.* Hours we spent talking about the plot developments, the characterizations, the ethical dilemmas—I think Richard found the ethical problems the most intriguing—boldly challenging in the beginning, but gingerly dealt with by the end of each show.

I speculated that the appeal might have something to do with *Star Trek*'s future world—a world free of disease, war, pettiness, sexism, and, for my black brothers in particular, racism. A fantasy world—beamed into our homes weekly—where those inescapable, annoying, infuriating slights and major injustices simply incurred due to the hue of our skins did not exist. A world where we could enjoy camaraderie and the wonders of the universe unsullied; a world—hell, a galaxy!—where freedom really did ring, in the cold vacuum of vast outer space.

My mother calls this pure escapism. Stuff and nonsense. But I beg to disagree. I think it is a bit more complex. I see it as ideological metaphor.

As a freshman at college, I had the great fortune to attend a lecture by the great African American historian Benjamin Quarles. I will never forget his talk. He argued that our African American forefathers and mothers had a particularly different view of the idea of America than that of the majority culture, that the words "freedom" and "liberty" were not viewed, among black folk in the eighteenth and nineteenth centuries, as currently attainable realities, but as something to attain in some imagined future. That Frederick Douglass and Sojourner Truth and Richard Allen were bullish not for the America that existed in 1863, or 1865 or 1890, but for an America in their minds. That, for the sons and daughters of slaves, "freedom" and "liberty" had on one level an apparent connotation, and on another level "the dream" and "land of promise" that was to be America in the future; it did not at that time exist—which was far from the beliefs and the rhetoric of white folk at the time.

"Hitch Your Wagon to a Star," Professor Quarles said, "was their motto." Indeed, what did they have to lose?

That other Ellison, Ralph, echoes this point of view in the epilogue to *Invisible Man,* when the narrator tries to parse out the meaning of the "principle," the idea of America:

> Did the man say "yes" because he knew that the principle was greater than the men, greater than the numbers and the vicious power and all the methods used to corrupt its name? Did he mean to affirm the principle, which they themselves had dreamed into being out of the chaos and darkness of the feudal past, and which they had violated and compromised to the point of absurdity even in their own corrupt minds? Or did he mean that we had to take the responsibility for all of it, for the men as well as the principle because no other fitted our needs? Not for the power or for vindication, but because we, with the given circumstances of our origin, could only thus find transcendence?

I saw the motion picture *Star Trek V: The Undiscovered Country* in Seattle, at a place named for York, the black servant of Lewis and Clark. (The subtitle of the movie comes from *Hamlet,* and the Danish prince was referring to death, which has absolutely little to do with this allegory about the end of the cold war.) Upon leaving the theater and thinking about the movie, I could not help thinking about how all these thoughts intersected, quite curiously, in Seattle.

> Time present and time past
> Are both perhaps present in time future,
> And time future contained in time past.
> —T. S. Eliot, "Burnt Norton"

Seattle. Seattle is a place defined in the American mind as a City on the Edge of Forever—as the American frontier knocks on the door of our own finitude. Think about it. Think about the ways in which Seattle's image burbles and froths in the American media imagination, from popular motion pictures like *Sleepless in Seattle* to popular television shows such as *Frasier* to tourist packets featuring green forests and coffee shops to the band Nirvana and the cultural phenomenon Grunge. For this is the American dilemma: from the very beginning, the concept of the "New

World," expansion and movement, westward movement, new-ward movement was at the center of our collective being. To be American is to not give up that infinite dream, that push for the next, the bigger, the better. We need a place where the frontier continues. And Seattle, wild and tame, simple and sophisticated, plain and complicated, remains fixed, like the New York of the famous *Star Trek* episode, in that constant state of yearning—regardless of the tawdry or quotidian reality of everyday Seattleans.

Not far from Seattle—relatively speaking—Lewis and Clark (and York) found the Pacific. Seattle is the hub of the economic Pacific Rim (though Vancouver is fast eclipsing it). Seattle rests amid Olympic timberlands and anomalous tropical forests. Seattle is home to Boeing—avatar of aerospace—and home of Microsoft—avatar of cyberspace. Without examining it, when we Americans imagine Seattle, we imagine our new frontier, both spatially and culturally. Where will we go? We are not really certain. But the idea remains: We will continue . . .

I have known a good many folk, over the years, who fled the East for Seattle. Some stayed. Many returned, disgruntled, disillusioned, vexed. Why?

First: Charles Johnson.

I was pleased and gratified that the novelist Charles Johnson took time off from his hectic schedule to have coffee with me at the campus of the University of Washington at Seattle, where he was a professor. Johnson was the author of several books of fiction; the last novel, *Middle Passage,* had recently won the National Book Award and had been a genuine national best-seller, and it was enjoying a cult status among young black men. I had always been fascinated by one of Johnson's creations, a tribe of African sorcerers, the Allmuseri, who kept showing up in different books.

When we discussed what I was doing, Johnson bewildered me for a moment when he said there was no way he could spend that much time on the road. It made me melancholy, thinking I really had not developed such a strong sense of attachment to any one place. Is that where home is? The place you don't want to leave?

Seattle was becoming more and more attractive to African American artists. Pulitzer prize–winning playwright August Wilson had moved there from St. Paul just a few years before, and it was home to renowned painter Jacob Lawrence whom I had wanted to interview. But, Johnson told me, there was one man it would be a sin to leave Seattle without meeting. Johnson described the man as a latter-day griot.

James W. Washington, Jr., had begun as a painter, and moved on to stone—he was often lauded as one of the very few living sculptors who worked directly with stone, no models, no casts. His work had been exhibited literally all over the world, and had been purchased by the National Gallery. He had lectured at major universities in the States and Europe and Asia, had been awarded numerous honorary doctorates and awards (one was named after him), and recently had been included in the Smithsonian's Oral History Project. In a catalogue of his work, *The Spirit in the Stone: The Visionary Art of James W. Washington, Jr.,* Paul J. Karlstrom writes:

> James W. Washington, Jr., falls somewhere in that engaging zone between schooled and self-taught, between sophisticated and naive. His painting and sculptures betray, despite his deprecation of technique as an end in itself, too great an awareness of formal and pictorial concerns to qualify entirely as the results of intuition, inspiration, or fortuitous accident.

His forms look like ur-things, demi-things, urges and totems, solid and abstract; they conjure the ethos of Africa and the Pacific Northwest and the American South—at times they look like long-buried relics of some ancient civilization, alien yet somehow touchingly familiar. One of my favorites of his pieces, *Obelisk with Phoenix and Esoteric Symbols of Nature,* which was completed in 1982, and now rests at the Seattle Sheraton Hotel and Towers, conjures up Egypt, with its etched symbols, arabic numerals and letters, hieroglyphics, ankhs, yet its phoenix at the top is almost enigmatic—the way it seems to emerge from the stone, fluid and captured, totemic and sacred.

The day I visited Mr. Washington at his home in the Central District, he seemed a contradiction: quick, full of energy, restless; yet spiritual and inward-looking, as if he'd discovered secrets to life and work years ago, but had to keep busy because time was a-wasting and he had miles to go before he slept.

Mr. Washington had recently had a corneal eye transplant, and his eyes were sensitive. We had to turn out a light so it wouldn't pain him. He was still recuperating, he told me. He could see colors, and "if I close my eye, I can see that picture over there. I can't see all the details yet."

Originally James Washington had been from Gloucester, Mississippi. In the '40s he had been in charge of the army's orthopedic department in Little Rock, Arkansas, "making adjustments according to the doctor's prescriptions." During World War II, when he came up for the draft, some of the brass colluded to give him a choice of exempt civil service jobs, and he was intrigued by a position in marine wiring. ("I'd done house wiring.") He was sent to Bremerton, Washington, as a journeyman.

Back in Little Rock, Arkansas, he had been a scoutmaster, and a group in Seattle approached him to become one there. At first he commuted, but after a spell, bought a home in Seattle. He had lived there ever since.

"We didn't have many black people residing here, but we had migrants that came from California looking for jobs. Like I did. It was only a few old-timers here when we came."

For years Mr. Washington had advocated the use of art, of culture, to educate, to smooth and connect people: "We had a pastor at the church up there at Mount Zion, which I'm a member of. I told him that I thought that we could solve some of the problems between blacks and whites. I thought we should have an art exhibition, since art is a kind of a catalyst. It is. And then it's the cream of all cultures. I thought if we had an art exhibition there, consisting of some of the main artists of Seattle, white and black, whatever, whoever qualified, that we would get the white element, who was out in the fringe, get them into the exhibition and our people could meet them, and they would become acquainted, and find out they're not too bad after all. So we did that. That was in the late '40s. First, to start it off, I borrowed paintings from the Little Gallery. And after that, I set up this invitational committee consisting of some of the professors at the University of Washington and we talked about different artists, and they sent out invitations to those artists, who were black and white. And then I had some of the art professors of the University of Washington to come out and speak. Then the director of the Seattle Art Museum, I had them out. We had a social before the exhibition. I had such artists as Mark Tobey, who's one of the best-respected artists in the world. And Morris Graves and Kenneth Callahan. The curator at the Seattle Art Museum, he said the caliber of this show that I was putting on was second only to the museum shows. And we had a wonderful time. Some of the blacks didn't take to it. The whites took to it more.

"So one Sunday, the minister let me announce that we were having this show, and that I would have some of the leading people of the city there.

And some of these blacks who were officers, they came round that afternoon, and peeked in the window, to see whether anything was going on around. They saw me and a professor of art at the university, hanging the paintings. And they had a clipping, I saw them, I could look through the window, and they looked at the clipping, and then they dropped it at their feet. I waited till they went off, and I went there and got it. And when six o'clock came, and those people began to pour in there with those big cars and long dresses and everything, and these officers, they were all peeping again. So they had to run home, get them some clothes to put on and come back. I say, 'These guys are stupid.' It's just too bad they're stupid. Several of them are dead now. One who died, he told me later on, he say, 'You know, Washington, I know they underestimated you.' I could have told him, I say, 'You was one of them.' But I wouldn't tell him.

"So I had to rely on the people who are inclined to consider culture. For instance I give you an example. Down at Vicksburg, I was painting a scene. A church scene on the streets one morning. Got up early. Church scene. It was a photogenic think-view and everything. I was out there painting, and here come some black guys, in a garbage truck. The wind was blowing. He was saying it to the fellows as he passed within 200 feet of me. 'What he think he doing?' You see what I mean? 'What he think he doing?' Then they'd giggle. I said, 'These guys are something.'

"But I was able to make some kind of an achievement under those conditions. It was a white who was able to help me in Mississippi. You see what I mean? That was during the Depression, and one day I was there at home, and two white ladies drove up and they wanted to see me. I was rooming, and they wanted to see me. They'd heard about me, and they wanted to see some of my work, and wanted me to bring a couple of paintings out to them in the car. And they were very impressed and they wanted me to work with them. So that was the beginning. The leading white artists knew me, and they would want me to help them with their exhibitions. And I would be around with them some, but it was against the law for me to show. See what I mean? It was against the law. They admired me for my work, the paintings, but they couldn't let me show. And they wanted me to help them put up the paintings."

I wondered how he got interested in art and learned and strived in such a discouraging environment.

"That doesn't mean nothing to me. But here's the thing about it: Most all of my life, I've been concerned, that we—each individual—is potentially somebody. Black or white. Potentially somebody. Now what gives you the potential of being an ideal individual? What is that something? It must be in you. If it's in you, then you search for that, and bring it out, regardless of what somebody else says. That was my plan. It's a sustaining force. I see a piece of paper on the ground, and I say, 'Well, if I turn that over, there might be a word on there that I can learn that I won't never have a chance to see again.' I turn and look at it to see if there's anything new or anything I can learn, see. So that's the way I had to advance under adverse circumstances. That's what it amounts to.

"You have to learn how to do that, and it's no problem. When things seem to be a problem, by your attitude and frame of mind, it automatically provides a solution, and when a solution is present, a problem can't stick around. The problems vanish, just like night. Just like when the room is dark and you bring the light in. Then the darkness must vanish. You offer solutions, and not worry about the problems."

I assumed the environment he found in Washington State to be more accommodating.

"Yeah, this is much better. Even though, there again, it wasn't much better with the blacks, but much better with the whites. See what I mean? Wasn't much better with the blacks because when I first came here, I was over in the navy yards, and I told another black man that I was going to have an exhibition over in Seattle. And he had showed me some of his work, and I told him if he'd get some things together, we could go ahead jointly and have an exhibition. And he never did get nothing more together. He had three or four pieces. Wouldn't get nothing. Some people are lazy or reluctant."

He told me that after his first show in Seattle—a two-man show with the artist Leo Kelly—the show was reviewed in the local paper, and "the paper say that I was a genius. So about a week after that I received a letter from a black preacher, and he said that he saw the write-up and it said I'm a genius. He say, 'All geniuses are from Satan.' I still have the letter. And he said, if I would join with him, he'd make me somebody. It's just ridiculous. The average black, he thinks the white man is his enemy. The church leader is more of your enemy than the white man. Because they keep you ignorant about your real potential and who you are. In order for them to rule over you. Not all of them, but a lot of them, too many of them. It's a sickness.

"By being superintendent at my church, it was necessary that I would attend an outing for the children, at a retreat. And I was supposed to address the children and young people. And I got up and told them that each one had great potential, that God had give them talent, and to find it and develop it. And the head preacher got up and he said, 'Mr.

Washington's wrong.' He said, 'That's not so.' This preacher had brought a guest who was a white person. And the white fellow got up right behind him and said, 'Mr. Washington's right.'

"I go to church," Mr. Washington told me. "But I go for a different reason. When I was a little boy of about ten, I had a saying, a little poem, that they'd asked me to come to church and recite. It's all about that same thing. The poem went:

> Some people go to church just for a walk.
> Some go there to laugh and talk.
> Some go there for an observation,
> Some go there for speculation.
> Some go there a time to spend,
> Some go there to meet their friend.
> Some go there to doze and nod
> And few for the Will of God.

"What should they go for? To help them find themselves is one of the things that is not being taught. 'How do I rate? How do I rate to this concept you're talking? How do I synchronize with the cosmos?' I never hear that very often."

I found Mr. Washington's philosophy enticing, as if he had found some mysterious truth. I wanted to know more. He had mentioned earlier that "you have to find yourself."

"Maybe I'm asking a naive question," I said, "but how does one go about finding oneself?"

"Well, this is the thing—it should be taught in school. In fact, it should be known at home. Inasmuch as each one of us has an abundance of innate ability, we have talents that boil down within us, and instead of schools trying to have you read so many pages, work so many problems, they should be instrumental in helping you find yourself. And you find yourself with this inner search. Unless they know it, unless their teachers know how it's done. Even to the extent of knowing whether you have one, two or three talents, they should be able to pick out the best one you have and make you cognizant of that. Not just them knowing. You understand? The one you pick out then, you pursue it and then you can reach your zenith. No doubt whatsoever. No failing, no nothing. You pick out the strongest one, something with which you can express your ideals, and it can teach you. You can excel. You can be an individual beyond the other.

So this is not known by a lot of people, surprisingly. In fact, I have spoken at the University of Washington, quite a few times. And one time I spoke, I said to the teachers, 'I perceive that many of you are laboring under the wrong assumption. First thing I found out is that in many instances, the teacher-pupil relationship is equivalent to the blind leading the blind. You seem to be laboring under the assumption that you have something they need. You think they came out here to get something from you. I submit to you that you have nothing they need. They didn't come out here to get anything from you. They came out here—whether you know it or not, or whether they know it or not—for you to help them find themselves. Unless you have found yourself, you cannot help them find themselves.' " James Washington told me he instructed everyone to go home and "scrutinize your curriculum." That the process was merely, "issuing it to the pupils, until they digest it, and you recommend them for a degree." "If you put the degree on the wall, and read it from top to bottom, all it says is, 'I'm certified.' Or, in other words, 'meal ticket.' That's all it means. I'm concerned about when you and your pupils become qualified. Not just certified.

"When I did my first sculpture, a bust for Philadelphia, six historical figures, I hadn't done any busts or anything. I got a book on art by some teacher back east, and I looked at the book and this guy was talking and telling the pupil, this here, and that, and it was illustrated plus the information. The first thing he said, 'No sculptor is going directly to the stone now.' He said he couldn't find one. He said they first go to plaster of Paris and then they make the plaster cast. I didn't want that. I didn't want that. I went inside. Created a spiritual environment—I did go to a photograph of King for a checkup on the anatomy. The proportion. And that was it."

I wondered if people asked James Washington about his visual inspirations.

"Those who are receptive to it, that have the audacity."

"Why is that audacious?"

"Normally, when you discuss things like that you have to rely on the feedback. You can give a little out, but if you give a lot out, the average individual really wouldn't comprehend it. So you don't want to flood them with something that's too involved. They say, 'Oh that guy's crazy, or something.' I made the same transition from painting to sculpting, so much so, that until after I made the transition, I prayed that I'd be uplifted in the art. That's all I ask. And I made the transition, I could look at a stone and tell its possibilities, spiritual possibilities. And I can take any stone, and in a few hours, I can have it ready for the museum. I'd have it mentally ready for the museum. I can tell its possibilities in a few minutes. But still it takes time."

"Hence the title? *The Spirit in the Stone*?"

"That's it. It's moving forces. I say they interexchange. Even though this member is between them. In our language we have to use a word that will be equivalent to osmosis. That's as close as I can get. I say, it's done by osmosis. I become saturated with it and as I feel my sculpture, that feeling is injected into my sculpture or painting. This is what the artist will do who is equipped or sensitive to it. The artist might choose his subject, he might also choose his palette. He might also choose his approach as far as modern or conventional style. But in the final analysis, in order to make it, to put it into high art, after you've done all of that, he must bring his inner self into it and let it live. And not until then will the subject move itself aright. Because the universality of art is life itself."

Despite what people say, I found everything about physical Seattle to be at once ugly and otherworldly. A warren of buildings, improbably built on a sloping slope from sea to hill, a city tilted and rising; held fast by concrete and steel and glass.

I was there a week before Christmas, and the quintessential ambiance of American commercialism, nostalgia and Yuletide romance peppered the very air:

Amazing scene on Madison Street. Once you come off I-5 between 6th Avenue and 5th Avenue, you can see straight down this immensely steep incline; into the great cavern of towers and huge buildings all the way to the bay, the ships on the lake, across to the other side. It's Christmastime here about, and lights are blinking: Starbuck's Coffee, Dilettante's Collection, Union Square Plaza, the library; mingled architecture, old and new, all the way down to the Alaskan Way. U.S. Bank; Sea First. Over and down to Pioneer Square, First Avenue becomes First Street, crossing Yessler, a huge totem pole in the middle of the street, Magic Mouse toys, Steam Bath South End: Rooms 75@ (don't know what that means either), Cowchip Cookies, Seattle Sport, Washington Street, the Old Butnik Manufacturing Company (don't ask me what they manufacture), Outerwear, Paul Bunyan, the Mission and Elliott Bay: and there's old what's-his-name on the street, smoking a cigarette. Pretty shops adorned for Christmas trade: evergreens about their windows in the Golden Horn Rug Shop, in Edward S. Curtis Vintage Photographs, in Seattle Quilt

Company, in International Interiors, Christmas trees are blinking; Reed's . . .

In the midst of it all is the Mission, down near Alaskan Way and Pioneer Square. The night before, when I had come by, folk were lined up around the Mission to get in, I don't know if they were getting in to eat, or to find clothing or shelter or what, but they were in full force.

For many years I have kicked around the idea for a play based on an odd meeting between Nobel prize–winning novelist Sinclair Lewis and noted sociologist Horace Cayton, Jr. In Lewis's novel about "the race problem," *Knightsblood Royal,* the young black scholar's work is mentioned. Deeply flattered, Cayton wrote to Lewis, in thanks, and received in turn an invitation to the famous writer's estate, Throvale Farm in Connecticut. When Cayton arrived, he found a paranoid, embittered old man, largely forgotten and alone, save for a retinue of black servants.

Cayton writes about his stay with Lewis in his autobiography, *Long Old Road,* and the account is all the more fascinating for the way it puts front and center the class tensions among black folk. He, the solidly middle-class black guest, being waited on, and treated as if he were "white" by the black folk; he, more than they, fixedly aware of the irony and the truths embodied in that long weekend, so unapparent to the lauded laureate.

Horace Roscoe Cayton, Sr., had come to Seattle sometime in the 1880s. He had been born in 1859, the son of a slave-master's daughter and a slave who, after emancipation, would go on to own his former owner's plantation in Clairborne County, Mississippi. After attending Alcorn College, Horace spent time in Kansas and Utah before coming to Washington State. Horace Junior's mother, Susie Revels, came in 1896. She was the fourth daughter of the first black senator in the United States, Mississippi's Hiram Revels (he had filled the seat formerly occupied by Jefferson Davis), also the president of Alcorn College.

Cayton worked for a while as a reporter for the Seattle *Post–Intelligencer,* but his ambition was to publish his own newspaper. He took over an existing black paper, *The Standard,* but apparently his editorials were so revolutionary, so vitriolic, that the black community itself had him removed. Undaunted, Cayton founded the *Republican* in 1894, which he published as a weekly for twenty-one years, with Susie as his associate editor. The pair were quite the firebrands. Both staunch Republicans, pro–civil rights, they were active not only in local politics, but Horace also served as a delegate for the 1898 Republican Convention, and he was secretary of the Washington State Editorial Association. At least twice Horace Senior was arrested for libel. At one point he punched a white man full in the face. (A black barber who declined to serve African Americans was called "puke of the lowest ilk.") Once he accused the chief of police of graft, and was subsequently taken bodily from his home, locked up without bail and was not allowed to talk even to a lawyer. He was never convicted.

Eventually the paper had to fold—his largely white advertisers became afraid to be associated with a newspaper willing to write a series of articles denouncing the Ku Klux Klan.

Without a doubt, the fiery Caytons set the tone for much of Esther Hall Mumford's 1980 *Seattle's Black Victorians, 1852–1901,* which is probably the best account of African Americans in the Northwest. (I spoke with Mrs. Mumford by phone, but for whatever reason, she declined to be interviewed.) And though the Caytons were certainly stars, they were but a bright pair in the firmament of black Seattle's history.

Imagine this isolated, outrageous, hilly, sailor-teeming, horsey town at the edge of North America's burgeoning democracy in the middle of the 1800s. Europeans had only first encountered the territory that would eventually become Washington State as late as 1788. (Interestingly enough, when Captain Robert Gray first brought his *Lady Washington* into the vicinity that year, he had a black crewman, Marcus Lopez, from Cape Verde, on board.)

Of course, when Thomas Jefferson said to Meriwether Lewis and William Clark, "Go west," the redoubtable York was among their thirty-man party. A lot of speculation surrounds York, both during and after his tenure as chief translator and man Friday for the journey. Some have written that he had as many as five Native American wives. Some write that he returned with the party to Missouri in 1805, and was given his freedom in 1806. There is even speculation that he actually returned to the West, where he got along well with the Native Americans. Some say he remained a slave until his death.

Then there was George Bush, a Pennsylvania freedman, who, in 1844, at fifty years of age, committed his wife and five children to the grueling trip along the Oregon Trail with 800 fellow pioneers. The seven-month journey took them to the Dalles in Oregon at the mouth of the Columbia River, only to find that the provisional Oregon government had just passed laws making that territory as inhospitable to black folk as that recently departed in Missouri. In response, Bush and a number of other settlers moved north of the Columbia and homesteaded there. Because blacks were not "citizens," Bush had to use a white man, Michael T. Simmons, to buy the land. The area became known as Bush Prairie (later Thurston County), and it was the first land settled by nonnatives of what would become the state of Washington.

Bush became known as a first-rate farmer, and even had a ship, the *Orbit,* built for $30,000, which he used to transport timber to California. His eldest son, William Owen, was also a successful farmer, so much so that he exhibited his produce back east at the Philadelphia Exposition during the Centennial. In 1889 he was elected to the first Washington State Legislature.

Similar to the accomplishments of Bush was the work of George Washington, who founded Centralia, Washington.

Probably the first black person to settle in Seattle was Manual Lopes, African by birth, who made his way west probably by ship—or at least he is the only black man of about 300 people listed in the 1860 census. But by 1880, the official population had grown to twenty-two people of African descent. With the completion of the railroad to Puget Sound, in 1883, Seattle's population began to increase rapidly, and among its numbers were black folk, though the numbers were never huge.

In fact, in ten years the city's population almost doubled: 44,748 in 1890; 80,671 in 1900—making Seattle the forty-eighth largest city in America. (Certainly the Klondike gold rush helped to boost Seattle's size and importance. Thereafter, it became the point of departure for travel to British Columbia and Alaska—a connection that remains.) The "black Victorians" worked on ships, on the railroad, as stewards, cooks, bootblacks, and in the burgeoning sawmills—by 1900 there were over forty mills in the Seattle area. There were 406 black people listed as living in Seattle that year, a number that grew to over 2,000 in ten years. But it was in the Second World War decade that the black population would burgeon from 3,700 in 1940 to 15,000 in 1950. By the eighties, there were close to 50,000 African Americans living in Seattle proper, 10 percent of its 500,000 people.

Another early and amazing Seattle personage was William "Big Bill the Cook" Grosse. At 6'4" tall, and weighing over 400 pounds, he came to Seattle in 1860, after serving in the navy and traveling the world, and participating in the earlier California gold rush. He helped form the western end of the Underground Railroad—and opened a restaurant and inn, in 1876, called Our House. In 1883 he built a three-storey hotel on the wharf, and bought twelve acres from Henry Yesler in what is now the

Central District for $1,000 in gold—in 1891 he was reported to have had assets of over $250,000. Grosse became the center of black middle-class Seattle, sponsoring a Grand Ball, and all-black productions of Shakespeare. When he sold one of his restaurants, and it burned down shortly afterwards, he refunded the money to its distraught owners.

Beacon Hill, Capitol Hill, Greenlake—in truth African Americans in the nineteenth century lived all over developing Seattle. By the turn of the century, the Madison section, aways from downtown, seemed to hold the biggest concentration. And despite what many folk kept telling me, about how the Central District or the central area was no longer, or never had been, the center of the black community, the fact remains that the southeastern and central areas are home to over 70 percent of African Americans who live in Seattle. And like any place in America where more than ten black folk live, the stereotypical expectations of unemployment and too many young black men loom, and the Central District, indeed, has a reputation among the general populace and the media as being somewhat tough, and drug- and crime-ridden. But to anyone east of the Mississippi who has actually witnessed a tough, unsafe and drug- and crime-ridden community, one wonders who's joking.

In 1990, Seattle elected its first black mayor, Norm Rice. By the 1980s, two of the nine city council members were black, "and 1,007 of 9,277 city employees are black. Blacks account for 10.4 percent of officials and administrators," said the Seattle *Times*. There were black professionals aplenty and black business owners were enjoying the fruits of the economic miracle of the Queen City of the Pacific Northwest.

But looking through a broader lens, one easily sees that Seattle—that city of our future—was in fact mirroring the rest of America: black unemployment was in the double digits, less than 4 percent of the Boeing workforce was black (let's not even ask about Microsoft); one year in the 1980s, fewer than 20 percent of Seattle's black high school students had grade point averages of C+ or better—compared to 70 percent for Asians and 54 percent for whites . . .

In short: same mess, different city.

Looking at the ostensible failures led me first into depression—in truth I had been sinking, sinking, for months now—for I had great hopes for Seattle: I wanted the hype to be true. Was there one city in America that defied trends, lived up to its promise? The chances were looking slim. Yet, upon reflection, looking at the entire landscape of time present, and time past, and time future, I told myself to have a little more faith. Were things really as bad as they had been for Horace and Susie Cayton? William Grosse? George Bush? Manual Lopes? York? I think not.

> There is a streak of defiant utopianism in the American imagination, and nowhere is it more boldly on display than in the belief, held in the very teeth of experience, that somewhere in this nation—just over the horizon, across the mountains, or down the interstate—lies the ideal city. Philadelphia was going to be heaven on earth, once. So was Los Angeles, when the Joad family packed their bags and headed west. So were St. Louis and Miami and Carson City, Nevada, and all those numberless little places with names like Harmony, Eureka, and Eden that time has boiled down to a defunct stoplight and an abandoned gas station. The country is littered, coast to coast, with dream cities that either came to nothing or came to something so monstrous that their names are now pronounced like those of Sodom and Gomorrah.
>
> Yet the dreamers go on dreaming and packing their bags. Ten years ago or thereabouts, a rumor started to go the rounds. In Cleveland, Ohio, and suburban New Jersey it was said (breathe it not abroad) that a civic utopia had just been discovered at the far western end of Interstate 90. There, life was sweet and green as in no other city, went the rumor. So, the bags were packed, the U-Haul trailers loaded; and the utopian pilgrims hit the road to Seattle.
>
> —Jonathan Raban, "America's Most Private City," 1991

At the base of Yesler Way, down off Pioneer Square, is one of the most impressive bookstores in the country—the Elliott Bay Book Company. Remarkable not so much because of its size—though it is quite large, like two old department stores—but because of its intelligently crammed shelves, filled with what seems to be every book in print. In this era of superstores, it is a treat to actually be able to find a place that has what you're looking for. Seattle is a book town.

Downstairs, along with a cafe, there is a good-sized reading room, and in that room, on December 12, 1991, I attended a meeting of the African

American Writers' Alliance. A good number of folk turned out that night, probably over thirty. Some wore dreadlocks, some sported kente cloth, and though my eye was caught by some funky color combinations, on the whole, they seemed like just plain folk. I noticed a fellow, waiting for the readings to begin, engrossed in a copy of *Hip Hop* magazine—I don't know why that latched into my consciousness, but it did. After a spell, individuals took the podium and commenced to regale us with their poetry and stories.

The first woman to read told us she had been in Washington since 1969. She read a story about a woman and the making of Turkish rugs—poignant and insightful—a story called "Ain't I'm Living." Michael Hureaux read his poems, "The Eternal Pack Rat" and "Let Me Hear"—a satirical, bitter, biting, vitriolic sermon using Hannah Barbera characters, especially Yogi Bear and the Flintstones, delivered with much verve and energy, and an ode to President George Bush—both comical and condemnatory. Gretchen Matilda read "Lioness and the Gazelle"—poems that ranged from lyrical animals to meditations on drug addiction; Charles Mudeda read about being broke in Seattle and watching folk in Pioneer Square—a comic and existential story; Randi Edens read from her play on abortion—monologues from women—and poems; Ed Holmes, (who had a fondness for rhyme) read "The Fight before Christmas." We heard from Demita Brown, and Chris Ware, who was dressed in desert camouflage—"Would You Speak to Me?" Ruby Daris read a poem on death and then one on love, "Straighten Them Out." Nagesta Abebe read a poem about the Middle Passage among others, and Bernard Harris ended the evening with an honest and tender love song to his newborn daughter.

I was roundly impressed. Never before in my travels, theretofore, had I encountered such a wellspring of creativity and eloquence and literary productivity in the form of a black writers' group. In fact, it reminded me of a literary church. Afterwards, I spoke with a number of the members—office workers, workers at Boeing, software companies, the social security office, bus drivers and writers. They told me how important the group was to them; how, despite the general atmosphere of artistry and poetry among the coffee shops and university milieu of Seattle, among like people—other black folk—they found not only an audience that could grasp the context out of which they wrote, but also one that did not require translation or defense. Regardless of the variousness of their backgrounds, there, nonetheless, they found common ground.

. . .

I got along famously with Rick Simonson, one of the managers of Elliott Bay, and his wife, Barbara Thomas, the painter. Rick was white; Barbara was African American, and a native of Seattle. They took me to a superlative Vietnamese restaurant, and then to their home for coffee, and I saw reproductions of Barbara's work, powerful, angular dreamscapes, awash with animals (especially chickens) and clouds and water. Thomas's work is sometimes twinned with that of Jacob Lawrence's and she admits to some influence—the approach to the human figure has a similar distorted and geometric sharpness—but her work seems to me less depictive and more involved with signs and symbols. Barbara was quoted in a brochure about her work as saying:

> I am obsessed with the mystery of relationships. In that obsession I am constantly watching myself and my fellow human beings to see how we deal with that mystery. The mystery, of course, is "what is it we are supposed to be doing here?" Or "how do we create that reason?" How we deal with those issues, both as individuals and as a group, are the essential elements, in my opinion, in the foundation which ultimately holds us together and links us as human beings.

Seeing the naked, interweaving, intertwined, and at times surreal figures in her paintings, it is easy to see that mystery loom.

We also discussed that city, Seattle, and they tried to help me get some grasp on understanding a little bit of what it was like to live there. Seattle was a very shuttered town, Barbara told me. Perhaps the reason it was difficult to find a black community, in the human sense, had to do with the fact that Seattle itself mitigated against community. She agreed with Jonathan Raban when he called it "America's Most Private City." This was a place of individualism. In fact, that's why many people had ventured here—to revel in their individuality.

How very American, I thought.

As fate (or is it faith?) would have it, on the day I arrived in Seattle, I happened upon an article in the Seattle *Times*' "Living with AIDS" section, the headline, "Black Churches, Community Need to Assist AIDS Programs." The article, by Robert O'Boyle, began:

> You couldn't tell Jeff Henderson's resume from the application of a candidate for a young executive at SeaFirst or the promotional material for a future politician.
>
> His papers, his presence, his speech and appearance glow with ambition and confidence. He looks good, sounds good and knows his stuff.
>
> In many ways, Henderson is not unlike many young people climbing the ladder. He joined all the right clubs, became an active volunteer, kept pushing ahead and liked to party.
>
> If you're a young, up-and-coming urban professional, you'll see a lot of yourself in Jeff Henderson.
>
> But Henderson, 33, is different. And the differences matter a lot now that he's fighting for his life. He's African American, bisexual and has been an intravenous drug user.
>
> I wanted to tell his story because he paints a different color on the face of AIDS. And, at the same time, he breaks all the stereotypes.

Boyle goes on to note most of the black folk who suffered from the disease were still practically invisible. "And when blacks or drug abusers happen to be gay or bisexual, they seem to be written off completely." He pointed out how that group deserved more attention as they "bear the highest risk of contracting and spreading HIV. . . and they are the people least likely to get critical education and health care." The writer pointed to Henderson as an exemplar for having taken a role as activist and spokesman and counselor, saying, "It's not easy to get the message of safe sex through to a drug addict. And news of HIV may only drive a drug user to further abuse."

Henderson also had strong words for "the black community" and for "black churches." Going as far as to say that they might even be blamed for the situation. "The churches are the most powerful institutions in the black community, but they are the most conservative. They are not supportive of gays."

"People are afraid of us," the article ends, quoting Jeff Henderson. "So we stay quiet."

To me, Jeff Henderson had an almost talismanic aura: at medium height, he cut a dashing figure, with pecan skin and jet black eyes—he charmed with his smile. Forthright, easygoing, articulate, crisp of mind, all the facts at his command—overwhelmingly so—and, just as he could be forceful, he could also be suddenly contemplative, loudly still, in that manner of people who at some point witness a great calamity, and are steeled by it, made to ponder larger things.

I visited Jeff in an apartment he shared with a friend in the Central District of Seattle. We got on well right off the bat; but at times, it seemed that Jeff was reminded of his role, of his mission, of his life, and would go into "activist mode," delivering preachments and statistics, stating the need for awareness and more health care, more money, more research.

At the time there was a lot of rhetoric in the air about AIDS awareness and education—front-page stories in *Time* and *Newsweek;* spotlights on news shows—and Jeff saw himself as a chief rhetorician for that cause, a message that still needs constant telling.

Jeff's odyssey began in Tacoma, Washington, where he was born while his father was stationed there, a command sergeant in the army. There were four brothers and three sisters. His father had been originally from D.C., and his mother from New York. His early memories of Tacoma were not all pleasant. "Real small place. Ours was one of the first black families to move into that area of suburban Tacoma. My father had to get permission from the base commander and local realtors to buy the house he got."

"I got along fairly well with folks. It wasn't until like I was in the sixth grade when I first experienced somebody calling me 'nigger.' You know? It wasn't until then that I started becoming race conscious. So it took a while, I guess, for me. Then, having to come from Tacoma, moving to D.C., that was a real culture shock for me, being around so many black folks. But I enjoyed it. It was a good feeling. It was a good feeling to be around so many different kinds of folks like me. People who were running things. People who were cleaning up the building."

Jeff had dropped out of high school at seventeen. In Tacoma, he had joined the National Guard, and had been going to Officer Candidate School. When he moved to D.C. he dropped out of OCS, and he was told if he wanted to rejoin, he'd have to start all over again, so he did six years in the army reserves. Also, while in Tacoma, he had been working with the Urban League's Youth Employment Center ("Stuff like CETA programs"). He wrote his first grant proposal for the center at seventeen. The grant was awarded, but Jeff was not available to take charge of the money. "I had an episode with LSD. I OD'd. I was in a coma for maybe three days. They thought I was brain-dead. I had other personal issues that I was dealing with. As in growing up, you know? Related to drugs and parents, and those kinds of things. Just growing-up kind of issues.

"I had gone to D.C. on an internship with a group called the Institute for Economic Development. And I basically felt like a kid in a candy store, because there was so much there for me to learn, to comprehend. I learned as much as I could. I had some hard teachers, but they were patient, and willing to spread the knowledge." He stayed with the Institute for four years, running a program with sixteen sites across the country—rural programs, housing programs, youth employment training programs—collecting data, visiting the sites, making the reports. He got involved "domestically" with a woman in Washington, a relationship that lasted for about a year. He worked in student loans and with housing and community development.

"That takes me up until '85. Eighty-five was when I got my HIV diagnosis. Things changed. I resigned my job. I came out here. I stayed for maybe three, four months. Just to get a base back, and some spiritual issues solved, and to get grounded. I went back, and I did some work with a community organization. From there, I was hired back at the Institute for Economic Development. That was '87. Took me into a period of homelessness; I was living in Richmond, Virginia, on the streets. How did I find myself on the street? I wasn't working; I was kind of just traveling and hanging out. I'd stopped in Richmond. I went through a drug treatment program there, and that kind of stabilized me a little bit. I didn't have people enabling me or assisting me through the process. I thought I'd do the things that I needed to do for myself, rather than for anybody else. I really didn't know people in Richmond, so it was just somewhere I could go and do what I needed to do. But I had to do it on my own. I stayed in Richmond maybe a year. I worked there. I did some work in the libraries. I worked for a student loan office there. I finished up in Richmond and went back to D.C., and had a relapse. D.C. wasn't the best place to be. I returned here in October of '89.

"The most important thing in my mind, at least, from the perspective of my own experience, before you can deal with HIV or AIDS, you need to deal with drugs."

That understanding came hard, he told me, and gave a rueful laugh. "It came *real* hard."

At one point, a counselor told him suicide might be a good idea. I asked if Jeff had considering murdering the man.

"It was kind of a flippant remark. 'If I had it, I'd do it.' A lot of people trained in chemical dependency aren't necessarily trained in dealing with HIV or AIDS, because one of the things that happens is your perspectives change. Your perspectives change on your life and how you're living it, and what you're doing. There are peaks and valleys in that, where some days you can just feel like, 'Fuck it, I'm dying,' or 'I'm alive today so I'm going to do everything that I can, or I want to do,' you know? It gives you a different perspective on life, and how you're living it."

Jeff took me for a spin around a very different Seattle than the one found on tourist maps and in guidebooks: not to say that it is an underground Seattle, but closer to a shadow Seattle, a Seattle easily missed, and intentionally ignored by visitors and residents alike.

We stopped at a needle exchange program in downtown Seattle, in what looked like a former dime store and had the feel of a thrift shop, with folk of all ages and hues and nationalities milling about. There I met JW, who described himself to me as a former drug dealer, originally from L.A., who had gone to UCLA. A powerful-looking fellow with a natural charisma, he could have been a former football player; his manner was at once jocund, avuncular and streetwise—speaking with him held a conspiratorial air. To my stretching credulity, he told me he had actually been recruited into drug trafficking by a dean at UCLA.

JW told me he had come to Seattle in 1983. "Profit potential" is what lured him there. But he wound up in the hospital by 1985: he had "crashed" on cocaine and heroin. Dealing drugs, he told me, was shamefully easy, and was so lucrative that it was difficult to make a case to smart, young black men not to get involved. He even knew of crack houses on federal land—land held up in bureaucratic red tape—"it's like a veritable invitation." Yes, he told me, there is excitement and fun and gobs of money and the exhilaration of being outside the law dealing in drugs, but there is also a sort of deprivation, a profound sense of emptiness—which is why so many dealers finally turn to their own product. And though he did not use the phrase, the idea of selling one's soul came to my mind. "People who get busted almost want to get busted," he told me.

Now JW was clean and on the board of several organizations, black and Latino adolescent treatment centers, and programs like this one, SOS: all centered on drugs and alcohol. He had dedicated himself to outreach work.

Jeff Henderson next took me to the offices of POCAAN—the People of Color Against AIDS Network—a multiethnic group set up in response to how some felt the larger, white-run AIDS advocacy organizations were not meeting the needs of people of color. "It sets us apart," Charles

Wilson, who ran the program, told me. "People of color primarily—it makes us unique." The organization's goals were to find funds for people, and to do outreach. It also networked heavily with other AIDS organizations to keep channels of communication and information open to all.

Charles was originally from New Orleans, and his father was in the military, so he described his growing up as going back and forth from the North to the South.

While Jeff and I spoke with Charles, one of the caseworkers, Kevin, also joined us. He had left New York to go to Rutgers University, and had been on the police force and had a "bad experience there," he told me. He had been in Seattle for four years.

Charles had been talking about the nature of black folk in Seattle. "There is a black community; in conscience, but not physically.

Kevin: "There is a strong black community here, though. It took a while to find. Seattle is like a big experiment. There are so many mixed people. It's really confusing."

Charles: "A community exists, but in terms of conscience."

Kevin: "Yeah, there are a lot of wanna-bes."

"And there are some who can look in a mirror and not see black," Jeff added.

Charles: "We're not a monolith. We're still a very diverse group—a subculture within a subculture."

Kevin: "There is a lack of an intelligentsia. Mayor Rice is just a good house boy."

Charles: "I understand that the media controls the city. Norm Rice was elected even with a small black population. But sometimes you can't be everyman."

Kevin: "Norm is always studying his way through things but he's not there yet."

Charles: "It's important that we are represented. I always hope that people will come through in the end. I always have that hope as long as there are people like us."

Kevin: "He's going to get up there and be a super–white man and suck up to people."

Charles: "We have a dichotomy. I have a lot to be thankful for for being in the position to help. If I came from the Panther era, I would have been violent, man. I feel that pain is still around. I have had a hard time becoming accustomed to mixed racial liaisons. I can't forget Emmet Till. White people in this country have benefited from slavery, racism. There's still a debt to be paid. So I'm for any black—even those who turn around.

I can't be against them. I just hope we can do something for our people. We can't just give up on them. We have to embrace them. We have to educate and support them."

Next Jeff took me to a group home for men with AIDS, where I met the ebullient and singular Holiday. He had once worked as a hairstylist, and was getting more and more involved with AIDS support work. This was the second home he had managed. Gravel-voiced, bearded, dark, and with a wry, down-home southern sensibility, he seemed to know where we both were coming from (and going, for that matter) upon first shaking hands. We sat on an enclosed porch for a spell, and he told me about his life and work.

He had done his growing up in Texas and Oklahoma and Louisiana. "New Orleans. Could never let me say Nawlins. It always was New Orleeens. Or it always is New Orleeens."

I asked him how he was holding up, living so closely, day in and day out, with this pandemic. "It's very difficult. I'm the oldest of six children; I'm from a very close family: my grandma told me I was gay when I was thirteen. And one of my brothers, I guess he's my favorite, we all have our favorites, he is so concerned about the fact that I work with AIDS patients, HIV positive individuals, because his first thought was that you're going to run into somebody that has super-AIDS, and you're gonna get super-AIDS. You're going to shake their hand, and you're gonna get it.

"That's why we need to educate people. You can't get it from kissing, you can't get it from eating after someone. You can't get it from drinking after someone. And it's very important that people understand, because, I mean, you're more at risk to get a common cold, which is what I have right now.

"This epidemic has been around a long time. To this day, since 1986, I have lost eighteen brothers. Some of them found out the day they were going to die. A lot of us knew each other from the church that we went to, and it's absolutely amazingly disgusting how African American heterosexuals behave. Just like run across the street, when they know that somebody is HIV positive or has AIDS. It really incenses me, because for all intents and purposes, we are all human beings. And whatever I do between the sheets, I still need to eat, and I need water, and I need a few dollars in my pocket, and I got to use the bathroom. What I'm very, very happy about is that Caucasians—I can't speak for everybody—have tried to help. You know? I mean, they've given up their money; they've given up their time. I have no money, all I can give anybody is my love and my support, and I have spent nights in bed with men that have had full-blown AIDS, not knowing whether they were going to be alive when we woke up the next day, and I'm in bed with them, or on the couch or sitting on the floor, only to let them know that I'm there for them."

I spent the balance of the day with Jeff, and after our little tour we talked some more. During my travels I found that I connected with people more and more easily—probably because I had been away from friends and family for months by this time, and latched onto emotional connection where I could find it. To be sure, asking someone to tell me about their life and their beliefs led to a certain intimacy. Whether or not that is superficial, I am not certain, even now. But speaking with Jeff I felt that sense of quiet intimacy, perhaps because he himself had no time for superficiality any longer. He shot from the hip.

"There's a lot of days where just the struggle of living becomes a lot. When I eat, I take maybe seven different pills, about three times a day. And it bothers me. You don't want to do that all the time, you don't want to remember to take your pills if you're going to go out and eat, you know? Or just simple things like, when you have issues of diarrhea, or you had an accident. Both are times, well, if I have to wear Depends, do they come in designer colors?"—he laughed—"Those kinds of things come up and when all the people you know are in and out of the hospital, dealing with that, that's hard."

Jeff had told me that he'd just gotten to the point where he could sleep. I wondered how he held it all together, psychologically, spiritually.

"I like to eat, drink and be merry," he grinned. "But even doing that, you have to watch for the obsessiveness, it suppresses the immune system. And nobody wants to wake up with a hangover, with your lymph nodes swollen, and you're in pain, and tired, and have a hangover on top of it. So I've learned some things about moderation. Moderation. It's a new word in my vocabulary. But I'm working on implementing it."

Aside from his volunteer work, Jeff was also involved in a support group ranging from six to twelve men. They would meet for a few hours and "get deep." "That's helpful. To do something informal without having to go into politics and explanations. The important thing is that you need to listen. So that there's some understanding." He told me that most of the men were originally from other parts of the country.

His family remained important to Jeff, which was one of the overriding reasons for his return to Seattle. Initially, he was more than a little worried about revealing his health problems, and the possibility of being rejected occurred to him. "It ran through my mind. You know: no more family. But I knew my family would be supportive. I just believed there's a risk that you take when you disclose your status. A risk that I took, based on the belief that the people that I disclosed to would use that information, and not against me, and not for me to get sympathy from anybody, but just to let them know where I'm at. Because I can be a riot sometimes, and that's part of the reality. And when you deal with any potentially fatal disease, you're going to go through some changes inside. But for the most part, people have been supportive, and I think that's because of the level of knowledge that people have now. A lot of the people who work in the field are friends of mine, that's helpful too. There are times when I felt really, really bad, and people have just been able to round up the rough wagons and put them around me so that I got through what I had to go through in my mental status. I've been able to do the same thing for others, especially with the group. I've had people who just came to hold my hand, for like a weekend until I could get through something. And I've done the same for a lot of others within the African American community. That's something I know I can draw upon when I need it, and that's helpful to me. It gives me a lot in terms of emotional support. It's not necessarily what happened to you that week, you know? But it's about what's happening now, with things. I can go to the phone and call up and say come over, I'm crying, I'm feeling really bad or, you know, fuck it, I just don't care. And there gets to be times like that in our lives. I'm thankful that I have this circle of people around me, that are as supportive as they are. For me it's a miracle that I'm alive. You know, I've been through the shoot-outs, the drug crises—I should have been dead. But I'm still here, so I believe there's a purpose with me being here. I've had real good friends who've died of drugs or drug-related causes, from AIDS. Why am I still here? I believe there's something for me to do, some kind of message to get across. There's a reason God has me here, you know? I believe that."

He told me he was in a relationship now, with a woman in Seattle. That relationship also became a source of support. "One of the things that was important was that I could never imagine, when I was nineteen, not having sex, like every day. I used to think, 'Gosh, if anything happened to this thing, I'd shoot myself in the head.' Because I was that much into it. But then having gone without it, and then with the reality of AIDS in my life, the impact on me, I had the education. Using condoms was not so nice. But my behavior hadn't changed. And it wasn't until I got in a relationship with somebody who said, 'Yes, I love you, but you *will* really use one of those things.' And through the practice of doing that, that became reinforced, and today I can say that everything that I'm doing is safe. It took some growth to get to that point, you know? Because I really felt like, 'No way. I'll shoot myself in the head. No way.' So it took a lot to change. It took a lot to change."

And also there was Gabriel Victoria Henderson, his then four-year-old daughter, back in D.C., with whom he spoke regularly on the phone. "Gabriel. 'As god, as strength, victorious.' She is the number one. And getting older, quicker. Awful quick."

Try though I might, I could not exorcise Jeff from my mind for the rest of my journey, which went beyond the traveling. His toughness, his mirth, his pain, so close to the surface, so vulnerable—all of which he clung to—haunted me; his ability to make meaning out of absurdity, and purpose out of existential void inspired me. Even I, the eternal romantic, could put no gloss and patina on so concrete a situation. Sentimentality seemed gross and thin in such harsh light.

In many ways, this voyage had taken me away from my own reality: a reality of funerals, of so many young men vanished and gone; away from New York and Washington and Chapel Hill and those I knew and know who must face an all-too-similar absurdity and void. Yet Jeff was in his here-and-now, as were the kind few who helped and the many who suffered. I think I felt lucky, a feeling which led to guilt; but I certainly know that I felt an enduring chill and wanted to feel warm. We all do.

Time future in time past. Time past in time future. Hitch your wagon to a star. To go where no one has gone before. Remember the future. What a work of art is man. It is our mortality that makes us. Surely Horace Cayton, one of my new quixotic heroes, had known these things, and very surely Jeff Henderson, one of my new flesh-and-blood heroes, knew this now. Perhaps it was that very knowledge that spurred on that former slave to come out to Seattle and attempt to make it into something Mississippi could never be. Perhaps he glared into the future and summoned up such formidable rage to keep him going for all those years. Perhaps the seeming futility, the apparent absurdity, the existential maw of his battle kept him focussed—he was not tilting at windmills, he was tilting at life. So was Jeffery Henderson, Cayton's descendant in this now and future time.

A wise friend once told me: It's not about hope; it's about faith.

As I left Seattle, over and over in my mind the words of Marianne Moore's poem "What Are Years?" played and replayed, and to this day, for some strange reason, remain the only true sense I can make out of this new and encroaching pall over us all:

> What is our innocence,
> what is our guilt? All are
> naked, none is safe. And whence
> is courage: the unanswered question,
> the resolute doubt,—
> dumbly calling, deafly listening—that
> in misfortune, even death,
> encourages others
> and in its defeat, stirs
>
> the soul to be strong? He
> sees deep and is glad, who
> accedes to mortality
> and in his imprisonment rises
> upon himself as
> the sea in a chasm, struggling to be
> free and unable to be,
> in its surrendering
> finds its continuing.
>
> So he who strongly feels,
> behaves. The very bird,
> grown taller as he sings, steels
> his form straight up. Though he is captive,
> his mighty singing
> says, satisfaction is a lowly
> thing, how pure a thing is joy.
> This is mortality,
> this is eternity.

Fifteen

# THE THERE THERE

## Or, Let the Work I've Done Speak for Me

*San Francisco, Oakland, Los Angeles and Allensworth, California*

I found I had an embarrassment of riches in the Bay Area: a goodly number of friends. Perhaps it is in keeping with the character of our most populous state that it is home, largely, to people from elsewhere.

There was my friend Larry Manning, whom I had known in college. A black fellow from Shelby, North Carolina, who had found a job in Oakland with the Social Security Department, he seemed to have had no trouble in making it home. He showed me all around downtown Oakland—that perplexing, ungraspable city that inspired the infamous comment about a lack of there-ness. Art galleries full of black and African art, and shops and parks, and a soul food restaurant whose owners I met, folk from Texas. He took me to a mall thronged with black teenagers—which, after months so far north, took me a little aback—suddenly I was in a true hub of black America again. Did it look different to me now? Did I look at it differently? Larry seemed to be prosperous and happy in Oakland. Here was a small-town southerner who had successfully made the transition to the big West, yet he carried a little bit of Shelby around with him.

There was Nina Harris, a friend from my New York publishing days. Hers was a different story. Drop-dead gorgeous, ferociously independent, unhappy in love, with a lacerating sense of humor (and a hilarious mimic), Nina did not possess the gene to suppress exactly what she thought, and was without the least bit of guile. Her world had been New York City and later Scarsdale and then Providence, Rhode Island, where she attended Brown. She had been in San Francisco less than a year, and it didn't fool her one bit, she told me. Just like everything else, she saw right through it. We spent the balance of a day together, and she let loose with all her grievances and disappointments with the Bay Area. Top of the list: Compared to New York, she found most people she met dreadfully dull. Life was slow, and the city was cold and wet, even in summer. Oh, there were some good things. I asked her to name one. She looked at me and laughed. Nina returned to New York a few months later.

And there were the Irvins.

Back in Maine, I had spent a night at Camp Armageddon, the summer home of my friend Nell Painter. In summers past, when I had visited her there, I had the great pleasure of meeting her parents, Frank and Dona Irvin. They were kind enough to let me stay in their home, high in the Oakland hills, for the few days I was in Oakland.

Like their daughter, they were both exceptional people. Mr. Irvin was a retired chemist who had taught at the university, and, in his seventies, was a marathon runner. He kept his head shaved clean, and he had the physique and energy of a man more than half his age. In fact, my first memory of him in Maine was seeing him chop wood. Mrs. Irvin had not long finished her first book, *The Unsung Heart of Black America: A Middle-Class Church at Mid Century,* about the Downs Memorial United Methodist Church, which would be published that summer by University of Missouri Press, and was at work on a memoir of her current years, tentatively titled *Dona Turns 70*. She was a dark vision of loveliness, sporting a silvery Afro, always elegant in dress as she was in speech—measured, thoughtful.

Their home was a reflection of their personalities and their experiences, a modern split-level, comfortable and large, each room filled with original works by African and African American artists. The Irvins had been collecting long before certain painters were in vogue, and now, as a result of their genuine enthusiasm, they possessed some important treasures. Of course, they never spoke of the art they owned in a commercial sense—it was always about the work itself, appreciation, joy.

Each morning the Irvins got up at about 4 a.m., drove to a local wooded area, and walked as the sun rose over the horizon. They invited me to join them, but I begged off due to the hour, feeling too feeble to match these two forces of nature; but I now regret it, wondering after the lost opportunity to hear their meditations as the sky waxed light.

The Irvins were always interested in nutrition and cuisine, and I delighted in some of their new dishes, many influenced by Nell's new forage into macrobiotics; some influenced by what they had learned from East African cooking during their stay there; some from motherwit.

The Irvins were originally from Houston, Texas, and came to Oakland at the beginning of World War II, Mrs. Irvin told me. "For two reasons. We did not, never did, like the racial situation in Texas, with all its restrictions; and then, there was all this war industry here. Recruiters were coming in Texas, getting laborers to come to California with promises of much more money than we were able to make where we were."

She told me the story of her coming to Oakland. Mr. Irvin had gone ahead, and when he had arranged housing for his wife and two children, he sent for them. "So we took the train and that was an arduous ride. From Houston to Oakland. Because at that time, of course, the trains were not as nice for one thing. Then they were segregated. And also crowded because it was wartime. I remember one very nice serviceman, black serviceman, gave us his seat. Here I was a young mother with a ten-week-old infant, and a four-and-a-half-year-old child. He gave me his seat, and he went and spent his time in the vestibule between the cars, because there were no other seats. Everything was crowded. So that was my entrance to California. And one incident that stays in my mind, on that trip. I had not had any thought of personal, friendly relations with whites before that, but on this trip, there was this very nice, friendly white woman, who had young children, just about the age of mine. She and I talked throughout the trip, and I thought she was very friendly. But it was a surprise to me, and an insult, a personal insult—when we got to Oakland, she left the train and didn't even say goodbye. I don't know. I think about it often, even after all these years. What caused that? Was it that she was so happy to see her family, and it had nothing to do with me as a black person? Or was it that here, 'I'm off the train, therefore this relationship of me as a white person with you as a black person, that's over.' But anyway, it was over. And it made an impression on me because to me it was a symbol of this new, racial freedom, that I could have a friendship with a white woman, based on our common interest of having young children, with what I thought was no racial interference."

The Irvins found Oakland different, better. The schools were not segregated, "but I can't say unqualifiedly better. Because there were subtle things. You could go into some places to eat, but the service may have been a little slower. Or the waiter or waitress might have been a little surly. And you never quite knew whether that was because of race or what. We were uncertain of the rules." Certain restaurants had signs in the window, saying, "We reserve the right to refuse service to anyone"; "we quickly found out that that meant black people. Even though it didn't say it. We learned that.

"But overall it was freer and easier. For one thing, we didn't have to sit on the back of the buses. Went to stores. You could try on hats, or clothes or dresses or anything you wanted to. And that was mostly forbidden in Houston. So, overall, the racial situation was better."

In the 1990s, Oakland had become a large, and a very complicated city. High in its hills lived a large and affluent white community; down in the valley, Oakland's large black population was marked, here and there, by a good deal of poverty and urban problems; and between the two was an extremely wide and varied middle class. All these worlds seemed to coexist, and yet they seemed as separate, to use the Booker T. Washington metaphor, as the fingers of the hand.

When the Irvins first came to California they lived in West Oakland. ("Which at that time was just about the only place black people lived.") They first went to Beth Eden Church, a Baptist church there. After they moved out of West Oakland, they stopped attending church for a while, until the early 1950s, when they found Downs, the church and the community that were the subject of her new book. "Nell was growing into a young girl. By that time our son had died. Just after his fifth birthday. Frank was working at UC Berkeley by that time, and he was getting more self-assured. We had made a niche here for ourselves in Oakland, had started putting down roots. We really became involved in the life of that church." The church offered youth programs, and Nell seemed to enjoy participating. They remained with the church until the early sixties. (They were now members of the Church of Religious Science.) But Dona Irvin felt compelled by the memories of the church, not simply as a place of worship, but as a social vehicle. In many ways it was a phenomenon and a dynamic of the black community. She spent years researching the founding of the church, and the members, and wrote a study, part history, part investigation, part memoir, about the institution as an agent in people's lives.

One of the reasons they had broken their ties with the Downs Church is that they went to Africa.

The Irvins had been watching the struggle for African independence with great interest. Through the university, Mr. Irvin had befriended a number of African students. "We really wanted to go." In 1962, Mr. Irvin was offered a position at the University of Ghana at Accra. Kwame Nkrumah was president then; the country was "on the move"; the infrastructure was being overhauled. ("One of my memories is standing on the street in Accra and waving my white handkerchief when Kwame Nkrumah was driven by in his big Mercedes. His flag on the front of the car. Oh, he was such a distinctive looking man. Very, very articulate.")

"But upon our arrival, we experienced cultural shock. We had read about Ghana. We'd read about Africa. We had talked to Ghanian students. We felt we were well prepared. But we were not. It was much different. We arrived after midnight, so we couldn't see anything. They took us right to the hotel, and they told us they would come and get us the next day to take us sightseeing. That was the worst thing they could have done. We saw things that we were not prepared for. People didn't tell us about the lepers. Friendly beggars who had withered limbs. People who were very, very lame. We were not prepared to see the communal waterspout where people would come with buckets to get their water. Young kids. We were not prepared to see barefoot people. Now it is true that Accra is, and even at that time was, a very large city. Had a lot of good things, but there were sections where the poor live. And that's where they took us. They shouldn't have taken us that first day. They should have eased us into that, you know. I went home and cried."

But she quickly righted herself—out of sheer necessity. She had to learn where and how to shop in the open-air markets, and how to deal with the periodic shortages. "We had what they call a steward. Some people call them houseboys. But I could never use that term. We preferred to call them stewards. His name was Adongo. He was from the northern part of Ghana. Could not read or write. A very sweet man. Became very fond of us, and did anything he could for us. He would walk from where he lived in another part of Accra to our house. We had to teach him, you wash your hands when you come in, before you wash the dishes. And of course we worked with him. His duties were to wash the dishes, clean the house. I did all the cooking. Some people had servants to do everything. But I wanted to do the cooking. Frank likes walking sticks. And he had a very beautiful walking stick that had been made for him by an African from Nigeria, very, very beautiful, and ebony. But Adongo took this walking stick back home on one of his vacation trips, and had medicine, religious-type medicine to protect us, put in that walking stick, and then had it covered up. Had it covered with leather. That was a very loving gesture. For years after that, anytime we went away, we carried that stick with us. If we went on an automobile journey, Frank would put it in the trunk. If we went on an airplane, we'd take it. For a long time, we enjoyed the protection of that stick. We still love the memories of what that stick meant to us."

The Irvins studied Ga, the local language spoken mostly by people in Accra, though they never fully mastered it. "I used to wear a Ghanian dress all the time. Now, the Ghanian dress was in three pieces. There was a skirt that was just a long piece of cloth, I guess about five yards wide. And you wrapped that around. It didn't have zippers or anything. And that's one piece. The second was a waist. But the distinctive thing about it was that it had a peplum that extended about five or six inches. This peplum could be pleated or it could be gathered, or it could be just straight. The third piece was a stole. Again, it was five yards just like the skirt. But you would fold it and usually the women would wear it just straight over the shoulder. And if it was cool at night, then you'd use it as a wrap. I had some very beautiful dresses. I can't wear them now because that was in the '60s, and even putting on five pounds makes a difference. But I loved wearing Ghanian dresses. And if I would go somewhere, nobody knew that I wasn't Ghanian, unless I spoke."

As we talked, memories of her time in Africa flooded her ("Oh, you're bringing back so many memories!"), of Independence Day spectacles, the physical carriage of the men and women, of concerts and dances and music and the people.

"We would very often hear at night, Saturday night, the drumming, which meant that somebody was having a party and they would be outside dancing and perhaps drinking, and just having a good time. One night we were in bed, and we heard this drumming, and it got to us, so we said, 'We'll just get in the car and go find that drumming.' So we did. We followed the sound, with our car. And we came upon a clearing somewhere. Ghanians had a fire, to give light. And they were just having a swell time. They welcomed us and offered us some of their drink. And we accepted it. And they invited us to dance, and we did. In those situations, you don't depend on a partner. If you want to dance, you just get up and dance. If you have a woman friend, if a man has a man friend, the two of you just go and join the dance. And just do whatever you want to do. There's such freedom. The main thing is keeping the rhythm of the drums. You know how drum rhythms can really get into your blood. And with circumstances like that, in Africa, you're outside in the night. I don't remember whether the moon was shining or not. But anyway, it was a very nice occasion. And we decided we wanted to go to one of the religious places, and somebody told us about a small town where they carried on religious celebrations every Saturday.

"Our stay in Ghana was very, very good for us. When we arrived there, we were met at the airport by two people from the chemistry department, one person from Britain, I think, and one from Canada. But the morning we left, they closed down the chemistry department and everybody came to see us off, the whole academic staff, the unskilled staff, the students. A crowd in the airport. And they loaded us with fruit from Ghana and everything. When we took off, I was sitting in the plane, crying. I didn't want to go. I didn't want to go. (That was our first experience of riding with a black pilot. Ghana Airlines.)

"I tell you one big impression that I still have. At that time, we heard a lot of talk, 'The Africans don't want to associate with African Americans, because they feel superior.' Well, we found that really was not true. I don't know whether it's conscious or unconscious but there's a division between Africans and African Americans. Where each one is thinking the same thing about the other one. We are thinking that the Africans think they're better, and the Africans think we think we are better. But we learned that when we showed that we identified with Africans, and respected them, they really went all out for us. But we had to earn that. That's another thing we had to deal with when we went there. We expected to be met with open arms. 'Oh, my brother, my sister.' That didn't happen. We had to earn their respect, because they had been told that we are coming with this superiority complex. So that they were wary of us. But once we let it be known that we identified, there was nothing they wouldn't do for us. So that preyed on us when we got back here, and saw that idea was still here, among black Americans. We weren't happy with that at all. And then the overall ignorance about it. We'd tell people we were in Ghana, and they don't know whether Ghana is a city, or a country. They have no idea whether it's west Africa, south Africa, east Africa. They don't know. So we felt that we were able in some cases, to give some education to people."

For a time Mrs. Irvin even worked as a consultant to the Oakland schools, sharing her knowledge of Ghana and Africa. "I felt that was my contribution."

Coming back, she told me, had also been something of a shock. "The culture shock that we got was going into the stores and seeing all these things displayed, like ten different brands of sugar. Who needs that? It took us a time before we could deal with that. It was almost equal to the shock that I felt when we went to Ghana. And then add to that, all this affluence. Drive a few blocks away and see poverty.

"In fact, even now, I sometimes think of that. Look at all of this. Who needs it? Like when I go to buy panty hose, it takes me a long time because I've got to find the kind of toe that I want. I've got to find the material that I want. I've got to find the color. I've got to find the size. And, oh, that's so much. The brand. It takes a half an hour to find a pair of panty hose. It worries me when I think of the fact that our priorities are probably not too well organized. I'm certainly convinced that it's possible to solve this poverty situation, in full measure. And find a cure for AIDS, and find a way of making schools more interesting to students. Not only to students, but to parents, so that parents will be interested in going into the schools and helping their children learn. We can do all those things. We—sounds trite to say it—we put a man on the moon. Why can't we find housing for our people? We found a cure for polio. Why can't we find a cure for AIDS? And the drug menace, where we see young men, young boys using that to make a living. Why can't we show them that this is not the way to earn a living?"

I spent the weekend just before Christmas Eve as a guest of a friend, Inderpreet, in San José. I had met Inder in New York where he did his internship and residency in medicine. He and his family had moved back to California when he was done. They had first moved to the Bay Area in the early eighties when they immigrated from India. Inder and I spent that Friday sightseeing, beginning in downtown San Francisco—a drive down Lombard Street (the crookedest street in the world), a stop at the Golden Gate Bridge, which was bright and blue; up to Sonoma Valley and a stop in Glen Ellen, where no one knew one of my favorite writers, M. F. K. Fisher, though I suspected they were protecting the eighty-nine-year-old maven (or at least I hoped that was the case, instead of their living day in and day out in the presence of the writer whom Auden said wrote the best prose of any living human being, and not knowing who she was), and where we couldn't make the cook understand, at a chichi pizza joint, that we wanted to take out a loaf of bread, so he forced us to sit and eat some spicy potato wedges and hot bread. We drove over the hills separating the Sonoma valley (valley of the moon) from the Napa valley, which was an excellent, winding ride among soothing blue hills—coming down, there were trees all covered in lightish lichens; a tour of a Robert Mondavi winery, which I found pleasant and even informative; and back to San Francisco to Marcus Books where Alice Walker read from her new children's book, *Finding the Green Stone.* Many children. And novelist Terri McMillan was also present. At the end of the reading, Alice commented on how she had written the book to typify the community she saw around her in the Bay Area—in which all peoples could live together. Inder asked, "Do you think she really believes that?" I didn't say anything. During the question-and-answer period, one young fellow asked, "What do you like to do best, read . . . or climb ladders?" Alice answered: "Well, climbing ladders is right up there; but I like best to walk alone in the woods and dream." We then went to the Castro—which surprised me with its small size and lack of frenetic energy and overall lack of funk, considering its saucy reputation. Then, to the end of the Pacific Ocean and a touristy place called the Cliff House, which nonetheless had a great view and good food (I had grilled tuna) and we took a night walk along the cliffs afterwards, and the ocean waters were loud like thunder.

The next day we visited Salinas and Monterrey, where I paid homage to John Steinbeck, and then Pebble Beach and Carmel-by-the-Sea, where we had warm cider in a bar owned by Clint Eastwood, The Hog's Breath. (We also went to a party at the home of one of Inder's doctor colleagues in Los Altos. I have been in larger, even more opulent homes in my life, but this place just stank of money, and though I greedily sipped wine all night, I felt like a cat on a hot tin roof.)

My time in the area made me understand why people would brave earthquakes and fire to live there. San Francisco's quaint poetry, the northern valleys' green and fragrant charms, Stanford University and Palo Alto and Silicon Valley's brainy hedonism, the earthy, aquatic peace down by the salty coast. This area was near to a paradise, and seemed a bit unreal compared to the rest of the country I had recently seen.

Remembering Chicago, I quickly decided to forgo attempting to plumb the depths of the Bay Area—too large, too confusing, too new in too many ways—which is really only partly true, since the history of African Americans in San Francisco and Oakland alone is amazing, dense and instructive. But after a little research (actually quite a lot), I realized it would require its own book.

Besides, I was tired, I finally admitted to myself. A few days as a tourist was just what the witch doctor ordered. Though there is one historical San Francisco figure—strange, improbable, extraordinary—who will haunt me to my very grave.

> You tell those newspaper people that they may be smart, but I'm smarter. They deal with words. Some folks say that words were made to reveal

> thoughts. That ain't so. Words were made to conceal thoughts.
>
> —Mary Ellen Pleasant,
> *San Francisco Call,* 1901

I had—and probably still have—a running argument with one of my closest friends. He is a historian. Though I think history is far from a waste of time, I do believe it is never able to know the "truth." Which is not a question of history, in the end, but of the way we think of history. Regardless, we spill ink, and study documents, and uncover documents, and chase down clues, as if the past were a crime, and we, each and all, Nero Wolfes hell-bent on bringing the perpetrators to justice. It's a diverting game, often a tedious and boring game, but an instructive exercise, and historiography has this paradox at its center—when we write history, we are telling future readers more about ourselves than about the past. We are laying bare our own souls, in the hope of illuminating the past, when what we are doing is merely adding another layer to the palimpsest of human records.

When I say things like that, my friend shrugs and says, okay, what the hell is that knowledge good for? What am I supposed to do with that?

I shrug and say, beats me.

But as a writer of fiction, I find that knowledge is at once tantalizing and liberating—the only person, other than perhaps God, who knows the truth about a human being is that human being. What Martin Luther King, Jr., thought as he stood before that crowd on August 11, 1963, what went through Jackie Kennedy's mind on the plane back from Dallas, how Hatshepsut felt upon being made pharaoh of Egypt, what David felt when he first saw Bathsheba, what any worker on the Great Wall of China dreamt at night—these are secrets taken to the grave. The heart of any human being, the thing that makes us, motivates us, moves us, comforts us. The known things are only a frame of our lives, a blurry and incomplete outline. Mary Ellen Pleasant knew these things, and used them with consummate skill.

When we look at the many things written about her, it becomes quickly apparent that everybody is guessing; no one really agrees. One man's fact is another woman's distortion. Mary Ellen Pleasant purposely dwelled in shadow—during one famous court case, she was said to arrive each morning "in an elegant carriage drawn by a team of bay horses," and to have "always appeared in unrelieved black. She pulled the brim of a huge black straw hat tightly down around her face so that it resembled a coal scoop more than anything else." Her comings and goings and doings were always shrouded in uncertainty. Did she? Could she? Perhaps? Maybe?

To both her contemporaries and to her interpreters, Mary Ellen Pleasant is too many, and often conflicting, things: "a civil rights activist," "a former slave," a "woman of mystery," "a very wealthy woman," "a shrewd old Negress," "a black housekeeper," "mammy," "a procuress," "the mother of civil rights in California," "a blackmailer," "cook, accountant, abolitionist," "madam," "voodoo queen," "prostitute," "boarding house keeper," and, my favorite—"this scheming, trafficking, crafty old woman." Perhaps she was all these things; perhaps only a few; even possibly she was none. Chances are, she did exist.

Was she born in 1814? Was she born a slave on a Georgia cotton plantation? Did her master find her so smart and fascinating that he sent her to Boston to study? Or was she born in Virginia? Or was she born in Philadelphia on August 19th to a wealthy merchant father from the Sandwich Islands and a freedwoman of color? Was she educated by the Hussy family in Nantucket? Or was her father a Cherokee? In Boston, did she come to know William Lloyd Garrison and other abolitionists? Was her first husband Alexander Smith, a wealthy black Cuban painter? Did he leave her an inheritance of $45,000? Did he insist it be used to help free black folks? Did she marry John P. Pleasant (or was it Pleasants?), a former overseer?

She and her husband probably came to San Francisco in 1849 at the time of the California gold rush; and it was during these years that she first opened a restaurant and boarding house. There are records that among her clients were some of California's—and the West's—most prominent men. Did she become a usurer and a madam during this period? She certainly came to own quite a few boarding houses and properties. Did she become a financial advisor and counselor to businessmen as well? But why did she leave in 1858? Why to Boston? Why then to Chatham, Canada? Is that where she met John Brown?

Did she give the militant abolitionist $30,000 to raid Harper's Ferry? If so, why was it not found when he was taken into custody? Did she, disguised as a jockey, travel around Virginia and other southern states to whip up potential black warriors for the raid? And what of the mysterious note found among John Brown's belongings? "The ax is laid at the foot of the tree. When the first blow is struck there will be more money to help.—W.E.P."? (Or was it an "M" as some speculate?) Did she flee north after impatient John Brown failed? To New York? How? But she did return, eventually, to San Francisco.

This time she appeared as the "housekeeper" of Thomas Bell, a man she had probably known from her earlier times in San Francisco. Bell had made a fortune in quicksilver, and was a banker. Some accounts say she connected herself to him "because she could get large sums of money from him for almost any reason." (Interestingly, most "accounts" of her life leave out the evidence that for years after returning to California, Pleasant ran businesses, ranches and farms. She opened Geneva's Cottage in 1869, and was selling produce at the Old Washington Market.)

Her relationship with Bell is also enigmatic. Were they lovers? Did she, like Pygmalion, remake Teresa Clingan, a white woman, to be his wife, or as a cover for their relationship? Clearly, everyone seems to agree that Mary Ellen Pleasant ran Thomas Bell's affairs, and many believe she planned and designed the three-storey, $100,000 mansion at 1601 Octavia Street in San Francisco that became known by the corny moniker "the House of Mysteries."

I also find it interesting how scandal dominates so many of the accounts of Mary Ellen Pleasant's life. The most famous being the *Sharon v Sharon* case, in which Sarah Althea Hill Sharon sued her maybe-husband, former Nevada senator who, along with Bell, had made a killing in the mines, for breaking their marriage contract. Pleasant was alleged to have been in on the doings from soup to nuts, to have hooked Hill up with Sharon in the first place, to have counseled her, and to have financed the trial—at fabulous expense. (Some say that's what broke her financially in the end.) Hill won her case, but lost in an appeal, and the judge pinned it all—on record—on "that crafty old woman."

She was also sued by the Bell family, after Bell died, but remained in the mansion until 1899, six years before she died.

What disturbs me no end, in reading the stories, and the stories of the stories, about Mary Ellen Pleasant is how much space is usually devoted to the salacious and the lugubrious (Did she meet the New Orleans voodoo queen Marie Laveau? Was she herself a practitioner of the dark arts?), as opposed to the courageous and the altruistic.

How little is said about how highly regarded Mary Ellen Pleasant was among the black people of San Francisco. How much aid she gave to black families trying to establish themselves in the area. How she "was responsible for securing more jobs for former slaves in San Francisco than anyone prior to 1900." How she was practically a one-woman employment agency. How she employed scores of black people herself. How, in the fifties and the sixties, she is said to have seen to the liberation of blacks illegally held in bondage in California. How she worked with the underground railroad and was rumored to have had "a price on her head." How she financed the case that in 1863 gave African Americans the right to testify in court. How the court case *Pleasant v. The North Beach and Mission Railroad Company* of 1868—when she had been refused admittance by a conductor—won the right for black folk to ride public transportation in California.

Mary Ellen Pleasant was a woman. Mary Ellen Pleasant was black. Mary Ellen Pleasant was uncommonly intelligent. Mary Ellen Pleasant had the courage of a lioness. She operated in a San Francisco famous for its rough-and-tumble Barbary Shore, and in a business community ruthless enough to engender William Randolph Hearst, and in an America that thought nothing of wiping out an entire group of aboriginal people, and enslaving another—her people—simply because they could.

A woman like Mary Ellen Pleasant was nineteenth-century America's worst nightmare, and one of its most extraordinary heroines. Is there any shadow of a doubt why the "official" stories of her life would be so heavily tinged by scandal? Is there any doubt why she felt the way she did about words, and couldn't have given a good goddamn? Is there any shadow of a doubt why a Negro like me would hold her in such high esteem, and want every man, woman and child, black, white, red, yellow, to know of her accomplishments?

I often think I would love to meet Mary Ellen Pleasant. To know the truth. To learn how she did what she did. Then it occurs to me that even if I were her best friend or her lover, I would never know the truth. And, just as I could never know her secrets, the men and women I encountered as I traveled around North America were equally and completely unknowable.

We leave behind us the residue of our deeds; our words are merely their shabby adornments.

Or, as the song my mother is so fond of quoting says, "Let the work I've done speak for me."

The Pacific Coast Highway. Already, I have waxed a bit too poetic a bit too often about the American landscape, but this drive from San José to Los Angeles was memorable, lyrical and varied, with the sun so forceful.

San Simeon was closed, but I spent time walking around Big Sur. On the road hugging the shore, I listened to Vinx's album, *Rooms in My Fatha's House,* the drums and the rhythms so African and diasporic, tum-tumming my syncopated way down, down, all the way down. On Christmas Eve.

I have seen the future, and it is not Los Angeles. Don't let anybody tell you different. Though all the evidence points to the contrary, in reality Los Angeles is a chthonic shape-shifter, a bloated, floating, centerless, arrogant, innocent factory of dreams and delusion and capital—capital especially. Its demographics are representative of no place but Los Angeles, and it can honestly be compared to no other place on the planet Earth.

Los Angeles looks exactly like what it is: an anomaly built on the desert, a futuristic nexus, a meeting place of far-flung cultures, an automobile-driven mecca of skin and celluloid, of high technology and Technicolor poverty.

Los Angeles was the product of a few madmen in love with money, a place now waiting, in narcissism, greed, vanity, death and lassitude, waiting to come to an end. Los Angeles is Sodom and Gomorrah, the tower of Babel and the New Jerusalem, El Dorado and the Fountain of Youth, all wrapped up in one, and yet none. If it does not kill you, it will make you rich. More than any other place I've encountered, Los Angeles is a state of mind. I love Los Angeles. I want to live there when I die. But why?

I like the color of light in Los Angeles in winter, especially as twilight approaches. The light becomes honey-hued and nuanced; it is not the overharsh light one would expect in the desert.

Being in Los Angeles is like being in a movie. A terribly fitting sensation. A constant feeling of being spatially, temporally within all those movies, and especially television dramas, about the myths, mores, manners, and machinations of the Golden State.

I set out on my first day to visit the California Afro-American Museum at 600 State Drive, in Exposition Park, located, essentially, in South Central Los Angeles.

I stopped across the street from the park to get some gas, and experienced an odd situation that I will always remember.

It was one of those self-service affairs, common throughout the U.S.

But around the pumps, like a murder of ravens, was a swarm of black men—I say swarm, but there were only five or six—perhaps it was the impression they gave. I can't say they were homeless, because I don't know that they were, but they were shabbily dressed, unclean, unshaven, creepy-looking, nervous-making folk. Like a Gulf station ad from the 1950s, they went about preparing to fillerup. I saw straightaway that they were not employees, and that they would be expecting a tip (already one of the fellows was harassing another man for money), just like those heartbreakingly annoying people at busy stoplight intersections who want to clean your windshield for change. Frankly, I simply wasn't in the mood, and frankly, I felt a little apprehensive about them, and talked the nozzle out of the man's hand, and served myself. In the store, I found four or five more men, hovering in front of the counter, behind which stood two Korean men who seemed to be shooing them away. The two Koreans seemed beleaguered, bewildered, yet somehow resigned to this state of affairs. I felt sorry for these fellows, one and all.

Cry havoc, I thought, and unleash the hounds of war.

Even before the apocalypse of April 28, 1992, South Central Los Angeles was a well-known place in the minds of most Americans, if not the world. Among rap music and *Boyz N the Hood* and L.A. Gear and the new gangsta–hip-hop romance and vivid pictures of gangbangers in *Time* and *Newsweek,* and shocking news reports that peppered national news as if to get the flavor of the news just right, South Central had become effectively notorious, socially quarantined. Forget how many people lived and worked there, day in and day out, honest, hardworking and nonpathological. South Central then existed as the archetypical urban badland—and moreso, cuz it was in Los Angeles.

Yes, yes, we know it was founded by a group of forty-four women and men and children of Native American, Spanish, and African blood. Yes, we know they came on September 4, 1781, or thereabouts, and that it was the first settlement the Spanish established in southern California—*El Pueblo de la Reina de Los Angeles sobre El Riò de la Porciuncula.*

People also know that the first and last elected governor of Mexican California had been a mulatto named Pio Pico. One of the main arteries in Central Los Angeles is named after him. During my stay in Los Angeles, I asked a number of black people who Pico was. Aside from two historians and one history buff, most people hadn't a clue. Perhaps "we" don't know these things about Los Angeles.

> Los Angeles, The "City of Angels." "If God made California, then Los Angeles was the compromise worked out between God and Satan," wagered the ubiquitous African-American savant. An unflattering comment certainly, but the man reflects the ambivalence held by a goodly number of African-Americans for the "City of Angels." Black playwright Paul Carter Harrison in his epically-proportioned theatre piece, *The Great MacDaddy,* represents Los Angeles as a nether world where Africans in America lose their ancestral minds, a ". . . room covered with a pliable plastic . . . a total environment" in which Black folk engage in all manner of social, moral, and political corruption. . . . And most recently, an African-American undergraduate commented on a series of photographs in the New York *Daily News* graphically illustrating the extraordinary lengths taken by a popular performer to cosmetically alter his appearance. "He's just deBlackifying himself. They do that kind of shit out there [in Los Angeles]." Interestingly, in an article written for this catalogue, Willie Collins suggests that ". . . it was common knowledge that a considerable number of Southern migrants to Los Angeles disavowed their Southern heritage . . ." For whatever reasons, it seems clear that a great many Black folk believe Los Angeles to be a place where forms of traditional African-American culture cannot survive.
>
> —Gerald L. Davis, Introduction to *Home and Yard: Black Folk Life Expressions in Los Angeles,* in a catalog for an exhibit at the California Afro-American History Museum

When I finally got to the museum, I took in the current exhibit, "Equal Justice Before the Law: The Civil Rights Movement in California, 1850–1950." The museum's mission, more than most such institutions, is seen as primarily educational. This admirable exhibit had a powerful narrative element, telling the story of black folks' struggle in pictures and words.

The show told how, two years after achieving statehood, the legislature passed a law saying that any "slave" living in the state before 1849 "who refused to return to his place of origin, could be thrown in prison." Another law had been passed making it impossible for any black person "one half or more Negro" to testify against a white man. A small exodus did occur in 1858, but the curator later told me, "A lot of them stayed. A few came back. Because with the euphoria of Emancipation, the end of the Civil War was like a new day. Okay, we can go and we can make a new start. They weren't necessarily eager to come back to California. A lot of the people who came didn't really come with the idea that they were going to stay. It was like: we go there, and maybe we can make a fortune, and leave. Go back to wherever we came from; that's where our real roots are. I'm not sure exactly of the numbers who came back. I don't think that's ever been really documented. Several hundred went, and there were very few who came back."

The exhibit documented the many African Americans who came to participate in the gold rush of the late 1840s, and how they prospered, and how many were men and women of learning. To fight the California legislature, they formed the Convention of Colored Citizens. They met in 1855, '56, '57, '65, and twice in '72. It seemed like a losing battle since the legislature wouldn't budge from its anti-black stance until after the Civil War and Emancipation.

If nothing else, these black pioneers had organized themselves. The next battle was over education. The California government had been particularly callous when it came to schools for Negroes, basing their funding solely on the number of white students enrolled in a given school. Even after a statute established support for nonwhite schools in 1865, it seemed that the legislators in Sacramento could have cared less. A number of black schools closed their doors due to lack of funding. Again, the black people of the state organized and petitioned and eventually sued. The 1873 case of *Ward v Flood* upheld the right to deny black children the right to attend white schools, but in 1890, *Wysinger v Cruikshank* made segregation illegal in California.

The images of Frederick Douglass and Booker T. Washington were prominent in the exhibit. Douglass's style of protest, and Washington's philosophy were said to have influenced the black civil rights activists of the state. (In fact, the Reverend J. B. Sanderson, first secretary of the Convention of Colored Citizens, was said to have been a friend of Douglass's.) And I was happy to see that Mary Ellen Pleasant had been included.

Afro-American Leagues were formed in the 1890s; this time the people were after economic participation. When land replaced gold as the drawing card to the Golden State, and California began its never-ending rapid growth, African Americans flocked to Los Angeles along with the rest of humanity. By 1920, there were over 20,000 black folk there, and the next battle came over restrictive covenants in renting and selling—that battle lasted over thirty years.

There was Frederick M. Roberts, who had been elected to the general assembly in 1918, and there was H. Claude Hudson, who fought the ban against African Americans on public beaches in 1925, and there was Augustus F. Hawkins, also elected to office in Sacramento in 1918. The exhibit followed the work of the NAACP and the Fair Employment Practice Committee through the Depression and the Second World War.

As I left, I thought over the Du Bois quote that had been cited. He referred to black Angelenos as ". . . full of push and energy and used to working together . . . the Black folk are fighters and not followers of the doctrine of surrender." I could not help but wonder what the sage from Barrington would have said of black Angelenos today. Those words were certainly still applicable, but the context—the battles, the permutations—had shifted more than slightly. I walked on to meet the museum's curator, with history heavy in my head.

Dr. Rick Moss was originally from McNary, Arizona, a very small town he told me, "maybe 30 or 40 percent of the population is black," the rest being Anglo, Navajo or Apache, with Indians in the majority. He reckons that his people had come there from Arkansas and Texas, but a lot was uncertain. His family moved to Los Angeles when he was quite young. I would be surprised, he told me, at the number of black families in Arizona, "families who had been there a long time. Quite a long time."

"If you look at any publication on civil rights, you'll see Alabama and Mississippi and Georgia, but you won't see California. This is important. You know there are folks here doing it. They weren't slaves. They were free black people and they were industrious. They were educated, trained. Many of them had abolitionist experience from the East, so they brought that with them. And the white folk here weren't quite sure how to deal with this. These black folks here in California weren't going to accept the kind of second-class citizenship and treatment they were receiving in the state. They weren't going to quietly acquiesce to attempts to proscribe their right to testify in court, for instance, or to homestead, or to get fair public education for their children. And so that's an important part of the history. Of course, most of that took place in northern California, prior to the 1880s when there was a shift in population to Los Angeles. But in small areas, places like Paris, east of Los Angeles, San Bernardino, what is now Victorville—you had all these little pockets of black folks. They were not really interested in coming to the city to rub shoulders, because I guess the closer they got to white folks, the greater the degree of racism.

Hostility rose in direct proportion to their proximity to this dominant class.

"I know of those isolated communities, and some very old pioneers there. People are surprised to find out about black folks living outside of Los Angeles. We're talking about as early as, I would say, the 1920s and 1930s, which is quite remarkable. Another area is around Fresno, California, where there are some old farming families. Something I have been thinking about doing some research about is the contribution of African Americans to California, to its reputation of being the bread basket of the country. There are a lot of black agriculturalists who did buy land, and who farmed in more than a nominal way. They had acreage and passed these lands down to their offspring. And some of them are still alive."

He told me he was keen to learn more about the black pioneers of San Diego ("There are a few areas where black folks settled in San Diego as early as the 1850s"), even in now-exclusive La Jolla, along the Pacific shore. That history is obscure, he told me. Though they were finding bits of information, little by little.

"Everybody was just funneled into California. Everyone brought their baggage with them. And so they developed what they call 'California culture.' But what's that? It's a synthesis of a whole lot of different cultures. There's no one—at least in terms of African Americans—no one place that you can go, and find a cultural legacy left intact. So you have to go to individuals, and piece together their stories. Then you start to get an idea. 'Oh, this is what Central Avenue was like.' Central Avenue would have been a place to go forty or fifty years ago. Because that would have been the hub. That's where you would have found a kind of cultural legacy, which would have come out of the South, because that's where those people came from. But that would have been where you found it in Los Angeles. Like Sweet Auburn Street in Atlanta.

"You would have gone to the Fillmore District in San Francisco, or Western Addition, in Oakland, to find that kind of thing in northern California. But those places, they're gone. As far as Central Avenue is concerned, definitely by the early '60s, it was gone, probably even earlier than that. The Fillmore District lasted maybe a little longer, but now with gentrification and urban renewal, no black folks there at all. Also, being able to, black folks moved throughout the city. You get ten of us together, then automatically you have to draw the boundaries and the lines. Can't move past this line. That happened in Los Angeles, and at least in the major cities in California, they had restrictive covenants. The red line where you can't move—west of Jefferson. Once you cross a certain street you're going to have trouble. And so we were forced to live in certain areas. Well, after 1947, and, with the Supreme Court decision *Shelley v Kramer* that struck down restrictive covenants, they became unenforceable. And when, two or three years later, they were declared outright illegal, then black folks could move. Once we could, we started moving out. And then you have the death of areas like Central Avenue. I mean, but that's progress. Right? I'm sure there are other reasons for it, but that was one of the major factors. And that ruling affected the other black enclaves in San Francisco, San Diego. You still had de facto segregation, of course. The projects and other places."

Places like the well-known exclusive enclave of Baldwin Hills, located in the hills above South Central, were "the remnants of restrictive covenants—how far black folks are going to be allowed to move. So you jump west of Crenshaw"—a major boulevard in South Central. "Black folks are going to have a place where the upper-class black people can live. That was one area where they could live. The other black enclave was the Sugar Hill area, West Adams district. They all had the same kind of legal battle to live there. In the forties, Hattie McDaniel, Ethel Waters, a few others, had to take their battles to court. Black folks were forming these organizations. These were celebrities. Just one of the sad stories of life in America. Life in Los Angeles. No other place you could go."

All during my traveling, I had become more and more struck by the vast amount of African American history that either lay gathering dust in hundreds of libraries or had gone unrecorded. I wondered if Dr. Moss, whose appreciation of the history of black California was clearly a living thing, felt that a greater knowledge of that history would work as a balm for young African Americans.

"I think you'd have to get this to them at a very young age. I think by the time they're seventh, eighth, ninth grade, maybe it's already too late. Because they've been fed all this other information. All the young people at risk, and the ones who aren't at risk who don't know, who are in these private schools. I would hope that it would make a difference not because it's separate history or because it's special history, but because it is history that is central to the development of this nation. That's the tragedy of not knowing. That we get an idea that there was just this one group of individuals who did everything, not only here in America but in much of world history, and therefore they're responsible for everything we have today. It gives people this jaundiced view of the contributions of other ethnicities. And that's the real tragedy. That directly translates in a real negative way; in the negative way we see ourselves, in the way we act towards each other, and it manifests itself in the kind of negative behavior that we see in gang activities, and, I think, high rates of teenage pregnancy. Just a real lack of self-esteem. Once you know this, my feeling is—maybe it's too idealistic and altruistic—but once you know this, it affects the way you act. You can't act a certain way, when you know what has gone on. You cannot. Something is triggered. And those people, those youngsters who are interested, they take it upon themselves to learn more anyway. No one really has to guide them. They will seek it out. They will come to places like this.

"Unfortunately, it's a very few who do it. Most don't seem to be interested. It's real ancient history. But it's very relevant now, today. History that very few people know about, especially California history. About the gold rush and everything. How many black miners there were. How many made their fortunes. How many who may not have made their fortune but made enough to purchase freedom for themselves and their families. And that's fascinating. That's the American dream. I mean, that's what we work for. It's the California dream.

"We're just oblivious to these individual stories. The stories not of great people, not Booker T. Washington, Frederick Douglass. We know their histories. But the histories of everyday people, leading ordinary lives, and through the course of leading their ordinary lives, they are making history. Because they did what they did, we are here today. I think if we could bring it down to that level, the kids might be more interested in it. But the kind of great-man approach to history maybe turns them off. This person was great. He made it, but what does that say about me?

"I would hope that they do appreciate the stories and the history. I feel obligated to continue to tell them. Maybe some will be affected by it. I don't know. There's a lot more to be discovered, even here in California. I don't know what we're going to do about it, with the kids. Especially in terms of stuff you thought they already knew. 'We fought that battle. I thought we understood all of this.' They know less now than I did. What's more, they don't seem to care."

> What Herodotus the Halicarnassian has learnt by inquiry is here set forth: in order that so the memory of the past may not be blotted out from among men by time, and that great and marvelous deeds done by

> Greeks and foreigners and especially the reason why they warred against each other may not lack renown.
>
> —Herodotus

> . . . It was for a long time the fashion to dismiss the Father of History as a garrulous raconteur, hoping to deceive his readers as easily as he himself was deceived by his informants. This "parcel of lies" type of criticism may now, fortunately, be considered extinct . . . But most scholars must now agree that even from the historical standpoint the world would have lost much of infinite value had Herodotus been more reticent, his "garrulity" is often proved to point the way to right conclusions.
>
> —A. D. Godley, Introduction to *Herodotus*

California is the most populous state in the union, surpassing the entire population of Canada by millions. The idea that I could address even a fraction of what it meant to be black in that state made me weak in the knees. To be sure, California proved my original point: it contained every possible element of African American diversity—descendants of pioneers, displaced southerners, Africans, West Indians, people of every possible mixture and hue; it had a north and a south and a middle; it had rich and poor and working classes. California was quintessentially American, yet America somehow distorted, somehow warped, somehow refracted. The mere breadth of current-day goings-on in Los Angeles alone defeated me, yet I was spurred by the conviction that I could come away with a better understanding of what it was about Los Angeles that made it at once the same and different.

To me, it seemed that in order to understand being black in California—whether one had been born there or not—one had to have a sense of the history that formed it. My travels were beginning to teach me how central history was to any such understanding; yet the more I read and thought about that history, the more it puzzled me.

Herodotus is considered by many western thinkers to be the "Father of History," the creator of the western historical tradition. However, he is also known to have outright lied and distorted and to have made up great fictions in the name of history. James Pierce Beckwourth, "trapper, hunter, guide, horsethief, Indian fighter, and Indian chief," discoverer of

Beckwourth Pass, and founder of what is now Beckwourth, California, dictated a most compelling autobiography, *The Life and Adventures of James P. Beckwourth: Mountaineer, Scout, and Pioneer, and Chief of the Crow Nation of Indians,* which has much fact in it, but the account has been proven also to have elements of the tall tale. Nonetheless, it is an arresting book, and I find myself inspired by it just the same.

On another level there is the not-so-well-written, but important, *Negro Trail Blazers of California,* by Delilah Beasley, published in 1910. Beasley could be described as being race-proud; she claimed to be of Zulu descent. She spent nine years writing her book, which is so monotonous and plodding that it is almost charming. But regardless of my literary criticism, the book is important to historians of California and the West and of African American history, for at the turn of the century Beasley knew many of the people who had been in California from the beginning of statehood and before. Her book is constructed out of reminiscences and anecdotes, newspaper clippings, and whatall. There are many inaccuracies and falsehoods, but that fact in no way diminishes the tremendous effort she made. So much of what we know of California history grows out of her Herodotus-like efforts.

This paradox is what stuck in my brain: the idea of the importance of that urge to create history, some history, some narrative of explanation. Like the famous and revered griots of western Africa who memorize entire codices of family histories and pass them on. What is that need? That urge? Why is it so important to know our history? What on earth would happen to us all if one day we were to forget?

I had a very pleasant supper with the novelist Trey Ellis at the Broadway Deli on the promenade in Santa Monica. In the mid-eighties Trey's novel *Platitudes* had been published to wide acclaim. He had even been featured in a PBS special showcasing young writers, reading from his work. He had been living for the past few years in Venice Beach, pursuing the celluloid market. After telling me of his travails and successes in the script-writing business and his upcoming novel, *Housekeeping,* we commenced to discuss "Black America." In my fumbling way, I tried to relate the many, multifaceted facts I had been learning about African Americans and history. I tried to explain my muddled thoughts on the "situation"—which almost to a one, folk regarded as precarious; and how the now too-familiar litany of ills seemed to be a tangle of external pressures and influences, exacerbated, often caused, by internal problems.

I was curious to discover that Trey was feeling pessimistic about those things about which I had been struggling to be optimistic—namely the spirit of African Americans. His belief was that, in general, black folk had internalized a belief in their own failure; yet he was surprisingly optimistic about those things over which I had been growing most pessimistic—some true governmental reform in the face of the Powers That Be—whoever they are. He told me that he had held profoundly radical views when he was younger, that he would even go so far as to have called himself a Marxist. At root, he told me, he still held on to those radical views, and he still believed that a grassroots movement could make great strides. But "could" and "possible" were the operative words. He did not feel sanguine about the early advent of such possibilities.

I felt that I had somehow in my thinking become both a Booker T. Washington and a Du Bois, an MLK and an X—seeing both sides, advocating for both sides, yet suspicious that arguments about African Americans could be bifurcated, as if there were only two sides to the debate of what must be done to deal with the problems of the great-great-granddaughters and the great-great-grandsons of the slaves. I wanted to believe in the indomitable spirit of black folk and in the wickedness of the great white father—while not dismissing the statistics of murder, drug addiction, and poverty, poverty, poverty; knowing full well that there exists an inherent contradiction in these simplistic views. I was seeing that I had grown up the son of Booker T. Washington, and wanted to run away and live with Dr. Du Bois. But I was getting to be a big boy: wasn't it time to build my own house?

I couldn't have it both ways; nor did I really want to have it either way; I longed for another, a fresher vision of the black American situation.

I was trying to come to terms with a desire to speak with hope and pride of black folk and of honestly assessing the problems that conspire to destroy us—yes us—rich, poor, educated and illiterate, a destruction based on color and nothing more.

Somewhere along the line, I had given up the question of whether or not a "we" existed—at least for me. The answer was yes. Of course it did. We exist because we see the need to exist. If someone chooses not to belong to us, that is all well and good, but we go right on existing, thinking, working, puzzling, asking, debating, crying, What then must we do?

The heroine of Oscar Micheaux's 1937 film, *God's Step Children,* is Naomi, a high-toned, light-skinned black

> girl who wants to be white. She frets, pouts, plots, whines, and well, *just plain acts up,* turning her tiny black community topsy-turvy. Finally, Naomi does everyone a great service; she throws herself into the river and, like a nasty stain on her face, is washed away. For white moviegoers during the depression, Naomi's trials and tribulations passed unnoticed. But for black audiences, Naomi's was a lopsidedly caustic and cautionary morality tale about cultural roots and loyalties, racial heritage and pride. It was only one of many such narratives told in a long forgotten branch of American movie history: race movies, independently produced films with all-black casts, made outside Hollywood, in an attempt to merchandise mass dreams for black America.
>
> —Donald Bogle, "No Business Like Micheaux Business: 'B' . . . for Black"

When I read that Oscar Micheaux was "a hardworking, bookish, somewhat priggish young man," I shuddered, for it reminded me of someone I knew too well who could be described that way; and there are more things about Micheaux, filmmaker extraordinaire, that bother me more than impress me—though clearly he was an impressive man.

His career as a cineast came about, one could say, directly as a result of America's greatest contribution and equally most shameful document in the history of film. *Birth of a Nation* remains one of the most visionary technical accomplishments, quite literally changing the way moving pictures were thought of, conceived and shot; and, at the same time, one of the most damnably racist pieces of celluloid to be run through a projector. The inflammatory story pitting the good guy Ku Klux Klan against the surly, drunken, murderous, raping Negroes of the Reconstruction era will always stand as an emblem of what is best and worst about America. To this day, it is impossible to view D. W. Griffith's genius without raging against his ignorance and bigotry and sheer and utter racism.

This was equally the case in 1915. As they should have done, the black folk of the day took it personally, with the NAACP in the lead, forming picket lines, organizing boycotts, and other forms of protest. Another strategy of talking back to Griffith's poisonous vision had been African Americans beginning to pick up the camera themselves.

This series of events led the Lincoln Motion Picture Company of

Nebraska to make an offer for the film rights to Oscar Micheaux's self-published novel *The Homesteader.* Micheaux was delighted but insisted he direct. The movie company decided to look elsewhere. Micheaux decided to do it himself. The movie version of *The Homesteader* was released in 1919.

Micheaux had been born in 1884 on a small farm not far from Cairo, Illinois. He had left home at age seventeen and worked for several years as a Pullman car porter, where he saw the West and developed a romance with the idea of the pioneer. He became one himself, after a fashion, when, in 1904, he purchased a farm in southern South Dakota. He self-published three novels: *The Conquest: The Story of a Negro Pioneer* (1913); *The Forged Note: A Romance of the Darker Races* (1915), and *The Homesteader* (1917). All are and were considered abysmal, nakedly autobiographical, and pitifully melodramatic. Kenneth Wiggins Porter, in the *Dictionary of American Negro Biography,* describes Micheaux's writing as "a literary disaster, with an unbelievably complicated plot, long-winded, pretentiously awkward writing, stilted conversations, and the grotesque misuse of words." Micheaux's vision was the vision of Booker T. Washington—though Washington certainly did not advocate going anywhere, certainly not to South Dakota—and cautions about race-mixing are often a powerful message in his works. Also, Micheaux had a very dim view, to say the least, about black folk in the South. In *The Forged Note,* one character makes the statement: "The Negroes in Effingham [Birmingham] are niggers proper. They think nothing about reading and trying to learn something; they only care for dressing up and having a good time." Shades of E. Franklin Frazier!

Chances are that such a writer would not gain a wide audience, especially among black folks. Wrong. Despite all his artistic and philosophical shortcomings, apparently Oscar Micheaux was a salesman *sans pareil.* Along with his wife, sometimes separately, Micheaux would drive into southern cities, and hawk his books with great gusto and flair, and success. He would bring this same capitalist verve to filmmaking.

During the same period, and into the thirties and forties, other black film auteurs arose: George and Noble Johnson, Emmet J. Scott (Booker T. Washington's former secretary), and Spencer Williams (who made a number of peculiar, though interesting and religion-laden, movies in the forties, *Blood of Jesus, Go Down Death, Dirty Gertie from Harlem, USA,* and *Of One Blood* among the best—sadly he will go down in history for his role as Andrew Hogg Brown of TV's *Amos 'n Andy*). But, from 1919 to 1948, Oscar Micheaux ruled. As a genre, "race films" enjoyed their heyday in the '20s, '30s and '40s, primarily because they had a relatively captive audience. These were the days of Jim Crow, of course, and in southern cities and in certain ones in the North, like Harlem, anywhere there were all-black or black-owned theaters, "all-colored casts" were in high demand. (There were close to 600 such theaters at their height.) With a few notable exceptions—like Williams—these films were not only mediocre and often poorly made, they increasingly became throwbacks to the minstrel era. It is no coincidence, then, that more and more of these films were backed by cynical white dollars.

However, as bad as most of them were, and no matter how P. T. Barnum–ish he became, Micheaux's pictures certainly stand out.

In all, he made over thirty films, cheap, shot on a shoestring, often in six weeks. He used every trick he could think of with productive results. (Porter: "He was even able to persuade white Southern movie-house owners to put on all-Negro matinee performances, and sometimes also special midnight showings for all-white audiences who were titillated by his frequent 'raunchy cabaret scenes.' ") From *The Birthright* (1924), yet another western pioneer story with black folk, to *Body and Soul* (1924), Paul Robeson's first film role, to *The Exile* (1931), his first talky, to *Underworld* (1937), Micheaux did his own thing. In truth, the films were diverse (many of the stories were "ripped from the headlines," as the hackneyed phrase goes), but certain themes recurred: the tragic mulatto, the problem of class difference, the superiority of the black bourgeoisie, issues of skin color. No poor working folk here; no Bigger Thomases or Janie Crawfords. Historically speaking, Micheaux's rough cuts represent two paradoxical notes. He showed a black middle- and upper-class world as if it were commonplace, when, in fact, it was, at the time, a particularly small and rarefied segment of African America. Yet he was bringing to the silver screen, however melodramatic or regrettable, many stories of black life, which have yet to be addressed again.

What are we to make of a figure like Oscar Micheaux?

As a businessman, he must be given his due as a trailblazer and entrepreneurial visionary, but jumbled up in that success is a boodle of stereotypical thinking, regressive philosophy, commercial cynicism, and bad-quality filmmaking easily passed over because of its shocking, prurient, titillating wrapping. Oscar Micheaux's story is a quintessentially American story. Or, in the words of one of his most successful descendants, boxing promoter Don King, "Only in America!"

Micheaux died in 1951 in relative obscurity. His film career came to an abrupt halt when *God's Step Children* was picketed by communists displeased over what it had to say about passing. He wrote more novels—*The Wind from Nowhere* (1941), *The Case of Mrs. Wingate* (1944), and *The Story of Dorothy Stansfield* (1946). He made one more film in 1948, *The Betrayal,* based on *The Wind from Nowhere;* it ran him into the ground financially.

Of course, in the perfect light of hindsight, it is a bit too easy to be harsh on ole Oscar. It is important to consider what the alternative was in his day (aside from the precious few other black-directed films) coming out of Hollywood. Blacks were minstrels, or varmints, or whores, or mammies—or they simply did not exist at all.

> It is said that the camera cannot lie, but rarely do we allow it to do anything else, since the camera sees what you point it at: the camera sees what you want it to see. The language of the camera is the language of our dreams.
>
> —James Baldwin, "The Price of the Ticket"

I love the movies. I am an inveterate moviegoer. If I don't see at least one movie a week, I become melancholy. There have been periods of my life when I've gone to the movies every day of the week. I have seen as many as five movies in one day. Movies are to me what heroin is to some people; I am a movie junky. But luckily for me, I am told it is a benign habit.

During this journey I saw: *Dead Again* in Vermont; *Mystery Train* and *The Doctor* in Maine; *The Commitments* and *Nightmare on Elm Street* (part whatever) in Buffalo; Chicago, *My Own Private Idaho*; *Batman Returns* in Madison; *The Addams Family* in Grand Forks and *Beauty and the Beast* in Coeur d'Alene. *Universal Soldier* (two times) in Anchorage. *Star Trek V: The Undiscovered Country* in Seattle, and *JFK* while I was in Los Angeles.

Though Akira Kurosawa and Orson Welles are probably my favorite filmmakers (in case you suspected I had absolutely no taste), I am omnivorous when it comes to actual moviegoing. Videotapes and television are okay, but nothing compares to going into this big, dark, cool auditorium and watching this big, flickering imitation of life, physically larger than life; moviegoing is not so much about art as it is about dreaming, fantasizing, perhaps even escaping.

James Baldwin loved the movies also. He wrote about it in *The Devil Finds Work,* a book that recounted his life through the movies he had seen as well as his brief and contentious encounter with the movie industry, and a whole lot more. His first and greatest novel, the admittedly autobiographical *Go Tell It on the Mountain,* has as an early and pivotal moment in the protagonist James Grimes's life, when he goes to see Bette Davis in *Of Human Bondage.* Grimes becomes entranced, disturbed and bewildered by the images before him. He, the son of a Pentecostal preacher, impoverished, psychologically tortured, waiting to be saved by Jesus in piety and in light, is confronted by opulence, elegance and, to him, decadence, beautiful in its expression and grace, damning in its other-making power. (Moreover, Bette Davis was a *"movie star,"* which equaled "rich," and most importantly, she was "ugly" and "she moved just like a nigger," confounding the lad, at once reinforcing positive and negative notions in his head. Later, Baldwin writes of himself, "I had discovered that my infirmity [what he saw as his ugliness] might not be my doom . . . my infirmities, might be forged into weapons.")

That same scene in the novel is a touchstone not only for Baldwin, but for generations of black folk, as empirically reasoned by Dr. Kenneth Clarke in his famous baby doll experiment, that these images, white images, have extraordinary power over the black mind. James Baldwin loved movies (one of my favorite essays of his is a piece about Swedish filmmaker Ingmar Bergman, "The Northern Protestant," in which Baldwin's great themes come together like a diamond—art, color, Protestantism, morality, history) but he also harbored a bitterness for what filmmaking was mostly used for in America.

Baldwin writes in *The Devil Finds Work:* "That the movie star is an 'escape' personality indicates one of the irreducible dangers to which the moviegoer is exposed: the danger of surrendering to the corroboration of one's fantasies as they are thrown back from the screen."

The truth is, we've yet to fully comprehend what we've done to ourselves with our movies. Many will scoff at the idea that motion pictures have any significant influence on our society, but I suspect they are fooling themselves. A movie may be trivial, but the impact the motion picture has in the world is far from trivial. Of all the things a film can be, one is that it can be dangerous—perhaps my habit is not so benign after all.

One of the most damning and continuing problems with American cinema is the representation of African Americans on the screen. I have already had the audacity to pin a lot of the blame for what occurred during the 1970s, regarding African American identity and culture, on blaxploitation films. What exactly were they?

To be sure, this movement began with the greater good of black people in mind. In the '40s, '50s and '60s, the question had been twofold: either it was, to quote Douglas Turner Ward, "Where de Nigras at?" or it was a matter of Stepin Fetchit, *Gone with the Wind*'s Prissy; liver-lipped, slow-witted, servile, pop-eyed train porters, waiters, butlers ("Yassah, Boss!"); or venal, murderous, soulless, oversexed criminals; or humble Old Man Rivers; or big-breasted Earth Mothers with a penchant for singing gospel; or high-yalla hussies looking for no good, and having a good time doing it. There were variations and riffs (and a few notable exceptions), but little deviation from that norm. Much has been written on the subject; perhaps the most eye-opening being the work of Donald Bogle in his landmark *Toms, Coons, Mulattoes, Mammies and Bucks: An Interpretive History of Blacks in American Films* (1973, 1989). Black directors and screenwriters were precious few and far between.

If we look at the chronology, it might be a little confusing. Ossie Davis, Gordon Parks and others were making excellent films about black life before 1971, and certainly extraordinary films would follow during the 1970s. But Melvin Van Peeble's *Sweet Sweetback and His Badass Song* was released in 1971, and, with mixed results, it set everybody's house on fire.

Van Peebles had been an American expatriate in Paris in the sixties who published four novels in French. He had been a boxer, and a great many other things. Even today, as a commodities trader and film producer, he would probably describe himself as a badass.

In a review of a film version of Baldwin's *Go Tell It on the Mountain,* critic Armond White writes of Van Peebles:

> Van Peebles understood—better than Baldwin—the value and liberating thrill of having your fantasies enlarged and electrified ("corroborated") onscreen. Van Peebles played directly to the black audience's urge to escape (through the uniquely cinematic pleasure of interwoven movement, music and fantasy), because he sensed how powerfully film could instill ideas and even, through escape, corroborate one's real-life sense of self-worth. He was after a better understanding of the angry, oppressed man's dream.

That he did. But perhaps more important than the inherent artistic merit of his film was his method. Very like Oscar Micheaux, Van Peebles, when it became quite clear that Hollywood wanted no part of his work, did it all himself. He was a one-man show: actor, director, producer, editor, distributor. He went over the heads of the studios and their networks, and cobbled together his own. The film was wildly successful financially—to this day it remains one of the highest grossing films ever made by an African American director. Of course, the scent of lucre was smelled on Wilshire Boulevard.

Now here is the fly in the ointment. Two lessons were taken from Van Peebles's feat: One lesson arose from the newfound sense of independence and artistic license that Van Peebles clearly saw as self-evident; he opened the way for new cinematic visions. More strident, bitter, satirical, honest, even surreal films would follow. Secondly, he discovered there was a lot of money to be made off black audiences. But Hollywood took away from Van Peebles's financial triumph the oversimplified concept that black folks would pay to see black folks who were, like Sweetback, badass niggers. Suddenly scores of films that would never before have seen the light of day over Sunset Boulevard were greenlit; some, like *Shaft,* actually had merit as social commentaries while being entertaining; others, like *Superfly, The Mack, Dolemite, The Legend of Nigger Charley, Blacula, Blackenstein, Abby,* etc., emphasized the bad in badnigger, glorified drug-dealing, pimping, and crime and violence in general; style over substance with the thin veneer of social worth by justifying any and all acts of defiance in the name of black rage, and railing against (and shooting at) the Man. Since the black man was hopelessly oppressed, the underworld was the only way to make it.

I do not mean to oversimplify the cultural dynamics that were aswirl during the early and middle seventies when these films were pouring out of studios like coins from primed slot machines. Other factors both made them salient and fueled their mis-message. One of many factors was that the Black Panther Party, long misunderstood in the mainstream media, had somehow been used to make being radical "chic" (as the writer Tom Wolfe once noted). But the Black Panthers' serious political intent and focus on voting, education, health and welfare was eclipsed as they were short-circuited from without and from within, while their style—Afros, leather jackets, guns—along with their bold talk and swaggering defiance, endured above all else. It is easy to see how that image merged so effortlessly with the new laissez faire of the black exploitation market.

There did exist a small Hollywoodized middle ground, like the black comedies made by Bill Cosby, and a memorable Western, *Buck and the Preacher,* starring Sidney Poitier and Harry Belafonte, or certain "wholesome" family entertainments, like *Sounder.* And Richard Pryor stands out, singular and alone, for making some lasting, and to this day unrecognized, masterpieces.

It was during this period, too, that Berry Gordy's powerhouse of music, Motown, made some memorable forays into the movies. Diana Ross—who at the time was the hottest thing in music after Elvis Presley and the Beatles, making her eminently "bankable"—starred in *Lady Sings the Blues,* a bio-pic about Billie Holliday, which Baldwin lacerates in *Devil* as being about anybody *but* Billie Holliday; and the camp classic *Mahogany,* about a black girl from Detroit who makes it big in the fashion industry. Motown also made a brave movie about the National Negro Baseball League, which about five people saw.

But the dominant movies, the ones Hollywood crammed down Black America's, and America's, collective throats, were the repetitions of stereotypes long held in the U.S. psyche—only now they wore an Afro and platform shoes. I firmly believe the residue of that nakedly exploitative period can still be felt in American society. It is reflected in my generation's attitudes, beliefs, choices of style, political conceptions, and, perhaps most important, in how we—my generation and the generation after us—conceive of black identity. It should not be a mystery why those films are enjoying revival cult status. They speak to teenage and preteen "corroboration" of what it meant, in the post–Civil Rights era, to be new Negroes.

Who says films are benign? By the late 1970s, the film industry had changed again. Steven Spielberg and George Lucas invented something called the blockbuster—films like *Star Wars* and *Jaws,* films which could single-handedly reverse a studio's fortunes. Relatively small films like those cheap two hours of black men shooting up other black men and treating women like trash had no such potential. By the time Ronald Reagan was elected, the American public saw only a few films with all-black casts. Interestingly enough, most of those were throwbacks to the *Cabin in the Sky* forties. *The Wiz, Sparkle, Thank God It's Friday* were musicals, vehicles for selling the disco music of Donna Summer and the like—an accepted and largely unquestioned role for African Americans.

Then in the mid-1980s, along came Spike Lee and *She's Gotta Have It,* a movie, to filmgoing audiences both black and white, that seemed to break all the rules. Shot in a retro and gorgeous black and white, it was comic, yet it dealt with "real" problems of "real," young, urban African Americans who were not desperate or desperately poor, not pathological, not angry at the Man; in fact, there were no white folk to be seen. More than being merely Woody Allen in black face, as some uncharitable critics have claimed, Spike Lee's first feature-length film came to black folk as a breath of fresh air. The political content (aside from gender politics and the politics of desire, which are not small matters) was minimal, if it existed at all. But that didn't matter, for, for the first time in a long while, African Americans had the opportunity to escape themselves into themselves. Revolutionary? Not really.

What Spike Lee did was simply reinvent what Oscar Micheaux and Melvin Van Peebles had invented and reinvented before him. He recognized a paucity and he filled it; he felt the itch and scratched it. When Hollywood declined to fund him, for his Morehouse College and Brooklyn-born vision had little to do with shoot-'em-up and show-me-how-bad-you-is, he just did it himself. After Spike Lee's second film, *School Daze,* about a historically black university, his films *Do the Right Thing* and *Malcolm X* became more and more politically charged, and interestingly enough, studio financed (*Get on the Bus,* about the Million Man March, was funded by African Americans, but it was distributed by a major studio). Despite Lee's status as an auteur, his real triumph came as an entrepreneur. This was black capitalism at its Booker T. Washington best.

Of course Hollywood paid attention again; they are great students when a balance sheet is involved. The results have been mixed. The spate of films for and by African Americans, particularly those funneled through the Hollywood system in the late 1990s, have reflected a definite and, I hope, permanent shift. Some have been better than good; others have been worse than bad. Perhaps more than the wares themselves, the most important shift is that now one needs more than one hand to count the working black directors and screenwriters. Now Sidney Poitier is not the *only* black male movie star (even in North Dakota and Vermont, Denzel, Danny, Samuel, Will, Eddie, Wesley, Lawrence and Cuba are household names—though Whoopi and Whitney remain, sadly, in a league of their own). And there are a handful of black women and men in positions of power in the big seven studios. (Or are there only four now?)

However—double, double, toil and trouble—you don't have to be Donald Bogle to see how the Hollywood product more often than not represents some vexing and deep-rooted problems. If one looks at the most successful and most hyped movies made by the studios, one sees disturbing trends: some see the demonizing of black males (*The Color Purple, What's Love Got To Do With It*?); others see the near-glorification of black male violence as being a cautionary tale (*New Jack City, Boyz N the Hood*).

(Intentionally, I neglected to mention the television industry, which is probably more powerful in the 1990s than it was in the 1970s in terms of influencing African American culture. In 1975, it was *Good Times, The Jeffersons,* and *Sanford and Son*—about which one could be cruel and say they were latter-day versions of *Amos 'n Andy.* By 1995, the field had become mighty complicated, involving new networks that cynically followed demographics, telling the major networks and hungry upstarts, Fox, UPN and WB, how to reach young urban black teenagers, and reinforced perceived notions of the marketplace. The motion picture industry mirrors that phenomenon, but its outlines are broader and are more clearly read.)

Perhaps I overstate my case. Black folk have been arguing for years and years about the above-mentioned films. A dialogue that I believe is actually rather healthy; it gets people to think. Moreover, we are in an era in which black actors are being cast in roles that have little or nothing to do with their being black. (*The Pelican Brief, Outbreak, Terminator 2, Soapdish, Clueless* come to mind.) And, once in a blue moon, Hollywood will even take a chance—God knows why—and produce a good film about black folk, even though that film's fate is usually obscurity.

Yes, Hollywood is changing, and rapidly (but into what?); and yes, America itself is changing along with it (I'm almost afraid to ask into what? but I must). Yet in the main, the movies Americans see have little to do with real folk; they are, by the time they reach a multiplex near you, mere products, store-bought, glossed, gussied, defanged, neutered, cleaned-up, polished, prettified and shrink-wrapped. They are like cotton candy or a Milky Way bar, good to the taste, but bad for you; and you forget you've had it, fifteen minutes after you swallow it.

Ever had an intense discussion or emotional experience over a chocolate bar? Ever had one change your life?

Charles Burnett was telling me about the day he learned he had been awarded a $275,000, five-year "genius" fellowship from the MacArthur Foundation. The year was 1988, and he had just finished making a film.

"I was at the studio—a one-room thing (people used to come over and they used to want to use the bathroom, I'd say, 'Well, the bathroom's in the hall.' So they'd go back and say, 'Where's the other room?' I said, 'You're looking at it.')—and a friend and I were sitting down. I had invested in my current film, and was just finished paying off everything. And so the phone rings, and here's this guy with this voice, like the IRS. I hear this voice, you know, so I said, 'Who do I owe now? I paid everybody,'—and on and on and on—'I can't possibly owe anybody else. So don't come asking me questions.' I had this attitude really. And so the guy says, 'Well, you know—' I didn't hear him at first, because everybody was making all this noise. And he said, 'Are you Charles Burnett?' I say, 'Yeah, yeah, yeah.' So he kept asking me all these questions. I say, 'Oh, God, who is this guy?' And so he says, 'Well, congratulations. You've won the MacArthur.' Or 'You received the MacArthur.' Something like this. I said, 'Oh sure. Okay. Yeah. Who's the joker?' He says, 'No, no. This is not a joke. This is very serious, and I assure you, you won a MacArthur.' I was very cynical. I said, 'Sure. When I get papers or letters saying I have a MacArthur, then I'll believe it.' You get to a point where you're like, hey, no more jokes. So he says, 'I'll get a letter out to you tomorrow.'" Then Burnett told his wife, still thinking it was a joke. "She just threw down her knitting, and put on her clothes and went out looking for a house. She was gone. She didn't even care that it might be a joke. She was, 'I don't care. Spend it before you get it.' The next day this letter came saying I won a MacArthur. Oh, wow. It was one of those kinds of treats, you know. It was really a good time."

Charles Burnett's very first feature film, the 1978 *Killer of Sheep,* a black-and-white study of a man who works in a Los Angeles slaughterhouse, had been among the first fifty films archived in the Library of Congress National Film Registry. The film won the Berlin International Film Festival Critics' Prize, and the U.S. Film Festival's first prize. He had since won a Guggenheim, an NEA grant, and a Rockefeller fellowship. Charles Burnett had been making films for over a decade. *Several Friends* and *The Horse* were two shorts he made in 1975; he had also written the screenplay and had been the cinematographer for Billy Woodberry's *Bless Their Little Hearts* (1984). *My Brother's Wedding,* made in 1983, was not released commercially until 1991. The film's milieu is very similar to that of Pulitzer prize-winning short story writer, James Alan MacPherson, whose stories often center around black men caught on the fault lines of the black bourgeoisie and the black demimonde. In the film, Pierce Munday is suspended between the worlds of his soon-to-be-married, prosperous lawyer brother, Wendell, and that of his running mate, Soldier Richards, an ex-convict who is the very embodiment of anger, rage, malice, rebellion, and dark charisma. And though it is set in Watts, and though there is some realistic violence, the film neither typifies one, nor sensationalizes the other. Rather, Burnett focuses on the modern-day dilemma—with grace and humanity and evident love—of Pierce's passage. Burnett does not take the easy way out, nor does he pose simple answers to complex questions.

The earlier film got its chance after seven years, because, in 1990, a major distributor picked up Burnett's next feature, *To Sleep with Anger.* This felicity was in large part due to the good auspices of actor Danny Glover of *Lethal Weapon* and *The Color Purple* fame. Glover's willingness to appear in a major role in the film, take a big pay cut, and even participate financially, assured not only that the film would be made, but that it would receive a larger audience than it might have received otherwise. The film was completed for less than $2 million.

When I first saw *To Sleep with Anger* in 1990, I had been thunderstruck by its mix of folklore and a modern-day setting, the blues, southern culture, dreams, mysticism and superstition, young men and women in love, the layers of generations, and, simply, a good story. The movie centers on a black family in South Central L.A. who, out of the blue, are visited by an old friend from the South, Harry Mention, a charmer with ominous overtones from his first appearance. Gideon (Paul Benton), the family patriarch, a hard-working gentleman, and Suzie (Mary Alice), his warm, worrying, though far from stereotypical wife, have two sons, Junior and Babe Brother (Richard Brooks). Harry is invited to stay, and it looks as if he is never going to leave. Over the course of the movie, the apparent trickster becomes more and more of a threat, as, little by little, his influence is felt throughout the household, most markedly on Babe Brother, who is chafing at the leash of his marriage and his father's insistence that he stand more on his own two feet. The dramatic tension is powerful, but Burnett keeps the pace slow, leaving time for a card game, or the fabulous scene when a group of old friends from back home come over for a party, and Burnett captures the world of southern immigrants in the West, and the mores, humor, vibrance and goodness of that culture.

Much to everyone's distress, despite winning awards at film festivals and receiving glowing reviews, the movie did not do well at the box office. In fact, though it gained some following at art houses (largely patronized by white moviegoers), *To Sleep with Anger* fared poorly in black communities. Double, double, toil and trouble.

. . .

I met Charles Burnett in a restaurant in a mall on South Central's Crenshaw Avenue, not far from his home in Baldwin Hills, still a black middle-class enclave, where he lived with his wife Gaye Shannon, and his two sons, then aged three and eight.

Burnett struck me as a shy, restless man. Unassuming, yet full of ideas and energy. At the same time, he had that wandering gaze and distracted air of the overtired. He is not a tall man, and he was dressed casually, comfortably. At one point the clichéd image of the director made famous by Fellini's 1950s films, sun-shaded, trench coat thrown over the shoulder, above all, aloof and arrogant, came to mind. I realized straightaway that even if one of Burnett's films were ever to outgross *Titanic,* he would never adopt that facade. He was a bit too real to put on airs; he didn't really have time to waste.

Charles Burnett was born in Vicksburg, Mississippi, but came to Los Angeles as a child, and had spent most of his life there. Los Angeles in the forties and fifties was "pretty much the South." It seemed to him that everyone belonged to clubs named after southern towns and cities and states from the South, like Club Alabama, or the Vicksburg Club. In those days Los Angeles was very segregated. "The police were oppressive. Worse than the South." But there was also a strong sense of community. "We all had chickens and rabbits and turkeys. All of that in our backyard. My brother had a horse. Then, the middle class and the poor were in the same area, all in the same boat, because they couldn't go anywhere else. It was like Soweto, the township. After the civil rights thing, people started moving out, moving to Baldwin Hills, Echo Park. The black community of L.A. disappeared with the riots." He thought the city government also had a hand in dispersing people, in collusion with the banks and their practice of redlining. Watts, he remembered, had a strong identity, but businesses gradually moved. "People were afraid to go there." Though he felt that bad reputation was largely a myth these days. "There are more rapes and mass murders in Hollywood than any place else."

He had originally been interested in electronics, and gradually got interested in filmmaking. "I was a poor English student. Awful at everything except track and field. Football. I don't know. I guess maybe because I had a speech problem"—Burnett has a pronounced stutter—"it really distanced you and set you outside everything. You could never really participate. I guess I became more of an observer. I lived in a sort of gang area. Watts. You had to know how to fight in those days. They had zipguns and guns. It was rare, but if you knew how to fight and stand up you weren't going to get stomped. That's why boxing became such a big thing. They had all these really weird names in those days like the Farmers, the Gladiators, with their martial arts—all these different gangs. It wasn't as crazy as it is today. We were brought up to see good guys dressed in white, bad guys dressed in black. Like cowboys in a sense. There's a limit to everything. These fools now, boy, they don't seem to understand anything. It's just destroying their lives, out of whatever frustration and their circumstances. You always wanted to make sense out of it then. That was one of the reasons I got involved in doing stories about the community."

Burnett had assumed he'd become an engineer, but during some of his classes, he got to know engineers who went back to school for refresher courses. "They'd be working at Aeronautics or Hughes or whatever it was. They weren't living in Disneyland. They were concerned about retiring, and about layoffs and other government ups and downs. They really depended on these things. They didn't have control over their own lives. I could see myself getting a job working there nine to five, and then getting one of these Winnebagos, and going fishing and coming back in two weeks, you know? and then at the end, you get a six-week vacation, and the gold watch. And I said, 'Oh no. I'm dead. No.'"

He had always been interested in photography, but never had a chance to pursue it. While he was working at the downtown library, he started going to movies more and more. Eventually, he decided to look into film school. He enrolled in UCLA. "I spent all that time working and going to school, which was a mistake. I was supporting myself, and they wouldn't give me financial aid. You really have to know where to go. I didn't. It wasn't a passion I had. I sort of backed in the door."

He would spend over ten years working and taking film classes, making his first short films in black and white. "It was a struggle. It was the only place where you could make films cheaply. They actually picked us out from undergraduate school and then forced us to go on to graduate school, and then forced us to get out of graduate school. We were taking everything from Russian, German, you name it, just to stay in class. It was only eighty dollars at the time. Eighty dollars a quarter. If you rented equipment for one day, that alone would cost you $200 for two days' rental. So you're getting all that, camera, lights and everything for virtually nothing. There was a bunch of filmmakers there who were good, and the sort of atmosphere where you can learn about film and work on other people's film—it was very popular."

When Burnett was at UCLA, there were few other African Americans, he told me. "They would only take ten out of the whole program of about 200 each quarter." He also remembered Ellis L. Taylor, a black World War II veteran who had studied economics in Germany and become one of the first black professors at UCLA. "He introduced a course on the film of social change. He also started a program to bring in minorities from other departments."

There were others: Basil Wright, Hugh Gray, the film theorist Art McCarty, John Adams, Lew Steuben. Big film directors like King Vidor and Josef von Sternberg came through. "But it was a funny thing. It wasn't the normal student-teacher relationship. It was irreverent. There would be these arguments. I mean, serious, bloody, four-letter-word kind of arguing. The teacher would tell you your film was a pile of crap—they wouldn't use those words—but tell you, 'You insult me by doing this,' and students would get on this same bandwagon. 'I've seen better movies by three-year-olds.' Whatever. It was very competitive. At the time, the film department was virtually only taking a few students a year. So people thought they were an elite group. At UCLA you had to come up with something original, because people were always guarding their stuff. It was an atmosphere where you had to outdo someone basically, that's what it boiled down to. It was just an extraordinary struggle to achieve this. 'Oh God, don't show it at the end of the quarter!' If it was slick or anything like that—forget it."

He told me these days had been a very good time to be a filmmaker. "It allowed you to develop a viewpoint. It wasn't like a commercial thing, where you had to satisfy all these people. You were satisfying potential artists. People who had done a lot of study in film, and had their own vision, so they can appreciate in a certain way other people's films. And then say, 'Hell, I got to do what I got to do,' and make them. It hardens you in a way."

Burnett never really considered making a living as a filmmaker. "Because it didn't exist like that in the '60s, like it is now. Kids now, boy, they do anything in order to get paid and get a three-picture deal. The unions were very strong, then. And we didn't have the independent market to consider; independent market wasn't like it is today. Unions kept you out." At one point, he considered becoming a cameraman, but he found out that if he even were to get in the union—which was difficult—it would have taken him "twenty years to move up the ladder, to become assistant camera, to be a first cameraman." But those were the rules of the cinema. "We grew up under those circumstances, you didn't have anxiety or anguish like the kids have today, you know, 'What? Wait twenty years!' I just got myself a Super8, and jumped up to shooting features. It wasn't really a conscious decision. Our expectations were different. We didn't have sense enough to use grants and stuff like that. We were working and *really* independent. We were making films for social change. Maybe a library or schools or some political group would be interested. As far as getting money from a bank, uh-uh."

Neither did Black Hollywood exist. Then came Gordon Parks with his *The Learning Tree* and *Three Day Pass,* and the trailblazing Melvin Van Peebles with his then-unorthodox and popular films. "All of a sudden you had the black exploitation film." By the middle 1970s, Parks would go on to make studio-backed films like *Shaft.* Sidney Poitier got behind the camera. But for Charles Burnett, it was "still remote in a way."

Serious black filmmakers were somehow left out of that explosion of exploitation. But they continued; Burnett continued. He credits Oliver Franklin, among others, for etching out a place for independent black films through organizing film festivals at historically black colleges, and in Europe, establishing tours. Groups of filmmakers emerged, though not in staggering numbers. "It was through word of mouth. Oliver and a few other people laid the foundation. Serious journalists started writing about black films. It was an evolution."

Burnett became more interested in "people dealing with a number of real-life matters on a more concrete level, changes, history. A lot of us were making films about kicking the dope dealer out, or whatever. Being like a Superfly, walking down the street, this narcissistic looking at themselves. Glorification of nothing. But these same people were doing some serious thinking about social problems. That was one of the good things. They had to do unconventional things in terms of cinema to encourage people to go on in different areas. They weren't concerned about entertainment value. The kind of conventional restraint that is automatically imposed on ordinary film. They'd have long shots, really long takes, some of it would be very didactic—most of it was—though they were really good. You saw some people who were serious, talking about changing the country's attitude. Here people were making films about tomatoes eating people, man-killers—just anything to take your mind off what's going on. You got out of that mode. Entertainment is not a dirty word. But what's more important is people's vision."

A developing artist, Burnett believed, must ask what is most important: entertainment or craft? Art or money? "Then you have all these accountants, people from law school, telling you how to make a movie.

You really can't have a police scene, 4,500 cops, and a budget of so-and-so and so-and-so. I mean you don't need those kinds of things. They don't like stories that are interesting stories, if they don't really fall inside a pattern. What they know, and are familiar with. That's why they keep making the same movie over and over again. When they talk about films, they talk about what's happening in the first act and the second act, and so you come with this stuff laid out. I can't talk about movies that way—as if entertainment is the common denominator.

"Looking at these kids today, you say, 'Well, what do they have?' Motivational speakers? Who are they? When times are bad, do you really put it in your heart? You wonder what they have to fall back on. I remember getting in trouble, and just remembering these guys who used to live up the street who did all this hard work, plastering and stuff—they kept on going. What does it take? I said, 'God, I'm in much better shape than they are.' It's drawing on other people. But these kids now, they're a product of babies having babies, and this generation watched movies that were very cynical and had this sort of anti-feeling. It's as if you're bashed for doing anything decent. It's the difference between sentimentalizing something and having good emotion. A sense of right and wrong. You find a lot of critics who criticize you if you take a stand. If you say, 'No, I don't think one should show some guy having an affair with a six-year-old, eight-year-old, nine-year-old. He doesn't have the right. What kind of business is this? You have to support someone who's decadent and immoral? This freedom is art? Freedom of expression?' It would be different if you were putting something back into the community. If we look at what's happening with this whole crack thing, and all this other violence in films, somebody will say, 'Well, it's not the guns that kill people, it's the people.' You say, 'Yeah, but you romanticize this stuff on the screen.' I remember I was doing this thing on the Black Panthers, and people thought that there should be a shoot-out; they thought that would be a commercial selling point. There's all this kind of dumbness. There's no sense that there are consequences to your actions. Films have had an effective role in creating this relationship between people. Critics will ask, 'Do you want to censor someone?' I say, 'No, I just want people to be responsible.' We live in a community. If you don't try to do something, you're going to be a victim. You can't just put bars up around the window and say, 'The hell with people out there.'

"I was trying to do a film that dealt with these things. About having a sense of value, right and wrong. How does it affect you when you don't have roots and deny the fact that you're from a certain place? How important are those things in people's lives? The fact that there is an oral tradition somewhere that is being lost. These were all the things that brought me around to *To Sleep with Anger.*"

Burnett found film audiences today "very strange." "They accept less, and have a different critical sense about them. I think black audiences have to demand more. I think this whole notion of entertainment just screws things up. Most films today are like roller-coaster rides. It's like wham-bam, and back in bed. Very little dialogue. I think we are yet to be able to tell our own story, mainly because when you have an executive over you saying, 'Well, I think we ought to do this and that because I don't understand this.' He went to Harvard Law School, whatever. Now what would he know? It prevents anything positive from happening. A lot plays on fear. Even in commercials. The audience responds positively to those kinds of things. We have a generation with no expectations. We have got to have expectations. It's not just showing the graphic side. It has to be a little bit layered and involved rather than showing someone getting their throat cut. A guy kills the guy, cuts the guy's throat, and the movie's over. They got revenge."

Many of the problems that beset African Americans were due to a dearth of positive images, all around, from history books to television, even to the "token Black History Month." It was a complex issue, he said, but "we're contributing to it by not being responsible."

"Most characters we see are one-dimensional. They're bad to bad. The stories are one-dimensional. You don't see a guy involved with other issues. We can count on this rut and that rut—someone killed a guy's brother, so he has to kill a half-dozen people to get even, and then he's satisfied. Then he goes and gets the girl. I was recently reading about Joseph Conrad and the complexity of his characters. It's not a question that these guys are good. They're people who are trying to define themselves as they go along and have all these contradictions." Black characters "can be positive. Not that they have to be a doctor, suit on, or something. But a guy who's struggling. He has these conflicts. He's struggling between good and evil. But he does wrong. One of the things about literature is that it is going to demand debate. Like Dostoevsky's *Crime and Punishment.*" Burnett liked the way the protagonist, Raskolnikov, becomes more of a human being—he becomes aware of his wrongdoing, "he ends with a moral point of view; it's redeeming in that sense, realizing that some things are not good. Which we all do."

"I think everyone looks at life very cheaply today. The way the papers and the media portray things. People laugh at people getting killed on screen. They cheer people getting killed. You see a homeless person, you just bypass him on the road. Everyone's concerned about making a living. Our values have changed. There's no longer that extended family. I don't think there is just one answer, one solution. Lots of things have to be done."

I first met Fletcher Gamble when I was a freshman and he was a sophomore at Chapel Hill, and we both lived in Grimes Dormitory. Thanks to Fletcher, I became involved in the Black Student Movement Gospel Choir, on campus—Fletcher was choir director—where I gathered fond memories and lifelong friends. Fletcher went on to medical school, and by the time I visited Los Angeles, he was living outside the city proper, and was well into his residency in pediatrics in Compton. I also found that he was still very much involved in church life, and directed a choir in a Compton church. I met up with him and attended church services one Sunday.

To me, Compton felt like a town that had once had an identity before being gobbled up into the megalopolis. The church was small though well kept, and the service was straight southern Baptist, and the folk all decked out in their Sunday-go-to-Meeting best (the absence of men my and Fletcher's age or younger was conspicuous). Watching Fletcher direct the choir, I felt transported back in time and across the country.

After church, we had lunch at a steakhouse nearby, and the place filled up with families, practically all black, dressed as if they, too, had just come from church.

Fletcher told me about his residency, and the sadly mixed fact that, for him, Compton was an excellent place to learn—the violence, the illness brought on by poverty and lack of education brought all manner of medical problems to his examination room.

Fletcher introduced me to Thierry,* another North Carolina native son, at a dinner party at his home, whom I found out was a teacher at a reform school in yet another Los Angeles suburb. I asked if I could visit, and he made the arrangements.

. . .

*The name of the teacher and the school and the students have been changed on request.

The Phoenix School, a residential school for the severely emotionally disturbed (SED), did not so much look like a low-level prison as the campus of a community college, peopled by more adults than students. There were 106 children. One social worker per twelve youths. There were seven teachers and a goodly number of aides. Though the head administrator was black, the only black teacher with the proper credentials was Thierry.

The class, aside from the presence of a guard, felt very much like the rambunctious classes of preteens and early teens I had been exposed to back in New York—though here the subjects were decidedly remedial, and it was clear these good-looking young kids had almost no attention span.

Most of the children were "refused" by the public school system, described as having "oppositional/argumentative behavior," "AWOL-ing from stressful situations," "impulsive," "verbally or physically abusive," "brief attention spans of five-minute intervals," known to "yell obscenities," "provoke peers through name-calling and physical fighting." Some were described as exhibiting "fighting, lying, manipulative behavior." As having "significant depression," "immaturity," "impaired self-esteem," "suspicious and distrustful of others," "lacks confidence," "acquires a detached facade." Some students—girls and boys—would behave in a "provocative, flirtatious" sexual manner.

The school operated six days a week, and though private (or "non-publicly funded"), was operated under the educational oversight of the State of California and the Los Angeles United School District. The school day went from 7 a.m. to 2 p.m. Classes started at eight.

"I have to respect these kids," Thierry told me, "even if I don't want to."

Ninety percent of these children were on probation and 10 percent were wards of the court—either "orphans" or their families couldn't be found, or they had been taken away from their families. Though I did not witness it, apparently it was not uncommon for youngsters to be restrained if they got out of control or were judged to be causing harm to themselves or others. Thierry told me that around Christmas time, these incidents were much higher. "Restraint," he told me, "is not pretty." Those children who had been physically or sexually abused were particularly problematic to deal with. They tended to want more attention, Thierry said. There was a danger of group sex, and students were "never to be left alone with any one teacher."

The sex offenders attended a group session with a staff psychologist once a week, and they had their own dorm.

Everyone worked, I was told; some received twenty-five cents an hour, others twenty cents. After graduation, many of the former students wound up in a drug rehabilitation center, halfway house, or YMCA, and not a few, simply on the streets.

In fact, one student—Thierry told me he had been his favorite success story—had worked off his court-stipulated restitution, $1,200 for robbery, and had saved $800. He was duly enrolled in a regular school and was doing well in physics, English, history. The boy had been from a smart family, and had a sister in college.

But his story was sadly rare. The majority of their stories were not so uplifting.

There was the boy whose mother tied him to a tree for three weeks, and beat him with an extension cord because he didn't do his homework; the idea of homework still "freaked him out."

There was the boy whose father was a minister and whose mother was in jail, a heroin addict. The boy's aunt had been killed, and the boy had no place to go since the father had disowned him.

There was the boy whose mother overdosed, and whose father had been working on getting custody. A week before the father was to come get his son, he died in a dentist's chair.

One boy had been a gang member and had been arrested. On the way to pick the young fellow up at the precinct, both his parents were killed by a speeding truck.

Another girl's parents had both died, and she was repeatedly convicted of complicity for major crimes committed by the gangboys she hung out with.

Thierry told me that only one student had graduated with straight A's. There had been a huge celebration—the newspapers covered the event. A year later, the young man was in jail for armed robbery.

Thierry said, "These kids are institutionalized and then go back to families who set no limits. The kid's self-esteem goes down. There is no praise at the end of the week for going to school, for staying out of trouble." Thierry believed in the behaviorist approach to education and training. "Kids need to be constantly reminded of these things."

He noted that most of the relatively few white kids at the school were in psychiatric care, watched for suicide, and had a tendency to run away; "black and Hispanic guys get their fun acting out."

Thierry said that roughly 80 percent of the kids were probably gang members. No signing was allowed in classes; no colors; no gang language. (The day before I came to the school, Thierry told me to be certain not to wear either blue or red of *any* type—blue for Crips, red for Bloods.) As Thierry saw it, gang members supplied "some love" for these kids in a world where they were liable to get none. It also brought the boys prestige. The younger kids were able to get close to older gang members, since the life expectancy for black males in Los Angeles was twenty-one, and the older members knew it and deliberately recruited the younger kids—as young as seven or eight. Those men who "escaped" their twenty-first birthdays were not expected to make it much past thirty-five.

"It is a cycle that creates a career criminal," Thierry said. "The system is designed to keep kids in the system. And the kids know it. Ask them, and they'll tell you, 'I'm going right back to jail.' Many of them have family in jail, and they *want* to be institutionalized."

Later I asked Thierry, "Why do you do it?"

He laughed, and then became pensive, and after a silence: "I don't know about the faith, but there is a hope. To see Mary laugh. Those little rewards—'cause it ain't the pay!

"As long as we have a society where adults shirk responsibility, we will always have need for these facilities."

But to my mind there was something more. Something deeply Christian in Thierry's attitude, commitment—inescapably. Fletcher, Thierry and I were all cut from the same black Baptist cloth. We had all received the same type of "home training," education, from black women especially, who had themselves learned at home and at historically black colleges and universities; we were all shaped by a community with American roots deeper than the Kennedys' of Boston or even the Chandlers' of Los Angeles; we had all been supported by those communities to go to the large "white" universities as ambassadors, something we were aware of every single day. There was no mistaking what kept Thierry's feet to the fire. I instantly understood, and admired and loved him for it. "*Here is a new commandment I give you: That you love one another.*" For better or for worse, regardless how I or anybody else felt about that church-haunted, Christ-haunted, sin-haunted background, that same background empowered us, and made us more humane than we realized.

By that same light, Thierry, Fletcher and, for that matter, Rick Moss, and Charles Burnett and Trey Ellis, as black men, were not so much exceptions as they were outnumbered. The question then became, how could that sense of sympathy, of empathy, and of self-worth be taught to the boys and girls of the Phoenix School? How could they be rescued?

Escape from Los Angeles? I have only been to Los Angeles a few times in my life, and I always find leaving it difficult. For some reason, in Los Angeles, rather than in Seattle or in Portland or in San Francisco or in San Diego, I feel as if I am truly on the edge of the continent—*Nowhere to run to, Baby/Nowhere to hide.* I am reminded of the main character in Robert Penn Warren's *All the King's Men,* who, in a moment of profound despair, gets in his car and drives west, until he arrives in Long Beach, and turns around and returns to Louisiana. Perhaps it is the feeling that something should be there, some answer. That after so many miles and miles, the landscape of the North American continent should offer up some reward for simply coming the distance. Perhaps, like so many present-day cults that make California their home, the feeling is merely the need for just such an answer. But the answer ain't coming; it just ain't there. The answer must be in us, not in the land.

Though it may scandalize fellow easterners to say so, I actually like the city of Los Angeles. Despite its urban problems, and the vast array of poverty, hidden so charmingly and effectively from the haute arrivistes of the well-heeled burbs and subs, I find the mishmash, the automobile-ridden, varied, congested, polluted, consumer-driven, architecturally challenged, laid-back, CHiPs-patrolled, desert-defying megalopolis appealing, in its dare, there on the edge of the Pacific. Engine of fantasy, warehouse of hopes, caldron of unrest, weaver of national spells. Unlike Seattle, evergreen and dreamlike and remote, puritan in its promise, Los Angeles is at the center of something in America that is at the precipice of what we all are, be we in a New England hamlet, a Georgia swampwater, a South Dakota range, or a midwestern efficiency. To be alive in the twentieth century is to have been touched by Los Angeles—it has invaded our dreams. Not merely the cinema, but the idea. Chandler, Otis, et al., were not simply building a private oasis out in the desert when they concocted the city where over 3 million people now live, they were making manifest what Manifest Destiny prophesied. They were enshrining that which was most big-shouldered about us, without Chicago's wind; that which was most empire about us, without New York's hard and driving ways and lack of space; that which was most sun-loving and gregarious about us, without the South's curse of the Civil War. Then Los Angeles fatefully metastasized, it outgrew even the dreams of its dreamers; it reached beyond its own destiny, and wrought a warped matrix of American ideals: loopy, lonesome and lone, Los Angeles, the crystal city, captures the many-spectrum light, and bends, separates, intensifies that light into our most colorful meanings. Los Angeles, the prism of our desire.

> In Southern California, in a small Negro community named in his honor, lives Colonel Allen Allensworth, a retired Army Chaplain, and his devoted wife. This community is located in the San Joaquin Valley, between Bakersfield, which is at the south, and Fresno, which is at the north, on the Santa Fe Railroad. The town is a little more than six years old. The people at Allensworth belong chiefly to an aspiring, self-respecting, self-supporting middle class—a class largely moved by the independent spirit to break away from the servant class and try their hand at agriculture and trade on their own responsibility.
>
> In all there are about 160 souls at Allensworth. They are all farmers, dairymen and traders. There is a hotel, with good accommodations and low rates; plenty of cool, refreshing water; several good country stores, a post-office, a railroad station with telephone and telegraph offices, and a large grain storage warehouse for the farmers of the district. The Negroes of this town are hard workers. They are prosperous, happy and contented.
>
> —Charles Alexander, *Battles and Victories of Allen Allensworth,* 1914

When we think of California today in terms of economics, most Americans first think of the movie industry, and then perhaps of technology, Silicon Valley, Hewlett-Packard, Apple, Hughes Aircraft, and the like. Surely those industries employ a great many people. But the thing that made California great, the thing that, in the unlikely event that the state should ever secede from the Union, would hurt us most, is agriculture. For the last hundred years, once transportation made it available and enough water was stolen to make it possible, the state has been an agricultural miracle. One of the key growing regions in California is the

Central Valley (which includes the San Joaquin), stretching from the mountains north of Los Angeles all the way to San Francisco Bay—literally some of the most fertile land in the world.

Delano is midway between Bakersfield and Fresno in the middle of the San Joaquin Valley. Oddly enough, the day I arrived, National Public Radio's *All Things Considered* did a piece on Delano and Tulare County. (California is, for all intents and purposes, the only place where people still talk about synchronicity—the Jungian concept that all coincidences are connected to a larger field of possibility; that nothing happens at random—with any level of seriousness. While there, I began to understand why.)

For the last twenty years or more, Caifornia's largely self-invented "problem" has been illegal immigration from Mexico. The valley has always needed cheap, mobile labor, and, since the Great War, has depended more and more on migrant Mexican labor. As Mexico's economy slipped, the population of Mexicans crossing the border increased, and as farm implements became more sophisticated, the demand for laborers decreased—but the Mexicans kept coming.

Tulare County had one of the highest percentages of Mexican nationals within the state of California, and, according to NPR, "the highest unemployment in California—30 percent," and it was suspected to be much higher due to the large number of "unreported persons." The report talked to people who spoke of eighteen or twenty-some people living in a two-room shack; of entire families living in garages.

Driving around Delano, I noted it was one of the few small towns I had seen whose downtown still functioned as a gathering place. On Saturday afternoon, the streets were full of people. I saw a few white faces and a few black faces, but most of the faces I saw were the handsome, dark brown faces of the descendants of the Aztecs and Maya, of Spain and of Africa.

Allensworth is not too far from Delano, the land thereabouts flatter than the Great Plains, sparsely vegetated, and even in December, at the height of the day, very warm—alkaline flats, full of weeds. I really didn't know what to expect as I headed toward Allensworth Historic State Park for my meeting with its chief savior and spiritual light. ("We're out in the desert. We're classified as desert because of the annual rainfall. Very little rain here. In the summer it's hot. In the winter it's cold . . .") As I turned off Highway 5 and crossed the railroad tracks, I began to see a settlement of trailers and houses back to the north, but the signs to Allensworth pointed in another direction, west. Allensworth was somewhere between an archeological dig and a few strikingly fresh, brightly painted structures. The visitor's center was housed in a mobile home.

Later, Cornelius Ed Pope would tell me that once upon a great time ago, much of the San Joaquin Valley had been covered by a saltwater lake, Tulare Lake. Shark's teeth had been found in the soil, as well as fossilized fish. He was also fond of speaking about the Alpaugh Indians who had lived in the area for centuries. Boat people, he told me, stellar cult people.

In 1908, when the black settlers came, they found four artesian wells. Water had not been a problem.

Mr. Pope told me that the state had been trying to develop this land for the past twenty years with limited success ("or at least not to the satisfaction of a whole lot of people"). Personally, he said, he felt that committed black folk would have to take charge and do it—it was their responsibility. "It irks me sometimes to see some very, very powerful folk—all of us—waiting for someone else to take our history and develop it: present it to us." What Allensworth needed was to be interpreted from a black perspective—it was a relevant history; a riveting history, he said.

Thus far, the eighty-acre historical site was dotted with only a few buildings. "We've focused on the main street. There'll be a string of houses going down both sides of this street. We'll build some twenty-odd houses. They'll tell the history of the first people that settled the town. We call them the Pioneering Black Families of Allensworth. We'll trace the history of those families from Emancipation right here to Allensworth. We'd done that with the little green house that sits over there. That's the Smith house. Through some historical research, we found out that that house was built by Frank and Laura Smith. They came off the Smith plantation in North Carolina. They came out and settled in Colorado Springs, Colorado, and immediately started off in business. They started a garbage business and a cleaning business for stoves and chimneys. Then Colonel Allensworth came into the area recruiting people, and they immediately sold their businesses and came to Allensworth.

"One day not too long ago, I was giving a tour to some people, and I told them about this house, and Frank and Laura Smith, first slaves to leave after Emancipation in North Carolina, and head out west, and this one lady says, 'My ancestors, my forefathers, my grandpas, they came from North Carolina, from the Smith plantation.' I said, 'Oh, yeah. Well, this was Frank and Laura Smith.' She says, 'Oh, those are my folk.' She had no idea. She said, 'Where do you people get your information?' I said, 'We interviewed a Winifred Smith. We got most of our information from one of the surviving sons.' She says, 'That was my grandpa.' That's the kind of history that we want to tell in these individual houses. We feel we're able to touch base with most of the large black families in the whole nation." And there were the Hacketts, and the Ashbys and so many other families, many of whom had yet to discover their connection to a place in the San Joaquin Valley.

Mr. Pope said that certain corporations were beginning to take an interest in the development of Allensworth. Kaiser Permanente was already involved. The National Heritage Foundation and Museum were said to be discussing getting involved. ("National Heritage has grand visions of growing into something sweet. They want to build a National Heritage facility right over in this area here, behind our campground. If they come in, that means a couple of hundred jobs.") Also direct fund-raising was on the horizon. ("We're talking about an eight-to-fifteen-million-dollar fund-raiser that's going to be taking place very, very shortly.") A new documentary was being made, which was to premiere in Los Angeles in a few months. A group called Friends of Allensworth was being organized, and there was talk of making the town private—perhaps a golf course: "a nine-hole course that would be north of town. We've already talked with people that are interested in putting up a motel-hotel, a small complex. We've talked about mini-malls. There's an awful lot of folk interested in moving in there." A bakery. A newspaper. Functioning livery stable and blacksmith attractions.

"Now most of the commercial private developments will take place just on the outside of the state parkland. We envision that to be a commercial area, going back about a quarter of a mile behind the park. All that land back there is virgin land, never been used before, and we expect to have homesites and stuff like that. That'll be where a lot of people will be living. They might even filter on back down to the old district. Land over there is all under ownership and pretty tied up. When we started off down here in 1969, I guess land was 200 bucks an acre, if anybody would buy it. A couple years ago, it started going up, it got up to about $1,000 an acre, and now it's 5,000, 6,000 bucks an acre."

To be sure, there was a sharp contrast between Mr. Cornelius Ed Pope's contagious, can-do, boosteristic, optimistic vision, and the denuded and lonesome landscape of Tulare County. Yet his talk was more than mere salesmanship; listening to him, as we stood on the platform outside the trailer that was the visitor's center, as he gestured to the few restored buildings, and saw beyond the flat and empty plain, I could not help but conjure up this future thriving Allensworth. Cornelius Ed Pope was something of a visionary, and his vision was catching.

Mr. Pope named the many festivals and celebrations held at the park, almost year round—from Juneteenth, the western Emancipation celebration, to black rodeo events. Since there were three debating societies in Allensworth, Mr. Pope dreamed of establishing an "old debating forum, getting participation from high schools, universities, things like that. Have teams of black debaters come and talk over some of the issues. I think that'd be nice." There was to be a site for black family reunions, and a group of ministers were discussing establishing a Baptist church—independent of the state, of course.

There was even talk of building an auditorium with an "animated" Colonel Allensworth giving some of his speeches. "We feel that it's just absolutely necessary that we begin to tell the story and do it in a dramatic way. That's what's happening now. That's about where we are."

Such talk had my head swimming. I could also see that Mr. Pope, so besotted by visions of a ghost-town-no-more, was perhaps even more besotted by visions of those ghosts. As he walked me around the town, his reveries were at times almost religious.

"Actually, what Allensworth is really all about was Colonel Allensworth and a group of his friends and business associates; they had been talking and planning for seven years, trying to find a spot where they could do this kind of experiment. To found a town, fund it, and manage it, and operate and run it, with black folk, all ex-slaves. To show the nation what the ex-slave was capable of doing. They had talked with Booker T. Washington at Tuskegee Institute. And they had discussed the brain drain that was taking place in California. Whenever a young, bright black person wanted a higher education, back in the early 1900s, they had to go somewhere else to get it, and they never came back. So all our bright lights were getting ripped off. And he said, 'Hey, let's build a Tuskegee-style institute right here.' That's what Allensworth was all about. 'We're going to take 50,000 of the biggest, baddest, blackest, smartest, wisest, most courageous, pioneering, adventuresome, successful black folk in the nation.' And isolate them from the whole world in a little colony here. And we'll show California and the nation and the world just what we are capable of doing. 50,000. Highest educated and skilled black folk in the nation. Now, when I think, that kind of frightens me even right now. All isolated out here in a little colony and dedicated to doing, to accomplishing one thing. That's a little scary. What a force that would be. That's what Allensworth was all about.

"So the first settlers, the pioneers that came, were all real accomplished people. Now they got off into the farming thing. They got off into a lot of masonry-type of work. They started little cement companies and well-digging, and they diversified. One of the first things they did, they went right over to a neighboring town, at Corcoran, and did the cement and brick work on a hotel. That's all they'd ever done in their lives, worked like that, so they could bid pretty, pretty reasonable. And they were master craftsmen. They built that doggone hotel over there in Corcoran, and people came from all around the surrounding communities to see this fantastic work that these ex-slaves had done, so then they were in competition for what little piece of the pie was available.

"That began to get a lot of people concerned about, 'Hey we got these black people over there. Instead of picking cotton and harvesting the fields, here they are coming into the towns and competing against the established white craftsmen of the area for what little work there is.' So that made it kind of risky. And that was another thing that contributed to their downfall."

The schoolhouse was the largest structure in town, then and now. "When they first started off, 300 families moved in almost immediately. They didn't have any school built at that time, so they took one of the resident's houses, and they started having school in their living room. So many kids were coming in that they had to go ahead." What would eventually become the library was originally built as a school. "They thought that would be good enough. The walls were bulging, because the town was just ballooning. Then they put almost all of their town resources into one puddle, and they came up with this school." The school was now a museum to those early settlers, the wood desks with the lift-up tops, the flags, the inkwells. Mr. Pope told me their display—pictures of Washington, Lincoln, Allensworth, and the first teacher, Professor Allan Payne, penmanship charts, the actual books the schoolchildren used—had won awards throughout the state, and was coveted by both the Los Angeles Museum and the Smithsonian. Even the cistern that stored rainwater for drinking had been restored. Walking about the schoolroom, Mr. Pope could have been a teacher there, in 1912. In fact, he had gone to school in this very building in second, third and fourth grades.

"All the kids from the first to high school sat on one side over there.

They could close this room off. Professor Payne and the teachers would do their teaching thing and then in the evenings, after the school kids would leave, they'd raise this partition up and they'd have the Women's Civic Improvement come in here. And all those sisters would come in. They'd make quilts. 'Welcome to Allensworth.' The Men's Progressive Association had their meetings in here. This was where all the debating societies would meet. There was no electricity in Allensworth in those days. No radio. None of that kind of good stuff. So there was pianos around. There was a girls' glee club, boys' singing group, a couple of church choirs, barbershop quartet. And a town orchestra, and there was a string band and a brass band, and a couple of groups, quartets—the music would be all over town. When I was a kid, '38, '39, and '40, well, we had radios and electricity in those days, but it was very, very similar to that. There was still a lot of music-makers in Allensworth. That was quite nice."

Stepping out of the schoolhouse, Mr. Pope walked me around the town, to the few restored structures, and to the sites of older ones.

"All of the streets in Allensworth were named after famous black folk—Paul Laurence Dunbar, Frederick Douglass." In fact Douglass had been one of the colonel's friends.

Mr. Pope pointed out what had been the Carter house. Mr. Carter had been the "entrepreneur of Allensworth." He started a livery stable with five or six horses and surreys, which he rented out. Also he was the town iceman, hauling ice from nearby Corcoran, which was eighteen miles away, by mule and cart. "Kind of a dangerous business trying to sell ice during the summertime in the desert. I understand that sometimes the sales would be low, and all the brother would wind up with was a puddle of water." Mr. Pope told me that—according to Delilah Beasley—the people of Allensworth built a 50,000-sack grain storage facility near the train track, "which was the largest between Los Angeles and San Francisco." According to Mr. Pope, between ten and fifteen trains stopped at the depot each day. This gave Allensworth an enormous boost.

We walked through what had been Allensworth's commercial district. Singleton's store, and Hindsman's drugstore, the Vickers' store, the Gross drugstore, ("Mary Gross was another of those fantastic sisters. As soon as she heard of Colonel Allensworth's student programs, she came here and opened up her drugstore, She became known as the town doctor. She delivered babies and took care of everybody that was sick and she'd go out in the fields and get the herbs and the natural medicines—she just did it."), the blacksmith, the town hotel—all of which were in various stages of restoration; some were standing and open, but many were just foundations.

He showed me the courthouse, which was fifty years old. Once enough people had settled in Allensworth, the town had been declared a judicial district. The first black judge and the first black constable in the state of California were in Allensworth. There was also a voting precinct.

Accounts I had read about Mr. Pope said that he had resided as a child in Colonel Allensworth's house. "Yeah. I lived in the library too. The library was a little old."

Mr. Pope's parents had been pioneers in the all-black town of Boley, Oklahoma. They had been originally from Kansas City. He had yet to be born, but his brothers told him stories of their trek from Muskogee to Boley. "By ox and wagon train. How they had the cow and the chickens and everything. Homesteaded. Down there for a long time.

"The town was almost abandoned when my family moved in here in '38 or '39, right in the midst of the Depression. The little library had been lived in as a house for some time. And we moved in there. Lived in there and later on we moved from there over to Colonel Allensworth's house. When I lived in Colonel Allensworth's house, there was an attic upstairs. And they had told us, 'Don't mess around in the attic, because there was a bunch of Colonel Allensworth's stuff stored up there.' But we little kids would get up in there anyway, and I'd dress up in Colonel Allensworth's uniform." He laughed remembering. "Oh yeah. I'd play Colonel Allensworth. I was a little one, second, third and fourth grade. And there was a lot of spirit-type contact. In fact, sometimes I almost feel as though I got chosen from all those kinds of experiences. But then Colonel Allensworth was a kind of a mystical guy, and in a speech, called the 'Battle of Life and How to Fight It,' he talked about the five manly virtues, a condensed version of the ten virtues of the African mystery system. They're the ten virtues that Socrates took and broke down into the four cardinal virtues. Know thyself. All that kind of stuff. I've studied the ten virtues in detail, and the way he talked about them was so far advanced, I'd say, 'Hey. He was a master. He was a master Mason.'"

When Mr. Pope lived in the town there were seventy or eighty other families there. All black. "All of the skilled labor had gone. The town was just hanging on. We became migrant farm workers. We left in '40. It was pretty rough. The war hadn't started off yet, and we moved into some farm labor camps and some tents, until the war started. After the war started, things picked up, and we finally settled in Tulare."

When he showed me the house, his already reverent mode intensified. It was as if we had just stepped into a temple, the Holy of Holies. Restoration had been completed, and the house dedicated in 1977.

"When we got the house, it was just flat. Nothing left. Nothing. We restored it and we made it a beautiful little old palace. This is Colonel Allensworth and Mrs. Allensworth's home. Now we have to be as careful as we possibly can once we enter this house."

Most of the furnishings were as authentic as they could make them. The chairs were the originals, as were the colonel's military paraphernalia. There was a piano of the same type that the Allensworths owned. ("Mrs. Allensworth was a classical pianist, and she would play the piano and people would come and sit on the lawns and recreate themselves, and he would give lectures.") The pictures on the walls were the "exact pictures" the family had hung, pictures of the colonel and his military cohorts, friends, their two daughters. ("Their daughters were very, very refined. Classic ladies.") The desks. Hatpins. Books. Replicas of the silverware. Certificates. And a United States flag with forty-six stars, which was the number of states when Colonel Allensworth was chaplain of the 24th Infantry. The kitchen, restored. ("We went so far as to get the old jack rabbit meat grinder—we've got some canned goods and things set around.") The bathtub. A fainting couch. The colonel's military trunk. Most of the actual artifacts came from the grandchildren of the Allensworths. The trunk had been in the military museum of the Presidio in San Francisco.

"We've been through a lot of experiences and an awful lot of research, just to get the history of it. What furniture was here, what furniture was there. They were lucky to find an awful lot of the artifacts that were original to the house. The state historian, this is his dream house. He calls it one of the finest houses in the entire state park system.

"Nothing has ever come up missing in this house. Everyone is a little spiritual when they come here; there is something that takes place here," Mr. Pope said, with something more than pride. "This is our little palace. Now we got this jewel right out here."

He took me into a smallish room in the front of the house. "I always called this room here the most important room in the house because this is where Colonel Allensworth did it all. This was his personal, private study. I call it the most important room in all of Allensworth." Mr. Pope showed me a letter on the desk addressed to "His excellency, Grover Cleveland, President of the United States. From Colonel Allensworth."

He pointed to an aged book in the center of the colonel's desk. "I call this the most important book in the town. This is a Webster's blue-back speller. Colonel Allensworth was born a slave. His master had a little son who was the same age as the colonel, nine years old. And he called this boy 'Master Tommy,' and they would play together when Master Tommy came home from school. So Colonel Allensworth's mother told him, she said, 'When Master Tommy comes home from school, you go play school with him, and have him teach you what he learned that day. You learn how to read and write.' So they did that. And Master Tommy was teaching Colonel Allensworth how to read and write, all out of this Webster's little blue-back speller, and they got caught. Master caught them. And the punishment in those days for a slave learning to read and write was to cut an ear off. There was a time when they'd hack a finger off, but that was destroying productivity—a guy could pick more cotton with five fingers than with four. They said, 'We're not going to cut your ear off, but we're going to sell you.' So they shipped him downriver, and sold him for 960 bucks. When he left his mother, she gave him fifty cents that she had been saving, and she told him, 'Son, go buy you a little book. And continue learning how to read.' And Colonel Allensworth did that.

"There's an irony to that story. Later on in life, Colonel Allensworth, when he was a big, high-ranking military official, and Tommy was doing a military career too, they ran into each other, and they just looked at each other and said, 'Hey, you Allen Allensworth?' 'And you Master Tommy?' And they laughed, shook hands, and talked about their childhood together—and the slave was outranking his prior master. There's a little irony to that. I always appreciate that, and the schoolchildren, they really like that because it shows that everyone wasn't just cruel and downing us altogether."

Later Mr. Pope gave me his theories about why the town had failed.

"In order for the town to be self-sufficient, there had to be extensive agriculture going on so they could have something to eat. And there were a number of small farms all located about two, three miles from here on back. They had five-, ten-, twenty-acre farms all around Allensworth where they were raising fresh produce, and a lot of the guys even got off into actual business, making some money. They raised a lot of sugar beets.

"There were big farmers all around here, and a lot of grain that was grown in the area, and a lot of cotton. And the big farmers, they looked on Allensworth as being a farm labor camp. A supply camp full of cheap labor to get their crops in. That was their conception of it, but that wasn't what it was all about. But they've always tried to keep it as that farm labor camp concept."

Indeed, the desire to remain independent of the other farms, as Mr. Pope saw it, became the mote in the eye of the surrounding white farmers. "That was pretty difficult for some of the neighboring towns to swallow. People that weren't supposed to know how to read or write or do anything. Plus they had a library, so many books poured through that library, that Tulare County put a special committee together to investigate, to find out what are those ex-slaves were reading? They read more books out of that library than any library of comparable size in the state of California." Mr. Pope gave a belly laugh.

Mr. Pope was not happy with the current "official story" of how Allensworth was a haven for escaped slaves. "I don't see anybody trying to escape from anything. I see it more as a gallant effort to jump off into something new. To show what we're capable of doing. A bold, creative and courageous step." He found equally unsatisfactory the "official" story of why the town became deserted. "Arsenic in the water, and then Tulare County declares the town a nonviable community and shuts off all county funding, and the town dies immediately after that.

"Once that kind of stuff got out, then the dismemberment, the fragmentation of the town began to take place almost immediately. This town was disorganized, was disassembled in almost exactly the same way as Boley, Oklahoma. And that includes all kinds of things to get rid of this town. External forces just said, 'Hey, got to go, got to go, got to go.' In later years, arsenic was discovered in the town water supply here; I haven't researched it yet, but I'd sure like to know how many towns in the state of California have had such a high concentration of arsenic found in their drinking water that they had to be shut down. I think this might be the only one, and it's the only black town. That's kind of coincidental."

The cemetery the settlers used was about a half mile out of town. No one had been buried there for fifty years until just the week before, when one of the surviving matriarchs of the town died. "And her family buried her in there. So we've reactivated our graveyard." But they were uncertain of how many people had been buried there. "The local farmers ripped off all the tombstones. Plowed it up and planted alfalfa.

"I tell you, we got here just in time to save the town. The school had actually been sold—for scrap lumber. The school bell was gone. They were going to plow the whole town up and plant cotton here. *Ebony* magazine ran a story on it a few years back and called it 'The Town That

Refused to Die.' Whenever I give tours and things, I always say that that's the thing about Allensworth. The town actually earned its reputation. It's been seemingly dead a whole lot of times. Sometimes I come over here, and I'm all alone in town, and I say, 'Hey, it sure does look dead.' And it always pops right back to life. Two weeks later, we had 6,000 people running around town; horses were running up and down.

"But as far as it happening, I'm absolutely positive it's going to happen. I just know it's going to happen. I know it's going to happen." And he laughed like Santa Claus.

Mr. Pope sent me to talk to one of the very few surviving original Allensworth people.

The Herring place was in Shakley, out from Bakersfield, so far out into the flat, cultivated country that no other house or structures caught my eye. The house itself was modest, and clearly had been added onto several times over the years; and the yard was full of machinery, and dogs, dogs that immediately barked and bared their teeth. But my granddaddy had taught me long ago how to deal with strange dogs, and besides, I had come much too far—from the other side of the continent—to be halted by a few cacophonous canines.

Gemelia Hall Herring reminded me deeply of my great-great aunt Georgiana: silver-tinted hair, large glasses—for a few moments she was a bit bewildered, for she had misplaced her purse, just like my Aunt Georgiana had often done. (By this time, I was acutely aware of how easily I framed people through other people I had known. Do all people do this?)

It was said that Gemelia Hall Herring knew Colonel Allensworth. "I don't remember what the colonel looked like. No, but someone wrote an article in some book—I got that book here now—about me going to the funeral with my mother. And that was a lie. I ain't never went to no funeral." She laughed at the apparent audacity. "Not to his funeral, because I didn't even know the man. I wasn't but six years old when he died. Now I have a sister that's four years older than I am. She remembers him. And she lives in Oakland.

"But to me, Allensworth, I thought, was a beautiful place. We'd go to our meetings, and one of the men asked the rangers, 'How long would it take before they could complete restoring Allensworth?' And he said, 'About twenty years.' The man said, 'Oh my God, I'll be dead in that time.' I said, 'Well, I won't be.' I said, 'I intend to make a hundred. And I would like to see that park finished.' But anyway, everybody was prosperous at that time, until the water began to recede and people couldn't make a living without it. Some stayed on, and some didn't. My dad was one that left. In 1916, he went back to Bakersfield.

"When my dad heard about this place, he came from Alabama—one of the worst places in the South." Apparently, her father had made an inflammatory speech in Alabama and had to leave town or risk his life. Eventually, most of his family followed him, his mother and father, five brothers and four sisters. They all bought land within a couple of miles of one another. She had been born in the house her father built there on Checker Road. "I did not want to sell that place when they died." But taxes and family disagreements forced them to sell the property. She had always wanted to reclaim her property there. Rebuild there. She would still like to go back to Allensworth to live.

In Bakersfield, her family seemed to prosper. "My dad grew alfalfa and he had cows and hogs. And my mother had her own chickens. She'd take her eggs to town. She had that many eggs, she'd take to town. Every week, to trade for groceries. She'd take them by the crates. And there's thirty-six dozen in a crate. We had them in Allensworth too, but not that number. Everybody had his own everything. Livery stable was there, and when we had picnics, they'd hitch the horses to the wagon, and go around and pick up everybody that wanted to go to the picnic. Everybody, a lot of the women, all the kids naturally, wanted to go on the wagon.

"And we'd be the last ones they'd pick up because we lived back down this way from the schoolhouse. We would wait and go on the wagon, with the rest of the kids. I never did know exactly where we went—it's back down this way, coming toward town. There was a lot of little streams of water running through there, and all kinds of little trees growing and everything. Nice shade and all. And that's where we would go. But I've never seen that place since I left. I guess people have bought it up, but I am going to find it one day—soon. Soon. Soon.

"My dad, after he'd get all his crops in—he raised sugar beets, alfalfa and grain—after he'd get his crop in, well, he'd go and work for other ranchers. One rancher by the name of Isaac. He was a fence rider, my dad.

"You know what a fence rider is? This Mr. Isaac had hundreds and hundreds head of cattle and horses, wild horses. He had some wild cattle too, and some that they milked, because he had to separate out the dairy. They'd churn butter and all. Well, my dad would ride the fence. To see whether there was any broken places in the fences, so if it was, he'd mend them to keep the cows and the horses in. And that's what you call a fence rider.

"And he also broke horses. But not for riding, to hook to the buggy. Or to plow, or whatever you wanted them to do. Sometimes he'd ride a horse home. We had horses of our own, but if we'd ask him, 'Papa, will that horse let you ride him?' He'd say, 'Oh, yeah, he'd let you.' So we rode that horse. And the horse's name was Major. And he was a big old Clydesdale. A big old foot-horse like that. You know, heavy. But he could run. And we'd get on him and we'd ride. And my mother would just holler at us, 'Get off that horse!' But if my dad said you could ride him, that's all we'd need. The ranch was about thirteen miles from where we lived. And in the summertime, my next to my oldest sister, she cooked out there for my dad, and some of the men that was working out there. So in the summertime, I'd go out there and stay with her. This was a great big old house. It had a porch all the way around, on the inside. And Miss Highbeck, the rancher's wife, she would come down there on the days that they would churn. She had a little boy, and she'd come get all the butter she wanted and take it home, and she'd bring a tricycle down there for her little boy to ride around in the house, because there was a lot of snakes and things, and she didn't want him out in the yard. So she'd leave the tricycle there. Then when she'd go home, I'd ride this tricycle out. All the way around this house. On Thursdays, when they'd churn, my sister kept all the butter she needed for the ranch. She'd send me home with a pan of butter, on this horse by the name of Major."

"By yourself?" I asked.

"Well how else? Who else was going to ride on the horse?"

"How old were you?"

"I was between six and eight, somewhere in there. Oh, I'd been riding other horses before I was that old." She laughed. "But we rode our own horses, you know. My three older sisters, they used to ride a horse by the name of Maude. And they was all three on this horse. We would always put the horse down in the ditch, and then jump on. The horse had to climb the ditch to come out. So the one sitting on the back, she was sliding off. And she held on to Helen, and Helen was in the middle, and she was pulling on the mane to keep from flying off and pulling onto Ethel to keep Ethel put. And they all fell off of that horse." Mrs. Hall Herring laughed again. "And the horse stopped right there. She didn't go another step till they all got up. And they pulled her on out of the ditch, and I don't know how they got to the house. But anyhow, I rode that same horse. And she was good. Wherever you fell off of her, she stopped right there. She wouldn't go another step. My dad trained his horses, I'm telling you, to take care of us—and him too. And so this particular horse, Major, when I rode him home, I couldn't run him. I couldn't run him because I had to hold on to this butter. I didn't want to lose any butter. He'd walk every step of the way. And jackrabbits would jump up out of the sagebrush, and he never batted an eye. These wild horses would come to the fence and neigh, and Major never missed a step. He just kept walking. And I'd come thirteen miles every time, every week. I'd bring that butter home.

"And so we left in 1916, coming back to Bakersfield. I'd never been back to Allensworth since then, until about seven or eight years ago."

These days Mrs. Hall Herring was having leg troubles. She had had an operation on her kneecap due to arthritis. Ever since the replacement, she had been forced to use a walker. She could not put much pressure on the leg, and she was extremely cross with the doctor who had promised better use.

"But now I wouldn't walk outside this door. Because you just never know who's around or what's going to happen, I wouldn't walk nowhere now."

Allensworth was a fresh memory for Mrs. Herring. "Everybody had his own piece of ground. You wanted five acres, you bought it. Ten acres, twenty, whatever. It was run by blacks all together. There was no whites. Only white people there were the man at the railroad station and his family. The white people, they went to school there, because there was only three white children; white people had two boys and a girl. They lived at the station. A train stopped six to eight times a day. It was a loading zone between San Francisco and Los Angeles. And there used to be a lady, she lived in Corcoran, a white lady, but she would load her own grain, sacks of grain on this wagon. I don't know how many horses she had pulling it. But we always called her the twenty-mule team. And she would come right past the school and go to the station to unload her grain on the boxcars. Did her own unloading. And whenever she would come through, Professor Payne would let us come out of our room and stand in a window and watch her go by. I don't know whether she had twenty mules or not, but she had a lot of them. She would drive this wagon right past the school, and we'd stand in the window and watch her go by. And she'd tell them, 'gee' and 'haw,' and 'get up' and 'move.' You know. Gee and haw. One means 'get up' and the other means 'stop.' But we'd always say, 'whoa' and 'get up.' They were just a sight for us to see. But she would haul this grain out of Alpaugh. Alpaugh had lots of grain. She would load her own wagon and unload it into the boxcars. Never asked nobody nohow."

Her memories of Professor Payne were also vivid. "He was a good teacher, but I saw him with three boys who had done something and he had him some switches, and he was switching those boys. One boy told him, 'Don't hit me with that stick.' He was a little old man. But he was a good teacher. My teacher was a lady teacher. She taught to the fifth grade, and he had the grades on the other side till the twelfth. There was a partition that you pulled down between the two rooms. And when we had a meeting, a program or something, you pushed it up and everybody was all together. In 1976, when we had the first program, the dedication of Allensworth to the state park, my teacher was there. She died the next year. She wasn't but twelve, ten or fifteen years older than me."

Mrs. Hall Herring had been a woman accustomed to farm life, and now, even in her eighties, she missed it, especially not being able to tend her garden the way she would like—though she still made the attempt with help from her daughter, who lived next door. Her curly mustard greens were popular. She sold them to local stores. ("People here in Bakersfield knew about them, and they'd tell their people. They'd come from San Francisco; they'd come from Nevada. Everywhere to get some greens.")

Aside from a man who leased the Herring land, they had been the only black farmers in the area. "We're the only blacks out here in the sun. We're the only two." The Herrings had been Methodist, but the closest Methodist church had been in Roscoe, so for years they had attended the Baptist church in Bakersfield. "Wasn't no black church outside of the Holiness. There are a lot of Baptists live around here. Not a whole lot of colored. One colored lady lived right over there, but she moved to Bakersfield. There are not too many blacks living around here in Shakley." So the little socializing her family did was at the Bakersfield church, or among their relatives elsewhere in California.

I wondered if Mrs. Hall Herring thought the downfall of Allensworth was conspired.

"Well, I don't know. The water was the main thing, and see, at one time, after they'd built the schools, they figured that's not going to be nothing to them black folks anyway. But when Colonel Allensworth wanted to build a university up here, then they wouldn't let him do that. Then everybody was on his own in Allensworth. But when the water begin to recede, the people couldn't do nothing without water."

Mr. Cornelius Ed Pope described himself to me as an ancestor worshipper. "When we've had a problem, we've always resolved it. Because there's been a lot of spiritual help. If there are any spirits out there, they sure as hell going to try and congregate around somebody who digs them, and adores them, and worships them and loves them. If there's any way to communicate, they're going to do that."

Among other things, Mr. Pope believed, the saving grace of Allensworth was history. "Their big mistake was allowing the history to be told. I shot from the hip." Popular interest, from church groups, local organizations, family outings, gave the town a stronghold. Today it would be very difficult to dismantle Allensworth. "Getting the right political voice has been a problem. We've got the right political voice now."

"You must be tired," I said to Mr. Pope. "Being the spearhead for this town for so long."

He nodded. "We've been at it for a little over twenty years. Almost twenty-five. All kinds of things were thrown against us. All kinds of vicious, vicious lies and stuff. Even when we first put our signs up, right on the highway. They'd shoot them down. For ten years, we couldn't keep signs up. And then about eight or nine years ago, when we put them up, they left them alone. Now no problems. The times have changed down here in the valley. It's changing dramatically. I don't think this park being here has been an influence; I think it's just a national trend. Just getting along better now."

"And the spirits have held on," I said.

"The spirits are definitely here. Getting it together. There's some visitations, advice from spiritual forces. And they have actually shown themselves in a weird way."

"Really?"

"Just to show there is an entity that's involved," he said, not gravely, but solemnly. "Yeah. Yeah."

When I asked Mr. Pope about his thoughts on the state of African America, he told me, as an ancestor worshipper, it did not bother him at all. He saw the problems, the drugs, the high number of black men in prison. But there existed, in black America, he said, an enormous potential, lying dormant, waiting. By and by, people would awake and arise. "We still got time. We haven't even started. We haven't even mobilized, jacked into our consciousness, pinpointed it right, focused it. We're still messing around. No. I see us as flowering. Getting ready to do it. We got to get some solid stuff, to begin to see patterns now. Change our pattern." That was what Allensworth was to him. That was why he was there. "I think it's going to be great. Going to be great. Its turn's coming."

I found it curious how much of my thinking came together in Ed

Cornelius Pope and his mission. Back in 1969, Allensworth was essentially dead as a doornail, it was kaput, or, as the saying goes, it was history.

What was left was less than the remnants of a dream. But therein was the rub. Regardless what Allensworth would become, an amusement park, a retirement center, a mausoleum, it didn't much matter. For the current building, the activity, the purpose had been born of a dream, the dream of a man, dead now almost one hundred years, a man who made a start, but effectively failed. Yet his dream lived on. *We are such stuff as dreams are made on.*

. . . Once upon a dream . . .

# V

# PROMISED LANDS

Sixteen

# THE AMERICAN CITY

*Las Vegas, Nevada*

I love Las Vegas in a patronizing and avuncular way. For only in Las Vegas did I realize that I was truly American, only an American. For in Las Vegas was the East that spawned me, contorted, enlarged, turned into an R- and X-rated amusement park of want and less visible need, a gateway to some fictitious other-world of blinding prosperity, bliss, heaven on earth. For in Las Vegas, the sin, the tawdriness, the sheer tackiness, and the vanity and the frailty and the banality, and yes, the humanity, of our country is front and center, so neon bright and unapologetic, that the only honest response can be love. Just as a father or a lover must accept unconditionally the twisted architecture and the physical manifestation of the beloved's soul, so must every American acknowledge, forgive, and pray for, the tortured and magical soul of our country. Whether we like it or not, on some level, Las Vegas is us.

I fell annoyingly ill on my second visit to Las Vegas. And, abed and reduced to too much TV watching, I beheld Julia Child again and again on her eightieth birthday, cooking with copious butter and salt and all those things we've now come to believe "evil," all with reckless and wonderful abandon. Las Vegas, surreal and curiously comfortable due to my illness, felt so much like home—this desert and Brechtian "Mahagonny," this money-hole and fleshpot—how lucky and damned it would be to be condemned here—lucky, wonderful: Las Vegas, yes. The American City.

Not too long ago, Martin Scorsese, after releasing his movie *Casino,* called it that, the American City. And I agree with him.

. . .

My first trip to Las Vegas had been in 1990. I had been sent there for a book convention and was put up at the newly completed Mirage. From my hotel window, looking out beyond the city to the desert, I had a sense I understood why Las Vegas's patron saint, Howard R. Hughes, lived the way he did. But then again, Howard Hughes, it is said, always kept the curtains shut.

When I unpacked on that first trip, I discovered that I had left my dress pants and belt at home, and I was to attend a function that very night. I fumbled through the Yellow Pages and found the address of a shop in a mall. I went downstairs and got into a taxi. Before we pulled out of the parking lot, the driver asked me where I came from. I told him. He then asked me what I did. I told him. Really? he said. You know, there's a plumbers' convention in town too. I allowed as how I didn't. After a pause, he said, looking into his rear-view mirror—"You don't mind if I ask how tall you are, do you?" A bit taken aback, I told him. He shook his head. Before I could ask him why he wanted this information, he volunteered: "See, there's been this black feller going around holding up taxi drivers. He hit three drivers this weekend and shot one of them. But seeing you're from out of town and everything . . . Besides, he's taller than you."

"Oh," I said.

"A lot of cabbies won't pick up a black guy now."

I didn't know whether to be vexed or amused. But I did worry about getting back to the hotel in time.

I cannot tell you how relieved I had been when the first taxi I saw had a black driver.

Because of the book convention, some of the world's most distinguished black men were in the city. Politicians, judges, executives, writers, musicians, television personalities. Ironically, the very next day, I would share a cab with Chicago millionaire mortgage banker Dempsey Travis. I wondered how many of them might be suspected of being a potential armed bandit. Moreover, if a white man had perpetrated such a notorious crime, would another white man have had a hard time catching a cab?

On my second trip to Las Vegas, I was in town on the third Monday in January, the federal, and in Nevada, state holiday honoring the Reverend Dr. Martin Luther King, Jr. The Las Vegas *Review Journal* had a special section, "The Dream Is Still Alive." They ran a number of brief articles on black residents. A twenty-three-year-old former gang member (a Blood), Anthony Burrell, who now worked in Caesar's Palace's kitchen; the forty-one-year-old Reverend James Rogers, pastor of the Greater Jerusalem Baptist Church in North Las Vegas; Wayne Carrington, a fifty-one-year-old Las Vegas police officer from New York City; Vanessa Thompson, a senior at Western High School.

And there was Edith Jackson, a tutor with the Las Vegas–Clark County Library District's literacy program. The article reads:

> As a young black student, Edith Jackson was taught that by working hard, you can have the same opportunities as the children in her school.
>
> But life did not turn out like that for Jackson . . .
>
> Many of her white counterparts went on to get the best jobs, while she was turned down for jobs over and over.
>
> "That was very, very discouraging because I knew I had the same skills and was as good a candidate," said Jackson, 40, the mother of a teen-age son and daughter.
>
> Jackson said she raised her children to be "super people," to achieve their goals. "It's not like it can't be done, but I hate to tell them that."

Later Jackson says: "My dream is that everyone who wants to know how to read, that somebody will come in their lives and show them until they've got it. Everyone should have that common right. If you can't read, how are you going to know what Martin Luther King had to say?"

I met Edith Jackson at her office in the library.

"I just like to talk. That's my big thing in life."

Edith Jackson originally came to Las Vegas in 1982, with her second husband who was in the military. "He was having problems, and I told him that I felt that any black who's going to make progress, or maintain their status needs to move. It's been my experience that whenever a black has a clash with the system, you don't win. Your best bet is to move on. Like when the slaves were going on the Underground Railroad. That Harriet Tubman thing. 'Keep moving. Don't stop.' So he got reassigned, and we wound up in Ankara, Turkey, in 1984, which was better."

She adored Turkey. "That was the first experience I've ever had in my life that I was not treated as a black person. I was treated as a woman. Those women had respect. They treated me much better."

It broke her heart to leave, two years later. "I knew what I was going to face. I didn't want to fight. I just want to be peaceful. I just want a family. I just want to have a husband. Nice little kids. A little picket fence. Let's live happy ever after. But it has never been like that. It's not going to be like that for a while."

Edith Jackson's great-grandmother was Lucy Dunham, a civil rights activist from Canada who worked on women's suffrage—as well as African American suffrage, through the Freedman's Bureau. Edith's mother had been born in Canada and came across the border. "Lucy traveled. It was the same thing. 'I will fight you, I will fight you.' And that's the only thing that works. It's too bad because people, especially women, don't have fight in their hearts, they don't. So when you see women fighting, things are bad. Because a woman, in her heart, she wants to nurture. And she wants peace and gentleness."

Edith Jackson was certified to teach in public school, but she never got a contract with the school system in Las Vegas. She applied, and waited for over six years. "All around here teachers were being hired." In fact, the school board had gone as far away as Mississippi, looking for minority teachers. "When there's plenty of unemployed minority teachers right here in town." Since she could not afford a lawyer, she filed complaints with the federal government—to the Equal Rights Commission—on her own. A preliminary investigation was made, and the case was deemed valid. At the time, they were "looking into" her claims, but the case was already four years old, and Edith Jackson had heard nothing. In the meantime, she worked as a substitute—with no health insurance, and no security. "They let us live like that.

"I'll say this. The opportunity is there. I don't think the quality of teachers is good. The opportunity is there for a teacher or a student to excel. Prejudice exists and everything like that, but it's not to the point where the child cannot excel. It was not like that in my day. I knew there were certain opportunities I would never get."

At the time, Edith Jackson was coordinating as many as forty adults who were looking for tutors. They came from "a variety, a mishmash," of backgrounds. She had a great deal of respect for these adults who came forth seeking to gain what they'd missed earlier in life, for whatever reason. They were bright, with bright personalities, she said, how otherwise could they have made it in the world without that basic skill; and they possessed the ability to adapt quickly. "They can zero in. They have a very clear eye for people, and for a lot of things that don't require reading. Mother wit. Being able to read, as black people would say, a situation. They can't read words, but they can read feelings. They're very sophisticated in their feelings."

When I asked the reason most of these adults couldn't read, she said, "A lot of the problem is lack of opportunity.

"People don't understand what racism can do in terms of devastating institutions. I understand it firsthand, because racism was used on me, to keep me from achieving. So I know the techniques when I see them, and these same techniques, if they're used on enough people, a lot of them will drop out of the education system because it was geared that way in the past."

She felt she had experienced that "technique." "Like in a classroom, when I had a question, they make sure they don't answer it. That trying to make you feel invisible. Making sure that you never get a leadership image. Making sure that the criteria is always at your weakest point. You know, say, for instance if they're going to have a science fair project, and all the kids pick the project that had to do with some book at the library. Now you did yours on a book at the library, and maybe you used a resource such as a neighborhood lab or an interview. A live interview. Then, instead of praising you for your use of variety and praising you for creativity, then the criteria would be set over here. 'We only wanted you to use a book. Now why did you go and do something different?' See, the criteria has shifted away from your choices. In certain settings, we will only choose to do what we see the whites do, because we know that there's going to be a change in the criteria. In the classroom, in a university classroom, the criteria for the paper on the curve is what the white people say. So you better say what the white people say."

I said, "Let me play devil's advocate. Some of my conservative friends would probably say, 'Well, that's not a matter of race. That's a matter of learning what the system's criteria are.'"

Edith replied, "But when the criteria never includes you, then it is racist. The cultural differences do exist between blacks and whites. But when you get in a classroom setting, those differences are never given any credence. Never. Just like in a writing class that I took. The examples of good writing were always Shakespeare and some white European. I asked this question when I was ten years old to my social studies teacher, 'Don't other cultures have shining examples of the written material in literature?' They told me, 'No.' See, I beg to differ."

This went beyond language, she said. Anytime a black person asserts an idea that is opposed to the thinking of "white culture," it is deemed wrong. "They're coming from a different cultural perspective. Everything sits upon conclusions that they've made. If you want to do learning outside of that criteria, then you're the one wrong." America does not have a holistic approach to learning, she said. "Public education is 'What did massa think?'

"This is the first job I've ever had where I've seen that the goal is really the goal. In most jobs, you are working against yourself. As a human being and as a black person, you're working against yourself. When you're a social worker, and you're working for the welfare system, and you do your intake, the criteria that you use is the criteria that massa used in London, whereas your head and your heart might tell you something different. What we have to implement in most jobs is what the white men say we ought to do, and that is the description of the job. What a white male has set down for the niggers to do, or the poor people to do, or the women to do, or the workers to do. So there is no room for critical thinking, and that is why I think the Clark County School District could see me as a person that shouldn't be teaching in the school district, because that isn't what I agreed with. That was not my teaching philosophy."

Edith Jackson told me that she thought a black community existed in Las Vegas. "Sad as it is." In general, she felt that blacks who came to Nevada from elsewhere were more progressive than native Nevadans. She called Nevada "Little Mississippi." They are shocked, she said, when they discover that inroads have not been made in establishing black folk in most areas of life, especially government. "The ruling class is mostly all whites here.

"Blacks in this town do not have a voice in anything that has to do with government. That's what is very upsetting to outsiders. They do have a black middle class here, but most of those people are southern and have a plantation mentality. They don't understand anything else. They have a certain silent agreement: 'Everything is fine. I'll just get mine. I'll get me a little house, in a neighborhood with other so-called middle-class black folk, and I will keep my mouth shut and not make white folk mad at me. I will live happily ever after.'

"Then there's this dip down to the underclass of blacks. Which is real widespread. You've got a lot of real poor blacks here. The ones that are the porters and the maids, and do the unskilled labor. There's a large unskilled labor pool here. And that was intentional because they had to have somebody to do the cleaning up on the Strip, so these people were imported here. Wouldn't even dream of owning anything, or making a decision that affected their neighborhood or blacks as a group. They're highly uneducated. That's why we got all these people coming in for the literacy program. They don't have a clue as to what's going on around them. Don't read the newspaper. Probably because they can't. This is where I've seen the highest number of uneducated black people in my life. And it is disgusting to me. Mainly because the middle-class blacks haven't addressed the fact that there's all these other unfortunate folk living right next door to them. You've got these principals who are living next door to folk who only went to the fourth grade, and there's no addressing that. It's just about the black middle class, 'Look at me, how great I've done; the white folk let me have this job and I'm slaphappy.'" Edith Jackson gave a mocking laugh.

"It's a very peculiar place, because these same middle-class black people that sit and say, 'I wouldn't be caught dead on the west side at night,' go to church there, get their hair done there. So they hold the same values as the whites that they work with hold, about their own people. If you hate them and you're so scared of them, why would you sit next to them in a church pew? God's sure not going to come down and defend you if they decide to stab you in the church. It doesn't make logical sense to me."

She pointed to Detroit as being the other side of the divide. "We are the judges. We are the mayor. We are the senate. We are the teachers. We are the street cleaners. We are everything. You don't have to worry that you can't get a job because the white man's going to tell you 'No, you don't get a job because you aren't qualified.'"

On top of everything else, Edith Jackson firmly believed that organized crime ("the Mafia") was instrumental in maintaining the status quo. "They've got an interest in holding anybody down." Back east she felt the power structure was controlled by Jews. "It's a clique type of thing. They're all the doctors, all the bankers. But here it's the Mafia."

And farther west? I asked. What about Los Angeles? Oakland? Seattle?

That, she said, was due to a conspiracy of drugs. "That was a concocted thing." Drugs were brought in for gangs to distribute. The gangs were allowed to flourish. Moreover, she felt that roles were being switched, in a psychological game of destruction. "Black males are now whores, and the female is the provider. Which weakens both people. The kids are caught in the middle, and they become gang members. They see that their mom is the provider, and also how weak she is. They see their dad as the whore, and they see how weak he is—All these men run from project dwelling to project dwelling, screw, have another baby, and say, 'I'm not responsible.' "

But this was not limited to Los Angeles, Edith Jackson felt. Nor was it imposed by a white power structure. In her eyes, it was the cancer that was devouring Black America. "Our own worst enemy. I think we are all the time. Because white people, from what I have seen, do not represent that big of a problem. I tell my boyfriend the same thing; because he's so bent on what white people have done. They haven't done that much. We've built America. They have not done that much. We are still looking for somebody to take care of us. We are still looking for somebody to answer for our own sins. Now that's really been my experience. My father built his house. The white man couldn't stop him from building no house. How could the white man stop him from building the house? If you're going to build a house, build a house. You know? We swam in a lake free of charge. We didn't have to pay to swim, or pay to have a pool. Why? Because my father and his family bought all the land around the lake. That's how you get a lake.

"Sometimes you have to take your opportunity and quit blaming people for what you don't have. And if you really find yourself in a situation that is racist, then do something about it. I tell my boyfriend the same thing when he complains. I say, 'Well, what are you going to do about it? That's a man's role. That's a man's responsibility to do something about it.' I resent that I had to take that much of a male role. To me, I shouldn't have had to say all the things that I've had to say. Because with all the opportunities that black people do have, they don't even take those. That's the mentality that drags black people down. Especially the men."

I began to question Edith's views on black men. Didn't she think she was generalizing a bit much? Weren't there a great number of black men who defied that stereotype? Wasn't that attitude, in and of itself, dangerous?

"I base it on everything that I've seen black men do."

"Nothing positive?" I asked.

Black men did not demonstrate their commitment to family, as far as she was concerned. When she went to the beach, when she went to museums, she saw white men with their families, and black women with theirs—absent the men. She saw white men pushing baby carriages at the mall. When she was pregnant, she said, her husband wouldn't even carry their two-year-old. "He turned to me and said, 'That is your baby. You carry it.' I was very angry, because I didn't understand that this is the black male mentality. It's still very slave oriented. 'I'm just a stud. I don't have to be responsible because massa's going to take care of all that for me.'" Black men weren't active in the lives of their children—as were white men, she said. "The black man needs to see himself as a leader."

This vision of black men, for obvious reasons, did not sit well with me, and I challenged Edith Jackson. After all, "all black men" included me, my grandfather, my mentor, my closest friends, and her son. She allowed as how there were "exceptions" to this rule, and mentioned a group of Kappas—from the Kappa Alpha Psi fraternity of black men—who had organized a group for young black men. "They do these things with the boys and introduce them to responsibility, in terms of being a man. What does a man do? A man studies in the library. A man reads the paper. A man knows his history. A man has a vision. He makes plans. This is what the Kappa League fosters them to do. That is the kind of guidance that teenage boys need."

However, in general, "most black men" behave as boys. "Little boys. It's obvious because black males don't own too much of anything. They don't provide service to their community. They're invisible. They're not adding anything to the quality of family life. They're pitiful." Maybe there were a few black male leaders, but this leadership was not exhibited in the family. The destruction of the extended family was maybe a good thing, she speculated, as it took the matriarch away from the boys. Yes, she said, black families were always matriarchal. "Grandma was always there to boost him along and to push him along. To me that is not what he needed. He needs to be like a lion, stick out his chest and say, 'This is what will happen with my family.' He never took that role."

I said this was far from my experience, especially in the South, in my family.

She said, that might be my experience, but she had never seen otherwise in her own.

In the end, Edith Jackson thought it all had to do with a situation in which black men were "all hung up by the balls. You are in a structure that had you hung up there."

I appreciated her metaphor, but I begged to differ. I pointed out how many black men I knew were neither metaphorically nor certainly physically "hung up by their balls." And she thought it was a lot of hogwash. Internationally speaking, she said, black men did not measure up. How many black men owned banks? How many were actually in the power structure in meaningful positions?

"There are Europeans and Africans and white Americans and Mexicans who own fleets of ships and airplanes. Black American men don't. Maybe we do own one or two banks. But I'm saying in comparison. The structure has it so that we are unrepresented in almost every area."

As far as she was concerned, black men no longer advocated for black women—regardless of their status. Whether they were Colin Powell, the president of the NAACP, school principals, bankers, doctors, lawyers, ditchdiggers—she never saw them standing up for the black woman. "They don't have a commitment to my plight or my community or my children. I have to do everything, the feeding, the earning, the advocating. That leaves me in a quandary." Therefore she felt it logical to conclude that they were, in truth, powerless.

I was still recovering from a sinus infection, and simply was not in the mood to sit and merely listen to Edith Jackson without challenging her ideas. We argued for a spell, good-naturedly, but it came to pass that I, at least, realized that we were just going to have to agree to disagree. At one point, I essentially threw up my hands and said, "Maybe we should reinvent our society along those lines. Maybe it should be a matriarchy. Maybe the women should control the equity and have leadership roles."

"I think that black women are leaning toward that," she said. "They're leaning toward that because in talking to all of my friends and associates that are female that have any kind of jobs, they are not thinking about a man. They look at them just like I do, as little boys. They're not going to leave the back door open for this knight in shining armor to come along. I think all of us really realize that he's never coming. Nobody's ever going to advocate for you. You are your own provider. He's nothing more than a novelty, and I think that women have accepted that. This is where your heartbreak comes in, because you don't want that to be the case. To have no one to advocate for you. The place where you find yourself is the place that you've dug out with your own hands. By yourself."

Despite my hardheadedness, Edith Jackson took a shine to me, and she invited me to her home later to meet her children and her current boyfriend, Tony. She lived north of North Las Vegas in an apartment complex.

Edith laughingly joked of her relationship with Tony—he was her "experiment." Was she trying to change him? Yes. But into what?

"Well, I'm not going to say I changed him, but I think that he was one of my experiments, like my kids were my experiments. I said, 'What would happen if I really try to meet the needs of somebody that everybody said won't work out.' And it worked out. I tried to be very, very, very kind to him. And he has just been that way back to me—lately. Because at first, he was real hostile. Real hostile. But now he's calming down. Then, I was pretty hostile too. I said, 'What am I doing?' Even my kids said, 'You don't act like that around us. Why are you acting like that around him?' I started consciously thinking about acting better, and acting like a model human being, instead of showing how ugly I could be. I think that's a trap people fall into. All you're doing is trying to protect yourself from getting hurt."

Edith Jackson had very strong feelings about the ways women should treat men. "I think that it comes from my father. I adored my father, and I regard all males like that. I adore my son. Everybody says 'Oh, you're just smothering him. You're just spoiling him.' I adore him. To me, males are very special. They're in another place. I'm over here, they're over there. It doesn't mean that they're higher or lower. It's just that I just admire them for their difference."

But men usually found it difficult to either accept or express the same emotion. "My second husband, he used to buy me a lot of jewelry. That was his way. I didn't want the stuff. I wanted him to take the garbage out. My first husband, his darn way of showing me that he adored me was to be there. To him that was a big accomplishment. He wasn't used to schedules and to coming home, and to him, to come home every day was, 'Wow, I must really love you.' It wasn't enough. I think that people are in the world to comfort each other without recrimination. If you're very consistent in loving a person, they can really flourish. That's what I think happened to my children. I just loved them and they are outstanding."

After a spell Tony dropped by.

Tony had been born and raised in Los Angeles. He had been mixed up in gang life, and he made the decision to get out while he could. He was now enrolled at UNLV studying sociology.

"I see more blatant prejudice here. I'm accustomed to black middle-class communities like Baldwin Hills. Black functions. They don't have that here in Las Vegas. They have the West Side which is the one poorer section of town that is primarily black. And I find that to be a difference, a big difference. Whereas L.A. is more open, you know, it's more spread out. Racially it's more spread out. I live in a white neighborhood right now, and I have a problem adjusting, just going to the supermarket, and getting dirty looks. I'm not accustomed to that. There's a lot of frustrations."

In the two classes he was taking, he was the only black person. "They have only one black professor there, but I never met him. He's real popular. He teaches ethnic studies, anthropology."

The famous gangs of Los Angeles, he told me, were slowly working their way into Las Vegas. "There's definitely a gang presence, but I think in a town that's built around tourism and gambling they're not going to allow it to get out of hand. It's mild compared to Los Angeles."

Tony had been a Crip. "I was there when it started. The inception. It was an offshoot from previous gangs, and previous prison gangs, like the Black Guerrilla Family, and car clubs, for the most part. This is after the Watts riot. After the Watts riot, I guess about four years, black youths in particular built up an enormous frustration with the society at large. And one reason why the Crips called themselves the Crips is because they feel society is crippling them. As far as trying to get ahead, and education.

"It just grew like wildfire. It started off on the east side of Los Angeles. It wasn't as violent as today. I think a lot of kids joined different gangs, Crips, Bloods, for security reasons. To get an education in high school, if you didn't belong to a gang, well, you're not going to make it. Without being intimidated and having a fear of intimidation going through. And it just started from one school to the next. It just took off from there. Then cocaine came into play. And I know a couple of guys were involved in that, and I think it was a plot myself.

"I do. I know some guys who were heavy cocaine distributors. And they went directly to the gangs. Some of them are doing time right now. But that's what happened, and once economics came into play, it really became more vicious. Just became real violent as far as street fighting. AK-47s and the guns. All this is a plot. You've been to Los Angeles, you know the pawn shops, liquor stores, and funeral homes on each corner. And being more educated now, I'm more aware. I can see what's happening in the black community. They say that all blacks are at fault. And they're trying to do away with affirmative action, civil rights and stuff, but it's needed. The black male, they're a dying breed. They're coming from dysfunctional families and they don't have any positive people to look up to. I use role models all the time. People always use that. But they don't have that positive influence around them. They need that. I think more of our adult black men need to take their sons and get back to their community and help these kids. Because right now, these kids don't know it, but they're controlled by this plot. Of drugs and guns and violence."

Tony told me he had become involved in the Phoenix School; he had first left Los Angeles for Bakersfield, and there he got more involved.

"They're starting younger now." The idea that these young boys and girls won't live very long has become an accepted fact. "They know that. They're living on the edge and it's a thrill for them. To be recognized, you have to live their life. To survive. Like I say, you don't have that positive influence around you to be determined to get an education or want to do something that's assimilating toward being law-abiding citizens, getting good jobs. They don't have that concept. They have that gangster mentality. And that's because they're frustrated. Their mother's on crack and their daddy's in jail, and it's too much of a negative for them to overcome."

Tony credited football legend-turned-minister and Republican, Rosey Grier, for his own escape from gang life. "He was appointed to a position at city hall. When he and Rafer Johnson captured Sirhan Sirhan at the Ambassador Hotel, they gave him a position to help black youths. And he's instrumental in my life, as far as helping me realize that this world, it's not about that. He kind of gave me a different outlook. And also my baseball coach. Sports kind of saved me. I've been in trouble before too, so I don't consider myself lucky. I still have my regrets. But I'm not giving up. I'm going to get my education, and I want to be able to someday look back at my life and say, 'Well, I didn't turn out the way you thought I would.' You know, and hopefully set a precedent or an example for other people, other men."

Tony had gone to Grambling University for a while, a historically black institution in Louisiana. "But I wasn't ready. I was seventeen years old. It was culture shock to me. Oh, it was terrible, man. I was like, 'Wait a minute.' Nothing but the woods, and I wasn't used to all that. Got this eerie feeling, and I just couldn't concentrate. But the blacks there, the southern blacks there, were proud to be able to get an education. Worked hard, whereas I, you know, I was just skating along. So it was too hard for me, and then if I went to school in California it'd probably been the same thing because California is so open, so much to get into. So you have to especially like Ramsey [Edith's seventeen-year-old son], he's so focused on his education. We don't see that in a lot of our young black kids. He knows what he wants to do now. And the frame of mind he has to have. I left school until I got mature enough to do it. I'm not ashamed to say it—you know, it happens.

"At Grambling, some were standoffish. Being called 'city slicker' and this and that. And then some of them were like, 'Oh, you from L.A.?' You know. So it was like a 50-50 deal. But like I said, on Sundays, the people were in church, and I wasn't used to that. I mean, the whole campus.

Everybody was there, and I thought it was beautiful, but I wasn't ready for it. The culture there was totally different than what I was accustomed to. You can be whoever you want to be in California. No one cares. And I believe you should have certain rules and standards, especially with black people. I think it's awful these kids don't go to church."

I wondered what had to be done to put an end to this dangerous cycle of violence and devaluing of life.

"Oh, God, that's a good, good question. I go over and over that every night. More government jobs and government job training programs would be a plus. Because I remember back in the '70s when they had the CETA program, and guys could get training and get paid for it. What I think needs to be done is basically—if you want to know the truth—is for black people at large to start concentrating on their communities. I mean, it's sad that other ethnic groups like the Koreans and Chinese have Chinatown, Koreatown, and how come we don't have a Black Town or Afro-American Town? We have no heritage, no culture. We're struck from it. So I think we need to go back to the basics. I think we need to quit mixing, racially.

"I do. I remember how it used to be. I feel that when people know their place, they act differently. But now, blacks have too much freedom. They're always raising hell, and white people are tired of that, and that's not going to get us no resources to help ourselves. Culturally. I think maybe we need to get back and identify ourselves. We generally don't have a culture or a heritage to be proud of. I just look at various applications, like when I used to go job hunting, and they'd ask, are you black, Afro-American, Negro. I didn't know what I was.

"We're strong, strong people, talented, and got a lot going for us. And I just think we just need to come back together and love one another as a group. Instead of living this class system, and just looking for status for our individual selves. I think that's a start. And I don't believe in interracial moving about. Until we get it together. That's just my personal position.

"I've talked to a lot of brothers out there, and they don't have no vision at all of what's going on, and what's going to happen. They're just living day by day. I think that's a major problem. They have all these frustrations. One thing, the system always keeps us down, keeps the frustration brewing in us, like the criminal justice system, the welfare system, the educational system. It's too much ferocity for black men to have. It's been said that we can't assimilate. Black men can't assimilate. But hell, you keep giving us all these obstacles, of course, we're not going to assimilate. I think we need more rehabilitation programs for the prisons. I don't believe in just warehousing these guys, just keep locking them up. Give them something to look forward to.

"These young black men, they look at this criminal justice system, and they're used to seeing a white judge, a white bailiff, twelve white jurors, a white prosecutor, a white public defender, a white, lily-white courtroom. And they say they don't have a chance. We need to build up more representation within that justice system and break that disparity in the penal system."

He felt integration should be halted. And that Asian grocers in black neighborhoods were keeping potential small black businesses from succeeding.

Black athletes should not be put forward as role models, Tony said. "Like Charles Barkley says, 'Don't call me no role model. I'm nobody's role model.' I agree with him. 'I'm just playing sports and getting paid for it. What can I change?' But a lot of these athletes, they get in there and get these white girls, and it's a new world to them, coming from the inner city, being up there and making all that money.

"We have to pay our dues. I used to feel the same way, that I always had something owed to me. But I had to learn the hard way. Life is not promised."

I mentioned Edith's earlier views about black men, and wondered how he felt about the state of black manhood.

Tony said, "We fight about that all the time. I just think black women are neglecting where they come from, and how they really need their black men. And they're blaming us. 'You guys are in prison or you guys are on drugs, or you guys are doing this or doing that.' But they're the ones that's getting the jobs. They're the ones that are being accepted in other communities. And the black man is not. And I strongly believe that the black woman should stick by her man through thick and thin. I don't care what kind of position she gets. She should still recognize her black man. But they don't, especially here. Most young black girls, they're making it. They're satisfied, and the hell with the black man. They're making it. But they don't know that they still got that emptiness within them. Still that voice is missing. I think black men have the vision, but they're just so frustrated. They're tired. They're tired of fighting. Once the black woman rises above him in social status, he loses a lot, his pride, his self-esteem. He needs to be on top. He does. I'm a traditionalist. I just believe in old values, and old moral standards as far as the man being first. The black man has never been in the household. Since slavery days, he was always out picking cotton. Fourteen, sixteen hours a day. He's never really been in the household. And as far as a black man's sexual nature, he's always cheating. He's always been a dog."

Edith responded, "You hear what I said about the whore and the provider? But that's the structure. That's the structure. It's not to say that you can't change it, or we won't change it, or that we should or shouldn't change it. That's the way it is."

Tony observed, "Well, I think the point is, when should you change it? Change it all of a sudden, and that's what's happening now to the black man. He doesn't know whether to look south or look north. He doesn't know if he's coming or going, a lot of these black men. They're seeing the women getting all these good jobs, and they're left behind. Black men are hard to assimilate to this western culture. But that's our African nature. The black man is wild, born to be wild. I'm sorry. Hey, I just tell it like it is."

Edith noted, "He sounds kind of opposite on some things from me, and then he sounds kind of the same on some things."

Tony said, "Right. Well, you know, like I'm developing more vision and more understanding as I further my education. I'm saying, 'Well, okay, maybe this just can work.' But you look at the poor black guys out there who don't have the education and come from southern backgrounds, they can't get used to this way of life. You can't just force them to do it. That's when problems arise." He went on, "I'm always optimistic. No matter what happens. My head is bloody, but it's unbowed."

Edith said, "Black people need to sit down and think, 'What are we going to do now?' That's the hope, that we can still think."

> "We were just having a picnic, a goddamn peaceful picnic," David repeated. Several kids stared hard, unblinking, in my direction. Someone lobbed an empty Colt 45 bottle into the sagebrush. Then a tall figure in a Georgetown sweatshirt grabbed my arm. "You'd better split, man. If you want an interview, come back tomorrow. I'll tell you anything you want to know about Lost Fuckin' Vegas." I asked his name. He laughed: "Just call me Nice D., Valley View Gangster Crips. Ok?"
>
> —Mike Davis, "Racial Caldron in Las Vegas," *The Nation,* July 6, 1992

When the Rodney King verdict was handed down, surely a lot of people, black and white, all across America thought their world was coming to an end. Call it a rebellion or call it a riot. We look at and talk about what happened in Los Angeles now, since that is where so much of it happened. But it happened to varying degrees in Seattle, WA, Racine, WI, Atlanta, GA, Washington, D.C., a great many other places. (I have yet to fully suss out why nothing of any consequence occurred in New York—perhaps if it had, our worlds really would have come to an end.)

Outbreaks of violence also took place in Las Vegas. In fact, in Las Vegas, the clash between young men and women and police continued for about a month until the sheriff—in an order creepily like the antebellum slave codes—banned groups of three or more people in West Las Vegas and North Las Vegas, essentially black Las Vegas.

The damage done to West Las Vegas was well over $5 million. Stores and a shopping mall were torched—including an AIDS clinic and the local NAACP headquarters. At least one person died.

When a local gang, the Kingsmen, held a party near the Gerson Parks project to celebrate the recent truce between the Bloods and the Crips, "A Metro squad car drove straight into the festive crowd," writes Mike Davis. "People went crazy. They started throwing rocks and bottles; then one of the homies opened up with his gat. The angry crowd burned down a nearby office of the Pardon and Parole Board, while other groups attacked stores and gas stations with Molotov cocktails." Over a hundred people were arrested. And there were rumors, later proven to be unfounded, that a black man had tried to kidnap a white baby. There were also a lot of blacks accusing police of misconduct. At one point, the police used an armored personnel carrier and shot wooden bullets at people. All this was happening less than a mile from the Mirage, the Circus Maximus and Caesar's Palace.

Clearly black folk in Las Vegas were angry.

I came to Las Vegas looking for black people in the winter of 1992, and returned later that summer, and, though the outright miniwars had stopped, people were still pretty out of sorts with the oasis of Nevada.

The reasons are, and were, glaringly obvious. Despite Las Vegas's astronomical growth rate, said to be the greatest in the union, and despite rapid expansion both in industry and gaming, the number of black folk in any job of consequence was pitifully few. Most were relegated to menial jobs as maids, dishwashers, cooks, and the like. Plus they were being crowded out of that sector by the influx of Latinos and poor whites who would take anything they could get.

Everyone I met kept making comparisons between Las Vegas and the Deep South—"Mississippi of the West," which is an inaccurate comparison. Mississippi's history and present are actually radically different from Nevada's. The number of black people in Mississippi is almost five times that of blacks in Nevada. The poverty rate in Mississippi was higher (higher for blacks and whites as well), yet there was much more black participation in government and business, and a significant black middle class existed in the larger cities such as Jackson and Hattiesburg; Mississippi also had a good number of historically black colleges; Nevada had none, and the number of blacks at the University of Nevada (even counting the basketball players) was disgracefully low. In many ways, Nevada seemed a less attractive place to live as a black person.

But I got the point.

Samuel Smith's Native Son bookstore is located in the heart of the business district of West Las Vegas—which has more in common with Delano than with the Las Vegas Strip. It was a smallish shop, the bookstore, and curiously stocked, and a few black men milled about and Mr. Smith was talking. He was talking about a great many things, interlocking, interweaving, rapid-fire. He was talking about African American history, American history, African history. He was talking about Richard Nixon and Richard Wright. He was talking about Las Vegas and astronomy. He was talking about fire fighting. Samuel Smith was also deputy fire marshal for the City of Las Vegas, and the prologue and epilogue and center of his talking, casually, yet intensely to one fellow in particular and whoever else was listening, was passing the exam for becoming a fireman. The test was notoriously difficult, and Mr. Smith, being essentially an expert in matters of fire fighting, wanted to share whatever he could to get more black men on the force; this also included psyching them up, encouraging them, cajoling them, pushing them.

The next day, I met Mr. Smith at the station—new, state-of-the-art, gleaming and Bauhaus in the desert sun—and he took me to lunch at a soul food restaurant not far away.

Samuel Smith came to Las Vegas in 1978. He got there after being born in Philadelphia in 1943, and being a New York City cop since age twenty-one. When the Las Vegas Fire Department hired him in 1980, he was only the third black man in the department.

. . .

In the 1950s, I was surprised to read, the legendary Eartha Kitt had been refused a drink of lemonade at a fast-food drive-in joint in Las Vegas. An *Ebony* magazine reporter had been denied a place to stay while writing a story about Louise Beavers. He had to fly in to see the show (from the wings) and then catch a plane back to Chicago. "No motels, hotels, casinos, or restaurants will serve the colored. The crummiest saloon in downtown Vegas will not let him buy a drink, nor will gambling joints permit him to make a bid," a 1955 account, *Las Vegas: Playtown, USA,* read. "Not in Las Vegas, or 'Lost Wages' as the Negro population mockingly call the town."

Ironies abound anywhere if we look long and hard enough. Ralph Ellison once warned writers not to depend too heavily upon irony. But one irony is too ripe for me to pass up. Las Vegas began as a colony of Mormons sent down from Utah in 1855 to convert the Paiutes and—believe it or not—raise cash crops in that valley. They called the little town Bringhurst (after their group leader, William Bringhurst). By 1858, they had all given up and returned to Utah.

When Nevada's famous Comstock Lode—that rich vein of gold and silver—was discovered in the 1860s, a town was desperately needed. One Octavious Decatur Gass bought the old Mormon settlement in 1865. He renamed the place—in a horrible lapse of Spanish grammar—*Los* Vegas.

Las Vegas has always been a crossroads, a place where people stop, a way station. When the Union Pacific line was completed in 1900, Las Vegas was the midpoint between Salt Lake and Los Angeles—plus Vegas had enough of a water supply to service locomotives, sealing its importance as long as western America depended upon trains.

Largely, Chinese and black folk built the railroad, and some were hired to work after its completion: men as porters and repairmen, women as housekeepers. By 1910, over forty black people lived in Las Vegas.

Las Vegas grew by squirts and spasms for the next twenty years. One of the biggest injections of growth came with the mammoth Hoover Dam project, just up the road. That project employed some 20,000 men. When it was clear that the Six Companies consortium had no intention of hiring black folk—in 1931, they had none—the local NAACP, now thirteen years old, went after them. Lip service was paid, but by 1936, no more than forty-four black men had jobs on the creation of Lake Mead.

The city, which had rather halfheartedly practiced segregation, stepped up its efforts during the thirties. Black folk were forced to live in a "block," next to the prostitution district. As gambling became more serious, blacks, who were once welcome, were banned. And no black man could enter a brothel. (In 1934, a license was given to the Idle Hour Club, a house of ill repute for blacks only.) By the same passage, African Americans became essential in growing Las Vegas—after all, somebody had to change the sheets and mop the floors and cook the food and serve it.

The Union Pacific line divided the town into east and west. Clearly the east was the more developed and had the most potential for growth. The west side looked unpromising, was shabby and rundown, called "ragtown" by the locals. A concerted effort was made to push the few black residents to the west. The white residents were neither subtle nor shy about their desire for segregation. By the mid-1940s, the black population of Las Vegas had expanded to over 3,000, many of whom worked for the Basic Magnesium Corporation, made lucrative by World War II contracts. Almost all of those black people resided on the west side. At one point, the housing situation was so bad that people were living in tents and cars. One historian suggests that the city's animosity was apparent, since a health crisis was imminent, but building adequate facilities might encourage the influx of African Americans to stay. The city fathers wanted them gone when the war was over. Of course, when black soldiers came to town, it was seen to that they remained on the west side. Violence broke out in 1943, in a fight between black soldiers and police, and again in 1944, at the Harlem Club. One soldier was killed, and Las Vegas became temporarily "off limits" for black military men.

By all accounts of West Las Vegas in those days, comparisons to the later townships of South Africa are probably not an exaggeration. "Many dwellings lacked toilets, and some even the basic amenities of running water, power and gas," says Eugene R. Moehring, in his *Resort City in the Sunbelt: Las Vegas, 1930–1970*. Roads were unpaved. Only with the good graces of Harry Truman and federal funding did the situation begin to turn around.

Just as in the South during the fifties and sixties, the civil rights struggle in Nevada was fractious, violent, frustrating, embittered, full of courage and ignominy. Bugsy Siegel's dream—if that old myth has legs—was commencing to flourish, and folk from all over the nation came to give away their hard-earned money and whore around, and have a good time. Southerners were among these numbers, and the city wanted to make certain they felt welcome. These people would pay good money to see Johnny Mathis and B. B. King and Lena Horne and Sammy Davis, Jr., and Eddie "Rochester" Anderson and Nat King Cole, but they did not welcome blacks beyond their immediate professional services. Most of these performers did not keep their mouths shut; some declined ever to return. (The Sands Hotel did relent in 1955 and allowed black performers to stay there.)

Also in 1955, the Moulin Rouge opened, the only integrated casino in the city, and it stuck out like a fly in buttermilk. It was the only casino located in a residential area: West Las Vegas. Black folk could stay there, but the establishment's history was fraught from the beginning with closures and boycotts. (Whites were said to have been charged less for drinks than blacks.)

Civil rights organizations battled on, forcing little, but some change. Then, not unlike the rest of the nation, it took violence to get the white folk's attention. In 1969, beginning at the Rancho High School, a fight broke out. The violence spread to other schools. When a black student was pushed through a trophy case, things really heated up. Two days later, over a thousand students got into such a battle that the school had to be closed temporarily. The situation only got worse. On October 6th of that year, the violence led to the streets, perhaps inspired by similar actions in many of the nation's cities the year before. Two people were killed, over a score hospitalized; property was vandalized, merchandise looted. The governor mobilized the National Guard. There was another situation in November. The year 1970 saw more violence.

Interestingly enough, the city and state government began to listen more closely to the leaders of black organizations. Bones were thrown to black folk. Fair housing laws were passed; unions signed agreements; schools implemented busing.

As skeptical as I am about the use and misuse of history, one does not need a crystal ball to predict the future. The patterns of the past look like a map.

My question became, Why did the city government persist with such blind, pigheaded stupidity? Maybe I was spending too much time trying to figure out the wrong people . . .

Lee Brown's father, Ed Brown, started a black newspaper, the Las Vegas *Sentinel,* in 1980. In the sixties, there had been the *Vegas Voice.* He bought out the *Voice* in 1981, and it became the Las Vegas *Sentinel Voice.* When I met his son, the publisher, editor, and general manager, Lee Brown, it was the only black publication in the state.

Lee had been born in Washington, D.C., and spent time in New Jersey as a young boy. The family moved to Las Vegas, "migrated" as Lee calls it, in the mid-seventies. His father had been radio station manager, first in

Washington, then in New Jersey. He became vice president and general manager of the only black radio station in Las Vegas at the time, KZOB. When the non-black owners began to talk about changing the format to all talk, Ed Brown decided it was time to move on. He used his media connections to get his paper off the ground.

"It was very tough going. Still is. It's very tough, very tough." His son, Lee Brown, at thirty-one, was the spitting image of the buppie executive—but that's an unfair shorthand, for with me, at least, Lee Brown, Jr. seemed laid-back, even a bit philosophical.

"At this point we're doing okay, but it was hard for probably the first five or six years. Just starting out was a lot of fun, because the interest was there. After that the novelty wears off. It was kind of up and down. It was really rocky."

When Mr. Ed Brown died in 1988, Lee took over. His mother, Betty Brown, acted as publisher emeritus. Currently, the paper had a circulation of 5,000 copies. Lee Brown estimated the black population of Nevada at between 85,000 and 90,000 people.

I asked if he saw a sense of community among blacks in Las Vegas. We had discussed the minor strain between those blacks who had lived in Nevada for generations—a relatively small number—and the large influx of blacks from other parts of the country. By the late eighties, however, that tension was moot. But now, he felt, especially after the violence following the Rodney King trial, there was more of a sense of solidarity. "It didn't really surprise me. And I wouldn't be surprised if it happened again. I think people are just fed up and they're looking for it. They're looking for a reason to make some noise. And that was the perfect opportunity. You know, same with Los Angeles, I think."

In many ways, he felt growing up in Las Vegas, for him, had been a disadvantage. "It's an adult-oriented city. Twenty-four hours of gambling. That's not too good for minors. There's very little for young people to do. They're starting programs now, but this has been going on for who knows how long. As far as, say, white Las Vegans, they may have a little bit more money to try to find things to do, but with a lack of funds, there's only hanging out. It seems like we have more problems during the summer, something about that heat, boy, that just makes you angry. It does. It makes you mad. When you're already mad, it can be explosive. In April, oh, now, it was very explosive. I guess they're lucky they got that out of their system then instead of now. It could have been bad."

We talked a bit about the riots. Lee Brown said that it was a big misconception—at least in Las Vegas—that the bulk of the destruction had been wrought upon black-owned property. "A lot of the businesses that were burned down were white-owned. Just because they're over in West Las Vegas, they think they're black-owned. A lot of white businessmen go over there—because they can get credit or loans from the bank—and they'll go over there and buy a little laundromat or something and let blacks run it for them. And that was the case for probably half, if not more, of the buildings that got burned down."

The idea that the rioting was merely "copy cat" activity was also a mistake. Police brutality had always been an issue in Las Vegas for black men. "We've always had this problem. Just as much as Los Angeles has. They had a march against police brutality maybe three years ago, when the cops had busted into a brother's apartment, put him in a choke hold and killed him, and got off scot-free. They said they thought his girlfriend or something was a prostitute, so they just busted into the apartment, no search warrant, no nothing. Three white guys, plainclothes, just breaking into your apartment, and he's in the bed asleep, butt-naked. Of course, he's going to resist. He doesn't know who you are, out of a dead sleep. They put him in a choke hold and he dies. And then they get off. That was the beginning of a lot of tensions here. So people still bring it up. The Rodney King thing, it may have been the straw that broke the camel's back, so to speak. Here anyway."

But in general, Lee Brown told me he felt racism in Las Vegas was well hidden. "I don't live in West Las Vegas, and I know when I'm driving home at night, and I go driving through some secluded areas, or I turn off from a main street to go home, through the back streets and all that, and the cop's behind me, he's just sitting there, he's watching. 'What are you doing over here?' And he's running my plates and everything. Everything comes up clean, and he just drives on by me. But I still go through that. So I think it's more of a subtle racism now."

West Las Vegas still felt very much like a segregated town to him. "There's still that stigma attached to it, of crime, and murder, and all that. It's 95 percent black, that little section of town. But what a lot of people don't realize, which I know for a fact, is that the majority of the blacks in the city no longer live on the West Side. They're scattered all the way through, I don't know what the exact number is out of the 90,000, but I would venture to say only half, if not less, live in West Las Vegas. A lot of that has to do with the popularity of Las Vegas. Two summers ago we went through such growth. There were three or four thousand people a month moving here. And of course, out of that boom, a lot of blacks were moving here from Los Angeles and from the South. But they didn't know about West Las Vegas. They just moved in, moved into the city somewhere. It kind of broke things up a little bit, that growth."

He noted a definite rise in gang-related activity—he felt it was approaching that of Los Angeles. "I don't understand that either. I guess it originated in Los Angeles. I don't know. But I think it ties in with poverty and the young brothers looking to belong somewhere. They want to have something to look forward to, and all they have is their partners, their buddies, and it turned negative. Until we get that turned around, it's going to stay the same, if not get worse. They feel like they're being kicked, while they're already down and impoverished. And they can't get a job, and they can't have nice things—especially, you've got to figure, living in a city like Los Angeles or even Las Vegas, where there's this money floating all over the place, and they can't get a piece of the pie."

In fact there had been a drive-by shooting the night before—in West Las Vegas.

But he said the *Sentinel Voice* would not be covering that story. "I try to stay away from all that negative stuff as much as possible. I don't like to report it. They get that on the news, and on radio, and in the major dailies. Why do I have to bombard them again? They already know. They live right there where it happened. They saw it. They know more about it than I do, so why should I try to tell them something they already know?"

After the conflagration, he said, the city and state governments had made promises. "Promises to try to help rebuild and find jobs. All the things that should have been done beforehand. They've started some programs, they've established two or three different committees to go in and see what needs to be done. There haven't been a whole lot of results. Probably the only positive thing that came out of all this so far is that after we tore it down, we went back in and cleaned it up."

In the national imagination, whether it was reality or fantasy, Las Vegas is a city controlled by organized crime. I wondered if that shadow hung over the lives of black folk there, day in, day out. "I don't think so. Maybe a select few men have a lot of power, maybe one or two top casino owners or something like that—there's always that little question mark. But as far as blacks, no, not at all. We don't have enough power for them to worry about us.

"It's been like that for so long that blacks have stopped worrying about it. It's just an accepted. Until one of us goes over and buys a major property on the Las Vegas strip, it's never going to change. And all that property's already owned by somebody else, who's not going to sell it. Our only other chance is building something in West Las Vegas, where we can get the property. Or use something that's already there, like the Moulin Rouge; but then, no one from outside of West Las Vegas is going to want to go over there for fear of crime and violence and all that. So it's like a catch-22. Almost a no-win situation. So they have to look for other things."

The irony, consistent with almost every city with a sizeable black population, was the large number of churches. "There's one on almost every corner in West Las Vegas. It should play more of a role than probably it does. The fact alone that we're in a city with gambling, drinking, women, and a lot of it—that's enough of a sin. But we have all the other problems on top of it. Maybe we should focus more on other things, maybe trying to uplift ourselves. I think they could do a better job."

But he was optimistic, he told me, overall. "It's going to take a while." He could see a day when black businesses thrived, when crimes decreased, when the kids would be off the streets and in the schoolrooms. "To do that, we've got to have money. It's a continuous cycle. I don't know if I'll see it in my lifetime. Racism will still be here, probably more hidden than ever. But I'm optimistic. Things may turn around." He laughed, as if to say his dreams were a long bet on a slow horse.

> "Las Vegas exists because it is a reflection of America," says Steve Wynn, the city's most important and interesting resident. "You say, 'Las Vegas' in Osaka or Johannesburg, anywhere in the world, and people smile, they understand. It represents all the things people in every city in America like. Here they can get it in one gulp." There is a Jorge Luis Borges story called *The Aleph* that describes the magical point where all places are seen from every angle. Las Vegas has become that place in America, less because of its own transformation in the past decade than because of the transformation of the nation. Las Vegas has become Americanized, and, even more, America has become Las Vegasized.
>
> —Kurt Anderson, "Las Vegas, USA,"
> *Time,* January 10, 1994

During my last stay in Las Vegas, I had enjoyed the help of Joseph Spears, the brother of Toni Scott whom I met in Grand Forks. He was a dice pit manager at the Dunes. He had come to Las Vegas during the boom of the 1970s, and started as a dealer. The money had been good: "A dealer could make over $50,000 in tips alone." In 1983, the IRS changed this situation, he told me, plus the industry itself began to change. That's when Joseph Spears became a manager.

Joseph was from Rhode Island. His mother was a full Narragansett; his father part black. Joseph Spears was a large, powerful-looking man, of a pleasant beige color, and with a gravel-deep growl of a voice, a voice that made his every sentence fascinating to hear.

He was very interested in the historic and present-day connection between black folk and Indian folk. He told me he had considered himself Indian until high school—he knew nothing of his black heritage until he became a teenager.

In school, and out, he studied anthropology, and he was interested in doing a book about the Narragansett. Now knowledgeable about gaming, he had his eye on the developing Native American casinos on the East Coast. He had formed a consulting firm and was looking perhaps to help establish a casino for one of the eastern tribes.

After talking about the cynical realities of Las Vegas, I asked if it was difficult to like Las Vegas, living there with such hard, ingrained, cynical knowledge.

He said, "After a year, I decided to live here. You learn to live with it; every place has something, here it is money."

Joseph Spears owned a bit of land just outside the city, and he took me there. On the way, he told me about his passion for bodybuilding, and that it came from his admiration for his father, a man who made Joseph look like a dwarf, he told me. And he was strong, his father, able to lift incredible weight. Joseph showed me a picture of this hulking man.

One of the fascinating things about Las Vegas to me is that it just stops. Some streets end, and there before you is desert; it feels as if you've just stepped out of a mirage. Going to Joseph's place contained this feeling, for after a while, the city was gone, and once again I was in rocky, barren, sandy, sagey desert. Presently we came upon a broad and small cluster of houses—four or five near the lot where Joseph Spears now had a trailer, and a little farm operation. One house was an opulent near-mansion on a rise, and another, where his friend, whom we visited later, lived, was humble, comfortable, like the man himself, a Californian who was so gentle and laid-back that I felt soothed just being around him. At the end of this settlement was a great hill, a tall, squat, craggy red rock of incredible beauty. I understood why Joseph Spears would want to one day build a house out there. He told me that when his son was born, he took the infant in his arms and climbed to the top of that great rock. There, both naked, they surveyed the world.

By this point, I had traveled across the length of this country: I had seen mountains' majesty and amber waves of grain, I had seen Maine's poetry and Alaska's epic sweep, I had seen the blue Pacific and the timberlands north of Lake Superior—but I can testify I have never been so moved as by this simple harmony of earth and man, red in the red sunset, but more, a place beloved.

Leaving Las Vegas in 110-degree dry heat, I listened to a recording of William Faulkner reading, and I could not help but fixate on one sentence from his Nobel-prize speech, for it resonated so strongly with that moment when I stood with Joseph Spears before his mountain. "It is easy enough to say that man is immortal simply because he will endure, that when the last dingdong of doom has clanged and faded from the last worthless rock hanging tideless in the last red and dying evening, that even then there will still be one more sound, that of his puny and inexhaustible voice still talking."

Man has a soul, the Sage of Oxford, Mississippi, goes on to say, man will not simply endure, he will prevail.

Seventeen

# UPON THIS DESERT

## Or, "Oh, Lord Jesus, How Long, How Long . . ."

*Salt Lake City, Utah*

Pierre Dale Selby had been put to death in 1987.

William Andrews had to wait another five years. He had been waiting for eighteen years—the longest, at the time, of any man on death row.

Without a doubt, the crime was grisly.

In April of 1974, six men drove two vans to the Ogden Hi-Fi Shop. At the time Andrews had been a nineteen-year-old airman, a helicopter mechanic, originally from Jonesboro, Louisiana. William Andrews and Keith Roberts had held five people for four hours. The hostages were bound. They were forced to drink Drano. Selby kicked a ballpoint pen into one man's ear. Selby raped one of the women. Then he shot them all in the head. Two people survived.

Roberts was convicted of aggravated robbery, and, after thirteen years, was paroled.

Andrews was convicted of murder and sentenced to death.

From the beginning, Andrews's lawyers contended that though Andrews poured the Drano into cups, he did not pull the trigger. He had left the room. (One of the survivors testified that Andrews had said, "I can't do it. I'm afraid.") But the appellate courts upheld the lower court's finding that people who play a role in a murder, regardless of whether they actually kill are eligible for execution. Prosecutors also argued that the Drano alone could have killed the victims. The jury had been all white and largely Mormon (the one black person in the jury pool had been excused early). A note had been passed to the jury—"Hang the Niggers!"—but the judge did not declare a mistrial.

Almost two decades of the appeals process followed—in the end, practically half of Andrews's life. The case reached the United States

Supreme Court six times. In a state with a black population of less than 1 percent, the issue of racism quickly raised its head. Though Andrews would be only the third black man executed in the state of Utah (the first had been in 1926), and he was only the fourth person in that state to be executed since Gary Gilmore's infamous case in 1977, the truth was that there were a number of white men who had been convicted of murder and were only given life in prison.

By the 1990s, the NAACP had been joined by Amnesty International and the American Civil Liberties Union in fighting to keep Andrews alive. The defense's appeal argued that a 1991 law giving the option of imposing life without parole in capital cases should be applied retroactively. Meanwhile blacks and whites held rallies and protest marches; nightly vigils were held outside the governor's mansion. Pope John Paul II sent a letter calling for clemency; a white, retired Mormon professor sent a letter to the Salt Lake City *Tribune* accusing the judicial system of racism.

Andrews, whose last meal was a banana split, had been strapped down when the Supreme Court ordered a stay to examine a new appeal. But Andrews only got one hundred minutes: the Justices voted 7–2 (Blackmun and Stevens dissenting), denying the stay.

The thirty-seven-year-old Andrews was administered a lethal injection on Thursday, July 30, 1992.

His last words: "Thank those who tried so hard to keep me alive. Tell my family goodbye, and that I love them."

The next day there was a memorial service at the Calvary Baptist Church in Salt Lake City. Alberta Henry, president of the local chapter of the NAACP, was quoted in the *Deseret News* as saying:

> People say, "How can you say it [Andrew's execution] is racist?" How can you not say it's racist? There will have to be changes. No more will we let all these injustices go by that have gone by in the past. He's the only one that's free. We who are left are not free because we've got to fight the racist and unequal justice here in Utah. We've got to fight on.

I arrived in great Salt Lake City the night of the execution.

Later, Alberta Henry would tell me she received as many as five complaint calls a day. Things are getting worse, she said, not better in Utah. Discrimination, slurs. She pointed to the complicity of the Church of

Jesus Christ of Latter-Day Saints. Their silence in such matters equaled approval as far as she was concerned.

Alberta Henry was a thin, fiery woman, with an intense and commanding smoker's voice. I attended a meeting of the seventy-three-year-old Salt Lake City branch of the NAACP at their building on West South Temple. Alberta Henry presided over the meeting with a controlled nature, though there was a hint of weariness and fatigue just beneath the surface; her eyes were quick, darting, busy, and they seemed to miss little.

Twenty-five people were present.

After the call to order, and the welcome and greeting, and a brief moment of meditation, and the reading of the minutes and the treasurer's report, there was a discussion of the "William Andrews Action."

Among the many things said, one of the first was from the minister of the Calvary Baptist Church, the Reverend France Davis. He expressed concern about people who took advantage of the vigils for negative publicity. The Reverend Janet L. Swift, pastor of the AME Zion Church, said that she had been worried about their "losing an edge." She was concerned about the black community becoming too moderate. Two white women who were present told everyone that they had been in L.A. during the riots (their point eluded me); and a black member exhorted the board to examine themselves. One young black man described himself as an agitator, and felt Andrews "had been agitated." A board member, a black woman, thought everyone should be congratulated for the work they had done. Another woman suggested an action discouraging people from bringing business to Utah. Another man said it was all about "Mercy v Equal Justice."

The body ratified the existence of a new committee, "Equal Justice for ALL." A three-part committee, with ministers, lawyers, and citizens interested in equal justice.

They moved on to discuss a march against the Aryan Nation on Labor Day. (That motion was defeated.)

It was agreed that they would create a Citizens' Review Panel of Police Actions. Other committees were heard from, old business discussed, and the meeting adjourned.

To be sure, I had expected more people, considering all the hullabaloo that had occurred just days (hours really) before. Perhaps folk had exorcised their feelings at the wake the day before? Or perhaps the problems facing the black community of Salt Lake City were deeper than one meeting could reach? I, one traveler, long I sat, and peered into the underbrush at the edge of the desert.

. . .

Desert. Deseret. Desert. You see the word *Deseret* a lot in and around Salt Lake. You will also see beehives all over the place. Deseret is the term, the metaphor, used in the *Book of Mormon* for the honeybee—it signifies and symbolizes industry.

I find it difficult to behold Salt Lake without feeling more than a little awed at how industrious that industry has been. Earlier I've commented on how Chicago seems to be the very embodiment of midwestern will, and how Los Angeles is a willed city, a city that was created by the sheer will of man over nature, and perhaps more by the will to make money. Salt Lake shares elements of those cities, the embodiment of Deseret will—the will of man over matter, and the will of manna—but I have yet to answer if Salt Lake is the will of God: Zion.

Brigham Young said, "This is the place." (In fact, in the south of the state there is a park called Zion, which is where the Latter-Day Saints were first thought to settle, but Mr. Young said, no, this is "Not Zion," which became the name of the future state park. Curiously, over the years, the "Not" fell off.)

An architecture and city planning critic recently told me that Salt Lake has one of the worst city plans in the nation, which is also the legacy of Brigham Young. He laid out the city in a massive grid, creating four quadrants, and also creating huge, undigestible city blocks. This, the critic said, made the intercourse between street and property, between man and destinations, difficult and complicated, and resulted in less contact.

With its great malls and centers, its Tabernacle and Genealogical Library, and, of course, its churches—all marked by Zion (as in Zion Mercantile Corporation, ZMC), or Deseret (as in the *Deseret News* or the Deseret Press), or LDS (Latter-Day Saints)—Salt Lake City is anything but a struggling town. Indeed, the city thrives, with low unemployment and high growth, both economically and population-wise (and its basketball team, the Jazz, has in a short time established itself as a formidable national presence). But the thing that stuck in my brain was the sense of ever-present dryness, aridity. It loomed over the city, in its summer heat, in the shallow, stinky lake, in the faces and gardens on the hills to the east. One is always aware that one is in the desert.

The thought lodged itself in my consciousness as I drove across the desert, up from Nevada to the city by the Great Salt Lake, my mind turning from sin to piety. This was the very same environment as that of the Chosen People, desert folk, rounded up in Egypt, set free across the Red

Sea, wandering like the followers of Joseph Smith's vision. The parched books of the Pentateuch are coded with the mores and necessities of the desert-bound. Those imperatives permeate every verse of that tome. Yet the land that Moses would not see, Canaan, had been described as the land of flowing milk and honey. And though Salt Lake City became the very model of an oasis, it seems that originally it would have been difficult to think of it as a "promised land," after you've seen Ohio, Illinois, Missouri, western New York (where Joseph Smith came from). Or was it a metaphor in the mind of old man Young—did he see the idea of a promised land as a state of mind, rather than a geographic state?

The Reverend France Davis was explaining to me the unusual level of cooperation that existed between Trinity AME Zion Church and Calvary Baptist Church, of which he was pastor. "When we disagree, we agree to disagree, but then we come together around common things and work toward achieving those goals." Trinity and Calvary, in particular, had become a center of African American activity in the state. "If I were in Oakland, California, I may not even speak to a Methodist preacher." He laughed, but I disbelieved him. One might say that the Reverend France A. Davis was a born diplomat. I found it hard to believe he could be spiteful.

The Reverend France A. Davis had been born and raised outside of Augusta, Georgia, and went to Tuskegee University in Alabama. He dropped out and joined the military, and eventually went on to UC Berkeley, and later seminary. He came to Utah in 1972, originally to teach communications at the university. The twenty years he had been in Utah were filled with positive change, he told me. When he came, he said, the average African American male had been born and raised there, and had little education; they either worked in the mines or at one of the refineries. "In 1972, African Americans were clearly outsiders in this community. Although they were here, they were not really welcomed. Since that time there's been a revelation from the Mormon church saying that we are full human beings, and that is now starting to trickle down in terms of people's attitudes." Now there was fair housing legislation, parks and monuments named after African Americans, more large corporations that made affirmative action an important policy—he named American Express and Delta Airlines.

But in order to keep that positive momentum, there were major problems yet to tackle. "This whole matter of access to the criminal justice system and fair treatment in the criminal justice system. This whole matter of how we develop economically. And politically. Three major obstacles that we still have to hurdle. But otherwise, I'm optimistic. I think we can make a difference, and we are. That we can survive here and do well."

He took the broad view when it came to the events surrounding the Andrews case. "The matter is probably the one major event bringing the community together in the last twenty years since I've been here. I've been here since the crime was committed. The community didn't come together at that time. I was here when they were tried and sentenced. It didn't bring them together, but the execution of William Andrews is what has brought, not only the African American community together, but sympathizers from every other part of the community. He did participate in a vicious crime, and we admit to that, but the sentence, we think, did not match his role. And that's what brought us together."

But there would be difficulty, he foresaw, in keeping that sense of community, "because the cause won't be as obvious. And secondly, some of the difficulty will be because there is no such thing as an African American community. It's scattered all over the place, and communication becomes a problem. So it'll be difficult. But we think that through our churches and through the NAACP and other organizations, we'll be able to keep the fight going. We think that the death penalty will be challenged, that there'll be bills introduced in the state legislature, and, we think, around those issues, there'll be sufficient interest to keep it going."

He wasn't positive, he said, but he felt that the runaround might be by design. With the exception of a single judge, there were no African American officials in Utah. There had once been two black state legislators, but they were no longer in office. Otherwise there was no one he could think of, either in city, state, education, "anything."

"By scattering us out in terms of where we live, you don't have a concentrated community to do any political action. I think that's a good thing, in terms of integration. It's a negative, though, in terms of political clout and social connectedness. So for Utah, then, the only place that you see large numbers of African Americans is at the ten African American churches in Salt Lake. There are another ten outside of Salt Lake, in Ogden and in Avis County. About twenty African American churches. And that's where the political clout operates from. As Frazier said in his book, *The Negro Church,* in Utah, the church is the center of power. Some people have actually likened Utah to Mississippi. They've called it the Mississippi of the West. They meant that discrimination here is probably as bad as any place else in the country. And there are two reasons for that.

On the one hand, we have lots of white people who are here from other parts of the country, the South in particular, and they brought with them their traditional beliefs and stereotypes of African Americans. And in addition to that, the dominant religious group here, until 1978–79, believed that African Americans were, in fact, cursed, and so they were treated as second-class citizens on a religious basis, as well as historic and traditional discrimination. So that exists. There were still, until just a few years ago, restrictive covenants in some real estate contracts. We just last year, for the first time in the history of this state, got a fair housing bill. So we've got serious problems, and the Andrews case demonstrates that to a large degree."

I wondered if the atmosphere, in a place so far from the East Coast power centers, so controlled by a single religious group, so noted for right-wing political resolve, held any intimidation for the reverend.

"There's no intimidation for me. There are threats and there are challenges, people saying what I can and cannot do. But for me that's not intimidation. I came from UC Berkeley, from Georgia, and lots of other places, and I brought with me a reputation as a person who was outspoken and would not take the backseat to anybody. I came as a teacher at the University of Utah—they thought as a token, but I showed them very quickly I was not just a token. Because I worked for the African American community as a pastor of a church, there's nothing that anybody can do to me to shut me up. I can say whatever I want to say, and I can't get fired from my job. I can go wherever I want, and nobody can tell me that you can't come in here, because I'm a clergyman, a pastor of a predominantly African American congregation. And that is my power base. Plus, because of my approach to dealing with things, I've been able to develop a respect in much of the larger community. Although people don't agree with my stances, they know that whenever I speak about an issue, I don't speak lightly, that I speak from an informed base, and I'm not intimidated by them."

First Baptist had a congregation of around 500 people the Sunday just before. His congregation was growing, by everything he could ascertain. Young professional African Americans were moving to Salt Lake City. Senior citizens. He thought a sense of community was developing, and a sense of involvement, and not merely spiritual, but social and economic as well. In the main, throughout the United States, he felt that the churches that actually spoke to people's deepest needs—"where people hurt"—tended to be growing. Ministers had to address "issues of black manhood, how to deal with boys, how to make sure that the single women, mothers and children are taken care of, and the senior citizens." As far as he was concerned, contrary to popular belief, the African American church was waxing, not waning.

> At the time of this writing a number of Negroes belong to the Church of Jesus Christ of Latter Day Saints and attend its services, but the great majority of the descendants of those early Negro pioneers now belong to one of the six Negro churches that hold regular services in Salt Lake City. The Negroes are a church-going people and most of those with whom we have talked during the writing of this chapter, attend the church of their choice regularly.
>
> —Kate B. Carter, *The Negro Pioneer*

I was interested to discover that James Madison Flake—also known as "Green"—had been born in Anson, North Carolina, in 1815. "In the winter of 1843-44," according to Ms. Carter, "the Gospel of the Church of LDS was brought to the Flakes by missionaries and they were baptised. To avoid persecution, the Flakes joined the Saints in Nauvoo. Three of the Flake Negroes remained with the family while Mr. Flake gave the others their freedom." The Flakes, Jordan and Faithy Elizabeth Hanna, had been "well-to-do plantation owners." Nauvoo, Illinois, had been, in the 1840s, renamed Commerce—the then-center and outpost for the much-persecuted Mormons. To be sure, the Flakes, black or white, had no idea what would follow. To be sure, the notion of a promised land was a part of their Bible- and Book of Mormon–laden thinking—but Utah? Indeed, to most white folk it didn't really "exist."

Where, when, who, why did it begin?

Joseph Smith, Jr., born December 23, 1805, in Sharon, Vermont, had more than a vision. First, God and Jesus appeared before him, standing on the air in the woods outside Fayette, in western New York, and they had a chat with the fourteen-year-old boy. According to Smith, as quoted in Arrington's *Brigham Young: American Moses,* the Lord said many things to him. ("Behold, none doeth good, no not one. They have turned aside from the Gospel and keep not my commandments. They draw near to me with their lips while their hearts are far from me, and mine anger is kindling against the inhabitants of the earth to visit them according to their ungodliness and to bring to pass that which hath been spoken by the mouth of the prophets and apostles, behold and lo, I come quickly, as it was written of me, in the cloud clothed in glory of my Father and my soul is filled with love.")

Later, on the night of September 21, 1823, after hours of prayer, the angel Moroni, "the last prophet of a vanished race that anciently inhabited the Americas," appeared before the twenty-one-year-old future church leader. The next night, the angel told him the location of the plates whereon were written the history of the long-gone people, a book written by Moroni and his father, Mormon.

Much of what follows is, on whatever level you read it, as holy writ or as historical strangeness, excellent narrative material about digging for the treasure of Captain Kidd, lost manuscripts, breastplates of gold, translations for the "Reformed Egyptian," the fate of the first *Book of Mormon*'s 5,000 copies, printed in 1830 for $3,000, a visit from John the Baptist, and the first initiates into the Priesthood of Aaron—all leading to the organization of the six-member Church of Jesus Christ of Latter-Day Saints on April 6, 1830. (Actually, it was first called the Church of Christ, then the Church of Latter-Day Saints—the current title was settled upon in 1838.) Miracles are purported to have happened; Mrs. Joseph Smith became "a Daughter of God." In 1831, Smith and his followers moved to a new "Zion," Kirtland, Ohio. By 1835, their numbers were around 1,500. A new revelation informed Smith that Zion was in Missouri, but the folk of Independence did not cotton to the Mormons. They were roundly persecuted—houses, churches were burned; at one point, Smith was jailed for six months, and several times tarred and feathered. So the faithful moved westward, eventually landing in their own Nauvoo, which grew to over 11,000 people by the 1840s.

Smith was a busy, busy man. He became lieutenant governor of the Nauvoo Legion, mayor of Nauvoo. He addressed the United States Congress about Missouri in 1844. He officially made a bid to become president of the union. He was arrested repeatedly. War practically broke out in Illinois between the United States and the Carthage Grays, a Mormon militia said to number over 5,000. Some of the hostility against the Saints had to do with their belief in marital polygamy; but most of it was fear and loathing of their otherness, their desire to form their own government, and their profound disregard for existing forms of civil government: theirs was to be a theocracy.

> 1844, June 27 (Thursday). A body of 200 armed Missourians, with their faces painted and blackened, broke into Carthage jail, and at 5 p.m. murdered, in a most cowardly and brutal manner, Mr. Joseph Smith and his brother Hyrum, and desperately wounded Mr. John Taylor; Dr. Willard Richards alone escaping"
>
> —Sir Richard Francis Burton,
> *The City of the Saints,* 1862.

The new president of the Quorum of the Twelve Apostles had been known as a powerful proselytizer who had had great success in Britain. Brigham Young, a Vermonter, had been born in 1801, and converted in 1832.

After the state legislature revoked the Charter of Nauvoo in 1845, the future governor of the State of Utah decided that the West was probably best. And, amid more bloodshed and fire, the Saints prepared to leave. (In fact, in September of 1846, after three days of fighting, the Mormons were kicked out of Nauvoo.)

From their new headquarters in Council Bluff, Iowa, 143 men set out to find, yet again, their new Zion. When, on July 24, 1847—now known to members of LDS as Founders' Day—Brigham Young arrived, he was accompanied by Green Flake, Hark Lay and Oscar Crosby—black men.

> Blacks have lived in Utah for more than a century and a quarter and in the United States for more than three and a half centuries. During these years progress has been limited to individuals and not to the race as a whole. In considering the historical experience of Blacks in Utah and the United States, encompassing the struggle from slavery and the continuing quest for human rights, one is reminded of words uttered by a female slave of the nineteenth century: "Oh, Lord Jesus, how long, how long . . ."
>
> —Ronald G. Coleman, "Blacks in Utah History:
> An Unknown Legacy"

Throughout the course of writing this book, I had occasion to discuss what I had been doing for the last several years. Two places always elicited the most predictable, and eventually annoying, response: One was Alaska ("What? Black people live in Alaska?"); the other was Utah ("What? Black people live in Utah? What? Black Mormons?").

One of the people who has written most about black folk in Utah is Ronald G. Coleman. In fact, to this day, his dissertation is probably the best and most comprehensive source on that history.

At the time I met him, Dr. Coleman was associate vice president for the University of Utah at Salt Lake City, and a large (former football star), frightfully energetic man. When I met him in his baronial office at the U, as the locals call it, he quickly told me that practically everything I wanted to know about the history of blacks in Utah could be found in his dissertation. At the moment, he was fired up to talk about the folk in general, not just in Utah.

"Professionals might have a very different worldview or nation-view of themselves as individuals and collectively—who we are—from someone who finds herself or himself earning less or not earning anything. When we talk about progress, unfortunately for too many African American people, there hasn't been any progress. The common expression that you hear day-to-day is trying to survive. When we say trying to survive, what we're really saying is, trying to cope, trying to deal, trying to maintain."

The stress of living in either world was tremendous these days, he said. Folk had bought into the "basic economic system"—material accumulation. "You find yourself accumulating and accumulating. We see this in the national debt. A large part of the burden of personal indebtedness is on us. We have signified as 'making it,' those things we have. I think in part the problems of crime within our community, drugs, and general attitude is a response to the desire to have things. And we have glorified and put on a pedestal people who have things. We don't often ask how they got those things. We have made heroes and sheroes out of the glitter, and we don't value those people who I like to think did it the way the old folks did it. They were honest, they had personal self-dignity. They had a work ethic, and they tried to instill that in those who followed them. How else were you going to make it? The access to anything good that white folks had was limited. An athlete? An entertainer? That's a very different world people in those professions have access to today as opposed to fifty years ago."

Even today, the vice president told me, he looked with pride upon men in the community who had held steady jobs for decades, and raised families, and "instilled them with values." However, these men were being overlooked.

"I really think that these are the people that need—deserve—recognition, because the odds in which they had to come of age are very different from what I've had to deal with. I'm forty-eight. I look at the generation that preceded me, my father's and my stepfather's generation, and say that the opportunities were limited. No matter how bright you were. And they did try to provide a sense of wholeness for their families."

Those were the men, back in San Francisco, from whom he learned, men who pushed him to go to school, to think about responsibilities.

"I went to college because I had to. There was no alternative. It was either that or move out of my parents' house. Now, at seventeen, I wasn't ready to move. I simply was not emotionally, let alone financially, ready to leave the nest.

"I thought I was going to be a printer or a plumber. I liked print shops. I was goofing off in high school with this dude, a white boy. He always knew what he was going to do. He was going to be a plumber. His daddy was a plumber. His uncle was a plumber. And he was going to be a plumber. And he said, 'And I'll get you on too.' I went home, and I remember telling my stepfather I was going to get in and be a plumber. He said, 'Ain't no niggers in the union.' 'What?' I didn't know anything about unions or anything. That went out the door right quick.

"But I think, with new rights and access, so many of us have an attitude that life owes us something. I think, with some of the more overt forms of racial discrimination in all of its manifestations, at least on the surface, appearing to fall aside, it's a kind of tricky thing to raise your kids to be assertive, and at the same time to be respectful. I don't know that we've modeled the way we should have modeled, some of us. Our behaviors. Many of us condone breaking the law. I'm talking about stealing. I'm talking about drugs particularly, without going out and doing an honest day's work. Even when you do get an honest day's pay. Some people will say that's blaming the victim. Well, you can wallow in that. I'm not blaming the victim, but I am saying that there are too many of us, particularly in my generation, whose children now are coming of age. I see it all the time. I've got nephews with this attitude, 'What is wrong with you, bro?' I think that's been like a cancer in our community. And I don't think we know how to deal with it, because we're so close to one another. We don't like to be critical of one another. Being critical of the individual appears as though you're being critical of all of us."

This attitude was a major fault he saw in the rhetoric of some of the current black conservatives. Many of those cultural critics, he felt, wanted to simply write off an entire generation of black youth. "We can't write off anyone. We have to be aware of the basis of the problem. How do you change the attitude that life owes you something? Or it's up to me to get mine? It's up to everybody else to get theirs. We've lost a little bit of that caring, that concern. That sense of involvement that I think used to be there. I've always felt so wonderful that I was nurtured by so many different people. I've thought about, 'How am I doing what I'm doing now and why?' And those women in that church. And being pushed, because that's where we got our first lessons. Those little rhymes and stuff and putting you out there. Unfortunately, within this generation coming of age now, a number of our children have given up. Some never had hope, real hope. None of us had anything, but I think we were less crablike."

Dr. Coleman found the Mormon Church as fascinating as I did. But he pointed out that one had to keep in mind that the Church of Jesus Christ of Latter-Day Saints was a relatively young religion: 1830. They wanted their "piece of the rock without influences. This was Zion." But eventually they found themselves a part of the United States. "The world of Brigham Young was a very different world.

"I remember reading an interview that was done in an African American newspaper of two former slaves here. One of the things that always struck me, even when I was an undergraduate student here in the early '60s, was the way they talked about the mountains. 'Where am I? What is it? Where am I and what am I doing here?' You start looking around and these mountains can appear to be pretty formidable. When I was a student, I used to look around, 'Wow!' I always knew I was going to be here temporarily. I was here to go to school, play football, and whew, I went home every chance I got. I took an extra week at spring break. I took a week at Thanksgiving. I'd never considered this home. I knew I could never live here because the place didn't offer me what I thought were the proper amenities. First of all, the racism was much more prevalent and overt, even though I didn't really experience it to any great extent. I was an athlete. My world revolved around the campus. But I knew enough about what went on that I said, 'Hmmm, not me.' So I was in a way kind of surprised when I came back in '73, but even then I saw it as temporary. 'I'll be here three, four years and then out of here.'" He seriously thought that way for eight years.

A number of things happened during that time—his children were coming of age; his wife graduated from medical school; his marriage broke up. He spent six months in San Francisco. And he began to think of Utah differently.

"When you start getting down into the day in and day out of things, I thought that the quality of my life was better here than it would be there.

"I've always asked in my own workshops, and I ask myself, 'How do black people stay in places like Salt Lake City, Utah?' In a way, if you look at us historically, we're a rural people who were transformed into urbanites. Within that rural experience, there's a certain amount of living with isolation, but you're not isolated when you're among yourselves. Historically, and even today, the thing that has enabled black people to stay here has been that they've always known that they were part of something larger. So there's a connectedness. Very important psychological connection and communications link with the larger African communities. So you reach out.

"Now I talk on the phone, and with modern transportation, I'm out of here enough so that I don't feel isolated. You have people who are coming through, who are saying, 'There ain't that many of us.' And some people couldn't handle it. But for me, I think I'm fairly secure; I think it's a good place for my kids to come of age.

"I figure I could do a lot of it at home. In terms of talking about culture and race and all that stuff, I can do that. But I made sure to plug them in. I knew they would be isolated in their schools. I guess, in a way, that took me back to having a distant association with church. I dropped them off. And my daughter, the youngest girl, she said, 'People say you drop us off but you never come.' Told her to 'Tell them to mind their own business.' But she pressed me. If I value this, why don't I demonstrate it? So I went, after I'd been out one Saturday night, and the Reverend France Davis preached a powerful sermon, a powerful sermon. You know, one that just broke through. Amen, I said, 'Oh, whoa.' I talked to him, I had some doubts and hesitations because I had not been raised in a Baptist church. My daughter said, 'Did you do that for us?' I said, 'No, I did it for myself.'"

> Negroes [are] not yet to receive the priesthood,
> for reasons which we believe are known to God,
> but which He has not made fully known to man.
>
> —The Mormon Church, 1969;
> *New York Times,* June 10, 1978

In 1971 Ruflin Bridgeforth, Darius Gray and Eugene Orr, three black members of the Church of Jesus Christ of Latter-Day Saints, received official sanction from the church's leadership to form the Genesis Group—an organization of black Mormons. It would be "administratively autonomous"—separate but equal in a way. Their unofficial goal: the institution of black priests.

Personally, I find the organization of the LDS the most Byzantine in Protestantism. Just like their symbol, the beehive, they are divided into a multiplicity of cells and units: regions, stakes, missions, wards, bishoprics, clerkdoms, presidencies, quorums, "assignments," associates, schools and societies—locally, nationally, globally. At the tippy top are the First Presidency (three men) and the Quorum of the Twelve Apostles. One might best think of the U.S. executive branch for one, and both the congressional and judicial (ecclesiastically speaking) branch for the other—though the analogy quickly breaks down since there are only fifteen people. There is also a church patriarch in charge of "special blessings."

Toiling within this massive behemoth of bureaucracy are two orders of priesthood. The Aaronic priests, "ordained" laymen, may administer basic rites: baptism, the eucharist; they are either deacons, teachers, or priests. The higher order, the Melchizedek, including Elders, Seventy Priests or high priests, tend to preside over entire churches or branches and on up. Members of both are qualified to preach.

When exactly the Mormon Church originally developed acute Negrophobia is unclear. It might be easy to conclude that it had been present at the very beginning. The territorial legislature of Utah made slavery legal in 1852; not all slaveholders manumitted their slaves when they first arrived in the 1840s—yet, strangely enough, though there were probably others, one black priest is well-documented.

Elijah Abel had been ordained as a Melchizedek Elder back in 1836, and then in 1839, he was made a member of the Nauvoo Seventies Quorum. He came to Utah in 1853.

No one can say—well, perhaps some can say, but they probably won't—why "He" changed "His" mind in 1978, as "He" appears to have done in "Letter of the First Presidency," June 9, 1978:

> He has heard our prayers, and by revelation has confirmed that the long-promised day has come when every faithful, worthy man in the Church may receive the holy priesthood, with power to exercise its divine authority, and enjoy with his loved ones every blessing that flows therefrom, including the blessings of the temple.

> Accordingly, all worthy male members of the Church may be ordained to the priesthood without regard for race or color. Priesthood leaders are instructed to follow the policy of carefully interviewing all candidates for ordination to either the Aaronic or the Melchizedek priesthood to insure that they meet the established standards for worthiness.

I reckon "He" has yet to make up his mind about women. Nonetheless, within two days, Joseph Freeman, Jr., who had been a part of Genesis, became the first ordained black Mormon priest in God knows how many years. (Freeman had earlier been quoted in the *New York Times:* "Many white people are hoping for change, praying that the blacks will hold the priesthood, same as the blacks are [praying]. But for now, we're on the right train. Maybe we're not the engineer, but it's better than missing the train." A few years later, he would entitle his autobiography *In the Lord's Due Time.*)

A cynical person might make hay of the uncanny timing of the First Presidency's "revelation" coming at the moment that the expansion of Mormondom in Latin America, Asia and Africa was considered paramount by the Church. And also that the revelation came with no theological amendation to the previously held doctrine that darker-skinned folk were "cursed." Had the curse been lifted?

Interestingly enough, all during the interregnum, there were significant—increasing—numbers of African American Mormons, throughout the nation and in Utah.

Isaac James and his sister, Jane, had worked for Joseph Smith back in Nauvoo. When they arrived in Utah, they were said to have been much esteemed by the Saints there. Isaac's son, Sylvester, probably took up arms back in Missouri, and was listed as a "prominent man" of Utah.

Nonetheless, despite these few revered colored folk—along with Green Flake, who Brigham Young himself seemed to hold in high regard—the organizers of Utah were not so moved to abolish slavery for people of African descent (even though there was a curious requirement that "masters" send their "servant or servants" to school "between the ages of six years and twenty years" for at least eighteen months).

This is how the Bankheads came to Utah.

I had been sitting by the phone all day, waiting for a call from a descendant of one of Utah's black pioneer families. But by midafternoon

I was powerfully hungry, so I slipped across the street to McDonald's hoping I wouldn't miss the call.

Walking back to my room with my combo in hand, a woman from the floor above spied me, and came in my direction in something of a huff. She was not too tall, Senegalese-dark, her hair augmented to flow down her back, Diana Ross–like, and, to be polite about it, her curves outdid Mae West's—worried, clearly on purpose, by the tightest, shortest, whitest, skimpiest slip of a garment I could recall seeing on a human being of her potent proportions.

She quickly asked if I had a car, and said she'd pay me to take her to her own car, not too many blocks away. And, being properly brought up, I could not refuse reasonable help to a young black woman in need. No charge, I said. I have spent little time as a rocket-scientist-in-training, so it didn't take me long to figure out what was going on.

Nice car, she said.

Thanks, I said.

She fiddled with her hair, and gave me directions, and complained about the police. Where are you from? she asked, and I told her. She asked what I did, and I told her. Damn, she said, that's good.

She told me she was originally from Lincoln, Nebraska. She'd spent a few years in Boise. I found it refreshing that she made no attempt to dissemble about her trade. She complained some more about the police and johns in particular.

I knew straightaway that I should ask for an interview, but I hesitated. My feelings about prostitution are mingled and commingled with my southern hang-ups about sex, with hard and fast views on feminism, with the belief in a woman's right to do whatever she pleases with her body, with a sadness that a human being would allow, be forced, or choose to use their body as a commodity, and with the realization that the sex industry is a legitimate one, despite governmental law and hypocritical social mores, with the awkwardness of looking at a sexworker and seeing her as just another freelancer—a person.

She told me her car was parked a few blocks ahead—the police recognized it. She offered to pay again. I said, no, thanks, and quickly gathered my wits. I explained that I was writing a book about black people in America, and that I would really like to interview someone from Nebraska. I paused and said, "I'll pay for your time, if that's a problem." And as the words fell out of my mouth, I felt like the perfect fool.

She neither smiled nor frowned or looked dismayed or bewildered, but there was something of disappointment about her face. I had been cool, up to that minute; now I was acting like another john.

Later the irony hit me. Here I was in the city of the Saints, worrying about being misunderstood by a prostitute; perhaps even more worried about associating with her.

I never heard from that woman again. In truth, I never expected to.

Susan Thompson's mother had been a Leggroan. It had been her grandmother's family who settled in the valley, in Cottonwood, Utah. They lived in Cottonwood for a year, and then helped settle Wellsville. The Bankheads also settled there. The Leggroans and the Bankheads intermarried, and most of their descendants were related. There was also the Perkins family.

Susan Thompson's maternal great-grandfather had been a horsetrader and translator for the Ute. A place, "Cookie's Hollow," had been named after him. "Those are things we just took for granted, as kind of insignificant."

I calculated that Susan Thompson's children were probably seventh-generation Utahans. "I don't know," she said. "I never counted.

"All these years, I keep saying, 'I should be writing this down.' It's so hard to retain all of this, the stories and the different things about my mother, and especially the things my grandmother told me, but because there are so many families, it's hard. I don't have the talent or the ability. But I keep thinking that somebody should be.

"I remember when Alex Haley came here. When he was researching his book. He'd come to do some genealogy, and they had him at the Tabernacle, and he was giving a summation of his book and his writing—but he told the whole little story. My sister and I went. I was so fascinated by it. When he started telling you about how this thing got rolling."

When Susan Thompson was younger, she told me she went to all the local churches, not exclusively LDS. "I did try the church. I guess my mother was raised in it, but she never ever forced it on me. I just kind of went a little while out of curiosity. I felt uncomfortable. So I didn't really pursue it. That was before they had the Revelation. That's what was messing with me. Not that I want to belong or anything, but before I felt I really shouldn't be there. I was going to primary and stuff there, around twelve or thirteen." Nonetheless, she told me, those blacks descended from the original black settlers who had connections to the vast LDS network felt they would be "taken care of" if they reached out for church support. "To this day. To this day. As far as my mom is concerned, it's like, once you belong to the church, it doesn't matter what color you are, or where you came from. Once you are truly a member, there's no discrimination. It was probably being raised here, but I had more discrimination based on the fact that I'm non-Mormon, as opposed to the fact that I'm black.

"If you're black and you're Mormon, you're in. My mother, who has been a lifelong member and has been active in the church, they constantly call on her, look after her, take care of her. Always reassure me that if there's anything that I need . . . They always have taken care of her.

"When our generation was coming up, it wasn't the popular thing to do. Most of us did not join. But now there's a resurgence—a lot of people are joining. I used to give my mother a hard time, mainly because I didn't understand. And I still don't understand. I've accepted it, but I keep telling myself, well, this is like slavery. Nobody liked slavery, but they had to go along with it. I think we were just raised in this religion, and there are certain things you didn't question as far as their attitude towards blacks and the curse and all of that. I used to rag on her all the time. 'How can you belong to this church?' She didn't respond, and then, of course I would feel bad for bringing it up. But what she did tell me one time was that there was a member of our family, Sylvester James, who held a position in the church that was the equivalent of a priest, but I don't think there's any documentation on it."

There was a small monument in Susan's neighborhood dedicated to the black pioneers. "Some things are very subtle. A lot of the older people, if they're still in that neighborhood, they know who the families are. You know, the names Bankhead and Leggroan and Perkins, that are very well respected. 'Oh yes, I've heard about your family. Oh yeah, we know where you live.'"

Susan Thompson said there was definitely a feeling of being watched, for her and the other black descendants in Salt Lake. Many people simply assumed she was LDS.

"A lot of people do. It's like the guy that I work with down at the barber shop. The people come in and he'll go, 'Oh yeah, she's one of our black Mormons.' So whether I am or not, I have that label. But nobody has questioned me on how come none of us really joined the church. I think it's kind of obvious. I think certain people realize where we stand."

Few, if any, of the original structures built by those first black settlers are still standing. One had burned down a few years ago, and the home of her grandmother had to be removed, due to a road and to city regulations. Instead of moving the house, it was torn down. "But I think everybody on the street has the stones. They're the cut stone. I've got them all in my yard, as walkways and things like that, some of the rocks that the house was made from. I was telling my kids about those rocks. 'If anything should ever happen to me, do not get rid of the rocks. Because these rocks came from Aunt Sarah's house.' My kids are going, 'Mom, you expect us to keep rocks in the family?' " Susan gave a chuckle. "That's all we've got left to pass on that came from the original black pioneer homes. 'Don't mess with the rocks.' "

Susan Thompson had two sons, then aged eleven and fifteen. I wondered if they had a sense of their local history. "They've heard so much about it; they just kind of take it in stride. And then, a number of years ago, my oldest one, I think when he was in sixth grade, he had to do a report on somebody famous or something like that. And I says, 'Well, why don't you do your great-grandma?'—because my grandmother, she died two years ago; she was a hundred years old. Nancy Leggroan. He's going, 'Well, not to be disrespectful, but grandma's not famous.' And I go, 'Well, of course she is.' He knew a little bit about the history, but I got books out that had her name in them. This was to show him. I says, 'Here's her picture, and here's about her mother, and here's about her dad.' So he was kind of fascinated by that, and he did a report and got an A on it. He did quite a good report. He really got into it, and he really learned a lot."

Susan Thompson told me that due to some negative past experiences her children now went to Catholic school. "I didn't like the attitude in the public school system. It's been the equivalent of private Mormon schools. I still live on the same street that I grew up on, and they would have gone to the same schools I went through. I felt very much an outsider. Sometimes I was the only black student, but that wasn't the thing, I was raised around whites all my life. It was more the Mormon versus the non-Mormon." Apparently it would not be uncommon for the Salt Lake City public schools to have the equivalent of Bible schools, and "little Mormon seminar classes." When she had been in school, she felt that this not only made her an outsider, but it also alienated her even more from the black kids downtown.

I wondered if Susan Thompson had ever considered leaving Utah. "No, no, no. I love it here. I married somebody from out of state thinking that would probably get me out of state for a while, but he came from Wichita Falls, Texas, so he was not eager to get back. After high school, once I started traveling and getting to other cities and being around blacks—you know, aside Salt Lake City, I'd never been anyplace where there was a large population of blacks. I went to Florida, Georgia, Virginia and California, and places like that, and it was really neat. It's wonderful, but I'm glad when I get back here. This is home. I would leave maybe for two or three years, but I would always want to come back."

Even when she was younger, she was aware of the differences and similarities between black culture in the West, and black culture on the East Coast.

"My family, not being from the South, our menu didn't consist of things like black-eyed peas, and rice and grits, and stuff like that. People here in Salt Lake ate it, but not within my immediate family. They were so far removed from the South, they didn't really eat like that. That was kind of a cultural shock for me. Whereas, my husband being from Texas, and myself acquiring a taste for that food, we introduced everything to my kids. But with my mom and them, I don't know. Maybe it was because when they were raised, blackness was not a priority. Color was never really an issue per se. I mean, they had gone through some trials and tribulations and discriminations, and they probably should have been a little bit more assertive, but then I don't see how they really could have prepared us for what was out there, because they didn't really know themselves. My mother would tell me about conditions all across the country, some of the laws, and not being allowed to go to school."

Today, Susan Thompson's children took black culture in stride, and she felt that they thought themselves very much a part of the mainstream. "They take things for granted. I took my son to Atlanta, last month. My youngest one. And I keep thinking, if I came down here at his age, I'd be breaking my neck. But he was oblivious to it. I think it is because of the media and the movies and things that we didn't have when I was a kid, you know. You just latched onto anything that was black, a picture in *Life* magazine or something like that. But well, he just blended right in."

While her children listened to rap music ("They're into the lighter stuff. Like Heavy D. They're not into it really, really heavy, which I'm thankful for. Like Public Enemy and Ice T. I just hold my breath."), she remembered listening to the Temptations and the Shirelles. Jazz. Sly and the Family Stone.

Susan Thompson felt very much a part of a larger, African American culture.

"I feel okay with it only because I have left here and gone to other parts of the country. I'm okay. I can fit in. It's surprising. Black people think that just because you're black, even if you've never been around black people before, once you get into that setting, that you're at ease because you're around your own folks. If you aren't accustomed to being around them, you can be just as uncomfortable as being a white person walking into a black church or a black person walking into a roomful of white people. Being uncomfortable. The same thing happens to blacks. When I very first left, I was maybe sixteen, I think. It was a shock. I went to West Palm Beach, Florida. It was interesting because it was like I needed a reality check. I had to see some white people. I don't want to say that, but that was my comfort level. I just assumed that once I went down there, I would have no problem. I was distraught. Because that's what I was accustomed to being around. I'm okay with it now. You have to get out there. I don't check myself anymore. I can pass. Instead of sticking out like a hick."

Nathan Gray:

"Back in the '30s, before World War II come on, you know, there were blacks who live in the town there. I could tell if you walked down the street, if you was a stranger. Everybody knowed everybody. Tell you where you worked, where you lived. Take you there. That was in the '30s. The late '30s. Then World War II come along, and the colored started coming in here. Before that, there wasn't too many colored around. I was born here.

"You take the pioneers. Now the first one come in, colored, was in the 1840s. My mother's people come in from Wellsville. That's where my mother was born, down there in Wellsville. She's a native, too, of Utah. And they come into Utah in covered wagons. She was telling me how they used to come in there. They settled in here. All black. I don't know where they was coming from before that. Because you take my grandmother on my mother's side, she was a slave. My grandfather, on my mother's side, he was part Indian. Where he originated from, I couldn't tell you that. And you take my father's side now; his mother was a West Indian. My grandfather, he was a Negro. He come from Kansas. That's where he originated from. But up until Wellsville, now my grandmother was a slave. She was freed when she was a young girl. I used to live with my grandmother. She used to tell us about the hardships they had. Coming from Wellsville and everything. Settling in here. My grandfather now, he liked to play the fiddle. They had the wood stoves in those days. They didn't have no gas like we got now. He used to get up behind that stove and fiddle. But he was quiet. Never get him to talk. No. He never did teach me how to fiddle. He used to teach my sister how to fiddle though, but she's dead. In fact, when he passed away, he willed the fiddle to her.

"You take now, around here at that time, some of them worked on the railroad. The railroad. Some of them worked out at the refinery, and some of them worked in these hotels.

"Klan's here, but they never did bother us. I mean, they'd burn a cross up behind the capitol there. But they never did bother none of the Negroes. Just burn a cross. I never did have no trouble with no Mormons.

"But you take Mormons. Now I'll tell you when the Depression was on, they'd come to you—I don't care what color you was—and wanted to know if you had enough to eat. Was your rent paid? Did you have fuel and all that? And they'd set there just like you see me talking. Next day, it'd be there. Bring you coal, if you burned coal. You'd have food. Black or white. That kind of people. But at that time, they didn't believe for black to preach, he'd still be a slave. Then they changed that around, because I have a friend, me and him worked together. You could go up to the temple grounds, but you couldn't go in the whatchacallit there. He was black. He's still black. He joined the Mormons. And he couldn't go in the temple. Blacks couldn't go in the temple at that time. So he joined the Mormon Church and him and his wife got married up there in the temple. And there's a big Mormon church down here, just a block from us, that's where they had his reception. We was invited, and you ought to see the presents they got. And he's the first black that's ever been married in the temple. That hasn't been too long. In the '70s. Me and him worked on the road together.

"I got a whole slew of relatives live up in East Side belong to the Mormon church. There was a little clan of them up there. And they all belong too. Now they all belong to that Mormon church. It's like they was white.

"I don't know. I could have joined up. I just couldn't see it. I like my own color, but of course I used to go with a white girl. Back then. That was it. When I was a kid, what I wanted. When you have to sneak around, you know it's bad. Whereas my own people, my own girlfriend, I could walk down the street with her, and nobody'd say nothing. But with this white girl, I'd have to sneak out and meet her someplace. And couldn't walk around. Wasn't too many colored girls around here at that time. You'd have to sneak around. But I remember one night—me and a little girl, and another white girl, and my friend, he was black. And it was the police. They come, and there was two officers in the car. My girlfriend sat up there with them. And they put me and this other girl and the other friend, in the back. She jumped right on in the back and got right on my lap and put her arms around me, stole a kiss. And they took us up to the police station. Just took blood tests though. See if we had anything. But that was it.

"But nowadays, it's nothing. You go out now, you don't think nothing of seeing a white and black. Plenty of them go past. Nobody don't say anything. If they do, they keep saying it to themselves. Not like it was in the old days. In the old days now, take the middle of the block here. Say here, now me and a white girl'd be out there talking, and wouldn't be nobody in sight. And the first thing you'd see somebody coming out of the house. And they'd be picking up something or watering the lawn, easing up towards you. Guess, trying to see what you was talking about.

"I got another cousin. He married a white girl during them years. He married a white girl. But they didn't bother them. They lived together till they had one boy, and then they separated. But they didn't get married here. At that time, you couldn't get married here. Blacks and whites. But you could go to Nevada and get married. They'd marry you. That ain't but 120 miles from here. But it's changed now. But in them days, well, they was better days than what they are now. Of course, people didn't have much money, but things wasn't as hard. A little money you made would go farther, and ten dollars, would go for, in them days, $100. Yeah. You could go to the store there in those days, get you a loaf of bread for a nickel. Like this butcher shop here, where you could go in, the meat's already cut. The butcher'd have to cut it for you. Butcher shop would be sawdust all over the floor and he'd take this big old round table and cut it for you. But those days, of course, then I was married and I had two kids. I'd take a little wagon, take five dollars and have to take the wagon to bring it home. Rent was cheap. Ten dollars a month for our house. Fifteen. Five-room house, fifteen dollars a month. In the '30s. We got another house over there on Fifth now, we're getting $400-$500 a month. It's six rooms. Now just figure that. This was just a five-room house and had a toilet, bath. Fifteen dollars a month.

"No, we didn't have no air conditioning. You'd have to take an old fan and do the best you could. But it wasn't as hot in those days as it is now.

"I've been all over the United States. Every state in the union. I was a Pullman porter. And I never did get accustomed to the South.

"I was down there in Hattiesburg, Mississippi. I was used to going in the station here and just walking through the station, going and getting my pass or whatever. Well, I wasn't thinking. Me and another porter, we was around there, and we'd taken a load down there, and unloaded. And they told us to pick up our pass in the station. Well, I forgot. I seen a "colored" sign over on this side, and a "white" sign on that side. But I wasn't thinking, and went up to one of those little old ticket windows. This old white fellow looks at me and says, 'What do you want, nigger? Get over on the other side.' Well, I just looked through there, and I seen colored waiting and colored over in this aisle. I went on out the colored way. Went all around, and come back, and that same son of a bitch who told me to go over there, he waited on me on that side. And he said, 'What do you want, boy?' I said, 'I want a pass for Gray and Sherrill.' He fumbled around and finally come up with a pass, and give it to us. And the same bastard come back on that side. I never did like the South. Never did care for it.

"The black people was friendly. But they could tell that we was from up north. Open your mouth. And they tell you, 'Oh, you're a northerner.' That was all over. I never did get used to it. We was up there in another little old place, and—oh, what's the name of it? Meridian. Bad place for colored. I had a load of white people, here, out in the East and West. Whole train of them. They were just on a tour. Anyhow, went up there to get me a newspaper. That bastard wouldn't sell me no newspaper. No. So anyhow, I went back to the train and one of these white passengers says, 'Did you get your paper?' And I said, 'No, they wouldn't sell it to me.' Well, he asked me first what kind of paper I wanted. Well, I wanted the Salt Lake *Tribune*. And he went right on over to that newsstand, and bought me a Salt Lake *Tribune*. And this old man was looking at him. He brought that paper right on and give it to me. That bastard. I said, 'He could have shot me, had me killed.' I never did like the South. Nobody liked to go there.

"I've been through Jackson, Mississippi. Let me tell you about Jackson, man. We unloaded a bunch of foreigners there in Jackson. It was a Saturday night. Well, there was a beer joint down the way. They was whooping it up, and having a good time. You could hear the music and everything. I guess it must have been about fifteen or twenty of us. And we went down there, to get something to eat, and get a beer or two. Nothing but blacks inside. We walked in to sit down, and everybody got up and walked out. About fifteen of us. Black Pullman porters. And all of them walked out. Just got up and walked on out. We could see the people through the window. So we ate and drank, got up and left. When we got about a half a block away, we looked back and all of them went back in and had dinner. It was a colored place. That's what I'm saying. All of them were black that was in this place. Black folk walked out. We never could figure it out. We never did figure it out. That was our own people.

"Only ever happened in Jackson, Mississippi. I don't know. I never did get used to the South. Because I was used to out here, you know, going in and out.

"I'll tell you now. You take around here, them times, there was places here, you'd go to a movie here, and you'd have to go upstairs and see it. Here. Here. Certain restaurants you couldn't go in. Segregated like that. All around here was that way. You take Utah, Idaho, Wyoming, and Nevada, it was all like that at one time. It was the same damn way over in Oregon. The only place that was more civilized than the rest of the country was up there in Seattle, Washington. You'd go in anyplace in Seattle, but get over in the Oregon side, and you're segregated. They had big signs in the damn window. 'We do not cater to colored.' That'd be in the window.

"It was worse down South—but up here, you wasn't used to it, like you was down South. Just some places. But I know we was up there in Laramie, Wyoming. Football team. We went in this place to eat. Now this is damn old Chinaman place. Chinaman place. He come telling, 'Feed you in the back.' I said, 'I don't eat in the damn kitchen in my home. I sure ain't going to eat in a Chinaman's kitchen.' And we walked on out. And we went all over town, trying to find a place to eat. And finally we found a Mexican restaurant. And they welcomed us, and we sat where we wanted. Then we was up in Idaho Falls, couldn't find no place to eat up there. I don't know. I guess the railroad got in touch with this restaurant, and made some kind of deal with them. Then they told us where to go eat. They'd feed us and they was nice there. But let me tell you about this one.

"We was down there in Nevada, picking up a load of soldiers, we were supposed to pick up a whole trainload. Oh, there was a whole gang of colored men. I guess there must have been seventy or eighty, ninety. They brought them in from all parts of the country, to go down there to make this movie, to make this troop movie. And they had this great big old café. Big old, big old place. So we went in there that morning for breakfast. Now they had all kinds of white waitresses in there. They didn't wait on us. They had two little old colored gals, worked in the kitchen, come in and waited on us. And we seen what the trouble was—sent two little colored gals out there to wait on seventy or eighty people. Some of the guys got up and helped them serve. So we got together, and everybody tipped them a dollar. So we went back that evening for dinner. I bet you know who waited on us for dinner. We didn't tip them like we did them colored gals. But up there in Yellowstone Park, we was up there one summer, and an old waitress up there, she said she wouldn't go wait on no black people. And the manager told her, 'Well, get your coat and your hat, and that's it.'

"But we had, I had, fun. If I had to pay for it, I never would have seen all these places. I made it through twenty-seven years, twenty-seven and a half. Retired when they went out of business. I retired in '65. Yeah, '65. That's when they went out of business.

"The last. After I got what they call 'whiskers.' I worked up to the number-two spot. And if I stayed in there long enough, man, I'd have been top dog. Number one. But they went out of business. That was the National. Picked up the tickets. I'd leave here at 4:30 like today, and get in Denver 8:30 the next morning. And that was where I'd be up all night. I never did get no sleep. I'd get seventeen hours."

"I got four children. Roy. He lives here. Then I got Myron. He lives in Las Vegas. And I got another son over there in Fairfield, California. And I got a daughter in Kansas City, Missouri.

"There was no complaint about school here. You had to go to school. Or you could go to reform school. So wasn't no problem about school here. No discriminating, no, uh-uh. They'd teach you the same as they taught the white kids. If you didn't learn, they didn't promote you and you stayed in the same grade next year.

"My wife, she worked thirty years. Supervisor for the Veterans' Hospital."

"I worked at General Motors until the war come on. And the old man called me in the office, and the lady said, 'This job is nonessential.' Said, 'I'm going to try and see if I can get you an essential job, like the railroad.' I said, 'Yeah, I'd like that.' So I went down to the club, and they was telling me about where they needed Pullman porters. Shoot, I don't know. They interviewed me over there. I still hung on to my job down at General Motors. I said, 'Hell. They ain't going to call me.' I was married then. One day, here come a man down there. Supervisor. He called me into his office, and he give me a slip for the railroad.

"So I went on up to the doctor and he examined me, and I passed that. And come on back down, showed them where I'd passed. And they told me, said, 'Well, you get ready tonight.' Los Angeles. So he said, 'You have to feed yourself because your room is paid for. But you take money to feed yourself. And take enough clothes because you'll be down there a week.' So I went home and told my wife, and asked her would she be all right? Had two kids. So I took off that night, twelve o'clock. Went on down there, and the next morning, they showed us how to make them beds. We worked two days making that bed. Hell, I got so I was making beds with my eyes closed. Making, then tearing them up and making them over again. That's the way we done it. And they'd give you a book to read and ask all these questions and that stuff. Worked down there for two days, and the third day, I took a trip with an experienced porter. Went on his run with him. We went down to someplace, some kind of beach, down in California. That's where the train runs, see, and that was his run. So next day, we went down to the train and worked on them damn beds. The next day, then, sent me out on another run with a porter to go from Los Angeles through Oakland.

"So I made that. That was a long run, a hot run, and well, it wasn't hot, but it was long. And he was a lazy bugger at that. He would let me make all the damn beds. Then when I got fast, he'd buy time. He had to shine shoes, and that's where you made tips. Let me shine all the damn shoes and everything—but he split the tips with me. I done the work. He split the tips. I was so tired when I got to the room. He went to drink and I was too tired. He told me, said, 'Fellow, you ain't going to do no drinking. You go on and go to bed.' Hell, I was glad to get to bed. So we left that evening, and come back to Los Angeles. I done the same thing. Made the beds, shined the shoes. They split the tips when we got to Los Angeles. Had a big old, what they called a sixteen-section car. That's thirty-two beds. I wrassled with them beds, putting them away and making them, and all. I said to myself, 'To hell with it.' That was what I was saying to myself. But I found out all them cars didn't have no thirty-two beds. Some had less, some had more. That changed the tune all around. 'I'm going to keep this job.'

"All over the country, all day and night. Yeah. Where you'd be here today, and hell, Omaha the next day, and down South. Then we'd go up to Washington—oh, we went all over, all over this country."

"I had some good old times there. Most of my old friends now have passed away. Just a few of us left, you know, the railroad porters. Only about four or five of us left. The rest passed away. But I had a good time on the railroad, but then, after you run all over the country awhile, you get monotonous. You get tired. The last few years, I was the conductor. Well, I liked that. Because I was my own boss. Nobody dared to bother me. I'd still be working, I guess, if they continued. There wasn't nothing hard. I just sat there and dozed off. I had a good old brakeman. He was always waking me up if anything happened. So I really enjoyed it. Of course, when I'd get home, I'd go to work someplace else or I liked to fish. And I had a buddy around here, he liked to fish too. We'd go out to the lake. But now there ain't no water out to the lake. The water's only up to here.

"Hell, water's down all over. All over. I think those spaceships have got a lot to do with this weather too. Something up there in the air. What the hell they doing? I don't know. Everybody want to live up there, but ooooh, I wouldn't want to live up there, floating around up there in the air. Shit. I guess they're trying to get to heaven. That's the only way I can figure it out. I don't think they'll ever make that."

Eighteen

# AND STILL I RISE

*Cheyenne, Wyoming*

I have a friend who says that one of the most desolate places on the face of God's green earth she has ever seen is Wyoming. I tell her I think she's crazy. I tell her Wyoming has one of America's most dramatic, shifting, and at times subtle landscapes, dramatic box canyons to the west, and vast high plains to the east. Wyoming is Yellowstone and buffalos, buttes and geysers, the flyfisher's dream and the environmentalist's hallowed ground, Grand Teton, Medicine Bow, Thunderbasin, Wasatch, the Black Hills, Shoshone, Targhee, mountains' majesty, bear, deer, pheasant, elk. Wyoming contains over a third of our nation's national forests. She tells me I'm crazy. She's city; I'm country. I was happy to find Cheyenne was still largely country.

Is there a man (or woman) living who, as a child, has not seen, if not fallen under the thrall of, cowboy Westerns? I had my period. And though I've long since realized that this mythology is one of the greatest lies Hollywood ever perpetrated, I still enjoy sitting with my grandaddy of a Sunday afternoon and visiting that never-never land of six shooters, hostile natives (even as a kid, I loved it when the Indians beat the devil out of the cowmen), saloons, ethical sheriffs, shoot-outs, faithful horses, ten-gallon hats, canteens, spurs, cattle runs. Of all the frontier towns, Dodge City, Silver City, Tombstone, none conjures up the romance quite like ole Cheyenne. Of course, nowadays, Interstate 80 runs right through the south of town, and Interstate 25 up its western spine. There is Federal Express and Kinkos, faxes and computer repair shops, Midas Mufflers, HBO and malls, and the neighborhoods, architecturally undistinguished, could be the suburbs of Seattle or Minneapolis or Las Vegas. And though the slip of a downtown tries a little too hard for that Peckinpah feel, for that quaint western mystique, and though perhaps the same can be said for the rodeos and the much-advertised Cheyenne Frontier Days Festival™ (which I missed)—"A ten-day wingding of street dances, parades, carnival rides, top-name entertainers, free pancake breakfasts, cowboys, Indians, and horses . . ."—Cheyenne, Wyoming, cannot help but remain that definite middle place, far from the middle. Just like Atlanta for the South, Cheyenne for the West can no more erase or deny its history than it can succeed in making people like me not want to know the reality behind the romance.

When I arrived at the Byrd home, Senator Harriet Elizabeth Byrd was in the middle of completing a mailing of fliers for her reelection campaign. As we talked, she enlisted me to help stuff envelopes. She could have been one of the church ladies I grew up around—reserved, polite, stolidly taking up the place she occupied and more than a little bit more of the room. But there was something else about Senator Byrd, something like melancholy, something like weariness—perhaps she was just preoccupied with her coming election.

She was one of only three women state senators in Wyoming. Her brother, Robert Rhone, had been in the Colorado state legislature before his death.

"Now, S. W. Harding was a mulatto," she was saying about the first African American in the Wyoming legislature, "and his father had already given him freedom. So he was not considered a slave. And many people did not know Harding was black to begin with." A very good friend—the wealthiest black man in the territory, the "Black Baron," Barney Ford—suggested Harding run for the first legislature in the territory. "And he did. Now, Harding was educated, and a very good speaker, and this was pretty hard to find in this area because Cheyenne at one time was known as 'hell on wheels.' It was a place where people brought cattle down to the railhead. Mountain men came, so it was a rough city. To have a very polished speaker like Harding—they said he was quite a ladies' man—and he was flamboyant and educated, so he was elected, and he served. He served two terms. But he was really caught up with himself; he married several times, and that was where he ran into some trouble. He had married a slave girl back in either Missouri or Kansas, and she was looking for him, because he had fathered a child by her. I think she came here. And then he was married to a Caucasian lady. In the meantime, some were not sure whether he was black or white. And when they began to find out that he was black, he lost a little bit of his clout. He did not pass to run in the legislature. He just didn't tell them what he was; some knew that he was mulatto, and some did not. In the legislature, they were trying to pass women's rights. That's why Wyoming is called the 'Equality State.'

"This was back in the 1880s. Wyoming did pass equal rights for women to vote. And they did it in the first territorial legislature, when Harding was there. (Of course, that happened to be Democrats who did that.) First they didn't think the bill was going to pass. They thought it was a big joke. So then, some of the men tried to talk to their wives about, let's repeal this thing. And the wives got mad and they said, 'Oh, no. You're not going to do that to us.' There's a statue that stands out in front of the capitol right now. That's the lady really responsible for voting rights in the state of Wyoming. She went to the different parties, and she said she didn't care which party got the bill through. Just get it through. So she pitted both parties against each other, but anyway, they got it through. The Republicans said, 'Well, we'll leave it alone.' And the Democrat men, they decided they wanted to repeal it. Wyoming was not a state at that time. The Democrats felt that it had to be repealed so that we could get statehood. Wyoming had applied for statehood once, and they said, 'Well, you have women out there voting. You can't have that.' Governor Campbell, who was one of the territorial governors, he told them back in Washington, 'You don't take our women, then you don't take Wyoming.'

"And that's one of the reasons why Wyoming was one of the last states to come into the Union, because we always had women voting. But when they did get voting rights, they still didn't let Indians and blacks vote. We were no different than blacks in any other state. You see, we had to get emancipated again, to get full voting rights. Now, in some areas, they'll say, 'Yes, blacks could vote.' In some areas, they would say, 'No, blacks couldn't.' The way my grandfather said, 'If there were more than ten blacks, they probably wouldn't let them vote.' If there were one or two, it didn't make any difference. They treated the Indian people the same way. And then when Indians were put on reservations, they really lost their right to vote. So Indian people and black people were treated about the same in the territory. Whatever happened to Indians most likely happened to blacks, except blacks had an advantage. They could own land. But sometimes the land was taken away from them. It depended upon what kind of land.

"Well, they never had any blacks in the legislature after Harding left.

Wyoming became a state in 1890. So I'm the first and only black legislator that has been elected to the Wyoming state legislature since 1890. And that's one of the reasons why I think Brian Lanker put me in the book *I Dream a World.* You see, he couldn't figure out, Well, if they didn't have any, how did I get there? There are a lot of extenuating circumstances about why and how I got in there. One thing was that my dad was born in Laramie in 1903. And he was the first black child born in Laramie, Wyoming. Now my great-grandmother came from Martinique. She was a gift to her master, who brought her over. And he fathered two children by her, who were my grandfather and his brother. They bought her from her master, more or less, and brought her here from Washington D.C. They brought my great-grandmother and her two sons with them here, to what they called an Indian outpost, which was between Laramie and Cheyenne. Then he had to go to the Philippines. The family did. But my grandmother could not take her two sons, so she left them here, with a man named Bonner, and they finished growing up here.

"Now, my grandfather was a young boy when Wyoming became a state in 1890. See, they came here before 1890. And his brother never did like the cold weather or the wind, and he always said when he got older, he was going to leave. And he did. His name was Will. And my grandfather's name was Charles. Now they're all buried over in Laramie in a little family cemetery. And my grandmother's buried over there and my dad. And my dad's brother. This cemetery is on the west side of the University of Wyoming campus, in the city cemetery there. So you can look at the dates and see how long we've all been here. My dad was the first generation born there. Then, of course, we were born in Wyoming. My brother Bob, and my brother Tommy, and me. (Dolores happened to be born in Texas.) That's the fourth generation. Then we had all of our children here. Which was the fifth generation and we have grandchildren."

Six generations in Wyoming was indeed rare—in fact, in most western states, among black or white. Senator Byrd was proud of her family history, but perhaps even more so of her own accomplishments. She had taught in the public schools for twenty-seven years, and had won awards and honors both statewide and national.

"I'm proud of my background in the public schools. The other thing is that I was the first black certified teacher to have ever taught in the state of Wyoming. And that's another long story, because, see, Wyoming being the Equality State and everything, when I graduated from college and came back here, I couldn't get a job.

"My whole family was very disappointed about that too. The state superintendent was the one who said that they didn't hire minorities. I had never really looked around to see whether they hired in the schools. I thought they did, and everybody else did too. This was in '49. Black people really didn't push too hard. We hadn't gone through the sixties, and we were just a step above where we had been, and we did what we were told. So my dad said to me, he said, 'Well, the government hires. Why don't you take a battery of civil service examinations?' And I did."

She wound up in the civilian personnel at Warren Air Force Base. She worked in the service dock, and base supply, accounting. Eventually, she was sent to train civilians, where she would be an instructor for ten years. When the base's mission was changed, the schools were phased out. In order to continue teaching, she would have to move to Amarillo, Texas, or go back to the warehouses—both of which were out of the question.

"So I go up to the Board of Education, ten years later, and the same old superintendent's still there, and she said, 'No.' But this time, I was a little smarter, and a little wiser, and didn't accept 'No.' So I walked from her office, down to the governor's office, and I asked the governor's secretary was he in? And she said, 'Yes.' And I didn't ask for an appointment. I walked right on back to his office. This is 1959. And the governor, Governor Hickey, went to our church. I'm Catholic and he was too. I told him I had sent letters to some other schools, and they said they needed teachers, but they did not know I was black. And I said, 'You know, Governor, you've known our family all of these years, and you knew my grandfather.' I said, 'Do you think I'm a really bad person?' And he said, 'No.' I said, 'Did you know that I cannot get a job teaching school here?' He said to me, 'Well, I've read about some of the things that you did at the base. Why can't you get a job teaching school here?' I said, 'Because your superintendent says I can't because I'm a minority.'

"Well, it just goes to show you that governors don't know everything. He said, 'I did not know this.' He said, 'There's no law. I didn't know that there was a policy that existed like that.' And he said, 'Come to think of it, I can't think of any minority teachers.' So he called the superintendent in. 'Oh,' she said, 'we've always had this policy, Governor.' He said, 'But I think that we ought to change it, don't you?' And she said, 'But Governor.' He said, 'But nothing.' He said, 'I'll take care of this.' So he called the principal of the school and said, 'I want this young lady to have a job in September.' The superintendent's jumping up and down in the office. 'But Governor,' she said, 'that's public school.' She said, 'Since the both of you are Catholics, why don't you have her teach over in St. Mary's?' Which was a private school. So he looked at me. He said, 'Do you want to teach at St. Mary's?' And I said, 'No, Governor. No offense, but I want to be a public school teacher like everybody else.' And he said to her, 'She wants to be a public school teacher like everybody else.'

"And I can guarantee you that I had a job when school started. From that day and for twenty-seven years, I really felt that I owed the governor one, and I worked really hard. And that first year was really tough. A sixth-grade teacher, he did some of everything to make me leave. But the principal himself, he was the greatest person on earth."

In 1963, she was awarded Teacher of the Year for the state of Wyoming. "It opened many doors." After that, the secretary of state appointed her to serve on the Marshall Scholarship Commission to select a scholar to study in England.

In retrospect, the senator felt that all these things helped her get elected. Not the least of which was the contact with the children and their parents. It would be safe to say she had one of the highest profiles of any teacher in the state. "The other thing was that my husband was working for the police department. He worked his way up through the ranks and became chief of police here—the only black chief of police they ever had. They really liked Jim down there." When he retired, he was appointed director of highway safety. During the Carter administration, he was appointed United States Marshal for Wyoming. (Because of its relatively small size, Wyoming has only one marshal.)

The fact that the Byrds were Catholics also helped her win elections, and that her husband served as district deputy for the Knights of Columbus. He also served on their national board. "So Catholics out in the West knew us real well. Holding public offices like that, we were always in the public eye, and we also traveled the state. You see, this will explain how it was easier for me to get elected. It is one of the reasons why I feel that we've never had another black legislator. Everything sort of fell in line for me. You know, just circumstance."

Senator Elizabeth Harriet Byrd was not particularly sanguine about her chances in the upcoming election. Her opponent was a Republican, and Wyoming was at that time largely Republican, though clearly, Republicans had voted for her in the past. Also the districts had been shifted, and she felt her new constituency might not know her as well as the people who had kept her in office for twelve years. "I don't have too many of my students living there. The people who live out in this new area, they have come from Florida and other states. It's going to be interesting.

"If I lose, I'll lose proudly. Say I did my very best."

How and why did Elizabeth Harriet Byrd decide to run for public office in the first place?

"Well, let me tell you—after I got into the school system and things started going better, and after I got the Teacher of the Year award, and had a chance to work on the Marshall scholarship, I became very active in the National Education Association and the Wyoming Education Association. I found out that those organizations really had clout in the state, when it came down to jobs and communities. I often wondered why black people never belonged. And to this day, they still aren't very active in it. It's a mistake. So I ran for building representative from my school. This is how I found out how the system really works."

She realized that advancement came only with knowing the system. She became determined to learn it. "I found out there was a lot more to it than just the Cheyenne Classroom Teachers Association." She got on one of the committees of the Wyoming Education Association, and then the National Education Association. "I ran as a delegate to the national council of the NEA. I was already sitting on the textbook committee. When I went to one of their legislative meetings, and saw the operation that they had at the national level with 10,000 teachers, I was amazed, you know, being from Wyoming, to see something like that. 'Whoo,' I said, 'these people are wonderful.' And I said, 'I shall always belong.' So I took out a life membership."

She got to see, firsthand, how education bills were passed, how lobbying worked. "I said, 'You know what? Those guys over there in that state legislature, they're ripping the teachers off.' I couldn't figure out why teachers couldn't get higher salaries, and all of these other things, you know. I came home and I told my dad about this. I say, 'Dad, you don't know what they're doing to these teachers. They're just treating teachers terrible. We're overworked and underpaid.' My dad said—my dad was a marvelous man. He was the most patient individual and he always had plenty of time for me—he said, 'You know, Liz, I believe you're right.' I'd been telling him about all of these things for a couple years, and he would encourage me to go on."

She took these issues to the legislature—literally. "That was the first demonstration teachers ever had. We went down from the junior high school and marched on the capitol. We all went up in the gallery, and they were watching us. The teachers all came out. I thought that was tremendous. That's the only way people can get anything, and I really became interested in how laws were made. And I said, 'No wonder they make such terrible laws. People let them.' And they never complain until the law is made.

"So when I came back, I was telling my dad. My dad said to me, 'Well,' he said, 'did you know that Governor Herster is going to tax coal, oil and gas, to put more money from severance tax in the state of Wyoming? Why don't you go up there and help the Governor?' I said, 'How can I do that?' He said, 'You run for the legislature.' I said, 'Dad, who in the world would vote for me?' He said, 'Oh, there would be a lot of people.' He said, 'I tell you what. You just get out and tell them everything you've been telling me.' So he reached down into his pocket (our filing fee to this very day is still only ten dollars, and you don't have to get into petitions or anything. You just file and run.), he reached down in his pocket and gave me ten dollars, and he said, 'Now there's your filing fee. You go up there and file.' He said, 'I want you to run.'

"I said, 'Well, I won't win.' He said, 'Don't say that. You've got five votes right here at this house. At least you won't have a big zero.' My dad had like a sixth sense. He could tell whenever something good was going to happen. And so I went up and I filed, and I came back afterward and I said, 'Dad, what in the world am I going to do?' He said, 'Well, just get you some material and go door to door and tell everybody what you've been telling me. They'll vote for you.'"

Just as with teaching, Elizabeth Harriet Byrd educated herself about politics; she joined the Democratic Women's Club. She knocked on doors. ("You know, it gets cold in November. I said, 'If I happen to get over to November, I'll give everybody snow scrapers.' And no one had ever used a snow scraper before.")

Being a native of Wyoming, she understood the importance of beneficial water use, so she added that to her platform, and other issues involving the environment, and, of course, education. She also made an issue of farms going into bankruptcy—farms that had been homesteaded. "My grandmother had homesteaded land, and we knew what it was to have to pay taxes, and how they almost lost their land. That was easy for me to talk about.

"I made that one of my issues, that we would save small farms and businesses. We don't have a lot of black ranches, but many of the white people were concerned. So when I was looking to help them with their lives, they thought, 'Well, gee, she's not just for black issues or for separating herself from us. She really is interested in schools and farms and ranches and saving water.' I went to senior citizens and of course my dad, he sat in on the first Senior Citizen Advisory Board appointed by the governor.

"See, that was another extenuating circumstance. Buck Rhone. Everybody knew my dad. They called him Buck, from the University of Wyoming, where he was a football player. He was on practically every committee you could think of down at the local level. He was president of the Quarterback Club for the University of Wyoming. He was very active with the Kiwanis. He worked with Model Cities. He got a couple of parks going here, and a lot of things. He helped in the community. See, that was another advantage I had, because they all knew my dad. They said, 'Well, that's Buck's daughter.'"

During the primary, it was discovered that her father had cancer. "My dad only stayed in the hospital for about a week, and he died. But let me tell you, I won the primary and my dad was still living. He was so happy for me, and he said, 'You will win the general election.'

"I came in first in that general election. You see. And ever since then, I've always been the top vote-getter in the county."

Senator Byrd's mother was still living, at eighty-nine, in Cheyenne. "She's in her own house, and she doesn't want to live with anybody else. She does fine. I hope I do that well if I live to be ninety.

"I'm at a point now. I'm retired from the school, and I have my grandkids. Jim has retired and we enjoy life. I figure after twelve years, maybe it's all right that I'm not in the legislature. But I feel sad that we have no black people that have tried. We've had a couple run, throughout the state, but they've never been able to get elected. I'm surprised. The few other minorities didn't run either. I don't know why. We have many intelligent black people in our city. We have seven-tenths of 1 percent blacks in the state of Wyoming. We don't even have 1 percent—out of 450,000. Most of them are here in Cheyenne and in Casper. Laramie has a good stockpile of intelligent black people. We have some blacks teaching out at the University of Wyoming. Most all black people that live in Laramie, they're highly skilled.

"Here in Cheyenne it's hard to find a poverty area. Blacks don't have a section of town. They live all over town. Blacks go where they want in Cheyenne.

"It's not always been that way. See, we went through different stages. When my grandfather was a young man, blacks lived almost anywhere. And that's one thing about the territory my grandfather liked. Runaway slaves, a lot of them came here. Some were outlaws with the Hole in the Wall Gang. We had a couple that even ranched and homesteaded land. One of the largest ranches in the state was owned by a black. When he died, he didn't have any kids or anything, and it reverted back to the state. They called him 'Nigger Jim.' His ranch was in two counties. It overlapped two county lines. He homesteaded it. There's a lot of black history in this state. And a lot of them intermarried with Indian people as well as Caucasians who lived here.

"Now usually, the white people accept you on your skill and your merit. But when they talk about black people as a group, they don't know whether they want to accept you or not. They don't want groups of black people. They'll take you on an individual basis, and they judge you by your character. But when you start grouping together . . . I really noticed this when I carried the Martin Luther King bill. It took me—well, I started out with a House joint resolution getting it as a national holiday. Then in '83, when we wanted to get it as a state holiday—whoo, I really had a terrible time.

"You ask most white people—they haven't been around black people, a lot of them—they don't know why they don't like blacks. They just know that most Americans don't like blacks. They're not supposed to. You ask some of the kids. Like I went to Newcastle, which hardly has any black people. I was on an educational program to evaluate the schools for a federal program. The kids just looked at me like I was out of Mars, you know. And they said, 'You look like somebody we've seen on TV.' I said to the principal, 'I'll read them a story.' I was down in the primary grades. While I sat there, they ran their hands over my arms and looked at their hands. The principal says, 'Is there any way that you would come up here and teach a year?' She said, 'The children are so excited about you being here. We'd just like to have a black teacher come.' But you can't get black teachers to go. We've had a few, but they said they just couldn't handle the wilderness. But the children wanted to see black people, and they wanted to go maybe to a black church and hear some gospel music sometime. That's what we don't have. We have black churches here in Cheyenne and Casper, but when you live in places like Smoot, you'll never hear gospel there, and you'll never have any soul food either."

In elementary school, Harriet Rhone and her brother had been sent to separate schools. "We played so much at school, my mother decided that we should go to different schools." They were both the only blacks in their respective schools. "It didn't bother us, because we had always been in a situation like that. It didn't bother my dad because he was the first black child born in Wyoming, and all his playmates were Caucasians—except for his sister.

"When we got into high school it was really different. Because that's when they get boyfriends and girlfriends, and there was one black boy in our school, and all the rest of the people that went to school were my cousins. Poor Sylvester. He just couldn't take us all out. Then there was one girl that came up there named Cortez. It just got so that you didn't want to go to the mixers or anything because they acted sort of indifferent. So that's why I went to West Virginia State College. It was a black school. I never knew how really locked up I was until I went to Charleston, West Virginia. And I tell you, when I went down there and I saw all those black kids, I thought I was in second heaven. I thought, Gee. It was just so different. I just felt free. I said, I can join any sorority. I can do all these things that I want to and belong to any clubs that I want to. They didn't really encourage me in high school to belong to anything, and there were some organizations that we just couldn't belong to. So I tried to join everything down there. I was so happy that I got to go, and I cried when I graduated. That really was sad. To know that I would have to come back to a community that didn't have very many black people. There's just something about being black that you enjoy being around your own."

In fact, she and her best friend, Dorothy, had reckoned they would teach overseas for a spell. Perhaps then move to New Jersey. Then she met Jim Byrd. He was an air force man and he was stationed, of all places, at Warren Air Force Base. Then he got a job on the police force. Things were too good to leave. When I spoke with the senator, the couple had recently celebrated their forty-fifth wedding anniversary.

"Junior high and high school were really my pretty good years, I guess. That's why I have such a close feeling for young people in junior high and high school because I remember what I went through. Mine was really a race factor of trying to always be adjusted. My first experience was when I was in sixth grade, or fifth grade. I wanted to belong to the Girl Scouts. I will never forget that mother saying, 'We can't take you, because of the color of your skin. You're not white.' And the Campfire Girls were the same. You know, I have always been very reluctant to support the Scouts because that was my first experience of segregation. I remembered in the sixth grade class, I just hated those Brownies. Simply because they wouldn't take me in, and having that kind of feeling, I've known how children feel when they don't like school. Or they don't like situations. Peer pressure. You can either make a kid or break a kid, in those grade levels. This is why I think we have so many teenage gangs and drive-by shootings in Los Angeles. These people are bitter, and we've made them that way. Society's made them that way. It's more than just being poor. It's a hurt inside that they can't get over. I still have inside of me a kind of hurt with segregation. I don't know whether all black people have that. I feel that black people who grew up in a black community are more stable than a black person who grew up in a white community like I did. They had something to rely upon. They had their churches to go to. The Catholic church is a white church. But I said to myself, 'Oh, it really is not.' But you know, I go to it, and there's white people all around me. I would not change my religion. But I didn't have any stability really in my growing up years, other than my family. And I was very lucky that I had a very close-knit family. But outside of the family, I really didn't have much going for me.

"I found out that black people had a society within the society, like in the South. Where we didn't have that in the West. I don't know how we survived, because we were all just hanging out there somehow or another. But we did. I've often wondered how many other black people grew up like I did, and do they feel the same? Well, I have a different kind of happiness. And I have a different kind of sorrow. I think I have more pity than sorrow, you know, about the people in the United States of America. I pity the people. I've always thought that they should never have treated black people that way. We built the country just like they did. I don't know why, but I'm like the kids in Los Angeles. I always felt they owe us something. We did more than our share.

"And maybe that's why I'm belligerent, in a way, and feel that more should be done. Maybe that's why in the legislature I've been able to survive, because when I go up there, I say it's my law too. They owe us this. I really feel that way. And I don't know whether other black people feel that way, but I always have. I had a lot of good things going for me, but I was sort of shortchanged too.

"Now my friend Ruby, who was Japanese, I guess Ruby and I were more alike than any of my friends. I never grew up with the experience of having what you'd call a real bosom buddy that was black. I could confide in Ruby, because she was like I was. She was happy but not happy. She was sad but not always sad. And when the war came, the government took everything that they had and put her family up here in Wyoming in a concentration camp. I can remember them. She was standing there with all her personal belongings in a suitcase. They just came and took their home. They said, 'You're not Americans anymore.' She wrote me a couple of times, and when she came back, she told me she was so bitter. It took years and years for her family to reclaim their property. She no longer lives in this country. She lives in Japan. She said she would never come back. Some of her family came back to reclaim the property—but she never came back.

"Now, that really never happened to black people. There were two things that didn't happen to black people: They didn't put us on a reservation, like the Indian people. And they didn't take our property away from us, like they did in World War II with the Japanese. I guess those were the moments that I really dislike the most. From that, I began to pity the people in the United States. I said, 'They speak with a forked tongue.' They don't really mean what they say. Being a teenager like that, I began to have less trust in what we had."

The Senator told me that her travels in India also affected the way she thought about her own country. Seeing Indian poverty, the homelessness, the illness, the faulty justice system, did not give her a false sense of American security and American superiority. Rather, she thought, "I better hurry back and try to make America a little bit better." In her opinion, the plight of the Native Americans was perhaps even more heartbreaking than that of African Americans. "Indian children have never been motivated, just like black children have never been motivated. They have never told their children, 'Yes, you can.' Because they felt they have never had the opportunity."

"What needs to be done? Very simple. It's so simple. And people will never recognize it. You see, if you bring a life into the world, you have to nurture that life and culture that life, to mold it into something that's good. But if you don't, it's not going to always turn out the way that you think it's going to. People have not been willing to give that much of themselves. If people have someone who cares, and someone they love, they're not going to abuse anybody. That's the only way to get through race relations. If everybody cares about each other, we won't have to worry about whether you're black or you're green or you're yellow. If they would respect one another, we could all get along. But we have a taking society. That's where I feel sorry again. We have to learn to give a little bit. Everybody has to give a little and share.

"They talk about health care. A lot of the health care is mental. I really feel if they go back in the schools, as well as in the family, in the homes, if they would really take care of these little children, they wouldn't have as many health problems. I'd like to see every school have a breakfast program, because we have so many hungry children that come to school. You can't teach hungry children. They're thinking about food. They're not thinking about three times five.

"I think that we can correct society. I really do."

"The Black Baron." Barney Ford. Senator Byrd was the first person I remember actually speaking of Barney Ford.

Mrs. Byrd was working on a children's book for the fourth and fifth grades, about Barney Ford. Like Mary Ellen Pleasant in California, Barney Ford captured my imagination. A figure I had never heard of, yet whose amazing story led me to wonder, Why? Every black child—indeed, every child—should know the story of Barney Ford.

"Barney Ford is such a wonderful character," the senator said. "Down in the Colorado capitol, in Denver, above the speaker's chair in the house of representatives, they have a stained glass window of Barney Ford. Very few people, black people, know anything about that. I thought he would be such a wonderful model for black children. Because I think that they need a model. He helped with the Underground Railroad in Chicago. And then he came out here to mine silver and gold. That's where he got his fortune. They're still looking for a lot of the silver and gold. They said he hid it all over Colorado and Wyoming, southern Wyoming.

"What happened was that he married a girl while he was in Chicago. Julia. And they had some children, but his son just dropped dead down here in Colorado Springs. I guess he had a heart attack or something. And then he had a daughter who was in the San Francisco earthquake and fire. And his other daughter, she married, but never had any children. So when he died, he had no heirs. He died in 1926, I think it was. He's buried in Colorado. And that man did some of everything. He was in politics. And he was the kind of guy that there was no limit when it came to money. He had the finest hotel in Cheyenne, called the InterOcean Hotel. They still talk about that hotel. And he built one in Denver. He also built the Ford Theatre and had a barbershop. It burned, this hotel. A place called the Eagle, which was next door, it caught on fire and then burned down the whole block, see. They did rebuild it, and a man named Chase, he tried to run it, but he could never run it like Barney Ford. So finally, they tore it down, and now the Hines Building stands there. They thought he had a lot of maps in his safe—but he didn't. His children said that he probably did have a lot of silver and gold, but they never knew where he really put it all. Some of it he put it in banks, and some of it he didn't. He built a beautiful home in Breckenridge, and now they've made that a historical site."

Barney Ford: the Stuff of Legends.

He had been an escaped slave. A conductor on the Underground Railroad. A hotel worker in Nicaragua. A barber.

In 1860, he and five other men struck it rich on a claim that Ford had purchased under the name of a white lawyer. When the word got out that the black men had found gold, the lawyer claimed the land was his; the men fled; no gold had ever been found. Until only a few decades ago, the site had been known as "Nigger Hill"—in 1964 it was officially named Barney Ford Hill.

Along with his friend, the gnomish Henry O. Wagoner (in a photograph of the man, his hair and long beard are snow-white, his thick glasses almost the size of his eyes), whom he met in his first days in Chicago, Ford established hotels and saloons in Denver and Cheyenne. After a time, back in Chicago, disheartened by the racist Colorado constitution, Ford was convinced by Wagoner to come back and fight. With support in the newly Republican congress, blacks in Colorado gained the right to vote. Ford helped establish an adult education center for black folks, and was the first black man to serve on a grand jury.

Wagoner became deputy sheriff of Arapaho County, Colorado.

As I made the drive down I-25 to Denver, I was strangely elated—and, to be sure, a little puzzled. But only a little. The puzzlement came from wondering why I had never known of Barney Ford. The fact is, if I had been a more diligent student of African American history, I would have stumbled across him. (In truth, I had read about him, but what I had read, for some reason, at the time, didn't stick or make a strong impression upon me.) Yet the fact remained that, throughout school and my twenty-nine years, lesser figures had been paraded before me with mind-numbing constancy. Was there something in Barney Ford's biography—perhaps in Barney Ford himself—that made burying him a bit more than advantageous?

Hence my elation: As I learned more and more, I was stumbling upon more and more of these extraordinary people (who also happened to be black): Montana's Stagecoach Mary, California's Biddy Mason, Henry Adams of Kansas, Robert Smalls of South Carolina, Edwin P. McCabe in

Oklahoma, and so many, many more. Moreover, I could see an interesting pattern emerging. So many of these now little-discussed people came of age during and directly after slavery. I don't mean to imply that along with Jim Crow black folk stopped doing great things, but it is one thing to be the scion of a great Atlanta family, and educated at the finest universities before standing before the people; and entirely another to free yourself, build a great fortune with your own two hands, and fight for rights barely imaginable. Surely, Martin Luther King, Jr., knew he was standing on the shoulders of giants.

Why was I elated?

We talk so much today about role models. The black women and black men of the nineteenth century had absolutely none: they were making it up as they went along. They knew that their destiny rested in their own hands and in their hands alone. What, I thought, might we accomplish if we took that same attitude? These men and women were, indeed, pioneers. What if we began to think of ourselves more and more as pioneers?

Nineteen

# DESTINY MADE MANIFEST

*Denver, Colorado*

They say, they reached the West through Denver,
a city much dirtier than I remembered.

—John A. Williams, *This Is My Country Too*

The Hue-Man Experience Bookstore is situated in two townhouses, on Park Avenue, in a working-class neighborhood, just beyond downtown. Odd, for a bookstore that specializes in African American books to be found in Denver; even odder that it has the reputation of being the best black bookstore in the country. That reputation is due to its indefatigable owner and operator, Clara Villarosa.

She was born in Chicago, and trained to be a psychiatric therapist. But doing therapy full-time was not enough of a challenge for her. She went on to train and supervise other therapists, and became more and more involved with administrative hospital work. She came to Denver in 1968 as the chief psychiatric social worker in the behavioral sciences department of the Children's Hospital. By the early seventies, she was running the entire department, and down the line she would be running fifteen of the hospital's departments.

"I stayed there, but I knew I couldn't go any further. Number one, I didn't want to take a hospital, and no one would give it to me anyway, with my credentials and my color. So now what am I going to do with the rest of my life? I decided to resign the position and went back to school." She began a doctoral program in social work and law. Just before beginning her dissertation, she ran out of money, and decided to take a temporary position and save. That temporary position became permanent, and before long, she was managing the human resources department for the United Bank of Denver. "At the time, it was the largest bank of the twenty-six affiliates. When I left Children's Hospital, in the back of my mind, I thought I wanted to own my own business. I didn't know what kind of business, but I wanted to start a business."

She had set up a consulting firm while she had been in school, but "I didn't know anything about it. I was a psychotherapist. It didn't work." This time, she decided to prepare better, and came up with a plan: a bookstore. "It was going to have a concrete product. I loved books. I knew about that product. Also I wanted a specialty bookstore. The largest independent bookstore in the country is located here in Denver, The Tattered Cover." She did her research. She crunched numbers on the demographics and the locations, the titles, the ins and outs of the bookstore business. When, in 1984, she experienced the proverbial glass ceiling, she used her years of management savvy to negotiate a sweet severance deal with the bank. ("I said, 'I'm not going to resign. You have to fire me.' There was one catch: All my performance appraisals were excellent. I had a good case. And they knew it. They weren't stupid. I wasn't either.")

Enter The Hue-Man Experience Bookstore. But a black bookstore? In Denver, Colorado? "The one thing that I learned is this is the hardest place to put an African American bookstore. Denver."

Clara Villarosa laughed. She is not a large woman, as her history suggests she might be, but she is formidable. The most prepossessing part of her—after her silver Afro, and bright, earthy, multicolored, multitextured African garb—are her eyes: large, luminous, intense, wise, cutting. And her laugh is raucous and like a crocodile's smile; you are not always certain if she is laughing with you or at you.

"Denver is not a town with culturally connected people. These are not your original migrants. They generally have been in other cities, and then have moved here. Some of them—not many—have been in the South. And they come here for a better quality of life, for jobs. I'm from Chicago. My parents were part of the great migration north. Very culturally connected, because two things happened: One, you band together because you're in a new place; two, you're in a very oppressive environment. Denver is not racially oppressive. It's a very comfortable environment. There are not too many of you, so they accept you. Denver's a place where they've had open public housing for years. You can move into any area. So they were moving into integrated areas before this was fashionable, or permitted. Therefore, people are spread out. Once they started to move, there wasn't that resistance to the moving. Then it's a pretty place. It affords you things you wouldn't get if you lived in Chicago. We have our ghettos, so to speak, but ghettos are houses here. With little lawns. And Five Points, which is considered the place where a large concentration of African Americans are, is not that bad. And besides, if you sneeze, you miss it.

"The people here came west to make their way, and they tend to be a bit more open. They're not as racist. Now it doesn't mean that racism isn't alive and well. But the form it takes makes it much easier to adjust to the environment, plus it makes it much easier to deny your own culture. That's what happened to us. Once we became integrated, we lost our culture. This city or state, represents that. So I have to come up with all kinds of creative ideas in order to penetrate the market."

Clara Villarosa paid a lot of attention to market data. She knew that her customers would be largely women, largely upscale. Highly educated. "So a perfect city. Yes. No. Not culturally connected. I'm not selling Courvoisier. I'm not selling cars, houses, furniture or clothes. Which these people value. I'm selling a cultural connection."

At the same time, she knew that she was a prime example of who she was marketing to. Eventually some people began to come to the store, and she discovered that word of mouth was a huge asset. "These people go to church. They're family oriented. At some point I said, 'All right, how do I penetrate that market? What do I do? What is it that they value?' I can't sell what they value, but what I *can* do is create a situation where it's prestigious to be associated with this bookstore. I go into a media blitz. I said, 'I want my name on everything.'" She got involved in community events and causes. National boards, associations, magazines. She became involved with the American Booksellers Association, and then became a member of the board. "If it's a black issue, they'd say, 'Call Clara Villarosa in Denver, Colorado.' I was just in the *New York Times,* the Washington *Post,* the Chicago *Tribune.*" First she created, and then she labored to get the word out, that this was the "best bookstore, the largest African American bookstore, in the country. Somebody said, 'Is it true?' And I said, 'I don't know, but tell me I'm lying.' My daughter was at a party and someone said, 'Girl, I just got back from Denver, and I went to this fabulous bookstore.' She called me at midnight and said, 'Guess what, Mom: It's working.'

"I have to make it so it's fashionable to be culturally connected.

"I wear African clothes all the time. All of that is part of the marketing strategy. When you see me, you associate me with the bookstore. And say, 'Girl, I got to get over there and get some books.' When you see me, you will recognize me. You don't forget me. We identify with people. It's hard to separate *Ebony* and John H. Johnson. That becomes important. The bottom line. It sells books. And it works."

Her sense of cultural connection did not exist only when she was among black folks, Clara Villarosa said. Even when she worked at the bank, she insisted on attending all the corporate events—not simply the ones involving African Americans. "They clearly understand that I'm Afrocentric. That I'm African American. My interests are there, my dress is there, and they admire it. They compliment me on my clothes. How I express and talk about my interests. They understand that.

"Sometimes buppies, when they go—particularly when they go into white associations or corporations—they may feel that being black is not acceptable, where it is. But if you don't feel that sense of comfort with that, then you won't get the respect. It's almost as if, since I know who you are, and you're proud of who you are, then I feel that's good. But when you're acting like you don't want to be proud of it . . .

"If they're not comfortable doing it, they're not comfortable with me doing it. Or they will say, 'All right for you to do it, but I can't do that.' And I say, it has to be with who you feel you are, and where you feel your commitment. It's pretty simplistic. That has to be reinforced in this society. It just doesn't happen naturally. Before integration, you were much more connected to your family. You were connected to the experience, because you were all together; it was constantly being reinforced. Even if nobody said anything. Then there was a lot of conversation about what goes on outside. What white folks do, and such and such. All of that was very insular. Once it becomes integrated, you stop that. You stop talking about it. You stop referencing it. And you become involved in an integrated situation, where people begin to say, 'I don't see your color.' I tell them they're blind. I say, 'Of course, you see my color.' 'No, I don't see color.' I said, 'Honey, yes, you do.' Don't tell me that. Now I will tell you what is correct. If they say, 'Of course, I see your color, but it does not matter to me. It doesn't make a difference to me.' But don't tell me you don't see my color, because then I say, 'Hmmm. I didn't know. Where's your blind man's stick? With the little red tip on it.'"

Clara Villarosa told me that, having been brought up in an all-black Chicago neighborhood, she was extra vigilant with regard to what her children were exposed to while growing up. She made certain that they were around black people as often as she could afford. "You see young urban African Americans who have not grown up around black people, and they freak when they see large numbers of us. They grab their purse, just like white people do. My children grew up around them, so that was good for them. But if all you saw was an integrated or all-white school, and people treated you reasonably well, you won't know what racism is."

As a result, some black folk don't know racism when they see it. Back when she was in human resources, she said, it was not uncommon for a black employee to come to her complaining of difficulties with certain managers. "And I said, 'Hmm. Racism.' They said, 'No, no, no. You don't understand. It has nothing to do with race.' Okay. Going to take them a little longer. Wait till he starts to beat up on them. Hmm. And they said, 'Well, you're paranoid, Clara.' And I said, 'Yes, I am. I sure am. Because they are out to get me. And don't ever believe that they're not.'

"Understand it. Understand it. That's fine. I understand it. I can still work with you. We can work together. We can cooperate. But I do understand who you are. And I don't forget that. I don't know when you're going to say 'Nigger' to me. I have no idea. But when you do, I'll know. Took you a little bit longer than the rest of them. But I don't ever delude myself into thinking that it can't happen. Of course, it can happen. Little black boy who ran into the house, he's been reared in a military family, all-white. He came home and said, 'Guess what, Mama. A nigger's at our school.' He did not know that's what he was. And the other kids said, that's what he was, this new kid. His mother said, 'Ohhh.' Ooooh. Then they realized what had happened. But it is hard to teach racism in an all-white environment. Because a lot of it you feel. I know what it looks like, though I may not be able to describe it. We see them come to the bookstore, and they really don't know. It's very tentative. One girl said, 'God, I never saw so much black stuff.' Living in an all-white suburb, it's true."

Listening to Clara Villarosa, seeing what she had accomplished, falling under her spell, so to speak, I was taken back over the course of my travels—Dora Grain, Dorothy Williams, Nellie Stone Johnson, Mahalah Ashley Dickerson, Dona Irvin—to how many powerful, courageous black women I had encountered. Not to say that I had not met black men of nigh-heroic proportions—Art Anderson, Major William Lee, James Washington, Jr. came quickly to mind—but black women seemed to outnumber them. I asked Clara about this perception.

"And I'm one of them," she said. "I know."

"Am I wrong even to say that? Am I playing into a trap?"

"Yeah, you are playing into a trap. That's true. People don't want to talk about it. I've often tried to think about why it's so. I want to take it back in many ways to slavery, because we come from a matriarchal society. Period. Africa. To start with. But then, what happened when we came here, it was an egalitarian working methodology for us. They didn't discriminate. They put women in the fields. We had to work alongside of men. And then the woman could be powerful. The woman was in control. Because men were separated from families, men were particularly vulnerable. Women were trying to protect the men. If a man naturally was assertive and aggressive, which is what men are, what would happen to that man? And the whole race would die out. So it was, in many ways, very protective to hold men back and to keep them down in terms of their own natural inclination.

"Plus white men were more brutal with black men, for a variety of reasons. That penis scared them shitless. And the assumption that it's bigger. 'It's bigger and it's better.' Because of the nature of the work and what was expected of them, and who they brought over. They were strong and they were bucks, but that's what they wanted, because they had to work. But it was extremely scary, because white men are perceived as being soft. They're aggressive and they're very controlling, but here you have blackness, which makes you look even more powerful. I mean, you can be little and black and still be seen as menacing.

"The color does so much to people. It makes you bigger, not necessarily better in their minds, but bigger, certainly bigger.

"So the women were working alongside of men. They could manipulate and get things done. They got into the house, and they had exposure. Women could read. They could move a lot more freely. Then, once they were free, black men moved up during Reconstruction.

"But then society became very oppressive again. It's symbolic. Wouldn't hire men to work. But women could work. Could work in the house. They moved off the plantation, but they were still on a plantation. Women got closer to the culture, and the society makes it a lot easier for black women to accomplish things. When I was at the bank, I could get a woman up the corporate ladder quicker than I could a man. I knew exactly what it was all about. It was much more difficult for a man. And it still is, because they're an endangered species. They're extremely vulnerable. If you really want to kill a group of people, you take away their breeders. Who's using the coke? Penetrate the market with drugs. You treat them a certain way, they're going to behave violently. Then you can throw their ass in prison. So there are all kinds of ways in which there's a repression or suppression of black men. And also black women, because it's a single-family household. They raise the men. They raise the girls, and they love the sons. They teach those girls to be strong. 'Hmm. Honey, you know you can't depend on no man, honey. Better take care of yourself. Better get yourself an education.' I saw it in my family. My mother spoiled my brother. But they made me strong. 'You got to take care of yourself.' But they didn't know that's what the message was. And I can function a lot better than my brother. He's a CPA, but I still function better than he does.

"Women got off the plantation sooner. Clara wants to own the plantation. This is the house niggers and field niggers. Oh no, no, no, no. Clara's going to own the plantation.

"So one of the things that happens, of course, is that you see this disparity. And then, over the years, generations, you see it continue. The women's movement came, then you had the Civil Rights movement. So these black women, Maya Angelou, Toni Morrison, Alice Walker, Terri McMillan—all of them, ride on that wave. All of a sudden, you didn't hear nothing about black male writers. There's a large number of black male writers, but there's no population for them. That's a cultural variable. Black men just don't read fiction. They don't read for entertainment. There's no Stephen King out there for them, writing in a style that's going to appeal to males. The closest one was Charles Johnson. *Middle Passage.* It was history. These men are reading this ancient African history. They're not interested in our history in this country. That's their way of empowering themselves. I think they are already empowered, but they haven't functioned as such, in a long time. When you compare the kind of work black men had with what white men had—it was so disparaging.

"But empowerment isn't lost. If you understand what it is, then you can begin to look at ways to work with it. I don't think anybody understands that. When you know you can do something about it.

"I like to think that I do understand. So my commitment really early on was to work with a large number of black men."

Though Denver is very far from being the cow town of a once-upon-a-time Sergio Leone fantasy, the humdrum reality was much grittier, grimier, homelier and more pedestrian than I had imagined. And though it is now a place of high finance, high commerce, with fancy suburbs and skyscrapers, high-tech industry, world-class universities, there is about Denver something dusty, something agricultural and plains-like clinging to its high-rises and its malls. It's not so much the ten-gallon Stetsons and the pickup trucks you see at the 7-Elevens and the Wells Fargo ATM—for you are indeed on the high plains, the foothills of the Rockies—but perhaps what I sensed is the blend of that very past with its outsized dreams of Manifest Destiny mingled with a new rugged and demanding yuppiism and the postindustrialization of the future. Perhaps Denver is leaping over the present, from a not-so-distant past, into a postmodern future. Perhaps what I sensed in Denver had to do with watching Denver invent itself right before my very eyes.

Both Barney Ford and Henry O. Wagoner lived in the Five Points section of Denver in a house on Arapaho Street. To this day, that part of town is described as the "black ghetto." In truth, there is no such thing, by modern-day (or is it postmodern-day?) reckoning. True, the Five Points section has for decades been the home of the bulk of African Americans in Denver. But as late as the early seventies, blacks had spread throughout the Mile High City. Comparisons with the Central District of Seattle are probably the closest and wisest—except Denver's black population is larger than Seattle's. But though Seattle's Central District has a few interesting sites, the Five Points area of Denver is architecturally distinct, solid, pre–World War II, elegant and tree-shaded. Though not exactly Harlem in terms of its underlying physical beauty, it is quite distinguished when compared to most American urban neighborhoods.

Carolyn Estes lives in the Five Points section. When I came to her home, in the early evening, she had been enjoying a drink with some fellows from the neighborhood. She seemed a little bit tired. Carolyn, who wore her hair in braids, and sported a gold tooth, was also wearing a cast-like bandage that went midway up her wrist and extended to the fingers with metal protrusions.

I saw a Stephen King novel on the table and asked if she enjoyed reading his books. She shrugged and just said she enjoyed reading. "I write poems, myself," she told me. When in school she wrote for the school paper.

Born in Amarillo, Texas, Carolyn Estes had been in Colorado for most of her thirty-three years. She had in fact just returned from a few weeks in Texas where her grandmother was ailing.

As Carolyn Estes saw it, black folk were being gradually moved out of the city of Denver, to the suburbs. "They got all these black people to sell their homes, right? These are good homes. They're built up, and they're made of brick." One of the new developments, she told me, had once been a city dump. "People's houses out there already have cracks in the walls."

"At the time that I started buying this house, I had a very good job. A very good job, paid very well. To where I'm paying for a car in two and a half weeks. It shocked the dealer. I mean, when I told him how much I was going to pay per week, you know, because they wanted like twenty-five dollars or fifty dollars a month. I said, 'No, I'll give you such and such a week.' And it shocked him. He's like, 'What, what, what?' 'Why? You trying to talk me out of it? I need a car.' I paid for my car in two and a half weeks, and it was like $1300. Which shocked the hell out of them. They probably think I was robbing banks. Really. They probably did. But like I say, I don't want nobody in my pocket no longer than necessary. If I can, I want to pay for it then. Get out of my pockets. I got too many people in there now. I be reaching in there, I snatch up the wrong person, I'd be like, 'Whoa.' They think their motto ought to be 'Reach out and touch.' Ma Bell. These public services ain't that nice. I just started in a program where they supposed to help you with your utility bills and everything. This is a really big house. Okay? And then I have three kids, which only one is here with me now."

One of Carolyn's sons had gotten in trouble, and the school had tried to have him removed from home.

"Yes, they did, hon. I went to that school, I told his principal, I swear to God, you all going to think Charles Manson was Mother Teresa, by the time I'm through. I'm not playing. You all leave my baby alone. So I had sat down and talked with them about his stuff, and I had seen all the little posters they got plastered in there about the Job Corps, where he can get his diploma also, plus a trade, or two.

"So I talked to him about it. So we agreed that that would be best for him. So that's why he's there. Okay, then I have a set of twins. They're fraternal, but they're of the same sex. Yeah, and I only carried them like five months. They weighed—the older, two pounds, two ounces, the younger weighed two pounds, three ounces.

"But the oldest, he'll be sixteen in October, and he got to the point where he was a wanna-be. You know, he was a Crip. But he wasn't a Crip because he wasn't really in the gang, but he was a wanna-be. And I said, 'Oh no, I really don't think so.' You know. I used to tear his ass up. I once had to whup him, and he went to school, and when he came back, they had a note on my door, saying they had him in a crisis thing. You know. And then, while I'm at the crisis center, they picked up them other two kids. Said I can't touch him. You going to help me raise him? I mean, he's out here. He's doing this, he's doing that. Are you going to tell me I can't touch him? 'Oh, it's my fault.' I really don't think so. I got like three contempts of court, because I read that judge. I told him first you say the kid belongs to the state. We can't touch him. Now that they're running amok, it's the parent's fault. If the child does this and this and that, you're all trying to put the parent in jail. I really don't think so. If you mind your own business in the first place, things wouldn't have got as far as they did. That was my second contempt. I was pissed. I said, 'Okay, you want to help me raise my kids? It's your turn now. It's your turn. You get him together, but you going to get him off the street, because I'm at work, okay? I don't think I have to pay for a babysitter, and my son's fourteen years old.' Get out of here. I'm only working part time anyway.

"You tell me you don't want me on welfare. I try to get off welfare. Everytime I try to get off welfare, you're fining me for something. The first time I tried to get off, they tell me, 'Report all your check stubs.' Okay I was getting paid like every two weeks, but you get this little redetermination paper in the mail once a month. So by the time I get paid again, I've already sent out the MSR, the Monthly Status Report. Okay. So I would just mail in the check stubs. Then they said I was defrauding the government, because I wasn't putting what I was making on this MSR. Now you tell me I got to have this MSR in by a certain date. Okay, you got it. But I get paid again in between that time. You got every check stub I ever made. And they started garnishing. I said, 'You guys got the nerve to garnish my welfare check.' They said, 'Don't call this garnishing, it's recovering.' I consider that garnishing. Whenever you guys get ready, they going to fine me and prosecute me. Well, do what you got to do. But I'm trying to get off. 'Okay, I got a job. Let me go.' Just help me up until I can get on my feet. But it seems like they didn't want me doing that. Every time I tried and tried. I spent half of my life in schools. And the other half working. I couldn't even go to school. I was in school for social work. I found out a lot of crazy laws that nobody has bothered to change but are still in effect. Today. But they don't pay no heed to them.

"I see people break the laws every day, but because they're so old and nobody's bothered to go back and change these laws, they're just like overlooked now. I learned that while I was in school, they stopped my food stamps, stopped my check. 'I'm not getting paid to go to school. What do you guys want me to do? What is it that you want? Get a job? I had a job. You made me quit. I'm trying to go to school and get another skill. You make me quit. What am I supposed to do? You all want me to sit at home and watch soap operas all day and collect this check every month? Okay, fine.'

"But I couldn't even stand it for too long. I couldn't stand it. I want to do something. Anything. I was painting. I didn't tell them that, since I was making pretty good money there, and self-employed, and anything over thirty dollars you got to report. Seems a whole bunch of trouble. That was during the summer, and I had my kids working with me. And we did real good, finally caught up. And then all of a sudden, my rivals, they got pissed because I was getting all the jobs, low bidding them, and so they turned me in. So they told me I had to pay $50,000 insurance for myself plus $25,000 for anybody working for me. Insurance.

"Oh yeah, right, sure I'm going to get all this money, okay. So which give me another brainstorm—you know, I have all these ideas. So I went to school to pick up welding. So I said, 'Now I know if I can do this, they make good money.' The school was fine. I learned to weld, but the blueprint, I'm a little short on. I can't do it in the field without taking my book with me. You understand me? Because there's so many symbols. Then, on top of that, my instructor got me into being a class reporter. He had me doing all four of these things, plus trying to weld at the same time. If you're going to be a reporter, you got to get all the news—how am I going to do all this, and still do my work?

"So I'm complaining to them, but they're going to extend me. The course was only supposed to last like eight to nine months, and I went for almost a year. It was like a week short of a year, because he had me doing all this other stuff, and I didn't have time to study. But I could write some good articles. My welding instructor told me I should get into journalism. I don't want to do that. I want to weld, okay. I don't see myself as sitting around in a chair all day, you know? I like to get up and do things with my hands. But recently now, I went to a birthday party and I fell. I hurt myself pretty . . . really, really, really, really bad.

"And then my doctor going to tell me I can't get no help. I can't even pass you the phone with this hand—you understand me? But they won't give me disability because they say that I be well in six months, and it's been six months. It's been over six months. And I have not changed. This is my range. They lay on my arm, and tell me my range is thirty. I'm about ready to whup their ass.

"I never got a chance to work as a welder. This happened February 9th. I had just quit my part-time, because they're working me like a dog, but feed me like an elephant. I was at St. Clair's gas station, and I had quit prior to hurting myself. And then I come to find out this was an experimental operation. They normally amputate. It was crushed.

"I tried to go and file SSI through the hospital social worker. He wouldn't sign the papers because he said I'd be well in six months. My question is, if this is your first surgery ever performed like this, how can you put a time limit on when I'm going to be better? If six months is up, and ain't nothing changed? I can't even pass you the phone. Somebody got to do something. I can't work. Although God knows I want to. And it hurts me. It hurts being stuck like this, to see myself like that.

"If I got a chance to meet with the mayor? First I'd like to know why the welfare system is so jacked up. Why do they make you have to be a criminal in order to survive? Why do they have to turn you into a liar and a cheat? When you try to be honest with them, they jack you up. And when you get jacked up with welfare, you're jacked up for months. I will ask him why it works that way. And I'd like to ask him about the school system and why don't they pay teachers enough? Teachers are having a hard time now. With all this gang stuff. I'd ask him why they push away our kids, instead of graduating them. Why you just push my kid right out of school and he can't read? I'd ask him about that. But that's only the two most important things. What I would ask him would probably take up the rest of July.

"I think about AIDS. I think that they mixed some stuff together, and they went and injected somebody and then somebody went on and passed it on, and it got it started. That's what I think. I don't care what nobody think. I believe the government—those chemical warfare people. I think they started this. World's overpopulated. Okay? We don't want no war, okay? They can't pop up with another war to get rid of a few more people. And United States, this is the only country in the world that I know that's got every nationality living in it. Every nationality living. I mean, man, we fighting in Vietnam, now they come down here, and they got sports cars. I've been here all my life, and I'm driving a little 1974 Gremlin. And government say, you got to have so many square feet per member of the family. That's what welfare say. You know, the housing authority.

"Let me hush my mouth. America take care of everybody but their own. And that's the problem. Charity begins at home, is how I was raised. America takes care of everything and everybody but its own. Which really pisses me off. We got all these empty buildings around here. I mean, there's five on this one block alone. Why do we have homeless? All these abandoned buildings. Why do we have homeless here and do nothing about it.

"I'd buy a big building and I'd turn it into a shelter. And I would pay everybody's first and last months' rent. I would give them thirty days to find them a job. You ain't got to worry about finding a job. I don't care if they flipping burgers or separating flies from black pepper. I don't care. Just get you a job. And I will rent this according to your income. You got thirty days to get your stuff together. And that's what I would do. Why can't our city officials do that? Get someone a chance. I don't see why they can't. You going to tear down a perfectly good building that someone could be living in so we can have a parking lot? Oh my goodness. And you wonder why the stereos are missing out of them? You wonder why you ain't got no hubcap, baby? Let me tell you. You wonder why you park your car, come out there, and it ain't there? Let me tell you. You got all those people out on the street. They are desperate. They don't care. When you get to that point, that is very dangerous. A point where you don't care.

"That ain't right. That ain't right at all. What can you say? That you can't fight city hall. You can give them a black eye, but that's about all you can do. No, you can't, you can't. You can't fight city hall. You can't even fight the police department. We all got to stick together."

John Tucker worked at the Hue-Man Experience, and, Clara Villarosa had told me, he had been turning a number of young black men on to books on African history, alternative histories, books about spiritualism, African empowerment. These books were popular and gaining a significant audience. (In fact, Haki Madhubuti had published a number of such books.) I was curious to talk to John about his impressions, his ideas.

John Tucker was born the year "King was shot." That's how he marked 1968. His family moved from Joliet, Illinois, to Denver, when he was four. Roughly every four years, the family would move back to Joliet, and then back to Denver. "So half my childhood was growing up here in this community. And the other half was in Joliet, Illinois. I actually know both cities. But really, there's no comparison."

Growing up, he found Denver to be more of a "racial mix." But ethnic and cultural groups stuck to themselves. "Mexicans were all doing their thing, and the blacks were doing their thing, and the whites were doing their thing." He had a few white friends in school, "but you never went over to their house after school." Some of the black men, especially the sports stars, dated white girls. Indeed, "that was really prevalent. Even though the groups never really dealt with each other." Back in Illinois, basketball had been a big deal—families went out to cheer family members. "School spirit. Here I hardly ever went to a basketball game. I really didn't care."

But in his senior year in high school, John did notice what he called the "advent" of gangbangers in Denver, Colorado. The GQs. The MOs.

"This is here in Denver. George Washington High School. They've even had cops shoot guns at the 7-Eleven, up the street from the school, and at lunchtime everybody's out there. Somebody busted a police car once with a brick. He got out of the car with his rifle and shot up in the air. And everybody just hit the ground. They locked us in the 7-Eleven. When they unlocked the door, everything was gone. People walked out with everything. It was wild. So we're ripe for that type of stuff. It's just that it doesn't really grab hold."

He predicted that Denver would see more such activity in the not-too-distant future.

I wondered, what makes gang life so attractive? What is it? Is it the peer pressure? Are young people forced into it?

"I think it's double-sided. On the one hand, it's that pressure from the peer group, or people in the neighborhood, or whatever. And then on the other hand, there's pressure from just your family situation. As I understand it, gangs are many times surrogate families. Something to believe in when it's not all there at home. And that's something that's even new for us, as African Americans, because many of us think that we were always like this, but even in the '60s, and the '50s, people your age and older can remember the strong family foundation, even when the mom didn't have a husband in the house. There was an uncle or somebody who lived with you or something. There was always that. But that's been broken down, I think. Not totally, but it can use a lot of repair.

"I've met people who are in gangs, and my general disposition is to befriend anybody until I have reason not to. And for the most part I haven't had any problems. A lot of them are in jail now. They go through their cycles. But I have come across and been friends with some gang members. They have to pull down the front to get to the person. The process gets you so engrossed, that things that you would have thought and done two or three years ago, you wouldn't do if you were a gang member. I mean, nice things. It would just indicate that you're soft or something like that. Generally, they had to be approached at a level that's nonthreatening, because they organize their whole defense structure against the world. What used to be threatening is no longer threatening, and what is not threatening becomes threatening. You see what I mean?

I've talked to them. I feel like I grew up in the fast lane here in Denver, so I had a balance, and I kind of understood where they were coming from. Sometimes, I didn't know what to ask them but the basic questions. 'Why are you doing this?'

"I understand a lot of the mentality. From living around it. But they generally don't change their minds upon my suggestion. But they do listen to other things that I say. And sometimes when I ask them, why do they do it? they say things that indicate to me that it's family. They don't say that this is my family, but it's like I'm down with my homie. A lot of times, people think that peer pressure is negative, but there's a positive side too, you know. If you have to go drive a car, and you're sixteen, you have peer pressure for that. And that's positive pressure to take on responsibility. Peer pressure to get a job when you get out of high school, or while you're in high school, because your friends are doing it. So there is positive peer pressure that can exist in gangs, but there's also negative forces that the gangs are used for. In my opinion, beer-makers, the malt liquor beers, target the teenage black population. Cisco is so bad, I mean, it's the worst rotgut you could get. And they call it liquid crack, on the streets. Liquid crack. And some people actually think they put crack in it. But it's not like any other liquor. I mean, it's just terrible. And they drink that, and there's a whole drug culture and alcohol culture and rap culture associated with gang members and gang violence and stuff. Though all the rap isn't necessarily gang related. That's just a young person's forte. That's something that they do.

"But in general, I think that gang members would change if someone would approach them on a level they could understand. I think too many times we come at them only one way. We give up because we don't know nothing else. That's a problem of ours, not theirs. If you listen to them, you know, they talk. They're not dumb. A lot of them are really intelligent. I mean, if you can count eighteen $400 transactions for some cocaine, in a matter of six hours, and keep track, and then take out your money to keep continuing the process, you got some intelligence. You could be working in a bank.

"It's just that they don't have the same American dream that the mainstream has. It's ironic because they still share in the value system of this American dream. In my opinion, gang members and gang mentality is just a microcosm of Wall Street and the political process of America. When you get rap groups—gang-related rap groups like NWA [Niggas Wit Attitude]—that's their attitude. They asked me the other day, 'Does a nigger have a master?' I had never thought about it. I was like, 'Yeah.' To even call yourself a nigger is to imply a master. Because that's something they created. And so when you're talking about 'I'm a nigger with an attitude/a nigger you'd love to hate,' and stuff like that, then you're telling the truth. Right? You're telling on yourself."

I wondered what John Tucker thought about the ever-increasing popularity of hip-hop music.

"I've watched them playing our music. The other races. In Denver. I think it's a vibe of—and get this, most people don't say this—but it's a vibe and a rhythm of African spirituality.

"It's actually on the same wavelength. It serves the same function. Just imagine if Africans didn't have music, even though drums were outlawed once. Imagine if we didn't sneak off in the forest, and we didn't sing or hum in the house late at night. If mama didn't hum to us when we were in bed. We would be crazy. We probably wouldn't even have made it. It's a part of us, you know, it really is. It's an expression of African spirituality that only gets to come out through limited avenues. We're so bombarded with negativity against ourselves, and the social structures that keep our spirituality and our humaneness from overflowing and being balanced. We have an armored shell on. And there's a hole and a couple of openings. We can see outside or something begins to escape, it's like we have those holes overflowing with our vibe, when it's restricted. So it's like a concentration of an outlet. That's what I really think it is.

"It appeals to so many young people, black and white, because of the level of creativity. Creativity transcends everything. People are attracted to that. Of all races, walks of life, they see something that's creative, they're really impressed by it. It has an effect on them. I think rap is much the same as Egyptian sculpture. It calls you to it, to understand it, to take it apart, understand what it's doing, and put it back together. I think it's an outlet. I know I learned plenty of things listening to rap."

"What'd you learn from rap?" I asked.

"I like radical rap. I really do like that. I like Sister Souljah. I think she's a remarkable young woman. I mean, she shows the fortitude of Fannie Lou Hamer. At Fannie Lou Hamer's age. I don't see that so often in black sisters in the media spotlight.

"I think each generation of music progresses with the political statements and adds to it. It actually stays the same, but rap is going back to the creation of man. With the knowledge that we were there first. See, that's a difference, you know, after all the twenty years of getting up, like Farrakhan would say. Making a lot of noise, and sit back down. Get up, make a lot of noise, sit back down. After years and years of doing that, over a long time period, we've developed and we've gained some things. We've lost some, but we've gained a lot more. Coming into this century we've gotten the record of our history written in our own languages. Back before white people existed. We didn't have those tools then. Certain times you cannot defy the truth. Or deny it, when we got it sitting here in front of your face. And you can't even destroy it, or you destroy your own. But I think rap fills a void, where public education fails. And where home education fails. Some of the songs talk about the original black man, and some of them take samples of political speeches from the '60s. Public Enemy is very good at that, and they're very politically attuned. But I like rap in general, because it offers me all of that. I don't think intellectualism will save black people anyway. That's linear, left-brained, Eurocentric thinking. We're not like that. We don't really understand that. That's our problem."

"To play devil's advocate," I said, "some people would say that to say such a thing implies that black folks can't think like white folks."

"No, that's not to say that at all. That's dysfunction. I think there's sometimes a balance, and the balance is the creativity that people don't know they have. It's not one way or the other. I think it can work both ways and in the middle.

"This is just my opinion. I think that if we turned inward, as a race and as individuals, turned inward to our roots, our history, our family, our culture, as our save-all, then we would discover many things that we'd never thought we were capable of doing, and that we are doing, and maybe not be aware of. Because after years and years and years of being conditioned, you have a predictable personality. You have a predictable set of values. You have a predictable life, basically. When you transcend that and go back to a record that's older than theirs, than white people's record, then you actually liberate yourself, personally, through the family and through the community. And so I think if we had our education coming from home about us, our complete education, not 1619 when we got here, that's not our education. We've been here for two billion, point five million years. That's not enough. You see what I mean? If we have a complete education, and dependence on each other, no one could stop us. We know that deep down, but we deny it, because we're following the American dream. We know that because we wouldn't be here now, if we didn't have that power, because no one else survived the atrocities they put us through. Not even Jews. I don't think they're telling the truth about everything. To say that their Holocaust, six million people, is the worst in the world, they forgot about the 200 million Africans, and the lost 70 million that nobody ain't even talking about, that have died through slavery, and the slave ships.

"We had people trying to keep the light on, like Garvey and Du Bois in his later years, about the African connection to the American. But, for the most part, that hasn't permeated into the mainstream. So we have this Negro mentality. Negro means black in Spanish. If you think about it, it's an adjective, am I correct? A descriptive term.

"If you write history for 400 years, as a Negro, then you're actually being written out of history, subconsciously, because the meaning of the word in the dictionary is black. Not a place, not a people, not a noun, a person, place or thing. So when you get to examine simple things like that, as far as the use of a term, to name yourself or to accept, it has a profound effect on what you do. Everybody knows that 'nigger' was substituted for the word 'Negro.' I even think people feel it; I felt it when I was a child—when I was called a Negro, I still felt like they were calling me a nigger. Now, I was a child, didn't understand nothing. It just was a tension then. I wasn't comfortable with that. And so when you use descriptive terms and capitalize them, that doesn't make them valid. The power to define comes when we can take that term and give it back to those who gave it to us. Now if they choose to call us that, that's fine. We don't have to acknowledge it or turn our head when they say it, and it'll die out. I think it's important that we reconnect with the African term, which we have. African American. This is a little radical in some people's opinion, but a lot of people claim to be African American. I don't even claim that. I say 'African, born in America,' because that describes my condition. And a lot of people have problems with that."

John told me he got into a discussion with twelve white teachers who insisted he was an American. "I said, 'I'm not American until I have access to college like your son. Till I own a house like yours, and until I can go to the country club when I feel like it. Then I'll become American. Until then, I'm African born in America because that's my condition. And it doesn't offend me for somebody to call me that. Because it always reminds me that this is not my home. That's what we forgot. We think this is home.' "

I asked John, What then do we do with the 300 years of history on the North American continent? All the blood, sweat and tears that have soaked in the soil here; the structures, the highways, buildings, railroads, and on and on from economics to science to art? "This America would not exist without the Africans," I said. "Is it really not possible to think of this as home—in whatever qualified a fashion?"

"Even though we've been here for a long time," John said, "it remains a universal truth that it was a forced home."

"Where does that leave us then?" I asked. "It puts us in a strange sort of limbo."

"It does. It puts us in a paradox. But see, paradoxes have a quality that people don't understand. When you get stuck in a paradox, you move to the other level. People don't see that. We have to make some hard decisions. What do we intend to do? What's our function here in this country? Up to now, we have been servile to the American system. Wal-Mart wouldn't have a chance. Right? We'd take 300 billion dollars. We're qualified as the ninth richest nation in the world. Just the black community. Ninety-six percent of our money goes out of the community. But if we left, it wouldn't, and neither would our labor go into the system.

"If we really wanted to realize that power, we could. And we need to determine an eternal optimism to follow. So what? Everybody wants to go back to Africa. We have to always know that we can. We can't never say we can't. When you say you can't, then all the time that we spent here learning, going through this hell, was for nothing, because this is how I consider it. And you know, I'm Americanized. Don't get me wrong. I'm just learning this African history stuff recently. But I always knew something was wrong. But if my great-great-great-great-grandmother lost her child—if they cut it out of her, like they used to do, for seasoning—the thing she longed for most in her heart was to go home. The thing she longed for for her children was to go home, and to return a free person. If we don't consider that, then we're willing slaves, marching to hell. On a silver platter.

"If we, in fact, built this country, the fact still remains: What is our responsibility based on our condition of being here in this country? If we were forced to do labor, and never got paid for 310 years of free slave labor, then our responsibility would be to tear it down, because it's wrong. No matter what anybody says, the advent of America and America now is wrong. I don't care how many people have those spiritual moments or those economic moments. You know what I mean?

"The underlying truth and reality is this is a very oppressive country. It may not appear so to us because, like some of the religious people say, we're in the belly of the beast—we can't see outside of the beast. When I was young, I never wanted to leave the country. America was great. I shouldn't have to wait till I go to work to find that out. So I am going to be this prestigious black guy who's just really making millions and don't care about the seventy million that haven't acculturated? No. I can't see myself like that at fifty, at sixty. I would be a broken person. My drive for success has nothing to do with America. It has to do with my people in America."

To be sure, John Tucker believed, a "we" existed.

"You may not be able to perceive it," he said. "Being inundated by negativity about your race, and the issues surrounding that, cause our dysfunction personally, and then permeate through the family, and the community. So there is a 'we' that exists. This is the question. If there's a 'we,' then why deny it? We need to understand that our cultural links, our links as a family, as a group, are not entirely based around oppression. That's really important. Our common bond is not oppression. You exhaust that, if you go for that route. Which is the Civil Rights movement.

"The goals that we have been setting just don't cut it. America's dream ain't enough. I mean, it's enough for maybe one generation, but as soon as people get old and ready to die, it'll be like 'Damn. I wish we would have done something different.' And we find ourselves saying this every generation. 'Rewind the tape. Stop. Let's look at this. Why do we keep doing these things?' Just that question would bring about change."

One of the people most responsible—at least in the public mind—for continuing to stir the pot of history of African Americans in the West is Mr. Paul Stewart. He had essentially started the Black American West Museum and Heritage Center, and was writing a projected six-volume series, "Black Cowboys." He lectured and visited schools. I figured I should certainly try to talk to him.

When I got Mr. Stewart on the phone, he seemed more than a little apprehensive, more than a little reticent. An interview? Well, he was writing his own book. He was a busy man, he told me. Most of the interviews he did these days were paid, I was told.

More than a bit disappointed, I thanked him and prepared to say goodbye, remembering the wise words of Mahalah Ashley Dickerson: "If one won't, another one will." But he said, before I hung up, be sure to go by the museum, now housed in the Justina Ford House. I said I had no intention of missing it. And, he said, the Bill Pickett Invitational Rodeo is in town. If I came to the rodeo on Sunday, he might find the time to talk with me a little and introduce me to some people.

A black rodeo! Hot damn, I thought.

When I was a little boy, when an uncle or an older cousin would give me a piece of candy or a soft drink, they would sometimes add, "Now you can't say black folks never did nothing for you."

I got lost on the way to the fairgrounds, well out of the city among ranches and grazing land and warehouses and highways. I couldn't find Mr. Stewart, and when I finally found someone who knew him, I was told that he might be around, but the fellow thought he might have already gone. I didn't let that spoil my afternoon: I'd never been to a rodeo before.

I went up into the bleachers and took my seat at the Bill Pickett Invitational. (I noted the sponsors were Wrangler, Nestle, BET, Lancaster Western Wear, and the radio station KDKO.)

Straightaway the emcee got on my nerves: a fairly obnoxious joke teller, insistent, misogynist, and unfunny.

But again, I had no intention of letting my day be spoiled. There I was, in this sea of beautiful dark faces (I don't remember any white faces), which had to number several hundred if not more—it's hard for me to tell in stadiums—and a multitude of children, raucous and having a good time. Clearly this was a family day. Everybody seemed to be eating nachos and chilidogs and boiled ears of corn. The crowd was like the cheering, restless, but attentive crowd at an Aggie football game or a Morehouse basketball game. Popular, mainstream hip-hop bounced from the speakers—they were particularly fond of "Jump, Jump" by Kris Kross that day, playing it a great many times—and lots of James Brown. All amid a profusion of cowboy hats.

Then there were the events.

Early on came calf roping, which was won by a minister from Prairie View, Texas.

Followed by bareback riding—the horses looked powerful and ornery, as one would expect. Two fellows from Oklahoma City and one from Port Arthur, Texas (his horse was called Funny Weed), rode the horses for all they were worth—which seemed plenty.

The staff seemed to spend an awful lot of time trying to control the livestock behind the gates, which at times proved as entertaining as the main event.

There was calf scrambling, where nine- to twelve-year-olds were invited to come down and form a single line out into the middle of the arena. Then they would charge two calves in order to snatch a tag off the calves' ears. The reward: "a crisp, new five-dollar bill."

Then came bull dogging, or steer wrestling—a sport invented by none other than the famous Bill Pickett. (It is said that one day in Tyler, Texas, while loading a stock car, a steer broke loose, and Pickett hopped on his horse, ran the critter down, jumped off the horse and single-handedly brought the animal to heel.) The contestants were expected to do it in the same time-honored fashion: a horn in each hand, turning the steer's neck till it went to the ground. One cowboy was from Muskogie, another from Tulsa, and the winner from Houston.

Of course, the people with the most dangerous job were the bull-distracting, bull-disarming clowns whom I eyed with fascination and awe.

Next came steer decorating, where a cowgirl (cowwoman? cowman?—no, just doesn't work, does it?) snatches a ribbon off a charging steer while she is atop a charging horse. The winner, Carolyn Carter from Oklahoma, did it in 1.4 seconds.

Then ladies' barrel racing, where three barrels had to be negotiated around the arena and returned to the starting place.

Ribbon roping was a team effort: A cowboy must rope a fleeing calf, and a cowgirl must snatch a red ribbon from the calf's tail and run to "home."

Bull riding—"the most dangerous sport today," said the emcee, as he cranked up Hammer's "Too Legit to Quit"—commenced as Dion Henderson of Wichita, Kansas, was rocked, bucked, buffeted, violently whipped about, all with the force of thunder and at the speed of lightning—but he stayed on. As he walked away, bowlegged and big, I thought, what on earth would get me on top of a bucking, murderous, agitated bull? Nothing, I thought, but dire, terrifying necessity—or insanity.

And as the kids all lined up at one end of the stadium and raced down to the other end to snatch up candy galore—I thought about what I had just witnessed. So much of it was a mixture of boyhood/girlhood fantasies of Pecos Bill and derring-do and the mythological mystique of the American-built notion of the hero in this large, strange, untamed, dangerous western land. But now that land had become tamed, domesticated, and, quite honestly, downright boring. For the men we watched that day, their skills were still needed to some extent; but for most of the watchers, these skills were no longer necessities. These acts spoke to us knowingly as athleticism and romance and anachronism, and there was a lot of testosterone in it as well. Why do we—men folk and women folk alike—do it? Continually seek to prove ourselves? Physically? What are we proving, exactly? To whom? Certainly, it has to do with more than being able to down a bull, and it certainly has to do with more than mere sport.

I was keen to speak with some of the cow folk, but discovered that they were to leave town the next day, and, understandably, they didn't have time to bother with me. But I was heading east; surely I could look some of them up in their towns, I rationalized. The road to hell . . .

> The trails end where fiction begins. As the records show, Negroes helped to open and hold the West. They explored the plains and mountains, fought Indians, dug gold and silver, and trapped wild horses and wolves. Some were outlaws and some were law officers. Thousands rode in the cavalry, and thousands more were cowboys. And, for a while, at least, some performed in rodeos and others rode on many of the country's major race tracks . . .
>
> Today, perhaps, ignorance of history is the most important reason that the Negro cowboy does not ride in fiction. Americans have assumed that because Negroes have not been in Western fiction they were never in the West. The prairie was different from the city, said one writer, for there the Jew, Negro and Italian never came. This attitude Americans accept as history, and what they learn is strangely incomplete.
>
> —Philip Durham and Everett L. Jones,
> *The Negro Cowboys,* 1965

In "The West as Fiction," the epilogue to their exciting and informative 1965 book, *The Negro Cowboys,* Messrs. Durham and Jones make an eloquent and sensible discussion of why there are almost no black folk in American western mythography. For 200 pages, they do an admirable job of documenting and enumerating the black men and women who actually made the West possible (many have estimated that as many as a third of the men involved in the "opening" of the West were black); then they lament that neither in the dime novel tradition of the middle and latter nineteenth century, nor in the archetypical Westerns that became the meat and potatoes for most of this century, both in the novel and on the screen, black folk virtually do not exist. I agree largely with their explanation of why. It was an intrinsic part of the justification for taking land to which the European marauders had no right. "He" had to be an "American folk hero," "with a superhuman personality." Neither Mormon, Catholic, nor Jew—"Like an 'ideal' Presidential candidate, he was expected to be a white, Protestant American with whom most Americans can identify." He was Everyman; he was great, "but not miraculous," "a symbol of the real or desired courage, independence and triumph of the ordinary American." This was successfully propagated. The authors then make a plea that "all Americans may someday share in the heritage of the West."

Thirty-some years later, the situation has not much improved, in terms of including African Americans, and other groups for that matter, in the mythic "Old West." Moreover, Hollywood has moved on to another battlefield. World War II gave movies a bigger, badder, more sinister Other—the Nazis and the Imperial Japanese. The West, now full of shopping malls and suburbs, is less strange. Westerns as a genre are so far out of favor that they are in the perpetual "comeback" stage, while World War II movies continue to flourish, as shown by the 1997 Academy Award winner for best picture, *The English Patient,* and the success of 1998's *Saving Private Ryan.* In recent years, of the cowboy pictures released, only *Unforgiven* had a major black character, and only *Posse* was specifically about black cowboys, and television had its integrated *Lonesome Dove* series. Otherwise, Durham and Jones's hope seems pinned to a dying genre.

All that said, the mythography created by Peckinpah and Louis Lamour et al. is still powerful, known to practically every American, and equally intimately in Japan, Argentina, Germany and even Polynesia. This vision of the West is part and parcel of our dream of what it means to be an American. But my real problem with that image of the old West has less to do with missing contributions than with cockeyed interpretations. A great many books have been written since *The Negro Cowboys,* and the lives and society of these men and women make for captivating reading—from the notorious shot Deadeye Dick (or Nat Love) to the law-abiding politician and Oklahoma pioneer Edwin P. McCabe; from the rich and enterprising Clara Brown of the Colorado mining towns, to Cherokee Bill, "the worst man in the West." Scouts, chiefs, trappers, town founders, lawmen, businesswomen—yes, they were colorful, and our national imagination suffers from their absence; just as it suffers from a lack of a space for those less flamboyant, struggling, farming, cattle-driving, soldiering folk, merely trying to make do.

Yet it is not enough, in my opinion, to merely list and tout their contributions, for I suspect that many of these people, many of them escaped slaves, had a very different idea of what their "new" land meant. Surely, some had dreams of becoming fabulously wealthy, and some were bad to the bone, but I suspect many also had a vision of a Promised Land much different from that of Andrew Jackson and Andrew Johnson and James Garfield and Theodore Roosevelt. They didn't need breathing space, they needed freedom space. Indeed, to truly insert an African American vision into the prevailing myth of the West would be to short-circuit that entire myth. Such a vision would bring questions of Native American rights and "coolie" labor and Mexican wars and criminal railroad barons to the fore, and reconfigure what "made America great." Remember, I do not write of ancient history, but of history as close as the television screen.

These questions are not just for African Americans, they are for all Americans. What is Manifest Destiny? What is Destiny? What or who makes it Manifest? Will the truth make us free?

I met Edward Gordon at the Justina Ford House, which housed the Black America West Museum. Located in the Five Points section, it was a handsome sturdy house, containing memorabilia, artifacts and documents of the black pioneers. Straightaway, Mr. Gordon impressed me with his knowledge of and fascination for the African American history of the West. It seemed that he was more than a docent; it seemed to be a significant portion of his life. After a while, when I asked about the Buffalo Soldiers, he volunteered that his father had been a member of that legendary group of black soldiers.

"After the Civil War, this was frontier. They didn't know what to do with those black Civil War soldiers. So that's where they sent them, out on the frontier. They served all over the West. Texas, Montana, Nebraska, and all over. That's the story that's just now coming out. They weren't the only blacks, the only soldiers out there, but that's where most of the black soldiers were sent. They helped tame the frontier. Guard the southernmost wagon trains and railroad lines, telegraph lines. Try to keep the Indians on the reservation. Of course, the blacks had nothing against the Indians. All they were doing was protecting their own, their rights, their homes, and their families. The Indian scouts always seemed to be separate. They had their families. They used them, in the earlier days on the frontier, on scouting missions to warring tribes. Now, some of those Indian scouts were part black."

Most of the men were southerners, Mr. Gordon told me. "They took pride in it. Even though they were treated meanly by the War Department and given poor equipment, they say their desertion rate was the lowest in the army. I think they had about twelve congressional Medal of Honor winners among them. High. About as high as they can go.

"Of course it's a romanticized tale about how they got the name Buffalo Soldiers, that the Indians gave them that name. But I've read that nobody really knows how they got the name. So many tales. One version is that the hair on the black soldiers looked like the hair on the buffalo. So that's why the Indians called them Buffalo Soldiers. But I can't concede that all over that frontier out there an Indian would look at a black soldier and say 'buffalo soldier.' That's a romantic kind of thing. But now it's generally accepted."

Mr. Edward Gordon's father had been stationed at Fort Huachuca, Arizona. He had been enlisted in the 9th Cavalry in Savannah, Georgia. Mr. Gordon's father spent more than thirty-six years in the military—1899 to 1935. "But it wasn't continuous," Mr. Gordon told me. "So many of those old soldiers would enlist in one regiment, and serve out that enlistment, and sometimes they'd take off and become civilians for a while, and go back in, maybe enlist in another regiment."

For a time, his father had been a prison guard at Leavenworth, Kansas, and also worked in a pharmacy. Edward Gordon, Jr. had been born in Fort Ontario, New York, in 1910, when his father was enlisted in the 24th Infantry. In 1918, they were sent to the Philippines. Mr. Gordon remembers living in houses, "up on stilts," near Camp Stattensberg. The 9th Cavalry had been the baseball champions. ("Many of those early black players in the Negro Baseball League came out of these army regiments.")

Mr. Gordon remembered that it took army transport ships thirty days to go from San Francisco to Manila. "About two weeks to get to Honolulu."

"It seemed to me just a few days after we left San Francisco, World War I was declared. We were out at sea, when we heard about that. And we proceeded on to Honolulu. And later on, I think from Honolulu to Guam. We were escorted by a battleship, because of the submarine scare. When we got to Guam, the allied forces had captured some Germans, probably from submarines. So they put them on the ship that we were on. Put them down in the hold, down in third class where we had been, so we got to go first class.

"We could look down in the hold there and see all these Germans down there. I was seven or eight years old. I can remember that.

"I do remember the atrocities. Some way or other you got hold of the atrocities. That's all the things that the Germans were supposed to be doing to people. And I can remember having nightmares about that. If I remember correctly, the song 'Over There' came out. It was just a big picnic for me. Really, the war didn't touch us so much over there in the Philippines."

When the family left the Philippines, they returned to Oswego, New York. In the 1920s, his father was assigned to the 10th Cavalry at Fort Huachuca in Arizona.

"The first job I got was as a temporary clerk over at Fort Huachuca in the commissary. I went out there a couple years ago. Went with the Elder Hostel program. Old folks. Right outside the reservation there. Sierra Vista City now. Wasn't there when we lived out there. Part of it was a history of Fort Huachuca, so that's why I went. I hadn't been out there since the '30s. They had preserved the old fort the way it was when we were there, except that the stables are all gone. They had a group of Indian scouts at that time. Well, they're gone. It's a communications center for the military now. The army. It's all built up. The old fort is like a museum, surrounded by modern communications equipment. They probably have another name for it. But I understand in Desert Storm, even now, it is the heart of the military communications system."

During World War II, the 93rd Division trained at Fort Huachuca—an all-black division.

Mr. Gordon had recently attended an unveiling at Fort Leavenworth, to honor the black soldiers, the Buffalo Soldiers. "Now the term is generally applied to all black soldiers, even those from World War II, because they were recognized there. That was so wonderful because there are very few living Buffalo Soldiers from, say, my dad's era." Former Chairman of the Joint Chiefs of Staff General Colin Powell had been there. "The first time I heard of a black man who got a nineteen-gun salute. And then they had a flyover, the formation flyers. And then they posted the colors of the four so-called Buffalo Soldier regiments. And also the colors of the 92nd Division, and the Airborne Brigade and the Tuskegee Airmen. It was really impressive. And I bet there were about 10,000 people there. It was so crowded."

The oldest living man there was 109 years old. "He enlisted the same year my dad did, but unfortunately there's no record that he ever served. I read one story that he joined the cavalry, and the men let him hold their horses, and probably he just lived with them. They just probably made a mascot out of him. Because there's no record of his service. But he was quite active. Every place I went, he was there. He was in good shape. Holding his children's children.

"They deactivated the 9th Cavalry and the 10th Cavalry about 1941. They no longer existed as such. In those old days, the black enlisted man, he knew he might make a warrant officer. In each regiment they have a warrant officer. They had several noncommissioned officers, and the next was the warrant officer. Now the chaplains and the bandleaders, as far as my knowledge is concerned, they might make warrant officer." Actually, there were a few commissioned officers like Colonel Allen Allensworth, but none were ever given a command.

I asked Mr. Gordon what he thought might have kept these men so strong.

"They became strong. When they first formed the regiments, some of them had fought in the Civil War. Most of them were illiterate. First time some of them had ever had a square meal. You have to give credit to those white officers that went there and trained them because it was on a volunteer basis, and there were many white officers who turned down the idea of accepting these black soldiers, and trying to make soldiers out of them. I don't think enough has been said about the white officers who did get in there. I mean, the Negroes didn't do it all themselves. We had help."

I was curious to know more about what it was like to have grown up on a military fort in the Arizona desert in the 1920s and 1930s.

"It was the most godforsaken place you'd ever see," Mr. Gordon said, and laughed. "Jackrabbits and rattlesnakes, sand burrs, sand. It was a wild country, a great playground. Down those hills.

"My mother and father were going to a dance one night, and it was rainy. And I had picked up an old dog, old hound, and got permission to keep him. Anyhow, I was sitting in the kitchen up there one night, and this dog kept barking and barking. And I kept hearing a buzzing. And I said to my dad, 'Isn't that a rattlesnake?' He said, 'Where? Where?' The dog had him at the door of the kitchen where I was. In the house. My dad finally shot and killed it. As I say, wild country. From our bathtub there was a pipe that ran out into a ravine. That's how primitive it was. They figured that this rattlesnake just went up that pipe, came out the bathtub. We still have a piece of that rattlesnake skin. One fellow skinned it for us. I still remember.

"When I used to be a kid—way back—my dad and the others, they got to telling tales, you see. Talking and all that. There was no radio and TV in those days. Sometimes they'd be out on maneuvers or out on target practice. And they'd live in the pup tents. And sometimes they'd wake up in the morning, be a rattlesnake in their bed. Come in someplace to get warm. Things like that.

"There were a lot of jackrabbits and rabbits out there and doves. People'd go out hunting. I never had a gun, but I'd go out with my dad or someone else, and I remember this woman out there. She used to take me out hunting with her, and that woman, I mean, she could walk. You'd be way out on the desert there, and you'd look back and you could hardly see the buildings at the fort. And it'd be hot out there, and you weren't supposed to drink a lot of water. I can remember that, going out hunting with this woman. They had a farm there, and my dad took all of us, my mother and sister and I out there. Once he was going to shoot some doves. And he's kind of a big man. And we were all curious, watching them get to the fence. He had a double-barreled shotgun and he laid the shotgun down. It went off. I don't know how one of us didn't get shot. Dad, he jumped about that far off the ground here. That's one thing I can remember." Mr. Gordon was laughing hard.

"Scared him, did it?" I asked.

"Scared all of us."

I asked Mr. Gordon more about his father. "He was stern. As far as I was concerned, he was just big." His father had been buried at Fort Leavenworth.

Mr. Gordon's mother had been from Oswego, New York, near Fort Ontario, where she met his father. "I know I had a grandfather up there from about 1850 or something like that. He was a gardener, found that out. It's rather fascinating because coming from up there, no one knew anything about black history, and you were reared in the dominant culture. I know when I came out of high school, I knew about George Washington Carver, Booker T. Washington. That's about all. It was during college in Emporia, Kansas. I was taking social studies. And I got to the place where I was writing a history paper. And there was a woman teaching there who was a faculty advisor, black woman. This is back when they had segregated schools. And she said, 'You act as if you're going to be teaching white boys and girls. You're going to be teaching colored boys and girls. But you never mentioned anything about their history, people who were outstanding.' I didn't know anything. And she made me do the paper over again. And that's where I got the study started, of black history. That was way back in the '30s. I'm still finding new things. So that woman did more for me—it wasn't in the course that I took—she did more for me, getting in that field, because you find something here and you find something there. Just not generally known."

Mr. Gordon had taught in the public schools in a small town near Leavenworth for nine years, but said he never felt that he fit in there. He moved to Denver in 1948, where he worked in the postal service until his retirement. "When I retired from the post office, I started working at the Adult Learning Center, volunteered, and I was doing volunteer work down in the museum. Last two or three years, they started paying."

I allowed as how Mr. Gordon had certainly seen some changes in his life.

"Comes with age," he said. "Better than where we used to be. The only hope that you had in the old days was maybe being a schoolteacher or being a janitor. A woman became a domestic. My parents, my grandparents, that's about the best they could do. But now, it's up to the individual. He can do almost anything he wants to do. Has to be part of himself. Nobody's going to come out and give you anything. You have to work for it. But that's what everybody else does. So I think it's all changed for the good, although we have some of these rabble-rousers, make you think differently."

I asked Mr. Gordon's opinion about the cultural losses due to integration. Were we, in fact, better off or had we lost a sense of community?

"Yeah. It's the price you had to pay."

"The price we had to pay?"

"Yeah. See the black businesses down in Five Points for instance, when you could go anyplace and get something at a lower price, and maybe of better quality, they went. The schools went—they had segregated schools, and they had black clubs. Colored Students Association. Almost each town had a little black high school. A colored high school group, athletics. You were separated. And they used to have a lot of fun, say, the black high school's basketball team.

"Now when they desegregated, those blacks who had a position in some of those things, why they were no longer needed as a separate entity. That's something I can't get over. When I go back to Kansas—it was so segregated there in Kansas—I never could see how it could be much different than the South was. You go back now, and everybody's buddy-buddy. I can't say it's all like that.

"They talk so much about your African culture. I can't see what the

African culture's done for us. I mean, you talk about black kings and so on. But what happened to them? No one ever became a king without taking advantage of someone else.

"And that's been the story all through history. You took advantage of other people. And they certainly didn't hang on to them. So-called black countries, I know they had opposition, but it seems to me they could have done something besides kill each other. Over in Somalia now. It's the other blacks that are keeping the food from getting in. For what, I don't know.

"I know there's so many things around being black now. Language and customs. Different things. And then there was an article in the paper last week on military brass. This is both white and black, that they grow in a separate group. They have a different perspective. The blacks that come from the South, blacks that come from the East. Blacks that come from states out here in the West, maybe just one or two black families within ten or twenty miles. They're not homogeneous. A large part of the things that they think about as black, are rural southern customs. But not all of us are from that.

"I'm not saying it's anything wrong with it.

"Say, somebody grew up in Nebraska, or Montana, you ordinarily don't think of any blacks coming from Montana. But there are blacks there. Their people came from Montana. They have an entirely different perspective than somebody who lived in rural Georgia. And you reflect whatever the dominant culture is in your particular area. I belong to the Episcopal church. Now they're searching for a minister. They want a black Episcopal minister. Well, heck, I was in my twenties before I knew there was a black minister in the Episcopal church. Depends on where you come from. Your ideas about things, your perspective about things. The military kids come up with a little different perspective from the general run.

"It's just not homogeneous. The only thing is the same, maybe, is the color. I got to go to Africa about ten years ago. And about the only thing that you had in common with some of those Africans was color. Because everything else was different. There are many things over here that you don't like, but you can do something about them. Over there, if you differ, in some cases, you may disappear and never be seen again. I remember, I was down in Dakar, and I got tired, and I sat down on the steps of a building there. Here came the gendarme with his gun and everything. 'Get up from there.' That's not what he said, but that's what he meant. Heck, if you go downtown here, if you're tired, you sit down, you don't see guns all around. And you never seen poverty until you've seen some of that poverty over in Africa, even in the better places. This was in Senegal.

"You see pictures, and not only in Moslem countries, with these great masses of people out there shouting and waving their hands. What do they do for a living? I mean, the only time you get groups of people like that, here in the United States, maybe would be at a football game or some athletic contest.

"But in Africa that seems to be an everyday thing."

> A still further step I was not yet prepared to realize must be taken: not simply knowledge, not simply direct repression of evil, will reform the world. In long, indirect pressure and action of various and intricate sorts, the actions of men which are not due to lack of knowledge nor to evil intent, must be changed by influencing folkways, habits, customs and subconscious deeds. Here perhaps is a realm of physical and cosmic law which science does not yet control.
>
> —W.E.B. Du Bois, *Dusk of Dawn,* 1940

In Denver I began to think more and more about history and, curiously, about destiny. For some reason, to me, that part of the world held a particular something with regard to African American history, something that was slowly becoming clearer to me. Something that included destiny as well.

Historians have written extensively about periods in black history, but as I see it, our history divides into six distinct, though sometimes overlapping, parts: Middle Passage, the break from Africa; the antebellum period, meaning, for black Americans, slavery; Reconstruction, including emancipation, manumission, and the chaos after the Civil War, allowing African Americans to begin to take a greater hand in inventing themselves; redemption, or the imposition of Jim Crow, a new kind of subjugation, ingenious in its insidious completeness and mimicry of legal slavery; the Civil Rights era—as opposed to the Civil Rights movement—which really began with the imposition of Jim Crow, even before the Niagara Movement, which sowed the seeds of the NAACP, A. Philip Randolph, Ida Wells Barnett, et al; and the now and unnamed, un-defined, un-understood period. It is important to understand each of these periods if we are ever going to understand anything about African American—black—identity. But it occurred to me that, of all these periods, the least familiar and perhaps the most remarkable was that of Reconstruction.

We so easily bandy about the word "pioneer" that it has become quaint and nearly meaningless, boring. But to have been a black "pioneer" in the West just after Sherman had destroyed the South, and so many poor white Mainers and New Hampshirites and Vermonters lay in graves in Pennsylvania and Virginia, and when Lincoln was looking for a way to reunite the country, and this great landmass beckoned, and the idea of being free, FREE, was as intoxicating as wine, and the hurt and the shame and the degradation of being held as chattel was more painful than a bruise—to be a "pioneer" was more than a notion. To have struck out for the western land was a bit more significant than climbing into a Chevrolet and heading west on I-40. For these men and women were literally taking their lives into their own hands. With only God and their own courage and wits and sinew and bones, they had no choice but to make it, or die trying. This is the genius of which I speak, this is the lesson I felt that I, personally, had to relearn.

Destiny. There is something about that word which has always bothered me, and yet the idea excites me just the same. Marianne Moore once wrote: "Think about this saying by Martin Buber: 'The free man believes in destiny and that it has need of him.' Destiny, not fate." I believe that those pioneers must have had a sense of their own destiny. How otherwise can we account for men like Barney Ford, women like Mary Ellen Pleasant? How otherwise could any black woman or man move forward into the gaping maw of chaos and uncertainty, and begin to build themselves?

Has it been lost? That ability, that belief, that grace? Could it be fashioned again? Is the news off the AP wire and Reuters and CNN and *USA Today* African America's destiny? How much of destiny is will, and how much, like the intervention of some Greek deity, is destiny writ by a higher power? In my thinking, I could clearly see two or more worldviews clashing: African and American, pagan and Christian, theological and scientific, John Tucker's and Edward Gordon's.

I left Denver when I left Mr. Gordon, and, as I headed east on I-70, I felt at once a sense of illumination and a sense of confusion. But this time it did not prick my consciousness as a terrible insoluble riddle. Instead, the mixture of certainty and doubt enveloped me more as a mystery. In many ways, Denver and the West had crystallized what once had been for me a gelatinous and semiformed notion about these questions of black culture, African American culture—indeed, American culture. But something in particular about my talks with John Tucker and Edward Gordon seemed to bring many of the overarching questions I had been asking into sharp focus: John Tucker, the ardent essentialist, seeing the connection among black folk as being more than mere science could explain, something ancient and bonding; and Edward Gordon, whose view of Africa held no romance, and whose wry view of what it meant to be black in America was shifting constantly, deeply linked to history and environment. ("Your old men shall dream dreams, and your young men shall see visions.")

In my mind, the Great Debate (though perhaps publicly less a debate than a discussion or an argument, broad and free ranging, diffuse and furious) became less and less about who is wrong and who is right. Nor did I seek to turn it into an exercise in trying to make both views work. (For, though in truth, I probably came closer to Mr. Gordon's way of seeing things, I cannot deny the pull and appeal of John Tucker's sense of a more mystical calling.) Rather, I began to think more about the future, the implications, the imperatives of either view, and how "we," whether "we" acknowledged it or not, were an unusual people on the face of the earth, transformed by a profound wrong many centuries ago; how we all, across this great landmass, were struggling still for satisfactory definition, definition beyond Middle Passage, definition for the coming age. And how, in the light of modern technology—cable television, fax machines, the Internet, jet planes, commercial distribution networks, Xerox machines, satellite dishes, fiber optics, laptop computers—it was not only possible to know what everybody else was talking about, but the Great Debate over what it meant to be black was being fussed over in hostels, houses, and hamlets from the Atlantic to the Pacific and back again, from the Gulf of Mexico to the Bering Sea. The truth was that I was not alone in asking this simple question, *What does it mean to be black?* An entire nation was asking. How, then, could "we" not know more about ourselves than any other "people" by the sheer fact of our restless, infernal, dialectical strut and boogie over the notion of what this identity meant?

And, with that great knowing, how could African Americans fail to achieve themselves? I was beginning to believe—despite the wisdom of the day—that destiny had something greater in store for the descendants of the slaves. But this was just a feeling, unscientific and personal—just a feeling.

# VI

# NIGHT SONG AFTER DEATH

The sun came up walking sideways.

—Zora Neale Hurston,
*Tell My Horse*

Twenty

# ZYDECO WHO?

## Or, Who is Creole?

*Lafayette, Louisiana*

> Say *Cajun,* and you're talking about the Cajuns in Southern Louisiana. Say Creole and you could be talking about any of a number of Creole cultures around the world. If there is a word that exclusively means *Creoles of Southwestern Louisiana,* I haven't heard it. Zydeco is about as close as you get.
>
> —J. F. Smith, *Creole,* August 1991.

New Orleans.

If I want to live in Los Angeles when I die, let me live in New Orleans while I still breathe. Yes, Louis Armstrong. I know what it means to miss New Orleans.

In one of my journals I once wrote: "New Orleans is not really a city." I have no idea what I thought I meant by that. I much prefer the less obscure and straightforward comment the novelist Louis Edwards made to me: "This city seems much older than it is."

I had visited New Orleans a number of times before I came there on the "official" visit. I'd had the pleasure of meeting Louis before. Author of the novels *Ten Seconds* and *N,* he was a native of Lake Charles, Louisiana, who had gone to Louisiana State University in Baton Rouge, and moved to New Orleans afterwards. Louis also worked for the famous New Orleans Jazz and Heritage Festival.

He broadened my sense of the Crescent City. Armstrong Park. Congo Square. The grave of Marie Laveau, where, if you make a cross on her tomb with a bit of brick, spin around and cast the fragment over your shoulder, the "Voodoo Queen" will grant your wish from beyond the pale. We visited the blues station WWOZ FM 90.1. At Faulkner House, the house in the French Quarter where the writer had lived as a young man, now a bookstore owned by a magically ardent and indefatigable bibliophile, we ran into novelist Richard Ford, who now spent most of the year in New Orleans where his wife worked as an urban planner. "Only place in the world," he told me. The campus of Tulane University, the Garden District, Charles Street, Magazine Street, streets with names like Tchoupitoulas and Burgundy (pronounced bur-GUN-dee). Louis took me to Treme (Ward 2), and we happened upon a funeral parade.

Maybe it's the food: trout almandine, gumbo, jambalaya, oyster po'boys, muffalattas, turtle soup with sherry, crawfish *étouffée,* shrimp Creole, oysters on the half shell, red beans and rice. I can say without a smattering of exaggeration that I have never, for breakfast, lunch or dinner, had a bad meal in New Orleans.

Another friend of mine, a native of New Orleans, describes the town as the asshole of America. The massive Mississippi ends its 2,348-mile journey here, bringing the dregs of the American continent along with it. The sight of that river is impressive, dramatic, vastly deep; at night Algiers twinkles sleepily over there on the other side.

New Orleans has a vague sense of menace about it. You have to go after this city, it just sits there, crumbling, bubbling in the delta mud; it does not come after you. Yet, unlike many another city, it is open, inviting—but you must find your own way within it.

The night after I had seen the funeral march, I was so excited I called a friend in New York to tell him about it. Joe sighed and said, "Come on, Kenan, you can do better than that. Everybody has either seen one or seen footage of one. Tell us something we *don't* know about."

He was quite right, of course. New Orleans existed, like only a few other American cities, in a realm of mythology and fantasy and history and romance that made it more than a mere city. Perhaps that is what I meant when I wrote: "New Orleans is not really a city." From Tennessee Williams to William Faulkner to Lillian Hellman to Walker Percy to Anne Rice; from Huey Long to Preservation Hall to Mardi Gras and *A Confederacy of Dunces* and *Angel Heart,* New Orleans is both part of and apart from the broad sweep of the American ethos. Like New York City, it is a center against which America defines itself; and, perhaps more so than New York, New Orleans is our most foreign city. There the loose, drunken, partying society we've come to think of as French and Catholic contrasts with the Protestant and the straitlaced and the early-to-bed/

early-to-rise English. It is all a myth. But in New Orleans's romantic decay, it is possible to project, and isolate, those antidotes to rectitude Americans want to have. We venture to New Orleans to party, to wallow in the muck and beer of licentiousness; to guffaw at the hijinks of corrupt politics; to eat too much, to drink too much, to fornicate too much, to laugh too much, to fall in love too much, to sing and dance too much, to make fools of ourselves too much—in short to enjoy ourselves too much. We Americans like to think we are neither excessive nor sinful, but we need places to exorcise our demons, or at least exercise them. Perhaps that is why we like to think of New Orleans as one of the places where voodoo still has a mojo working, where the black folks are mysterious, the white folk drunken, neurotic aristocrats under the thrall of some wistful, antebellum bygone time—and all remains chaotically well on Bourbon Street, as long as sacrifices are made to Damballah, Legbah and the governor.

Please don't get me wrong. Life for average black folk in New Orleans is rough. The projects, Desire among others, are perhaps some of the most crime-ridden in the nation; gang warfare is alive and real there, as if it hopscotched its way over the great middle. Across the Mississippi in Angola Prison, once one of the scourges of the American penal system, are still hundreds of black men whose proportion to white prisoners screams for examination. Underemployment is high. And, not only are relations between blacks and whites, generally speaking, regressive compared to places like Atlanta or Memphis or Charleston or Savannah, but also there still exist rigid color codes and color barriers between light-skinned and dark-skinned folk. New Orleans has had several black mayors. I defy you to find one as dark as I am. Coincidence?

When John A. Williams visited the city in 1962, he said he had been disappointed, for he suspected it might be a better place than other southern cities. He recounts episodes of dealing with segregation that are almost comic in their absurdity—almost. Nowadays, sadly, conditions for too many black folk in New Orleans are worse than in Jackson or Birmingham or Charlotte or Little Rock. Some might say that's not saying much, but the gains in those other cities are significant; the gains in New Orleans should simply be greater.

Nonetheless, perhaps paradoxically, I have never felt more at home, more welcome, more a part of any black community in America. More at home than at home, alas. Once, after I had raved and raved about the joys and magic of New Orleans, my family decided to take a vacation there. When they returned, they had not one good word to say about New

Orleans: hot, loud, the people behaved badly, the food was too spicy, the black folk seemed backward. I looked at them and said, "You are all just a bunch of bourgeois Negroes." They looked at me blankly and asked, "What's your point?"

Clearly, I love New Orleans too much to write about it in any way that would rip my romantic vision away. Clearly I see through it and love it all at the same time. Perhaps what I love about that city at the bottom of my country is the lack of hypocrisy about its Americanness. Perhaps, for those who don't live there, New Orleans issues a license to leave one's guilt at the border and enjoy the fact that your time on this globe is brief. Perhaps, as a writer of fiction, I am attracted to the impossible density of its skein of history, politics, culture and mythology.

All told, I realized it would be better to go out into Louisiana to a place where the gravitational pull was less acute; a place where the history and the romance were not quite so heady and overwhelming.

Don Cravins's insurance office in Lafayette was a big, red-brick block, and, the morning I arrived to see him, surrounded by cars. Within, workers and visitors bustled about. I sat in the lobby by the Coke machine, and looked down the long, open expanse—full of women clacking typewriters, faxing, phoning, calling "Line 4!" stapling, rustling, printing—through a partial lattice wooden fence. At the very rear, behind opaque golden windows, sat the senator.

His office was surprisingly small—or smaller than I expected—squarish, dominated by a large desk and a print of Tanner's "Guitar Lesson." Don Cravins was a handsome man of tannish complexion with immaculately tended, graying hair. Charismatic. A smoker. All during our conversation, the phone rang and rang and rang; I was impressed by his concentration because he never seemed to lose his train of thought after hanging up.

Senator Cravins graduated from Southern University in 1970 with a degree in political science. "Got married, had three children. Got in the insurance business in the early '70s. Seventy-one to be exact. Lived in Houston for several years. Didn't like it worth a damn. Too big. I'd never live in New York. It would kill me." He had returned to Lafayette in 1981, and started his own business. When I met him, he had been a state senator for two and a half years.

"It's something that I had thought about most of my life. I guess I had gotten very disillusioned with the system as I saw it. One that was not very responsive to the needs of people, particularly poor people."

For decades, the eastern part of Louisiana—New Orleans, Baton Rouge—had sent black members to the state house, but, except for Don Cravins, the southwestern portion of the state had had no African American representation "since Reconstruction." According to Senator Cravins, not being from a metropolitan area "brought something tremendously different. I saw that people were suffering, regardless of whether they were black or white. My focus has been one of economics."

Louisiana has long been famous—or perhaps infamous—for its homegrown political program, one part style, one part socialism, one part capitalism, one part corruption. From Huey Long to incumbent Governor Edwin Edwards, the system seemed not only byzantine, but immune to voter initiatives.

"The reputation it has built, unfortunately, is basically true. It's insensitive, in that those in power have always taken care of those in power. It continues today. But it's changed tremendously, because people are now demanding accountability and responsibility. The new era, new breed of politicians are saying, 'I'm not going to be there long. Doesn't matter.' You know, one of my favorite sayings is, 'I don't give a damn if you don't reelect me.' Politics is not my career. I really just want to make my contribution and get out. Unfortunately, that has not been the mood of most people in politics. The bureaucracy and the politics feed on itself. It is what you've heard about Louisiana—even though they would jump up and down and say it's a damn lie. Most of it is true. Now it's changing because people are scrutinizing politics and politicians very, very closely. The press I think has done a real good job—some of the press. Those that are not part and parcel of that same group. Out of necessity we have shifted our emphasis from people to economics. I know the future will demand that we go back and reinvest in people. For a lot of reasons. Number one is, we have a generation of kids that we have basically lied to and told that they can do a lot of things, and they find that once they get into the system, they can't be part of it because there's really nothing there to offer them."

Recently, former Grand Imperial Wizard of the Ku Klux Klan David Duke—newly coiffured and tailored—had made a credible bid for governor. Don Cravins found the race "interesting."

"A lot of things happened. One thing is that racism became very pronounced. You could see it. I think it polarized the state to a large extent.

On race. That was the vehicle for a lot of people to vent frustration over a system that had failed them. And on the other side of the coin, it also put people together. It empowered the grassroots.

"It inflamed people," he told me. African Americans sent a message "loud and clear." In some precincts, voter turnout was as high as 90 percent—unheard of in all the country.

"The masses turned out in numbers, saying, 'We are not going to stand for David Duke. We're going to show that we mean business.' I don't think politics will ever be the same in this state as a result. Because we have come to the realization that indeed we have power in the ballot. Because we make up a large percentage of this state."

He could see, all about him, signs of a reenergized, grassroots politicized black community. "This community lived the Civil Rights movement of the '60s. It really did. But I think you have probably more activism, right now, than you did in the '60s." The NAACP was attacking the school system, "this organization, that organization." Independent voices were speaking out. " 'Why is it that we are not part of that particular group?' they are asking. People are finally rising and saying, 'We have to do something about it.' But in order to correct the problem, we got to beat the system through the political process."

About eight years earlier, Don Cravins had been invited by the manager of radio station Z-100, KAG, to do a Zydeco program. He had never done radio before, but welcomed the chance. He emceed the program with an engineer, and eventually they fell into an on-air conversation that became very popular with the audience. That led to a local television program. "Has a very wide audience. But I don't do it for money, I do it simply because I enjoy it. For me it's a break from the regular routine.

"Radio offers me an opportunity to talk to people and they can't talk back to me." He laughed. "But it also gives me an opportunity to keep a sense of the community, because we get phone calls. It has proven to be something very rewarding for me. From a political vantage point, it was an extremely useful tool in my quest for office. I became very well known in the community. They always said, 'I knew you from the show.' "

For him, Zydeco music was a part of the culture that produced him. "Part of something that I truly enjoy, because I think it's very unique. It's a combination of a lot of things. Joys and sorrows and food, and I guess religion and a little bit of everything. It has been one of the rewarding experiences of my life."

That said, I wondered if Don Cravins felt black folks from this part of the world saw themselves as being separate from the larger black culture.

"To some degree. It's really a different culture. I mean, if you took me, for example, and brought me into New York City, to Harlem—I think as similar as we are, and we are truly brothers—I think that there's a very distinct difference in our culture. I was brought up in the Catholic Church. I come from a community that has been Catholic forever. And French. 'Let the good times roll.' I mean, that kind of thing. The food and I guess even in the way we do things, and our feelings, to a large extent, may be very different. We know that Africa is our motherland, and we're still black and we're African Americans. But there is a difference."

One particular distinction in that part of Louisiana had to do with the stress—at least in the not-too-distant past—placed on skin color among African Americans. The senator was very polite in referring to "certain factions, certain groups within the black community, that would not associate with other groups. I mean, separation, even within the community. It's abating. There was a settlement near Baton Rouge. There was certainly one in Opelousas. In Iberia Parish. Where actually they would only marry their own. That hasn't been many years ago. Now people are kind of blending more, and it's changing, slowly. I remember that so vividly when I was growing up. And even as a young adult."

Certain terms still confused me, I explained to Mr. Cravins. Was there a distinction between "Creole" and "black French?"

"Creole and black French? Well, I guess you probably would call the Creoles black Frenchmen. There's not really a whole lot of distinction. I think that Creole was maybe more of a perception, because it was those people of African heritage who spoke French, basically. I think that people look at Creoles as those who spoke French, and not so much based on skin color. You have communities now that you could go to, and I bet you wouldn't understand what the hell they're saying.

"My mother and dad speak French. That's their language, even though that particular part of the heritage is beginning to die. The young folks don't know the language at all. It has also something to do with food. Different kinds of cuisine. Real hot and spicy food.

"Tell you what was very similar to it. I was in Martinique a few years ago. Found the language to be very, very similar, because they do have a Creole dialect there, and they speak a French dialect that is very similar to the Creole that's spoken here. As a matter of fact, I had the good fortune to serve as the interpreter for the group that I was with, my brother and I, because the others didn't understand a damn thing. Even the appearance of people there. There's a very similar appearance, and the way people look and talk was very, very similar. You have different segments. New

Orleans, for example, claims a large Creole population, which I've never been able to identify."

Despite the media love affair with quaint, exotic, down-home, Cajun-flavored, alligator-infested, bayou-scented Louisiana—the cooking shows of Justin Wilson, Paul Prudhomme, Emeril Lagasse; the movies and the television shows set in the Big Easy, even the plays of Lillian Hellman and Tennessee Williams—the foundation of my thinking about the state had been influenced by a few excellent books: Robert Penn Warren's *All the King's Men,* T. Harry Williams's biography, *Huey Long,* and the novels of Ernest Gaines.

Like most Americans, I had first learned of Ernest Gaines through the award-winning TV movie adaptation of his novel, *The Autobiography of Miss Jane Pittman,* starring Cicely Tyson. To this day, most folk think of it as an "autobiography" and not a work of fiction, and this is testament to the prowess of the author.

Later, while in college, I would read his lesser-known, though far from lesser works, the four novellas of *Bloodline,* the novels *Catherine Carmier, A Gathering of Old Men* (also made into a television movie), *In My Father's House,* and the most recent, *A Lesson Before Dying,* which won the 1995 National Book Critics Circle Award for best novel.

I find it interesting that, with the exception of Louis Edwards and poet Brenda Marie Osbey, Gaines is practically the only African American writer of and about Louisiana to gain a national, and in his case international, recognition. All his novels are set in St. Raphael Parish—very like the Pointe Coupee Parish where he grew up in the quarter of Riverlake Plantation; it was still called, and in effect still was, a plantation in those years. That is the milieu about which Gaines writes: a few white planters, a multitude of blacks. It is a feudal world, an antebellum world; a world where, in the middle of the twentieth century, little has changed. That stasis had been shocking when I first read Gaines's work. In its outward dress, the world of these characters did not seem, at first, too different from my own rural background, but then there were layers (French, Catholic) and the sense of time having stood still for all these people living not too distantly from slavery. And then the introduction, as if an anachronism, of something quintessentially modern (like the militant son who returns to the plantation in the story "Bloodline"), which unnerves and angers. Gaines is a subtle, tight writer, who, like Flannery O'Connor, situates his meanings in such a way that they are omnipresent throughout a story, as obvious as the light of the sun—always there in the sky, yet never calling attention to themselves. His themes—dignity, honor, manhood and womanhood—are at once bedrock and large, so much so that one would assume them to be self-evident. But clearly, to a large segment of the population of southwestern Louisiana, they are not so apparent. That is the point of his work.

Until the summer of 1993, when I visited Lafayette for two weeks, Ernest Gaines had split each year between San Francisco and Lafayette, where he was a professor at the University of Southwest Louisiana. But that year, the sixty-five-year-old MacArthur Award winner had married a woman who lived in Florida, and was spending the summer there with her. I regretted not having a chance to speak with him. I was curious to know why, over the decades, he chose to keep coming back to that area, despite what he, without a doubt, saw to be its deep-rooted problems. What was it about the idea—the reality?—of home that compelled him to keep up his ties here? I suspected I knew, but I was keen to hear his own answer.

That which is Spanish and that which is French is apt to be Catholic. When these two empires enjoyed their greatest expansion, they were Catholic monarchies. Southern North America was essentially a Catholic domain long before the Puritans got their act together in the North. Therefore it is no mystery why the southwest holds the largest concentration of black Catholics in the country. But there were black Catholics long before the invasion of the New World.

It is said that there were three African Popes: Victor I, Melchiades and Gelasius I. St. Benedict the Black and St. Martin de Porres were dark-skinned Africans. It was Pope Pius II who declared slaveholding a grievous sin in 1462. Black priests and nuns existed in Africa long before the slave trade even began. In most of the islands of the Caribbean, Catholicism is still the main religion of black folks.

KJCB Radio, Lafayette—jazz, blues, R&B, gospel—770 AM. Motto: "Knowledge is Power."

The station was located in an old store on Jefferson Street—the former main drag in town—across from Abdulla's Department Store. I found it surprisingly open, space-wise, and unlike a radio station; more like, well, an insurance office, a government agency, a tax accountant's office, or a jewelry store on Main Street, USA, turned into a radio station—which is what it was. In the windows were signs for an "Annual School Supply Drive and Radio-Thon!"

Jé Nelle Chargois was general manager of KJCB, a post she had held for almost two years. Originally she was from Lafayette. Prior to coming to work for the station, she had been a lobbyist in the nation's capital. She had started, she told me, working on the local level, then on the state level for business, and then she got "tied up with some people in the Republican Party."

She had worked on "all types of issues. There were two black Republican lobbyists. Thelma Duggan and myself. We tried to do more sensitizing on the issues, and actually convince them that issues were right or wrong. It was interesting. You know, there are a lot of issues, family issues, things that I think we can do better on. I think where we separate the waters is on issues of education, issues of civil rights, those issues work more on the contradictions."

Chargois graduated from Holy Rosary Institute in 1967. She told me that that eighty-year-old institution was one of the few remaining places of significant African American education left in the area. In March of that year, the bishop of the diocese decided to close the school due to low enrollment, lack of funds, and the sorry condition of the physical plant. A group of alumni had gotten together to oppose the closing. One of the biggest local problems was the large number—27 percent—of African American boys suspended or expelled from public schools in the parish, who then went to Holy Rosary. What would happen to these young men in the coming years? "Are we preparing ourselves for another generation of illiterate youngsters?

"As we began to analyze what had occurred at Holy Rosary, we came to the conclusion that its closing was premeditatedly calculated by the diocese, purely for finances. Holy Rosary Institute sits on some forty-seven acres of prime land in the city. The logical way to address this is to raise money to recruit students and to get the community involved in repairing the physical plant. We sent a number of letters to the bishop of the diocese indicating that we wanted to discuss a plan for community control of the school since we understood the diocese could no longer financially support it. He wouldn't agree to talk with us."

The bishop finally did meet with them, but was indifferent to the group's proposals, and essentially said it was his decision, and his alone. "So that paternalistic attitude was a real turnoff for us."

But they were continuing to fight—even if it meant going to the Pope, which they were in the process of doing. "I think the whole Rosary incident is like a catalyst for a number of problems that have been arising, not only out of the Catholic Church, but across this country. But I also see, now more than ever, a willingness of the community to unify. And to stand up and be counted. That's the good thing that has come out of all this, that all walks of life, various socioeconomic backgrounds have stood up and said, 'No, I don't think it's going to be that way.' It's regrettable. It's regrettable because the bishop has really not offered us a real reason why he's closed the school.

"The sad part of it is that I don't think the diocese cares whether black people leave or not. If you have half of your major churches empty on Sunday, if you had 700 Catholics (they say 700; it's actually 897) who decide not to go to church, that should cause you some concern. But they have not expressed any concern, other than this paternalistic letter that the bishop wrote. 'We have always been good to the coloreds.' The manner in which the Church is run, from Rome down to the local dioceses across the country, I just think that they're insensitive. They really don't care. For the bishop of the diocese to show up at a meeting in the heart of the black community with police officers—my God.

"It makes the potential for the demise of black Roman Catholic churches a strong possibility. A strong possibility." To be sure, there were integrated Catholic churches, but they were "integrated by default."

There were no black ministers at white churches. No predominantly white congregations had ever actively recruited African Americans. "I don't think that race relations are any different here. I think there's a decline in race relations across this country. I think it has to do more with economics, though. Anytime the economy is bad, we look for people to blame it on. And so over the last twelve years, or maybe even longer, during the economy's steady decline, we saw the rise of the skinheads, and the renewal of the Ku Klux Klan. It was people who felt that economically they had lost and somebody was taking what was theirs. And who was the most vulnerable to blame but us?"

Another reason Jé Nelle Chargois lamented the potential closing of Holy Rosary was that it had always been a training ground for young people, for leadership. Since the advent of integration, she said, that component had gone sorely lacking. "You have this big, vast majority of teenagers who are just standing in the middle of the road, not knowing where to go, and none of them have the tools or the skills to say, this is the way you should be going. When we were coming up within the segregated process, before you even learned how to read and write, you learned how to lead. You learned how to stand up and articulate your needs and the needs of others." This was the job of the church, of the community, she said.

"We are a product of the extended family. We were made to think, somewhere about twenty years ago, that the extended family concept was bad. We began to portray our community as being a community of single parents. But that is nothing new for us. See, we always had grandma, grandpa, aunts and uncles, the lady down the street, who contributed to that family learning process. Suddenly we became distant, and we also began to internalize the 'me' values. That broke up what conceptually our black family is. What American society defines as family—mom, dad, children—is not necessarily a definition of our family. We've gotten away from taking care of business as a family."

> And what about the color issue? Through my research and contact with various individuals, I have discovered that much hostility and resentment is harbored in many a black person's soul in regard to the conceptions which have arisen from the term Creole. For example, among members of the white community, the word Creole conjures up images of mammies and praline-makers. On the other hand, one black female historian accused me of basing my work on the notion that the Creole of color is strictly a light-skinned, upper-class individual with little desire to maintain an identity with the greater black community. Eventually, I convinced her that my mission was to dispel the myth that Creoles were all light-skinned as well as to show that many nineteenth century Creoles were both large land and slave-owners as well as carpenters and blacksmiths.
>
> —Helene Goudeau, "Importance of Preserving the Creole Culture," *Creole,* January 1991

However, I can prove to you that the promotion of Cajun/Acadiana is a form of white colonialism, promoting white superiority and white people are making us pay for it by using taxpayers' funds. Imagine the reaction and attitude of white people if black people change everything tomorrow that is now Cajun/Acadiana to Nigger/Niggeranna. How many white persons do you know would send their child to USL, home of the Ragin' Niggers? Do you think white people would allow the building on Congress Street to remain there if it was named the Nigger Dome? . . . How many white folks you know would stop in this area if they read a billboard sign on the highway that read "Welcome, this is Nigger Country." Now to add insult to injury, we tell white people we used their tax dollars to create our selfish world. Then say to them, "Don't worry, be happy."

White people would not sit still for such foolishness. They would declare bloody war within 24 hours. Brothers and sisters, you could not colonialize white people under a good black label—much less a racial slur that they gave us. If you say you are not a Nigger—then you should also reject being called a Cajun. Remember Cajun = Acadiana too.

—Takuna Maulana El Shabazz, "Promotion of 'Cajun/Acadiana' is Colonialism," *Creole,* December 1992

Ironically, the language and culture of the Cajuns and the black Creoles overlap a great deal and in important areas. The two communities have enjoyed considerable contact through much of their history together here in south Louisiana. It is no accident, for example, that both groups make gumbo (from African tradition) and etouffee (from French tradition), and that Cajun music is bluesy and old-time Zydeco is sung in French. Even during the worst of Jim Crow segregation, neighbors helped each other across color lines in times of need. Yet the two groups toward the bottom of the economic and social ladders often found themselves competing for the second-to-last rung, especially after the Civil War, and this competition has fueled an unhealthy amount of tension, resentment and racism throughout the years. The recent David Duke phenomenon was fueled in part by this ongoing class struggle to stay off the bottom of the pile. And no one wins when the fighting gets that dirty.

—Barry Jean Ancelet, "Ragin' Cajuns: What's in a Name?" *Creole,* December 1992

Louisiana is one of the most confusing (and confused) and complex cultural stews in the country. Take for example, three terms: Cajun, Creole, black French.

These three terms are at once emblematic of the state's rich past and the source of great misunderstanding and misinterpretation, all rooted in cultural, political and color issues.

Cajun is the easiest. "Cajun" comes from "Acadian." The current Cajuns are descendants of those French-speaking settlers of Nova Scotia and New Brunswick who the British had deported in 1755, and who arrived in French-controlled Louisiana in the mid-1760s. When the Acadians arrived in Louisiana their culture was different from that of the Quebecois and the French nationals—they had been in the maritimes for over a hundred years and had social intercourse with the Micmacs and the British. Louisiana would further inject their culture with cultural influences from Spain and Africa. Mostly, the Acadians settled west of New Orleans. Theirs is a distinct culture.

Creole is neither so straightforward nor as clear. So very much depends on geography, and who you ask. In New Orleans, it has two very distinct meanings: (1) the "white" aristocrats who are directly descended from the original French settlers, who came after the Spanish, whose tongue therefore is an admixture of New World French, some Spanish, and a smattering, of course, of African dialects; (2) the mulatto, self-perpetuating, self-generating, self-marrying, self-justifying society suspended somewhere between black folk and white folk. Theirs is a society they claim, for all intents and purposes, rightly, to be over 400 years old. Not a few New Orleans Creoles will tell you, despite what the law says, that they are not black. Many will not marry black or white. Many will say that old way of thinking is silly and regressive and racist. Regardless, it still exists. They inherited a language, similar yet slightly different from, the "white" Creoles.

Then there are the black French, mostly to the west. Black men and women, light, dark, middle, who also call themselves Creole. For them it is a language, a culture, and of course, a way of thinking. Being Creole is about language, Catholicism, food, Zydeco, rituals, customs.

Is there no such thing as a black Cajun? Even more, if your mother is Cajun and your daddy is half black French and half Creole, are you then a black French Cajun Creole?

I have looked long and hard. No one is an authority, and yet everyone seems to be an authority. Some folk couldn't care less, and some folk get into great ire if the term is misapplied.

Who is right? I decided to ask the editor of *Creole* magazine.

. . .

Ruth Foote was then editor and publisher of *Creole* magazine. She described herself as an army brat. She had been born in Altsburg, Germany, and the family had lived in Munich and Frankfurt, and Seattle and Tacoma, Washington, and later Georgia before returning to Lafayette, which she considered her father's town. She had been in Lafayette since the age of nine.

She founded *Creole* in 1990, with Emmette Jacobs, Jr. She had freelanced for the *Times of Acadia,* and had worked for four years on the Opelousas *Daily World.* She had spent eight months on the Sarasota *Herald Tribune* in Florida, but she disliked Florida.

"Our goal was to provide an informative newspaper and magazine for the African American community here that was professionally done. We wanted to cover a wide range of issues that were affecting the community. Blacks read the regular paper, but the issues aren't targeted to them. Like AIDS. We did a series on AIDS and what it means to the black community. We did a series on the black male crisis. And issues like that."

For their first issue, they produced 10,000 copies, and their circulation rose as high as 20,000—though it now hovered at around 10,000.

"It's free with advertising. And we have about 200 to 300 subscribers across the country."

Ruth Foote's goal was to make the magazine more subscription-oriented. Finding advertisers for the monthly was becoming increasingly difficult. She still did freelancing on the side.

"We're struggling. Put it like that."

Surely Ruth Foote would be the person to shed light on the word "Creole."

"In my first column, that's what I wrote. I said, 'Creole means a lot of different things. There's a million different definitions for it.' I put it as the culture that we grew up with. What we're used to, our food, our music. So I kind of gave it an umbrella definition. I mean, there's so many different definitions.

"I named it *Creole* and I remember I had a friend who said, 'Are you sure you want to name it "Creole"?' And he said the only reason he was saying that was because of the thing with skin color. There were in the past—and I guess there still are—those who discriminate because of their skin color. He said, 'Well, maybe in Lafayette it's not the same.' He lived in Opelousas. But another reason we named it *Creole* was because everything at that time was being marketed as Cajun. And a lot of things that are Creole were going under the Cajun banner. Cajun is really a term they're promoting for tourism. They're even calling some people black Cajuns, which is illogical.

"So that was another reason to promote the black French culture too. Whether or not you consider yourself a Creole. Because a Creole can mean a pitch-black person or a light-skinned person. It can mean a person who grew up speaking Creole or it can be a person that's mixed down with a French/Spanish/African background. It can mean somebody from Haiti. Or New Orleans Creole. There are so many different definitions."

She told me that even out in the western parishes, skin color mattered in some places. People she had interviewed remembered being subjected to the famous paper bag test in nearby clubs. (You passed the test if you were lighter than the brown paper bag.) And she told me about "the comb test." "It had better go straight. We still have people like that." Some people still intermarry to insure that the "color line" remained "pleasing."

"That's a problem I just think you have in the whole culture. I don't think it's just the Creole, but in the mulatto, going back to slavery, the lighter-skinned people, you still have that. There's a movement in California right now, to have Creole separated on the census. They want it distinct. There's people who are pushing that. My view is that the black race shouldn't be separated. There's already enough to separate us."

Was black French culture surviving? "It's not predominant here. I remember, I had a friend who was living in New Orleans, and I ran into him. I was telling him about the magazine and he went, 'Oh, Creole. I just really don't like the term.' He's fair-skinned, straight hair, and he started explaining to me how he went to dance with a friend who was getting married, and her mother told him, 'Oh, she should be marrying you instead of that black person.' So you still have that. I guess it's the older generation.

"I remember seeing *The Maury Povich Show,* and sometimes other shows, which will have these light-skinned people on, and they'll say how they're passing for white. And we look at them. 'If you came to Louisiana, we'd all know you're black.' Where people up North just do not realize. I remember in college, I had a girlfriend who was fair-skinned, and she was working as a manager in a restaurant, and they just assumed she was white. This boyfriend of hers came in who was pitch black and the next thing she knew she was fired. I guess they suddenly made the connection, 'Oh, she must be black.'

"Zydeco is reaching more and more young people. It's ingrained into the community. But as far as the language, that has been totally lost, I would say."

"Totally lost?"

"It's been more or less practiced among the forty year olds and above, but the next generation hasn't received it. In the old days, you were ridiculed if you spoke Creole. It was kind of stigma-like. You're country. It's not a written dialect."

She had been in touch with people who were working on a Creole dictionary, which was proving to be more than a notion, since there were so many subdialects. Lake Charles was different from Lafayette which was different from Baton Rouge, which was different from Haitian, which was different from Beaux Bridge. She found it sad that while so many young African Americans, especially during the sixties and seventies, were talking about returning to their roots, this root was neglected.

"Sometimes I'll get calls from young people who have done their history project on Creoles, and they want, maybe histories, or they want sources or something. So I see there is interest with the young people but as far as the language, I don't know. The generation that spoke it fluently, or who couldn't even speak English, they did everything to send their children to school and to college, so they wouldn't be in a rural area. That generation remembers it from their parents, but they didn't pass it on."

I found it clear that a huge part of black French, or Creole, culture was Catholicism. But it was shifting now, Ruth told me. "I'm not Catholic, but I feel that it's happening more and more. I know I did this anniversary booklet for a black Catholic church in New Iberia. They did their whole anniversary in African style. I remember some of the members telling me other members of the church were kind of in shock about it, but they went forward with it. I think in each Catholic church there's groups that want to be more Africanized. I know people that have left the Catholic Church searching for a more—I don't know if the word is 'spiritual setting.' I did go with the Ladies' Altar Society of a black Catholic church, on a retreat in Bay St. Louis. We visited a church out there, and there was a priest who had been in this area, and everybody was clapping and real excited, and I remember when we got back on the bus, the women all said, 'Wow, if we could only have that. I'm tired of going to church and just feeling like I didn't get anything.' I think there's a definite change going on."

She had seen figures stating that that part of Louisiana had the highest concentration of black Catholics in the country. But she questioned the extent of the Church's authority in the lives of black folk today. "I feel like a lot of people just remain in it, and then there are those who break. But I think there's a group that feels really comfortable within it."

I mentioned the number of black people out West who claimed roots in

Louisiana, which seemed like an Old World to the New West. "It's almost as if Louisiana's their roots. Everybody's roots. I would say that we're like everybody else, but we've been enriched with a flavor. I don't know how to describe it. More down home. I don't mean countrified, but maybe a respect for our roots, that we know where we came from.

"I remember when I was living in Florida, I just didn't sense that. I think we have more of that—I hate to say it—'let the good times roll' atmosphere. You don't realize that it's not there until you leave it. You take things for granted, until you go somewhere else, and you realize that something's gone.

"I think blacks here are just as concerned with the different issues that are going on worldwide. There is this sense of people wanting to be in tune. I think that's happening with black people nationwide. It's all part of the Afrocentric movement."

I found this line of thought interesting, and asked Ruth Foote to define black for me: "It's very much like the question about Creole, isn't it? Is black cultural? Is it in some way genetic? A biological thing? Or is it merely a political construction, having to do with history?

"I would say all of the above," she said. "We're all composed of everybody else. A lot of times people have interviewed me, and asked, 'Oh, do you consider yourself Creole?' I want to say, 'I consider myself an African American first,' because of the misconceptions about Creole. We're a unique type of black. But I think we all share a common bond, and need to keep the unity.

"I think it's political, definitely. It can't help but be political, because we have so much catching up to do. Economic standards for black folks are not up to par, not where they should be as far as being represented in power decisions. Racism still exists, probably will always exist. When I say 'culture,' we have a background and even though maybe some of our heritage has been lost, and we can't all trace our roots back to Africa, we still share the common thread, and I think that's what makes us, you know, a cultural group, because of our heritage, what's brought us this far.

"It's funny. Sometimes, when I say 'race' it's not skin color. Sometimes, in groups you'll find that you'll have somebody who's pitch black, who's anti-black, and then somebody who looks white, who is as pro-black as you can be."

Recently *Creole* did an issue devoted to "the black male crisis." This was something that preoccupied Ruth Foote.

"I mean, they are like walking time bombs. They're frustrated. They don't give a damn anymore. They want to vent their anger, and it's bottled up, and they're going to explode one day. Right now I'm pessimistic. I'm realistically pessimistic. I'm romantically optimistic. I don't know. I feel the only solution is a drastic one, which can't be done. Those children have to be gathered up and taken out of the poverty-stricken areas—the drugs, the violence—and put in schools, boarding schools, that teach them pride and their African heritage. The young people are not teaching their children. The parents are too tired. It's not like the extended family where you can know grandma raises the children."

Recently, Ruth had done volunteer work in a tutorial program designed to counter the high dropout rate among black teenagers. "It was so doggoned depressing. Fathers in jail. Fathers on drugs. Fathers selling drugs.

"They put a little girl in my group, because she was cutting up in the other group. I told her to write her name on her paper. She reached down and lifted up her knapsack, to see how to spell her last name. This little girl was about seven or eight. I just looked at her, and I said, 'You're too old not to know how to spell your name.' And I think what's happening is a lot of these children are being passed through school, and the reason they become frustrated in later years is because they're really helpless, and they don't know they're helpless, so they become angry. They're sitting up in classes, and they don't know what the hell is going on. They are just pushed on till they can be pushed out, or they get pregnant, or they drop out, or they are suspended or expelled.

"It dawned on me that this little girl was cutting up and screaming, and I could see her. She was a miniature eighteen year old. I felt the reason she was angry was that she didn't know anything. She couldn't even spell her last name, and she was probably sitting in a class where a teacher didn't understand. She hadn't even got the doggone basics. We're doing multiplication but you never learned your times tables.

"It's kind of like the things that made you, you no longer think are important. You know what I'm saying?"

Every now and again, Ruth Foote taught as a substitute in the public schools. One group of black boys almost drove her crazy one day, she told me. "I talked to about twelve of them, because I was telling them about competing in the world and our jobs going overseas and that they'd better get their minds together and start studying, and the importance of education, and some of them seemed like they were grasping what I was saying. I kept them after class, and I remember I told them, 'You know, I'm not trying to be mean, but you just don't understand what's out there. The world is out there. It's a tough world.'

"One of them said, 'Yeah, what you're saying makes sense.' But I knew a lot of what I was saying was going in one ear and right out of the other."

Unlike the most dour existentialists of the 1950s, I basically enjoy life. There are many small pleasures I truly love, without which life might indeed be hell, and not worth the pain of birth. One such pleasure, if you haven't guessed it, for me, is food: I love to eat.

I had eaten well most of the summer of 1993, and my weight proved it. I found one humble fish place in Lafayette that I went to practically every day I was there. Darrell Borque, of the University of Southwest Louisiana, had taken me to a small restaurant, named Mama's, that served the spiciest collard greens and the biggest, most succulent turkey wings in creation—so large they had to belong to mutant turkeys. Ed Renee told me the best crawfish *étouffée* could be had at a restaurant outside of Opelousas, and asked me if I would like to join him there for dinner.

I said, What time?

Ed Renee taught high school at Eunice Junior High School. He taught Spanish and English. He had majored in journalism and was working on a masters in creative writing.

"I think the meaning of Creole is based solely on color, not so much the language. Also people who don't want to identify themselves as blacks or African American, they'll say, 'Well, I'm Creole.' Okay? They don't want to attach that stigma of being black.

"On occasion, I hear people say, 'Well, I speak Creole French.' I really don't pay too much attention. From what I understand, Creole French is like broken down French. There are some shortcuts in it, and African Americanisms, right? From here in the South. And most southern blacks speak what they refer to as 'Creole French.' Now, how different that is from the French that Cajuns speak I don't know. Because I don't speak French. My father speaks it. My mother can understand it. In the household they did not speak it all the time. In the house it was not stressed. It was not the language that they used. My grandmother and my grandfather, that's all they spoke. Until their kids went off to school, then they learned how to speak English, and they also taught their parents. My father's family, who are mostly light-skinned people, they consider themselves Creole. Before they will marry someone dark-skinned, they'll marry somebody in their own family, a distant relative. To keep that Creole blood in the family. Now my dad is the only one strayed away from that.

"Nobody ever talks about what Creole actually is," Ed said. "And you know, some people identify it differently. But the people that I've been around, it's basically black. Even in Gaines's book—I think it's *Catherine Carmier*—he actually referred to white men who were speaking Creole. Basically that's all I know about Creole. I really have never even given it any thought before."

Ed thought it was easy to still find examples of people marrying along color lines. "It's not as monumental as it once was. Because most of your older people are dying off, so this younger generation is not inclined to give in to what was. They've started to change. But there are still some of them who will go and seek out other mulattoes. And they'll marry them. But it's not practiced too much anymore with relatives." He laughed. "Not that much. But when they do, from what I understand, they marry distant cousins. I heard a lady I used to work with, and she considers herself a Creole, she always talks with the foreign guys or white guys. And one time I asked her, Why? She must be about forty-something. She told this to me and another guy, that her mother and her grandparents taught her not to like things that were black, people that were black, because they were bad and evil. Then she started talking about the symbolism of the badness of black. 'Why, when someone dies, do we have to be in black? Why are kids scared of the dark? Okay? Why is everything that's black associated with bad stuff?' But it backfired because to this day, she's a very unhappy lady. Very unhappy.

"Another case in point. There's a coworker of mine. She has a son who's in the seventh grade, going into eighth grade. And she does not want you to say that he's black. He will fight you if you say he's black. And they're black. They're black. Well, he could pass for somebody white. Easily. Some people know that he's black. And if you identify him as being an African American, he will fight you. He does not want you to say that. Okay. It stems from the upbringing in the household. His parents told him their definition of what he was. And that's a big problem right now, because he has a lot of discipline troubles in school. His mother and father are the cause of it. They really think they're white. When we have open house in school, his mother never comes by black teachers. She stays with the white teachers. And there's another coach, a black guy, who, to be facetious sometimes, he'll say, 'Hey, come here, black boy.'

And the boy will just get upset. And one time his father came to school and reprimanded a teacher for calling his son 'black.' So you see what I'm saying. It's still prevalent in that area where the parents will teach the child not to identify with being black."

Ed Renee told me the high school where he taught had a population of about 670 students, and that about 70 percent of them were white and roughly 30 percent black, essentially the demographics for the state itself.

Black and white students are establishing a good rapport, he said. "Now three years ago, at the same school, there was a lot of rioting. Lots of fights, racial things." The principal at this school was a black man. "He's come a long way. When they first started to integrate the school, he told me how tough it was. They had problems, about two or three years ago, fighting, because of race. All it takes is one student to start it, and then it feels like a chain reaction."

I was interested to know Ed's opinion, from his point of view as a high school teacher, of why so many young black men were dropping out and essentially disappearing from the educational system.

"The eighth grade, that's really the level where it's time to decide, 'What am I going to do? Will I stop here? Or will I continue to go on?' And many of them see school as unnecessary. 'I can go work on my uncle's farm. Or my dad's.' And a lot of them do quit school. A lot of them drop out. Around that age, eighth and ninth grade. It's usually those who have not been successful academically. They're beginning to think they're men and women, so 'Now I have to make this decision. Do I want to struggle and continue going? But it's so hard, and I don't want to do it, and I have my uncle. Or, I can do the trade school, and I can learn a trade and get a good job. I can get paid better than you. You're a teacher. And I'll make more money than you.' So that's true. Okay?

"A lot of them have that attitude. Especially when we're going over grammar. 'Well, Mr. Renee, I don't know why we need to know this, because when I go look for a job, am I going to actually need to know what is a preposition?' Really. That's what they question you on. 'Why do I have to learn what this is?'

"One thing I noticed, with parents of today, is that they're very, very selfish. They don't spend enough time with their kids. When I was coming up, I was fortunate in that I had parents who were not selfish. They weren't fortunate. They could not finish school. So they sacrificed a lot of things for their kids to achieve something. But parents these days want what they want. On weekends, most of them go to the mall, or they go to their friend's house or something. The parent of that child is not bad, but the thing is, the parents do not spend that much time with the child. I think you have a whole new breed of parents. It's basically become very selfish."

As far as Ed Renee was concerned, everything stemmed from the home (something I had been hearing time and time and time again), even attention span. He seemed to loathe the term Attention Deficit Disorder, ADD. "If there's something wrong with the child, you can't holler at them. You can't fuss and you can't correct them. Really, what it comes down to is that your teachers and administrators, they're working for the parents. They have to please the parents. And the parents are not pleased when something has to be done. So the teachers are really against the wall. I mean, out of 135 students, I probably had about 6 or 7 of them like that. Most of them really try. And those who don't, you try all kinds of intervention, and then, when you see it's useless, and well, as long as they don't disrupt the educational process, you just let them slide, and then when they get their report card, they have Fs; usually those type parents, they don't come. They just let it go. Some of those kids say they'll go get their GED, and they'll go into the army or something.

"What happens a lot with black students is the school board might put them in special education programs. You put them in Special Ed, and you get them out quicker. They'll have this little certificate. So you see what I'm saying? That's very wrong. Because these school board officials are telling these parents, 'Well, your child, blah, blah, blah. He'll get out earlier. He'll have his certificate.' They don't try to see what's wrong with that child. They immediately put him into Special Ed. And you don't do that. You're cheating a child. But school officials are more than willing to do that. I read an article about two years ago, about how there's a huge proportion of blacks in Special Ed. When they have discipline problems, they immediately put them in Special Ed.

"Let me tell you. I had a student my first year teaching, and he became friends with me. They put him in Special Ed. I started talking to him and finding out what was wrong. What it was, he was all alone, because everybody's been putting him down. Nobody gave him attention. All he wanted was attention in class. And that's why he was rude. He wanted that attention because he wouldn't get it at home. And lo and behold, he turned out to graduate. He proved them wrong."

Sitting where he sat, seeing as he saw, I wondered if Ed Renee was at all optimistic about the future.

"I'm very pessimistic. With the whole world for me. Honestly. I don't know. I just see things, bad things, continue to happen. Every time you put on your radio, or your TV, you read the newspaper, the bad things that happen. I think until African Americans, well, young African Americans really, stop valuing money and material items the way they do, I think we're doomed. There's this big drug thing, and a lot of my students, I hear them. They're going to be a drug dealer."

"You mean, they actually say that?" I asked.

"Yes. Lo and behold, it does occur. Because when they go home, their parents don't care, so they stay on the street corners, maybe selling drugs. And if they want nice things, Air Jordans, Nikes, they want these things, and they'll do whatever they have to do to get them. Unless something drastically changes with the black male, something bad's going to happen. I hate to be pessimistic, but I don't see anything changing. Things are only getting worse. I don't know what the future will hold. I really don't."

I wondered aloud where and when the notion of delayed gratification gets lodged in a person's brain.

"The younger generation, they want it right then and there," Ed said. "They don't want to wait. I think that it's the society and also the media assault. I hear a lot of kids saying, 'Well, tomorrow I might not be here, with all the things that happen, so I gots to get mine. I gots to get mine before it's too late. I might not be here tomorrow.'

"They hear it in the news. They see the newspaper. And these rap songs don't add anything to it. One of them said something the other day, he said, 'The man is out to get us.' So they're going to use that. 'I got to steal from the rich and give to the poor.'

"I really think we've lost our morals. Our ethics. Our discipline that we once had. It's like everything is in a rush. I talk to my grandmother and she says, 'Time passes so fast. Time is moving so fast.' And I think it's our fault, because we've technologized everything. Everything seems to be moving so, so fast. Used to, you would sit down as a family, you'd eat. That rarely happens today, because everybody's got to do what they got to do."

Of course hip-hop culture had found its way into that part of Louisiana, but Ed told me the young folk, many of whom still had those Creole accents, were adapting it to their own, rich, Zydeco, French-influenced, bayou slang. "There's a rap song that they listen to, 'Get the Gat.' Now 'get the gat' really means 'get the gun.' And they Creolized it to: 'Get the gat bebee.'

"There's a lot of things they learn from the media. They learn from TV. Watching these videos and things like that. Or magazines. The stores will bring them here, you got a whole new fad. Everybody else wants it. This guy at this school will call his friends at school. 'Man, guess what's happening here? We got this in.' And one'll get one, and they all want to have that, what's in style.

"They'll say things, and I'm like, 'Well, what are you talking about?' And everybody'll bust out laughing. 'Mr. Renee, you don't know what's happening.' I don't know what's happening."

Ed Renee told me that his best friend was his mother, Juanita. He was the second of three children. Two boys and a girl. He lived at home, and took me to visit his family. "I'm not ready to move from home yet."

The place they lived outside of Opelousas was an area called Belle View, surrounded by grazing fields, full of cows. It was night, and I couldn't really see anything. Ed's mother was a Jehovah's Witness, and had been one for three years. Only one of her other family members seemed to be interested in that religion. That one aunt was "studying" to become a saint. Ed told me he was not necessarily a churchgoer but believed in God.

We went to meet his grandmother who lived two doors down from Ed's mother and father and him, and his sister and her little girl. His grandmother struck me as a very sweet and gentle lady. She had been brought up very much in the French-speaking culture, and I was taken by her appearance. Her eyes had sort of veiled upper lids, slightly pinched at the corners, and her nose reminded me of pictures I'd seen of the southwest plains native people. She had had fifteen children, all living except the oldest, who had been killed. Her husband had died about three years ago. All of her children lived in the area except for three, and they lived in Texas. Ed took me around the house to his room, and talked a lot about his mother. I was very taken by his relationship with his mother and his sense that he should not leave home, and I was deeply affected by his sense of place, and his sense of his place within the place—how connected he was to home.

Ed's centeredness led me to wonder about the concept of home, and how foreign his close attachment was to me; it led me to wonder about what started this whole project. The idea of geography defining a self, and beyond that, a sense of identity—who you are. I was very moved by how fervently he had a sense of who he was, and how much that was inextricably bound to where he was, and how he drew a certain sustenance from that knowledge; how much a part of Opelousas he was and felt, and how Opelousas defined him. These thoughts led me to think about whether or not I had indeed become rootless. Was all this driving and meeting all these people, actually bringing me closer to home, or taking me farther from my roots?

I began to think how curious a thing it was to ask these questions about identity, because in truth, for those who don't give a lot of thought to the idea, that understanding is simple. It simply is. You are who you are, whether you think about it or not. But I could not help believe that to bother is better, or as Socrates once said, an unexamined life isn't worth living. It seemed incumbent upon me to figure out the American ingredients in the soup we call identity.

Leaving Opelousas that evening, I felt that necessity weighing heavily between my shoulder blades.

With regard to music, the best way to keep them straight was, Cajun equals white, Zydeco equals black.

Sometimes, while in Louisiana, outsiders make the ignominious mistake of confusing the two. A warning: This does not please native Louisianans.

Cajun music is centered around the fiddle and the voice. Usually it is set to either a driving and straightforward 3/4 or 2/4 time. Sometimes the songs are done a capella. The songs are often hymn-ly, folk tunes, like the Acadian anthem "Evangeline." Sometimes a pianoforte is used.

Zydeco is the Creole word for snap beans. An old Creole song went, "The snap beans are not salty," and people would ask for "the Zydeco song." Nowadays, Zydeco should be quickly recognized by the brassy, fluty sound of the accordion, and the gritty, scratching *frottior* or a washboard or a rub board. The songs are blues-influenced, or more specifically, jazz and rhythm and blues, for there is syncopation. (To syncopate is to stress the rhythmical or metrical "weak" note instead of the obvious note [as in one-TWO, one-TWO, as opposed to ONE-two, ONE-two], and it is a staple of African American music). This is the music made famous by Clifton Chenier, "the king of Zydeco."

If the two modern forms, Cajun and Zydeco, are first cousins, then their uncle is La-la, from which Zydeco evolved. Cajun and Creole fiddlers were always distinctive because of their sound. "What I think makes our fiddle sound different," said fiddler Canray Fontenot, "is a special crying sound. Like a baby. I remember how the old men used to shout at me, saying, 'Make it cry like a baby, Canray!' Only a Cajun or Creole fiddler can do that." The father, Adam Fontenot; the son, Canray Fontenot; Alphonse "Bois Sec" Ardoin; and Bebe and Eraste Carrier were the forerunners of Chenier, themselves making the folk music of southern Louisiana popular throughout the gulf states during the '40s.

At present, especially in northern states where Zydeco is exotic and different, folk don't bother much with the distinction, and they think, Zydeco is Cajun is Louisiana music. (Paul Simon's 1987 *Graceland* album, with his tribute to Chenier, is a good example.) This confusion is complicated further by "Cajun" bands borrowing elements of Zydeco. Which is not to say anything is wrong with their sharing and adapting—that's what made them both in the first place, this, more often than not, genial sharing. Indeed, this borrowing and mixing is a very American phenomenon, the very dynamic that informs American popular music, from Big Mama Thornton to Elvis Presley, from Little Richard to Jerry Lee Lewis, from Tina Turner to Madonna.

In 1993, the Southwest Louisiana Zydeco Festival was eleven years old. It took place each September in Plaisance, not far from Lafayette and Opelousas. That coming September the roster was to include: Corey Arceneau and the Zydeco Hot Peppers, Bois Sec Ardoin, Zydeco Force, Preston Frank and the Zydeco Family Band, Roy Carrier and the Night Rockers, Rockin' Sidney Simien, and a host of others. I briefly met one of its founders, Wilfred Guillory, who was from St. Landry Parish.

Back in 1982, the fear had been that the music would be forgotten and disappear. But now Mr. Guillory was convinced that Zydeco was more popular than ever. The problem was just making certain the festival could stay afloat. "Money breaks organizations," he said.

The mother organization of the festival was the Southern Development Foundation, and its scope went beyond music—its goal was the documentation and exhibition of "Louisiana's black French folk culture." Like the festival itself, the foundation was concerned with arts, crafts, regional cuisine, workmanship. The foundation's role, perhaps its most important one, was to supply money to these musicians and craftspeople by employing them. The foundation saw to it that city arts councils, parishes and churches did their part as well.

Mr. Guillory was also involved in a number of the organizations. Most seemed centered on young people, like the Manhood Development Camp for African American males, which took place each summer in Chicot State Park in Ville Platte, Louisiana. It had been in its fifth year. One week with forty boys, aged twelve to sixteen. The young men formed their own city, and city government, electing a mayor and officials. There were physical exercise and classes; a seminar on teen sexuality was mandatory. The boys were given a twelve-page African American history reader, and were told they would be tested on it at the end of the camp. They made a trip to the infamous Angola state prison, where they met inmates and saw the execution chamber. At the end of the week, the boys went through a "Rite of Passage" where they burned their red, black and green bracelets to signify their leaving boyhood behind and entering manhood. ("When I was a child, I spoke as a child and acted as a child; when I became a man, I put those childish things away.")

The center of the camp, it seemed, was Father A. J. McKnight, its official spiritual director. The priest was refreshingly unconventional, with a long white beard and given to wearing African garb. Mr. Guillory said the priest's rapport with the boys was uncanny—this was the sort of Catholicism these boys need, he said. "So much of the imagery of the Catholic Church is white. I hope this program grows into something vital. Young black males need so much at that age. There is a need for better parenting. The school system needs to do a better job. These boys have a desire to learn."

Mr. Guillory also worked with the Youth Group of the Church of the Holy Ghost. He told me it was probably the largest Catholic church in the country: 3,000 families, 10,000 members. If such organizations could not make a difference—who or what could?

Chemical dependent the lyrics are the stimulant
There's no need for the crack pipe, the mike is the implement
A force to be reckoned with, I got a gift
Rhymes deadlier than Tyson when he drops the fist
Can you withstand the power of a lyrical explosion?
Divinely chosen, mind depth like the oceans
In motion, a locomotive mind on track
That can't be derailed, letting off steam, I'm leading the pack.

—Poets of Power, "Let the Track Attack"

So much is said these days about the detrimental and hateful effects of hip-hop—especially gangsta rap—misogynist, homophobic, glorifying violence, perpetuating bad nigger attitude. Demographically speaking, the truth of the matter is that hard-core rap's main constituency is suburban white boys and college undergraduates. Black ballads and dance music—now merely flavored with a hip-hop track—have far outsold rap music among black consumers. So while Dolores Tucker and others try to bulldog international corporate empires like Time Warner to the ground, and make them responsible for Ice T's lyrics about cop-killers, and while Niggas Wit Attitude (NWA) try to convince folk that they are more relevant than novelist John Edgar Wideman or astrophysicist Neil Tyson, and while we all wait for Tupac Shakur to return from the dead with Elvis—it's a crying shame that more of that energy is not directed at supporting positive hip-hop music.

I was surprised and delighted to find, in the heat and heart of Zydeco land, just such a group.

Michael Pikes and Antoine Broussard both grew up in a section of Lafayette, the Rufus Peck subdivision, known to locals as "Fightingville." The two had been involved in other groups, but saw the advantage in teaming up in the fall of 1991. The result was called RAGE, "Retaliation Against Genocidal Elimination." Later they changed their name to Poets of Power, the title of their first cassette, which was produced by New Orleans musician Darryl Johnson of the Neville Brothers. They had a manager in New Orleans, too.

Both were then students at USL. Pikes, twenty-three, was a junior in business; Broussard, nineteen, was studying broadcast journalism. From the beginning, they wanted their music to stay away from the "bitches and ho's" mentality, no cop-killing; neither did they want to do ear candy and vacuous jumping nonsense. The two wanted to talk about the contemporary scene. As Pikes told *Creole,* they were "trying to improve" themselves and "escape the ignorance that plagues our race."

I met Mike at the Dupree Library on the USL campus. He was a tall, healthy-looking fellow, light-skinned, his hair cut in a sharp fade, high on the top. Around his neck hung a leather gold, black and green amulet in the shape of Africa. He had been born in Los Angeles, but had spent most of his life in Lafayette.

He told me the story of how he and Antoine got together, and how their first demo, "Coming in from the Cold," got them a deal. Now they had started their own label, Bos Gold Records. Mike now worked part-time at a copy center.

Mike told me how he got interested in rap music, and how, like for so many others, Public Enemy really got his attention. (When he told me this, I reflected that when Public Enemy first came onto the scene and began challenging everybody in the mainstream about the possibilities of rap music, Mike Pikes was ten.)

We talked generally about the movements in the so-called youth culture. Rap stations, BET, music on jukeboxes, magazines—this is how black kids across the nation, East and West, South and North, kept up.

Though Mike had been brought up Baptist, he now considered himself a follower of Islam. "Reading the Koran is all it takes." The stress on economic independence that was championed by the Nation of Islam appealed to him. Knowledge of self was of the utmost importance, he told me. He was also involved with a group of about sixty black men, who were of interreligious faiths. They met regularly and discussed literature and history. The group tried to promote unity, Mike told me. The problems with black folks today were rooted in the problems within the educational system, Mike was convinced, and the fact that it "doesn't teach, doesn't *really* teach, history." That and external forces weighed down on African Americans, making it hard. "It's a constant struggle."

When he got his business degree, Mike told me, he had every intention of remaining a rap artist, taking it to the street.

> I believe success lies in the struggle along the way. If I can leave a person with a spiritual enlightenment in his life, that will mean more than any painting I could create.
>
> —Dennis Paul Williams,
> in a catalog of his paintings

Rain. August rain. Louisiana August rain. Hard rain. He was showing me the shed behind his mother's house where he stored his artwork, and we were walking through the sudden thundercloud that had just hit St. Martinville. Dennis Paul opened the door, and I ran in. A cat, like quicksilver, to escape the rain, darted in as well. The feline hid amid the stored clutter, and we couldn't find it. We spent the better part of half an hour searching. Unsuccessfully. "Damn, cat."

After the rain stopped, we walked down the road apiece, in front of the small, neat houses, with their love-cared-for lawns, to the house Dennis Paul used as a studio. He showed me the bed he was working on: rich mahogany, a twisted, surreal, fantasy bed: he pointed out an Arabic letter in the headboard, central to the overall design. Stained glass, he told me, would complete the project.

Dennis Paul Williams's ethereal, lyrical dreamscapes and visions—bright, angel-allusive, magic in their lithe, blithe drifting—have been shown in exhibits in Atlanta, New York, Okinawa, Los Angeles, Quebec, New Orleans, and, of course, St. Martinville, and his work had found homes in some impressive personal collections. A premier literary journal of African American arts and letters, *Callaloo,* would soon dedicate a special issue to his art.

It would not be hyperbolic to say that Dennis Paul Williams was a remarkably handsome fellow, compact, pantherine, mocha-colored, and had the sort of laid-back charm that could have easily made him the head of a cult. His power was not so much intensity as it was a certain grace. In his presence, even when chasing a cat, I felt a sweet and easy peace.

Dennis Paul Williams's family had all been from St. Martinville. His family had been connected first to the local St. John's plantation, then they became sharecroppers. "We were ten in the family. One girl, and I'm in between."

Though he had been brought up as a Catholic, he described himself as "universal." "I practice the Catholic faith. That's the faith I was born into. But I've studied Hindu to Buddhism to liberal religions of the world. Sufism, because I'm into that kind of stuff. My work involves that. I try to be ecumenical about my subject matter, because it involves a lot of different religions and cultures. I'm very careful about it. I'm into spiritualism. I'm not into religion. That's the difference. It's not so much what you believe, as how you practice. You see?

"It's the walk, not so much the talk. It's better to live it than preach it. Because when you live it, your light is shining. There's an old saying that St. Francis said, 'It's not for us to wonder why but by the grace of God.' In other words, don't worry. Just get your light, get that big beam out of your eyes. Persist in what you're doing. Be conscious. Recognize those shortcomings. It takes a lot of time just to better your own character. I spend more time trying to work on Dennis's character, and trying to be a role model. Not because I want anybody to follow me, or choose my way or my perspective, or even to agree with me.

"Coming from a large family—my father died when he was thirty-eight years old. Mama brought us up by herself. And we didn't have anything. I mean, we lived in a little shotgun house and after that, we were kicked off the property and so we had to stay with grandma, and she had a small house. As a child, I sort of learned the laws of self-preservation right quick. There was nothing that took long for me, because I was experienced right then and there, and I had no alternative, because I had to rise above that situation. It was either do or die, because mama could only do certain things. Mama had good principles and values and everything else. That was better than money, but she could only do certain things and that's it. As a child, I always did paint and draw, but she could never afford to buy art supplies. So I got me a job early on. When I got promoted to seventh grade, I was already working. I had two jobs. I worked at an office supply store, and I worked at a pet shop. At the office supply, the man would give me brushes; and at the old pet shop, that man would give me the scrap paper. And there was enough for me to draw. And the other things I couldn't afford, like quill pens and stuff like that, what I would do is I'd improvise. I'd get little young twigs, and dry them out and I'd make quill pens with them.

"One day, my grandmother sent me out there to pick some figs. And when I brought the figs, I noticed that there was like a milk, the sap from the fig, the white sap that comes from between the fig and the branches. I said, 'What would happen if I dry it, and use it as a drawing pen? Would it hold the ink?' And I learned a way of cutting it, where when I would dip it in there, it would soak the ink. The ink would go into the fig twigs. It'd be like an ink stick. You see."

In the beginning, Dennis told me, "the library was my art teacher." When his father was living, the young boy had been sent to Catholic school, a place Dennis remembered with little fondness. He had been deemed uneducable, and had been given jobs like handling heavy metal crates to keep him away from the other children, "to keep me occupied with anything other than learning." After his father's death, Dennis's mother could no longer afford to keep her children in parochial schools. "She had no choice."

"It was a blessing in disguise. When I went to this public school, they retested me and put me in my normal grade. But I was already two years behind. When I got there, when I got to sixth grade, I'll never forget. It was around recess time, and I sort of left, and I walked up to this little metal building, and there was this white art teacher, drawing on the board. And I was trying to get his attention, to get in, just to try to get in there. Distract him some kind of way. So I interrupted his class. I said, 'Mister, sir, I heard about your art program from one of the teachers. And I can do that, what you're doing on the board. I've always wanted to draw.' He was real nice. He was almost saintly in a lot of ways. He wasn't ugly with me.

He was real nice, and he just stopped me, just shocked that I would do something like that. And one of the things he told me, he said, 'I'll tell you what, son. If you can pass from sixth grade to seventh grade, I'll make sure you get into the art program.' So when I got promoted to the seventh grade, they had put me in the French class, automatically, I went in, talked to him and I said, 'Mr. Arnold'—his name was Mr. Rufus Arnold—'You told me that if I got promoted from the sixth to the seventh, that you would let me into your class.' And they talked and they talked, and he finally got me into the art program. That was the beginning of a long relationship, because he was more like a father to me and everything else. And a white man. But he was an unusual man.

"I think he was from Opelousas originally, but he's living in Lafayette. I turned out, man, I would work, and I was part of his art program. Mr. Arnold was a big influence on my life, and I worked real hard to try to get a scholarship, and from Mr. Arnold's exposure, I went to college, and I would draw from the models and things like that when I was in seventh grade. I was drawing at USWL before I even got to high school. Every summer. I worked with models and stuff like that. And I would audit a lot of the classes and stuff. I would ride my bike from St. Martinville to Lafayette. I didn't have a car. I did that for about twelve or thirteen years. It would take a couple of hours, it depends. I would walk, when my bike was broken. I did that for a long time, man.

"Oh, I've always wanted to do this. And you know what? I tell you, I had a lot of opposition. Because coming from a small town, first I had to contend with my own people, because they thought I didn't want a job, I didn't want to work. Because all they knew was manual labor. They didn't think of art as being something that you can profit from. They were more interested in me doing something where you would get a direct result. So I had that challenge, but my mother was with me. Through all of that, my mother was with me.

"Some days I would leave home, and it'd be so hot, like today, even a hot day like yesterday, I'd walk or I'd ride my bicycle early in the morning, be fog in the morning. Mama would give me a dollar or fifty cents. I'll never forget. I'd get to Lafayette, man. They used to have a Fat Albert Fried Chicken Stand on the corner of University and St. Mary. It just opened. It was the new thing in town almost. I'd go there and get chicken wings, get what I can. I'll never forget. One day the lady told me, she said, 'You know you're here every day, so I'll throw in another wing. You don't get tired of eating chicken?' Said, 'No, ma'am. I'm thankful to have that chicken.'

"Now sometimes at the university, when the professors would be in a bad mood, they would get upset when I came in late, and wouldn't let me use the printing press. For a long time, they didn't know I was walking and hitchhiking. Then one day, I told the printing professor at the university, I said, 'Man, sometime it takes me all morning, till the evening almost to get here. I've been walking for years, and I didn't want to tell you that. I've been hitchhiking.' "

Dennis Paul would carry his art supplies around in an old burlap sack slung across his back, looking "like an old bum," he told me. "I'd sew my blue jeans and everything else."

As is bound to happen with anyone who starts so young, has such a fire in the belly, and works so hard, by the time he got to high school, Dennis Paul Williams's work had achieved tremendous proficiency. He became more and more bored with traditional approaches to fine art, and wanted to explore other avenues of artistic expression. Here, he ran up against more opposition in the form of an art teacher he describes as "an ex-nun. I was too aggressive for her; she saw that aggressiveness and was intimidated. When she would give me one or two drawings to do, I'd do twenty or thirty. When she told me to go learn a few things about the muscles of the body, I would learn all 400 of them.

"I wanted to learn. I wanted to learn, man. So there was a burning desire. I knew that if I did well in school, that would be an opportunity for me, but she made it as difficult as she could for me. And she succeeded in her own way. She succeeded in getting me out of the art program. The university professors knew me already, and they were waiting for me to come over, but they needed her recommendation. I didn't get the scholarship. It broke me down into the smallest thing, and I felt like an insignificant fly. I felt like there was no reason for me to live. You know what I'm talking about?

"So man, I went and talked to the black teachers, and then tried to get them interested in supporting me and helping me, not for them to give me anything. I didn't want nobody to give me anything. I was willing to earn it by the sweat of my brow. I kept at it. And I couldn't get no blacks that was willing to put their profession on the line. None that was willing to help me. Stand out of the way and say, 'I'm going to support this young man.' I don't know. It felt like they didn't want to jeopardize their position. See what I mean? And it turned out, man, that I got kicked out of the art program. And everything went down.

"To me it was worse than the Crucifixion. I think I would have felt better if I was nailed to concrete, man. I felt like my soul was removed. Out of all the energy I had put in, man, it just went down. But there was still a grace that kept me, man, kept me going strong. And one day, there was a Marine Corps recruiter at the campus. And I went and talked to him. But I knew about my physical problem in the beginning."

Dennis Paul Williams had been diagnosed at an early age with a congenital heart defect.

"I prayed and asked the Lord. I said, 'Lord, I have no way out. I need a hand. Can you hide me in your most tender wound? Can you spare me, Lord?' Said, 'Lord, I need a definite healing. Because I can't pass that physical without Your healing, man.' Went to take the physical. I passed."

For a long time, Dennis had been intrigued by Japanese art, but the prospect of ever going to Japan, for that small-town boy from southwestern Louisiana, had been so remote as to have been unthinkable. Suddenly here was his chance.

"I was eighteen. And I left St. Martinville and went immediately to Japan. They said, 'You mean, you want to go to the Rock? Okinawa?' 'Yeah.' When I got there, all the free time I had, I was up there either near the temple or wherever I could learn something. And I just kept looking, kept hunting, kept fighting, and I just sort of built my strength up. I got this wonderful book about the life of Mahatma Gandhi. And there was a passage in there, in that book, that sort of helped me out. He said that our strength doesn't lie in our physical capacity but in the indomitable will. And every time when I felt kind of weak, I would think about that. The will, the will. And I had that will to keep on, even though the opposition, the challenge, was great.

"You know, it's when the task, the enormity of the task, poses the challenge, when it seems so impossible. But I found there was something in me that wouldn't let me quit, just something in me, and I held on to my rosary, I held on to my prayer. I kept seeking elsewhere too. God started teaching me things. And eventually I learned, once I left St. Martinville, left this little small town, I realized that there were people like me elsewhere, that had that burning desire to learn. I met more progressive people, and more people that were cultured. The only culture that I experienced over here was culture I read about. See.

"And when I was in lower grades, I couldn't read at all, basically. But I fought with that, and I rose, I just fought myself above that, and I taught myself. And I took the time with myself, and I had to develop a lot of patience, because nobody else would have patience with me. When I came back from the Marine Corps—I was three years in the Marine Corps—I kept on with my same drive. I got me a bike. And I started doing the same thing. Back and forth. Building things, hustling, I'd work for a while, I'd paint for a while. Make a little money. The Lord kept telling me, said, 'Dennis, if you sow that seed, you shall reap. Dennis, keep sowing that seed. Don't worry, don't wonder. Keep sowing.' Something in me said, 'Keep drawing.' No matter if they laugh at you, no matter if your brother would call you a bum, or neighbors would say, 'Oh, you're weird,' and everything else. Keep going. Because I knew there was something, something in there. There's a parable and God, God in everybody's journey, everybody. Some recognize the parable. Some make a correlation with it. You know what I mean?

"And others, they sow and they're not conscious. They don't study themselves. The only thing they know about themselves is what friends tell them. They never have the time to create the environment that's in themselves. But I had to create environment in myself. I didn't need a pat on the back, because my audience was here. I learned at a young age that the knowledge that man wants to give me was limited.

"So who else could I give the credit to? You know? But something in me? So I learned. It didn't matter to me. You know when you do all that, it's like exposing yourself naked. It's an intimidating thing. For example, when you get through with your material and it's all personal, and everything else, and you submit it, do you realize it's like showing people the interior of who you are? For some people that's too much of a stretch for them, because they're going to have to deal with the critics. They're going to have to deal with what their family's going to think of them. But the Lord had put that armor on me; it's an armor, and it just protected me, man. I knew that lady art teacher couldn't stop me. She could bury me in the ground, but my spirit would never rest. That's how much I believe. She couldn't hold me, and I wasn't going to let her defeat me. Any defeat would come, it would be by my own hand, but not her hand.

"So when I got out of the service, I didn't have a place to draw. I got me a job at the mill in St. Martinville. I just hustled, man. Odds and ends. I remember meeting an art gallery owner when I was in the seventh grade, when I was in junior high school, and I would just go to her, the Heritage Gallery. That was my first gallery, in the seventh grade. From that gallery there, I learned the mechanics of the business aspect. Of course, I was doing a lot of black images and things like that, so that was sort of a funny thing. She was more into Audubon and that kind of stuff. I was doing a subject that I saw. People that I was around. So she didn't particularly like it, right off the bat. But I kept at her, and I would do odds and ends. I'd clean her yard. Whatever it would take. I'd walk from St. Martinville and ride my bike, to go clean her yard. Leave early in the morning. After ten years of knowing me, she said I must be all right.

"Eventually, she was buying me plane tickets to big cities. She and her husband, they knew I was sincere. They'd give me money to go look at museums and shows. I couldn't afford it. Chicago. California.

"I would go and I'd look at the galleries and see what other people were doing. (Of course, I had hitchhiked to Chicago too.) Just look around. I went to Atlanta to see the Monet show and that kind of stuff. I always revel in that kind of stuff. But that was the first gallery that I dealt with. I just kept fighting with it. And now I've had shows in New York and other places like that, and publications and television, and have done soundtracks, recordings. Couple of albums."

Dennis told me he became interested in music after he was "kicked out of the art program. I had to do something because the semester was still there. So I met the band teacher at the high school, and he gave me some Wes Montgomery albums to listen to.

"Wes Montgomery. I had never heard of jazz, or heard anybody play a guitar like that. I'm left-handed, and when I got into the guitar program I used to borrow people's guitars and play the strings upside down. The man that had the printing shop, one day I went to him, and I told him, 'You know, I was so depressed about the art program.' He knew what happened, and just took a liking to me as a person. His name was Mr. Bailey; he told me, 'Man, why don't you get you a guitar?' I said, 'Well, Mr. Bailey, I can't afford a guitar.' He said, 'I tell you what.' He used to listen to classical music all the time. He said, 'Dennis, I want you to hear a musician. I want you to hear a guitar player. When you can play like Julian Bream, I'll be happy. That's who I want you to listen to and play like.' I said, 'Well, I never heard people play guitar like that either.' So he started me out with a classical guitar. I started copying stuff like this Spanish music and stuff, and learning on my own, and just picked up listening to sounds and imitating sounds. He bought me my first guitar. At the printing shop."

Dennis Paul Williams played for me a spell that afternoon. The rain had gone, and the sun blazed in through the windows of his home. Like his personality, his music was mesmerizing, the melodic embodiment of faith, charm, strength, beauty and grace.

"I knew I was going to do something," he told me as I left him that day.

. . .

Now, along with his art, and his acoustic compositions, Dennis Paul Williams was a guitar player for Nathan and the Zydeco Cha-Chas. "Nathan" was his brother Nathan Williams. Three years before, Dennis's younger brother, who had always been interested in La-la and Zydeco accordion, had formed a band. It was only logical, "and economical," that his older brother Dennis, who had a reputation for his guitar playing ("I used to go play at the art cafés. Classical kind of stuff. Go play for the white folks. Every now and then have a bongo with me. Make some extra money."), join the band. Their third compact disc, *Go Chicken,* had just been released. The band had done tours across the country, from New York to Los Angeles, wherever Zydeco had an audience.

I was lucky enough to catch Nathan and the Zydeco Cha-Chas in concert in Lafayette at the El Sid O. The nightclub was long and rectangular, with concrete floors. The crowd, as it trickled in, looked very southwestern in their cowboy hats and jeans and boots and shades.

The band struck up, by and by. Feet started tapping, hands to clapping, and directly folk to dancing.

Nathan was a big, square man, with a smile that could light up a billboard chart, him all loosey-goosey and bowlegged, with his accordion going strong. There was something disarming about the sight of that big man and his accordion, and the frenetic wild man, Mark Williams, wearing the *frottoir* (when he got to going, that sound was akin to a hundred rattlesnakes dancing). This music was sassy. I especially liked their Creole rendition of Stevie Wonder's "Isn't She Lovely" (*"Elle est jolie"*).

The house commenced to rock after a while to "Follow Me Chicken" and "Zydeco Road" and *"Tout Par Tout Passe"* and "Hey Maman." They were doing the two-step, these folks, and line dancing. I smiled big at a man, surely in his seventies, swinging a young woman about the floor. Then a smartly dressed woman about the older gent's age took to the floor and attracted everyone's admiration. As my grandfather would say, "I ain't never seen nothing to beat it."

I had to leave town the next morning, so I said my good-byes to Dennis Paul at about half past one in the morning, and the folk seemed to just be getting started. I said thank you and laid blessings upon the place, and vanished into the night.

I felt as if I were leaving home.

## Twenty-One

# WALKING ON WATER

*Atlanta and St. Simons*
*Island, Georgia*

> The water brought me here, and the water will take me back.
>
> —attributed to an Ibo Shaman

On the 29th of April, 1992, I was in Atlanta promoting my new book of stories. That afternoon I had decided to take a tour of the CNN Center, the former OMNI complex, a vast brick and glass and steel minicity, with atriums and inside-outside elevators—an uneasy marriage of shopping mall, corporate complex, and town square. In the midst of the tour, the young tour guide interrupted her speech to answer a ringing phone. After a moment, she announced that the entire center had been closed off indefinitely. No one could enter or leave. A "mob" of teenagers were rioting outside.

Everyone, except me, happened to be white, and a flurry of whispering overtook the group. I remember the looks on the faces: disbelief, fear, worry, bewilderment. But mostly I remember my own sense of excitement and wonder and amazement, primarily for a particular irony to which I think only I noticed. Here, amid this dawn of new race riots, we watched, bewitched, on the monitors covering the pandemonium in Los Angeles and San Francisco and, indeed, Atlanta, locked into the very heart of this monster news network. We peered down at that moment, to look and listen to Bernard Shaw, this dark, elegant man with his smooth, baritone voice, telling us how it all was. That image said so much to me, about the marked advances wrought over thirty years, yet at the same time, how very like many past eras the situation remained. That was 1992.

Some folk would argue that African American militancy began in the sixties. Anyone who believes that fallacy desperately needs a history lesson. There is practically no decade in American history unmarked by "race riots": the teens, the '20s, the '30s, the '40s, the '50s, the '60s, the '70s, the '80s. And well before the Civil War, even decades before the famous slave uprising of Nat Turner, there had been the insurrections of Gabriel Prosser and Denmark Vesey; a war in Florida alongside the Seminoles, and countless unrecorded incidents. American history has been pockmarked by black men and women not only taking to the streets, but arming themselves against people who oppressed them. Uprisings over lynchings and myriad horrible acts of injustice are a surprisingly little-acknowledged fact in the American mainstream memory. Everyone knows about the radicalism of the sixties thanks to the pervasive crystal ball of television. Moreover, those images were sexy and charismatic and dramatic—never mind that the reality behind the images was also deadly and brutal. So much for what the camera sees and refuses to see. To this very day, I encounter people, black and white, who think the Black Panthers and SNCC were the first organizations of their kind. A form of selective amnesia?

"So what you're saying is that there is a difference between the revolutionary man and the revolutionary woman?"

We sat on quilts and blankets on the Morehouse College campus. Mid-November. 1993. Leaves dusting the still-green sward in front of John Hope Hall and Charles Merrill, red brick eminences both, beside a tiny chapel.

"You're not listening to what I'm saying, Sherri," Lawrence Jeffries debated, defending an article he had just published in *The Liberator,* the official newsletter of SAAE, Students for Afrikan Amerikan Empowerment. He served as its editor.

"Okay," Sherri, a Spelman College student, yielded with a somewhat challenging air. "Okay, I just want to understand."

This was a karamu—the ki-swahili word for festival—and amid the ten or fifteen students from the Atlanta University Center who came and went was a jumble of tuna salad, popcorn, nachos, tabouli, bananas, cookies, watermelon, juice, soda . . .

"All I'm saying is that there are things that the revolutionary man is better equipped to do and there are certain things that the revolutionary woman is—"

"Now hold up, hold up." Omar Freilla, SAAE's minister of economics, wanted there to be no mistake, wanted to be certain Lawrence was not making a sexist statement.

The crepuscular ever-darkening light made it hard to see the faces of our fellows; we huddled in the bracing chill before a shanty. In fact the shanty, made of plywood and blue tarp and ropes and cinder blocks and bricks and plastic and tape, was the point of this meeting. After a fashion. A true eyesore, this shanty (the members of SAAE refer to it as the "shantytown"), but of course that was the point. Graffiti splattered in red and green proclaimed: SAAE, FREE SOMALIA!

A month before—in mid-October—thirty students from the five colleges that make up the AUC—Clark Atlanta, Morris Brown, the Interdenominational Theological Center (ITC), Spelman, and Morehouse—led by SAAE, had marched from the AUC main library to the Morehouse campus, and around midnight put up the shantytown to provoke consciousness about the United States' and the United Nations' action in Somalia. According to Clayton Collie, SAAE's minister of information, it was motivated by an interest in oil deposits, imperialist aspirations, and African real estate, and he had some convincing documents to make his case.

On that night, the campus police were none too happy with the shanty and threatened to move in on the group of huddled students if they didn't take it down. Soon, said Jeffries, they were confronted by about twenty-five or thirty police officers ("it always seems like more when you're in a situation"). The police gave them an ultimatum. "We were very tightly packed in there, and it was real cold too. And so we went right back to SNCC 1960, singing old Negro spirituals, and locked arms and locked legs and started praying real loud so that they could hear that we were getting God on our side against them."

The police called the Student Government Association president, Walter White, down. "He started talking to me," Jeffries said, "the worst representation of this Negro apologist bullshit I've ever heard in my life . . . 'What are you doing? This isn't going to help anything.'" In frustration, White gave up and told the police to do what they had to do. The police were about to move in; the students stood their ground. "Though we may be singing and praying," Lawrence recalled he told the cops, "this is not 1965 or 1962 and we are not SNCC, and we will not allow you to brutalize us." The students reminded the police of the potential negative publicity that might arise, and suggested they call the president of the college. Dr. Leroy Keith, the president, instructed the officers to leave them alone, perhaps expecting the shanty to be gone in a week.

A month later, the shanty still stood.

So we sat on the ground before the shanty—despite the cold, an altogether pleasant gathering and setting, reminiscent of a simpler time—debating gender politics in language that at times would have made Foucault or bell hooks blush with its intricate qualifications and terminology. I could not help but think of all the minds that had been formed at these very institutions: Martin Luther King, Jr., Maynard Jackson, Julian Bond, Tina McElroy Ansa, James Alan McPherson, Spike Lee, and so many others. And how any one of these young women or men may be future Nobel laureates, senators, captains of industry, radical professors, revolutionary leaders . . .

Nevertheless, I must confess that I had come to Atlanta somewhat prejudiced against what I had heard about this particular radical, militant, activist group. At the grand old age of thirty, I had settled into a comfortable cynicism. Retro-radicals, I expected. Knee-jerk romantics after the dream of Malcolm and Huey and Angela and all those Afroed, articulate, arch-demons for change and Black Power. I suspected that these younger folk had only a superficial knowledge of a movement that even I was too young to have participated in; and that they were only interested in finding a neo–radical chic vehicle to vent their neo–middle-class black-and-blue blues.

I was soon to learn how very wrong I had been: They quickly taught me that cynicism is the refuge of a lazy and fearful mind; that some movements die hard, and others just don't die at all.

Since their inception in the spring of 1992, SAAE has gotten a goodly share of media attention. Their members had been on the Oprah Winfrey show; a multitude of articles had been written about them in the regional press, their images flashed on the evening news. Reporters even sought them out for sound bites. And among their more famous detractors numbered the Reverend Ralph Abernathy, head of the Southern Christian

Leadership Conference, and the governor of the state of Georgia, Zell Miller.

What did they stand for? Why had they caused, and were still causing, such a rumpus?

The organizational principles for SAAE were quite simple. There were only four, a page long, published in each issue of *The Liberator.* It began: "We are first and foremost Afrikan people, the Alpha and the Omega!" The second principle says: "We are the masters of our fates and the captains of our destinies!" It went on to state that "liberation is the highest value," and borrowed a phrase from Malcolm X, a phrase used nearly to death by SAAE's members—"and shall employ *any means necessary* to free and protect our people from the evils of imperialism, capitalism, classism, racism, and sexism!" The third point condemned racism and its origins; and the final, perhaps most controversial pronouncement stated: "We do not wish to be 'equal' to, or necessarily integrated with any other group . . . We demand cultural autonomy! We demand freedom to practice our unique Afrikan traditions . . ."

Perhaps too many exclamation points, but certainly their points could not be mistaken.

SAAE rose up from the battlegrounds of Atlanta's Rebellion of April 29th and 30th, 1992, after the verdict in the Rodney King case was announced in Los Angeles.

In Atlanta, on the night of the verdict, young people—among them many students from the AUC—marched downtown and proceeded to explain what they knew in a visceral way, as one Atlanta daily put it, "throwing chunks of concrete, bottles and pieces of metal through storefront windows." Cars were overturned. People were injured.

That same daily, *The Fulton County Daily Report,* also talked to students, one from Spelman who "decried the violence." "We can't account for the few who did what they did."

The article goes on, "However, one young black man holding a megaphone and standing on the Capitol steps exhorted the crowd to do whatever was necessary to enforce black rights. 'I hope you all know what revolution means,' he said. 'If we are going to have liberation, we have to take something from them they are not prepared to give up.'" That young black man was Lawrence Jeffries.

The very next day, the students at the AUC, still incensed by the verdict, planned to march on the university campuses and in nearby neighborhoods. Needless to say, the college administration, the city administration, even the state administration (Atlanta is the capital of Georgia), were on pins and needles. The media buzzed with reports of impending riots, creating a Battle of Britain–like tension.

"The minute we stepped out of Morehouse's gate, the police were there in riot gear and shields," Jeffries remembered. "And they're like, 'You can't come off campus.' And we're like, 'What the hell are you talking about we can't come off campus?' " And the students pushed through literally hundreds, by most accounts, of Atlanta police, the state patrol, the Fulton County Sheriff's deputies, and the Georgia Bureau of Investigation (GBI) agents. The National Guard was waiting only a few blocks away. Helicopters circled the campus.

The students marched a little ways, wanting to go into the black communities that abutted the AUC campus: Vine City, the John Hope housing projects, University Homes. The battalion of officers blocked their way. The students settled for simply going back to the campus. "I said, 'Look, everybody knows that they are going to try to say that we started something to give them justification to come and attack us.' " Jeffries told the students to put up their hands. "And the police take their billy clubs and start jabbing people in the ribs. So I say, put your hands down."

Buses were pulling up. The students said they just wanted to get back to campus. "The officers don't even talk, they stand there with their shields and their helmets, and they don't say anything. At one point they just snatched two people, people who had dreds in their hair, whom they arrested." The students sat down in unison, trying not to resist. Then, in the words of many students, the police attacked.

Clayton Collie, SAAE's minister of information, told me: "I was pretty much in the middle of it, of police officers taking women to the side of the building and beating them. Then the police shot tear gas canisters into the dorm, into an enclosed area. One of the crowning indignities was that the police were circling in a helicopter and proceeded to drop tear gas, from the helicopter."

Over sixty students were carted off to jail, Lawrence Jeffries among them. By and by, Maynard Jackson, mayor of Atlanta, imposed a curfew. Fortunately, surprisingly, no one had been killed.

A few days later, SAAE was formed.

. . .

The day after the karamu, I met with Jeffries at a restaurant called Delights of the Garden. Founded by recent Morehouse graduates, this restaurant was not only vegetarian, but served everything raw.

Lawrence Jeffries was a gentle, ginger-colored man with wavy hair. Within him, you cannot help but see, to varying degrees, a little Che Guevara, a little Huey Newton, a little Mao, a little Gregory Hines. At twenty-two, he had only a few credits to go before he completed his degree at Morehouse; but he seemed to be in no particular hurry. He worked for an anti–white supremacist organization based in Atlanta, and appeared to be fully focused on "the struggle."

We lunched on kush, cracked bulgur wheat, marinated, wrapped in seaweed sheets, bean sprouts, nori rolls, carrot tuna, nutmeat, salad, and avocado goulash. I, who relish the taste of cooked blood, found the meal surprisingly memorable and good.

Lawrence talked. And, if I had not seen the fruits of his labors, or known the circumstances that motivated him, or seen his hectic schedule, I would have found him a little suspect. Not that he was either humorless or pompous; rather, he was so extraordinarily intense, and at times his rhetoric was so incendiary, it caused me to look at him harder, to see if he was, in fact, joking. He wasn't.

"I think labels are just not a good thing. When you give someone a label, then people relate to the label rather than the individual. For me revolutionary nationalist is maybe a good phrase. Pan-Africanist in scope. Socialist in economic orientation. Anticapitalist, antiracist, antiimperialist, antisexist. But labels—think you should judge people more by what they do."

Jeffries got off to an early start as a radical, a label he gladly claimed. Born in D.C., he spent thirteen years in Anderson, Indiana, and his family moved back to the D.C. area when he was fifteen. His mother was a teacher, and had been a member of SNCC. In high school, Jeffries had been involved in the Democratic Party, and was a student member of the board of education. Then he came to Morehouse. "I then determined what it meant to be a radical. I saw people who were very political, but were talking about concepts and theories and leaders that I was only vaguely familiar with." He argued a lot in that first semester, he told me, and during Christmas break he read a great deal about the Black Panther Party, about Marcus Garvey. He read the African historian Cheik Anta Diop, and many others. "So eventually I got to the point where I understood everything they were talking about. Now I find myself challenging those same people who challenged me to take their level of consciousness and their level of commitment to another level."

This level is quite high. Before taking over the *Liberator,* he had been the minister of politics for SAAE, as one of its founders. Though he seemed a lightning rod for the organization, with his charisma and his articulate forthrightness, he disavowed being the leader. Though it was clear to an observer that he was the strong link in the chain of students. "We want to make sure that we don't allow the media to encapsulate everything into one individual," said Malika Saunders. (Saunders, a Spelman senior, daughter of an Alabama state senator father and a political activist lawyer mother, was minister of politics.)

Prior to the events of April 1992, Jeffries was making himself into an enemy of the status quo. As a freshman, he was among those who instigated a takeover of a student assembly, which all the AUC college presidents would attend, to demand changes in curriculum, tuition, housing, food services, and other concerns. Someone snitched beforehand. "They sent campus security to my room at six o'clock in the morning to pick me up." He was taken to the dean of students' office where heated words were exchanged. The takeover went ahead as planned. Jeffries was suspended, along with a number of other students. They were reinstated shortly thereafter, after the administration caved in to a number of the students' demands.

Listening to Lawrence Jeffries, understanding more and more where he was coming from, I could not help but get a sense of paranoia. Long-suppressed fears of oligarchies and conspiracies and imperialist cabals loomed large when he spoke. This was how Jeffries saw the world.

"Regardless of the fact that we have a black mayor in the city of Atlanta, regardless of the fact that the black middle class is assimilated into various institutions in American society, those institutions have remained the same. Anyone who tries to preserve the status quo is anti–black people. Because the status quo is killing black people. En masse. And that means congressmen, that means mayors, that means . . ."

Nonetheless, the evidence for Jeffries's caution seemed quite apparent. Not once, but twice, SAAE found undercover police officers in their midst. On one occasion, they even gave the suspected infiltrator false information about an "intended" march, and got a call from the mayor's office the very next day.

Whether or not the government was out to get SAAE—and there seemed to be compelling evidence pointing in that direction—these young black folk seemed undeterred. The fact that they guarded their membership numbers jealously and went through elaborate security measures with new members pointed out not only how serious the group was, but also how they had learned from the mistakes of their predecessors, especially the Black Panther Party of California, in whose history Jeffries had more than a passing interest. "The Black Panther Party was the organization that brought to America the ideas of meeting the needs of the people first. That was a Maoist concept." But Jeffries and other members of SAAE were aware of the Black Panthers' faults. "They didn't really understand the nature of the beast, and how their organizations were going to be disrupted and destroyed. They didn't understand the real capacity of their perceived enemies to do harm."

Not so SAAE, or at least that is what this organization tried to guard against. Before anyone could become a full member, after an extensive background check, that person had to attend political education and self-defense classes. "Before we are even qualified to try to go out and work for our people, we have to have an understanding of why we are doing it, and what we need to do."

What was the key to a successful organization? Jeffries asked. The key to heretofore denied longevity? Ideology. "If you don't have a sense of direction and a sense of principles, you can easily be taken off into different directions." Hence the overarching mistakes of the Civil Rights movement, according to Lawrence Jeffries: "They just wanted to get that hamburger. They just wanted to have the right to sit at that lunch counter and leave a tip if they wanted to, you know. And they wanted to be assimilated into American society, but never really had their own system of beliefs, other than what America said they believed . . . So what happens is that later, America says, 'Okay, we're going to give you the Civil Rights Act of '64, and other bills. Come on in the house.' But once you're in the house you don't know how to survive."

Survival was the cornerstone in Jeffries's vision—not a let's-go-to-the-woods-and-give-up-on-civilization survival, nor merely a hunker-down-and-we'll-get-by survival. Rather, a survival after the apocalypse. That's what he was calling for—apocalypse now, the razing of the American empire, total overthrow, true revolution. "I am a revolutionary," he said. "I believe that the system of oppression that we face today is fundamentally corrupt, cannot be saved, cannot be reformed or reshaped to serve the people. I think that the existing system that we live under must be completely deconstructed, and we must build a new one which affords our people freedom, justice and self-determination."

Somewhere during my conversation with Lawrence Jeffries, I began to disassemble, bit by bit, my skepticism. The truth was that I was not very much older than these college students, though, since I taught at universities, in the front of my mind I expected myself to be older, and, God forbid, wiser than these younger folk. Only later, when I examined the truth about myself, did I see that I was dealing with a guilt and a fear, and an inchoate sense of confusion. When I was younger than Lawrence Jeffries, I had fancied myself a "radical." I read Mao's *Little Red Book* and Anwar Sadat's memoirs, and accounts of Che Guevara. I even tried to read *Das Kapital.* I had studied the Black Panther Party, read *Soul on Ice* and the *Autobiography of Malcolm X.* I revered, and still do, Angela Davis and Fannie Lou Hamer and Bayard Rustin and James Farmer and, of course, James Baldwin. My dilemma, and I only came to reckon it more rightly years after I had left Atlanta and those undeniably courageous black students, had to do with what I had become—a BUPPIE down to my socks—when I had once dreamed I would become a revolutionary. Had I become, to use Ellison's term in *Invisible Man,* a "spy in the enemy camp"? Or just another bourgeois Negro, running after his share of the American dream? Paying lip service to the "need for change" while I was looking to "get paid." Such critical thinking must cut both ways.

In Atlanta, after a few days, I no longer expected to find little clay feet upon kente cloth–wearing princelings. I commenced to replace that doubt with worry, worry for these self-styled, modern-day, rifle-toting and Mao-quoting knights errant for this new African American dream.

Despite my suspicion that SAAE had flowered in the tense aftermath of the Rodney King uprising and would wilt, day by day, and was soon to die out, I discovered that they had been more than true to their aims.

In February 1993 about 300 people—composed of roughly 200 AUC students and 100 onlookers—burned the Georgia state flag on the steps of the capitol, chanting, "Burn, baby, burn." Since the mid-1950s that flag had borne the emblem of the Confederacy, the "stars and bars." The Atlanta *Daily News* reported: "The group, Students for African American Empowerment (SAAE), called the flag a symbol of 'racist hatred, oppression, white dominance and slavery,' and said they would do everything in their power to change it." Lawrence Jeffries was quoted as saying, "Today we burn the flag, tomorrow we burn the racist institutions in this country—by any means necessary." The Atlanta *Journal–Constitution* quoted Governor Zell Miller: "The only thing that's ever resulted from burning things is just more hostility."

Eighty black students at Georgia State University, "augmented," reported the Atlanta *Journal–Constitution,* "by ten Atlanta University Center students in a group called SAAE," successfully staged a twelve-hour sit-in at the school's financial aid hallway, ultimately winning five key demands agreed to in writing by the administration. The incident, sparked by a racial slur and racial epithets stenciled on a garbage can, began in the president's office. Lawrence Jeffries is quoted as saying: "My people here today discovered their inner courage."

Clearly I was mistaken, or as the folk say, "My bad."

Clayton Collie met with me in McPhetter-Davis Hall on the Clark Atlanta campus, the building that houses, among other things, the computer science department. Now a graduate student in that field, Clayton received his undergraduate degree at Morehouse. As SAAE's minister of information, it was his job to inform me about how the group was organized around a central committee composed of ministers of education, information, politics, defense, justice, outreach and economics; and how each minister chairs a respective committee; about the various enterprises SAAE operates: the Children's Breakfast Table, a newsletter, a political education class, self-defense classes, voter registration; about how SAAE was instrumental in the establishment of a new political party, the Black POWER (People Organized to Win Empowering Representation) Party, which ran A. Amen-Ra A as a mayoral candidate, among others; and about the plans for the future: community-based cooperatives, prison outreach programs, and an Empowerment Institute, "to make black business accountable to the community."

At twenty-six, this native of Nassau, the Bahamas, was unexpectedly soft-spoken. There was about him an air of frightful intelligence, masked by an almost adolescent awkwardness, as though he trusted his mind infinitely more than his body; or perhaps he merely gave the impression of a man of science at war, with his quasi-military cap, the MASH-like couture: a doctor coming out of triage.

He surprised me when I asked about the level of current activism on the AUC campus. "It seems that people on both sides of the issue have essentially settled down to business as usual. In the absence of that crisis, perhaps there's not as much motivation. After the public weeping and gnashing of teeth, there always seems to be a period in which those pronouncements become substitutes for substantive action." Now people were talking about "healing," which in Clayton's eyes was "something like justice on the cheap." He felt an opportunity had been missed among the students as a whole; that, in the wake of such naked aggression by the establishment, a more meaningful dialogue might have occurred. "Beyond the usual dry rhetoric about police brutality, the myth of black male criminality, we should begin to look at the economic and social underpinnings of police brutality."

Nonetheless, out of that turmoil, SAAE had emerged, and continued in its intention to be "in the forefront of those issues."

"SAAE is a revolutionary organization, and ultimately what we are striving for is the deconstruction of the system as it stands in terms of power relationships. Reconstruction in terms of the construction of a new society that allows us to be more genuinely human." Despite rhetoric that some may find a bit grandiose, or helplessly, hopelessly improbable, I found Clayton Collie to be a surprisingly pragmatic soul.

He told me about how Governor Zell Miller wrote letters to the college presidents when he got wind of SAAE's intention to burn the flag on the Capitol steps. Members, once again, were called into President Keith's office; visits were made to students' rooms at two o'clock in the morning. ("We knew when we were doing certain things that there were places that we need not be.") And even how the fabled Johnetta B. Cole, president of Spelman, had insinuated that "Spelman women were being led around by" the men in the organization. "Though Dr. Cole happened to be more of a diplomat," Clayton Collie adds, "and is able to articulate her objections in a much more palatable way, the sentiments were exactly the same as Dr. Keith's."

On the matter of SAAE's involvement with the city council ordinance to ban the sale of drug paraphernalia, I questioned the efficacy, and the philosophical integrity, of a radical organization cooperating with the government in such a fashion.

"Don't be mistaken," the minister of information quickly told me, "that we have any illusions that legislation can bring anything substantive in terms of improving the quality of life for black people. And while ultimately, we say that the solution is indeed revolution, there are certain things on ground level, day-to-day, that you have to deal with before you can get people where they can begin to deal in the abstract."

Spoken like a true minister of information. Or, I teased Clayton, a minister of propaganda. He didn't mind in the least.

"The minister of information is responsible for the preparation and dissemination of propaganda. I use the word 'propaganda' myself because it says up front that the intent of this broadside, or this flyer, is to persuade and that it can very well be considered biased. And I have no problems with that."

I could not help but think of the seriousness of our discussion, the "concrete" implications of not only his words but of his actions, while immediately right outside, several thousands of young black women and men were going to class, engaging in all the traditional collegiate folderol and tedium of getting an education, as well as the nonsense of growing up. I thought about the overwhelming burden these comparatively few students had lugged upon their shoulders, surely not alone in their fight, but essentially inviting a dragon over for tea. I wondered about W.E.B. Du Bois, who had taught at Atlanta University, and his notion of a Talented Tenth of black intelligentsia. I wondered about things spiritual, things hoped for, and things yet to come.

"Are you optimistic about the future, Clayton Collie?" I asked.

He didn't even—didn't have to—stop and think. "It's really not a matter of whether or not I feel optimistic, but really, given what I know, what other choice do I have? Do I resign myself to the fact that African people in this country are in very dire straits? Virtually in the throes of death? Or do I take the position that I am an agent of change? I don't think I have a choice."

What choice, indeed.

On a Saturday afternoon, students walked to and fro on the Morehouse campus. Going to the library. Doing laundry. Going downtown. A wedding was about to happen in the little chapel; men and women dashed in, late, in their white finery.

In front of the SAAE shantytown, in the nippy air, five students were taking a requisite self-defense class—in order to become full-fledged members of SAAE. The class was run by Lawrence Jeffries and Clayton Collie, who acted as a "sensei" of sorts. That day the students learned how to disarm a gun-toting aggressor; later, how to lay flat a knife-bearing assailant. Breath visible, panting, partners went to the ground, again and again. Getting the moves right.

Later, they did drills for security maneuvers during rallies and such. They spread out in a circle of about twenty-five or thirty yards in diameter and went over the roles: what to do if this or that happens; how to talk to potential disruptors; how to communicate across a crowded area.

Students continued to walk by on that cold afternoon, and ask, What are they doing? ROTC? Drill Team? Fraternity moves? Some smiled mockingly. One or two pointed and laughed, muttering something to their friends. Some stopped and watched.

On the night of the riots, Lawrence Jeffries remembered Maynard Jackson's exhortation to the students at the King Chapel: "And so this is what he came in and said: 'If we want to fight, we have to fight with the Ballot, the Buck and the Book.' Not even the ballot and the bullet. He said, the Ballot, the Buck and the Book."

Lawrence Jeffries and SAAE took bullets very seriously.

We were in two cars—Lawrence; Clayton; Malika Saunders; Tommy, a Morehouse freshman from California; Harold, a Morehouse junior from Atlanta; Ina Solomon, a Spelman senior from New Haven and the minister of outreach—and we were heading for a shooting range. Out past the immediate suburbs of Atlanta, which is quite far since Atlanta is merely one large suburb with a downtown on steroids, we went. Over twenty miles, easily, out on I-20, up on Highway 124, to Lithonia, into a rural landscape. Atlanta's robust economic influence was visible in the immense size of the homes perched on long, autumn-touched lawns.

The day before, Lawrence had said to me, while discussing the very real problem of black men killing black men, "It's not the violence that's the problem; the problem is who the violence is being directed against. Violence in and of itself is not a bad thing. I mean, violence has served many righteous causes, if you look at revolutions across this globe. If you look at birth, birth is a violent process. Blood is shed when a child is born. It's who the violence is being directed against, and how it's being directed."

Be that as it may, I had profound misgivings both about his syllogistic argument, and about the very real presence of guns.

At the shooting range, we signed waivers not to sue the range if we unfortunately got in a bullet's way. Then, we collected foam ear-plugs, and marched down a number of spots from a father, a white man, earnestly instructing his two very young-looking sons. Lawrence took out three guns: a futuristic-looking, matte black Tech .9; a Chinese assault rifle; and a .38 handgun.

By threes, they shot at black-and-white bulls'-eyes, twenty-five yards away, propped against a wall of red Georgia earth. I thought of war.

Lawrence: "I want you guys to think of the police when you fire." Ironically. Jokingly. But seriously.

"I want you to see that they are not toys."

Overall, the group seemed to be below-average shots, which did not cheer me in the least.

"Today I hope you just get a feel for these things," Lawrence said. "So that you can get an idea of the potential, the danger you can do, and the damage that they can do to you."

On the way back to the college campus, I asked Ina Solomon—an ostensibly pleasant, sane, kind, intelligent woman, who could probably do pretty much whatever she chose with her life—whether the potential danger of guns and the inherent paradox of guns for peace at all bothered her.

She paused. "No, not really. When you consider that they might be used against you, I think it's a good idea to know how to defend yourself with them."

Logical, I thought. Sound. Perhaps I was simply being naive and sentimental and reactionary and just plain dumb. Perhaps the logic of their situation—these students putting themselves in danger's fickle way—dictated that they take seriously the idea of potential retaliation with equal force. What did I expect, really, for them to do? Disarm police and national guards with flowers? The way Corazon Aquino and the women of Manila did in 1988?

Bright and early each Saturday morning at the Hariand Boys' and Girls' Club just off the AUC, children gathered. They followed a drum there. Like a Pied Piper, a young man walked through the community beating a drum to an African beat, calling the young ones to SAAE's Children's Breakfast Table.

The atmosphere was a warm combination of kindergarten and vacation bible school and camp. They all sat down on the floor and watched as the university students donned masks: Brother Rabbit, Brother Fox, Sister Fire, Brother Possum enacted the folktale "Who Ate the Cheese?" Among the children this was a roaring success.

Later, the children separated into groups by age. The younger ones colored pictures to represent "Black is beautiful." The older students, twelve and up, had history discussions. That day, the teens went to the Shrine of the Black Madonna, a black bookstore in the neighborhood. Usually, there are around forty children participating, and about fifteen or twenty SAAE members involved. Ina Solomon said of the program: "We try to foster a sense of the community. We try to hug them as much as we can.

We tell them they are beautiful. They are certainly not going to get this in school. We teach them about their African heritage. Breakfast is just an aside."

I asked Salah (aka: Jason Ross Brown), a freshman at Morehouse from Buffalo, and the chair of the breakfast table, about the program's goal. "The other day," he told me, "we sat down and told the kids stories. I was reading them a book, and in the book there were pictures of many different colors of kids. I asked them how many thought the black one was pretty, and all the children said, She's ugly. And I say, Why? And all the little kids in unison said, Because she has a black face. So we're here to give them breakfast, but we are also here to start to combat the stigma that society is placing on them at such a young age."

To me, this was the most profoundly revolutionary act SAAE had embarked upon. Some might see this, next to their stated aims and more "glamorous" escapades, as being tiny or of limited consequence. But in its simple, selfless beauty, its unaffected directness, its immediate connection, this shepherding struck me as the most effective and powerful and farsighted action of all.

Before I left Atlanta, I spoke briefly with one of SAAE's elders. There are a number of older radicals whom the students trust and whose counsel they seek. Among them was Kathleen Cleaver, former Black Panther and ex-wife of Eldridge Cleaver. Another, with whom I spoke, was Hisan Crockett, a political science and African studies professor at the AUC. He had been involved with SNCC while a student in North Carolina in the 1960s.

I asked him to help me gain some more perspective on SAAE. Was their rhetoric, perhaps, a little too hyperbolic?

"I think if we look at the 1960s, at SNCC or the Freedom Democratic Party, or the Black Panther Party in California, I think that the rhetoric was harsh. The program was activism, and there was a question of, 'Are you people that serious *right now?*' There's a language there that links. It's a conscious effort to continue a radical dialogue that is necessary when you try to present a picture to the people of your society, particularly an oppressed people." He went on to say that African Americans are an aural people. "Language is one of the things that lifts our spirits and helps us to make it."

After talking with Professor Crockett, I began to see more clearly, though perhaps a little through a glass darkly, how SAAE was, in fact, as he put it, "a continuum of the '60s." Lawrence had earlier said to me, "We had a '60s, the '60s brought us here, to the 1990s. Now we have to build something new and something different." And better, I pray.

There is something ironic about the fact that Atlanta's seal is the phoenix and its motto is *Resurgens,* in memory of being burned to the ground in 1864 by Sherman's troops. I find it ironic, since—without the national hoopla and international attention and popular galvanization among black people—in Atlanta, a movement may well have been reborn.

After all my traveling, after seeing the good, the bad and the indifferent, I found this movement to have been undeniably one of the most encouraging and exciting developments among African Americans. I thought of Nat Turner, Gabriel Prosser, Denmark Vesey, Cinque, Harriet Tubman—men and women who had no alternative but to fight, to use violence against a system that would listen to no other appeal. I thought of Ida B. Wells, Mary McCleod Bethune, Frederick Douglass, and perhaps most forcefully, Thurgood Marshall—warriors all, irreducibly and irrefutably, locked at times in mortal combat with a wicked government and a wicked people who would keep them in de facto slavery at any cost, yet men and women who nonetheless held firm to the belief that to sink to the methods of the enemy, to use the enemy's weapons against them, would be to rend from the African American people the only thing to which they could securely cling in their disenfranchisement: a sense of their own humanity.

The strength of African Americans has always been that their position was (is) a moral one. When morality is taken away from black folk's struggle for parity, we are left with only economics and the politics of might. "All is fair in love and war"—what a silly statement. Love without caring is lust; war without a just cause is thievery. The question then becomes, Is America at war with itself? Scattered evidence—scattered? no, accumulated—would suggest that this country is battling with itself, without a doubt, and the situation could get dramatically worse. I am convinced that the outcome is not inevitable. The possibility still exists for America to take the high moral ground, to listen, as one of our presidents once admonished, "to the better angels of our nature."

Are you people that serious *right now?*

> You have to learn how to do that, and it's no problem.
> When things seem to be a problem, by your attitude and

> frame of mind, it automatically provides a solution, and when a solution is present, a problem can't stick around. The problems vanish, just like night. Just like when the room is dark and you bring the light in. Then the darkness must vanish. You offer solutions, and not worry about the problems.
>
> —James W. Washington, Jr.

While I had been in Alaska, during the summer of 1992, I happened across an article in *USA Today* about a young black woman who had sold her first novel while in high school. Over a year later, in the fall of 1993, while giving a reading at Emory University in Atlanta, I was lucky enough to be introduced to the young Lorri Hewett, author of *Coming of Age,* then a sophomore. Before I left Atlanta, I took her out for coffee.

Lorri had a bubbly, sparkling, girlish presence. But there was also an intensity and profound seriousness, surprising in one so young.

She had grown up in Littleton, Colorado, a suburb of Denver. "We lived in the middle of nowhere, really. Only recently have they begun to build up the area where we lived. I remember really loving lightning. Before our house was finished, we lived in an apartment that faced the Table Mountains; it's one of the foothill ranges before the Rockies. I used to sit outside, and in the summertime, you'd have lightning storms every day and the sky would turn this really deep purple and the thunder would be really loud, and the lightning would just split the sky, most every afternoon. So that was one of my earliest impressions of Colorado, just the lightning."

She remembered trips to the mountains to watch the aspens turn color, and going skiing at fifteen. ("I love it. I am probably the world's worst skier. Can barely stay up on my feet, and I've never taken lessons. It would probably do me really well to take some lessons.")

Not until Lorri reached high school, she told me, did she realize that practically all her friends were white. "I really didn't have a context for it to matter. That's just the way it was; my friends liked me, I liked them. I think I'm one of the few people who's never experienced any overt racism. Nobody's ever called me anything. I think that was sort of a sheltering thing too, because I never really had anybody tell me who I was, or really make me see who I was. It wasn't until I started looking for myself that I started thinking, 'Wait a minute. There's something more here than what I'm experiencing.' When I went to high school, more so, understandably, when dating started to come up. That whole issue. I went to high school with 1,700 kids. There were seventeen black students, and of that number, maybe six or seven were male, and all of those six or seven dated white girls. That was really what I started to notice. There was a group of black girls at my school, Hatfield Senior High, some of whom I'd known since I was in elementary school, and some of whom I didn't really speak to very much, and they didn't speak to me either. They thought I was stuck up because I was really involved in the high school. I was on the dance team. I was a cheerleader for a year. Yes, I admit it, a cheerleader!" She gave a self-mocking laugh. "But I was really involved. I was on the track team. I was in student council. I just did all that student stuff. So they thought I was stuck up. Something like that. Until I got to know one of them really well, because we were both on the forensics team. When I got to know her, she was my entree into that group of girls. They would go to Denver, go to parties in Denver. That type of thing. Because I was also realizing that I really didn't like any of my social options. Like I didn't like heavy metal music. I didn't like going to parties and just standing around drinking. I mean, that just didn't interest me."

Until that time, Lorri never really had a boyfriend, she told me. "I don't know why. I really wasn't all that interested I guess. The guys that I knew were my friends, so I didn't really see them as guys. They were just friends. And I was always involved in everybody else's love life, like putting people together and matching them up and counseling and all of that stuff, so, but I was too involved with other people to really be involved with myself. When I started to go to parties in Denver, where people would dance, listen to different kinds of music, that's when I started to date, and when I started to meet more people. But even still there's one difference I've noticed. I don't know if it's just the young people or people in general, between Denver and here, but interracial dating is a lot more acceptable in Denver. I don't necessarily believe it's because people are more tolerant. I think that people at times, not all the time, because I don't like to categorize people as a whole—but a lot of times, interracial dating is a way to escape identity rather than to be with someone you really care about. When you see people completely go out of their way to date only certain people and only certain white people. I had a friend who'd only date blondes with blue eyes."

A lot of young black men she knew were very color conscious; she credits them with her own awareness of "the light skin–dark skin issue."

"I just didn't even know about that before. The lighter the better, or whites, basically. Really color-struck." She began to notice black men, "upscale black men," in the company of white women, and the number of local sports figures and the like who had white wives.

"Maybe it's in the air. Or the lack thereof. So that really gave me a sort of negative impression of black men."

Lorri admitted that she and her friends had experimented with white boyfriends, but that the entire process left "a negative impression." And it was an issue that never seemed to occur to her parents, for whom such a situation had been unthinkable when they were her age.

"In fact, they don't really deal well, with conflict, with problems. What my parents would do is that they would take us to the library; my father especially would take us to the library and he'd get us books about different figures. I had a book about Marian Anderson, a book about Booker T. Washington, W.E.B. Du Bois, Martin Luther King, and so I knew all these things. I knew a lot of history. But I wasn't really given a chance to experience black life. I think my parents thought that they were doing enough, just by that. 'Just making sure she knows what's up.' But that wasn't really enough. Even though I was able to befriend more black people in Denver. Just the whole tension between my white friends, my black friends, my identity at school, my identity when I was with my other friends. I really felt it strongly, and that was a difficult thing to deal with a lot of times.

"When I had black boyfriends, that was the thing that they always found the most amusing about me. The way I spoke. And they just thought it was hysterical. Then my parents realized what a problem it was for me. I was unhappy. Frustrated. So we switched churches. We'd been going to a white church in Littleton. Methodist. We switched to an AME church, actually the largest AME church in Denver, in Park Hill.

"I think that was a really good move for my parents. Because it really enabled them to get back in touch with the community and with what was going on in the community, and they both got really involved. They both taught Sunday school. They went to services every week. They were on this board and that committee and this and that. So they were having a good time. I'm really glad that they switched, and I think it really became something that was for them. But for me, I'm not all that much of a religious person anyway. So that really didn't do it.

"What did I do?" She laughed. "I wrote. I wrote. I wrote." When she said this, another light seemed to come on in Lorri Hewett's eyes, and I understood instantly. "I just kind of kept at it. I'd been writing way before then, but my writing started to focus on that."

What would become Lorri's first novel centered on these very issues,

issues of race, skin color, social distance, isolation. One central issue was a main character's—a protagonist not unlike Lorri Hewett—wanting to move from the suburbs to be amid the denser population of black folks in Denver.

"Part of her character came out of 'Would I really be welcomed with open arms? Would I all of a sudden feel I were at home?' As I was writing the book, I think I really wrote through what I thought really would happen if I did switch schools. It probably wouldn't be the wonderful, easy transition that I thought it was. And it wasn't, for this character. She ends up actually doing the same thing that she did in the suburban school."

That is to say, remain involved in school activities, and be the perfect model of an overachiever. "She ended up having white friends, even in the school that had a substantially larger black population." Which becomes one of the main tensions in *Coming of Age.* There was also a character of mixed parentage, and the psychological hurdles born of that circumstance—white mother, divorced from a black father. A third character is an athlete, a heavily recruited football player, dealing with those pressures, as well as a family struggle. Each of these characters' voices alternate to make up the novel.

Lorri Hewett was fifteen when she began to think seriously about getting published. "I sent a manuscript that I wrote to a Delacourt fiction contest, something about young adult first novels. The manuscript got lost. It wasn't even read until after the contest was over, but when it was read, one of the editors wrote me back and said, 'We think you have a real future in the field. Most of the problems in this manuscript have to do with style.' I was like, 'Well, what's style?' 'There's a book called *Elements of Style.*' 'Okay, I'll buy that, and I'll read that and maybe that'll tell me what style is.'" She bought other books and studied on her own; there was no one around to discuss her project with, really.

"I wanted the book to really lift off the pages, as far as dialogue, as far as the plot, that type of thing. That's why I wrote it in the first person. I really couldn't be writing it in any other way. And one of the ways that I used to differentiate characters was the way they spoke, so I took my own liberties with the English language in writing the way people speak. I did a lot of those things that really aren't all that sophisticated to do. To write phonetically.

"I was seventeen, and that's when I started *Coming Of Age.* It had a couple false starts, and then it wrote itself, basically. I wrote it in something like six weeks. I had like a 450-page manuscript and I went through a long revision process all spring of my senior year and then all summer.

"Then I came to Emory. I was a freshman. And probably the first week or so, I mailed it to Holloway House because I saw them in *Writer's Digest.* Said, 'Black experienced publisher.' I didn't expect anything to happen. I just wanted to know if it was publishable. Because it wasn't a conventional young adult novel, but it wasn't quite an adult novel either. I thought it wouldn't fit any niche, as far as publishing goes. In November, I got a phone call from the editor-in-chief. Said they wanted to publish it. Of course, I was ecstatic. And everybody was just like, 'You did what?' It came out August of 1991."

At the time, Lorri was working on the revisions of her second novel, which was to be published by Dutton.

"I don't think there is anybody who can't teach me something." Black women writers like Toni Morrison, Alice Walker and Terri McMillan she watched and read very closely. "I don't think there's too much made of the success of black women writers. They're brilliant. They're just so lofty to me. Their work is so dense and so rich. I can just do nothing but admire." She also admired Charles Johnson, and many other writers, various, diverse.

"What I write about is a particular black experience. It is not *the* black experience. It is a particular young adult black experience. And that was one of the reasons why I wrote it, because I didn't feel that there was much out there that really talked about contemporary experiences as they were, without editorializing. Without resorting to the rhetoric that we hear every day. That just talked about ordinary people, not heroes. People and their lives, and what's going on. That's where I really feel that my work has had the most value. When I talk to young people, at high schools, at universities, who tell me that this was really what got them to read. Because they didn't think there was anything out there that pertained to them specifically. I was just like, whoa."

Lorri found that a great many of the black students at Emory had backgrounds similar to her own—upper-middle-class black youths who had grown up in places largely isolated from black culture. A circumstance she had not given much thought to before, and which now led her to look at her situation with new eyes. "I thought that, since we were a small group on campus, that we would stick together more, and that didn't happen. That really disturbed me a lot until I realized what it was. Most of the black students had gone to all-white schools or prep schools, boarding schools. Coming to Emory, when you've been raised in a predominantly white culture, you go through a period of rebelliousness at some point or other, where you want to disassociate yourself from everything white and just really grab on to black culture.

"It's not a thing to grab. Once I realized that, a lot of things made sense. People do funny things. 'Everything western is bad.' I think it's important; it's fine to go through that. It's like a cycle, and then you come around and realize, this is who I am. This is where I fit in. I can't say that I can identify with everything black because black isn't a thing.

"There are how many million blacks? Twenty million, thirty million black people. So that means there are thirty million black experiences. There is no one black experience. So if you're looking for a black experience, you're not going to find anything. You're just going to be frustrated. I feel like I've really come full circle, and that I can disagree with things. Like I don't have to put in a black opinion. I don't have to fit myself into any specific categories. I can be myself. I am a black woman. I am an African American woman. I don't try to assign any more to that than what there is. In a lot of ways, it's the most important thing about me, and in a lot of ways it's the least important thing about me, but I don't think you can really say that it's one thing, one way, all the way either way."

"'It's not a thing to grab,'" I quoted. "I really like the way you put that."

What did Lorri Hewett think about the future?

"It's so tough. I think I can really say that I am who I am because I had a family behind me, who supported me in what I did. They didn't have a lot of money. They didn't really have much of anything but that support. I think everything goes back to family and it's really difficult to find a solution because that's such a personal thing. You only have control over yourself. You could create an atmosphere where it's more conducive for people to fully experience family and to make family valuable. But I don't really know how you can do that. I don't really know that institutions can do that. Economic power helps a lot, but economic power, I think, equals political power in a lot of ways. Communities really have to get themselves back on track. I can't say exactly how to do that.

"I'm too young to be jaded, but I think I'm a cynical person in a lot of ways, and that bothers me. Well, sometimes and sometimes not. I think it can also be an excuse, to stand back and just think everything's horrible instead of figuring out what you can do. I think it's a way of evading responsibility. That kind of romantic cynicism, you know, 'Oh, the jaded writer.' We've seen that before."

"How optimistic am I? I don't know. I mean, sometimes I'm optimistic and sometimes I'm not. I don't think I'm ever really pessimistic. But sometimes, I'm just not optimistic."

After graduation, Lorri Hewett was considering making a two-year obligation to Teach For America, which would place her in rural areas or in urban city schools. Or perhaps she would apply for a Fulbright to Ghana. She wanted more exposure to the world, she told me.

"Are you going to keep writing?" I asked.

"Oh, yeah," she said. "That's always in the program."

The idea made my heart glad.

Lorri Hewett published her second novel, *Soulfire,* in 1996, and her third, *Lives of Our Own,* two years later.

> ". . . They just turned, my gran' said, all of 'em . . . and walked on back down to the edge of the river here. Every las' man, woman and chile. And they wasn't taking they time no more. They had seen what they had seen and those Ibos was stepping! And they didn't bother getting back into the small boats drawed up here—boats take too much time. They just kept walking right on out over the river. Now you wouldna thought they'd of got very far seeing as it was water they was walking on. Beside they had all that iron on 'em. Iron on they ankles and they wrists and fastened 'round they necks like a dog collar. 'Nuff iron to sink an army. And chains hooked up the iron. But chains didn't stop those Ibos none. Neither iron. . . . They feets was gonna take 'em wherever they was going that day. . . ."
>
> —Paule Marshall, *Praisesong for the Widow*

Live oaks. Spanish moss. Resurrection ferns. Tina McElroy Ansa pointed those out to me, for though I had grown up in the country, I had never been able to tell a resurrection fern when I saw one.

Tina was a native of Georgia, born in Macon, a graduate of Spelman, a former reporter for the Atlanta *Journal–Constitution,* and at the time, author of two novels, *Baby of the Family* and *Ugly Ways.* She and her husband, Jonée, had moved to St. Simons Island, off the coast of Georgia, in the archipelago known as the Golden Isles, some years before. To them, this swampy, marshy, estuarial, alligator- and crane-infested, verdant, history-laden isle was a near paradise. Walking its beaches and marshes, I briefly glimpsed why.

Tina told me that in the early 1980s she took some young black children to the beach for their first time, when the couple had first moved to the island—even though they had been desegregated, black people didn't go to the beaches. She said there was a lot of passivity around.

Jonée came off initially as a modern-day hippie, laid-back, low-key, unpretentious, dreadlocked. He was another lesson in how deceiving appearances can be, or in truth, how we all carry stupid stereotypes in our heads.

Jonée Ansa was a Vietnam veteran. He had received his doctorate in music from Julliard, and had been a vice cop in Atlanta. He had been a cameraman for CBS and had freelanced for other networks. He had spent time as a sailor. He graduated in the early eighties from the prestigious American Film Institute in Los Angeles and had directed videos and commercials (TV watchers would know his eye-catching DeBeers diamond spot, in which a shadow wears a diamond ring). At the time, he was working on a movie called *Drive By,* (which became *The Crossing Guard*), for which Sean Penn was the executive producer. Jonée was also a black water diver (diving in water with zero visibility), and sunken treasure hunter and, accidentally, an amateur paleontologist. In the opaque waters around St. Simons, he and a friend discovered the fossilized skeleton of a prehistoric sloth—twenty feet deep in the Altamaha Rim. He made a documentary of his efforts for National Geographic. Jonee had an extensive and nigh-priceless collection of movie memorabilia.

Talking with Jonée, I came to realize that he loved danger, being a militant and living as an artist—and he seemed to know *everyone.*

After meeting and marveling and talking with Jonée Ansa, I gave up wondering where all the remarkable black men of the past had gone.

One of the most intriguing and fresh films in recent years, and practically the only film made about the Gullah (or Geechee) of the Sea Islands, is *Daughters of the Dust,* made by the director Julie Dash.

The film takes place sometime around the turn of the century, and it is lush in its evocation of Africans off the coast of America, going about their lives in what feels like pastoral simplicity. There is sea, surf, fish and shellfish, fruits and vegetables aplenty. The film's narrator is the unborn child of the two main characters (very like in the novel *Christopher Unborn* by Carlos Fuentes). There are a muezzin's calls at dawn and dusk; there is a love affair between a black girl and a native boy; there are visitations from the dead; and, in a key scene at the site of the 1803 mutiny at

Ibo Landing, the narrator's father walks on water while a fanciful passage regarding the event is read from Paule Marshall's novel, *Praisesong for the Widow*.

Ossabaw. Saint Catherine's. Sapelo. Sea Island. Jekyll. Cumberland. Saint Simons.

Actually, in the 1500s, the Jesuits, with the help of the Spanish, had named the island San Simon; before that, the Yemassee, the Waccamaw, the Yacamaw and others had given it a name. That all changed in 1736, when the British decided they wanted Georgia for themselves, and all the offshore islands, too. James Edward Oglethorpe, first colonial governor of Georgia, had Fort Frederica—the "most expensive fortification built by the British in North America" to that date—erected on the island. Named in honor of Frederick, Prince of Wales, the son of George II, and father of George III, who would see the whole thing lost. (It amuses me no end to read in so many accounts of the "Spanish Invaders," as if the English had been born and raised in Georgia.) In 1748, the Treaty of Aix-la-Chapelle assured the British of their claim. The fort on St. Simons was abandoned shortly thereafter, and the island turned to less militaristic pursuits.

It would remain something of a backwater for decades, if not centuries. Plantations were established by people named Spaulding and Couper and Butler and Kenan and others. (Yes, the Kenans of St. Simons were related to the Kenans of Duplin County, North Carolina, to whom I am no longer "related," by writ of manumission.) Corn, peas, beans, sweet potatoes, sugar cane, rice and ole cotton were their yields. Slaves for a long time outnumbered whites in some places in the area by an extraordinary ten to one (like Georgetown, South Carolina, in the 1830s). Most of the structures built on the islands were made of a substance called "tabby," equal parts sand, lime, oyster shells, and water, which was mixed into a mortar and poured into forms, and, after being lashed into place by wooden pegs, was finished with stucco made of lime and sand. The word tabby, and probably the concept for making it, is believed to have come from an Arabic African word which means "a wall made of earth."

In 1863, Frances Anne Kemble published a book about daily plantation life in the islands, *Journal of a Residence of a Georgia Plantation, 1838–39*. "It throbs and burns with a fine hatred of slavery, and is said to have caused more criticism of the South than any book that was ever written except *Uncle Tom's Cabin,*" writes Margaret Davis Cate in *Early Days of Coastal Georgia* (1955).

Cate also writes about Rufus McDonald, still living in the 1950s, in Pennick, another part of Glynn County.

> Rufus looked like 'Uncle Remus' and it seems entirely proper that there should be a child and he told him the old stories which the Negroes brought from Africa and which have been handed down from generation to generation. Joel Chandler Harris preserved the folk tales of the Middle Georgia Negro while here on the coast where the dialect is entirely different, these old African tales were collected and published about a quarter of a century after the war by Georgia's eminent historian, Charles Colcock Jones, Jr., under the title, *Negro Myths from the Georgia Coast.*

St. Simons shares a symbiotic relationship with the onshore town of Brunswick, the seat of Glynn County, and now where most of the black folk who work in the hotels and restaurants of the island actually live.

The Honorable Orion Douglas was an extremely tall, self-possessed man, with a devilish smile. The judge was one of those rakishly handsome mid-life men, who could pass for younger, but who didn't care to do so. He seemed to understand that living his life had led him to a secure and enviable position; and his exuberance grew from not only a sense of satisfaction, but also a sense that he had only just begun. And he probably knew how to enjoy it much better than a wet-behind-the-ears greenhorn such as myself.

His Honor agreed to meet with me in his chambers in the Brunswick courthouse, a spanking new building of handsome brick and glass.

The city of Brunswick—with a population of 20,000—had a black majority. Glynn County, population about 80,000, was 22 percent African American. Judge Douglas had been appointed to be judge of the municipal court, where he had served for eleven years. In 1983, he had been elected, with a majority in all twenty-three precincts, to the county bench.

Orion Douglas had originally grown up in Savannah. "I think as a kid, growing up, there were only three beaches we could go to. Even though we lived on the coast. We could go to Hilton Head. We could go to the south end of Jekyll Island, which is the island right next to St. Simons. And we could go down to Florida. Hilton Head, when I was a kid growing up, you had to take a ferry boat. And it was all black on the island. There were many, many black families in Savannah who owned lots on Hilton

Head. By the time I returned to the South, Hilton Head was no longer black owned. They had a bridge that would get you there and few blacks go out there now. And on the south end of Jekyll Island, only reason we could go there is because the millionaires gave the island to the state, which allowed blacks to use that portion of the beach. Had they not done that, there would have been no beaches in Georgia that black people could go to. In Savannah in 1964."

The judge had spent time in the Northeast and the Midwest, before he returned to the area. "I found the South a much better place, opportunity-wise. The North is very bigoted. Very bigoted, but it's bad manners to call somebody a nigger. It's very, very entrenched, the racism up there. And I really saw no future there.

"I consider myself the first wave of blacks to come back home. In the old days when we were growing up, it was, 'I'm getting the hell out of here. I'm going to live in New York or someplace. I'll never live in the South again.' A lot of my peers felt that way too. Till we got up there. I saw big differences between black and white relationships, and black-on-black relationships. Differences between the southern black and a northern black. In terms of their interaction with whites. Forgive me and allow me to generalize. I found northern blacks more inclined to segregate themselves. Southern blacks were more inclined to open themselves up. I don't want to use the word 'integrate,' and I don't want to say 'assimilate,' but there's a word around there someplace.

"I found that opportunity is much greater for blacks down South. Whites might be more willing to accept, with confidence, black expertise. And you're less likely to be stereotyped, particularly if we're professionals. Absolutely.

"The South has been taking a bum rap for a long time. And they asked for that bum rap by maintaining a society that enforced Jim Crow laws. For those of us who grew up here in the South, we know that these were bad examples. There were people like Emmett Till who were killed and all that, but as a child growing up, I was very happy. My life was very well rounded, and I was materially sound. As a kid growing up in Savannah, I remember there were three black movie theaters. I had a choice of three black movie theaters. There were black-owned motels. When Louis Armstrong and Lionel Hampton would come to Savannah, they would stay at the black motel, and since my mom knew them, they would come over to my house. We had black doctors, black professionals. We had supermarkets, fish markets, black-owned businesses.

"I never saw that up North in any substantial degree. And, as a result of desegregation down here, I haven't seen it down South since. Life was pretty secure for me here. I knew how I could prosper. And many blacks did prosper. But when I went up to Holy Cross, the images up in New England were always the ones that were portrayed by the media. For a year or two, I played into it, but after that, after seeing South Boston and what you have up there in New York, Crown Heights? Bed-Stuy? And in St. Louis, after seeing what they did in East St. Louis, I realized that, whoa, the South wasn't that bad. It really wasn't. It never was like that on a persistent and pervasive basis. I think I've done better here than I could have done anyplace else. Really. Helped a lot to be trained up North though. When I think of the educational quality of the institutions, I have to give credit for having been trained up there. We bring the skills back down South, where I had a better chance of really being who I could be.

"In this community, there are no glass ceilings, because there are no opportunities. There's no room. So as a professional, if you come here, you really got to hang out your own shingle, and be self-reliant. I mean, nobody offered me a job as a lawyer here. I came in and hung up a shingle. But once I did I was able to prosper. Over half my practice was white. I ran in an election in a county which was only 22 percent black. Whites supported me against two other whites. So no, there's no glass ceiling in that sense. I could run. But in terms of the initial entry-level opportunities, no, it's not here.

"Our people have a tendency to concentrate in the urban centers. They want to be in the New Yorks and the Atlantas. They don't realize that just by going a little bit out of town, there's a large black market that's untouched."

The judge pointed to a number of businesses in the area, black-owned restaurants, saying that in Chicago, where two of the owners were from, they wouldn't have stood a chance.

"I actually love the South. I mean, after living in New England and the Midwest, this is it."

I was curious, speaking with a judge, to know Mr. Douglas's views on the much-bandied-about statistics on black crime.

"Drugs. If you took the offense of possession out, I don't think you'd find a great disparity between white and black crime. If you look at the impact of the illegality of drugs, then you'll see a huge disparity per capita. Of all these city task forces, these metro drug forces, well, all they're doing is going to the local corners, and busting the dude that's out there selling five-dollar, ten-dollar pieces of crack. They're not cutting off the source at all.

"So these people get arrested every Saturday night. If you want to go arrest somebody on Friday and Saturday night, you can. Just drive around the projects, sit there long enough, and you going to see a dude out there trying to sell some drug? Okay? So you can build up your arrest record. And if you make black people look like they're just intent on being criminals, in that sense, then your numbers are correct. But if you eliminated those types of arrests, there is no great disparity between white and black. They talk about Wayne Williams in Atlanta, but I haven't heard about too many black serial killers. I mean, is something wrong with white people that they have such a high proportion of people that like to kill ten and twenty of them, and then beat them and slice them up and put them in a freezer? Is it fair to say whites are depraved because of that? I think not.

"People arrested on possession of drugs, they're not trying to take another person's property or hurt someone. A person wants some release. He wants to alter his mind and take his focus off the world around him. Alcoholism is very strong too. Why do we do this? Because of the world we live in. Some individuals feel that there's a need to escape, for a period of time. Some of them just never want to come back. The need, the desire to alter one's mind, that's been here as long as man has been here. Except we've got a real pernicious drug that's been flooded into our community. Heroin didn't do what crack does. Before 1985, nobody ever heard of crack. All of a sudden, in one year, crack was in every city in this country. But nobody's arrested anybody that's bringing the stuff in. Just the brother that's standing on the corner, selling it."

Given what the judge was saying, I pointed out that his line of reasoning seemed very close to one of the most prevalent "conspiracy theories"—that the drug-use epidemic was actually a planned and administered plot.

"I do believe that the heavy producers of drugs like heroin, cocaine—not so much cocaine, the white people like that a lot—but heroin and crack, didn't give a damn about the fact that they were hurting certain people because they were black. Let's assume it was the Italian mafia doing it, I don't think they would have allowed this drug to be distributed in the Italian communities in New York or whatever. I don't think they would have imported it and sold it to their children. I know black people are not importing drugs into the country. I know that. They're just distributors of it.

"I think those who are bringing the drugs in didn't give a damn, and they chose their well-being over the well-being of a certain segment of people. Because we are black and very gullible people.

"I go back to the debate between Du Bois and Booker T. Washington, and the debate between Malcolm X and King. The urban northern black and the southern black. I think you would say the southern blacks were gullible. Booker T. says, 'No, don't try to integrate. Just learn the skill and be good farmers.' Right? Was it Garvey or Du Bois that said, 'No, hell no. Let's take a vote and go back to Africa.' He was more militant. Malcolm says, 'Hell no. If he does it to me, do it back to him.' I guess you would say King was teaching us to be gullible. 'Turn the other cheek and love thy brother, even though he's putting a foot up our butts.' Were we always gullible? Willing to accept the treatment whites imposed on us? It all depends on what school we, as black people, came from, because we were never uniform on that. Going back to the Civil War. There's a group that wanted to be more militant, and wanted to pull away and do their own thing. White man came in there, shot them.

"There was another group that says, 'No, let's forget it. Let's just go on and become a part of the system. Let's be good helpers.' So we've never agreed. We never had a consensus on that. We will never function as a 'we' again."

Of course that had been my original question, months—now years—ago. And though I thought I had answered that question for myself some time back, I was not quite satisfied with my formulation: Is there such a thing as "we"?

"There's a 'we' in terms of, we suffer from common threats, and that kind of thing, how we choose to deal with the situation. I'm not saying if you're from New York, I'm not certain you and I would agree on what's necessary for young children to grow up and prosper. I'm not sure we would agree. One of the things they did in the '70s in colleges was demand a black floor in dorms to live on. They wanted a table, a soul food table. That was the thing in those days. Some blacks were opposed to that. To them it was Jim Crow. The folks up North were saying, 'We want to close into ourselves.' And I've seen it with the kids at Holy Cross; I've heard of several conflicts between the southern and the northern black as to how they respond to white America. Then we start calling each other names. Uncle Tom and all that. Those are the symptoms of conflicts about black strategy, overall strategy, and we differ."

The judge blamed it, largely, on the media.

"You don't remember the first time *Soul Train* came on, do you? When it was in Chicago, Illinois. At the same time there was *American Bandstand.* All right. Now during that period of time the media began to reach uniformly among blacks nationwide. And this rap thing is sort of the extension of this. Because when I was a kid growing up, I would go to Nashville to find out what the dances were in Nashville. And I would go to Atlanta, and Atlanta was doing the Shingaling, and Orlando was doing something else. But each city had its own thing.

"So when you came back to Savannah, you could say, 'Hey, this is what they're doing in Nashville. This is what they're doing there.' Black communities having a different flavor. That doesn't exist anymore. When *Soul Train* hit the TV, everybody did what everybody was doing on *Soul Train.* So it didn't matter whether you went to New York City, or if you went to Hattiesburg, Mississippi. They would do the same dance. During the days of Jim Crow, we didn't see ourselves on TV. But there was a strong communication network, and an intercourse among all the black communities. *Ebony* magazine, *Jet,* and all would tell us about these things.

"We lost all that. When the media finally allowed blacks access. I don't say access. Allowed blacks to see themselves, then we all began to respond and possibly to think the same way. I think it's a plus and a negative to all sides of that, because there was a richness. They used to call a dance the Philly Dog. You remember the Philly Dog?"

"I do not remember the Philly Dog," I allowed.

"The Philly Dog was the baddest dance. In the late '60s. I mean, it was together. It was the Philly Dog because there was a dance called the Dog. But the folks in Philadelphia had a different flip to it. And it was real cool. So they called it the Philly Dog, and somebody would call it the L.A. Hop and da, da, da. Each town had its own flavor, which we've lost. And now we are all looking at that boob tube, and we all want to be like Mike.

"My parents always thought that we, the younger generation, were going to the dogs. Well, I'm in the same boat now. What's happening with this younger generation? They're going to the dogs. I feel comfortable relying solely on black cultural growth. And the richness it brings. I'm very comfortable with black professionals, and anything of that nature, because I remember that for hundreds of years that's all we could survive on, and it was good. And I look at our schools and our teachers, and they're not getting the quality education today that we got in segregated schools.

"Even categories like Behavior Disorder. It makes it sound like you have a psychological problem. Then you wonder why the kid in second grade's B.D. Now white kid jumps up in the classroom. 'Oh, he's just slightly hyper.' That's the way the integrated system began to deal with a black child who might look you in the eye and challenge you. Whereas in the segregated days, if you got out of place, they'd just take you outside and jack you up on the wall. When you came back in that classroom, you sat there.

"I went to Catholic school all my life. Segregated Catholic school. And if you didn't do the homework, you had to leave school and go to the convent, and sit there until you'd done it. Can you imagine sitting till six, seven o'clock at night, at the convent? You're hearing them sing and doing Mass and all, while you do your homework? The next day, you did your homework. Now they don't take time with you. They just write you off, track you out. And so we're really hurt tremendously in our educational systems. You might want to count the number of black colleges that have lost their accreditation in the last ten years. You'll find most of them in the South. Barbara Scotia, Knoxville College—there's a bunch of them. Produced class graduates. Closed up, because black kids don't want to go there anymore. They want the University of Georgia, and we're losing our institutions quickly.

"Be careful what you ask for. You might get it.

"Even though we lost control of our educational institutions in the South, in the North you never did have any. What we're beginning to see down South is what you have always had up North. Mainly there's going to be a group of kids that's going to do well. They'll go to Harvard, Yale or Princeton. There's going to be a strong underclass, dropouts and all that crap. Now that's happening to us now. Was it all for naught? Honestly speaking, for me, I'm better off because of integration. But several of my friends are worse off because of it. They would have survived; they would have prospered. There would have been somebody who would have mentored them through had the schools not been desegregated."

Though his outlook might appear dire—some would say clear-eyed—the Honorable Orion Douglas was nonetheless working with young black men. He was a charter member of Fourteen Black Men of Glynn—a group of black professional men who had "adopted," at that time, twenty-one youngsters, beginning in the tenth grade. "To try to get the idea across that the black male is responsible for the black male. The black man must say you must subdue your passions. The black woman cannot do that—only men can do that. Even with money she can't replace the black man. When that boy turns into a teenager—fourteen, fifteen—he ain't going to listen to her anymore. The problem with black men is other black men."

. . .

To put it kindly—today St. Simons Island is largely a tourist trap.

*The Official Guide to the Golden Isles* (St. Simons, Little St. Simons, Sea Island and Jekyll) reads:

> WELCOME TO THE GOLDEN ISLES
> Southerly winds softly caress your face, turning you see the sun setting over the horizon while the surf gently laps against your feet on cool, wet sand. As you take in the view, your [sic] become aware of a sense of presence, an idea that this landscape has not been altered all that much from the way generations past may have viewed it and enjoyed it as you are.

I often wonder if anyone of driving age would actually read and fall for such rhinoceros dung. Please don't misunderstand: much of the island is inspiring, the salt marshes, the beaches, the dense forests with oaks the size of small houses. Luckily Sapelo Island is still pristine due to the good graces of R. J. Reynolds, Jr., who bought the island and gave it to the state with the proviso that it and its black inhabitants be left the heck alone—one of the best things North Carolina tobacco money ever did; the Rockefeller family did the same thing with Jekyll Island. St. Simons and Sea Island, which you reach either by boat or by driving through the larger St. Simons Island, have been developed and developed, country-clubbed and hotel- and golf course–resortified. Sea Island is practically choked with expensive, exclusive houses, and all the beaches are private.

Sea Island is also the home to the five-star, "ever grand" Cloister. With 264 accommodations "in all," that "range from $262 to $420 for a party of two, per day." "At the Cloister traditions never die." And for those who care, "the hotel orchestra plays for dancing, year round."

All said, I still understand why Tina and Jonée choose to live there. In fact, despite its being yards from one of the most congested places on the island, their house could be hundreds of miles from civilization. The socialist and romance novelist Eugenia Price had lived there for decades until her death in 1997, as well as novelist William Diehl among others.

Perhaps my reaction to the ever-threatening consumerist rot on St. Simons had less to do with conspicuous consumption, and more to do with my very acute awareness of what had happened on that island. Georgia had Atlanta, one of America's bastions of African American success on every level, and it had St. Simons, which seemed in a way to be regressive. Yes, it seemed that the "traditions never die."

That bothered me no end. And still does.

. . .

"I was born quite some years ago," she told me. That event occurred in a small town called Wrightsburg, Georgia.

Mrs. Joanna Stevens Allen was kindly and demonstrative in her speaking, and graceful with hands and arms.

All together, her parents had nine children.

"All of us are past seventy years old."

Her father operated a grocery store and ran a farm. "My dad was a deputy sheriff. Whites used to come to him for information. He didn't have a high school education, but he had common sense. Which went a long way. And they took his advice in a lot of cases.

"We'd go out in the woods, and haul wood, and my dad planted cotton. Not that much. Rice. We didn't ever buy rice, because he planted all the rice that we ever used. I know all about wading in the water knee-deep to work in the rice fields. And also harvesting the rice and bringing it home and stacking it and different things like that. Sooner or later, we beat the rice. That's the way they do to get the chaff out. You'd be surprised how easily it's done. I wish I had the money for the time I have spent knocking the rice off the seeds. Put it in the mortar, and beat it, and take it in the house and cook it. We did that. I finally got away from it, and they stopped farming, they don't farm like they used to do out there."

After graduating from Dorchester Academy ("it was built by some people out of New York, because in Liberty County, Georgia, they didn't have a high school for blacks"), she came to St. Simons.

"I came over here in 19—I believe—35. And I started working. The work that you found over here then was mostly domestic. In the homes. They didn't have hotels and motels and all that over here then, like they have now. Everywhere, every other step you make, you can find either a place to stay or a place to eat. But then, there were boarding houses. They would have guests come, and they'd put them up in rooms. I would be the maid, waitress, help the cook. Combination. They weren't rich people so much. I had worked for people that came down here just for the summer, because you didn't find a lot of entertainment around here in the winter. They had a saying that after Labor Day, the swallows on the wire, that's about all you could see. The people would go, and you'd come back again in May or June.

"I guess it was in the '40s, more motels and hotels were being built. You got two dollars a week, two-fifty a week. Fifty cents a day. Like that. And the people that worked over on Sea Island they used to get seven dollars a week, a dollar a day. And that was big bucks. A dollar a day. Seven dollars a week.

"People coming to spend the summer, they would bring their help with them, and they had a little house or something built on the outside, for these servants or whatever, but not in the house. That is being done sometimes now. I don't hear about it as often, but just a few years back, a lady would bring her help, I think she was from Ohio. Frankly, the way sometimes you were treated, you felt like giving up.

"You felt like giving up, the way some of your employers would treat you. I tell you, the part that really is true. It really was downgraded because I told a lady something that one lady did. That's when I was coming over here in the summer, going to school. And that was way back. You would do all your work that's supposed to be done. With the cook in the kitchen, you'd set the tables up and prepare to serve the guests when they came. And after all of this then, the maids or the help, they had their food, and cleaned up the kitchen, and they have a break, a little break in between, then they have to fix lunch. And then they'd go home and stay about two hours, and then come back and fix dinner at night. But this one incident, I ran into a couple of incidents.

"Now after it was time for me to eat my breakfast, toast, bacon, or whatever, and you have at certain times, like preserves, to go on your toast and whatnot. (When I think about it now I don't know where that lady is, but I hope she's in heaven.) But I got a little strawberry preserves and put on my toast because that's what I wanted to have. And that lady came to me, and she said, 'Oooooh. Did you have this on your toast? You can't have this.' She came and took that toast off of my plate, and took the preserves off and put them back in the jar. Believe it or not. Now these things happened. That's right. And then another woman I worked for, she had a way of demanding and yelling and saying, 'You do good. You're working for me.' And I guess they were saying, 'You're bad. So you do what I say.' I was setting up the table, and she was telling me what to put on the table, some things like the silver and the napkins and all that stuff together. And this is the way I answered her, I said, 'All right, Miz Rose. I will do that in the future.' 'How dare you talk to me? You get in there, and you do so and so.' Now I don't care. I've always been firm. And I stood by her and I said, 'Yes.' I said, 'Yes.' Had my apron on. I started untying my apron, and out the door I went. And she looked at me. Guests were sitting up there in the living room waiting for food. I walked out the back door, and I had my umbrella, and I was kind of furious. So I went on out and I remember by the time I got around to the front house, I had forgotten my umbrella. So I turned around, and she had already come to the back door, and she was looking for me, and she spied me, and she went back in the house like a streak of lightning.

"So I just walked on out. That lady is dead, and she hasn't paid me for my last week's work. Everytime I'd go by there, if she was in the house, she didn't answer. But there are good people and there are terrible people. I used to stay in a little house down there with a friend of mine. Her mother had a house, and I stayed there with her. We all stayed in the same room because it was hard to get a place to stay. After I had been home for a while, these people came looking for me. The guests that were supposed to eat. They'd heard the conversation. And they came and knocked on my door. And back then if you got a two or three dollar tip you were doing good. And they came and brought me a tip because I used to be the one to wait on them. They just said nonchalantly, 'Are you going back to work?' I said, 'I don't know. I'll think about it!' I just said, 'You all on your way home? Back up to the northern states somewhere? You have a safe trip.' But I thought that was so nice of them to come to find me because they knew I was mistreated, see. But anyway, that is just some of the things that I found."

Mrs. Allen's first memories of St. Simons were that it had been mostly owned by black folk. "Way back, because my dad came over here. They had a terrible storm in 1898, I believe. And they had to come and rebuild the place and plant grass over at the golf course and all that. They didn't have any open way to get here. You had to travel by boat. I know people need more, but some I don't think really was thinking when they let their property go for almost nothing. If they tried to buy it back, they couldn't get it. That street down there, they got a lot of condominiums. It's fenced off now. And only black people occupied it. And the name of it was Harlem. And that was Harlem Lane for a long time until a young man asked for the name to be changed in honor of his father-in-law.

"Some people think if they go up to a northern city, they have more rights. I've been in New York. I've been to a lot of places. You are black all over the world. That's right.

"But as far as segregation, yes, there's a lot of segregation over here. Go on that beach and put your feet in the water, you did not swim on that beach. No blacks. No, no. You did not swim. Blacks did not swim. No. You did not go out there, unless you were nursing a little child or something. These things I know for a fact. This happened since I was here. But the law and the NAACP worked to get a lot of this done.

"Now I worked over at Sea Island at the Cloister for a long time. I worked at the King and Prince a long time. And I met the Prince from the Netherlands.

"I worked at the King and Prince for about twenty years, and I worked at the Cloister for about twelve. I retired from there about thirteen years ago. And one thing about what they're doing on St. Simon's now with blacks, I think it's because it has to be done. They're putting blacks in places, in offices and whatnot, that they hadn't ever been before. If there's ten whites, then you'll have one black. And that's an advance. But you know, they could put more than one.

"I was supervisor at the Cloister. And we worked so many different maids, porters, and the bellmen, you got to know all the people. I'm supposed to issue certain orders, you know. Okay? Most of them were black women and black men. Now, you can't get work in these hotels because whites have almost taken over. Oh my, in the last five years, I would say. Even before I left, there were some of them there, but they're a bunch of them now. They didn't do that kind of work, because that kind of work was for blacks. That's what they thought. They wanted the white-collar jobs and all that. And they found out if they worked and made five dollars, it's just like the five dollars they made out of a main office. Five dollars is five dollars. I had problems in a way, but then the executive housekeeper told me, 'Joanna, you keep them all under your wing.' I tried to work in a way that I will not do anything that would cause them any kind of bad conduct on their job. I talked to them. I said, 'I'd rather talk to you. Now, you don't do the things that I asked you to do, and it doesn't get done, then I have to go to the person that's over me, because I need my job.'

"Sometimes they would go and whisper behind my back. One girl left there one day and she told me everything she was big enough to say. Yes, because I told her what she was supposed to have done. She said she wasn't going to do it. I told her 'You do it, because it's supposed to be done.'" The housekeeper suspended the woman for a few days, in essence causing her to lose three days' pay. "The day she came back to work, she come in about nine. I'd get there about eight and get everything together. And she ran in that office. I was sitting at the desk. She said, 'Oh, Mrs. Allen, ain't I a fool.' That's just the way she said it."

There were other matters, like the time a maid drank all a guest's whisky. ("So I asked her, I said, 'I heard that you just drank some whisky that didn't belong to you.' 'Yes, ma'am, I did.' And started crying. I said, 'Don't cry.' 'I told him I would buy it back.' I said, 'Now, listen, if you had the money, and you knew you were coming to the job, and you'd be drunk, why didn't you buy your own whisky?' Ain't I right? Buy your own. That man could have asked for her to be fired. Hmm-mmm. Hmm-mmm. Yes.")

"Yep, yep, I had more incidents than one, but there's no use in going through all those incidents, because I stayed over there twelve years. I encountered a lot. Sometimes they come in and they were too drunk to come to work, some of them. Some of them may often lie, say they're sick, and they're not sick. I can understand all that, but if you're not coming, let somebody know in time, then you'll try to get somebody else. Be honest with yourself and with your coworkers and what not. I think as long as you go behind somebody's back, you're not going to ever move in the way you should.

"So these are the things, in these hotels and motels. I don't know. I don't know. Sometimes I told them, I said, 'You know what? I'm telling you all what's supposed to be done. But if you stop and look at yourself, you all are not ready for black on black. You all are not ready for this. You all want a white person to breathe down your throat.'

"I think it's good to work together, but I think honesty is the best policy. It's easy. But you just have to practice it. You got to practice it. And just like I tell these kids, around here. I have seen children grow up from this place. Ever since little babies. Play in my yard, get all in my flower bed and all that stuff, and I'd chase them out, but I haven't had any problems with any of the kids that grew up around me. I respect them and they respect me. If I see them doing something that's wrong, then I tell them. I don't tell them in a way like, you know, hard and mean. Call to them and talk to them, like they're human beings. Because I have seen some of them, you know, rough girls and boys, rough and ready. And I'm still doing it, you know.

"But the kids have grown in a way now, you don't know exactly how to approach them. I pray for the whole nation. Because the nation is in turmoil. That's true.

"I don't know who's at fault, but I tell you one thing, it's bad. The kids go away and they come back. Some of them's grown, they come back and bring their children and their children's children. All they know around here is Miss Joanna. Miss Joanna. If I can't tell you something that is of some value, I'll just be quiet.

"That's what I try to do, and I do that in church. I've been a member of the Emmanuel Baptist Church, oh my God, I guess for about fifty years. Almost fifty years."

Mrs. Joanna Allen was involved in a bible study group—"bible sharing" she called it—and donated time to the Mary House Ministry

Daycare. "It's day care and ministry. They have about forty children right back over there, and they go to kindergarten from this day care. I volunteer and I'm on the board. One or two white children." Recently, she had been honored as United Way Volunteer of the Year. "You know what? I try to keep busy. I don't want to go crazy. I try to keep busy. If I stay in this house all day long, I'd be crazy."

"Well, I'm a native of St. Simons. Been here all my life. I've traveled extensively, domestically and also several places abroad. And, in spite of the difficulties that one might have encountered, I still think Glynn County is the best county in the United States. I won't say that for all of Georgia, but Glynn County. Because we never had the extremes either way. There wasn't any intermarriage between the blacks and the whites, but there was always that respect there. And I've seen the island change an awful lot since it was really an island. When there wasn't a causeway here. And people had to go back and forth by boat."

Mr. Jasper Barnes—distinguished, lion-looking, water-brown eyes, gray at temple—spoke in a measured, almost military way.

He told me that at the base of the causeway over in Brunswick there was a restaurant called Emmeline Hessie. It had been named for the two boats that ferried people back and forth, the Emmeline and the Hessie, at that time the only transportation on and off the island. "I've seen the contour of the land change considerably from nature's way of taking it away and bringing it back."

He told me about Neptune Park, named after a black man, Neptune Smalls. He had been the slave of a family whose sons had gone off to the Civil War, and he kept watch for their return on the shore where the park now stood. "Because he was a 'good nigger,' as they would have said at that time, in gratitude for how loyal he was to the family, they donated this place to him. So it's not named for King Neptune of the Sea," he laughed. "It's named for Neptune Smalls. Now I have documented facts to that effect. And incidentally, he was my great-grandaddy. So my roots are here. I was here when there was very few automobiles, and horse and wagon and buggies was the main source of transportation. Over the years I've seen the population explode. We got an airport just down the street there. It doesn't accommodate the big commercial planes. But then you got a commercial field just over in Brunswick, called Glen Cove, where the commercial planes come in."

In Mr. Barnes's opinion, the "greater amount" of discrimination had disappeared on the island. "But there's still some around." And he attributed most of that to the "old diehards." "I think they would like to see it go back to the 'good old days,' like people usually say. I hear a lot of blacks say that. I don't agree. The good old days when you worked for a dollar a day or something like that. Hell, was that different from what it is now?"

I was curious about ownership of the land. From what people had been telling me, most of the islands were owned by black folks. What happened?

"What really happened was during the Reconstruction days, when Sherman marched through to the sea, most of the white people got away from here as fast as they possibly could. He took the land and gave the bigger portions to blacks. During my lifetime, I've seen a lot of property that was owned by blacks that's now in the hands of the bigger companies. Predominantly white. This tract of land wasn't one that was given to slaves; my grandfather bought this property here. Twenty-five acres of it for $300. Back in 1903."

So much of why black people left the islands had to do with the economy, and not being able to earn a decent livelihood in this essentially remote archipelago. "But during my lifetime, the original owners' children migrated to the big cities like New York, Chicago and Detroit. City-minded people. And they forgot about this property. Just didn't mean anything to them. And most of the property was confiscated for taxes. The bigger portion of Sea Island Park, going back down to the bridge, was confiscated for taxes. It's a funny thing, they have discriminatory prices on the property in the predominantly white areas. Blacks don't move in because they can't afford it. But when the opportunity arises, there are many whites that move into the black community, into the black neighborhood. We have neighborhoods now that's whites and blacks. Only the most exclusive places like Sea Island, I don't think there's a black who's over there. Because of the financial level. A lot of the blacks came back, to find out that they had some property down here, and they probably sold out to the whites because they didn't have any use for it. The island wasn't near as populated as it is now. They didn't know what it meant to live by the ocean or by the rules of the marshes or whatnot. I think that's what happened."

Like neighboring Jekyll Island, St. Simons had been one of the "last places for preparation for the saltwater Africans," Mr. Barnes told me. "These people coming from Africa was thrown off, because they were sick or something. Thrown off to die. They separated the good ones from the bad ones, and got them cleaned up for sale, at the market. The last ship that brought slaves over was called *The Wanderer.* They have a hotel complex on Jekyll now. It's named the Wanderer.

"I've seen the island when it didn't have any electricity. People used wood for heating, and kerosene for lighting. They had one ice house over here, but I know the ice was made in Brunswick and brought over on the ship. On the *Emmeline.* And for lights down there in the village, they had what you call a dynamo, generates electricity. And each of the places had electricity. That was true of white and black. All of us."

Rice plantations dotted the coast to the east and north, between Brunswick and Bailmouth, amid the marshes and swamplands. St. Simons produced a great deal of cotton as well as timber, wood that was legendary for its quality. Mr. Barnes told me that the famous battleship of the War of 1812, the *Constitution,* had been built from St. Simons oak. ("I can't back it up, but I'm inclined to believe that some of those oaks were cut right off our property here.")

Someone had told me that after the cotton market collapsed, lumber became St. Simons' big industry, and blacks found work in the mills.

"This was the Hilton and Dodge sawmills," Mr. Barnes said. My maternal grandfather was one of the head sawers down there. His name was George Morrison. That was a main source of employment here, during that time. They fastened these logs together and bring them down to Altamaha, down to Frederica Road. To this mill. That's the way they made their living. I've talked to one man who did this a number of years ago. The way they used to survive, they'd build this raft; they'd fasten these logs together, float them down. And they also build a platform, where they could have a little something to cook and eat. It's a tidal river."

Mr. Barnes told me that a tsunami had once crippled the island. "The water covered St. Simons. 1898. Biggest catastrophe they've had here. Tidal wave. Covered St. Simons. Except this, this was one of the high ridges. Some people were destroyed, and a lot of people were saved. Everything was washed up."

I wondered if Mr. Barnes often got to Sapelo Island, and I asked what it was like.

"Well, if you don't have facilities over there, you have to stay with somebody, rent or pay something. That's why I always see those mobile homes. That's about five or six of them over there, and we stayed in one. We had a ball. We carried what we wanted over there, and then we'd have one of the ladies from Sapelo prepare food for us. There's no segregation over there so far as the beach is concerned. R. J. Reynolds fixed it to furnish transportation. They have boats that go back and forth. They say you can't go over there, unless you're invited. That's not true.

"You go anytime you want, and you don't have to ask anybody. At one time, you could go for free. They charge a dollar now. A dollar going and a dollar coming back. They also have tours that go over there. They'd take you all around the island and show you.

"People over there are not backward people. There are some over there that's probably never left that island. The very oldest people. But they're not backward people now. Most of them are progressive people."

Mr. Jasper Barnes had served in the military during World War II. "Hawaii, the Fijis, the New Hebrides, Bougainville, New Caledonia." Over the years he developed a passion for travel. ("After I got out of the service, I never knew I was going to be able to retire, so I used to work for about eleven months and take the other one month, and travel.") He had traveled extensively in the West—Nevada, California. In fact, recently, while he had been in Los Angeles, attending a taping of *The Price Is Right,* "they stole my Cadillac. I don't know how. It had 38,000 miles on it. Had like thirty-five when I left here. And I was devastated."

"The only states that I haven't been in, that's the states of Alaska, Washington, Oregon, Minnesota, Montana and South Dakota. All the rest of them I've been there many times."

Mr. Barnes "played around with real estate" these days. He owned property on the island, and had holdings in Arizona. "They call it 'entrepreneur.' I don't name it." He gave a chuckle. "I'm just doing what I feel needs to be done."

I asked: "In your opinion, being a travel-minded man, how does the South differ from other parts of the country?"

He took a long, serious, thoughtful pause. "I can't vouch for all of the South. Places like in Philadelphia, Mississippi, during the '60s, during the Martin Luther King era, where they killed all those people. I've been there too. There are certain places in Georgia that I will pass by, according to what the paper says, the media. But I think the northern states, while the support of segregation was supposed to be minimized, it hardly was minimized. There was still segregation there. They had a different way of hiding it. In other words, the Yankees, so to speak, was people who throw bricks and hid it in their hand. In the South, he'll tell you up front how to handle him. When the slaves was freed under Abraham Lincoln, it wasn't his desire to free the slaves, he was trying to bring the union together. And incidentally, the slaves was free, but I think it was one of God's plans for this thing to happen, so it happened.

"These southern people. The North had the know-how and manufacturers and whatnot. The South had the know-how and food production, farms and textiles. So I still think, in spite of the difficulties that one had encountered, I think the opportunity for the black man, advancements in the North are no better than in the southern states at that time. When I think about the things going on back in Booker T. Washington days, and the finest school, Tuskegee Institute. A lot of things come out of that as wasn't expected. They figured a black man didn't have sense enough to fly a plane. (I done some flying myself. Flying a plane is not as hard as running a car. I think navigation is probably the biggest thing about it that's complicated.) Mississippi had more black people than any state in the union. And Georgia was next. There are more educated black people came out of the state of Mississippi than any other state in the union. I guess because more and more is there.

"Now you was old enough to remember the Martin Luther King days, and that started the whole ball. It's much better now than then. I think the Negro race as a whole made more progress from slavery to this point than any nation in the world. We have black men doing anything that a white man did. Doctors, lawyers, teachers, preachers, you name it. And now we have black mayors in the biggest cities. We had one governor up in Virginia. So when you stop to think of it, from the slavery to today, we was in slavery 300 years or more, and during that time I think the white man has been able to destroy the unity. Sometime I think he has destroyed unity, and then sometime I don't know. I know he abolished all the history of the black man. Because some of these slaves, some of them were daughters of kings and rulers. I think about those things seriously sometime. It was no way the man could own thousands of slaves and half a dozen bosses to keep control over those people. So what he done, he taught them to conspire against each other. He'd take one or two of them in the house, he'd treat them better than the others, every damn thing. That's the way he controlled them, and the way I think he's destroyed quite a bit of the unity. It took us 200 years before we could read. What the hell's going on?"

I came, more and more, around to the idea that it all had to do with Middle Passage.

In many ways, these islands were where it all began. Of course, there was Annapolis, New Bedford, New Orleans, St. Augustine, Richmond, Providence, the ports of entry, and then there were the slave markets.

Many African Americans will chastise me that it all began in Africa. I, too, like the *Roots* notion of my connection to Africa—but that connection is only a part of the modern-day reality of an African American, a romantic and at times irresponsible notion. My history, as an American, began with Middle Passage, and the end of Middle Passage. Only in dealing with that historical trauma will I ever accept my Americanness, my blackness, my humanity.

This is the sticking point: The appellation "African American" is all the more curious, as "we" have allowed the specter of slavery to dim and recede. Is it out of shame? Or is it fear? The fear of accepting that our connection to Africa is so traumatically severed that it becomes incumbent upon us to begin anew: here. Perhaps even to accept that Africa was never the land of paradisical freedom that has been part and parcel of Afrocentrism.

I read about the current struggles in paradoxically named Liberia, with dismay and a bemused disquiet. Those repatriated former slaves named their country's capital Monrovia, after the American president who sent them there, and I pray that the descendants of these freedmen are no relation to me. (When I write this, I am fully aware that many of the monstrous regimes that replaced the colonial rule were themselves largely proxies for the two superpowers, two empires that cared about little else but winning their geopolitical war of ideologies and dominance. However, and regardless, the watchdogs and madmen, from Idi Amin Dada to Robert Mugabe to Joseph Mobuto, were willing, sub-Saharan black pawns, backed by millions of black policemen, soldiers, officials et al, who knew exactly what they were doing, and were not, historically speaking, sui generis to the continent, the place my foremothers were kidnapped from, often with the cooperation of their dark-skinned brothers.)

This is the wound. We talk around it, we sing around it, we dance around it, we joke around it—but we do not really confront it. The hurt simply hurts too damn much.

How do we heal such a hurt and move on? I am not entirely certain. Perhaps it lies in confronting, head-on, the meanings encoded in the history of those Africans—new, frightened, defeated, demoralized, naked, cold, angry. Perhaps it lies in taking their pain and confusion into our breasts and never forgetting. Perhaps, at the end of the day, we, like those who built and maintained the Underground Railroad, who took up arms, who rediscovered what had been expunged from them, now struggling on the computer-vexed, crime-prone, cancer-plagued eve of the twenty-first century—must relearn that fierceness, that same intelligence, that same dignity and pride.

So much is up to us. So much depends upon choice. So much remains to be done. So much can go wrong. So much can still go right.

> In the olden days no Negro would drop a hook to fish at Ebo. It was "ha'nted!"
>
> —Margaret Davis Cate, *Early Days of Coastal Georgia*

> And now, at dark of the moon, they say, when the water laps on the old landing and the breeze sighs across the marshes, one can catch again a faint echo of the rhythmic chant of the Ebo tribe.
>
> —Burnette Vanstory, *Georgia's Land of the Golden Isles*

> Another spot that they avoid is Eboe's Landing, between Gascoigne's Bluff and Frederica. The slave ships were said to have landed their cargoes here, and there is a tradition that a slave who had been a chief in his native land led a band of slaves through the woods to death in the sound, in preference to slavery.
>
> —Caroline Couper Lovell, *The Golden Isles of Georgia*

> Heahd bout duh Ibo's Landing? Das duh place weah dey bring duh Ibos obuh in a slabe ship an wen dey git yuh, dey ain lak it an so dey all staht singin an dey mahch right down in duh ribbuh tuh mahch back tuh Africa, but dey ain able tuh get deah. Dey gits drown.
>
> —Savannah Unit Georgia Writer's Project,
> Work Projects Administration, *Drums and Shadows:*
> *Survival Studies Among the Georgia Coastal Negroes*

The state of Georgia banned the importation of African human chattel in 1798. Ten years later, the United States government did so as well. This did not stop slavery, and it certainly did not stop new shipments of kidnapped Africans.

They had been taken by the people of Arochukwu, probably from what is now Nigeria or Ghana. They were Ibo (or Ebo or Igboo or Egbo—the spelling, to me, seems immaterial as they would have used very different notation). They were sold through a broker at a seaport on the Gulf of Guinea. They landed at Skidaway Island, near Savannah. Seventy-five were sold to Thomas Spaulding of Sapelo Island, and to John Couper of St. Simons. (Both men had been in the state legislature and had put ink to paper in support of the 1798 law.) They paid $500 for each slave. The transport schooner was called the *York,* and it arrived at Dunbar Creek in May of 1803.

I wonder now exactly how it was done. Did it begin with a plan? Was it spontaneous? Did they fight with their chains on? Shackled one to another? Or were they without chains? Did someone snatch a gun or a sword? How long did it last? It is said that two sailors also drowned, but what happened to the others? Killed? Fled to tell the tale? And what went through the minds of those Ibos in the hour of their liberation?

When the mutiny was over—some say a shaman, some say a chief, some say an official—led them to the creek. *Orimir Omambala bu anyi bia. Orimiri Omambala ka anyi ga ejina,* they sang. *The water spirit brought us. The water spirit will take us home.* If the god Chukwu wanted them to die, then they would die, H. A. Sieber writes. Perhaps they thought they could make it back.

By most accounts ten to twelve Ibos drowned that day, and however many survived were taken to their respective new "homes."

Matter, physical matter as we know it, exists in four states: solid, liquid, gas, plasma. All matter consists of molecules made of atoms made of electrons and protons and neutrons made of Lord knows how many smaller, and infinitely smaller particles. According to the laws of physics, the reason a human being is unable to walk on water is due to the fact that his molecules, being in a solid state, move more slowly than those molecules in liquid (water)—they are out of molecular sync.

I learned this in school and through books. It is not inconceivable that I am the descendant of one of the survivors of that day back in 1803. But that is one knowledge.

Another knowledge came from my Uncle Roma who taught me Sunday School at First Baptist Church. I remember one Sunday school lesson about the day Jesus the Nazarene walked on the Sea of Galilee. He told his disciple Peter to step out of the boat, and Peter did, standing on the water, but by and by, the fisherman began to sink below the surface. The carpenter said to him, "Your faith is sinking: believe."

Uncle Roma told us that morning, "If you have faith, you can walk on water."

That is another kind of knowledge.

Ana Bel Lee Washington had a smile that simply raised the spirit. It had less to do with the upward lilt in her apple cheeks, than her eyes. She had smiling eyes.

Mrs. Washington was a painter. Some hoity-toity folk like to draw distinctions between "trained" artists and "untrained" artists. They use terms like "primitive" and "naive." Frankly, I despise such categorization. Training has nothing at all to do with artistic expression. Some may have more book learning, more knowledge of technique. But the importance lies in the effect the piece has on the observer. The paintings of Ana Bel Lee Washington move me deeply.

I met that most gentle of women at her apartment in a modern complex on St. Simons, and she showed me her many paintings, and we spoke over a table where she was working on one of those 1,000-piece puzzles. I told her how much my grandmother loved to work on those very same puzzles too, and how I, as a boy, on Saturday evenings, would help her.

Mrs. Washington gave me that smile again.

We fell into talking about the way things were and the way things are. She pointed out how little black folk went to church nowadays, how integration had made black resorts disappear and so many small black businesses vanish. "We thought that was going to be a solution, but it turned out it wasn't. Now that I can go anywhere I want to go, then I don't have to go to this safe haven.

"You can't think of what was being wasted. I'm thinking of the area that I lived in—of course, you always went downtown to the big stores—you were always looking for bargains, you know. But integration changed a whole lot of stuff that we had. If you desire to, you can go to a mixed church, oftimes, especially if people go up the ladder, as they say, they change. Their wants change. They want a different social group.

"And churches, when you had your bake sales and your chicken frys and whatnot, and Miss Jones raised so much money, and that was the prestige that you got. Through your efforts. You could proudly stand up because they called your name in church and whatnot. I think that integration played a bigger part in the downfall of the group. It's strange, down here, now there's two or three restaurants that are run by blacks. But they're a passive sort of people here. You know, 'Mister Charlie's always taken care of me, and Mister Charlie don't take care of me.' I see it. Of course then I, how can I say that when I'm not around that many of them?"

Mrs. Washington noted the ongoing struggles between blacks and white developers on the island for land, and how the African American community tried to defy the attempts to seize their land. "But bit by bit they began to lose the land. That's all through the South. You know how the developers would come in and blacks just lost land. So I just went to one meeting and I said, 'I didn't come down here to go through the same stuff I went through up in Detroit. I'm retired. And I'm retired from the whole thing.' I'm not a property owner. So I backed out of it, and I don't go."

Watching people force other people off their land made her angry. "Money talks wherever you are. You can defeat them today, and whatever the time limit is for them to come back, they'll be back. But I don't know what the world is coming to. You listen to TV—I had to stop listening to some. I look at CNN and I like to listen to talk shows. Debates, you know. And CNN had me so mad. I'd sit here and I'd be fussing at the television, 'How can you be so stupid?' and whatnot. I cut it out. I said, 'I can't listen to this.'"

Ana Bel Lee Washington moved from Detroit, Michigan, to St. Simons Island after she retired from the welfare department in 1983. Her brother and sister-in-law had made the island where the sister-in-law had grown up their home. When Mrs. Washington's brother died in 1990, she had no desire to return to the North. "No reason."

Mrs. Washington told me it took her a while to adjust to St. Simons. "Oh, the quietness, laid-back lifestyle, but after a number of years I began to make more friends among the artists. The people are rather clannish and cliquish. If you're sick, they'll knock down your door. And if there's trouble in your family, they're very kind in that respect. But as far as say building a bosom buddy, no. Not going to happen. I understand, though, it's a common thing, even among whites.

"I think it's a southern thing, although my sister-in-law said when she came to Detroit, she found Detroit the same way. So now, I don't know.

"We don't get that many invitations anymore. That's not southern. That's worldwide.

"But it's just a lovely place to live. As long as you're not dependent on others. And as long as you're not looking for a finger-popping good time and all that kind of stuff, which goes on, but it's mostly the younger people, you know. We do have some social affairs, the arts center does.

We give a great, big Christmas party and everybody has a nice time and whatnot. But I just love it, because I don't have the fears I would have in a big city. I don't think I'd ever want to live in a big city again. Won't say 'never' because you never know what might come up and you'd have to. But I'd prefer to find me another small area. Except for the humidity in the summertime, the weather's gorgeous."

We discussed Julie Dash's film about the area, and I wondered if Mrs. Washington saw remnants of that culture still on the island.

"Not really. Not like Julie Dash's movie, no. That was a beautifully shot movie, but I was disappointed in it. The story, to me, was a little vague. But I don't see any of that way of life here now."

Once on St. Simons, Mrs. Washington volunteered at the Arts Center. In a way, it was an attempt to combat the sense of being an outsider, she told me. She watched people paint and eventually decided to try her hand at it. The only painting she had done theretofore had been a little paint-by-the-numbers in the 1970s.

"Got to be an obsession after a while. Let's see, I started in '84, in September. And by '87, I got my nerve up to do an exhibit. And any artist can tell you, that takes nerve, to watch people look at your work, talk about it and whatnot. Then I began to sell a little bit. But in '89 Tina and them asked me to do the Sea Island Festival. And I didn't have any idea whether I could do it or not. All my life my first words are, 'I don't know if I can do it.' Or, 'I can't.' So I gave it a try, and I got it done, within about a month's time, I think. That opened all kind of doors. I went into a gift shop and that lady really liked my work, so I sold quite a bit. And as time went on, it's just become something I love doing."

Jacob Lawrence was a painter she admired "greatly." "I went to Seattle in '90, and I talked to him on the phone. That was a thrill. The teacher wanted to know if I wanted to paint like him. But I had sort of settled into my own little thing. I had told him, 'No.' I had wanted to do it the way I was doing it. The teacher used to give me a lot more attention and then he explained to me that he didn't want me to progress to the point that it got too sophisticated; that I would lose, you know, the uniqueness of it."

"I think it has its own sophistication," I said.

"As they say, there's a difference."

Ana Bel Lee Washington liked to work from photographs, but, she told me, "Most of it I've made up. Except the buildings." She showed me pictures of churches in the area she had painted. A cotton field.

"You like the color green," I said.

"Yes, I guess I do. Greens and blues. I guess the island is green. I've done some sea things. They aren't too popular. The ruins over there of the hospital. Hospital ruins. I did this—" she showed me a recent painting. "Those are supposed to be ghosts. It's strictly my interpretation.

"A lot of pictures I get attached to, like this one. I made this one, I had it on the wall for I don't know how long. I did that in '88. It doesn't get sold, and I just bring it back home and put it back. This is the church right up the street, but then the scene I just made up. Because there's no trees like that up there now.

"I'm prolific, as they say. But that's my first inside church. It hasn't been out too much. I think it's been out once. I had two paintings that I just love, and I took them out for a show, and put an outrageous price on them and they sold. I could have cried. I said, 'Oh no.' And Jonee is responsible for that, because somebody asked him, 'Which are her best paintings?' And he went, boom, boom, boom, boom, boom. And she bought all of them. Then he was mad, because he had always said, 'Give me first choice.' It was an oyster row, see. I said, 'Sure. If I ever decide to sell it.' But I didn't put 'not for sale' on it. I wished I had now. It was a night scene, with the people with the oysters, and the house, the tabby house. I had put lights, it was lit up, the windows, I had the fire in the tin, and that's what fascinated a lot of people. Well, I used to almost cry when something would get sold. I guess there's a lot of me in it."

Another favorite, a wedding scene, the bride about to throw the bouquet, she donated to Spelman College.

"It's a shame, but I do get attached to them."

"Why do you say it's a shame?" I asked.

"I'd be glad when they get a good home, but I feel sad too. Because no two are alike. None of my paintings are alike. I can't copy. I may use the same houses, churches and things, but the scene is always different. And it just happened."

"Do you do many baptisms?"

"Hmm-mm. Quite a few. And this one, I'm just making up as I'm going along. I drew people on there, then I decided that I'm going to make it like a fair or something behind them. I had a road coming down here that I painted out today because I didn't like it. It wasn't doing what I thought it was."

"Does it work that way?" I asked. "Trial and error or . . . ?"

"Hmm-mm. That's one thing about oil. You don't like it, you can paint it out. Sometimes when I try that, then I end up changing. Because one time I had a bunch of people standing on the banks, and when I got to painting, I just changed to mountains and started over."

"Like something possesses you?"

She said, "I'm always saying, sometimes I don't do the painting. Something else is, somebody else is doing it, I think. I don't know, it just comes. Because the style I used in painting that one, I used the big brush on the sky, which was something new for me. The teacher asked me why didn't I use the same method for another part? I said, 'Don't feel like it.' One lady said to me, she was an artist, that she hadn't thought of using the yellow and green. This shade of yellow is a pure yellow, with a green that's about that color, and the two colors mixed together. But you're always looking at something saying, 'I wonder if I should fix this and fix that.' If you do, if you touch it, you're going to change the whole thing."

"When do you know you're done?" I asked Mrs. Washington.

"You just stop." She laughed.

Mrs. Washington showed me her rendition of Ibo's Landing. Oddly, it was divided into two panels, in both sides the dark, stoic men and women peered out in all their dignity, despite their enslavement. Though by the colors, the dark blues, the painting clearly was much more somber than the others. Yet the narrative scene of the two panels was confusing. Were they back in Africa in the right-hand panel? Had they walked on water?

"When I first came down and began to paint, I did a lot of reading. The interpretation of Ibo Landing at that time was that they put the slaves in this dense woods by the creek, Dunbar Creek. And that they walked out of the woods, into the water. Purposely. 'The water brought me here, and the water will take me home.' Later on, as time passed, I understand it has been documented that they went off the ship. But last February I think it was, I was up at Statesburg College for an exhibit. One of the professors and I were walking across the campus, and I talked about it. I said, I had such mixed emotions about doing the painting. Am I supposed to be happy? Because they're not going to be slaves? Or sad, because they drowned? So I just casually mentioned to her, I said, 'I don't think I'll ever do that painting again, unless I can show them in Africa.' And there it is.

"And one day I just split the canvas in half, and I had them going into the water, and coming out, and not only coming out, but being greeted. When I told people what I was going to do, they got hysterical.

"Because they thought that was silly, some people did. A fantasy. Well, it is a fantasy, but why not? You know? It's mine, and I won't sell either one of them."

She did that painting in 1988 or 1989, she remembered.

"What does the story mean to you?" I asked.

"Ibo Landing? It's fact," she said. "I think that there was a group of people that didn't want to be slaves. They had been uprooted and brought over here from their own homes and whatnot. And I think they really believed that when they went in the water, since the water brought them here, they could just swim home. That's what I like to think, as opposed to 'I'd rather kill myself than go.' I guess it means whatever you want, whatever meaning a person would want to put on it. 'I'm committing suicide because I don't want to be a slave.' Or, 'I'm going back home to where I came.' You know."

Jonée Ansa went to Dunbar Creek to take photographs for an African scholar, and Mrs. Washington accompanied him. She showed me a black-and-white photograph of her staring out at Ibo Landing.

"Jonée took that. While he was taking his pictures and thinking, I was standing just about like this, and looking at it, and I didn't know he had taken a picture of me looking at it. There was a bend that was a horseshoe bend in the creek, you know. I was impressed because my imagination made me put it in.

"It was after I had done that picture. I had painted that in February. From where we stood on the dock, and in looking down, the creek was shaped like this, but it has so much undergrowth around it now, and trees and stuff, and the dock was about right here. And the creek went past where we were standing. But just that little item. I said, 'Well, who would have thought it?' "

I asked Mrs. Washington if she believed in ghosts.

"I understand people that have lived there have. . . . well, one lady had an apartment that was over on the other side of it, and she swears that she hears, heard chains, and noises in the night that were unusual. That's part of it, legend and myth, but who's to say that she didn't hear it. And she's a supersensitive person. So . . ."

"But you don't hold stock with any of it?"

"I don't believe or disbelieve. That's why I say, 'Who can say?' You know? I wasn't there. I haven't lived over there. I'm not going to say she didn't hear something, because how do I know? I guess a part of you wants to believe in the spirituality of it. I think that's part of wanting to say, 'Well, maybe.' "

Clarise Lumpkins was born and raised on St. Simons; she was eighteen when I met her. She possessed an extraordinarily smooth and deep complexion, and she was also remarkably soft-spoken. We talked about

TV and music. ("Whatever comes on FM 101.5. I listen to it. Rock. Black music. They basically play like rap and R&B. That's what I listen to. Like MTV and BET. I will not spend my money on a tape. If I can't get somebody else to record it for me, you know, I'm going to listen to the radio. Fine with me.")

She had recently seen the Hughes brothers' film about black kids in South Central Los Angeles, *Menace II Society*. "They don't show everything on TV. I mean, I want to, like some people going to say that most black people are like that, because they had the movie. But I don't think so. They're just showing a part of where these guys are from. And how they have to grow up with things they have to go through. That's the way I see it. It seems to me they're always, like on the news and stuff, always about the bad parts of black people. They always have black people who don't know how to use correct English on TV. You see that like all the time. That's all you see. Maybe once in a while, they'll have something good, but basically it's all bad."

Clarise told me she didn't go out much. "I just go to my classes. Do what I have to do and come back home. I'm a freshman in college. At Brunswick College."

She told me: "I don't know what they do. Other people. I really don't do anything. You know, I spend time with my son, because he's almost seven months. Really, I stay home, or go to my grandmother's house. I really don't go out. You know, it's different when you have a child. What did I do before? I don't know."

We talked about the current situation with young people and drugs.

"There was a show on drugs on *Montel* or *Jerry Springer* the other day. I believe it starts in the home. A lot of black people don't have what the white people have, so they start doing things to get them by. If the situation was reversed, white people would be doing more drugs. But black people don't own anything to get in over here. And there are white people selling. They just don't show it. There are a lot of white people using drugs too. Rock stars and everyone else. There is always a reason. They see other people doing it, and they just can't stop and it becomes an addiction."

Clarise was thinking of becoming a CPA. Both her sisters were in the armed services; one was coming out that next year. Clarise had also considered going into the military. But she didn't really want to leave home. And there was her son, Devon. But so much depended on the job situation. "Depends on the job I can get with an associate's degree." Nor was she interested in heading North. "I'm not used to city life."

She talked more about hip-hop: "It's not about being black, it's about being in style."

I asked her what she thought being black was about.

"I don't believe there is such a thing," she said. "White people have used that to describe things. You can't define what is being black, because everybody is different."

About racism she said, "I don't care where you go, you are always going to find white people who are prejudiced. But that's something they have to deal with. In school it's not outright. But if you watch you can tell." Clarise said there were more white teachers in her school than black.

"There is always going to be hostility between the races. I've heard black people say, 'I can't stand being around white people.' I have white friends."

Clarise was indifferent to black and white romance. "I see more black and white people getting together. I don't care. I'm not prejudiced. If you get in a black and white relationship, you are going to get some looks.

"I will say the word 'cracker.' I think a cracker is a person who doesn't like black people. Wants to see a black person whipped. I found out the origin of the word—it came from the word whip. That's what I consider a cracker. But I don't say all white people are crackers. Same as calling a black person a nigger."

I asked Clarise how she thought things could be fixed.

"I don't think they can be fixed. The only way is through individuals, and they have to broaden their minds. We're all here. We have to forget color. When we turn off the light we're all the same anyway.

"More people should think about going to college. Learn more. Unemployment is just everywhere. Somebody is going to be unemployed. Somebody's not going to work. The basis is education. Family values. A lot of people don't spend enough time with their kids. And these days you have to start earlier.

"I'm fairly optimistic about the future, though I am maybe just an optimist."

Now, by all rights, intents, purposes and expectations, anyone who has read this far would have expected me to ask Clarise Lumpkins, an eighteen-year-old single black mother, more specifics about her situation, about Devon, and Devon's father, and perhaps even what advice she would give to other young women in her situation. But I did not. Sitting with Clarise in the dark living room of her mother's home, the television flickering, I not only sensed her very real vulnerability, but my own. I was myself very like Devon, and Clarise, very like my own mother. I see now that if I trod lightly around the subject, it was because I brought a particular sensitivity to the circumstance, and regarded it not with judgment, but with compassion. To have asked such questions, I felt, would have been intrusive and disrespectful, and downright rude; it was simply none of my business. To have asked such questions would have been to exploit the young woman, and there was enough exploitation going around for everybody. Here was my mother: too young, too beautiful, dealt a biological blow that society neither protected her from, nor prepared her for. Like my own mother, she was inventing her life, her destiny, day by day. What she needed was an understanding of her burden and her humanity in her coming travails.

I left with nothing but good wishes for Clarise Lumpkins and her baby; I prayed that, like me, Devon would find support and encouragement in an extended family, a community; that he would discover words, numbers or faith, or all, as I did; I prayed someone would teach him, and he would believe, that there was power in knowledge, and that, when married to faith and courage and will and work, he possessed all the grand possibilities of life.

Or, as the old folk say, I left it lay where Jesus flung it.

Albert Gary was so handsome with his dark, bright eyes, so eager, so full of energy and spunk that I envied him. Oh, to be seventeen again!

He played point guard on his high school basketball team, and was one of the participants in the Fourteen Black Men of Glynn program—"The Torchbearers and the Dream Team" they called themselves.

"You have like your hard-core rap. It's like Ice Cube or IceT. His whole tape is about the riots. Songs are about the riot, about what happened in the Rodney King case. He talks about how some black people feel, how they felt right then. That's what he's rapping.

"We like reggae here. Reggae is pretty popular here. Everybody listens to some sort of reggae. Then you have rappers that make like dance music or something. That's something you go to a party and hear. You ain't go to a party and hear something by Ice Cube. A lot of songs might express the way other people feel. I guess here we don't usually take music like Ice Cube that seriously. Nobody would do nothing like that. Go out and just shoot a police officer. Would have to pull a gun on them first in order for them to shoot.

"I guess we have so many different types of music. It's kind of weird. I mean, because everybody listens to the same radio station. You know HOT 101.5. Everybody listens. And if you go to almost any black teenager my age, and you say 'What's your radio station?' he's either going to be on 92.3 or HOT 101.5. And they both play the same type of music. It's all mostly black music. Myself I like to listen to some other music. You know, if I'm feeling kind of stressed out or something I might listen to music just to mellow me out or something. It depends on the occasion."

Albert and I talked for a while about the importance of popular culture for teenagers, for him and his schoolmates. Comedian Martin Lawrence's situation comedy *The Martin Lawrence Show* "made a big difference on campus lately." It was a must to watch every episode and then discuss it the next day. If you didn't watch it, you were accused of not "doing your homework." Ever interested in language, I asked Albert about some choice phrases making the rounds. One, at the time, was boys calling each other "doll," as in: " 'Hey, doll, what you doing this weekend?' And he'll say like, 'Well, I ain't doing nothing.' Now we have a thing, we get a girl, 'She trying to play my heart like a Nintendo.' So you just leave her. You should kick her to the side of a curb like a pile of trash. That's what you ought to do."

The 1991 movie *Boyz N the Hood* was still popular among black teenagers on St. Simons, Albert told me. "Some people have been renting the movie, watching it, and they started quoting him and stuff. 'You'll always be black.' You know, stuff like that."

I wondered if the fact that the movie had been set on the West Coast, and in one of the most urban settings on the planet Earth, made any difference to rural Georgia boys and girls.

"It don't matter where it's set. It's like this here now. If they come up, it's a racial thing. If I was to go to Los Angeles, let's say there are three white guys beating on a black guy, and I was the only black guy there, and I stood and watched. Next month, I might be in the hospital because I ain't jumped in. They going to fire me. There's always going to be like, 'Well, you black and I got to get you back.' They did awhile back, they had a thing for the Florida guys who come in here, and the guys here are getting upset, and they get mad, so if you're from Florida, you just better get off, or somebody going to get beat down here. It was like that for a while though. But then everybody started calming down, you know. I think, another thing got something to it was rap.

"When the gangs and stuff started getting together, and the rap groups started coming together, like you had the East Coast and West Coast, the songs, Doctor Dre and Snoop Doggy Dog in Long Beach coming together. So then that brings the people from Florida together with people from anywhere else. They sort of unified at the same time. Like now, you can go to Florida, like Daytona, on spring break. You saw people you knew from here, and you saw people from everywhere, just about. Everybody was just out there to have a good time. There were no fights, nothing like that. No threats. No, everybody was like 'Hey, if you going to mess with it, go ahead.' Nobody cared.

"I wouldn't exactly say there ain't no gangs here. See, you have your drug dealers that hang together, see. You have the Fourth Street Gang and Eight Ball Posse. You knew who they were, because all had like the same color eight-ball jackets. It's a jacket that you can buy, and it's got a pool ball with an "8," and it's usually black. Theirs are all black with a red ball. Fourth Street hated the Eight Ball Posse. So for a while they were going to stab each other in the street and stuff. They had that going on for a while. But that's sort of desisted now."

I wondered how Albert Gary got involved with Fourteen Black Men of Glynn. His father had died in September of the year before. Albert had read about the organization in the paper. One day during school, when he was in ninth grade, he was called to the principal's office, and there were eight or nine of his friends. His guidance counselor handed him a set of papers.

"It had all these questions: 'How old are you? What do you want to become in life? What do you want to do when you grow up?' Asked parents' names. 'Do you plan on going to college, or do you have any specific college you'd like to go to?' Questions about stuff we wanted to do in the future. We had no idea what that was for." Two weeks later, he got a letter inviting him to join the program.

"We were all wondering what we all have in common. It was like were we selected behavior-wise or because of academics? I mean, we weren't the perfect students or nothing. It's not like they just wanted kids who made straight As, who they know weren't going to get in trouble. Originally, we started off with twenty-one young men my age. I think now we're down to like fifteen. They picked average kids. I'm the only one from the island."

Already some of the young men were speaking to groups of other young men. "Some of my friends have spoke. I haven't gone to speak yet. But they say my time is coming up, so I'll probably be going out pretty soon. It's like a boy's club. They introduce the program, what the program's about, and then they introduce us and then we get up and we talk to them about thirty, forty-five minutes, you know, what our life has been like since we've been in the program, and what we have tried to achieve.

"When we first got into the program, we were like, 'Well, who are some of these black men? These are the black men who made a difference in the community. I mean, not all of them are judges and lawyers, not all of them make lots and lots. We have some who work out at Georgia-Pacific. We have others who are school counselors. We have a probation officer. My mentor, Mr. Carl Brown, works out at customs. We have a Mr. Bailey, who's the vice president of the fourteen; he is a schoolteacher. Really, it's just a mix. They come from different perspectives or points of life. They brought us together, and asked what are your goals in life?

"We have Saturday morning seminars. We'll go like ten o'clock in the morning. They'll lecture us. We'll look at statistics about things that are happening in the neighborhood and stuff. They kept emphasizing that the black man has so many negative statistics in America. I mean, highest prison population. And stuff like that."

The men provided tutorial sessions for the boys and study groups. Also the Fourteen Men of Glynn wanted to engender a sense of giving back; to help the boys realize "we are not just out for ourselves."

"We help with the United Way. There was a lady that was getting evicted from her house, Memorial Day weekend, and it was raining that day, and I think about three or four of us went with Doctor Culbreth, and we helped her move out of her house to another house that was about a mile away and we did that. We cleaned up one of the streets. I think it was Martin Luther King Boulevard. And we did that. We do so many different things. A boy named Demetrius Johnson is also in the group. They sent him to a seminar up in middle Georgia, and he came back and he gave a lecture on the seminar and stuff. And they were like really impressed that he was able to come back and do that."

Representative Jack Kingston, from that district, had been so impressed with the program that he instituted an internship for the boys in his Brunswick office. Albert Gary wound up working in the congressman's office for the summer. Albert Gary was getting a taste not only of how government works, but of how the world works.

"Some of the mentors take some of us to their jobs with them. Like my mentor, Mr. Brown, took me for almost a day out to the Federal Law Enforcement Agency. FLEA. It's over in Brunswick. We tour colleges. Going to colleges is fun. What they do is they'll rent two vans, and they pay for the hotel and food.

"Doctor Culbreth said, 'I thought when I was taking them black boys in there, they were just going to embarrass me. So when we got there, they made me feel proud. They went in there like gentlemen. They greeted people, shook their hands, they talked to them. It made me feel proud to be with them.'

"We were also taken to visit the jail. We went to the county jail also. Judge Douglas took us there to visit the courthouse. It was like what you see on TV, like you see the lawyer come up and he'll ask questions. And they were mostly doing traffic cases."

All told, I wondered how being in the program had affected Albert's perceptions of things, of his life.

"After seeing what these men've achieved, and how people in the community look at them, I guess it's made me a little bit more enthusiastic to go out there and do it. I plan on going into either law enforcement or some area of law. I don't want to work in accounting because you can't move up the ladder. Recently I just came out of a youth police academy. I went three weeks and we did everything basically that most any police officer would in the academy. You went through the fire rangers, from working radar, cars, you did everything. Just about. Doing paperwork. How to do murder investigations. We went out to the firing range. We did everything."

"You used the word 'success' earlier," I said. "How do you define success? What would success be to you?"

"I guess success would be to have the things that I wanted. To know that I've achieved something. 'Hey, look how far you've gotten in life.' To be able to look back and see where I came from, see what I've done, and say it's all paid off. I guess success would be to look and see how many people look at me, and to see how many people badmouthed me and said I'm worthless, and see how shamed they would look. Saying, 'Well, he did all this, and I didn't, and I wish I could have done that.' "

The idea that Albert Gary had lived all his brief life on an island whose history was so provocative and rich, and in a way emblematic of the mythos of Middle Passage, haunted me. Was he aware of how extraordinary the history of African Americans was there?

He remembered that parts of *Roots* had been filmed on Jekyll Island. "You think about how far you've come to where you're at now. I guess you would think about how slaves were beaten here, transported up and down. Probably went the same road going through here at Demere. Travel up and down that same road. Now you don't have to get beaten to travel up and down that road. You might get run over, but you don't have to get beaten to go down that road."

Albert told me that when he was ten or twelve, he thought a great deal about how, if he were to throw a quarter up a tree, "Somebody a million years from now might find my quarter." He thought a lot about time capsules. What I was doing, talking to people, talking to him, reminded him of the idea of "archives." "What if people found this in a million years? That's kind of dumb."

No, I said, that's history.

Somehow or other Albert Gary gave me a stronger sense of faith (*The evidence of things not seen and the substance of things yet to come*). "Got to keep the young ones dreaming," said Mr. Anderson back in Buffalo. *Got to keep the young ones dreaming.* This next thing I had to do was to keep this faith, and that was a personal mission.

> The past is never dead. It's not even past.
>
> —William Faulkner, *Requiem for a Nun*

There is no real marker at St. Simons Island commemorating that bizarre and resonant action of May 1803, when a group of "saltwater" Africans discovered that they were locked onto the American continent. Instead there is Neptune Park, a reminder of how the hegemony of slavery was rewarded, and how the ancient African ways had been largely erased from the minds and the hearts of their descendants. I could leave the matter at that, but that twisted skein of circumstances represents the state of our present condition. Black folk and white folk alike.

If black folk were ever to control this country, I should hope—in that vein of humanity that feels it must make history concrete—that a monument would be erected somewhere at that weeping bend in Dunbar Creek. But then, I ask myself, in that someday fantasy world, would it be built, or simply forgotten, like some of white America's more emotionally complex monuments? And if such a monument were to be built, how would it interpret that mysterious event?

Sometimes, I worry that the only difference between Americans descended from Europeans and Americans descended from Africans, is simply that there are more white folk, and that a few white folk have and control literally trillions of dollars, and they are scared to death of me and my kin, and, to insure that their control is maintained, they must, through collusion and by deliberate acts, make certain that their control is never seriously challenged. Then I consider that if the situation were reversed, and black folk were in power, they might simply do the same thing; that, in the end, this is how human beings behave. They always have done this, and they probably always will. Such thinking chills my spine.

But I am convinced that this ongoing political, social, cultural, economic and philosophical struggle is not merely about the Haves versus the Have-nots, despite what Professor Marx once said. My job, as a member of the minority, the opposition as it were, is to critique the majority culture, to point out when it is wrong, to cry when I am pained, to scream when I am angered, to fight when I am wronged. This is a moral battle, a battle to make humankind better, responsive, responsible, aware, just, fair, respectful, perhaps even good.

I felt uneasy driving past all the opulence and affluence of St. Simons Island today, aware of the poverty of most of the black families, overwhelmed by the feeling of inevitability, regardless of gains made here and there: Where there was wealth, especially in the South, there are still poor black folk. Slaves were expensive. The ten who probably died at Dunbar Creek cost Couper and Spaulding $5,000—well over $100,000 in 1990s money. I thought, How much would I have been "worth"? The thought brought a wave of nausea. And anger.

For me at least, this was a place of high emotional tension. In the air. Creepy.

How do the white folk deal with these chain-rattling, mutinous, homeward-looking, water-walking ghosts? I wondered, as I headed back home. I heard them. Did they?

# VII

# HOME TO A VERY STRANGE PLACE

Yes, the also and also of all that also; because the oldness that you are forever going back again by one means or another is not only of a place and of people but also and perhaps most often of the promises that exact that haze-blue adventuresomeness from the brown-skinned hometown boy in us all. There must by now be at least yes one thousand plus one or more tales all told of the underlying sameness; and whether retold by wine drinkers or beer drinkers or bootleg-whiskey drinkers, and whether in fire circles or by firesides, and whether in barbers' shoptalk or ten o'clock Latin or in blue-ribbon anthologies twelve-plus year advanced, the implications of self-definition, self-celebration, and perhaps not a little self-inflation and self-designation are nevertheless quite as obvious in each of us for all and since forever: when you are talking about somebody come from where us folks come from you talking about somebody come from somewhere. You talking about people been through something, you talking about somebody come out of something.

And is therefore ready for something. Because self-nomination after all has perhaps as much to do with promise and fulfillment as with anything else; and promise and fulfillment probably have at least as much to do with self-discipline as with anything else; and the thing about self-discipline (which is to say dedication which is to say commitment which is nothing if not self-obligation) is its conditioned unforgetfulness which is perhaps as good a reason as any why even the most frivolous-seeming good-time music of downhome-derived people so often sounds like so much rhapsodized thunder and syncopated lightning.

—Albert Murray, *South to a Very Old Place*

Twenty-Two

# WHERE AM I BLACK?

## Or, Something About My Kinfolks

*Cyberspace, North Carolina*

During the academic year of 1994–95, I was honored to be a guest lecturer at my alma mater, the University of North Carolina at Chapel Hill, and its perpetual academic rival, Duke University. It was a bracing experience. Or, to paraphrase Marianne Moore, I laughed too much and was afraid of snakes.

Many revelations presented themselves to me that year, and some were daunting, and some were tender, and some I would like to forget, but probably never will, not without work. I became reacquainted with my family in a way that geography heretofore had made not possible; and I became reacquainted with a young black man, really a boy, ten years in the past, who made the first important move of his life, when he left a small village on the coastal plains of North Carolina, and matriculated at a major university, in an area later described by the national news media to be among the most civilized in the country. And not the least of all my discoveries and rediscoveries was my fervent return to the computer.

The reasons I never got any good at basketball are fourfold: (a) I didn't really have a place or anyone to play with; (b) I didn't play and practice when I had the opportunity; (c) I was so pitiful when I did attempt to play that I was roundly discouraged and ridiculed; and (d) I really didn't care. Actually I did, but it helped me deal with the fact that I was so bad, by feigning indifference until that feigning became real. In fact, not playing basketball gave me as much identity as it gave those black teens who did. If they were to become superb dribblers, slam dunkers, passers, shooters—I would become superb as something other. Or that's what my twelve- and thirteen-year-old mind told itself. My being drummed out of the corps of future NBA wanna-bes was so draconian. And it is for a great number of black males. Mine was in junior high school during school tournaments. We had a varsity high school player as a coach for a week. I was at the bottom of the lineup. I played for two shakes of a dog's tail near the end of the game when the outcome was inevitable, and even then I got laughed at and eyes rolled at by fellow players. For a while, I carted around something like contempt in my heart for all athletics, seeing supreme hypocrisy operating under the guise of sportsmanship. And being a boy, I could not get my mind round the conflation of commerce and recreation and "education" and, let's just face it, fun. I had not yet developed the ability to see and think on more than a few levels and could not understand how a particle could contain the truth and a lie and remain whole. I was a sensitive lad.

Now many will say that this trial by fire, as harmless as it is, ultimately builds character, not unlike what some folk say the military will do for adolescents. I don't know about that. But I will weigh in with the observation that to be a young black male in the public school system is to experience a weird, outsized pressure to excel at this now-national pastime. Young boys such as myself are weeded out of the process early. Most, unlike myself, try and try again, and deepen their affection and admiration for the sport and for the Michael Jordans and Dennis Rodmans and Horace Grants of the world. And, to quote B. B. King: "I'm not saying it's wrong; and I'm not saying it's right." Suffice it to say that today I watch my fellow schoolmates from UNC burn up the court and amaze the world (and draw down huge checks) with the rest of them. I cheer the Bulls and lament the Knicks. I see the game whole and for what it is. No longer is my ego bound up in my sorry inability to put a big orange ball through a metal hoop.

It was on this very subject that I would stumble upon what was to be my penultimate inquiry into the nature of blackness: haphazardly and unexpectedly, a discussion of basketball on the Internet.

Someone said it takes a village to raise a child. I do not doubt that piece of West African wisdom. But in my case, it was largely done by four people, with a village to back them up.

I was born illegitimate and male and black to a poor woman in Brooklyn, New York, in 1963. Luckily for both of us, my father acknowledged me as his issue, and he happened to possess a kindhearted father, who offered to raise me with his family in Wallace, North Carolina. My grandfather had been born in 1914, and had by the early sixties built himself a thriving dry-cleaning establishment; his wife was a seamstress. From the very beginning, they doted on me. I came to live with them at the age of six weeks.

My grandfather's sister, Mary Flemming, still lived in my grandfather's hometown, just fourteen miles east of Wallace, a village called Chinquapin, unincorporated and rural, largely tobacco fields and cornfields and hog farms.

My great-aunt Mary took a shine to me straightaway, and would often take me from Wallace to Chinquapin on the weekends, to spend time with her and her husband who ran the family farm. I'm not certain how many weekends she did take me back to Wallace, but one weekend she simply didn't bring me back, and there I remained. My grandfather, who drove one of his own delivery trucks, came by Chinquapin every Monday, so he saw me each week.

Three years later, on a mild September day, my great-uncle Redden died of a blood clot. I remember this vividly, for he died right next to me, on the porch of a pack-house, where my great-aunt and other women were grading cured tobacco. My grandfather suggested, now that my great-aunt Mary was a widow and alone, that I remain with her, which I did for the next fifteen years. I did, and I continue to call her Mama.

It took me years to appreciate the accident of my winding up in a place like Chinquapin during my developing years. For in many ways, Duplin County, fairly remote, off the beaten path from any metropolitan area of consequence, forty miles from the ocean, rich with history, was in a time warp. During the years that I was learning the English language, and figuring out the basic realities of the world, the United States was going through some of its most tumultuous events: Vietnam, Woodstock, Watergate, rashes of assassinations, civil rights marches and boycotts and sit-ins, the Black Panther Party, free love, flower children, Kent State, Jackson State, men walking on the moon, the Great Society. In Chinquapin, all those events could have been happening in Thailand. Not to say that folk were ignorant of the goings-on in the wide world; rather, folk were simply focused on more pressing matters: getting crops in, getting their children fed, grown and married, caring for the elderly, going to church and trying to be good, with occasional missteps. Chinquapin from 1963 to 1981 could have been Chinquapin in 1920, with the exception of a few welcome new gadgets. Mama had an old Admiral television set, which was situated in a handsome walnut cabinet, the screen about the size of a letter; a set which broke down before my uncle died. She didn't get a new one until I was in kindergarten—something on which I always blame my addiction to print, although she, who worked in kindergarten, taught me to read when I was four.

Moreover, I was surrounded by folk who had been on the planet for the entire century, and their view of the world began before any of these new-fangled machines were even invented. There was my cousin Norman, who lived right across the dirt road from us, who was in his seventies when I was born. He knew an awful lot about the land and raised hogs and chickens, and had an admirable orchard adjacent to his and his wife, Miss Alice's house. There was my great-great-aunt Erie, who was the youngest daughter of my great-great-grandfather. (Only years later did I discover how rare it is for a person to know a great-great aunt. Indeed, both my maternal great-grandmothers were living when I went to high school.) Aunt Erie had over ten children, most of whom were away, but all were colorful people, and they would descend on Chinquapin during the holidays and the town would feel like a festival. There was my aunt Lillian, who lived in a big two-storey house down the road, and her multitude of daughters, and her sons, Herman and Irving, who had worked to send many of the girls to college, and Herman's nine children with whom I went to school . . . and that's just one limb on one branch of one side of the tree of the extended family in which I grew up, surrounded by stories and antics and foibles and gossip and artifacts and something like love, though the many feelings engendered by life in a small town are much more complex and tangled than most people who've never lived in one, belonged to one, could ever imagine.

There was church. Two churches in fact. First Baptist and St. Louis. Both Baptist, and to this day I cannot say why Chinquapin never had an AME church. My mama was zealous about my going to church, and I remember too many sermons to be in my right mind, and the pastors Hestor, and Lassiter the younger, who succeeded Lassiter the senior. There were revivals in September and Vacation Bible School in June, when the blueberry season came, and Sunday school each and every Sunday—even on fifth Sunday when nobody had church services. Church remained an indelible mark on my growing up, and, no matter how far or how fast I run, the lessons of Baptist protestantism and southern Calvinism will be etched on my brain—probably my soul—the way circuits are hardwired to a motherboard.

There was school, which I truly enjoyed. And all the black women who taught me (I actually had more black teachers than white teachers before I went to high school), women who had known me and my mother their entire lives; women who watched me and all the other black boys and black girls like sentient hawks, and who would report any crime or misdemeanor with the rapidity of lightning. Getting away with wrongdoing or occasional mischief was doomed to fail. I remember feeling completely watched, and always felt that was one of the many reasons I couldn't wait to say goodbye to the hamlet. Not that I wanted to do anything particularly evil; I just didn't want my business known to every Myrtle, Blanche and Willie Earl.

I will not be romantic about Chinquapin. From as early as I can remember, I always wanted to get the hell out of there. After all, it was what it was: a very small backwoods North Carolina village. The schools were not desegregated until 1969; a great many roads were unpaved; medical care was twenty-five miles away and then not particularly competent; water was pumped from private wells, and many folk had no running water. As soon as I could read newspapers and magazines, I had a clue that the world was wide and far different from what I had seen day in and day out in Duplin County, and something like resentment grew in my breast. I resented people who were elsewhere. Though I would not know the phrase for decades to come, like Milan Kundera's poor artists in the novel *Life is Elsewhere,* I figured real life was going on somewhere else.

Of course that was a boy thinking, feeling. And though I think that this feeling, inchoate and arch, was the origin of my wanderlust, I now see those elements of Chinquapin that were so fundamental in making me a fairly good citizen, a fairly decent person, a fairly respectful human being, and, probably, a writer. Though, in truth, all those years, there was nothing I wanted to do more than become a scientist.

In 1994, Paramount Communications launched a new television network called UPN, and one of their flagship shows was *Star Trek: Voyager.* Apparently the success of their cash cow franchise was so irresistible—after *Star Trek: The Next Generation* and *Star Trek: Deep Space Nine,* and the string of movies—that they couldn't resist the moneymaking urge.

The remarkable thing about this new series was not the fact that this super-duper new starship had been flung to the other side of the galaxy, and that it would take its crew more than their lifetimes to get home—no. What I found arresting was that the security officer was a Vulcan, one of those pointed-eared, green-blooded, utterly logical aliens from the planet

Vulcan, whom Mr. Spock had made a part of American pop culture, and he was black. Mr. Tuvok, played by the actor Tim Russ, was the logical, honor-rigid, emotionless embodiment of all of Gene Roddenberry's peculiar psychosexual hang-ups about the id and cognition, which, as the young folk say, blew my mind. This series was clearly made to address all the cultural, ethical, ethnic bugaboos that had been haunting the franchise since the sixties. The captain was a woman, the first officer was a Native American, the science officer was a Korean, and the chief engineer was a woman—half-Klingon.

Too much can be made of this minor historical development, I am well aware. But, for a while, what Paramount had unwittingly done—in a sheer and utter and bald attempt to pander to people like me—made me ponder many a thing.

A black Vulcan. For me, in high school, besotted and beset by science fiction, and watching the original *Star Trek* religiously, and fantasizing about being on a starship, it was not imaginable—or at least I did not imagine—the convolution or the notion of "race" in conjunction with alien life, let alone on the planet Vulcan. Moreover, this purely monetary gesture on Paramount's part was rife with a huge cultural irony which tickled me no end.

Vulcans, for those who don't know, are a species who, centuries ago, decided that emotion was a bad idea, so they essentially eradicated it from their society. In emotion's place, they elevated the philosophy of logic, to which they subjected everything. This premise, the notion of a "humanoid" without the petty, messy, irrational baggage of feelings, was what made Mr. Spock so compelling for so many folk. He became a built-in device for examining emotions in a new way—in a way that only science fiction, really, can successfully achieve. Moreover, Vulcans are bound by rigid codes of honor; filial piety is paramount as are duty, dedication to science, and they only mate once or twice in their life, and that act is seen as something of an embarrassment and is shrouded in solemn ritual.

The irony comes when you consider the image of the black man in popular media, indeed, long before popular media existed: emotion-less? logical? honor-bound? sexless? One could take this cultural juxtaposition as a joke. But, in 1994, when this new media phenomenon was presented, blatant and subtle in its various permutations, and admittedly minor in the scheme of things, it nonetheless made me wonder. Was our society finally, so close to the turn of the century, coming round the bend? Were we ready to begin to reimagine our deepest prejudices, and come closer to that Martin Luther King and Rodney King vision? Were we starting to climb to the mountaintop and get along?

> Always keep Ithaca fixed in your mind.
> To arrive there is your ultimate goal.
> But do not hurry the voyage at all.
> It is better to let it last for long years;
> and even to anchor at the isle when you are old,
> rich with all that you have gained on the way,
> not expecting that Ithaca will offer you riches.
> Ithaca has given you the beautiful voyage.
> Without her you would never have taken the road.
> But she has nothing more to give you.
>
> And if you find her poor, Ithaca has not defrauded you.
> With the great wisdom you have gained, with so much experience,
> you must surely have understood by then what Ithacas means.
>
> —C. P. Cavafy, "Ithaca"

In 1994, Chinquapin had finally been thrust—more like yanked—into the heady whorl of the postmodern era. The ambulance was state-of-the-art. The town had city water. There was cable television and a supermarket and two convenience stores, at which one could rent videos of movies that had, in some cases, been released in the last six months. Less than twenty miles down the road was Ellis Airport with a landing sleeve and a rotating luggage belt. Interstate 40 had been completed only a few years before, which effectively created a line all the way from Barstow, California, to Wilmington, North Carolina, and, for the good folk of Duplin County, cut an hour off the drive to the Raleigh/Durham/Chapel Hill area, which in that year had been assessed by *Money* magazine as the most livable place in the country. My grandfather now used a microwave, and cultivated a taste for *Die Hard* and *Lethal Weapon,* while my mother watched *Montel* and *Oprah* and was receiving medical care that, in 1963, would have been essentially the stuff of science fiction.

To be sure, these things seem minor to most folk in the country, but the way they changed the complexion and the quality and the quantity of life bewitched me. For in my mind, Chinquapin was still backwoods and out of step, yet, thanks to satellite dishes and faxes and e-mail, was not so far away from the rest of America, and not so quaint and Tobacco Road.

Nevertheless, for me, Chinquapin was very much a land of specters, so many of the people I had known as a boy now dead and gone. I could not help but hear their ghosts about the rooms and fields and barns, now empty and relic-like. And, as sentimental and shamefully nostalgic as it may sound, groups of folk no longer sat about on porches and just talked; now they watched HBO and Cinemax. Most farms had been bought out by larger farms; church congregations seemed sparse. The old folks who remained seemed older, more frail, halting, almost ethereal, some from Alzheimer's, some from neglect and being forgotten. My running buddies were practically all gone, like me.

All of which is not to say that any of these changes are in and of themselves bad, and I am the last person on the planet Earth who will lament the passage of an era. Chinquapin did, and probably still does, abound with a multitude of hateful truths, dirty laundry, murders, substance abuse, strife of every manner, small-mindedness, racism, boredom, and downright inertia.

During my year back home, I could make the drive in less than two hours, go from Chapel Hill's squeaky clean, high-tech, Ph.D.-laden opulence, to Chinquapin's postmodern present, where hog farms were running riot, and the chopped barbecue was good, and I could get chitlins and run from snakes and attend the Daughters of Zion's annual event at the church, and go home and watch BET, and check my e-mail after calling a friend in Japan.

I was not so much bothered as disquieted by the changes that were occurring in Chinquapin, for in a way, those changes were at the foundation of the changes that were taking place in America. Chances were that the young folk in the elementary schools and the high schools of Duplin County were not having the same sorts of experiences that I had had in school. In fact, their experiences were probably very close to those of young folk growing up in Alaska or Maine or Wyoming or Arizona. Yes, there was a local flavor, a local color, but the information they were receiving, there in no-longer-quite-so-remote Chinquapin, was not very different from the information being received by kids, black kids, in Seattle and Madison and Salt Lake City and New York.

More to the point, those things that I had taken so for granted about being black, which had come from my mama and my grandfather and Uncle Roma and Aunt Lillian and Aunt Mildred in third grade, and Reverend Raynor and Miss Ruth, were now being dictated by the *Martin Lawrence Show* and *Moesha* and Snoop Doggy Dogg and Dr. Dre and Russell Simmons and *Vibe* magazine and, yes, Paramount. Chinquapin was becoming more like the rest of America. It was being absorbed by the vast cultural soup of consumeristic we-think.

The problem, as I saw it, had to do with the idea that blackness was not so easily beamed through a satellite or through an optic fiber. After all this travel and bother, I had, in many ways, arrived back in Chinquapin with the same question: What is blackness?

> I have argued that Internet experiences help us to develop models of psychological well-being that are in a meaningful sense postmodern: They admit multiplicity and flexibility. They acknowledge the constructed nature of reality, self, and other. The Internet is not alone in encouraging such models. There are many places within our culture that do so. What they have in common is that they all suggest the value of approaching one's "story" in several ways and with fluid access to one's different aspects. We are encouraged to think of ourselves as fluid, emergent, decentralized, multiplicitous, flexible, and ever in process. The metaphors travel freely among computer science, psychology, children's games, cultural studies, artificial intelligence, literary criticism, advertising, molecular biology, self-help, and artificial life. They reach deep into the popular culture. The ability of the Internet to change popular understandings of identity is heightened by the presence of these metaphors.
>
> —Sherry Turkle, *Life on the Screen: Identity in the Age of the Internet*

I had a revelation one day in the library in Phillips Hall, the math and science building, back when I was a junior: Sentences are very much like equations.

Why did I want to become a scientist?

People in Chinquapin considered it, me, a little weird or just plain strange, my pursuit of science. But then again, in Chinquapin, in general, I was considered a fairly strange child.

I always believed the desire stemmed from my fundamentally intense sense of magic and the supernatural. From a very early age I had been fascinated by tales of ghosts and vampires and werewolves. Witches, sorcerers, wizards, warlocks, to my preteenage mind, were the ultimate. Perhaps it was the ability to affect matter, to change the world. (Psychologists might say that such a strong interest in what can only be called magic actually comes from a deep-seated dissatisfaction with regard to the way things are; a desire to actually change a world one feels powerless to change. That may also be so.)

Nonetheless, somewhere about third grade or so, the more I learned about the world, and was able to distinguish fact from fiction, I settled on the notion that the real, modern-day sorcerers were those men in white lab coats who sent people into outer space, and designed lasers, and made experiments into the nature of atoms and electrons. They could affect the physical world, change it. I don't know if I made the connection, though I probably did, that "witch" means a wise woman, or a person of knowledge, and "science" means knowledge. In both cases, knowledge meant power. For a poor colored boy living on a dirt road, with an overly fertile imagination and strange ideas, the concept proved to be irresistible.

Thus science fiction, thus *Star Trek,* thus notions of teleportation and warp speed and solar-powered cars and gravitational fields and Maxwell's equations; thus the ambition to become a black Arthur C. Clarke or Isaac Asimov, a Ph.D. in the physical sciences and a writer of science fiction—for I had always written, knew I always would write; thus Chapel Hill, on a track for a B.S. in physics; thus computers.

When I came to Chapel Hill in 1981, the personal computer craze was essentially in its infancy. Apple had yet to introduce Macintosh, and kids like me, who were weaned on BASIC in high school, were dying to learn the more sophisticated, more powerful languages. As a physics major, I was required to take a course in numerical analysis in my sophomore year. The professor was an experimental nuclear physicist from New Zealand, who wore khaki shorts, and boots and socks, and who essentially made us learn FORTRAN on our own, for that was, in his opinion, the best way to learn it. I remember staying up for thirty-six hours, most of that time in Phillips Hall, creating a program that would translate Kepler's Laws of Planetary Motion into a graph. All this was done on a big mainframe computer. In the laboratory where I reported as a work-study student, the physicist who worked with the microbiologist there was going to teach me the latest version of PASCAL, which was one of the hot new computer languages.

Most of my comrades-in-arms in those heady and headache-provoking years were from backgrounds of a little more financial substance than my own, and a few had their own personal computers. They knew much more about hardware and wiring and circuitry than I, largely due to the fact that they had had a head start. I had only been able to work on a computer when I attended North Carolina's Governor's School in 1979. Duplin County high schools had no computers in those days. (And some still don't.) Nonetheless, I had no intentions of letting any of that stop me. I was well on my way to becoming a computer geek in the grand, nerdy fashion. (Back then, the word "geek" was not as widely used as it has become today. Science folk were known as "nerds," but a "geek" was a badge of honor: it meant you knew machine language, the stuff of the future.)

Somewhere in my sophomore year, my designs went badly astray: I got distracted by literature and writing. I found a mentor in a kindly and loveable old curmudgeon named Max Steele, who was then the head of UNC's creative writing department. And he wasted no time in informing me that most of the science fiction I so deeply regarded was essentially trash. I bristled with resentment. He said that my background was rich and fecund and just made to be written about, and that I didn't know what I was wasting if I neglected it. He suggested I read some real literature. Fully intending to prove him wrong, I did just that. I discovered he was right; I also discovered something that I can only describe as vital about the process, and the danger and the possibilities of writing. I came to know the work of James Baldwin and Richard Wright and Alice Walker and Toni Morrison. I fell in love with Isaac Bashevis Singer and Yukio Mishima and V. S. Naipaul and Henry Dumas and a man named William Shakespeare.

The truth is, I would have made a dreadful scientist. I was a disaster in a laboratory, a bit too dreamy. My academic advisor told me this. I took more and more English classes; Gaussian matrices annoyed the hell out of me; and thermodynamics, as fascinating as they are, made less sense than Buddhist koans. By the summer of my senior year I was hell-bent in the pursuit of language; differential calculus and I said good-bye.

To this day, I feel that I've failed in some way by not pursuing my original goal. To be sure, we all have such naggings in the back of our heads, though I am happy with my choices. But the relevant thing here is that after 1985, I not only turned my back on science, but I turned my back on the computer. I would come to tamper with computers and programs in the most innocuous way after the personal computer revolution, but only with games and word processing.

Ten years later, however, back at Chapel Hill, the computer and I became reacquainted.

. . .

My granddaddy is one of my heroes.

He was born on his father's farm in Chinquapin, and his mother was the local schoolteacher. He worked at various jobs as a young man, including shipbuilding down in Wilmington, but in 1942, he and another man bought the equipment to open a dry cleaner. When he began, he would walk to people's houses in the community of Wallace, and ask if they needed anything cleaned, and he would tote their clothing to and fro. By and by, he bought his partner out, his business grew, and he was able to build a two-storey red brick house, with a lovely terrace in the back, and next door was his cleaners and my grandmother's seamstress shop.

He sent his youngest son to college, and paid for it himself. His older son joined the air force. By the time I was in high school, my grandfather's routes went into three counties, and for a time he employed a number of delivery trucks. My grandfather also sold clothing and bought houses that he would fix up and rent out, and for a time even dealt in scrap metal.

My uncle, George Edward, suffered from epilepsy and other ailments, and came to live with my grandfather and grandmother after he had been discharged from the military, and needed to be looked after. I remember this period as a particularly troubling time, and I helped my grandfather on his route, down to Maple Hill and Beulaville. I would sometimes drive his truck through those narrow highways and secondary roads. What struck me and stuck with me long after was first of all how hard he worked, and secondly, how many people he knew and how much he was trusted and respected. Even at that age, it never occurred to me how difficult what he had accomplished must have been for a poor boy from Chinquapin, North Carolina. Indeed, all the products of his labor I essentially took for granted; to me, my head full of stuff and nonsense, my grandfather was a wonderful man, but nothing about what he did made him remarkable. He was simply a small businessman.

My grandmother died when I was in college, and for a time, my grandfather was understandably depressed. They had been married for almost fifty years. I still miss my grandmother. In the mid-eighties my family had a rash of trouble. My mother's house, the ancestral family home, burned to the ground; my mother's son-in-law, who had become very like a father to me, came down with a mysterious ailment that almost caused him to die; and my grandfather suffered a horrible burn accident.

I then lived in New York, and I flew down straightaway. He was in the Burn Center at Chapel Hill's Memorial Hospital. Initially, the doctors said his chances were grave; he was not expected to live, he had been burned on 75 percent of his body, much of it third-degree burns. We would make the trip from Chinquapin to Chapel Hill each day, and to watch him in such pain was enough to make us despair. At one point, he told his sister that he wished he could just die.

My grandfather remained in the hospital for three months. He was, at the time, seventy-four. Each week, his prognosis got better and better, and, much to the doctors' amazement, he recovered enough to go home. He was not 100 percent, as he would say, but he was alive. The doctors suggested that, though with therapy they could help him regain his full walking capacity and the use of his limbs, he would never regain the full quality of his life. He went through months of painful therapeutic exercise and changes of dressings.

Within two years, not only had my grandfather recovered almost completely, not only had he regained his ability to walk unassisted by a cane, not only had he gone back to his six-day-a-week, fourteen-hour-a-day schedule, and gone back to tending his massive garden of peas and collards and mustard greens and okra and sweet potatoes, but he also, at seventy-eight, married a woman ten years his junior.

> John educated himself so fast that within a few months after he bought his modem, he was on track with the other MOD [Masters of Deception] boys. For one thing, John figured out that some rules are the same, whether you're on the street or in cyberspace. If you want to get ahead, no one is going to just *let* you. You have to take what you want and get there yourself. He played a little game sometimes. He called it Let a Hacker Do the Work. Like the time he called a hacker named Signal Interrupt in Florida, and sweet-talked the kid out of all *kinds* of information, just by claiming to be a member of the Legion of Doom.
>
> Another way cyberspace was like the street was that it helps to have friends.
>
> —Michele Slatalla and Joshua Quittner,
> *Masters of Deception*

John Lee was essentially a poor black boy from Brooklyn, who, with a $299.00 Commodore 64 computer, became one of the most brilliant and most notorious hackers in the country. He had been a member in good standing of a group of boys who called themselves the Masters of Deception, a high-brain-powered bunch of bad boys who were breaking into private computer files, rewiring phone lines, stealing a look at the credit histories of the rich and famous, and other crimes that had the FBI nervous and frustrated, and AT&T hopping mad.

Interestingly enough, the Masters of Deception had been formed in response to another group, the Legion of Doom, whose members were well-heeled white boys from all over America. The Masters of Deception were the sons of blue-collar folk, largely living in New York.

In their book of reportage about these fancy going-ons, *Masters of Deception: The Gang that Ruled Cyberspace,* Michele Slatalla and Joshua Quittner write about one fine day in 1990 when several hackers were yakking on-line:

> "Yo, dis is Dope Fiend from MOD," the newcomer says in distinctly non-white, non-middle class, *non-Texan* inflection.
>
> One of the Texans (who knows who?) takes umbrage.
>
> "Get that nigger off the line!"

Needless to say, John Lee did not take the comment without offense. In fact, the MOD and the LOD "waged war," which led to all sorts of high-tech shenanigans, involving security companies and serious offenses, and an FBI sting operation that showed the old folk how the new folk were changing the world, with bytes and bits and data gone mad. At one point, an entire grid of AT&T's eastern seaboard service went completely down. These boys were trouble, but a new kind of trouble.

John Lee appeared later on magazine covers and on *60 Minutes.* He wore dreadlocks, and had gold capped teeth, and appeared "down," as they say in the "hood." And he was indicted and ultimately sentenced to a year in jail and three years of suspension, and two hundred hours of community service and a fifty-dollar fine. By this time, he had been a student at Brooklyn College, and seemed in many ways unrepentant. Who can say?

Nonetheless, I followed the news reports of these guys I had left behind, or who had left me behind. (Who knows? I might have become a hacker had I remained in the wonderful world of computers; I certainly had the interest and the inclination.) It struck me how the cause of this "war" between these two groups of pubescent hotshots had been precipitated by the onslaught of a very low-tech ideology, something that Texas hacker had inherited from a country almost 300 years old, and a culture over 400 years old, where a boy with the intelligence to bulldog multinational corporations and government agencies in cyberspace was reduced to being just another nigger.

The term *cyberspace* actually had been invented in, of all places, a science fiction novel, published in 1982. *Neuromancer,* by William Gibson, was a departure from most science fiction of its day, which had, over the decades, become dominated by space operas of little green men and postapocalyptic danger-scapes. In truth, the late Philip K. Dick had been the prophet for the sort of writing that Gibson would almost single-handedly create, called cyberpunk. But it was Gibson's crystal-clear vision of a world not destroyed by the bomb but overrun by international conglomerates that have gobbled one another up, and megalopolises that covered entire coasts, and of the gap between rich and poor becoming a chasm, and of artificial intelligent life, of the hacker-like specialists called "cowboys" who "jacked" into an electronic world of data where information was in some way seen, and where one could lose one's life. This man-made world of the data-stream Gibson dubbed "cyberspace," and the phrase stuck.

Nowadays it is hard to find someone who has not heard of cyberspace or Vice President Al Gore's information highway; hard to find someone not impacted by personal computers and Windows and Macintosh and e-mail and the Internet and the World Wide Web; hard to find someone who is not, as William Gibson had been, more than a little skeptical about the whole evolution of technological might.

I particularly like the phrase created by cultural critic Scott Bukatman, "Terminal Identity." Image addiction, media-scape, virtual space. Already most Americans live most of their lives virtually: through television, or through a screen, or at a terminal, or over the phone. This way of living is not new news, it is self-evident; moreover, these modes and manners are reshaping what it means to be American, and, in some ways, what it means to be human, and yes, what it means to be black.

Call it Terminal Blackness.

William Jordan, Jr., an electrical engineer, and his brother, Rodney, a software designer, wanted to test their concept of "the uncut black experience"—blacks marketing to blacks and controlling the experience.

And what better way to do that than to use the Internet's World Wide Web? It offers small black businesses an inexpensive way to market goods and services to a vast audience of blacks and others. An estimated 10 million to 30 million people worldwide use the Internet.

—"Black Businesses on the Internet:
A Market that was 'Invisible Until Now,'"
*New York Times,* September 4, 1995

For many Americans, the expanding universe of computers lies somewhere in the imagination between Buck Rogers and "Mr. Rogers' Neighborhood." Wondrous and neat. But if you happen to be an African-American, the same gadgets may evoke less benign images. Try racially segregated schools, back-of-the-bus seating and town halls buzzing with angry white males.

Farfetched? Well, consider this: blacks spend several billion dollars a year on consumer electronics, but relatively few plunk down for computers. As PCs rapidly rewire the ways this country works, plays, learns and communicates, blacks are simply not plugging in to what feels like an alien, unwelcoming place. Certainly economics and education are also powerful handicaps to computer ownership. The average household income for blacks is $25,409; for whites, it is $40,708. But dollars and diplomas don't fully explain why some black professors let their university-issued computers gather dust. There are other important causes of this computer gap, reasons that are rooted in African-American history, culture and psychology.

—"CyberSoul Not Found," *Newsweek,* July 31, 1995

What, some will ask, does this have to do with being black?

There exists a company called "It's a D.C. Thang" that sells tee shirts with "an African American flavor" over the World Wide Web. There is Carlos A. Howard Funeral Homes, "the first funeral home on the Internet," whose owners are black. There is Melanet and there is NetNoir and there is Sphinx Communications and Black News Network and Afrinet and AfriTech and the African American Information Network, and an entire host of other local bulletin boards and forums. Many of these online companies belong to what is known as the BPON, or Black Pioneers of the Net network. Organizations like the National Urban League have set up training centers across the nation, to teach black folk computer literacy, as have mammoth computer firms like AT&T and Microsoft.

The truth of the matter is that the cost of a computer, for a family, for an individual, in the last few years of the twentieth century, is affordable. Indeed, most poor folks in the U.S. own a car—for it is a necessity in most parts of the country, and the cost of a computer is a fraction of a used car. Moreover, libraries and schools make access to computers easier and easier every day. The question then shifts to the user: Does a person value the machine enough, and the learning and the skills needed to use one? Already, people I know who work for any large corporation or university or college or library or museum or bookstore, etc., communicate through e-mail and record invoices. What are we saying when we dismiss that percentage of African Americans who do value the power of this Brave New Cyberworld? Are they any less black? And, according to all the numbers, they are getting more and more company, day by day.

I am not eager to say that any of these new ways of existing on the planet are bad, nor am I quick to say that they are all good. A person always runs the risk of being either a reactionary or a booster, when the prosaic truth usually runs somewhere towards the middle.

All that said, I nonetheless find this development not only tantalizing, but at the heart of my original question(s) about identity. This thing we call being black, does it exist outside of our bodies? Where, indeed, am I black? On my skin? In my mind?

Originally I did it for writing.

I wrote my first novel out in longhand, and then typed each page up on an IBM Selectric typewriter, and then entered the final copy onto an old Xerox computer. My second book was also written first in longhand, on yellow legal pads, but I then entered the changes on a secondhand IBM knockoff that had no hard drive. In 1991, I purchased what was then a state-of-the-art portable computer on which to write and take notes. One day, three years later, out of the blue, this computer gave up the ghost, and I was forced to buy a new one because I had become habituated to the damned thing, functioning as a fancy typewriter. This new computer was a sleek laptop that amazed me with its elegance, its small size, its speed, its Windows operating system; I was slowly seduced out of my stance as a pseudo-Luddite.

I returned home, to Chapel Hill, the year the media machine discovered the Internet. TV shows, magazines, books practically yelled about the new "computer revolution." In ten years, what had been essentially the province of geeks and scientists and hackers had become, in the words of politicians and marketeers, "mainstream." I was then in North Carolina's triangle, Raleigh/Durham/Chapel Hill, one of America's most congenial brain trusts, the area situated between the University of North Carolina, North Carolina State, and Duke University, known as Research Triangle Park, the gift of North Carolina's forward-looking, long-time Democratic governor James B. Hunt, who created this enterprise zone to lure large corporations to build laboratories and factories, taking advantage of the atmosphere, the forests, the universities and the Ph.D.s.

At dinner parties, everybody was talking about the joys and hardships of e-mail; friends were telling me about staying up all night surfing the Net; I was hearing strange things about being "on-line." After a while, I was beginning to feel left out, and intrigued.

Ten years after I had thought my computer use was going to be minimal at best, and I would never again learn a computer language, I was back in Chapel Hill, owning yet another computer, this one faster than fast, with massive storage, a modem and three Internet accounts; I bought loads of books that told me all sorts of information about FTP and Gopher and Veronica and Mosaic and Listservers and Usenet and Telnet. I sat amazed, for this was far from the days of a monochrome screen, with awkward, unattractive type flashing at your bewildered retinas at 3 a.m. No, this was a multicolored world of pictures and images and bells and whistles and information, information, information. I was fast becoming drunk with the stuff.

Presently, I found myself on-line, and what an amazing world that was, all fresh and new and cyber-wonderful. I explored, I lurked. I visited chat rooms, my eyes aflash with curiosity; my mind afire with the possibilities of this humming new mechanism. Here I was in my room in Carrboro, North Carolina, talking to folk in New Zealand, in Nigeria, in China, in Passaic, New Jersey. I say talk, but what we were doing was typing at one another; who they were, who I was, was largely immaterial; in truth, at the time, I deeply believe we were all, essentially, in love with the concept. We were netizens.

One fine night, I found myself on America Online, chatting with a man who said he was black and living in Los Angeles. We fell into a typersation about this and that. By and by, why I don't now remember, we began to discuss basketball. I allowed as how I was no good at the game, and probably went on too long about my feelings of insecurity, especially after having gone to a basketball-crazy place like UNC. Without preamble or warning, this cyberNegro typed: "Well, I got to get outta here and git wit some real niggas." And blipped off on his merry way.

Now objectively there is nothing remarkable about this minor incident. Folk on the Internet tended, and still tend, to be ruder to folk than they would be face to face; there is something about the electronic anonymity engendered by the beast that makes people insensitive. No, the thing that got my goat, stuck in my craw, angered the hell out of me, was the content of his aspersion. Here, after years of seeking out the nature of blackness, after talking to so many black folk, after reading, discussing, debating, investigating, the nature of blackness, here I was being accused of not being black. That stung. That hurt.

But what fascinated me—after I realized how silly it had been to allow my feathers to get ruffled by somebody I did not know—was how quicksilver and fast was my reaction; how subjective the idea had been on the one hand; and how, on the other hand, the very nature of what this cyberfellow expected to be black had fallen into question. Indeed, how could you be black on a computer screen? To be sure, he meant more than skin color, but how, qualitatively, could anyone adjudge how black you were or even if one were black? This silly incident led me once again, like a snake chasing its tail, right back to my original dilemma. What is blackness? Where does it exist? How can one person be more authentic in his being than another?

My grandfather is now eighty-four. He rises each morning between six o'clock and seven. Most months of the year he first goes out and tends his garden, which is almost half an acre. He still works six days a week, and his hobbies are still renovating houses and restoring furniture, and he cleans carpets sometimes on the side. George Washington Kenan seems to have more energy every year.

He owns a 1964 Park Lane Mercury, which is red, has less than 100,000 miles on its odometer, and runs like a dream. That car is one of his most prized possessions.

I enjoy sitting and talking with my grandfather for hours, and he seems to enjoy waxing nostalgic. I was surprised to learn a few years ago that he almost regrets not having become a farmer; he learned many things about farming as a teenager, and knows in his soul that he could have produced bountiful crops. Once, in the 1950s, he owned a farm for twelve years, and farmed while he ran his business. He sold the land at a profit in the 1960s. (Ironically, that land is now the site of a new luxury housing development.)

My grandfather tells me stories of his father and his father's father, of his days working at the shipyard, and of building his business from practically nothing; he talks of Chinquapin, which, in his day, was home to more people than it is now. Much of today's technology baffles my grandfather, and he coexists in a world with it, paying computers and faxes next to no attention. Air travel astonishes him, and new cars amaze him, but he knows his old Park Lane remains something special; and he only flew on a plane once when his older brother was sick and dying, and otherwise has no real use for flying.

I remember once discussing nursing homes with my grandfather, who remains grateful that at his age he has maintained his independence. He marvels at the paradox of how much medical science has done to prolong life; and yet, once when a member of the family fell sick, he or she became the focus of an entire family, not the nuclear family of the 1950s television dreams, but of uncles and aunts and cousins. He remembered when his own father fell ill, how people would take turns sitting by his side, the women taking care of him.

"No," he said, "it ain't like it used to be. People just don't seem to care about people the way they once did."

The truth is that I am very different from my grandfather, and we both know this for a fact. I can no more imagine such a world as he describes, than he can imagine jacking into cyberspace. I am a creature of network television and books and music and cyberdreams; I am the inheritor of not only his vision, but of the ultimate dream of the American: individualism. I am not surrounded by family and bound by codes of caring and closeness. At the age of thirty-four, I am as itinerant as the fabled Wandering Jew. I have changed my address more in one year than my grandfather has in his entire life. I could easily live in California or Brazil or Japan or Ireland or South Africa. My friends come from all over the world, and some of my closest friends I have not seen for years, though we keep up over the phone and through the computer.

In this way, in many ways, I am emblematic of my generation. Despite my rural background, I am now a netizen, a paradoxically rootless American whose home is reluctantly the world. We have exchanged the village for the globe, yet, despite what Mr. McLuhan predicted, the global village can be a cold, impersonal place.

And whence blackness in this strange happenstance we find ourselves? After this long march across the country, I now see that the era in which I came of age was the era in which the concept of being black or Negro or African American changed indelibly. During my grandfather's time, the construct was at once political (Jim Crow), cultural (language, food, clothing, music), and spiritual (black Baptist). Now Jim Crow is no more, one can bridge the distances between Protestant, Catholic, Islam and agnostic, and this thing called culture, once specific to so many regions, has become a postmodern amalgam of this and that, borrowings and findings and newfangled creations like Kwanzaa, and media manipulations of street lingo, innocent of its origins and only interested in style, newness, the expression of being other, being black. But what is black anymore? Who is authentically black in a country, within a culture, where one's very existence has always been the shifting identity of survival?

Black American culture was always a Creole culture, a mixture of remembered African ways, of European impositions and influences and inflections, of Native American wisdom, and of the stubborn will to survive. Long before the term was coined, black culture was a postmodern culture; folk made it up as they went along. Therefore, who can be authentically black, when every black person holds the codes and the blueprints of that blackness?

Not only do I march to the beat of a different drummer, but sometimes I fail to make out the beat. It seems at times I'm making it up as I go along. I think of those black folk in the 1860s who had none of the modern baggage my contemporaries and I lug around. As deprived as they were, they were also lucky. They knew exactly who they were. There was no jangling television set, no blasting boom boxes, no candy-colored magazines, no Wal-Marts, Tower Records, Web pages, billboards. Marketing had yet to be invented, and consumerism was a mere glint in Rockefeller's eye. We—black, white, indifferent, but American—must now disentangle ourselves from the garbage of the information age; we must pioneer a new way of seeing ourselves; we must reinvent humanity.

Who I am and who the world wants me to be will not jibe. So much of this disease is caused by peer pressure, the perceived notion that one is not "black" enough; the hints and clues that somehow I, he, she, wishes to be other than other, and therefore a traitor.

Traitor. A strong word. But a traitor to what? Traitor to the race? Most countries punish treachery by the most severe means available. But how do you betray that which has yet to be truly defined?

Going back to Chapel Hill resurrected a great many of my personal spectres, many of which I was certain I had laid to rest years ago. But walking down the halls of the English building, down the long green mall, down Franklin Street, into the massive Davis Library, I was accompanied always by the kid from Chinquapin, ten years before, and, like those patients of charlatan psychotherapists, I began remembering those things that I didn't want to remember.

After polyglot and polycolored Brooklyn and Queens and Manhattan, it struck me how homogeneous and largely white Chapel Hill was in 1994, and how much more it had to have been in 1984. All those Scots, Irish, English and German faces, blond, brunette and red hair all seemed to weigh on me more, and I wondered then how I had coped with that sea. I remembered how often I joined groups of black folk out of the sheer need to see black folk; how I volunteered at soup kitchens and tutored black kids, perhaps more out of a personal need than out of a desire to help.

I remembered incidents of being singled out as a Negro, like the time I was almost ejected from a frat party, being the only black person there; or the time the police stopped me while I was running down Rosemary Street near a number of sorority houses, because I "fit the description" of someone who had mugged a woman the day before. I remembered trying to express my outrage to my white housemates at the time, and their baffled inability to say anything at all, which made all of us feel inexpressibly worse and alienated from one another.

I remembered, as a freshman, having gone to a mixer at one of the tony North Campus female dorms, and being introduced by one of my roommates to a young lady friend of his. She asked me where I was from, and I said, Chinquapin. Her eyes grew wide, and she exclaimed, "Oh, you mean in *Africa?*" Everyone laughed, primarily at her profound ignorance, but somehow I felt the laughter aimed at me. I felt marked.

Perhaps, most damningly, the thing that came back to me with such a wave of psychic force was the remembrance of how very much I disliked myself. I was not white, rich, socially in; I felt excluded, and subconsciously unacceptable.

I never wanted to be white; I never felt ashamed of being black.

Indeed, until my school had been integrated in the first grade, it never occurred to me that anyone was any different from me and my folks. Over the years, increasingly, as I watched more television, read more, thought more, became exposed to more and more of the insidious social microcosm of high school, I did become more and more dissatisfied with my own personal lot. I believed everything my family told me about what one had to do to succeed in this world, that, as a young black man, I had to make certain my house was in order, that I had to eschew the more frivolous activities my white contemporaries indulged in, I had to hit the books; I had to prove myself.

By college, I remembered ten years later, this pressure had become acute. Often, in those years, I was not only uncomfortable but depressed. I now remembered that I did not often have a good time as an undergraduate. I felt myself on the outside looking in.

Many of the black guys I knew in those years made a fetish of whiteness. They coveted white women, and cultivated white attitudes, white clothing, white manners and mores. Was I one of those misled young men?

Sometimes I think I was; sometimes, most times, I know I was not. This conundrum being, at its base, the basis of my questioning. The question becomes not whether I, a young black man, an "affirmative action baby" (whatever that means), a child of the dream, wished to shed my skin, exchange my nappy head for blond tresses, expunge my chitlins and collard greens past, and adopt a New England clenched-teeth speech, eradicate all folkways and knowledge of the Veil, and blissfully slip into a country-club future unhampered by the shadow of the Other. No, the question becomes: Did I, in my attempts to learn and to experience another world, somehow lose, divest, mitigate or disavow who or what I was? Did I, in mingling and comingling with white folks, dilute or pollute or weaken my legacy as a son of a son of a son of a son of slaves stolen from Africa?

By 1994, I had moved a long way from that way of thinking. Like Lorri Hewett, I had come to realize that being black is not something to grab; like the Reverend Swift in Utah, I understood that being black was more than love, peace and hair grease. I had remedied the confusion of politics, economics, social class and skin color; I had come to understand that other people's notions of me could only influence me as much as I allowed them to do; I had come to the unshatterable conclusion that being black was indeed a willed affirmation, a recognition of my past, my beliefs and my most secret dreams.

> We Americans have lived in a country that's been very successful technologically, and we instinctively think that every problem must have a technological solution.
>
> —I. F. Stone, National Public Radio, April 12, 1983

I met Richard Elias Wimberly, III, the first day I arrived at Chapel Hill as a freshman; he roomed right across the hall from me in one of the older dorms on what is called the North Campus of the university.

The first black student was admitted to Chapel Hill in 1951 to the medical school; in fact, Chapel Hill was the first southern university to voluntarily accept black students, though it did not gracefully tear down the barricade for most black folk for decades. In 1981, most of the 800 or so black students (out of 20,000) lived in what was known as South Campus, at the southernmost edge of the school, where four of the newest, high-rise dorms had been erected. It was understood that South Campus was where the black folk were largely housed, and those who chose to live elsewhere were considered somehow different. And though it was not an instant badge of oreo-dom (for instance, Michael Jordan and most of the other basketball players lived on a special floor of a privately owned and operated "dorm" called Granville, north of North Campus), one was open to being suspect. Or, to be more specific, folk would wonder where you were at.

When I chose Grimes Dormitory, I was blissfully ignorant of all these territorial imperatives; it merely seemed logical to be close to most of my classes. There were a number of other black guys in my dorm, twelve or fifteen out of about a hundred students. It took me a while, but gradually I came to realize what some of the folk on South Campus thought of the black folk who lived on North Campus. The truth is they were right about a number of those people; that is to say, some of those black men and women who sojourned on North Campus did so because they wanted little if anything to do with other black folk, while for some there were other reasons; and some, like me, had given it little, if any, thought.

For many people on South Campus, the few who knew him, Richard Wimberly fell into the former category. Richard was from a prosperous upper-middle-class family from Raleigh, which belonged to one of the oldest and most affluent black churches in the state; his father owned his own business, and Richard had gone to one of the more competitive high schools in the state capital. Richard was beautiful, athletic, articulate, a gentleman and a preppie; funny, good spirited, a history major. Richard enjoyed playing basketball, and was good at it. He had an eye for the ladies, and loved pepperoni pizza, and Richard was deeply, deeply religious.

Richard had white friends, Richard had black friends, Richard had Chinese friends, Richard had Japanese friends. And fairly quickly, the two of us became fast friends. I often wonder if the proximity in which we lived for a year was the basis of our friendship, plus the fact that being black together, surrounded largely by white folk, forced us to seek one another out. And of course, the answer is partly yes. However, we had so much in common that I feel it was inevitable that we would get along so famously. Our interest in history, sociology, theology, and in *Dungeons and Dragons,* led us to spend hours just talking. And yes, our interest in *Star Trek* and science fiction as well.

In the fullness of time, we spoke more and more about our specific circumstances, about the speculations folk had made about him, about us. One of our mutual friends actually told Richard to his face that for months he had assumed Richard to be an "uppity nigger"; one who didn't want anything to do with black folk; one who thought he was better than other black folk; one who had few black friends by design. This friend later asked for Richard's forgiveness, saying, after getting to know him, that Richard was "all right." These ideas intrigued both Richard and me, and we shared our feelings of insecurity, of doubt, of the possibility of self-hate, of the doublethink that goes on in one's own mind when people who don't know you cast aspersions about your inner self; the second-guessing that breeds discontent. These ideas led us to ask questions about blackness. What is it?

I remember one night in particular, one which seems too good to be true, though it is true nonetheless. Richard and I had started talking after studying late; somewhere around ten or eleven, we were in the hall, on the landing, talking. At one point, we looked up, and the sun was peeking up. Neither of us was tired. We talked about many things that night: personhood, faith, history, economics, Hegel, Martin Luther King, sex, death, manifest destiny.

At one point, Richard said something to the effect of:

I would love to just travel all over the country and study black people. Try to figure out what exactly it is we talk about when we talk about blackness.

I remember, as the sun came up that morning, as we said good night and went to our own beds, agreeing with him, thinking, somehow, I would try to do just that.

Richard went on to Duke Divinity School, and then on to become an ordained minister, and then chaplain at Central Prison in Raleigh. When I told Richard my plans, to do what he himself had suggested, he was perhaps more excited than I. I suggested that for the final chapter, I would go with him to the prison and interview him and some of the inmates. He thought that would be a grand idea.

Richard married a beautiful black woman named Denise in the summer of 1993. He died almost exactly a year later of cancer.

Life, love, work, service, death.

I remember most fondly how fervently Richard Wimberly applied his mind to the conundrum of being. The issue of being black was no singular, isolatable question for him. He saw it always within the context of faith, of humanity. It never mattered to Richard what others thought of him; rather, it mattered what he thought of himself. He refused to allow himself to be dictated to about what or who he was, for, like Ralph Ellison's Invisible Man, he stubbornly examined each and every particle of his life; he questioned it, not on the basis of what he was supposed to think about it, but on the basis of what he actually thought of it. This, of course, is a wearisome, tiring, frustrating exercise, and when anyone questioned him or became impatient with his dogged analysis, he would just smile his infectious smile, and say, Now just bear with me . . .

Now just bear with me . . .

> Now you've been told, so you ought to know. But maybe, after all the Negro doesn't really exist. What we think is a race is detached moods and phases of other people walking around. What we have been talking about might not exist at all. Could be the shade patterns of something else thrown on the ground—other folks, seen in shadow. And even if we do exist it's all an accident anyway. God made everybody else's color. We took ours by mistake. The way the old folks tell it, it was like this . . .
>
> —Zora Neale Hurston, *Dust Tracks on a Road*

Twenty-Three

# BLACKNESS ON MY MIND

*New York, New York*

There's a crow flying
Black and ragged
Tree to tree
He's black as the highway
That's leading me
Now he's diving down
To pick up something shiny
I feel like that black crow
Flying
In a blue sky

I took the ferry to a highway
Then I drove to a pontoon plane
Took a plane to a taxi
And a taxi to a train
I been traveling so long
How'm I ever going to know my home
When I see it again?
I'm like a black crow
Flying
In a blue, blue sky

—Joni Mitchell

During this sojourn in America, I came to develop a strange romance with the motel. To be sure, it was not a part of my original intent, but this romance became, in the end, part and parcel of my journey.

The sun-splashed bed and breakfasts, too quaint for comfort; the tawdry and broken-down rooms ghosted by truck drivers, prostitutes and johns; the hunting lodge with the black-and-white TV; the depressing, dull dungeons on the edge of a megalopolis, like something out of a Fritz Lang nightmare; the happy inn run by the Indian family on the shores of Lake Erie. The coffee shops. The laundry rooms. The front desks. The sunken beds. The corporate logos. The free books of matches.

I understand that the filmmaker David Lynch made a documentary about American motels. I have not seen it. But, from what I gather, he concentrated on the kitsch and the unusual, which is abundant and interesting enough. However, I am compelled by the quotidian and the lackluster, and the vague promise of rest proffered the wayfarer. But, in truth, what can the motel offer? A warm, clean bed. A safe and convenient place to park the car. Shelter from the elements. A place to bathe and rest your suitcase. Fresh towels. A boob tube. Fresh towels. All well and good, but how far these several things are from home; how far they've come from providing actual rest. As Frederick Douglass once said, "You may not get what you pay for in this world, but you will certainly pay for what you get." My question, then, perhaps: What price is home?

Whether I like it or not, my time in motel rooms is as much a part of my years of travel as the people and the landscapes and the histories. For there is something about living in motels, about being in an *American* motel room, that is an experience in itself. I find that in a motel room, I become a person apart from myself. I have entered a strange limbo, a quasi-world, ruled ruefully by corporate demographic studies, stingy owners, American tourist demands, and the American psyche of what it means to be a human being away from home. Home, that ever-elusive intangible mythology of self and place. I found it difficult, if not impossible, to write about these experiences without taking myself back to that room in Atlanta where I scribbled notes, or read articles and books; that place in Lafayette where, after a day of chasing this person, this book, this fact, this lead, I would return with a sigh, and reenter a beige or off-white womb of sorts, with a newly made bed, and a freshly vacuumed carpet, and a clean bathroom; this place in Anchorage where I sat waiting for a confirming or a returned phone call, and picked up that most benign but universal of habits, television watching, after having gone over eight years without owning a television set. (I became so addicted to CNN that I would seriously think of passing up a motel when I discovered that they did not carry that monotonous station.) For there is something about being in a motel room, alone, with that big cubic receiving device, a device you know hums and glows and flickers with pretty pictures and multifaceted sounds, with just a snap of a switch, that makes it a necessity: this illusion of company, this promise of connection; this unflagging desire to mitigate loneliness. Impossible, yes, for me to think of these days abroad in my own land, without thinking, fondly, of my times in these sundry homes away from home. For as I left other people's homes, I could not but acutely think about the idea of what composed, comprised, configured a home.

So it was, that when I finally returned to New York, when it had hit me like a boulder that this trip of trips was indeed over for me, that I reemerged from this period of intransigence, and began again slowly to think of myself as a person who was of a place, and in a place, and able to make a home. And in many ways it was fitting for me to think of New York, and not North Carolina, as home, for, in the most basic of senses, it was my home. It was the place where I was born; it was the place where I had made my living and the bulk of my life for the last eight years; and it was a place I mysteriously, deeply loved. And though I was not a true New Yorker, having been stolen away at six weeks old, and having grown up a true country boy, New York could bewitch me as it never could someone for whom the asphalt and the concrete and the noise and the grime were commonplace. Like Thebes for Oedipus, who had to rediscover his heritage, beyond his heritage, New York seemed to hide secrets and dreads and conjurations wherein I might find some lurking truth about myself. But that is, of course, the myth of New York, from the dancers on Broadway to the investment bankers on Wall Street, from the Israeli cab drivers to the Hungarian waitresses. The monkeys in the zoo, and the pigeons too, New York, New York, they all want you.

> And then the voyages, the search for the happy land. In his moment of terrible vision he saw, in the tortuous ways of a thousand alien places, his foiled quest of himself. And his haunted face was possessed of that obscure and passionate hunger that had woven its shuttle across the seas, that had hung its weft across the Dutch in Pennsylvania, that had darkened his father's eyes to impalpable desire for wrought stone and the head of an angel. Hill-haunted, whose vision of the earth was mountain-walled, he saw the golden cities sicken in his eye, the opulent dark splendors turn to dingy gray. His brain was sick with the million books, his eyes with the million pictures, his body sickened on a hundred princely wines.
>
> And rising from his vision, he cried: "I am not there among the cities. I have sought down a million streets, until the goat-cry died within my throat, and I have found no city where I was, no door where I had entered, no place where I had stood."
>
> —Thomas Wolfe, *Look Homeward Angel*

I know I romanticize New York. I always have and I probably always will. I feel sorry for people who are not in love with the place where they live. For many people, sadly, such a happy marriage of geography and emotion is not possible. I count myself among the lucky.

Trey Ellis once told me he believed that certain folk were born hard-wired for certain cities. He knew two brothers, he told me; I think he said they were twins. One brother was laid-back, sybaritic, open, fun-loving—he wound up in Los Angeles. The other brother was an A-type personality, driven, neurotic, constantly on the move, frantic, busy, busy, busy—he lived in New York.

Utterly un-American, deceptively kind, beset by blizzards and exploding towers and the worst traffic in the nation; home to the Irish, the Jewish, the Indian, the Pakistani, the Haitian, the Senegalese, the French, the German, the Dutch, the Italian (ah, the Italian), and the highest concentration of Chinese outside of China, not to mention the Greek and the Spanish, which include Puerto Rico, Honduras, Equador, El Salvador, Belize, Costa Rica, Mexico, et al, and don't forget Spain.

North Carolina's favorite native son novelist came to New York. Thomas Wolfe wrote a story, "Only the Dead Know Brooklyn," that will probably always do the city proud. One of this century's most influential writers of prose, Joseph Mitchell, was also a North Carolina boy. As was the roving Charles Kuralt, and so many others. Call it tradition, call it coincidence, call it what you will, but I believe in some strange and mysterious link between my home state and the place I now think of as home. True, the great city draws folk from all over the world, yet curiously Carolinians seem to love it most by writing about it.

> One may well ask at once whether a travel book is an appropriate place for an investigation into the heart of a region. In some respects, travel writing is a shallow form of serious literature, the only form in which ignorance is pure bliss. W.E.B. Du Bois once wrote scornfully, perhaps quoting someone, about "car window sociologists," who view their human subjects mainly from a comfortable distance, then write about them with confidence and, no doubt, consequence. No matter how long he or she lingers in any one place, filling notebooks or tape cassettes, the travel writer must surely be most often a car window sociologist, a car window psycholo-

> gist, and a car window writer, however plentiful or intimate are the interviews or chats with members of the native population.
>
> —Arnold Rampersad, "V. S. Naipaul: Turning in the South"

At one point, after I knew it was over, the traveling, the talking, the searching; after transcripts and notes and diary entries were organized and placed in order, I looked at a mound of over 5,000 pages of stuff, words upon words, undigested, needing digestion—and I panicked.

The manuscript-to-be was my bone; I had to chew on it.

There was a horrible psychological terror involved with bringing this project to a close. I was beginning to see the truth. Every article, every movie, every television show, everything about black people I encountered gave me an upset stomach. It couldn't be done, this task I had set for myself. Already I was aware of all the lacunae in my travels. I could hear ardent voices asking: Where are the Muslims? Where is hip-hop? Where is jazz? Why didn't you go into the prisons? Why did you leave out a large chunk of the South? Where is the Negro Baseball League? What! No football, basketball, hockey, soccer players? Not enough about food! Not enough about language! What about black insurance companies, newspapers, plumbers, undertakers, oil magnates, physicists, engineers, state department officials, singers, patent attorneys, shipbuilders, jockeys, drug addicts, trumpet players, botanists, skateboarders, marine biologists, violinists, ornithologists, midwives, candy makers, comic book authors, karate black belts, Jews, chiropodists. . . .

I looked upon what I had done, and all I could see was what I had not done.

One day, in the summer of 1996, at the Black Arts Festival in Atlanta, I had the honor and pleasure of finally meeting the award-winning writer Octavia Butler. I had interviewed her over the phone the year before I had set off on this odyssey, and I was pleased, six years later, that she remembered me. After a while, she asked what I was working on now, and, as succinctly as I could, I told her. She chuckled. "That's like saying you're writing a book on what it means to be human."

It was.

New York was going to be the *pièce de résistance* for *Walking on Water.* I had worked it all out after a lot of heady deliberation. I would interview Afrika Baambata, the man considered to be the father of rap music, and I would interview Mrs. Joyce Dinkins, the former first lady of New York and descendant of an old New York family; I would interview a homeless man, and I would interview an AIDS patient at a hospice, and I would interview the writer and thinker and now–Columbia University Professor Manning Marable, and I would interview the kids who were selling illicit substances on my corner, and I would interview the astrophysicist Dr. Neil Tyson who had recently been made head of the Hayden Planetarium, and I would interview a friend of mine who was a gay Episcopal priest . . . and I knew there was no way in hell I would finish this book before I was ninety-seven at the outside.

If Chicago defeated me, and California consumed me, and Louisiana kidnapped me, New York would surely kill me.

By this point everything was redundant and everything was new.

I phoned my editor and told her New York was out. I think she thought I had lost my mind. You're writing a book about African America, and you are going to leave out New York City? The place that got you involved in the first place?

Yep.

I realized later that my dream was undoable and yet done, for on my table rested not interviews and notes and thoughts, but a record of my personal history of the last six years. No longer was this about gathering facts—though I had facts aplenty. It was about feeling and interpretation and ways of seeing the world and of being in the world. The truth is there are over thirty-six million ways to be black, from the curious guy who raises pigeons on the roof across the street from me, who wears the same jacket 365 days of the year, to the Tennessee mountain minister who teaches Greek and Latin to high school students, to the NBA player from Lake Charles, Louisiana, who loves his mother to death, to the matriarch of an apple orchard in Washington State who hates to see her children go off to school, to the crack addict in some Philadelphia alley, with a hard-on and thirty-seven cents to his name, just wanting to stay up and UP, to the congresswoman, to the cowgirl, to the fisherman to the dogcatcher to the young lovers, at this very moment, engaged in that ancient act that will undoubtedly bring, nine months hence, yet another brown-skinned girl or brown-skinned boy into this world, into this country, into this city, into this block, into this building, into this room where they shall learn their own uniqueness, and, one fine morning, say softly, I am.

To accurately accomplish what I had originally set out to do would have made it necessary to go and talk to thirty-six million people—but the truth is, even if that feat were humanly possible, the end result would be the same: inconclusive.

But to bear witness I need only one soul, and my soul is a witness.

> He lived there for years, and New Yorkers even named a street in his honor. But these days would dapper Duke Ellington feel at ease taking the A train 2 1/2 miles north from midtown Manhattan to black Harlem? Not if he believed the vision this New York City community conjures up in the minds of apprehensive whites: a post-nuclear landscape of poverty and blight, where crack dealers plan gang wars in cratered tenements. To most Manhattanites from the wealthy southern part of the island, Harlem hardly exists, except as an old, obscure head wound—the beast in the attic, a maximum-security prison for the American Dream's unruly losers. Why would a white person go to this Harlem, except to buy drugs? . . .
>
> Harlem is certainly not a harmless place for residents or itinerants, but neither is it the city's worst crime area. In any case, fear is no excuse for missing out on Harlem's cultural and historical bounty. . . .
>
> —Richard Corliss, "Welcome to New Harlem!"
> *Time,* April 24, 1989

I can be honest about Harlem now. Or at least I think I can. Or at least I certainly want to be. After my time on the road, I found a place right on the edge of the traditional beginnings of Harlem. One hundred and Tenth Street, and was happy there. Over time, I came to see my original aversion as only natural, and frightening in the sense that I might never have worked out those conflicting and warring factions that threatened to split me apart. I speak of my identity as a black person and of the representative truths that have everything and nothing to do with me. So easy it was to only associate Harlem with poverty and crime; so easy to figure that to love and to come to understand Harlem would be, in some way, tantamount to embracing those elements: to become them, that media-driven entity. But I saw through a glass darkly, and with the weight of many generations on my shoulders, the loud whispers to not become a criminal or poor or hopeless or helpless or homeless or a victim of society's blind hatred and malice. Overcome, these voices said, and, in my simple mind, Harlem had rejected the proud commandments of those dark Ur-daughters and dark Ur-sons not long out of the Jim Crow–haunted south; in my mind I found it necessary, physically, to separate myself, to disassociate myself from the horny possibility, from the place and image the national consciousness seemed to possess, not simply of Harlem, but of what it meant to be a Negro. I, lacking the imagination, the sense of real history, the sense of self, and the understanding to combat society's presumptions, fell victim to a silly, though prevalent, way of thinking.

Can anyone reading this, even today, black or white, say that they are immune to these forces? Say that any of their everyday choices are free from these looming judgments?

But we must become immune. We must work at becoming. We must begin to see more deeply, reason more soundly, indeed to reason at all about these ideas of color and "race," begin to disentangle the lies from the reality.

What does it mean to be black?

I know now, after a great deal of work and worry, that none of the obvious answers to that question hold much water. Yes, to be black is to be composed of three essential ingredients: political, cultural and emotional. You don't need to look long at the history, and the present, of Black America to be convinced of the ongoing political necessity for some unity among black folks, if nothing else, to band together against discrimination, to fight for parity, to safeguard against injustice inherently aimed at a person solely because of his or her skin color.

At the same time the culture of being black, great or small for some, but present for practically all, remains fascinating and elusive, multifaceted and ever-changing, problematic and profound. Despite its Old World origins, black American culture, the language, the art, the music, the customs, ad nauseam, is a New World creation, as varied as the geography of the Americas, and belonging to all. It is a part of America.

And most vexing to come to terms with, for me at least, on an intellectual basis, is that emotional condition called being black. To be sure, it was created by people who wanted to create an Other, black folk, for sinister purposes. But out of that damnable imposition sprung something I'm certain they never expected, and something which has grown into its own state of being: being black. It is a desire toward some spiritual connection with some larger whole. To me this yearning is at its root an existential construct: Who am I? Where do I belong? To whom do I belong? When Zora Neale Hurston cries, "My People, My People," this is the construct she addresses. This "willed affirmation" is the sense of identity that leads to people intentionally embracing the idea of "race" as a fact. And though I still do not hold with the idea of "race" as a scientific concept, I cannot easily dismiss that belief as an active force among folk, for better or for worse. Dr. Du Bois's essentialist, mystical connection to some mythical Mother Africa still holds profound emotional energy, even for me. Indeed, that mysticism bound many black folk to decades of positive service, to the race; it brought us through Middle Passage; it brought us through slavery; it brought us through Reconstruction and Redemption; it brought us through the twentieth century, and it will assuredly bring us into the future.

Yes, when I call another black man "brother," or a black woman "sister," I mean it. But being able to hold conflicting, complex views in my head does not cause me to short-circuit; rather, it leaves me with a rich concoction to look toward, with pride, with wonder, with awe. To paraphrase Whitman: Do I contradict myself? I contain multitudes.

Oddly enough, to finally understand—like the rest of black folks, like the rest of America—that I am a work in progress brings me a strange peace.

> Not enough can be enough and being enough quite enough is enough and being enough enough is enough and being enough it is that. Quite all that can be what it is and all of it being that, quite all of it is all there is of it.
>
> —Gertrude Stein, "A Long Gay Book"

Chinquapin, New York, Chapel
Hill, New York, Rome,
Oxford, Memphis, 1992–1998

# ACKNOWLEDGMENTS

First of all, this book could not exist without the trust and cooperation of over two hundred and scores more people who actually took the time out of their lives to sit down and talk with me, and to share their experiences, thoughts and ideas. My gratitude and memories of them will be everlasting.

I had the life-enriching opportunity to speak with a number of people who, alas, are not all mentioned in the final draft. Nonetheless, the lack of their contribution would have made this book less. Undoubtedly I will miss a great many people who helped and simply offered kindness, but I would like to extend special thanks to the following: *New York*: Art Anderson, Estelle Anderson, Ken Holley, Tim Smith, Leslie Auerbach; *Massachusetts*: Zita Cousens, Jackie Holland; *Vermont*: William Osiris Caldwill; *Maine*: Duff Gillespie, Beverly Talbott; *Nova Scotia*: Charles Saunders, Gale Saunders, Craig Smith; *Quebec*: Fred Ward; *Ontario*: Leslie Saunders, Cecil Foster, Ayanna Black, Gary French, Winston Smith; Linda, Adrienne and Robert of Two Black Guys; Adrienne Shadd, Marva Jackson, Norm Richmond; *Ohio*: Darlene Brown; *Michigan* : Audrey Bullett, James Cox; *Wisconsin*: Nathan Adams, Samantha Fenrow, Nellie McKay, Joel Gershman; *Illinois*: Brent House, Bob McCurdy, Tom McRuer; *Minnesota*: Tanya Bransford, David Taylor, Charles Sugnet, Patrick Sculley, the Rev. Dr. Earl F. Miller; *North Dakota*: Toni Scott, Christine Hoper, Reuben Harris, George Strickland, Steven Schmidt, Sharon Carson; *Idaho*: Tony Stewart, Frances Heard; *Saskatchewan*: the Nelsons; *Alaska*: George T. Harper, Bruce Merrill, Linda Pennywill, Evelyn Bailey, Cornelius "Bo" Walden; *Washington*: Charles Johnson, Randi Edens; *California*: Frank & Dona Irvin, Inderpreet Dhillon, Nina Harris, Blanche Richardson of Marcus Books, Steve Barnes, Trey Ellis, Les Wills, George Jenkins, Quincy Troupe, Margaret Troupe; *Nevada*: Sam Smith, Carl Holmes, Joseph Spears, Rudy Garland, Clifford Garland; *Utah*: Tamara Taylor, the Rev. Janet L. Swift, Willard D. Samuels, Curley Jones; *Wyoming*: James Byrd; *Colorado*: Rajer; *Louisiana*: Louis Edwards, Darrel Bourque, Peter Smith, Aaron Walker, Mary V. Murray,

Doris Barrow, Paulette Raymond, Mrs. Charlie Moutons; *Florida*: N. Y. Nathiril; *Georgia*: Walter White, Tina McElroy Ansa, Jonée Ansa.

Again, I am overwhelmed by the kindness and encouragement I've received from absolute strangers. To all those I've neglected to mention, I remain in your debt.

The actual seven years of traveling throughout America—and the subsequent writing—could not have been possible without the financial support of the following institutions: the Simon Guggenheim Memorial Foundation, the Mrs. Giles Whiting Foundation, the University of North Carolina's Carolina Institute for the Arts and Humanities, the Trustees of the Sherwood Anderson Estate, the Trustees of the Mary Hobson Estate, the American Academy of Arts and Letters, the American Academy in Rome, and the support of John and Renee Grisham, who funded my year at the University of Mississippi.

I was blessed to find support and encouragement at all the institutions I've been involved with while working on this book. I'd like to thank at: *Sarah Lawrence College*: Barbara Kaplan, Linsey Abrams, Myra Goldberg, and the memory of Jerry Badanes; *Columbia University*: Alan Zeigler, Richard Locke, and the memory of Doris Jean Austin; *Duke University*: Reynolds Price; *University of North Carolina, Chapel Hill*: Jim Seay, Lawrence Avery, Beverly Taylor, Ruel Tyson, Lloyd Kramer; *American Academy in Rome*: Adele Chatfield-Taylor, Caroline Bruzelius, Pina Pasquintonio; *University of Mississippi, Oxford*: Dan Williams; as well as Richard Howarth of Oxford Square Books, and Charles Rowell of *Callaloo*.

As teachers and friends for whom I remain a continuing student, I thank Max Steele, Daphne Athas, Doris Betts and Lee Greene for continuing instruction. And Nell Painter for continuing inspiration.

To quote a certain British rock band, "I get by with a little help from my friends." In truth, it was a lot of help, advice and moral support, and I will forever be grateful to: Sheila Anderson, Don Antrim, Don Belton, Joseph A. Cincotti, Connie Christopher, Nick Christopher, Karen Latuchie, Alane S. Mason, Richard Morrison, Randy Page, Mohan Ramachandran, Zollie Stevenson, Jr., Denise Journer Wimberly, Yoji Yamaguchi, and all the 1996–97 AMAR fellows.

I especially want to thank Patrick Guilfoyle for going well beyond duty in the name of friendship and support.

Even more important was the support and tolerance of my family, who saw me come and go—and sometimes disappear—for close to a decade. My love and gratitude to Mary Kenan Hall, Edythe Kenan Brown, John

W. Brown, Nakia C. Brown, Ayesha C. Brown, Matthis Sharpless, Cassandra Sharpless and George W. Kenan.

For their diligence and support and protection I'd like to thank the folk at the Wylie Agency, especially Andrew Wylie, Sarah Chalfant and Zoe Pagnamenta.

Wherever he is, I tearfully acknowledge all the guidance and support I received from Eric Ashworth, who got the ball rolling, and literally got me rolling.

To Mary Carroll, transcriber extraordinaire, I will never forget your magic with over a hundred tapes.

I gratefully thank my editor, Ann Close, who encouraged me with my very first manuscript over a decade ago, and who did not throw a fit when I gave her over 1,400 pages to vex her for the next year of her life. I'll always be thankful. And to her assistant, Asya Muchnick, for her swift, smooth help.

Lastly, if this book were a starship, its chief engineer would be Douglas Smith Munro, researcher and miracle worker. Thank you for keeping the warp drive on line.

It goes without saying that I take all responsibility for any mistakes.

I could do no better; I could do no worse.

# SELECTED BIBLIOGRAPHY

*Chapter One: Prologue: Come Out the Wilderness*

BOOKS

Adams, Henry. *The Education of Henry Adams.* Boston: Houghton Mifflin Co., 1918, 1973.

Baker, John R. *Race.* New York: Oxford University Press, 1974.

Davis, F. James. *Who is Black?: One Nation's Definition.* University Park: The Pennsylvania State University Press, 1991.

Dewart, Janet, ed. *The State of Black America, 1990.* National Urban League, Inc., 1990.

Dyson, Michael Eric. *Reflecting Black: African-American Cultural Criticism.* American Culture Vol. 9. Minneapolis: University of Minnesota Press, 1993.

Ellison, Ralph. *Going to the Territory.* New York: Random House, 1986.

———. *Shadow and Act.* New York: Vintage, 1964.

Fields, Barbara J. "Ideology and Race in American History." *Region, Race, and Reconstruction: Essays in Honor of C. Vann Woodward.* Edited by J. Morgan Kousser and James M. McPherson. New York: Oxford University Press, 1982, 143–177.

Goldberg, David Theo, ed. *Anatomy of Racism.* Minneapolis: University of Minnesota Press, 1990.

Gosset, Thomas F. *Race: The History of an Idea in America.* Dallas: SMU Press, 1963.

Gould, Stephen Jay. *The Mismeasure of Man.* New York: W. W. Norton & Co., 1983, 1981.

Hemenway, Robert E. *Zora Neale Hurston: A Literary Biography.* Urbana: University of Illinois Press, 1977.

Hernton, Calvin C. *Sex and Racism in America.* New York: Grove Press, 1988.

Hurston, Zora Neale. *Dust Tracks on a Road: An Autobiography.* Edited by Robert E. Hemenway. Urbana: University of Illinois Press, 1984.

———. *I Love Myself When I am Laughing . . . and then Again When I am Looking Mean and Impressive.* Edited by Alice Walker. Old Westbury, NY: The Feminist Press, 1979.

———. *The Sanctified Church.* Berkeley: Turtle Island, 1983.

Lewis, David Levering. *W.E.B. DuBois: Biography of a Race, 1868–1919.* New York: John MacRae-Henry Holt and Co., 1993.

Mintz, Sidney W., and Richard Price. *The Birth of African-American Culture: An Anthropological Perspective.* Boston: Beacon Press, 1992, 1976.

Murray, Albert. *The Omni-Americans: Black Experience and American Culture.* New York: DaCapo Press, 1970.

———. *South to a Very Old Place.* New York: McGraw Hill Book Company, 1971.

———. *Stomping the Blues.* New York: Vintage-Random House, 1982, 1976.
Omi, Michael, and Howard Winant. *Racial Formation in the United States: From the 1960s to the 1980s.* New York: Routledge & Kegan Paul, 1986.
Terkel, Studs. *Race: How Blacks and Whites Think and Feel About the American Obsession.* New York: The New Press, 1992.
Williams, John A. *This Is My Country Too.* New York: Signet, 1966.

ARTICLES

"A Nation Apart." *U.S. News and World Report,* 17 Mar. 1986, 18.
Begley, Sharon. "Three is not Enough: Surprising New Lessons From the Controversial Science of Race." *Newsweek,* 13 Feb. 1995, 67–69.
Boas, Franz. "Review of *The Rising Tide of Color.*" *The Nation,* CXI, 8 Dec. 1920, 656.
Cose, Ellis. "One Drop of Bloody History: Americans Have Always Defined Themselves on the Basis of Race." *Newsweek,* 13 Feb. 1995, 70–72.
Fields, Barbara Jeane. "Slavery, Race and Ideology in the United States of America." *New Left Review,* May/June 1990, 95–118.
Fineman, Howard. "The New Politics of Race." *Newsweek,* 6 May 1991, 22–26.
Morganthau, Tom. "What Color Is Black?" *Newsweek,* 13 Feb. 1995, 63–65.
Verhovek, Sam Howe. "One Man's Arrival in Town Exposes a Racial Fault Line." *New York Times,* 27 Feb. 1993, L7.
Whitaker, Mark, et al. "A Crisis of Shattered Dreams." *Newsweek,* 6 May 1991, 28–31.

## *Chapter Two: Martha's Vineyard, Massachusetts: Once Upon an Eden*

BOOKS

Birmingham, Stephen. *Certain People: America's Black Elite.* Boston: Little, Brown, and Company, 1977.
Cromwell, Adelaide M. "Afterword." *The Living Is Easy,* by Dorothy West. New York: Feminist Press, 1982.
Feagin, Joe R., and Melvin P. Sikes. *Living with Racism: The Black Middle-class Experience.* Boston: Beacon Press, 1994.
Frazier, E. Franklin. *Black Bourgeoisie.* New York: Collier Books, 1962.
Fussell, Paul. *Class.* New York: Touchstone Books, 1992.
Platt, Anthony M. *E. Franklin Frazier Reconsidered.* New Brunswick: Rutgers University Press, 1991. 111–169.
Shange, Ntozake. *For Colored Girls Who Have Considered Suicide When the Rainbow is Enuf.* New York: Bantam Books, 1980.

ARTICLES

Bamberger, Michael F. "Dora Grain Views Prejudice, Beauty Side by Side on Island." *Vineyard Gazette,* 21 Jan. 1983.
Benjamin, Playthell. "The Black Bourgeoisie's Burden." *Emerge,* Feb. 1991, 58–61.
Clark, Edie. "A Slave's Daughter." *Yankee,* Mar. 1991, 78.
Cromwell, Adelaide M. "The History of Oak Bluffs as a Popular Resort for Blacks." *Dukes County Intelligencer,* 26.1 (1984): 3–25.

Forrest, Leon. "Harlem Sings America: The Legacy of Harlem Renaissance Endures in Lyrical Novels and Prescient Poetry." Rev. of *The Wedding*, by Dorothy West. *Los Angeles Times*, 26 Feb. 1995, sec. Book Review, 1.

Frisby, Michael K. "The Economics of Disparity: Gap Among Blacks Widening, Study Says." *Boston Globe*, 9 Aug. 1991, 1.

Garreau, Joel. "The Integration of the American Dream: Not Millennium, but a Historic Change." *Washington Post National Weekly Edition*, 8–14 Feb. 1988, 6–7.

Hardman, Della Taylor. "Slave Trade in New England: A Scholar on Myth and Truth." *Vineyard Gazette*, 4 Mar. 1988.

Holland, Jacqueline L. "The African American Presence on Martha's Vineyard." *Dukes County Intelligencer*, 33.1 (1991): 3–26.

Hopkins, Ellen. "Blacks at the Top: Torn Between Two Worlds." *New York*, 19 Jan. 1987, 20–31.

Kilson, Martin. "*The Black Bourgeoisie* Revisited: From E. Franklin Frazier to the Present." Dissent, Winter 1983, 85–96.

"Moving Up at Last?" (Based on forum discussion among Glenn C. Loury, Julian Bond, Frank Mingo, and Paula Giddings, moderated by Juan Williams.) *Harper's Magazine* Feb. 1989, 35–46.

Nelson, Jill, and John Pinderhughes. "Martha's Vineyard: Summers Spent Off the Coast of Massachusetts." *American Visions*, Jun. 1991, 26–31.

Railton, Arthur R. "The Indians and the English On Martha's Vineyard: Part III: Thomas Mayhew Sr." *Dukes County Intelligencer*, 33.1 (1991): 27–63.

Sege, Irene. "Mass. Black Population Growing, but Progress Lags." *Boston Globe*, 9 Aug. 1991, 11.

Stradling, Richard. "Program Tells the Rich Story of Island's Black Community." *Vineyard Gazette*, 26 Feb. 1988.

Towley, Lewis. "Review of *The Black Bourgeoisie*." *Social Work*, Vol. 3, No. 1, 1958.

Updergrave, Walter L. "Race and Money." *Money*, Dec. 1989: 152.

Usdansky, Margeret L. "Success Dividing Blacks: Growing Economic Disparity." *USA Today*, 9 Aug. 1991, 3A.

West, Dorothy. "Cottagers' Corner." *Vineyard Gazette*, 31 Aug. 1971.

———. "Fond Memories of a Black Childhood: Oak Bluffs Had Band Concerts, Lemonade, Cookies and Whist." *Vineyard Gazette*, 25 Jun. 1971, 1E.

———. "Stepping Back Into Divisive Times: Sad Memories of Color Barriers." *Vineyard Gazette*, 2 Mar. 1990.

———. "To Cottagers: A Plea for a Vital Program." *Vineyard Gazette*, 2 Feb. 1990.

———. " 'The World Was Not Lost . . .' " *Yankee*, Mar. 1991.

### *Chapter Three: Burlington, Vermont: Where Two or Three Are Gathered in My Name*

#### ARTICLES

Bandel, Betty. "Social History in the Land Records." *Vermont Historical News*, no. 30, 1979, 72–73.

"Biography of a 5-term Governor." *Burlington Free Press* (Extra), 14 Aug. 1991, 4.

"Black Population Rose in Booming Areas." (*Washington Post*, excerpted in *Burlington Free Press*) 21 Jun. 1989, 2A.

Decher, Laura. "Blacks Say Population Growth Is Good for Vermont." *Burlington Free Press,* 21 Jun. 1989, 1A-2A.
"Diversity University: Statement of Purpose." N.p.: Privately published, n.d.
Hileman, Gregor. "Iron-Willed Black Schoolmaster and His Granite Academy." *Middlebury College Newsletter,* Spring 1974, 6–26.
Lickteig, Mary Ann. "Together in Prayer: State's First Black Church Organizes in Burlington." *Burlington Free Press,* 6 Feb. 1989, 1A.
Maurice, Maggie. "Vermont Blacks Sing Hallelujah." *Burlington Free Press,* 2 Jun. 1989, 1D, 3D.
Mitchell, Robert W. "Biracial Activity in Vermont: As Old as the State Itself." *Rutland Daily Herald and Times Argus,* 4 Jul. 1976, B-41.
Nicolosi, Vincent. "Twilight Mystery." *Yankee Magazine* Jun. 1986: 174.
Older, Jules. "Uneasy Peace: The Black Experience in Vermont." *Vermont Sunday Magazine,* 9 April 1989, 4–5, 14–15.
Randolph, Laura B. "How Blacks Fare in the Whitest State in the Union." *Ebony,* Dec. 1987, 44.

## *Chapter Four: Bangor, Maine: Many Hundreds Gone*

### ARTICLES

Austin, Phyllis. "Blacks in Maine." *Maine Times,* 3 Dec. 1976, 2–7.
Brown, Gewoffery F. "At Maine's Colleges: Black People are Not White People with Black Faces." *Maine Times,* 1 Mar. 1974, 8.
Hoose, Shoshana. "Black History Elusive." *Maine Sunday Telegram,* 17 Feb. 1991, 2F.
———. "Crossroads." *Maine Sunday Telegram,* 24 Feb. 1991, 1F–2F.
———. "Proud Roots." *Maine Sunday Telegram,* 17 Feb. 1991, 1F–2F.
Maine. Governor's Task Force on Human Rights. (report) Aug. 1968.
Matheson, Ed. "Bangor's Black Community." *Register* (Bangor, Maine), 8 June 1988, 1.
———. "Bangor's Black Community." *Register* (Bangor, Maine), 15 June 1988.
Sharp, David. "Black Youth Describes Growing Up in Maine." *Bangor Daily News,* 23 Aug. 1991, 1.
———. "Maine Blacks Seem to Lack Strong Sense of Community." (AP) *Bangor Daily News,* 22 Aug. 1991, 1.
———. "Northern New England Racism Has Many Faces: After Vermont, Maine Is the Whitest State in the Union." *Bangor Daily News,* 21 Aug. 1991, 7.

## *Chapter Five: Buffalo, New York: Lake Effect*

### ARTICLES

Allen, Carl. "The Old Families of the Black Community." *The Magazine of the Buffalo News,* 15 Jan. 1984.
Bashō. *On Love and Barley: Haiku of Basho.* New York: Penguin Books, 1985.
Trollope, Anthony. *North America.* New York: Da Capo Press, 1951, 1986.

### *Chapter Six: Idlewild, Michigan: The Snowbirds*

BOOKS

Chestnutt, Helen C. *Charles Waddell Chestnutt: Pioneer of the Color Line.* Chapel Hill: University of North Carolina Press, 1952.

ARTICLES

BeVier, Thomas. "Idlewild Shakes Free of Past." *Detroit News,* 3 Mar. 1991.

DuBois, W. E. B. "Hopkinsville, Chicago and Idlewild." *Crisis Magazine,* Aug. 1921, 158.

Hart, John Frasier. "A Rural Retreat for Northern Negroes." *Geographical Review,* Apr. 1960, L.2, 147–168.

Wilson, Benjamin C. "Idlewild: A Black Eden in Michigan." *Michigan History,* Sep./Oct. 1981, 33–37.

### *Chapter Seven: Madison, Wisconsin: Something Like the Future*

ARTICLES

Marable, Manning. "Black America in Search of Itself." *Progressive,* Nov. 1991, 18.

### *Chapter Eight: Chicago, Illinois: My Own Private Chicago*

BOOKS

*DuSable Museum of African American History, 1961–1990.* Chicago: DuSable Museum, n.d.

Lemann, Nicholas. *The Promised Land: The Great Black Migration and How It Changed America.* New York: Alfred A. Knopf, Inc., 1991.

Madhubuti, Haki R., ed. *Black Books Bulletin, Volume I: The Challenge of the Twenty-first Century.*

——. *Black Men: Obsolete, Single, Dangerous?* Chicago: Third World Press, 1991.

———. *Earthquakes and Sunrise Missions: Poetry and Essays of Black Renewal, 1973–1983.* Chicago: Third World Press, 1984.

———. *Killing Memory, Seeking Ancestry.* Detroit: Lotus Press, 1987.

Terkel, Studs. *Chicago.* New York: Pantheon Books, 1985.

ARTICLES

Ward, Francis. "Dusable Museum: The Spirit of Chicago's Founder Lives On." *Push Magazine,* 1991, 20–23.

### *Chapter Nine: St. Paul/Minneapolis, Minnesota: What Is the Question?*

BOOKS

Fairbanks, Evelyn. *The Days of the Rondo.* St. Paul: Minnesota Historical Society Press, 1990.

Scott, Walter R., Sr., ed. *Minnesota's Black Community.* Minneapolis: Scott Publishing Co., 1976.

Spangler, Earl. *The Negro in Minnesota.* Minneapolis: T. S. Denison & Co., 1961.

Taylor, David Vassar. "The Blacks." *They Chose Minnesota.* Edited by June Drenning Holmquist. St. Paul: Minnesota Historical Society Press, 1981, 73–91.

ARTICLES

"About Our Church," ts. Pilgrim Baptist Church, St. Paul, MN.

Chin, Richard. "Minnesota Minority Population Grows Much Faster Than Whites." *Saint Paul Pioneer Press* 1989: 1A.

———. "79% Growth Rate Posted by Metro Black Community." *Saint Paul Pioneer Press,* 9 Apr. 1991, 1A.

———. "Twin Cities Now Home to Increasing Number of Middle-Class Blacks." *Saint Paul Pioneer Press,* 23 Jun. 1991, 1A.

Kelly, Sean T. "Selby Avenue Is Expecting Better Times." *Saint Paul Pioneer Press,* 24 Jul. 1991, 3NE.

Millet, Larry. "Close-Ups Track Shifting Tides of Racial Diversity: Black Residents Settle Throughout St. Paul and into the Suburbs." *Saint Paul Pioneer Press,* 3 Mar. 1991, 8A.

———. "6 Sites With Black Ties Nominated for Historic Register." *St. Paul Pioneer Press,* 17 Feb. 1991, 1 B.

"Nellie Stone Johnson Scholarship Program." (brochure). Minnesota State University System: privately published. N.p. n.d.

Ojeda-Zapata, Julio. "Minority Teens Under More Stress Than Whites in Survey." *St. Paul Pioneer Press Dispatch,* 9 Feb. 1990, 1A.

Perry, Steve. "The Good Fight: Nellie Stone Johnson's 70 Years in Minnesota Politics." *City Pages* (Minneapolis-St. Paul), 29 May 1991, 8–12.

## *Chapter Ten: Grand Forks, North Dakota: "How Old Would You Be If You Didn't Know How Old You Was?"*

BOOKS

Sherman, William C., and Playford V. Thorson, eds. *Plains Folk: North Dakota's Ethnic History.* Fargo: North Dakota Institute for Regional Studies, 1988.

Thompson, Era Bell. *American Daughter.* St. Paul: Minnesota Historical Society Press, 1986.

## *Chapter Eleven: Coeur d'Alene, Idaho: Fight No More Forever*

BOOKS

Oliver, Mamie. *Idaho Ebony: The Afro-American Presence in Idaho State History.* Boise: privately published, 1990.

ARTICLES

Bateman, Nancy. "Neo-Nazi Convention Quiet." *Coeur d'Alene Press,* 16 Jul. 1990, 1.

Olson, Rev. John. "Are Racial Tensions Likely to Lead to a Race War and an Attempt to

Establish a Separate White State?" *Spokesman Review* (Spokane, WA), 21 Apr. 1985.

Paul, Irving. "Decision Cedes Ground to Aryans." *Coeur d'Alene Press,* 10 May 1991.

Stewart, Tony. "Civil Rights Legislation in Idaho," Press release. 12 Sep. 1990. Coeur d'Alene Public Library, Pamphlet file: #40.

Stoddard, Ken, and Ann Stoddard. "An Appeal to Common Sense," ts. Letter. Coeur d'Alene Public Library, Pamphlet File: #5.

Yarbrough, Gary Lee. "Are Racial Tensions Likely to Lead to a Race War and an Attempt to Establish a Separate White State?" *Spokesman Review* (Spokane, WA), 21 Apr. 1985.

## *Chapter Twelve: Maidstone and North Battleford, Saskatchewan: By the Big Gulley*

### BOOKS

Cruikshank, Julie and Angela Sidney. "The Story of Crow." *Coming to Light: Contemporary Translations of the Native Literatures of North America.* Edited by Brian Swann. New York: Vintage, 1996.

*North of the Gulley.* Maidstone: North of the Gulley History Book Committee, 1981.

### ARTICLES

Fisher, Mathew. "Last of Black Homesteaders Celebrate 70 Years in Alberta." *Globe and Mail* (Toronto), 3 Jul. 1989, A1.

Lieber, J. "The Saint from Shiloh." *Sports Illustrated,* 17 Aug. 1987:50–2.

Zeman, Brenda. "Canadian Black Doesn't Fit Stereotype." *Saskatchewan Report Newsmagazine*, Summer 1989.

## *Chapter Thirteen: Anchorage, Alaska: Cold Hands and Fiery Hearts*

### BOOKS

*The Alaska Almanac: Facts about Alaska.* 18th ed. Anchorage: Alaska Northwest, 1994, 1976.

Cohen, Stan. *Alcan and Canol: A Pictorial History of the Two Great World War II Construction Projects.* Missoula, Montana: Pictorial Histories Publishing Co., 1992.

———. *The Trail of '42: A Pictorial History of the Alaska Highway.* Missoula, Montana: Pictorial Histories Publishing Co., Eighth Revised Printing 1994, 1979.

Hunt, William R. *Distant Justice: Policing the Alaskan Frontier.* Norman: University of Oklahoma Press, 1987, 274–275.

Lopez, Barry. *Arctic Dreams: Imagination and Desire in a Northern Landscape.* New York: Scribners, 1986.

McGinnis, Joe. *Going to Extremes.* New York: Plume, 1981.

McPhee, John. *Coming into the Country.* New York: The Noonday Press, 1976.

Overstreet, Everett Louis. *Black on a Background of White: A Chronicle of Afro-Americans' Involvement in America's Last Frontier, Alaska.* Fairbanks, AK: Alaska Black Caucus, 1988.

ARTICLES

"Alaska: Bonanza For Blacks? Oil Windfall Heralds New Rush for Wealth." *Ebony,* Nov. 1969, 123.

Anderson, George C. "Alaska Frontier . . . Attracts Negro Pioneers: 'Anchorage Is My Home.' " *Color,* Apr. 1953.

"Blacks In Alaska History." *Heritage,* Jan.–Mar. 1987, 1-2.

"Colored Folk to Have Big Dinner." *Daily Alaska Dispatch* (Juneau, AK), 5 Sep. 1918, 4.

Jordan, Nancy. "Black Perspectives of Anchorage." *Anchorage Times,* 15 Feb. 1991, E1.

Naske, Claus-M. "Blacks Blocked by Bureaucracy." *Alaska Journal,* Autumn 1974 1.4, 8–10.

Neuberger, Richard. "Alcan Epic." *Yank Magazine,* 10 Feb. 1943, 20–21.

Skerrett, Joseph, Jr. "Michael Healy: Mulatto Sailor." *Negro History Bulletin,* Jul.–Dec. 1978.

## *Chapter Fourteen: Seattle, Washington: City on the Edge of Forever*

BOOKS

Cayton, Horace R. *Long Old Road.* New York: Trident Press, 1965.

Ellison, Harlan. *The City on the Edge of Forever: The Original Teleplay That Became the Classic Star Trek Episode.* Clarkson, GA: White Wolf Publishing, 1996.

Karenga, Maulena. "Nguzo Saba." *Kwanzaa: Origins, Concepts, Practices.* Los Angeles: Kwaida Publications, 1977.

Karlstrom, Paul J. *The Spirit in the Stone: The Visionary Art of James W. Washington, Sr.* Seattle: University of Washington Press, 1989.

Kilian, Crawford. *Go Do Some Great Thing: The Black Pioneers of British Columbia.* Vancouver: Douglas and McIntyre, 1980.

Morrow, Theresa. *Seattle Survival Guide: An Essential Handbook for City Living.* Seattle: Sasquatch Books, 1990.

Mumford, Esther Hall. *The Man Who Founded a Town.* Seattle: Ananse Press, 1990.

———. *Seattle's Black Victorians, 1852–1901.* Seattle: Ananse Press, 1980.

———. *Seven Stars and Orion: Reflections of the Past.* Seattle: Ananse Press, 1986.

Satterfield, Archie. *The Seattle Guidebook.* 8th ed. Chester: The Globe Pequot Press, 1991.

ARTICLES

"Does Seattle 'Work' for Blacks?" *Seattle Times,* 28 Aug. 1983, A16–A17.

Fry, Donn. "A Brother's Challenge." *Seattle Times,* 8 May 1988, L1.

Gwinn, Mary Ann. "Statistics Show Seattle Still Has a Way to Go." *Seattle Times,* 26 Feb. 1985, C2.

Hayes, Janice. "Social Struggle." *Seattle Times,* 13 May 1987, C1.

Henderson, Jeff. "AIDS and African-Americans: the Compound Challenge." *Spring Board,* Mar.–Apr. 1991, 6.

———. "AIDS and the IV Drug User: Addicts Face Tougher Odds for Survival." *Spring Board,* May–Jun. 1991, 1.

Johnson, Charles. "A Kind of Promised Land." *Pacific Northwest,* Jan./Feb. 1986, 25.

Katz, Dean. "... Years of Change." *Seattle Times,* 26 Feb. 1985, C1–C2.

MacDonald, Sally. "Minority Status." *Seattle Times/Seattle Post–Intelligencer,* 27 Sep. 1987, sec. Pacific, 10.

Mumford, Esther. "Seattle's Black Victorians—Revising a City's History." *Portage,* Fall/Winter 1980–81, 14–17.

O'Boyle, Robert. "Black Churches, Community Need to Assist AIDS Programs." 8 Dec. 1991, L3.

Powell, Ronald W. "A Speck in the Milk." *Pacific (Seattle Times/Seattle Post–Intelligencer),* 7 Aug. 1988, 8.

———. "Black and Blue." *Pacific (Seattle Times/Seattle Post–Intelligencer)* 7 Aug. 1988, 6.

———. "Deep Roots: City's Blacks Come Home." *Seattle Times,* 7 Jul. 1985, A1.

Raban, Jonathan. "In the Cool, Green Archipelago of Seattle, Seclusion Reigns and Every Home is an Island: America's Most Private City." *Travel Holiday,* Nov. 1991, 60.

Simon, Jim. "'A Terrible Loss: Not Knowing All That History.'" *Seattle Times/Seattle Post–Intelligencer,* 27 Sep. 1987, D1.

## *Chapter Fifteen: San Francisco, Oakland, Los Angeles and Allensworth, California: The There There*

### BOOKS

Alexander, Charles. *Battles and Victories of Allen Allensworth, A.M., Ph.D. Lieutenant-Colonel, Retired, U.S. Army.* Boston: Sherman, French & Co., 1914.

*Allensworth: An Enduring Dream: February 7–September 27, 1987.* Los Angeles: California Afro-American Museum, 1987.

Baldwin, James. *The Price of the Ticket: Collected Nonfiction, 1948–1985.* New York: St. Martin's/Marek, 1985.

Beasley, Delilah Leontium. *The Negro Trail Blazers of California; a Compilation of Records from the California Archives in the Bancroft Library at the University of California, in Berkeley; and from the Diaries, Old Papers, and Conversations of Old Pioneers in the State of California.* Los Angeles: n.p., 1919.

Bonner, Thomas D. *The Life and Adventures of James P. Beckwourth as Told to Thomas D. Bonner.* Lincoln: University of Nebraska Press, 1972.

Crouchett, Lawrence P., Lonnie G. Bunch, III, and Martha Kendall Whitaker. *Visions Toward Tomorrow: The History of the East Bay Afro-American Community, 1852–1977.* Oakland: Northern California Center for Afro-American History and Life, 1989.

Daniels, Douglas Henry. *Pioneer Urbanites: A Social and Cultural History of Black San Francisco.* Berkeley: University of California Press, 1990.

Davis, Mike. *City Of Quartz: Excavating the Future in Los Angeles.* London: Verso, 1990.

Herodotus. *Herodotus: Books Five Through Seven, Loeb 119.* Translated by A.D. Godley. Boston: Harvard University Press, 1992.

Holdredge, Helen. *Mammy Pleasant.* New York: G. P. Putnam's Sons, 1961.

*Home and Yard: Black Folk Life Expressions in Los Angeles: November 7, 1987–April 3, 1988.* Los Angeles: California Afro-American Museum, 1987.

Irvin, Dona L. *The Unsung Heart of Black America: A Middle-Class Church at Mid-Century.* University of Missouri Press, 1992.

Logan, Rayford W. and Michael R. Winton, eds. *Dictionary of American Negro Biography.* New York: W. W. Norton & Co., 1982.

Rieff, David. *Los Angeles: The Capital of the Third World.* New York: Simon and Schuster, 1991.

*The Spirit of Allensworth.* (videorecording) Producer, director, and writer, Danny L. McGuire. Host and narrator, Greg Morris. San Jose, CA: KTEH-TV, 1980, 1976, 29 min.

Wheeler, B. Gordon. *Black California: The History of African-Americans in the Golden State.* New York: Hippocrene Books, 1993.

## ARTICLES

Benson, Sheila. "A Magical, Mystical Tour of South-Central." *Los Angeles Times,* 24 Oct. 1990, F1.

Bogle, Donald. "No Business Like Micheaux Business: 'B' . . . for Black." *Film Comment,* Sept./Oct. 1985, 31–34.

Canby, Vincent. "Scene: Black Middle-Class Home. Enter a Comic, Lost Demon." *New York Times,* 5 Oct. 1990, C10.

Cerone, Daniel. "Awakening to the Realities of Black Life." *Los Angeles Times,* 12 Aug. 1989, sec. V, 1.

Drummond, Tammerlin. "Descendants Bring Back Memory, Glory of Former Mecca for Blacks." *San Jose Mercury News,* 18 Dec. 1991, D1–2D.

Evans, Rowland, and Robert Novak. "No Insurrection in Los Angeles." *Washington Post,* 4 May 1992, A23.

Fraser, Isabel. "Mammy Pleasant: The Woman." *San Francisco Call,* December, 1901.

James, Caryn. "After Pizza and Polite Squabbling, a Film Wins." *New York Times,* 29 Jan. 1990, sec. C, 17.

McAllister, Bill. "Call for a Panel on L.A. Unrest Echoes Historical Response." (Plus 2 charts), *Washington Post,* 4 May 1992, A21.

Moss, Rick. "Equal Justice Before the Law: the Civil Rights Movement in California, 1850–1950." Museum Exhibit, October 12, 1991–May 17, 1992, California African American Museum. N.p.: privately published., n.d.

Sterrit, David. "Making Movies That Fill a Vacuum: Charles Burnett Wants to Correct Stereotypes by Conveying Black Society's Uniqueness and Moral Sense." *Christian Science Monitor* (Boston), 2 Oct. 1990, 11.

Thomas, Kevin. "Burnett's 'Killer of Sheep' to Open Watts Commemoration." *Los Angeles Times,* 6 Aug. 1990, F3.

Wallace, David. "Burnett—Telling a Story on a Shoestring." *Los Angeles Times,* 24 Oct. 1990, F1.

White, Armond. "Telling It on the Mountain." *Film Comment,* Sept./Oct. 1985, 39–41.

Wilmington, Michael. "'Wedding': A Vision of Watts as Anywhere, U.S.A." Rev. of *The Wedding,* by Charles Burnett. *Los Angeles Times,* 26 Apr. 1991, F6.

## *Chapter Sixteen: Las Vegas, Nevada: The American City*

### BOOKS

Best, Katharine and Katharine Hiller. *Las Vegas: Playtown, USA.* New York: David McKay Co. Inc., 1955.

Moehring, Eugene P. *Resort City in the Sunbelt: Las Vegas, 1930–1970.* Reno: University of Nevada Press, 1989.

### ARTICLES

Green, Marian. "The Dream Is Still Alive." *Las Vegas Review Journal,* 20 Jan. 1992.

## *Chapter Seventeen: Salt Lake City, Utah: Upon This Desert*

### BOOKS

Arrington, Leonard J. *Brigham Young: American Moses.* Urbana: University of Illinois Press, 1986.

———, and Davis Bitton. *The Mormon Experience: A History of the Latter-Day Saints.* New York: Vintage Books, 1980.

Bloom, Harold. *The American Religion: The Emergence of the Post-Christian Nation.* New York: Simon and Schuster, 1992.

Burton, Sir Richard F. *The City of the Saints and Across the Rocky Mountains to California.* Niwot: University Press of Colorado, 1990, 1862.

Carter, Kate B. *The Story of the Negro Pioneer.* Salt Lake City: Daughters of Utah Pioneers, 1965.

Coleman, Ronald G. "Blacks in Utah History: An Unknown Legacy." In *The People of Utah.* 2nd ed. Edited by Helen Z. Papanikolas. Salt Lake City: Utah Historical Society, 1981, 115–140.

Freeman, Joseph. *In the Lord's Due Time.* Salt Lake City: Bookcraft, 1979.

### ARTICLES

"Black Group Clings to Mormon Church Despite Restriction." *New York Times,* 30 April 1978.

Brown, Mathew, and Linda Thompson Oberg. "Mourners Eulogize Andrews as Martyr." *Deseret News* (Salt Lake City), 1 Aug. 1992, B1–B2.

Lundgren, Linnea. "Ethnic Studies Center Prepares U. Students to Live in Modern, Pluralistic Society." *Daily Utah Chronicle,* 4 Mar. 1991.

## *Chapter Nineteen: Denver, Colorado: Destiny Made Manifest*

### ARTICLES

Edwards, Audrey. "Leaving the Corporate Nest." *Executive Female* Jul./Aug. 1992, 32–37.

*Chapter Twenty: Lafayette, Louisiana: Zydeco Who?*

BOOKS

Brasseaux, Carl A. *The Founding of New Acadia: The Beginnings of Acadian Life in Louisiana, 1765–1803*. Baton Rouge: Louisiana State University Press, 1987.

Hall, Gwendolyn Midlo. *Africans in Colonial Louisiana: The Development of Afro-Creole Culture in the Eighteenth Century.* Baton Rouge: Louisiana State University Press, 1992.

Rushton, William Faulkner. *The Cajuns from Acadia to Louisiana.* New York: Noonday Press–Farrar, Straus and Giroux, 1992, 1979.

Taylor, Joe Gray. *Louisiana: A History.* New York: W.W. Norton & Co., 1984, 1976.

ARTICLES

Ancelet, Barry Jean. "Ragin' Cajuns: What's in a Name?" *Creole,* Dec. 1992, 42.

Baudouin, Richard. "Standing Tall: Ernest Gaines' Novel with Familiar Message May Be His Best Yet." *Times of Acadiana,* 14 Jul. 1993, 15–17.

"Black French-speakers Seeking Recognition." (AP) *Sunday Advertiser* (Lafeyette, LA), 12 Nov. 1989, 6.

Coulombe, Charles A. "Creoles and Catholicism: A Cultural Connection." *Creole,* Mar. 1991, 9.

———. "Legacy of Zora Neale Hurston—Revisited." *Creole,* Mar./Apr. 1993, 22.

———. "Zora Neale Hurston: A Genius of the South." *Creole,* Sep. 1991, 30–32.

El Shabazz, Takuna Maulana. "Promotion of 'Cajun/Acadiana' Is Colonialism." *Creole,* Dec. 1992, 43.

Fontenot, Donna. "'Uncajun Committee' Gives Plan." *Advertiser* (Lafeyette, LA), 14 Aug. 1987.

Foote, Ruth. "Creoles of Color Exhibition Premieres in Lafayette." *Creole,* Jan. 1991, 16–17.

———. "Part II: Opelousas Police Chief Larry Caillier—Target of Murder: Black Male Crisis: Fact or Fiction?" *Creole,* Mar. 1992, 15–17.

Goudeau, Helene. "Importance of Preserving the Creole Culture." *Creole,* Jan. 1991, 18–19.

High, Kamau. "A Camper Tells His Story." *Manhood Development Camp For African American Males: Chicot State Park Ville Platte, Louisiana* N.p.: privately published, n.d.

Huggs, Katrina. "Rage's 'Poets of Power' Cassette Released." *Creole,* Aug. 1992, 21.

———. "Remembering the Creole Culture: An Interview with Fiddler Canray Fontenot." *Creole,* Nov. 1992, 20–22.

Hunter-Hodge, Katherine. "Black Artists Have Gotten Bad Rap." *Daily News* (New York), 7 Nov. 1993, 21.

Mills, David. "It's a White Thing: Is It Serious Hip Hop Or a Pale Imitation." *Washington Post,* 14 Jul. 1991, G1.

Porter, Tissa. "A Zydeco What?" *Creole,* Sep. 1991, 5–8.

Reedom, Jackie. "Blacks Contributed to Rich Louisiana History." *Creole* Feb. 1993, 4–8.

Smith, J.F. "Zydeco Drawing Big Crowds in New England." *Creole,* Aug. 1991, 24–26.
"Southwest Louisiana Zydeco Music Festival: 10th Anniversary: Saturday, September 5, 1992: Plaisance, Louisiana." Grant proposal, n.d.
Tate, Morris. "Zydeco: Music that Generates Lots of Excitement." *Creole,* May 1991, 7.

## *Chapter Twenty-One: Atlanta and St. Simons Island, Georgia: Walking on Water*

### BOOKS

Downes, Olin. Introduction to *Slave Songs of the Georgia Sea Islands,* by Lydia Parish. Athens: Brown Thrasher-University of Georgia Press, 1992, xxxv–xxxix.
Georgia Writers' Project. *Drums and Shadows: Survival Studies Among the Coastal Negroes.* Athens: Brown Thrasher Books: University of Georgia Press, 1986, 1940.
Jones, Bessie, and Bess Lomax Hawes. *Step It Down: Games, Plays, Songs and Stories from the Afro-American Heritage.* Athens: University of Georgia Press, 1987, 1972.
Jones-Jackson, Patricia. *When Roots Die: Endangered Traditions on the Sea Islands.* Athens: University of Georgia Press, 1987.
Kemble, Frances Anne. *Journal of a Residence on a Georgian Plantation in 1838–1839.* Edited by John A. Scott. Athens: Browen Thrasher-University of Georgia Press, 1984, 1961.
McFeely, William S. *Sapelo's People: A Long Walk into Freedom.* New York: W. W. Norton & Co., 1994.
Price, Eugina. *At Home on St. Simons.* Atlanta: Peachtree Publishers, 1981.
Wightman, Orrin Sage. *Early Days of Coastal Georgia.* Photos by Orrin Sage Wightman, story by Margaret Davis Cate. St. Simons Island, Ga: Fort Frederica Association, 1955.

### ARTICLES

Ansa, Tina McElroy. "Artist Ana Bel Lee Washington Captures the Festival on Canvas." *Georgia Sea Island Festival, Neptune Park, St. Simons Island, Georgia, Aug. 19–20, 1989.* Georgia Sea Island Festival. N.p., 1989: 3.
———. "Georgia Sea Island Festival—1989." *Georgia Sea Island Festival, Neptune Park, St. Simons Island, Georgia, Aug. 19–20, 1989.* Georgia Sea Island Festival. N.p., 1989: 2.
Bailey, Cornelia. "The World of Sapelo Island," in *Sapelo Stories* by Cornelia Bailey. (Reprinted from *High Tide Guide to the Golden Isles.*) *Georgia Sea Island Festival, Neptune Park, St. Simons Island, Georgia, Aug. 19–20, 1989.* Georgia Sea Island Festival. N.p., 1989: 18–19.
Bell, Malcolm, Jr. "Memories of a Coastal W.P.A. Project." *Georgia Sea Island Festival, Neptune Park, St. Simons Island, Georgia, Aug. 19–20, 1989.* Georgia Sea Island Festival. N.p., 1989: 12–13.
Black, James T. "St. Simons From Dawn to Dusk." *Southern Living,* Jul. 1993, 12.
Blake, John. "Never Again the Same." *Atlanta Journal Constitution,* 27 June 1992.
Daniels, Lee A. "The Future of Black Colleges." *Emerge,* Apr. 1991, 28–32.
Griffin, Charles W., III. "Riot Rips Court District." *Fulton County Daily Report,* 1 May 1992.

Jones, Sandy. "Neptune Small's Story." *Georgia Sea Island Festival, Neptune Park, St. Simons Island, Georgia, Aug. 19–20, 1989*. Georgia Sea Island Festival. N.p., 1989: 4–5.

Murphy, Carla. "Demonstrators Burn Georgia Flag at Capitol." *Atlanta Daily News,* 15 Feb. 1993.

"Ranking Black Colleges." *Emerge,* Apr. 1991, 36–37.

Sherman, Mark. "Banner Burns at Capitol Rally." *Atlanta News Weekly,* 18 Feb. 1993.

Sieber, H. A. "The Factual Basis of the Ebo Landing Legend." *Georgia Sea Island Festival, Neptune Park, St. Simons Island, Georgia, Aug. 19–20, 1989*. Georgia Sea Island Festival. N.p., 1989: 26.

*The Official Guide to the Golden Isles,* Vol. IV, Issue 10.

## *Chapter Twenty-Two: Cyberspace, North Carolina: Where Am I Black?*

### BOOKS

Bukatman, Scott. *Terminal Identity: The Virtual Subject in Postmodern Science Fiction.* Durham, NC: Duke University Press, 1994.

Cavafy, C.P. *The Complete Poems of Cavafy.* Translated by Rae Dalven. New York: Harcourt, Brace, 1961.

Dery, Mary, ed. *Flame Wars: The Discourse of Cyberculture.* Durham, NC: Duke University Press, 1994.

Harvey, David. *The Condition of Post-Modernity.* Cambridge, MA: Blackwell, 1989.

Slatalla, Michelle, and Joshua Quittner. *Masters of Deception: The Gang that Ruled Cyberspace.* New York: HarperCollins, 1995.

Turkle, Sherry. *Life on the Screen: Identity in the Age of the Internet.* New York: Simon & Schuster, 1995.

### ARTICLES

Slatalla, Michele, and Joshua Quittner. "Gang War in Cyberspace." *Wired,* Dec. 1994, 146.

## *Chapter Twenty-Three: New York, New York: Blackness on My Mind*

### ARTICLES

Corliss, Richard. "'Welcome to New Harlem!': the Intrepid Tourist Can Find Charm, Spirit and Soaring Music in New York's Most Notorious Ghetto." *Time,* 24 April 1989, 68–74.

Rampersad, Arnold. "V. S. Naipaul: Turning in the South." *Raritan,* Summer 1990, 24–27.

Stein, Gertrude. *Matisse, Picasso and Gertrude Stein with Two Shorter Stories.* Paris: Plain Edition, 1933.

## *General Reference Works*

Barringer, Richard, ed. *Changing Maine.* University of Southern Maine, 1990.

Callwood, Jane. *Portrait of Canada.* Toronto: PaperJacks, 1983.

Cantor, George. *Historic Black Landmarks: A Traveler's Guide.* Detroit: Visible Ink Press, 1991.

Chase, Henry. *In Their Footsteps: The American Visions Guide to African-American Heritage Sites.* New York: Henry Holt and Co., 1994.

Dillard, J.L. *Black English: Its History and Usage in the United States.* New York: Vintage Books, 1973.

Drake, St. Clair, and Horace R. Clayton. *Black Metropolis: A Study of Negro Life in a Northern City.* Chicago: University of Chicago Press, 1993.

DuBois, W. E. B. *An ABC of Color.* New York: International Publishers, 1989.

———. *Dusk of Dawn: An Essay Toward an Autobiography of a Race Concept.* New Brunswick: Transaction Publishers, Fourth Printing, 1992.

———. *The Souls of Black Folk.* New York: Signet–New American Library, 1982, 1969.

———. *Writings: The Suppression of the African Slave Trade; The Souls Of Black Folk; Dusk of Dawn; Essays and Articles.* New York: Library of America, 1986.

Foner, Eric. *Reconstruction: America's Unfinished Revolution, 1863–1877.* New York: Harper and Row, 1988.

Franklin, John Hope, and Alfred A. Moss, Jr. *From Slavery to Freedom: A History of Negro Americans.* 6th ed. New York: Alfred A. Knopf, 1988.

George, Nelson. *The Death of Rhythm and Blues.* New York: Pantheon Books, 1988.

Giddings, Paula. *When and Where I Enter: The Impact of Black Women on Race and Sex in America.* Toronto: Bantam Books, 1984.

Hacker, Andrew. *Two Nations: Black and White, Separate, Hostile, Unequal.* New York: Scribners, 1992.

Harding, Vincent. *There Is a River: The Black Struggle for Freedom in America.* New York: Vintage–Random House, 1983, 1981.

Harris, Middleton, Morris Levitt, Roger Furman, and Ernest Smith. *The Black Book.* New York: Random House, 1974.

Katz, William Loren. *Black Indians: A Hidden Heritage.* New York: Atheneum, 1986.

———. *Black People Who Made the Old West.* Trenton, NJ: Africa World Press, 1992, 1977.

———. *The Black West.* Seattle: Open Hand Publishing, Inc., 1987.

Levine, Lawrence W. *Black Culture and Black Consciousness: Afro-American Folk Thought from Slavery to Freedom.* Oxford: Oxford University Press, 1977.

Major, Clarence, ed. *Juba to Jive: A Dictionary of African-American Slang.* New York: Penguin, 1994.

*The Milepost,* 44th ed. Spring 1992–Spring 1993.

Quarles, Benjamin. *The Negro in the Making of America.* New York: Collier Books, 1969.

Roberts, Sam. *Who We Are: A Portrait of America Based Upon the Latest U.S. Census.* New York/Toronto: Times Books–Random House/Random House of Canada, 1993.

Smitherman, Geneva. *Black Talk: Words and Phrases from the Hood to the Amen Corner.* Boston: Houghton, 1994.

———. *Talkin' and Testifyin': The Language of Black America.* Detroit: Wayne State University Press, 1977.

Sowell, Thomas. *Race and Culture: A World View.* New York: Basic Books, 1984.

Spencer, Jon Michael. *The Rhythms of Black Folk: Race, Religion and Pan-Africanism.* Trenton, NJ: African World Press, 1995.

Steinberg, Stephen. *The Ethnic Myth: Race, Ethnicity, and Class in America.* Boston: Beacon Press, 1989.

# INDEX

# PERMISSIONS ACKNOWLEDGMENTS

Grateful acknowledgment is made to the following for permission to reprint previously published material:

*Barry Jean Ancelet:* Excerpt from "Ragin' Cajuns: What's in a Name?" by Barry Jean Ancelet (*Creole* magazine, Dec. 1992). Reprinted by permission of Barry Jean Ancelet.

*California African-American Museum:* Excerpt from the Introduction by Gerald L. Davis to *Home and Yard: Black Folk Life Expressions in Los Angeles* (California African-American Museum exhibition catalog, 1987). Reprinted by permission of the California African-American Museum.

*Violet M. Copeland:* Poem "Negro Pioneer Church" by Violet M. Copeland. All rights exclusively held by the author and may not be reproduced in any form without her permission. Reprinted by permission of Violet M. Copeland.

*Takuna Maulana El Shabazz:* Excerpt from "Welcome to Nigger Country" by Takuna Maulana El Shabazz (*Rising Seed,* Dec. 1992, also published in *Creole* magazine as "Promotion of 'Cajun/Acadiana' is Colonialism," Dec. 1992). Reprinted by permission of Takuna Maulana El Shabazz.

*Harlan Ellison:* Excerpt from the Introduction to *The City on the Edge of Forever* by Harlan Ellison, copyright © 1995 by The Kilimanjaro Corporation. Reprinted by permission of, and arrangement with, the Author and the Author's agent, Richard Curtis Associates, New York. All rights reserved.

*Helene Goudeau:* Excerpt from "Importance of preserving the Creole culture" by Helene Goudeau (*Creole* magazine, Jan. 1991). Reprinted by permission of Helene Goudeau.

*Harcourt Brace & Company:* Excerpt from "Ithaca" from *The Complete Poems of Cavafy,* translated by Rae Dalven, copyright © 1961 and renewed 1989 by Rae Dalven. Reprinted by permission of Harcourt Brace & Company.

*Harcourt Brace & Company* and *Boodle Music/Otis Lee Music:* Excerpt from "Live Where You Can" by Lee Breuer and Robert Telson adapted from the text *Oedipus at Colonus by Sophocles,* copyright © 1941 by Harcourt Brace & Company, copyright renewed 1969 by Dudley Fitts and Robert Fitzgerald. Lyrics reprinted courtesy of Boodle Music/Otis Lee Music. Adaptation reprinted by permission of Harcourt Brace & Company.

*Johnson Publishing Company, Inc.:* Excerpt from "Zula Swanson: Alaska's Richest Black" (*Ebony*), copyright © 1969 by Johnson Publishing Company, Inc. Reprinted by permission of Johnson Publishing Company, Inc.

*Newsweek, Inc.:* "CyberSoul Not Found" (*Newsweek,* July 31, 1995, pp. 62, 64), copyright © 1995 by Newsweek, Inc. All rights reserved. Reprinted by permission of Newsweek, Inc.

*Penguin Books Ltd.:* Excerpts from Haiku No. 67, No. 97, and No. 132 from *On Love and Barley: Haiku of Bashō,* translated by Lucien Stryk copyright © 1985 by Lucien Stryk (Penguin Classics, 1985). Reprinted by permission of Penguin Books Ltd.

*Michael J. Pikes:* Excerpt from "Let the Track Attack" by Michael J. Pikes and Antoine J. Broussard, copyright © by Michael J. Pikes and Antoine J. Broussard. Self Publishing Co. (Ghetto Funk Muzick, B.M.I.). Reprinted by permission of Michael J. Pikes.

*Putnam Berkley:* Excerpts from *Praisesong for the Widow* by Paule Marshall, copyright © 1983 by Paule Marshall. Reprinted by permission of Putnam Berkley, a division of Penguin Putnam Inc.

*Jonathan Raban:* Excerpt from "In the Cool, Green Archipelago of Seattle, Seclusion Reigns and Every Home is an Island" by Jonathan Raban (*Travel Holiday,* Nov. 1991), copyright © 1991 by Jonathan Raban. Reprinted by permission of Jonathan Raban.

*Random House, Inc.:* Excerpt from William Faulkner: Nobel Prize Speech, copyright © 1965 by Random House, Inc. Excerpts from "The World and the Jug" from *Shadow and Act* by Ralph Ellison, copyright © 1953, 1964 by Ralph Ellison. Reprinted by permission of Random House, Inc.

*Simon & Schuster and Marianne Craig Moore, Literary Executor for the Estate of Marianne Moore:* "What Are Years?" from *The Collected Poems of Marianne Moore,* copyright © 1941, copyright renewed 1969 by Marianne Moore. Reprinted by permission of Simon & Schuster and Marianne Craig Moore, Literary Executor for the Estate of Marianne Moore. All rights reserved.

*Third World Press, Inc.:* Excerpt from "Possibilities: Remembering Malcolm X" from *Killing Memory, Seeking Ancestors* by Haki R. Madhubuti, copyright © 1987 by Haki R. Madhubuti. Reprinted by permission of Third World Press, Inc., Chicago, Illinois.

*Time Life Syndication:* Excerpt from "Welcome to New Harlem" (*Time* magazine, April 24, 1989), copyright © 1989 by Time, Inc. Reprinted by permission of Time Life Syndication.

*University of Nebraska Press:* Excerpts from "The Story of Crow" by Angela Sidney as told to Julie Cruikshank from *Life Lived Like a Story: Life Stories of Three Yukon Native Elders* by Julie Cruikshank, copyright © 1990 by the University of Nebraska Press. Reprinted by permission of the University of Nebraska Press.

*Vintage Books:* Excerpt from *Les Blancs* by Lorraine Hansberry, copyright © 1972 by Robert Nemiroff. Excerpt from *South to a Very Old Place* by Albert Murray, copyright © 1971 by Albert Murray. Reprinted by permission of Vintage Books, a division of Random House, Inc.

*Warner Bros. Publications U.S. Inc.:* "Black Crow" by Joni Mitchell, copyright © 1977 Crazy Crow Music. All rights reserved. Reprinted by permission of Warner Bros. Publications U.S. Inc., Miami, FL 33014.

*John A. Williams:* Excerpts from *This Is My Country Too* by John A. Williams, copyright © 1964, 1965 by John A. Williams. Reprinted by permission of John A. Williams.

## A NOTE ON THE TYPE

The text of this book was set in Times Roman, designed by Stanley Morison for *The Times* (London) and introduced by that newspaper in 1932. Among typographers and designers of the twentieth century, Stanley Morison was a strong forming influence, as typographical adviser to the Monotype Corporation of London, as a director of two distinguished English publishing houses, and as a writer of sensibility, erudition, and keen practical sense. In 1930 Morison wrote: "Type design moves at the pace of the most conservative reader. The good type-designer therefore realizes that, for a new font to be successful, it has to be so good that only very few recognize its novelty. If readers do not notice the consummate reticence and rare discipline of a new type, it is probably a good letter." It is now generally recognized that in the creation of Times Roman, Morison successfully met the qualifications of his theoretical doctrine.

Composed by Stratford Publishing Services,
Brattleboro, Vermont
Printed and bound by Quebecor Printing,
Fairfield, Pennsylvania
Designed by Anthea Lingeman